Industrial Relations
in Britain

For Hugh Clegg
Teacher, Colleague, Friend

Industrial Relations in Britain

Edited by
George Sayers Bain

Basil Blackwell

First published 1983
Reprinted 1983
Basil Blackwell Publisher Limited
108 Cowley Road, Oxford OX4 1JF, England

British Library Cataloguing in Publication Data
Industrial relations in Britain.
  1. Industrial relations—Great Britain
  I. Bain, George Sayers
  331'.0941   HD8391

  ISBN 0-631-13138-8
  ISBN 0-631-13295-3 Pbk

Phototypesetting by Katerprint Co. Ltd, Cowley, Oxford
Printed in Great Britain by T. J. Press Ltd, Padstow

Contents

Contributors

John Addison, Associate Professor, University of South Carolina, Columbia S.C.

George Bain, Professor of Industrial Relations, University of Warwick

William Brown, Director, Industrial Relations Research Unit, University of Warwick

Robert J. Davies, Assistant Professor, University of British Columbia, Vancouver

David Deaton, Research Fellow, Industrial Relations Research Unit, University of Warwick

P. K. Edwards, Research Fellow, Industrial Relations Research Unit, University of Warwick

Bob Hepple, Professor of English Law in the University of London at University College

Richard Hyman, Reader in Industrial Relations, University of Warwick

Roy Lewis, Senior Research Fellow, Industrial Relations Research Unit, University of Warwick

Robert M. Lindley, Director, Institute for Employment, University of Warwick

David Marsden, Lecturer in Industrial Relations, London School of Economics

Ken Mayhew, Fellow, Pembroke College, Oxford

Peter Nolan, Research Associate, Industrial Relations Research Unit, University of Warwick

Chris Pond, Director, Low Pay Unit, London

Robert Price, Lecturer in Industrial Relations, University of Warwick

John Purcell, Fellow, Centre for Management Studies, University of Oxford

Keith Sisson, Senior Lecturer in Industrial Relations, University of Warwick

Michael Terry, Research Associate, Industrial Relations Research Unit, University of Warwick

David Winchester, Lecturer in Industrial Relations, University of Warwick

Figures

Tables

Preface

This volume provides a comprehensive, systematic, up-to-date introduction to the study of British industrial relations. It is intended primarily for students doing a basic diploma, undergraduate, or graduate course in industrial relations at colleges, polytechnics, or universities as well as for those doing courses in industrial sociology, labour economics, labour law, and personnel management. It should also be of interest to those in adult education, to those seeking membership of professional bodies like the Institute of Personnel Management, to practitioners in both unions and management, and to the general reader who simply wants to find out more about industrial relations in Britain today.

The book draws upon the insights offered by the major disciplines that contribute to the study of industrial relations. It has seventeen chapters, covering trade unions, management, collective bargaining, industrial conflict, the labour market, labour law and state intervention in industrial relations. Each chapter is an original essay that brings together in a coherent fashion the most relevant theoretical and empirical work. Each is stamped with the author's own views. Each emphasises analysis and explanation as well as description. And each focuses on trends over the past two or three decades (unless a longer time perspective is required to develop the analysis) and says something about likely developments during the 1980s.

The material is presented in as non-technical a fashion as possible. Technical jargon and mathematical notation are kept to a minimum; where they are used to advance the analysis, an attempt is made to translate their meaning into everyday English. References are fully listed in the bibliography at the end of the book and a parenthetical reference in the text to the author's surname, the date of publication, and the page reference (if any) directs the reader to the appropriate item in the bibliography.

Many people assisted with the preparation of this book. Several friends and colleagues gave helpful comments on the drafts of chapters: John Bowers on Chapter 10; William Brown on Chapter 3; Jon Clark on Chapter 15; Hugh Clegg on Chapters 9 and 17; Simon Crine on Chapter 8; David Deaton on Chapters 8, 11, 12, and 17; Linda Dickens on Chapter 3;

Patricia Dutton on Chapter 14; Paul Edwards on Chapter 3; Ben Fine on Chapter 12; Emma Maclennan on Chapter 8; Paul Marginson on Chapter 10; Gregor Murray on Chapter 2; Charlie Nelson on Chapter 10; Peter Nolan on Chapters 3, 8, 10, and 11; Kathy O'Donnell on Chapter 12; Fran Rowley on Chapter 13; Bob Simpson on Chapter 15; Keith Sisson on Chapters 3, 9, and 17; Jill Sullivan on Chapter 8; Mike Terry on Chapter 9; Lord Wedderburn on Chapter 15; and Stephen Wood on Chapter 11.

Thanks are also due to Janet Godden for meticulously copy editing the typescript and removing numerous stylistic infelicities; to John Bennett and Annemarie Flanders for compiling the bibliography; to Judith Auty for helping to correct the proofs and for compiling the index; to Margaret Morgan for helping to compile the data used in Chapter 1, for verifying much of the data used in other chapters, and for helping to correct the proofs; and to René Olivieri of Basil Blackwell for his faith in the project. Finally, the editor is grateful to all the authors for agreeing that the royalties earned by the book should be placed in a fund at the University of Warwick for promoting teaching and research in industrial relations.

The book is dedicated to Hugh Clegg. He has been a colleague and friend of the editor and most of the contributors for many years and he has taught all of us either directly through tutorials, lectures, and supervising our research or indirectly through his many publications. Among the most important of these are his textbooks. The most recent, *The Changing System of Industrial Relations in Great Britain* (1979), is a lineal descendant of a series of volumes which stretch back to the first systematic textbook of British industrial relations, *The System of Industrial Relations in Great Britain* (1954), which he and Allan Flanders edited thirty years ago. If our text accomplishes as much as any of his, we will be well satisfied.

PART I
Trade Unions

1 Union Growth: Dimensions, Determinants, and Destiny

George Sayers Bain and Robert Price

Data on union growth do not provide a precise quantitative index of the industrial or political power of trade unions. Nevertheless, union growth and union power are broadly related: at the very least union growth is a necessary condition, a prerequisite, for the exercise of union power (Bain and Price, 1980:160–3). Hence the study of union growth is a starting point for any assessment of union influence and involvement in the decision-making processes of British industry and society. More generally, it is also an essential basis for any examination of the representative quality and of the contemporary role of British unions.

The chapter begins by presenting some basic data on various dimensions of union growth in Britain. These data reveal considerable variations over the years in the rate of change of unionisation and hence, at any particular moment, in the level of unionisation between different groups, occupations, sectors, and industries. The chapter attempts to account for these variations, especially since 1948, and, by so doing, to isolate the strategic determinants of union growth. Then, in the light of this analysis, it assesses one aspect of the destiny of the trade union movement in Britain by predicting the course of union growth during the 1980s.

DIMENSIONS OF UNION GROWTH

The concept of union growth refers to a change in the number of union members. It can be measured either absolutely or relatively: that is, either by the number of union members or by this number taken as a percentage of the number of potential union members, a ratio known as the density of union membership. Union density is generally the more convenient measure to use when, for example, comparisons are being made at a single moment across different industries or occupations with widely varying potential union memberships; for by taking variations in potential union membership into account, it enables the most obvious determinant of union growth to be controlled for. In general, however, the two measures of union growth are complements rather than alternatives, for they impart different pieces of information. Changes in union density need not necessarily imply anything about actual union membership or vice versa: for example, union density may be increasing while actual union membership is decreasing. Hence a complete description of union growth requires the use of both measures.

Given the nature of these measures, any attempt to obtain data on them raises three basic questions. What is a trade union? Who is a union member? And who is a potential union member? Different answers can be given to each of these questions, because the various conceptual and practical problems each of them involves can be solved in different ways. The nature of these problems has been discussed elsewhere (Bain and Price, 1980:1–12), and there is room here only to make clear the way in which the above questions have been answered in compiling the data presented in the following tables.

The data are, with a few additions, those compiled by the Department of Employment. They cover organisations of employees which try to regulate their members' relations with employers. Each union's definition of who its members are has been accepted, but retired members have generally been excluded where they constitute a significant proportion of a union's total membership. Potential union membership is the labour force, including the registered unemployed, but excluding employers, the self-employed, and members of the armed forces. In the process of compiling data on union growth there are numerous points where errors creep in, but the data are generally no less reliable than data on, for example, strikes or unemployment. And so long as they are interpreted carefully and in conjuction with other quantitative and qualitative information concerning the nature and extent of unionisation in the area in question, they provide a reasonably reliable measure of union growth.

Aggregate Unionisation

The data presented in Table 1.1 reveal considerable variation from year-to-year in the rate of change of unionisation. The upper half of Figure 1.1 illustrates the pattern traced by the short-term variations in union growth and demonstrates that over the years for which data are available the annual rate of change in union density in the United Kingdom has fluctuated between −20·8 and +21·3 per cent. In short, union growth is characterised by cyclical fluctuations of varying amplitude and duration.

If attention is focused on the long-term trends which underlie the short-term movements in union growth, as in the bottom half of Figure 1.1 which plots the level as distinct from the rate of change of union density, the broad outline of union growth in the United Kingdom can be easily summarised. It increased fairly steadily from 1909 to 1920 when union density reached 45·2 per cent; this was followed by a substantial slump which bottomed in 1933 with union density at 22·6 per cent; then another upsurge occurred, peaking in 1948 with union density once again at 45·2 per cent.

TABLE 1.1: AGGREGATE UNION MEMBERSHIP AND DENSITY IN THE
UNITED KINGDOM: SELECTED YEARS, 1892–1981

	UNION MEMBERSHIP		POTENTIAL UNION MEMBERSHIP		UNION DENSITY	
	Number (000s)	Annual % Change	Number (000s)	Annual % Change	Level (%)	Annual % Change
1892	1,576		14,803		10·6	
1900	2,022		15,957		12·7	
1910	2,565		17,596		14·6	
1913	4,135		17,920		23·1	
1917	5,499		18,234		30·2	
1920	8,348		18,469		45·2	
1921	6,633		18,548		35·8	
1926	5,219		18,446		28·3	
1933	4,392		19,422		22·6	
1938	6,053		19,829		30·5	
1945	7,875		20,400		38·6	
1948	9,363		20,732		45·2	
1949	9,318	−0·5	20,782	+0·2	44·8	−0·9
1950	9,289	−0·3	21,055	+0·3	44·1	−1·6
1951	9,530	+2·6	21,177	+0·6	45·0	+2·0
1952	9,588	+0·6	21,252	+0·4	45·1	+0·2
1953	9,527	−0·6	21,352	+0·5	44·6	−1·1
1954	9,566	+0·4	21,658	+1·4	44·2	−0·9
1955	9,741	+1·8	21,913	+1·2	44·5	+0·7
1956	9,778	+0·4	22,180	+1·2	44·1	−0·9
1957	9,829	+0·5	22,334	+0·7	44·0	−0·2
1958	9,639	−1·9	22,290	−0·2	43·2	−1·8
1959	9,623	−0·2	21,866	−1·9	44·0	+1·9
1960	9,835	+2·2	22,229	+1·7	44·2	+0·5
1961	9,916	+0·8	22,527	+1·3	44·0	−0·5
1962	10,014	+1·0	22,879	+1·6	43·8	−0·5
1963	10,067	+0·5	23,021	+0·6	43·7	−0·2
1964	10,218	+1·5	23,166	+0·6	44·1	+0·9
1965	10,325	+1·0	23,385	+0·9	44·2	+0·2
1966	10,259	−0·6	23,545	+0·7	43·6	−1·4
1967	10,194	−0·6	23,347	−0·8	43·7	+0·2
1968	10,200	+0·1	23,203	−0·6	44·0	+0·7
1969	10,479	+2·7	23,153	−0·2	45·3	+3·0
1970	11,187	+6·8	23,050	−0·4	48·5	+7·1
1971	11,135	−0·5	22,884	−0·7	48·7	+0·4
1972	11,359	+2·0	22,961	+0·3	49·5	+1·6
1973	11,456	+0·9	23,244	+1·2	49·3	−0·4
1974	11,764	+2·7	23,339	+0·4	50·4	+2·2
1975	12,026	+2·2	23,587	+1·1	51·0	+1·2
1976	12,386	+3·0	23,871	+1·2	51·9	+1·8
1977	12,846	+3·7	24,069	+0·8	53·4	+2·9
1978	13,112	+2·1	24,203	+0·6	54·2	+1·5
1979	13,447	+2·6	24,264	+0·3	55·4	+2·2
1980	12,947	−3·7	24,171	−0·4	53·6	−3·2
1981	12,182	−5·9	23,879	−1·2	51·0	−4·9

Source: Price and Bain (1983: table 1).

Three broad periods can be identified in the aggregate pattern of union growth since 1948. The 'plateau' period, 1949–68, in which union potential increased more quickly than union membership with the result that union density stagnated and slightly declined; the decade of exceptional union growth, 1969–79, in which union membership increased by 3·2 million and

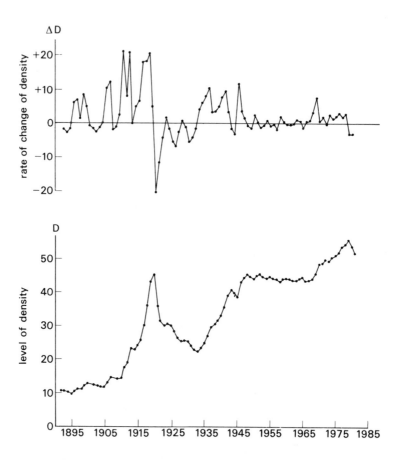

FIGURE 1.1:   The Rates of Change and the Level of Union Density in the United Kingdom, 1892–1981.
Source: Table 1.1, and Bain and Price (1980: table 2.1).

union density increased from 44 per cent to 55·4 per cent, a level more than 10 percentage points higher than the previous peak of 45·2 per cent reached in both 1920 and 1948; and, finally, the years of decline, 1980–81, in which the trade union movement lost about 1·3 million members, almost 40 per cent of the number it gained during the period 1969–79, and in which union density declined by 4·4 percentage points to 51·0 per cent.

TABLE 1.2: UNION MEMBERSHIP AND DENSITY BY SEX IN GREAT BRITAIN: SELECTED YEARS, 1896–1979

	MALE			FEMALE			TOTAL			Female Union Density/ Male Union Density (%)
	Union Membership (000s)	Potential Union Membership (000s)	Union Density (%)	Union Membership (000s)	Potential Union Membership (000s)	Union Density (%)	Union Membership (000s)	Potential Union Membership (000s)	Union Density (%)	
1896	1,356	9,652	14·0	116	4,230	2·7	1,471	13,882	10·6	19·3
1910	2,330	11,326	20·6	275	4,935	5·6	2,605	16,261	16·0	27·2
1911	2,799	11,436	24·5	331	5,002	6·6	3,129	16,438	19·0	26·9
1920	6,937	11,891	58·3	1,316	5,227	25·2	8,253	17,118	48·2	43·2
1933	3,637	13,040	27·9	713	5,915	12·1	4,350	18,955	22·9	43·4
1948	7,468	13,485	55·4	1,650	6,785	24·3	9,118	20,270	45·0	43·9
1965	7,610	14,777	51·5	2,132	8,119	26·3	9,742	22,895	42·6	51·1
1968	7,428	14,452	51·4	2,265	8,251	27·5	9,693	22,703	42·7	53·5
1970	7,994	14,177	56·4	2,634	8,363	31·5	10,628	22,540	47·2	55·9
1973	8,036	13,945	57·6	2,899	8,790	33·0	10,935	22,734	48·1	57·3
1974	8,151	13,809	59·0	3,062	9,010	34·0	11,213	22,820	49·1	57·6
1975	8,272	13,920	59·4	3,329	9,122	36·5	11,601	23,042	50·3	61·4
1976	8,492	14,069	60·4	3,462	9,257	37·4	11,954	23,326	51·2	61·9
1977	8,675	14,085	61·6	3,608	9,431	38·3	12,283	23,516	52·2	62·2
1978	8,940	14,074	63·5	3,639	9,561	38·1	12,579	23,635	53·2	60·0
1979	8,866	13,979	63·4	3,837	9,708	39·5	12,702	23,687	53·6	62·3

Source: Price and Bain (1983: table 3).

Note: This and all subsequent tables in this chapter refer to Great Britain rather than the United Kingdom; in other words, they exclude Northern Ireland. As can be seen by comparing Tables 1.1 and 1.2, union density is slightly higher in Northern Ireland, and hence in the United Kingdom, than in Great Britain.

Male and Female Unionisation

The increase in the extent of female participation in the labour force since the end of World War II is reflected in a substantial increase in female potential union membership. The data in Table 1.2 indicate that female potential membership increased from 6·8 million or 33·5 per cent of total potential membership in 1948, to 8·3 million or 36·3 per cent in 1968, and to 9·7 million or 41·0 per cent by 1979. In contrast, male potential union membership was less, both relatively and absolutely, in 1979 than in 1968, having reached a peak in 1965; in other words, female workers accounted for the entire increase in total potential union membership between 1965 and 1979.

Actual union membership among women increased even more rapidly than potential union membership, with the result that female union density increased from 24·3 per cent in 1948, to 27·5 per cent by 1968, and to 39·5 per cent by 1979. Male union density declined from 55·4 per cent in 1948, to 51·4 per cent by 1968, but then rose to 63·4 per cent by 1979. Although union density increased by about 12 percentage points among both sexes between 1969 and 1979, the proportional increase was much greater among women than men. Nevertheless, union density among women is still only about 60 per cent of that among men. Although the levels of unionisation among men and women differ considerably, there are many similarities in the way in which union growth among these two groups fluctuates over time; one indication of these similarities is the close correlation ($r = +0·93$) between the male and female union membership series over the years 1896 to 1979.

White-Collar and Manual Unionisation

As can be seen from Table 1.3, the potential union membership of manual workers has declined more or less continuously since 1931—being less in 1979 than it was in 1911—whereas white-collar potential membership has been growing rapidly throughout the twentieth century. As a result the white-collar share of potential membership has increased from about 20 per cent in 1911, to 25 per cent by 1931, to 31 per cent by 1948, and to 49 per cent by 1979. Although the rate of transfer from manual to white-collar employment began to slow down during the 1970s, the white-collar share of potential union membership has already passed the 50 per cent mark and will continue to increase throughout the 1980s (Institute for Employment Research, 1982:71).

During the period 1949–68 actual membership among manual workers declined more rapidly than potential membership, whereas among white-collar workers potential membership grew more rapidly than actual membership; hence union density declined slightly among both groups during this period. In contrast, in the period 1969–79 union density

TABLE 1.3: MANUAL AND WHITE-COLLAR UNION MEMBERSHIP AND DENSITY IN GREAT BRITAIN: SELECTED YEARS, 1911–1979

	MANUAL			WHITE-COLLAR			White-collar Union Density/ Manual Union Density (%)
	Union Membership (000s)	Potential Union Membership (000s)	Union Density (%)	Union Membership (000s)	Potential Union Membership (000s)	Union Density (%)	
1911	2,730·9	13,141	20·8	398·3	3,297	12·1	58·2
1920	7,124·1	13,271	53·7	1,129·2	3,847	29·4	54·7
1931	3,544·0	14,157	25·0	1,025·4	4,639	22·1	88·4
1948	7,055·7	14,027	50·3	2,062·1	6,243	33·0	65·6
1968	6,636·9	13,322	49·8	3,056·0	9,381	32·6	65·5
1970	7,095·0	12,852	55·2	3,533·0	9,688	36·5	66·1
1973	6,968·9	12,468	55·9	3,966·3	10,266	38·6	69·1
1974	7,082·3	12,362	57·3	4,130·8	10,458	39·5	68·9
1975	7,112·1	12,327	57·7	4,488·8	10,715	41·9	72·6
1976	7,321·6	12,322	59·4	4,632·3	11,004	42·1	70·9
1977	7,445·3	12,265	60·7	4,837·9	11,251	43·0	70·8
1978	7,549·7	12,168	62·0	5,029·1	11,467	43·9	70·8
1979	7,577·5	12,035	63·0	5,124·7	11,652	44·0	69·8

Source: Price and Bain (1983: table 4).
Note: The following occupational groups have been defined as white-collar: foremen, overlookers, and supervisors; scientists, technologists, and technicians; clerical and administrative workers; security personnel, including the police; professional workers; salesmen, shop assistants, and commercial travellers; government administrators and executive officials; and 'creative' occupations such as artists, musicians and entertainers.

increased dramatically among both groups: from 49·8 to 63·0 per cent among manual workers and from 32·6 to 44 per cent among white-collar workers. The rapid increase in union membership among white-collar workers was particularly remarkable: they accounted for slightly more than two-thirds of total union growth during this period, and this meant that by 1979 they constituted about 40 per cent of total union membership in Britain compared with 32 per cent in 1968 and 23 per cent in 1948. In spite of this rapid growth of unionism white-collar workers are still not so well unionised as manual workers: in 1979 white-collar union density was about 70 per cent of manual union density. But, as in the case of male and female unionism, there are many similarities in the way in which union membership among white-collar and manual workers fluctuates over time ($r = +0·86$ over the years 1892–1979).

In 1964 there were forty-three purely white-collar unions and nineteen partially white-collar unions, with a white-collar membership of about 1,711,000 affiliated to the TUC; thus about 65 per cent of all white-collar trade unionists were in unions affiliated to the TUC and they represented about 20 per cent of the TUC's total membership in 1961. In 1979 there were forty-one purely white-collar unions and twenty partially white-collar unions, with a white-collar membership of about 4,366,000 affiliated to the TUC; thus in this year 85 per cent of all white-collar trade unionists were in unions affiliated to the TUC and they represented about 36 per cent of the TUC's total membership. In 1964 about 33 per cent of white-collar trade unionists belonged to unions which were affiliated to the Labour Party; by 1979 this figure had increased to about 40 per cent.

Unionisation by Sector and Industry

Table 1.4 describes the pattern of union growth across five major sectors of the British economy since 1948. It reveals that union density decreased during the period 1949–68 and increased during the period 1969–79 in all these sectors except agriculture, forestry, and fishing where, in contrast, it increased in the first period and decreased in the second. A striking feature of the later period is the concentration of union growth in the already well unionised manufacturing and public sectors; they accounted for about 85 per cent of the increase in total union membership during the years 1969–79. The poorly unionised sectors showed little sign of producing a significant expansion of the base of unionisation in Britain in this period; in particular, although union membership in private services increased by close to 60 per cent during 1969–79, its level of union density increased by only 4 percentage points to 16·7 per cent, a level only about 2 percentage points higher than that prevailing in 1948. In 1979 the poorly unionised sectors—agriculture, construction, and private services—accounted for approximately 40 per cent of union potential but for only 15 per cent of union members.

Two features of union growth in manufacturing during the period

TABLE 1.4: UNION MEMBERSHIP AND DENSITY BY SECTOR IN GREAT BRITAIN, 1948–1979

	1948			1968			1979		
	Union Membership (000s)	Potential Union Membership (000s)	Union Density (%)	Union Membership (000s)	Potential Union Membership (000s)	Union Density (%)	Union Membership (000s)	Potential Union Membership (000s)	Union Density (%)
Public sector[a]	3,278·5	4,637·4	70·7	3,661·0	5,536·9	66·1	5,189·9	6,297·2	82·4
Manufacturing[b]	3,720·1	7,290·4	51·0	4,138·4	8,285·9	49·9	5,157·4	7,385·8	69·8
Manual	3,566·5	6,123·9	58·2	3,808·1	6,139·9	62·0	4,234·6	5,273·5	80·3
White-collar	153·6	1,166·5	13·2	330·3	2,146·0	15·4	922·8	2,112·3	43·7
Construction	611·2	1,325·8	46·1	472·0	1,570·7	30·1	519·7	1,415·2	36·7
Agriculture, forestry, and fishing	224·4	988·9	22·7	131·1	516·8	25·4	85·8	378·3	22·7
Private services[c]	664·8	4,578·4	14·5	767·5	6,042·0	12·7	1,214·5	7,283·6	16·7

Source: Price and Bain (1983: table 5).

Notes: Road transport and sea transport are not included in any of the sectors. See Table 1.5 below for data on these industries.
[a] Comprises national government; local government and education; health services; post and telecommunications; air transport; port and inland water transport; railways; gas, electricity and water; and coal mining. The nationalised iron and steel industry is included in manufacturing.
[b] Manufacturing includes the first sixteen industries listed in Table 1.5 plus other mining and quarrying.
[c] Comprises insurance, banking, and finance; entertainment; distribution; and miscellaneous services.

1969–79 are particularly noteworthy. First, potential union membership declined, particularly among manual workers, but even slightly among white-collar workers. Second, union density increased dramatically among white-collar workers: from 15·4 per cent in 1968 to 43·7 per cent by 1979.

Table 1.5 extends the analysis by giving the level of union membership and density by industry for 1948, 1968, and 1979. As can readily be seen, the level of union density varies greatly between industries: for example, in 1979 union density was 99·9 per cent in post and telecommunications, 79·6 per cent in metals and engineering, 65·3 per cent in glass, 36·7 per cent in construction, 14·9 per cent in distribution, and 7·3 per cent in miscellaneous services. But the rank order of each industry in terms of its level of union density has remained fairly stable over the years: the rank correlation coefficient for the thirty-seven industries listed in Table 1.5 is +0·8 between 1948 and 1979.

In spite of this stability, union membership and density in each industry tend to vary over time. During the period 1949–68, nineteen of the thirty-seven industries listed in Table 1.5 registered a decrease in union density; in contrast, during the period 1969–79 all but four of the thirty-seven industries recorded an increase in union density. The density level was above 75 per cent in eighteen industries in 1979 compared with ten in 1968 and eight in 1948; whereas the density level was below 30 per cent in five industries in 1979 compared with six in 1968 and three in 1948.

DETERMINANTS OF UNION GROWTH

The questions raised by data on union growth, though numerous, are broadly of two kinds. First, what factors account for variations in the rate of change of unionisation from one year to the next or, more generally, from one period to another? Second, what factors account for variations at any particular moment in the level of unionisation between different groups, occupations, sectors, and industries? The following discussion attempts to answer both types of question. In particular, why did union density decline, slowly and slightly, in the twenty years before 1968 and, swiftly and sharply, after 1979? In contrast, why did union density increase markedly not only in aggregate but also among males, females, manual workers, white-collar workers, and in almost every industry in the period 1969–79? And why was the level of union density in, for example, 1979, higher among men than women, among manual than white-collar workers, in the public than the private sector of the economy, and in some industries than others?

These questions are not approached with a *tabula rasa*. The literature on union growth has listed most of the possible determinants of unionisation. For the purposes of the following discussion, they can be conveniently grouped under six headings: the composition of potential union membership, the business cycle, employer policies and government action with respect to union recognition, personal and job-related characteristics, industrial structure, and union leadership.

Composition of Potential Union Membership

Since the level of union density is higher among men than women and among manual than white-collar workers, changes in the relative share of potential union membership held by each of these groups affect the level of aggregate union growth for purely arithmetical reasons. Similarly, changes in the industrial distribution of potential union membership can affect aggregate union growth. For example, between 1948 and 1979 the share of potential union membership taken by the eighteen industries in Table 1.5 with a density level above 75 per cent in 1979 decreased from about 47 per cent to 43 per cent, whereas in the same period the five industries with a density level below 29 per cent in 1979 increased their share of potential union membership from about 26 per cent to 30 per cent. In short, the industrial tide was running against the trade union movement between 1948 and 1979 and this worked to undermine aggregate union membership and density.

One way to assess the impact of changes in the composition of potential union membership upon union growth is to measure how much larger aggregate union density would have been if these changes had not occurred (see Price and Bain, 1983). If the female share of potential union membership had remained constant since 1948, then total union density would have been higher by 0·7 percentage points in 1968 and by 1·8 percentage points in 1979; if the white-collar share of potential union membership had remained constant since 1948, then total union density would have been higher by 1·8 percentage points in 1968 and by 3·6 percentage points in 1979; and if the industrial distribution of potential union membership had remained constant since 1948, then total union density would have been higher by 2·4 percentage points in 1968 and by 3·7 percentage points in 1979. Since changes in the sexual, occupational, and industrial composition of potential union membership are interrelated, the separate effect of each of these changes cannot simply be added together to obtain the total impact of the changing composition of potential union membership upon aggregate union growth. Nevertheless, the figures indicate that all three effects worked against the maintenance of aggregate union density; indeed, whereas the negative impact of the industrial effect was about the same throughout the whole of the period 1949–79, that of the sexual and occupational effects was greater in 1969–79 than in 1949–68.

The negative effects of these changes in the composition of potential union membership are probably sufficient in themselves to account for the slight downward trend in aggregate union density during the years 1949–68. By their very nature, however, they do not vary sufficiently to account for the year-to-year movements around the trend in union growth

TABLE 1.5: UNION MEMBERSHIP AND DENSITY BY INDUSTRY IN GREAT BRITAIN, 1948, 1968, AND 1979

	1948			1968			1979			Change 1949–1968			Change 1969–1979		
	U.M. (000s)	P.U.M. (000s)	U.D. (%)	U.M. (000s)	P.U.M. (000s)	U.D. (%)	U.M. (000s)	P.U.M. (000s)	U.D. (%)	U.M. (000s)	P.U.M. (000s)	U.D. (%)	U.M. (000s)	P.U.M. (000s)	U.D. (%)
Food & drink	247·2	575·3	43·0	252·0	729·3	34·6	444·3	685·4	64·8	+ 4·8	+154·0	− 8·4	+192·3	− 43·9	+30·2
Tobacco	26·1	43·7	59·7	26·7	34·7	76·9	30·0	31·3	95·8	+ 0·6	− 9·0	+17·2	+ 3·3	− 3·4	+18·9
Chemicals	141·5	401·0	35·3	186·9	474·6	39·4	288·6	490·5	58·8	+ 45·4	+ 73·6	+ 4·1	+101·7	+ 15·9	+19·4
Metals & engineering	1,913·7	3,514·4	54·5	2,410·4	4,249·8	56·7	3,033·9	3,809·4	79·6	+496·7	+735·4	+ 2·2	+623·5	−440·4	+22·9
Cotton & man-made fibres	274·3	350·1	78·3	146·3	180·6	81·0	112·1	114·1	98·2	−128·0	−169·5	+ 2·7	− 34·2	− 66·5	+17·2
Other textiles	201·3	511·8	39·3	165·6	478·1	34·6	170·5	359·9	47·4	− 35·7	− 33·7	− 4·7	+ 4·9	−118·2	+12·8
Leather, leather goods, & fur	23·5	71·6	32·8	14·8	52·1	28·4	11·6	41·0	28·3	− 8·7	− 19·5	− 4·4	− 3·2	− 11·1	− 0·1
Clothing	146·0	387·2	37·7	119·7	359·6	33·3	127·7	307·2	41·6	− 26·3	− 27·6	− 4·4	+ 8·0	− 52·4	+ 8·3
Footwear	92·8	120·0	77·3	75·6	106·4	71·1	65·2	80·3	81·2	− 17·2	− 13·6	− 6·2	− 10·4	− 26·1	+10·1
Brick & building materials	58·4	164·4	35·5	56·1	194·3	28·9	83·5	133·5	62·5	− 2·3	+ 29·9	− 6·6	+ 27·4	− 60·8	+33·6
Pottery	44·0	71·5	61·5	41·1	57·0	72·1	43·1	59·9	72·0	− 2·9	− 14·5	+10·6	+ 2·0	+ 2·9	− 0·1
Glass	29·8	66·7	44·7	40·2	76·7	52·4	46·6	71·4	65·3	+ 10·4	+ 10·0	+ 7·7	+ 6·4	− 5·3	+12·9
Timber & furniture	122·2	273·0	44·8	95·3	294·9	32·3	92·6	266·5	34·7	− 26·9	+ 21·9	−12·5	− 2·7	− 28·4	+ 2·4
Paper & board	60·8	163·9	37·1	98·4	244·0	40·3	116·2	205·3	56·6	+ 37·6	+ 80·1	+ 3·2	+ 17·8	− 38·7	+16·3
Printing & publishing	206·7	272·8	75·8	292·2	368·4	79·3	326·0	347·7	93·8	+ 85·5	+ 95·6	+ 3·5	+ 33·8	− 20·7	+14·5
Other manufacturing	89·6	228·8	39·2	95·7	331·2	28·9	143·0	330·4	43·3	+ 6·1	+102·4	−10·3	+ 47·3	− 0·8	+14·4
Coal mining	691·4	800·1	86·4	398·9	443·8	89·9	297·6	306·6	97·1	−292·5	−356·3	+ 3·5	−101·3	−137·2	+ 7·2
Other mining & quarrying	42·2	74·2	56·9	21·4	54·2	39·5	22·5	52·0	43·3	− 20·8	− 20·0	−17·4	+ 1·1	− 2·2	+ 3·8
Gas	101·1	137·6	73·5	90·5	129·5	69·9	95·5	105·8	90·3	− 10·6	− 8·1	− 3·6	+ 5·0	− 23·7	+20·4
Electricity	101·0	157·4	64·2	181·5	242·3	74·9	178·3	179·9	99·1	+ 80·5	+ 84·9	+10·7	− 3·2	− 62·4	+24·2
Water	16·7	29·3	57·0	33·5	47·5	70·5	61·4	66·2	92·7	+ 16·8	+ 18·2	+13·5	+ 27·9	+ 18·7	+22·2
Construction	611·2	1,325·8	46·1	472·0	1,570·7	30·1	519·7	1,415·2	36·7	−139·2	+244·9	−16·0	+ 47·7	−155·5	+ 6·6
Distribution	325·8	2,089·1	15·6	294·5	2,762·9	10·7	428·3	2,872·2	14·9	− 31·3	+673·8	− 4·9	+133·8	+109·3	+ 4·2

	1948 U.M. (000s)	1948 P.U.M. (000s)	1948 U.D. (%)	1968 U.M. (000s)	1968 P.U.M. (000s)	1968 U.D. (%)	1979 U.M. (000s)	1979 P.U.M. (000s)	1979 U.D. (%)	Change 1949–1968 U.M. (000s)	Change 1949–1968 P.U.M. (000s)	Change 1949–1968 U.D. (%)	Change 1969–1979 U.M. (000s)	Change 1969–1979 P.U.M. (000s)	Change 1969–1979 U.D. (%)
National government	375·3	709·1	52·9	457·1	602·7	75·8	583·8	639·5	91·3	+ 81·8	−106·4	+22·9	+126·7	+ 36·8	+15·5
Local government & education	860·9	1,241·2	69·4	1,366·8	2,221·2	61·5	2,232·0	2,879·9	77·5	+505·9	+980·0	− 7·9	+865·2	+658·7	+16·0
Health services	222·5	521·9	42·6	369·8	976·3	37·9	971·2	1,317·9	73·7	+147·3	+454·4	− 4·7	+601·4	+341·6	+35·8
Post & telecommunications	283·1	324·1	87·3	400·6	408·5	98·1	427·6	428·1	99·9	+117·5	+ 84·4	+10·8	+ 27·0	+ 19·6	+ 1·8
Railways	474·6	535·3	88·7	228·9	274·5	83·4	204·2	208·9	97·8	−245·7	−260·8	− 5·3	− 24·7	− 65·6	+14·4
Road transport[a]	481·8	520·3	92·6	432·6	521·0	83·0	451·0	449·6	100·3	− 49·2	+ 0·7	− 9·6	+ 18·4	− 71·4	+17·3
Sea transport	112·7	150·5	74·9	90·4	101·4	89·2	83·8	87·2	96·1	− 22·3	− 49·1	+14·3	− 6·6	− 14·2	+ 6·9
Port & inland water transport	140·0	150·7	92·9	92·3	128·1	72·1	59·8	71·9	83·2	− 47·7	− 22·6	−20·8	− 32·5	− 56·2	+11·1
Air transport	11·9	30·7	38·8	41·1	62·5	65·8	78·5	92·5	84·9	+ 29·2	+ 31·8	+27·0	+ 37·4	− 30·0	+19·1
Insurance, banking, & finance	137·1	352·3	38·9	250·3	583·0	42·9	395·3	720·9	54·8	+113·2	+230·7	+ 4·0	+145·0	+137·9	+11·9
Entertainment[b]	96·4	135·6	71·1	97·7	113·7	85·9	128·7	114·8	112·1	+ 1·3	− 21·9	+14·8	+ 31·0	+ 1·1	+26·2
Fishing	11·0	23·0	47·8	5·7	13·1	43·5	2·3	11·2	20·5	− 5·3	− 9·9	− 4·3	− 3·4	− 1·9	−23·0
Agriculture, horticulture, & forestry	213·4	965·9	22·1	125·4	503·7	24·9	83·5	367·1	22·7	− 88·0	−462·2	+ 2·8	− 41·9	−136·6	− 2·2
Miscellaneous services	105·5	2,001·4	5·3	125·0	2,582·4	4·8	262·2	3,575·7	7·3	+ 19·5	+581·0	− 0·5	+137·2	+993·3	+ 2·5

Source: Price and Bain (1983: table 6).

Notes:

[a] The union membership and union density data for this industry are considerably overstated. The potential union membership data include only those employed in road haulage firms. But the union membership data include the entire membership of the commercial road transport group of the Transport and General Workers' Union, which contains not only workers employed in road haulage firms but also employees engaged in driving duties within firms in manufacturing and other sectors of the economy (e.g. in engineering and distribution).

[b] The union membership and union density data for this industry are also considerably overstated. The pre-entry closed shop is widespread in this industry, and a large number of persons who are primarily employed elsewhere belong to entertainment unions so that they can seek employment within this industry.

during this period. And since these negative effects persisted and, in most respects, were accentuated after 1968, there is a need to explain why union density nevertheless increased markedly during the next eleven years and then in 1980 began just as markedly to decline. To begin to answer these questions the focus of the analysis must turn to the business cycle and, in particular, to such components of the cycle as retail prices, wages, and unemployment.

The Business Cycle

An increase in the rate of change of retail prices is likely to encourage workers to become and to remain union members because of the threat which it poses to their standards of living. If workers think in real as distinct from money terms, however, they will not perceive their standards of living being threatened by rising prices if money earnings are rising even faster. Hence the relationship between prices and earnings is also likely to be important. But regardless of what is happening to prices, an increase in the rate of change of money earnings may encourage workers to unionise, for they may credit such an increase to the efforts of unions and become or remain union members in the hope of doing as well or even better in the future (Bain and Elsheikh, 1976:62–5).

The 'threat' and 'credit' effects associated with rising prices and earnings provide a good deal of the explanation for the contrasting experience of union growth between 1949–68 and 1969–79. As Price and Bain (1983: table 7) have demonstrated, the behaviour of prices and wages also contrasts sharply between the two periods: both rose slowly in the first period and rapidly in the second. Moreover, although increases in earnings generally exceeded increases in prices in both periods, the gap between them narrowed considerably during the later period; in other words real earnings increased much more slowly during 1969–79, and, in some years during the last half of this period, they actually declined as prices increased faster than earnings. White-collar workers were particularly hard hit. Whereas increases in white-collar earnings generally kept up with and even exceeded increases in manual earnings prior to 1968, the reverse was true during 1969 to 1979. The white-collar/manual earnings differential was severely squeezed—primarily as a result of the flat-rate characteristics of a series of incomes policies—and a non-indexed, progressive tax system produced 'fiscal drag' and a 'wage-tax spiral' which caused an even greater erosion of real disposable income during 1969–79, particularly for higher-paid white-collar workers (Wilkinson and Turner, 1972; Taylor, 1980:38). Hence there can be little doubt that the behaviour of prices and earnings during the period 1969–79 encouraged large numbers of workers, particularly those in white-collar jobs, to unionise in an attempt to defend or to improve their standards of living. By the same logic, union density stagnated and declined in the period 1949–68 because the relative stability of earnings and prices meant that the positive impact of the 'threat' and 'credit' effects was not sufficiently large to counteract the negative impact of the changing composition of potential union membership.

The impact of unemployment upon union growth is less clear cut than that of prices and earnings. There are several reasons for expecting unemployment to have a negative impact upon union growth. Unemployed workers may have little incentive to become or to remain members because there is usually little that a union can do to get them employment; also, the benefits of collective bargaining have little relevance for them, and the cost of union subscriptions is greater in relation to income. Moreover, when unemployment is high or increasing, employers may be more able and willing to oppose unionism; for in so far as unemployment reduces the level of aggregate demand, production lost as a result of strikes and other forms of industrial action will be less costly to employers. And if they wish to maintain production in the face of industrial action they can more easily do so by recruiting an alternative labour force from among the unemployed. Indeed workers who are not unemployed may be reluctant to join unions in periods of high unemployment for fear of antagonizing their employers and thereby losing jobs which are in short supply. Finally, inasmuch as unemployment reduces the ability of unions to win collective bargaining advances, the benefits of membership are reduced even for members who are not unemployed, and some of them may come to feel that union membership is no longer worthwhile.

But there are contrary forces which may reduce the negative impact of unemployment on union growth. Some unemployed members may for social and political reasons be reluctant to cut their links with the union movement and, since many unions waive or at least reduce subscriptions for unemployed members, it often costs them little, if anything, to maintain their membership. There may also be economic reasons for workers, especially those in skilled trades, to remain union members when unemployed: they may obtain unemployment benefit, maintain their eligibility for other union 'friendly benefits', receive information about job openings, and acquire access to those which exist in closed trades. More generally, and probably of greater importance, as Hawkins (1981:84–5) has argued, the threat, as distinct from the experience, of unemployment may encourage employees to join a union for 'basic self-protection' in case they are faced with redundancy.

Given the conflicting influences which unemployment may produce, its overall impact upon union growth is difficult to predict. But it is probable that when the level of unemployment is low and changes in its level are small, it will have little impact one way or the other upon union growth, because its positive and negative effects are likely to be small and to cancel each other out. Another reason for expecting an insignificant relationship when unemployment is low is that most unions permit members to be in arrears for several months before dropping them from membership; hence, except in periods of severe recession, most unemployed members are likely to be re-employed within this period and to be back in 'good standing' before their membership has lapsed. When the level of unemployment is high and changes in its level are large, however, it is likely to have a significant negative impact upon union growth, primarily because unemployed non-members will have little incentive to join unions and unemployed members will have little incentive to remain in unions as their attachment to the labour force is broken and they endure long spells out of work.

The evidence is consistent with this reasoning (see Price and Bain, 1983: table 7). During the period 1949–68, when the annual average level of unemployment was 1·9 per cent and the changes in its level varied from −0·9 to +0·9 percentage points, it appears not to have influenced union growth; as already indicated, union density stagnated and declined during this period, and this is adequately accounted for by the relative stability of earnings and prices and by unfavourable changes in the composition of potential union membership. Even during the period 1969–79, when the annual average level of unemployment was 4·1 per cent and the changes in its level varied from −1·1 to +1·6 percentage points, it appears to have had little influence upon union growth; at most it may have slightly dampened the growth-inducing effects of the accelerating pace of price and wage inflation during this period (Price and Bain, 1983). Unemployment appears to have had no significant impact upon union growth in the post-war period until 1980, since when its magnitude has increased substantially. Unemployment increased by 1·7 percentage points to 7·4 per cent in 1980 and by 3·9 percentage points to 11·3 per cent in 1981 and, in spite of large increases in earnings and prices in 1980 and, to a lesser extent, in 1981, union membership and density declined sharply in both years. There can be little doubt that unemployment is the major reason for this decline.

Employer Policies and Government Action

Economic factors are clearly critical in determining whether workers decide to become and to remain union members. But how workers decide these questions will also be significantly influenced by the attitudes and behaviour of employers. The greater the degree of recognition which employers confer upon unions the less likely employees are to jeopardise their jobs and career prospects by being union members, the more easily they can reconcile union membership with their 'loyalty' to the company, and, most important, the more effectively unions can participate in the process of job regulation and thereby offer employees services and benefits which will encourage them to become and to remain union members (Bain, 1970: 122–3; CIR 1974c:68). In short, the greater the degree of union recognition the more likely workers are to join unions and to remain in them. Union recognition and union growth are mutually dependent, however, because the degree to which employers are prepared to recognise unions is at least partly dependent upon their membership strength. Hence union recognition and union growth combine together in a 'virtuous circle' of cause and effect in which the more unions obtain recognition and succeed in participating in job regulation the more they are likely to grow, and the more they grow the more they are likely to increase their recognition and deepen their participation in job regulation.

One of the factors which affects the willingness and ability of employers to resist union organisation and participation in job regulation—the extent of unemployment—has already been mentioned, and other factors will be referred to later in this chapter. But one factor—the government's role in promoting union recognition—needs to be dealt with here because it is important in accounting for the pattern of aggregate union growth in Britain since 1948. In World War II, as in World War I, the government fostered union growth by introducing policies which, directly and indirectly, tended to neutralise or at least contain employer opposition to unions (Bain, 1970: ch. 9). In the years following the end of World War II public support for union recognition and the extension of collective bargaining became much weaker. But the publication of the report of the Donovan Commission, the White Paper *In Place of Strife*, and the Labour Government's Industrial Relations Bill in 1968–9 greatly improved the climate for union recognition. All these documents affirmed the principles of freedom of association and union recognition, and the Commission on Industrial Relations, established in 1969, strongly reaffirmed these principles in a series of reports recommending the recognition of unions and the development of collective bargaining. Many of the Commission's recommendations were ignored by the firms to which they were directed (James, 1977), but its reports nevertheless had a significant impact upon union growth by encouraging employers and managers to attach more importance to industrial relations principles and procedures and to view the growth of union organisation among virtually all levels of employees as, if not desirable, at least inevitable. As a result, many employers recognised trade unions as part of a more general restructuring of industrial relations within their firms and industries.

With the defeat of the Labour Government in 1970 and the passage of the Industrial Relations Act in 1971, the climate for union recognition became less favourable. Although the Act provided a mechanism by which unions could obtain recognition from recalcitrant employers, only registered unions could make use of this mechanism and most TUC unions decided not to seek registration. Moreover the whole tenor of the legislation was restrictive rather then permissive. At no point did the Act or its accompanying Code of Practice stress the desirability of extending union recognition. Thus union growth received little help from the Industrial Relations Act (see Price and Bain, 1976:352–3), and it expanded less rapidly in 1971–3 than in 1969–70 and 1974–9.

The legislative framework for union recognition became more favourable again after the return of a Labour government in 1974 and the consequent repeal of the Industrial Relations Act and the passage of the Employment Protection Act in 1975. The new Act provided both voluntary and statutory procedures for promoting union recognition, and by 1979 these had directly extended collective bargaining in one way or another to approximately 133,000 employees (Price and Bain, 1983). In addition, as the Advisory, Conciliation and Arbitration Service (1981a:100–2) has pointed out, the Act indirectly promoted union growth and extended collective bargaining by making employees more aware of the feasibility of collective representation and by encouraging employers to recognise unions voluntarily in order to obtain orderly bargaining structures and to avoid the public scrutiny which would result from a reference under the statutory procedure.

This procedure was increasingly undermined after 1977 by a series of unfavourable legal decisions (see Lewis and Simpson, 1981:140–7), and in 1980 it was abolished by the newly elected Conservative Government. But the Employment Protection Act had other sections which indirectly promoted union growth. Its provisions for time off work for carrying out trade union duties and training, for facilities for union lay officers, and for disclosure of information by employers encouraged union growth, particularly in areas where unions were already recognised, by strengthening their organisation at the workplace and increasing their depth of participation in job regulation. The provisions of the Health and Safety at Work Act 1974 providing for health and safety representatives had a similar effect. So did those provisions of the Trade Union and Labour Relations Act 1974 which, by removing the legal restrictions the Industrial Relations Act had placed on the closed shop, made possible a large increase in the number of formal union membership agreements, thereby helping to extend the closed shop among both white-collar and manual workers in both the public and private sectors of the economy (Brown, 1981:54–9; Gennard et al., 1980:16–22).

Nor were these the only pieces of legislation which promoted union growth by strengthening union organisation at the workplace and increasing the depth of union participation in job regulation. Virtually all of the much-increased volume of government intervention into industrial relations in Britain throughout the whole of the period 1969–79 tended to have this effect. It did so—as is demonstrated elsewhere in this book, particularly in Chapters 3, 4, 6, and 7—by directly and indirectly encouraging employers in both the public and private sectors to adopt a more professional approach to industrial relations. Among other things this involved them in placing greater emphasis on collective bargaining as the preferred method of job regulation, reforming and formalising bargaining structures and procedures, and underpinning these with greater union stability and security by supporting the spread of shop steward organisation and facilities, the check off, the closed shop, and other union membership arrangements. These processes were further encouraged in the private sector by the steady increase in the size of enterprises, and in the public sector by the reorganisation of the health service and local government, and by an increased emphasis on productivity and efficient manpower utilisation.

The above discussion leads to the conclusion that the impact of government action upon union growth during the period 1969–79 arose not only from public policies which were expressly designed to extend union recognition into areas where it was previously absent but also from public policies which, by encouraging employers along the path of reforming, formalising, and consolidating collective bargaining, helped to strengthen union organisation at the workplace and to increase the depth of union participation in job regulation in areas where union recognition had been conceded many years earlier. The data presented above in Tables 1.4 and 1.5 support this conclusion. Even allowing for the general framework of white-collar union recognition which had existed in engineering and newspaper publishing for many years before 1969–79 (Bain, 1967:31–73), the size of the increase in union membership and density among white-collar workers in manufacturing industries generally during this period suggests that unions must have expanded considerably in areas where they had previously lacked recognition and strength. A similar conclusion is suggested by the substantial increases in union membership and density among both white-collar and manual workers in such industries as food and drink, chemicals, and, to a lesser extent, insurance, banking, and finance. But about 50 per cent of the increase in union membership during this period occurred in the public sector—especially in health services and local government and education which between them added almost 1½ million members to union ranks—where generally unions have been recognised for many years, and a further 20 per cent occurred in engineering and metals, where the recognition problem is confined primarily to small firms which are not members of the Engineering Employers Federation. Hence, although unions were successful during 1969–79 in extending their representative base into areas in which they were previously unrecognised and weak, most growth during this period resulted from unions 'topping up' membership in areas where they were already recognised and moderately well organised.

The data on the distribution of union growth during the period 1969–79 underline the duality which exists in the industrial pattern of unionisation in Britain—between the well organised sector of public services and manufacturing and the poorly organised sector of private services, construction, and agriculture—and, by so doing, point to the important interrelationship which exists between the economic and political determinants of union growth. In both sectors price and wage inflation provided a common backdrop to union growth: the erosion of real incomes encouraged workers to turn to unions, and the unions' apparent success in defending their members' economic interests reinforced this process. In the well organised sector, however, the unions were sufficiently well established to take advantage of the benefits offered by public policy, and, in doing so, they were frequently able to obtain the support of professional and relatively sophisticated personnel managers who seemed, in the context of the reforming and restructuring of collective bargaining which was going on in the 1970s, to have taken to heart Flanders's well known aphorism that they could 'only regain control by sharing it' (1967:32). In contrast, in the poorly organised sector there was much less scope for building upon existing union organisation and recognition. Moreover employer policies, relatively untouched by the new 'professionalism' and usually unchallenged by workers, remained generally hostile to collective bargaining, and public support for union recognition was not sufficiently strong to overcome them. In short, in the well organised sector economic factors, employer policies, and public support for union recognition combined to produce a major expansion and consolidation of union membership and organisation. In the poorly organised sector neither economic factors nor public support for union recognition were felt sufficiently strongly to overcome an environment which was generally hostile to unionism; put simply, union density in this sector was below the level at which a 'virtuous circle' between union growth and union recognition could begin.

This conclusion raises the question of why some sectors and industries are more highly unionised than others. Greater public support for union recognition of the type discussed above tends to apply across all industries, and hence does not help to account for differences in unionisation between industries. Similarly, an increase in the cost of living is a general factor which tends to be the same across industries. Earnings and unemployment do vary between industries, however, and, as Bain and Elsheikh (1979:148–50) have shown, these factors account for some of the variation in the inter-industry pattern of union growth. But most of the variation is explained by other factors.

Personal and Job-Related Characteristics

Several writers have suggested that the inter-industry pattern of union growth is significantly influenced by certain factors which are associated directly with individual workers and the jobs they hold. The factors mentioned include age, sex, part-time employment, labour turnover, and occupational status.

Age. Shister (1953:421–2) has claimed that younger workers are likely to show a greater propensity to unionise than older workers because, among other things, younger workers' shorter lengths of service will make them feel less 'loyalty' towards their employer, their greater mobility and relative lack of seniority and superannuation benefits will make employer victimisation for union activities less costly to them, and their generally higher level of education will make them more resentful of arbitrary treatment by employers. There are other reasons, however, for expecting the reverse relationship to hold: for example, older workers have fewer opportunities than younger workers to improve their terms and conditions of employment by changing jobs and, if they are in jobs in which productivity tends to decline with age, they may have more need of union protection as they get older. In any case, the level of unionisation is determined not only by the propensity to unionise but also by the opportunity, and, in general, older workers will have had more opportunities to join unions and unions will have had more opportunities to recruit them because they will have been in the labour force for a longer period than younger workers. Hence even if Shister is correct in asserting that younger workers have a greater propensity to unionise than older workers, the 'exposure effect' may result in a higher proportion of older workers actually being union members.

In fact empirical studies in the United States (e.g. Blinder, 1972; Moore and Newman, 1975) have found that older workers are more likely to be unionised than younger workers. Similarly, in Britain Bain and Elsheikh (1979:148) and Richardson and Catlin (1979:378–80) have shown that the higher the proportion of older workers in an industry the higher its level of unionisation. But more highly unionised industries may have a higher proportion of older workers because the benefits brought by unions reduce labour turnover. Moreover, many of the highly unionised industries are old and declining and have relatively few new entrants each year. Hence the direction of causation may run from unionisation to age rather than from age to unionisation and, as Richardson and Catlin point out, 'show more about the kind of industry that employs old workers than about the propensity of old workers to join unions'.

Sex. Many writers have argued that women have a lower propensity to unionise than men because of the nature of female employment: women do not participate continuously in the labour market because of marriage and family responsibilities, and they are often secondary earners whose pay is not the family's main source of income. This argument suggests that the higher the proportion of women and, in particular, married women in an industry the lower its level of unionisation is likely to be.

Bain and Elsheikh (1979) found little evidence to support this argument in an empirical study of the inter-industry pattern of unionisation in Britain, a finding confirmed by Richardson and Catlin (1979). Similarly, Bain (1970:40–3) found that the proportion of women in the labour force does not·exert a significant impact upon the inter-industry and inter-occupational patterns of white-collar unionism in manufacturing, a finding which agrees with that obtained in a later study of the inter-establishment pattern of unionisation in manufacturing (Elsheikh and Bain, 1980). But this same study indicated that the proportion of women does have a significant negative impact upon the inter-establishment pattern of unionisation among manual workers. The reason for this conflicting result is not clear, but it may be explained by the distribution of female employment: female manual workers are much less evenly spread across establishments than female white-collar workers, and the establishments in which female manual workers tend to be concentrated may have other characteristics, not controlled for in the study, which make them more difficult to unionise.

Be that as it may, differences in the way in which men and women are distributed across industries and occupations—differences which, as Chapter 13 points out, may partly result from discriminatory behaviour by employers and male-dominated unions—largely explain why women generally are not so highly unionised as men. The distribution of female employment is skewed to a greater extent than male employment in the direction of industries characterised by small establishments and of occupations characterised by small work groups, and these characteristics—which, as explained below, tend to inhibit unionisation—rather than any intrinsic characteristics peculiar to women account for their lower degree of unionisation. Similarly, changes in the distribution of female employment are largely responsible for the marked increase in female union membership and density during the period 1969–79. Almost 60 per cent of the increase in female potential membership in this period occurred in the public sector, and this sector contributed almost 50 per cent of the increase in total union membership and about 65 per cent of the increase in female union membership during 1969–79. Thus the factors which caused unionism to grow in this area—of which some have been discussed above and others will be discussed below—also account for a large part of the increase in female union membership and density during this period.

Part-time employment. This practice is closely associated with female employment and is rapidly growing (MSC, 1982:23–5). Work and such work-related matters as trade unionism are likely to be less central to the life interests of part-time workers than of full-time workers. Hence, other things being equal, the larger the proportion of part-time workers in an industry the lower its level of unionisation is likely to be.

But Bain and Elsheikh (1979) found that part-time employment is not a significant determinant of variations in the inter-industry pattern of unionisation in Britain, a finding confirmed by Richardson and Catlin (1979). The explanation for this lack of significance is provided by the way in which part-time employees are distributed across industries. Of the five industries with the highest proportion of part-time employees, only two—distribution and miscellaneous services—are poorly unionised; the other three—health services, local government and education, and entertainment—are well unionised. Distribution and miscellaneous services are poorly unionised not so much because of their high proportion of part-time employees as because they have other characteristics—in particular, a large number of small establishments—which are unfavourable to the organisation not only of part-time employees but also of full-time employees. Similarly, the other three industries are well unionised because they have characteristics—for example, public employers, large employing units, and widespread closed shops—which are favourable to organising not only full-time but also part-time employees. Indeed, as the success of such unions as the National Union of Public Employees in organising part-time employees in the health service and in local government and education demonstrates, where the characteristics of an industry enable a substantial degree of unionisation to be established among full-time employees, the organisation of the part-time employees is likely to follow fairly readily.

But in areas where these characteristics do not exist a large proportion of part-time employees is likely to impede unionisation. In a study of the inter-establishment pattern of unionisation in manufacturing, Elsheikh and Bain (1980) found that part-time employment had a significant negative impact upon white-collar unionism but not upon manual unionism. This difference probably occurs because union density is about half as great, whereas the proportion of part-time employment is about twice as great, among white-collar as among manual employees in manufacturing. Thus unions are much less able in white-collar than in manual areas in manufacturing to use prevailing social norms and closed-shop arrangements to persuade part-time employees to become and to remain members. Similar considerations apply in sectors such as distribution and miscellaneous services. Thus although the extent of part-time employment does not help to account for the variation in unionisation *between* industries, it may nevertheless be an important factor in explaining the low level of unionisation *within* a particular industry or occupation.

Labour turnover. A high degree of labour turnover is another factor which is closely associated with female employment, but is also characteristic of male employment in certain areas. The higher the degree of labour turnover among employees the more difficult and more costly will unions find them to recruit and to keep in membership. Moreover, many of the advantages of unionisation are only forthcoming after several years of continuous pressure upon employers, and hence workers may be reluctant to take the time and trouble to organise themselves into unions unless they expect to be employed in their present work long enough to enjoy these advantages. Indeed a high degree of labour turnover may indicate that workers are leaving unsatisfactory work as an alternative strategy to improving it through unionisation. Be that as it may, these arguments suggest that the higher the degree of labour turnover in an industry the lower its level of unionisation is likely to be.

Bain and Elsheikh (1979) found that labour turnover had a significant negative impact upon the inter-industry pattern of unionisation when considered by itself but not when the effect of other factors was controlled for, a finding which was confirmed by their inter-establishment study of manufacturing (Elsheikh and Bain, 1980). This result also appears to be explained by the way in which employment is distributed across industries. The industries in which employees have the highest degree of turnover—distribution, miscellaneous services, construction, timber and furniture, health services, and clothing—are with one exception—health services—

characterised by small establishment size and private ownership, whereas industries in which employees have the lowest degree of turnover—railways, water, port and inland water transport, coal mining, post and telecommunications, electricity, and air transport—are characterised by large employing units and public ownership (Bain and Elsheikh, 1981: tables XI and XVI). In short, although labour turnover appears to have a significant negative impact upon unionisation, it tends to be associated with other, more powerful factors which overshadow its effect.

Occupational status. Although craftsmen have historically been the vanguard of the trade union movement, the extent of skilled status among manual workers no longer has a significant impact upon either the inter-industry or the inter-establishment pattern of unionisation in Britain (Bain and Elsheikh, 1979; Elsheikh and Bain, 1980); the reason is that unskilled and semi-skilled workers now tend to be as well unionised as skilled workers. As Table 1.3 demonstrated, however, white-collar workers are generally less well unionised than manual workers, and, perhaps not surprisingly, the higher the proportion of white-collar workers in an industry or an establishment the lower its level of unionisation tends to be (Bain and Elsheikh, 1979; Elsheikh and Bain, 1980).

The question arises, however, as to why white-collar workers are generally less well unionised than manual workers. The answer most often advanced is that the different social positions which the two groups hold in the system of social stratification produce different ideologies: manual workers have an ideology which is favourable to trade unionism in that it stresses conflict and collectivism, whereas white-collar workers have an ideology which is inimical to unionism in that it emphasises harmony and individualism. This answer has been shown to be deficient in several respects (Bain et al., 1973). As indicated earlier in this chapter, there are many similarities in the way in which white-collar and manual unionism fluctuate over time, and the factors which affect their growth are also broadly similar. Some of these have already been mentioned above: the relationship between prices and earnings, and the relationship between employer policies and government action. The latter relationship is particularly important in explaining the generally lower level of unionism among white-collar employees: employers have generally been much more opposed to recognising and negotiating with unions on behalf of such employees, and government action has often been necessary to help overcome this opposition (Bain, 1970:ch. 9). Another part of the explanation is provided by the lower degree of employment concentration among white-collar employees: in most firms they tend to be found in smaller numbers and in smaller work groups than manual workers. And, as is indicated below, the degree of employment concentration is of crucial importance in determining the extent of unionisation among both white-collar and manual employees.

Industrial Structure

The above discussion has made it clear that the impact of the various personal and job-related determinants of union growth is very much affected by the way in which employment is distributed across and within industries. Indeed, Bain and Elsheikh (1979:153) concluded from an analysis of the inter-industry pattern of union growth in Britain over a twenty-year period that 'as unions are increasingly accepted as part of the structure of British society and union membership becomes increasingly widespread, it becomes less dependent upon the self-selection of individuals with similar personal characteristics and attitudes and more dependent upon the characteristics of the firms and industries in which individuals work'.

An important characteristic of an industry is the extent to which the employment of those who work in it is concentrated in large groups, and a number of studies in a variety of countries have demonstrated that this factor is closely related to the extent to which an industry is unionised. In Britain Bain and Elsheikh (1979:146) found that the degree of employment concentration, as measured by the average size of establishment, accounts by itself for about 40 per cent of the variation in the inter-industry pattern of unionisation in production industries. It also accounts for a considerable amount of the variation in the occupational and industrial patterns of white-collar unionism in manufacturing (Bain, 1970:72–81). And within individual manufacturing industries, it is significantly related to the inter-establishment pattern of both white-collar and manual unionism: in general, unionisation tends to increase as establishment size increases, but it does so at a decreasing rate so that an establishment which is twice as large as another does not, other things being equal, have twice the level of unionisation (Elsheikh and Bain, 1980). Finally, although adequate data on employment concentration do not exist for the public and private services sectors of the economy, this factor is clearly important in explaining their very different degrees of unionisation (see Chapter 8; Lockwood, 1958:141–50).

The strong positive relationship between the size of establishments and the extent to which they are unionised is fairly easy to explain. To begin with, the larger the establishment the more interested unions are likely to be in organising it, for the lower the *per capita* costs of doing so and the greater the return in subscriptions and bargaining power. More important, the larger the establishment the more interested its employees are likely to be in joining trade unions. For the larger the number of employees the more likely they are to be treated not as individuals but as members of groups, to have their terms and conditions of employment determined not by the personal considerations and sentiments of their managers but by bureaucratic rules which apply impersonally to all members of the group to which they belong, and hence to come to the conclusion that the most effective way of modifying these rules in their favour is by collective rather than individual bargaining. In short, the larger the number of employees in an establishment the more likely they are to feel the need to unionise because of the bureaucratic manner in which they are governed on the job, and the more easily trade unions can meet this need because of the economies of scale characteristic of union recruitment and administration.

Establishment size may also be linked to unionisation by another causal mechanism: the impact which it has upon the willingness of employers to concede union demands for recognition. Initially, almost all employers, for reasons which are understandable if not commendable, are opposed to recognising unions and bargaining with them. As unions develop in large, bureaucratically administered firms, however, employers may increasingly offer less resistance because they come to realise that 'if the bureaucratic rules are to be acceptable and friction in their operation is to be reduced to a minimum', they need to be 'formulated in consultation with organised groups representative of all the main interests involved' (Kelsall et al., 1956:322). In short, as Flanders (1974:355–6) has observed, large employers have an interest in obtaining union 'assistance in managerial control, in making and upholding rules to regulate work and wages for the sake of gaining employee consent and cooperation and avoiding costly strikes', and this interest may encourage them to extend recognition to unions and further their participation in job regulation.

Some employers also have an interest in obtaining union assistance in market control, in 'taking wages out of competition' by reducing disparities in labour costs between firms. Their interest in regulating wages is derived from their interest in regulating prices in competitive product markets, and the higher the proportion of labour costs to total costs the greater their interest in regulating wages and the more such regulation contributes to the regulation of prices and the control of competition. Thus in industries where labour costs make up a large proportion of total costs *and where* unions can develop sufficient strength to enforce collective agreements, employer opposition to them is likely to be less severe and less sustained and hence the level of unionisation is likely to be higher, other things being equal, than in industries where these conditions do not exist. The evidence for Britain is consistent with this reasoning: in production industries—the only sector with data on labour costs—the more labour intensive an industry or an establishment the higher its level of unionisation tends to be (Bain and Elsheikh, 1979; Elsheikh and Bain, 1980; Beaumont and Gregory, 1980).

Regardless of its size and labour intensiveness an establishment may be easier to organise if it is owned or controlled by a large enterprise than if it is a single independent unit. Even if the establishments within a large enterprise are administered in a decentralised fashion they are in institutional, and perhaps physical, proximity to each other, and for all the reasons which Shister (1953:422–4) sets out, this proximity may make unionisation easier. Its effect is likely to be much stronger, however, if the enterprise has a centralised personnel policy. In this case, regardless of how few employees there may be in a particular establishment, they are likely to become aware of their common interests because their terms and conditions of employment will tend to be determined in a bureaucratic fashion by formal rules which apply impersonally throughout the whole enterprise. Multi-establishment enterprises are also more likely to employ professional personnel managers (Brown, 1981:30), and if they, rather than paternalistic managers in individual establishments, formulate the policy on union recognition it is likely to be more favourable to trade unionism and collective bargaining. Indeed, if the enterprise wishes to bargain on a company-wide basis, a union may be recognised in an establishment where it has only a few members. Within a single independent establishment a paternalistic style of administration is more likely to be applied to white-collar than to manual workers and, within a multi-establishment enterprise, company-wide bargaining and personnel policies are more commonly applied to white-collar than to manual employees (Brown, 1981:14). And, interestingly, Elsheikh and Bain (1980) found that the level of unionisation tends to be lower among white-collar employees, but not among manual employees, in single independent establishments even when their size and labour intensiveness are controlled for, than in establishments which are part of a larger enterprise.

The above discussion of industrial structure has been largely based upon the private sector of the economy. But similar forces operate within the public sector. The large size of employing unit and the high degree of bureaucratisation characteristic of the public sector have clearly fostered among employees, including those in managerial and executive positions, an awareness of their collective interests and of the need to advance them through collective organisation (Lockwood, 1958:142–5). Bureaucratisation has also made employers in the public sector more willing to recognise unions and, indeed, to encourage employees to belong to them. For example, the Treasury informs new entrants to the civil service that

> besides being a good thing for the individual civil servant . . . it is also a good thing for Departments and for the Civil Service as a whole that civil servants should be strongly organised in representative bodies . . . it is hopeless to try to find out the wishes of a scattered unorganised body of individual civil servants each of whom may express a different view. When they get together in representative associations, their collective wish can be democratically determined and passed on to the 'management' with real force and agreement behind it; the 'management' know where they stand and can act accordingly (cited by Bain, 1970:124–5).

Most local authorities and nationalised industries have made similar pronouncements. Indeed the government has placed the various industries it has nationalised under a duty to recognise and bargain with appropriate trade unions. In short, the greater degree of employment concentration and bureaucratisation and the greater degree of union recognition in the public as compared with the private sector of the economy go a long way to explaining its greater degree of unionisation.

Union Leadership

So far nothing has been said about union leadership. Shister (1953) has claimed that union leaders have an impact upon union growth through the organising techniques which they devise for recruiting employees, the structural and governmental forms which they design for the union, and the nature of the collective bargaining relationships which they forge with employers and governments. Shister made this claim with respect to the United States, but Undy et al. (1981:163–6,349–50) have recently advanced a similar argument for Britain.

Few people would quarrel with the basic contention that union leadership has an impact upon union growth. Leadership is likely to be an important factor in determining the particular time and place of a union's emergence. And the importance of leadership style and policies for 'the union *incidence* of growth—that is, which union succeeds in organizing a given group of workers—is', as Shister has pointed out, 'too obvious to need comment'.

But how important is leadership in influencing aggregate union growth? This is a difficult question to answer. When an attempt is made by examining the growth of unions in areas in which they have sharply demarcated spheres of organisation and other unions are effectively prohibited from recruiting, the problem is to isolate the independent effect of leadership by controlling for all the other factors which directly, as well as indirectly through their impact on leadership styles and policies, affect union growth. When an attempt is made to assess the importance of leadership by comparing the growth of unions in areas where they are competing with other unions to recruit the same group of workers, the other determinants of union growth are controlled for, but then the problem is to demonstrate that a particular union's growth in this area occurred at the expense of continuing non-unionism rather than at the expense of another union which, in spite of having different leaders and policies would, in the absence of the successful union have recruited the workers in question; for workers who join one union rather than another when presented with a choice of leadership styles and policies might nevertheless have joined the other in the absence of such a choice.

These problems are well illustrated by the work of Undy et al. Even if they are correct in asserting that 'ASTMS's and the TGWU's selective recruitment efforts in areas of non-unionism . . . almost certainly positively affected their membership growth without depriving other unions of an immediate membership increase'—although since both are general unions which generally recruit in competition with other unions, there is no way of knowing whether this is so—special recruitment campaigns depend for their success not only upon the way they are pursued and the charisma and policies of union leaders but also upon the determinants of union growth discussed above being broadly favourable. Special recruitment campaigns may have attracted a significant number of members when the climate for union growth was very favourable, as in the period 1969–79, but they generally do not appear to have done so when the climate for union growth has been unfavourable, as in the period 1949–68 (see Bain, 1970:92–100) and in the years since 1979. Similarly, although Undy and his colleagues are undoubtedly correct to claim that by adopting policies favourable to the extension of such practices as the closed shop and the check off, certain unions influenced their growth in areas in which other unions were not capable of recruiting, these practices cannot be attributed solely, or even mainly, to union leaders and their policies. While these practices would not exist if unions were opposed to them, their introduction and extension during the late 1960s and the 1970s was, as indicated above, critically influenced by employer policies and government action.

Since only a very small amount of union growth can be unambiguously attributed to the independent influence of union leaders and their policies, and would not have occurred in the absence of these leaders and policies, Undy and his colleagues surely dramatically overstate their case when they speak of 'the critical role of leadership'. Unions and their leaders basically act as catalysts in the recruitment process. Before a group of workers can be successfully organised there must be some irritant resulting in a widespread feeling of dissatisfaction. Unions and their leaders cannot create this antipathy, they can only discover where it exists, emphasise it, and try to convince the workers that it can be remedied by unionisation. Their role in aggregate union growth, as Hyman points out in the next chapter, is vigorously to exploit the opportunities which are generated by the determinants of union growth discussed above, but it is a role which is tightly circumscribed by these determinants. Indeed, given the other determinants of union growth discussed in this chapter, most of the increase in union membership and density during the period 1969–79 and most of the decrease in union membership and density since 1979 would have occurred regardless of which union leaders were in office, because 'union leadership is dependent upon and constrained by the same socio-economic forces which motivate or enable workers to join trade unions' and, 'as such, it is very much a secondary and derivative determinant of aggregate union growth' (Bain and Elsheikh, 1976:23).

THE DESTINY OF UNION GROWTH

Now that the strategic determinants of union growth have been identified an attempt can be made to predict its future course in Britain during the 1980s. Such an attempt has to start with the existing pattern of unionisation. As can be seen from Table 1.4, despite the high density levels attained in the well organised sector of public services and manufacturing, there are still substantial numbers of non-members, especially among white-collar workers in manufacturing, whose recruitment would greatly increase the strength of the trade union movement; indeed, if the 3·3 million non-members in this sector in 1979 had been unionised, aggregate union density would have been about 70 per cent rather than 55 per cent. But further union recruitment in this sector is likely to be constrained by the 'saturation effect': the greater difficulty of further increasing union membership as union density rises, partly because there are fewer workers left to recruit and partly because those who are left have less propensity and/or ability to unionise (see Bain and Elsheikh, 1976:67–8). For example, many of the non-members in manufacturing are located in small establishments and, in the case of white-collar workers, in managerial grades. The scope for further union growth in the well organised sector is also likely to be limited by future employment trends: forecasts suggest that public employment will remain at roughly its present level throughout the 1980s, whereas both manual and white-collar employment in manufacturing will continue to decline substantially (Institute for Employment Research, 1982: table 3.1).

The largest untapped potential for union growth in Britain is in the poorly organised sector and, in particular, among the more than six million unorganised workers in private services. Although union density increased in private services during 1969–79—especially in insurance, banking, and finance, and, to a lesser extent, in distribution— in general, the gains were very limited. They were limited primarily because, as Chapter 8 indicates, private services are characterised by a large number of small establishments, part-time working and high labour turnover, and employer opposition to union recognition and collective bargaining. These characteristics are unlikely to change in the near future, and hence private services will remain a major obstacle to union growth for some time to come.

Even if unions are able to make modest membership gains in private services in the 1980s as they did in the 1970s, aggregate union density will probably still decline, other things being equal, simply because employment in this area is expanding so rapidly. This expansion is merely a particular example of the negative impact which the changing pattern of employment predicted for the 1980s will have upon union growth. Even if unions maintain throughout the 1980s the levels of union density reached in all areas in 1979, aggregate union density in 1990 will nevertheless be lower than in 1979 by, other things being equal, 0·7 percentage points as a result of the relative increase in women workers, 1.0 percentage points as a result of the relative increase in white-collar workers, and 2·0 percentage points as a result of changes in the industrial composition of the labour force (Price and Bain, 1983).

But the assumption that other things will remain equal does not hold for long in the real world. Many of the other determinants of union growth have already changed dramatically since 1979 and in such a way as to reinforce the negative impact of the changing composition of the labour force. The rate of wage and price inflation has moderated and the earnings differential has widened in favour of white-collar workers (Price and Bain, 1983: table 7). In addition the Conservative Government elected in 1979 repealed those sections of the Employment Protection Act which enabled a union to make a unilateral reference under the statutory procedure for obtaining assistance with a recognition dispute. It has also passed legislation designed to curb the closed shop. Perhaps most important, unemployment has increased dramatically and, as the recession has deepened, some employers have adopted a much tougher stance towards trade unions.

Economic forecasts suggest that the decline in the rate of inflation and the increase in unemployment will continue, with both trends levelling off in the mid-1980s (Institute for Employment Research, 1982). Greater public support for union recognition is unlikely to be forthcoming until a Labour government is returned to power and the prospects of this happening in the next few years do not appear good at the moment. It remains to be seen how effective the Conservative Government's labour legislation will be, but, even if it does not undermine existing closed shops, it will almost certainly restrict the growth of new closed shops. And the changing composition of the labour force will continue to work against the trade union movement. Thus trade union density is likely to continue to fall over the next year or two, to stabilise when unemployment stops increasing and then, assuming inflation continues at a moderate rate, to fluctuate slightly around a declining trend as it did during the years 1949–68.

How steeply declining this trend will be, however, will largely depend upon how employers behave. As this chapter has made clear, union recognition was greatly extended and deepened during the 1970s, with the result that trade unionism and the collective bargaining which it makes possible are now more deeply embedded in the management process than ever before. This greater degree of union recognition may act as a ratchet which will prevent union membership slipping away on the scale which, for example, occurred during the mass unemployment of the inter-war years. But the present government is questioning the desirability of collective representation and is attempting by legislative and other means to shift the balance of power in industrial relations more firmly in favour of employers. If employers take full advantage of the opportunities with which they are now being presented to reduce the extent and depth of union recognition, then the relationship between union growth and recognition will be reversed and become a 'vicious circle', and the downward trend in union density will be much steeper. Hence union growth has reached a watershed, and its direction during the 1980s will depend, as in the previous decade, upon the crucial inter-relationship between economic forces, employer policies, and government action.

2 Trade Unions: Structure, Policies, and Politics

Richard Hyman

British trade unionism is famous—or notorious—for its complexity and diversity. Both features must be appreciated if the dynamics of union development are to be adequately grasped. Accordingly this chapter consists predominantly of empirical detail, even though the account presented is necessarily selective. Issues of interpretation and theory, which in a more extended treatment would bulk far larger, are correspondingly compressed.

Description and analysis are presented within three main sections. The first examines changing trade union structure; the main interest is in the connection between industrial and occupational shifts and the organisational evolution of unionism, and the mutual interrelation of external pressures and opportunities and the course of official strategy. The subsequent discussion of policy and democracy focuses on diverse tendencies towards centralisation and decentralisation of control in different unions and the experience of organised opposition; the emphasis is on the complex interaction of membership activists and officials. Some elements in this interaction are pursued specifically in the context of the changing role of women in British unions. Thirdly, the developing political involvement of unions—reflected both in the status of the Trades Union Congress (TUC) and in the relationship with the Labour Party—are considered against the broader background of the interplay of the state, the economy, and industrial relations.

The concluding section of the chapter attempts to connect, in summary form, three themes: the boundaries of common organisation and identity, the sources of differential involvement and control within unions, and the links between internal and external politics. Recent literature is critically but selectively considered.

CHANGING STRUCTURE OF BRITISH TRADE UNIONISM

Two decades ago the pattern of British union membership differed little from the structure consolidated around the turn of the century: dominated by a handful of general, ex-craft, and single-industry organisations;

composed overwhelmingly of male manual workers in staple sectors of nineteenth-century British capitalism. Unionism in the 1980s is far more broadly based: a reflection in part of the decline of traditional strongholds and the growth of 'tertiary' employment, in part of increased density in areas of former weakness, particularly in the public sector. Occupational shifts in employment and unionisation have led to the current prominence of 'white-collar' organisations. The number of women trade unionists has doubled; out of every ten union members today three are women as against two in 1960. Union structure is even more complex than in the past; mirroring trends within British capitalism, the leading unions have grown more concentrated and more diversified. After the stabilisation of membership patterns in the 1950s the environment has become far more competitive. The fortunes of the major unions have become increasingly dependent not merely on employment trends in their traditional terrain of organisation but also on their success, relative to their rivals, in grasping new opportunities. Policy and strategy have become salient factors in structural development.

In 1960 there were 651 unions in the United Kingdom, with a total membership of 9,835,000. Of these 183 were affiliated to the Trades Union Congress, with a membership of 8,299,000. Seventeen organisations registered a membership greater than 100,000; all but two (NALGO and the NUT) were TUC affiliates. Together these seventeen unions contained 6,332,000 members, or 64.4 per cent of all British trade unionists.

In 1980 438 organisations were officially recorded, with an aggregate membership of 12,947,000. TUC affiliates numbered 108, their combined

TABLE 2.1: MAJOR BRITISH UNIONS, 1960

Transport & General Workers' Union (TGWU)	1,302,000
Amalgamated Engineering Union (AEU)	973,000
General & Municipal Workers' Union (GMWU)	796,000
National Union of Mineworkers (NUM)	586,000
Union of Shop Distributive & Allied Workers (USDAW)	355,000
National Union of Railwaymen (NUR)	334,000
National Association of Local Government Officers (NALGO)	274,000
National Union of Teachers (NUT)	245,000
Electrical Trades Union (ETU)	243,000
National Union of Public Employees (NUPE)	200,000
Amalgamated Society of Woodworkers (ASW)	192,000
Union of Post Office Workers (UPW)	166,000
National Union of Printing, Bookbinding & Paper Workers (NUPBPW)	158,000
Civil Service Clerical Association (CSCA)	140,000
National Union of Agricultural Workers (NUAW)	135,000
Iron and Steel Trades Confederation (ISTC)	117,000
National Union of Tailors & Garment Workers (NUTGW)	116,000

Source: TUC Report 1961 or individual organisations.

membership 11,601,000. The number of major unions had risen to twenty-seven, with a membership of 9,992,000, or 77.2 per cent of the total. Again, only two were outside the TUC (the RCN and the Police Federation, the latter not unambiguously a trade union and legally precluded from TUC membership).

TABLE 2.2: MAJOR BRITISH UNIONS, 1980

TGWU	1,887,000
Amalgamated Union of Engineering Workers – Engineering Section (AUEW–E) (previously AEU)	1,100,000
GMWU	916,000
NALGO	782,000
NUPE	699,000
Association of Scientific Technical & Managerial Staffs (ASTMS)	491,000
USDAW	450,000
Electrical Electronic Telecommunication and Plumbing Union (EETPU)	405,000
Union of Construction Allied Trades & Technicians (UCATT)	312,000
NUM	257,000
NUT	232,000
Confederation of Health Service Employees (COHSE)	216,000
Civil & Public Services Association (CPSA) (previously CSCA)	216,000
Union of Communication Workers (UCW) (previously UPW)	202,000
AUEW – Technical & Supervisory Section (AUEW–TASS)	201,000
Society of Graphical & Allied Trades (SOGAT) (previously NUPBPW)	197,000
NUR	170,000
Royal College of Nursing (RCN)	162,000
Banking Insurance & Finance Union (BIFU)	141,000
Association of Professional Executive Clerical & Computer Staff (APEX)	140,000
Post Office Engineering Union (POEU)	131,000
National Association of Schoolmasters & Union of Women Teachers (NAS/UWT)	124,000
Amalgamated Society of Boilermakers, Shipwrights, Blacksmiths & Structural Workers (ASB)	124,000
National Graphical Association (NGA)	116,000
Police Federation (PF)	112,000
Society of Civil & Public Servants (SCPS)	109,000
ISTC	100,000

Source: TUC Report 1981 or individual organisations.

Despite the substantial rise in union membership since 1960, the number of unions has fallen by more than a third—even though many new organisations were created during this period. Thus the average size of British unions has doubled, from 15,000 to 30,000. This trend reflects the growing preponderance of a few giant unions: by 1981 well over half of all British trade unionists were concentrated in seven organisations.

TABLE 2.3: SIZE OF BRITISH UNIONS, 1960 AND 1980 (in thousands)

Number of Members	1960				1980			
	Number of Unions	Total Member-ship (000s)	All Unions	Percentage of: All Member-ship	Number of Unions	Total Member-ship (000s)	All Unions	Percentage of: All Member-ship
below 500	308	51	47·4	0·5	187	32	42·7	0·2
500–9,999	249	661	38·3	6·7	165	427	37·7	3·3
10,000–24,999	44	718	6·8	7·3	28	474	6·4	3·6
25,000–99,999	32	1782	4·9	18·2	33	1749	7·5	13·5
100,000–249,999	10	1742	1·5	17·8	15	2518	3·4	19·5
250,000 and over	7	4848	1·1	49·5	10	7749	2·3	59·9
Total	650	9803	100·0	100·0	438	12947	100·0	100·0

Source: See, for example, Employment Gazette, XC (February 1982), 54–5.

The trend to concentration has been particularly strong within the TUC. The number of unions affiliated has fallen much more rapidly than the number outside; but affiliated membership has risen by more than half while the membership in non-TUC unions has fallen. In part this reflects the affiliation during the period of most of the major organisations formerly outside—a process discussed in a later section. The reduction in the number of unions is largely attributable to the many mergers and 'transfers of engagements' which have occurred during the past two decades: up to twenty a year, roughly four times the rate in the 1950s (Buchanan, 1974 and 1981).

The process has been assisted by the Trade Union (Amalgamation) Act of 1964, which abolished previous statutory requirements that a majority of members should actually register their votes in a merger ballot (Elias, 1973). But there have also been several positive stimuli. Of general importance has been an apparent rise in the threshold of union solvency: the expanding range of activities undertaken by British unions today—in research, education, and legal services in particular—has involved increased administrative costs, while subscriptions (on average roughly 6p per week in 1960, 10p in 1970, and 30p in 1980) fell behind the rate of inflation in the 1960s and did little more than keep pace during the 1970s. In addition a variety of more specific factors has helped to push unions into surrendering their autonomy. Stagnant or declining membership can entail financial difficulties: as in the textile trades which have contributed a substantial proportion of union amalgamations throughout the post-war period, the traditional multiplicity of local and occupational associations having lost all viability with rapidly dwindling employment. Similar though less drastic pressures have led, for example, to the Vehicle Builders in 1973 and the Agricultural and Allied Workers in 1982 merging with the TGWU, and to the fusion of the main building unions to form UCATT in 1971 (Druker, 1980; Undy et al., 1981).

Changes in technology which threaten strategic skills or erode traditional occupational demarcations have provided an additional impetus towards union amalgamation. So has the rapid concentration of industrial ownership, reflected in the growing dominance of multi-plant and multi-national companies, and the consequential shift in the balance of power in collective bargaining. Mergers in engineering, in shipbuilding, and in printing have owed much to such factors.

A further reason for the amalgamation 'wave' was a deliberate policy of expansion pursued by some unions, often trying to tempt potential partners with attractive terms. The TGWU—which with its trade group structure has always allowed distinctive occupational and industrial interests among the membership to exercise significant autonomy—made special arrangements to accommodate such unions as the Plasterers (1968), the Chemical Workers (1972), and the Vehicle Builders (1973), each of which might otherwise have amalgamated elsewhere. ASTMS—itself the product of a merger in 1968 between the Association of Supervisory Staffs, Executives and Technicians (ASSET) and the smaller Association of Scientific Workers (AScW)—has likewise allowed unions which transfer engagements to retain much of their independence. In this case, amalgamation has permitted a remarkable diversification of membership coverage.

In the past, amalgamation has often been viewed as a means of simplifying Britain's notoriously complex structure of trade unionism; and at times this has indeed occurred. The formation of the ASB brought together the main metal-working crafts in shipbuilding; the NGA has transcended many of the previous occupational and geographical divisions among printing crafts; to a lesser extent UCATT has had the same effect in construction. In textiles, clothing, and leather trades the reduction in the number of unions has also simplified union structure. But other amalgamations have resulted in an even more disordered pattern of unionism. Expansionist unions—otherwise inhibited by the TUC 'Bridlington' rules from entering new territory—have been able to extend their scope of recruitment as a result of mergers. Political sympathies among key union leaders, or guarantees of enhanced status or generous pensions, seem to have been important factors behind some otherwise bizarre partnerships. The overall outcome has thus 'not been rationalization of trade union structure but increasing complexity due to the further diversification of the conglomerates' (Clegg, 1979:177).

The extent of the amalgamation process since 1960 has made it very difficult, in appraising the changing balance of membership among the major British unions, to distinguish the effects of merger from what Undy et al. (1981) term 'natural growth'. The two phenomena are often mutually reinforcing: a union which is already successfully expanding may well appear an attractive partner for amalgamations, which in turn can provide the springboard for effective recruitment initiatives in new areas.

Unions may grow by extending the 'job territory' within which they recruit, through an expansion of employment in their existing recruitment area, or by increasing density among those eligible for membership. Because of TUC restrictions on new recruitment activities where an existing affiliate has already staked a claim (as is the case in most areas of employment), amalgamation—as indicated above—has been the principal means of expanding a union's 'membership market' (Undy et al., 1981). Most of the organisations absorbed in amalgamation have been small: the largest being the NUAAW with 85,000 members and the NUVB with 80,000 (both taken over by the TGWU). (In 1971 the Draughtsmen, with 105,000 members, became the Technical and Supervisory Section of the AUEW, but it remains an essentially autonomous member of a federal organisation, and attempts at full amalgamation have so far proved unsuccessful.) Only four other 'junior partners' in mergers have had over 50,000 members; by contrast, almost 80 per cent of those absorbed have held fewer than 2,500 members (Buchanan, 1981). While a few unions—notably the TGWU—have gained substantial membership directly through amalgamation, the effect has often been more indirect by providing new recruitment opportunities.

The changing fortunes of different unions have owed much to alterations in the pattern of employment. Most notable has been the expansion of public sector services and the financial and commercial sector; and, more generally, the growth of occupations classified as white-collar. These sectoral and occupational trends have been a key facilitating factor in all the fastest growing of the major unions, with the partial exception of the TGWU and the EETPU (though the latter has itself primarily benefited from the expansion of its particular job territory). Half the unions with over 200,000 members recruit principally among white-collar employees, the public sector services, or both. Or to express the same tendency by different criteria: of the twelve unions with a membership of 100,000 in 1981 but not in 1960, six organise in the expanding sectors of public employment, and four others among private-sector clerical, technical, and managerial staff. In the two remaining cases, growth is attributable to amalgamation: the NGA's membership is only slightly above the combined numbers in its component organisations, that of the Boilermakers' Society actually below the original total.

As argued in Chapter 1, increases in union density since 1960 owe much to such general influences as trends in the labour market, in price levels and in the willingness of employers to bargain collectively. Yet the success of particular unions in membership terms may be in large measure the result of bold expansionary policies or at least the vigorous exploitation of externally generated opportunities. As Undy and his associates have argued, while some unions (such as NALGO or POEU) benefited automatically from rising employment in their field of organisation, others worked hard for expansion. This largely explains the contrasting records of (at least partially) rival unions: The TGWU as against the GMWU across a wide range of industries, ASTMS as against APEX in the white-collar field.

Conversely, both external and internal influences may be identified in those cases of significant membership decline over the past two decades. Unions locked within a contracting 'job territory', such as mining, railways, iron and steel, clothing, or agriculture, must struggle even to stand still. But this cannot explain all cases of decline or stagnation in recent decades. For example, despite rapid growth of employment of schoolteachers the NUT has failed to benefit (apart from expanding the number of its student 'associates') and actually lost members in the 1970s. The contrast with the progress of the NAS/UWT, which has grown almost sixfold over the same period, is only partly attributable to the latter's base in the more rapidly expanding secondary sector of education: in part it must be regarded as evidence of a failure of strategy.

POLICY, ORGANISATION, AND DEMOCRACY: DIVERSE TRAJECTORIES

Trends in union membership, in amalgamations, and their impact on trade union structure, can be readily tabulated or at least outlined with relative simplicity. Trends in internal union organisation, in relations between and among full-time officials, lay activists and ordinary members, in the policies and strategies adopted, cannot be similarly assessed or quantified. Whatever the formal affinities between unions in their systems of government, the actual patterns of control, initiative, and influence differ substantially. Changes in these patterns are likewise subtly varied and often contradictory. British trade unions, in H. A. Turner's words (1962:14) 'are historical deposits and repositories of history . . . Every union possesses a personality of its own.' Generalisation thus confronts enormous problems.

An essay of this scope and character cannot offer a comprehensive summary of the shifting internal politics of even the major British unions during the past two decades. (For some systematic assessments see Clegg, 1979; Undy et al., 1981; and Eaton and Gill, 1981.) This section has the more modest aim of assessing three main areas of development during this period: the distribution of power and character of interrelationships between different hierarchical levels within unions, the nature and extent of internal conflict and the range and forcefulness of policies and activities pursued, and the representation of women and their interests.

Devolution and Centralisation

Many recent commentators have stressed 'the radical democratisation of relationships in many unions, particularly those organising the unskilled and semi-skilled in the public service and in private manufacturing industry' (England, 1981:27). More specifically 'the adjustment of methods of union government to meet the growth of workplace bargaining' has been identified by Clegg (1979:209, 226) with 'a growth in democracy in British unions'.

The most notable—or at least the most often noted—internal trans-formation has occurred within the TGWU. Under Ernest Bevin and Arthur Deakin power was centralised in the hands of national trade group secretaries and above all in the general secretary himself. Independent action among the membership was regarded with hostility by a leadership eager to treat dissent or discontent as evidence of communist subversion. The election of Frank Cousins as general secretary in 1956 (following the deaths of both Deakin and his successor in the previous year) heralded a change of direction, symbolised industrially by the London bus strike of 1958 and politically by the union's support for nuclear disarmament. But the union remained dominated at every level by 'men appointed and sustained by the Bevin-Deakin regime' (Goodman, 1979:114), and the pace of internal change was slow.

After 1960, 'devolution' became the keynote of union policy. In national negotiations, local officials and workplace representatives were brought on to negotiating committees, and reference-back procedures were intro-duced or extended (Undy, 1978); while shop floor bargaining by stewards was actively encouraged, particularly with the movement towards 'productivity' agreements. The 1968 rules conference introduced a range of organisational changes, in particular encouraging the formation of district committees. An important sponsor of reform was Jack Jones, whose career had been blocked under the old regime but who rose rapidly under Cousins, succeeding him as general secretary in 1969. By then most of the key officials of the Deakin era had retired or been otherwise replaced; their successors were more attuned to Jones's express aim of 'a system where not a few trade union officials control the situation but a dedicated, well-trained and intelligent body of trades union members is represented by hundreds of thousands of lay representatives' (1969:6). In line with this principle the number of full-time officials actually declined during this period even though the union's membership was growing rapidly.

'Devolution' in the TGWU may be seen, at least in part, as a pragmatic response .to the position which workplace representatives had achieved 'unofficially' in many areas of the union's membership. The changes were less a surrender of power to the shop floor than a formal accommodation to the reality of decentralisation which had occurred during the post-war years. Providing lay representatives with an officially recognised place in the union's government has matched the philosophy of the Donovan Report by ensuring greater congruence between the 'formal and informal systems' (though for Donovan this was to involve an expanded role for full-time officials). Adapting the union's organisation to changed industrial reality involved 'a general weakening of the traditional TGWU national bureaucracy' (Undy et al., 1981:94); but paradoxically the reforms were sponsored and pressed through by the resources available to the official at the pinnacle of this bureaucracy. As part of the process Jones, as general secretary, bolstered the role of the general executive council in initiating policy.

The unstable balance between devolution and central leadership was exposed in 1977 when the union's delegate conference rejected Jones's own advocacy of continued support for incomes policy. Moss Evans, who became general secretary the following year, inherited an office deprived of much of its traditional unquestioned authority. Today the locus of power in the TGWU is fluid and uncertain.

Less dramatic but still significant changes have occurred within the other main general union, the GMWU, in which a conservative organisational bias traditionally complemented an authoritarian (and nepotistic) leadership and right-wing politics. This pattern was shaken by the rise of workplace activism. In 1969 the union's Halewood membership transferred *en masse* to the TGWU in protest at the GMWU's refusal to back the Ford strike; the following year the protracted strike of 10,000 members at Pilkington culminated in the formation of a breakaway union. Less dramatically, the union's growth compared unfavourably with that of the TGWU, while opportunities for expansion among the growing number of public service workers were being grasped far more effectively by NUPE and COHSE; and the GMWU was also singularly unsuccessful in the competition for amalgamation partners.

The successful campaign of David Basnett for general secretary in 1973 emphasised the need for change, and the gradual retirement and replacement of officials with roots in pre-war industrial relations permitted modest internal reform. National and regional industrial conferences, tentatively introduced in 1969, received rulebook endorsement in 1975. In the same year the machinery of government was altered to provide a 'lay' majority on a new executive council. Organisationally the union has devoted considerable resources to research, education, and health and safety representation, while politically the attempt has been made to modify the traditional image of the GMWU as a pillar of right-wing orthodoxy. Nevertheless, pressure for more radical change has been largely deflected by the traditional power of the regional secretaries.

NUPE, a union heavily dependent on the work of full-time organisers in recruitment and negotiation, provides a third example of devolution. Precipitating factors have been a particularly rapid growth of membership, the reorganisation of local authority boundaries and the structure of the NHS, and moves towards workplace negotiation over work arrangements and bonus payments. In 1973 an academic research team was commissioned to study the union's organisation; its report (Fryer et al., 1974) stressed the need to strengthen workplace organisation and to extend the role of lay representatives. It also emphasised the need to promote greater participation by women members, whose numbers had almost quadrupled since 1960 and who now constituted over 60 per cent of total membership. A special conference in 1975 approved rule changes defining the role of union stewards at workplace, branch, and district level; instituting an interlinked structure of service-based committees from district to national level; and reconstructing the executive council with a fifth of its places reserved for women.

While workplace organisation was in large measure sponsored from above, and in many cases remained dependent on support and servicing by full-time officials, there have been intimations of greater autonomy. The most notable instance was in the winter of 1978–9 when grassroots pressure, channelled through to executive level, resulted in the rejection of a provisional agreement which had the backing of general secretary Alan Fisher.

Yet despite such evidence of the impact of workplace power in union government since the 1960s, Undy et al. rightly insist (1981:88) that 'the devolutionary shift was by no means universal'. During the same period long-established restraints on centralised control have been substantially weakened in a number of unions, particularly those with craft backgrounds. At times amalgamation—by providing a 'natural' occasion for revisions of rule—has facilitated such changes.

This has been true, for example, of building trade unionism. The ASW constitution long represented an uneasy tension between national leadership and local activists. The general secretary and full-time executive council, sustained by a right-wing electoral machine which successfully tapped the support of the craft conservatism of the union's fragmented membership, maintained exclusive control over the national direction of union policy. But at local level a key role was performed by district management committees, often composed of left-wing lay activists, with responsibilities for recruitment and for monitoring employment conditions and with powers to control district organisers. Since the 1940s, the union's national leaders had sought, unsuccessfully, to abolish these committees; but merger in 1970 with the Painters and Decorators allowed the ASW leadership to win a narrow majority for a change of rule. District committees were replaced by regional councils meeting infrequently and with few powers; officials were brought under central control; and the regular re-election of local organisers was ended. In the following year UCATT was set up on the basis of these new rules, which 'obviously had the intended effect of strengthening the EC, through control over regional secretaries and organisers, at the expense of the activists in the branches' (England, 1979:10; see also Druker, 1980).

The new structure proved unstable. Amalgamation weakened the hold of the ASW right-wing electoral machine, and in the 1970s the UCATT executive became evenly divided on political lines. The abolition of district committees left a vacuum which was filled by unofficial forms of organisation, most notably the Building Workers' Charter which campaigned for an ambitious programme of demands and helped to inspire the national strike of 1972. In 1974 the national delegate conference displayed a militant temper, defeating the executive on major policy issues. National leaders could not realistically attempt to suppress the new local activism, since this was associated with a rise in membership after the decline of the 1960s. Revised rules agreed in 1975 represented a compromise between conflicting interests and pressures. In particular, local joint committees of branches and shop stewards were instituted; lay involvement at regional level was strengthened, and regular re-election of organisers was restored (England, 1979).

Centralisation proceeded far more decisively in the EETPU. In the 1940s, members of the Communist Party won election to key national offices and a majority of executive seats in the then ETU. Their control was sustained until after the Hungarian rising of 1956, when a number of members resigned from the party and opposed the incumbent union leadership. Allegations of ballot-rigging culminated in a court case in 1961 which invalidated the 1959 ballot for general secretary and declared the anti-communist John Byrne elected. This was followed by the defeat of most sitting members of the executive and the election of Leslie Cannon as president.

For a time the rules were liberalised. The limited powers of the conference were extended, and a final appeal court composed of lay members was introduced (an important safeguard against abuse of the executive's considerable disciplinary powers). But more restrictive changes followed in 1965: area committees were abolished; the executive was made full-time, its members' tenure increased from two to five years; communists were banned from union office; and the executive was empowered to close or amalgamate branches and to appoint full-time secretaries.

In 1967 Byrne was succeeded as general secretary by Frank Chapple. The partnership of two seasoned ex-communists Cannon and Chapple in the key national offices coincided with increasingly right-wing and authoritarian tendencies. After the merger with the Plumbers to form the EETPU in 1968 the appeals court was abolished, and the regular local election of organisers was replaced by executive appointment and control. After Cannon's death in 1970, Chapple was eventually elected president; the runner-up Mark Young (another of the ex-Communists of the 1950s), who had campaigned against some of the centralisation of power, was soon afterwards dismissed from his post as national organiser. Before an election was held for the vacant general secretaryship it was agreed in 1974 to abolish the presidency; the powers and duties of both national offices were concentrated in Chapple's hands.

More recently the executive's power to close or amalgamate branches has been used to discipline or smother dissident branches and their officers, a practice condemned at the union's 1979 conference. Opposition candidates in executive elections have been faced with substantial obstacles; in particular, allegations of technical breaches of rule have been used to disqualify successful challengers or to invalidate elections. Disciplinary action against internal dissidents and litigation against external critics have become regular features of the EETPU under Chapple. The election of his successor, which took place in 1982, does not seem likely to lead to major change.

Trends in the internal politics of the former AEU, now the AUEW-E, have been particularly complex during the past decade. Traditionally, central control within the union has been limited by three factors. District committees, composed of representatives of branches and district shop steward meetings, enjoy considerable formal autonomy; and localism is reinforced by the regular re-election of district and divisional officials. At national level a system of checks and balances is designed to inhibit concentration of power: there is a division of functions among president, general secretary, and full-time executive council; the policy-making national committee, 'probably the most assertive conference in the entire Labour movement' (Minkin, 1980:179); and the final appeal court. Finally the requirement of regular re-election of national and local officials generates frequent campaigns in which competition between right and left-wing factions plays a prominent part, entailing continuous opposition to the incumbent leadership.

Despite rulebook recognition of workplace representation, and active shop steward involvement in the machinery of government (Boraston et al., 1975), for half a century the formal constitutional arrangements have diverged from shop-floor reality. The main cause has been the growing autonomy of domestic bargaining and pay determination, the virtual elimination of district-wide agreements, and the decline in relevance for most members of national negotiations. The union branch—normally encompassing a number of workplaces—has been eclipsed in significance for most members by shopfloor organisation, the basic unit of union government failing to involve the large majority of members; and active participation in union affairs outside the workplace has remained largely confined to a skilled stratum which was once the sole source of the union's membership but now accounts for only a quarter of the total.

The past two decades have seen intensified divisions within the union's internal politics; a change in the ground-rules of electoral activity which has markedly affected the political balance of power; and a shifting environment in which national policies have regained their relevance to workplace industrial relations.

Given regular elections for officials in which well below 10 per cent of members normally participated, organised political groupings sought to coordinate nominations so that politically similar candidates did not 'split the vote', and to ensure a high turnout on voting night at 'reliable' branches. A disciplined right-wing faction began operation in 1952 with the aim of displacing the impact of communist-led left officials. It proved highly successful, particularly in the aftermath of Hungary: by 1960 the right held both leading national offices, six of the seven executive seats, as well as a substantial majority of lower-level positions. Helped by constitutional provisions which under-represented large urban districts in which the left was strongest, the right also dominated the national committee. Control over the union journal, edited by the general secretary, was used for blatantly partisan purposes; while the prerogatives of the president, William Carron, were applied with idiosyncratic deviousness (giving rise to the epithet 'Carron's law').

During the 1960s an opposition 'broad left' organisation was formed to counteract the right-wing electoral machine (Armstrong, 1978). Internal politics became increasingly polarised, and for a time the two 'parties' were relatively evenly balanced. The left won a major success in 1967 with the election of Hugh Scanlon as president. By 1973 it also held two executive posts (as against two committed right-wingers and three 'floaters'), both assistant general secretaryships, and half the national organiser positions; in addition the national committee was almost equally divided between right and left.

This advance by the left doubtless reflected important shifts in membership opinion and a changing material environment. Carron's insistence on committing the union to unqualified support for the 1964–70 Labour government—and in particular its incomes policy—was increasingly at odds with membership disenchantment with the government's record. In national collective bargaining, the 1965 'package deal' (involving a three-year settlement, 'productivity' concessions, and implicit reaffirmation of the 1922 procedure agreement) provoked discontent which clearly helped the broad left. But its successes also rested on the narrower organisational ability to mobilise higher than average voting in relatively few branches whose officials were united in support of left candidates, rather than in broader campaigning among the membership (Armstrong, 1978; Undy, 1979).

Such a strategy was, however, vulnerable to alterations in the procedure of election itself. At its rules revision meeting in 1970 the national committee voted 26–25 (with one abstention) to replace balloting at branch meetings by postal ballots. There followed a series of election defeats for left-wing candidates, including some incumbent officials: a demonstration of the shallow roots of the organisation established in the 1960s. A series of press campaigns favoured right-wing candidates, particularly significant where members voted in their own homes in the absence of branch discussion. The right's organisation also proved effective in campaigning at workplace level, often with employer assistance. But in addition, the Scanlon presidency was no long-term electoral asset for the left: the failure of the 1971 pay claim and the consequential sit-ins in 1972, and Scanlon's subsequent support for social contract wage controls which squeezed craft differentials, eroded much membership support and led to divisions within the broad left.

By the end of the 1970s the right had regained the presidency, held all seven executive seats, and could normally command a comfortable majority on the national committee. Its hold on the union's government is thus even firmer than two decades earlier. Even more significantly, tighter factional discipline now ensures on most issues homogeneity of policy across the different institutions of union government. This has permitted the approval of further rule changes in 1981. Branch ballots have been abolished in the two contexts where they remained important: TUC and Labour Party delegates now being elected by postal ballot, and final appeal court members chosen by divisional committees (which appoint the members of the national committee). The national committee has itself been enlarged and its composition altered, consolidating the position of the right wing. More than at any time in the union's history, then, the internal constitutional checks on leadership control have been largely attenuated.

This remarkable concentration of power within the formal machinery of union government is the more significant because of the marked decline in the independence of workplace organisation which has occurred during the same period. 'Reform' of procedures and payment systems has narrowed the scope for fragmented bargaining; changes in labour and product markets have forced shop stewards on the defensive; multi-plant companies with centralised industrial relations strategies are increasingly the norm. Ironically the traditional autonomy of the union's districts is a major handicap in responding to such changes: for representatives in one plant of a company cannot constitutionally collaborate with others in a different geographical location except through the formal channels of district and national officers. Both in rule and in practice, steward organisations in the AUEW-E have become increasingly dependent on the leadership provided—or not provided—by national officers and executive (as in 1979 when the executive sabotaged resistance to the victimisation by British Leyland of Longbridge convenor Derek Robinson). This unprecedented concentration of power in the hands of the AUEW-E leadership could well be further consolidated if proposals for amalgamation of branches under full-time secretaries (on lines similar to developments in the EETPU) are carried through. A closer integration of some or all of the components of the wider AUEW, or merger with other right-wing unions, could well reinforce such centralising trends.

Policy and Conflict

Many unions have experienced organised opposition between politically based factions in elections and decision-making processes. These divisions have often developed from challenges to the political stance and bargaining strategies of an incumbent 'moderate' leadership, in which growing assertiveness and discontent among the membership was successfully tapped by 'rank-and-file' movements.

One notable example is the National Union of Seamen (NUS), a union with a long tradition of authoritarian leadership and collaborative relations with employers, bolstered by joint control of the industry's employment register. Dissatisfaction with progress in national negotiations in 1960 erupted into a series of localised unofficial strikes, and local activists formed a National Seamen's Reform Movement. Reformers opened a campaign within the branches, secured growing influence at the annual general meeting, and from 1962 won seats on the executive council. Pressure for more ambitious demands and militant tactics resulted in the official national strike of 1966. Arguments for democratisation of the union's decision-making structure—which involved a bizarre system of plural voting in elections, and gave full-time officials considerable power in policy determination—proved successful at the rules revision meetings of 1967 and 1972. Organised left-wing pressure culminated in the election of one of the Reform Movement leaders, Jim Slater, to the post of general secretary in 1973 (Hemingway, 1978:ch.4).

The NUM has a long tradition of politically-informed divisions and oppositional activity, but factional conflict has recently sharpened considerably. A complex interrelationship between regional identity, pit-level militancy and political commitment has received explosive force from the changing economic fortunes of the industry and hence the shifting terrain of industrial strategy.

Despite the militant reputation of mining trade unionism, many of the regional associations (which until 1944 functioned independently) were committed to conciliatory policies. After the old Miners' Federation was replaced by the NUM and the industry itself was nationalised, co-operation became the keynote of national policy. The rapid contraction of employment (virtually halved by redundancies and pit closures during the 1960s) was accepted as inevitable while pay claims were moderated for fear that high labour costs would result in even faster job loss. The relative decline in miner's pay was particularly severe in traditionally higher-paid areas, since the union pursued a policy of eliminating geographical differentials: a policy reflected in the national day-wage structure of 1955, and culminating in the national power-loading agreement of 1966.

Paradoxically, the years of 'moderate' official policies were also those when mining dominated the statistics of the number of British strikes, with a multiplicity of pit-level stoppages over local payment issues, or working conditions which affected piecework earnings. But the progress towards a national time-rate payment system removed the scope for earnings improvements through fragmented militancy, directing miners' wage aspirations unambiguously towards their national negotiators. At the same time an organised left-wing tendency began to urge resistance to pit closures and a more ambitious wages policy. Drawing support from such traditionally militant areas as South Wales, Scotland, and Derbyshire, this loose left alliance also managed to displace the right-wing leadership in Yorkshire—by far the largest area of the NUM (Allen, 1981; Watters, 1981). The successful campaign to elect Laurence Daly as general secretary in 1968, on an overtly radical platform, reflected both growing pit-level assertiveness and effective left-wing organisation; so did the decisions of annual conference from the late 1960s, committing the national executive to explicit and ambitious pay targets. The shifting internal politics of the NUM were reflected in extensive unofficial strike action in the course of the 1969 and 1970 national negotiations followed by the official national disputes in 1972 and 1974. The continuing grip of the right was demonstrated, however, in 1971 when Joe Gormley was elected president by a 5–4 majority.

Throughout the 1970s there was a 'trend towards open internal American-style factions' (Edelstein and Warner, 1975:251). The left has normally been able to command a majority at annual conference, but the right-wing president, favoured by the built-in bias towards right-wing areas in the composition of the national executive committee, demonstrated considerable ingenuity in outmanoeuvring the left.[1] The introduction of incentive payments in 1977, despite their rejection by annual conference and a membership ballot, exemplified such factional struggle, as did Gormley's public opposition to the executive's strike recommendation in 1981. The election of Arthur Scargill as his successor, by an unusually large majority, may however entail a significant shift in the political balance.

Factional activity is a novel development in public sector white-collar unionism. Here the upsurge in factionalism reflects in part the general trend towards more abrasive public sector industrial relations, as incomes policies and curbs on public expenditure in a period of rapid price inflation have transformed the context of pay determination. Given the central determination of salaries, members' sense of 'relative deprivation' has inevitably led to pressure on the national negotiators. As in the unions discussed above, sharp controversy over both the level of pay demands and the use of strike action in their pursuit has been a growing feature since the 1960s. In some unions, however, internal conflict over such issues has interconnected with divergences of sectional interest, accentuated where patterns of employment hierarchy are mirrored within union government.

Both features have been evident in NALGO and the NUT, where such conflicts have both encouraged and been intensified by the emergence of organised oppositional groupings. In both unions, too, key issues of internal controversy in the 1960s—strike action and affiliation to the TUC—were vital political symbols for entrenched conservatives and leftist activists alike; but change in official policy owed much to a more pragmatic shift of attitudes within the membership and among politically less committed officials and lay representatives.

The complex internal political repercussions can be clearly seen in the case of the NUT. After a feeble flirtation with militancy in 1961, largely in response to the challenge of the NAS (R. D. Coates, 1972:64–7), unrest resulting from government pay restraint provoked extensive strikes and other sanctions in the late 1960s. In part this militancy reflected the changing structure of teaching employment, as educational expansion increased the proportion of younger staff on the lowest salary scales.

---

[1] On the formation of the NUM in 1944, each area was guaranteed a seat on the executive. Today the twelve smallest areas, with only a fifth of NUM membership, hold half the seats; Yorkshire, with a larger membership, has only three. Overall, right-wing areas are substantially overrepresented in relation to their membership; see Allen, 1981.

A Young Teachers' conference was launched by the executive in 1960, but soon caused embarrassment by pressing vigorously for narrower differentials and more aggressive action (Undy et al., 1981:254). Internal controversies of the 1960s and 1970s highlighted the paradox of the NUT as a union whose members are predominantly women and teachers on lower salary scales, but whose executive is dominated by men in senior positions. Demands for improvements in basic pay as an overriding priority, and for reductions in the authority of head teachers, thus challenged the distinctive interests of the union's leadership.

After the strikes of 1967 this challenge was coordinated by an organised group, led by members of the International Socialists (IS), around the journal *Rank and File*: a paper launched in 1968 'by a small self-appointed group of IS members and ex-CP members, most of them with some sort of base and history of activity in the union and all of them in London' (Hallas, 1974:18). The movement won a significant presence at the union's conference and eventually gained a foothold on the executive. But the Rank and File group failed to achieve a major impact among the membership outside London, and on much of its programme was forcefully opposed by an executive majority containing a substantial proportion of 'militants' of an earlier generation (many of them members of the Communist Party). In the 1970s the union's official leadership—having established its 'progressive' credentials through affiliation to the TUC and occasional initiatives in controlled militancy—had little difficulty in containing pressure for more radical reform.

Several unions experienced active opposition factions which emerged in the late 1960s, but declined or disintegrated by the end of the 1970s.[2] Five reasons can be suggested for this trajectory. Firstly, the centrifugal tendencies on the left have typically weakened the coherence of factional challenges. In particular the differences between communists and those further to the left have rarely permitted more than temporary alliances. Secondly, 'rank-and-file movements' have typically been based upon a small cadre of activists (sometimes, as in ASTMS, embracing a few full-time officials). Except during phases of generalised discontent or militancy, these have rarely represented the mood and commitment of the majority of members, and in key controversies union leaders have been able to appeal over the heads of such activists or simply ignore them. A third and related point is that such movements were a feature of unions and industries without a tradition of workplace negotiation and organisation; this has helped opposition movements to direct membership protest over wages and conditions to the national level of union policy, but has deprived activists of a continuing organic link with their constituencies.[3] Fourthly,

---

[2] A major exception is the CPSA, where the left faction dominated the executive elections in 1978, was routed the following year after a change of electoral procedure, but regained control in 1982.

[3] Demands for the introduction of a shop steward system have been part of the programmes of movements in several of the unions, and in some cases—notably NALGO—have been adopted as official policy. But the practical consequences have been limited and uneven.

incumbent leaders have in the main proved adept in accommodating sufficiently to membership assertiveness to undercut support for leftist activists and hence isolate opponents. Finally, the general decline in industrial struggle after 1975, and the rightward shift in the national political climate, undoubtedly favoured a re-assertion of 'moderate' control in a majority of unions.

Women and Trade Unionism

The rapid increase in the proportion of women trade unionists in the past two decades has been noted earlier. This has been paralleled by growing and critical attention to the (in)ability of traditional trade union mechanisms to represent women's distinctive interests. Changes in union organisation and strategy have come about as a result; but their precise significance cannot be easily evaluated.

In the 1960s Hughes (1968:31) noted the lack of 'a consistent or a generally accepted approach by British trade unions towards the rights and participation of women members'. In some unions women were explicitly second-class members. Even where formally equal, their participation in decision-making processes and representation in union office were typically well below that of men. And tacitly or overtly, collective bargaining strategies typically endorsed discriminatory treatment.

In some respects the situation has changed in recent years. Government action—the Equal Pay Act 1970 and the Sex Discrimination Act 1975, both in part a reflection of general European moves in the field of anti-discrimination law—has inevitably affected collective bargaining strategy and, in the case of organisations with discriminatory constitutions, trade union rulebooks. Legislation coincided with broader debates on women's social and economic position. Among women activists who formed part of the expansion of union membership since the 1960s, particularly in the 'white-collar' area, were many whose experience in the feminist movement informed an assertive and articulate challenge to traditions of male dominance in trade unionism. And institutions which had long performed a largely token role—notably the annual TUC Women's Conference and the Women's Advisory Committee of the General Council, both established in the 1930s—developed a more vigorous campaigning posture.

There have been three main areas of change. In wage determination the formal attainment of equal pay in the public services in 1961 was followed by ritual trade union insistence on the principle for women workers generally. But no serious action on these resolutions took place until 1968, when the Ford sewing machinists' strike against the low grading of their work in the company's job evaluation scheme provided 'a lead for all women workers' (Lewenhak, 1977:284). The trend towards more vigorous activity by women at workplace level was reinforced by the passing of the Equal Pay Act and subsequent discontent at its limited impact on pay disparities. Attention to the question of women's pay within trade union policy has expanded substantially in the 1970s, and has included extensive demands for the strengthening of existing legislation.

Given systematic gender-based inequalities in employment opportunities and experience, it is now widely accepted that the formal introduction of 'equal pay' is of limited effect. This has been reflected in a broadening range of equality-related issues discussed within the trade union movement. The 1963 TUC Women's Conference approved a six-point 'Industrial Charter for Women', which has been regularly revised and expanded. The 1977 version, now entitled 'Aims for Women in Work', includes fourteen items. Demands for maternity leave and for crèche and nursery provision contrast with the assertion of the TUC Women's Committee in 1963 that 'women with very young children do not wish to work unless forced to do so by financial strain'. Since 1975 TUC policy has included 'adequate services for contraception and abortion on request, available free of charge on the NHS'; and in 1979 the TUC organised a national demonstration against proposed restrictions on legal abortions. Latterly, union policy has recognised the need to go beyond the negative prohibition of overt discriminatory practices and to generate positive initiatives to overcome women's disadvantages in employment. A special conference on 'positive action', held by the TUC in 1980, resulted in a policy statement which pointed to trade union responsibility for continuing inequalities.

The structure of union representation has itself come under scrutiny. After the 1967 TUC Women's Advisory Committee called attention to women's underrepresentation in responsible positions, most main unions established equal opportunities or women's advisory committees. In 1979 a TUC Charter set out ten proposals for equality within unions; while in 1981 a 'Positive Action Programme' was published with detailed suggestions for the organisation of meetings, training courses and publicity material; and for reserved seats on executive bodies. As noted earlier, NUPE created five women's seats on its executive in 1975; while the traditional two women's places on the TUC General Council were increased to five in 1981.

In the past, women have generally been regarded as a problem for trade unions; now there is a growing awareness that trade unions are a problem for women. Yet it is far from clear what the changes in official posture entail in practice. The gap between male and female earnings, having somewhat narrowed proportionately in the mid-1970s, has widened again; job segregation remains entrenched; the proliferation of advisory committees for women trade unionists has not been associated with any major increase in their representation on executive and policy-making bodies. The unemployment rate has risen faster among women than among men, while cutbacks in state welfare provision increase the obstacles to women's participation in unions and in employment. For some observers, trade union commitment to equality has been essentially a token movement, which cannot offset the divisive tendencies of a period of economic adversity: 'it seems that women's economic equality has to be a no-cost benefit, which can only be sanctioned in a period of economic growth' (Coote and Campbell, 1982:152; for other discussions of women in British unions see Mackie and Pattullo, 1977; Hunt and Adams, 1980; Coote and Kellner, 1980; Robarts, 1981; Aldred, 1981; Ellis, 1981; Hunt, 1982; and the historical studies by Lewenhak, 1977 and Boston, 1980).

UNIONS, POLITICS, AND THE STATE

In Britain, 'politics' and 'industrial relations' have long been clearly distinguished: a demarcation in turn reflected in a firm separation of functions between the 'political' and 'industrial' arms of the labour movement. These dichotomies, so potent in their impact on trade union ideology, have always been misleading (Hyman, 1975 and 1981); but they have lost much of their superficial plausibility in the past two decades.

Since 1960 major transformations have occurred in the relationship of unions, both individually and collectively, with the processes and institutions of government on the one hand, and with the Labour Party on the other. This section examines each set of relations in turn. The two areas of transformation necessarily interconnect: not least because Labour has itself formed the government for the majority of the past twenty years, a circumstance without precedent in British history.

State Intervention and the Role of the TUC

Encroachments on the tradition of 'voluntarism' during the past two decades have had important repercussions on the role of the TUC as central representative of British trade unions. By international standards the TUC has differed from most other central confederations in two respects. Firstly, its position has never been seriously rivalled. For a century, virtually all major unions have been affiliated and those outside have rarely contemplated, and never accomplished, the formation of an alternative trade union centre. But secondly, in other key respects the TUC has been unusually weak. It was created, initially for very limited purposes, by unions many of which boasted long traditions of autonomy and all of which were jealous of their independence. The slow historical accretion of its functions and influence has occurred often against considerable resistance and only in response to overwhelming force of circumstance (R. M. Martin, 1980). It remains a body with meagre resources, few powers over the affairs of its affiliates, and, in particular, minimal jurisdiction in the sphere of collective bargaining.

Yet the balance between the TUC and its member unions has shifted perceptibly with increasing state involvement in industrial relations. Firstly, governments have assumed responsibilities for the planning of both overall economic development and labour market strategy. Initially framed optimistically in terms of 'planning for growth'—the perspective underlying the creation of the National Economic Development Council (NEDC) in 1962 and the early phase of the Labour Government of 1964—such intervention has been intensified as a result of economic crisis and decline. Secondly, the expansion of public services (especially health and education) and the nationalisation of an array of 'lame ducks' have made the state, together with other public sector institutions, a massive employer in its own right. Thirdly, a specific aspect of government intervention has been the operation of wage controls, almost continuous since 1961 and particularly important for public sector unionism. Fourthly, judicial anti-union inventiveness, together with government exploitation of trade unions' electoral unpopularity, has made labour law a major interface between state and unions. If the trade union 'problem' was initially defined largely in terms of shop-floor 'anarchy' which official trade unionism might help contain, during the 1970s trade unionism as such— official as well as unofficial—was increasingly regarded as a threat to government (and employer) objectives.

The increasing challenge from state and employers—so obviously general in its implications—has stimulated closer coordination among British unions, and governments themselves have at times encouraged centralisation by fostering the status of the TUC. Anxious to gain union support for the creation of the NEDC in 1962, the Conservative Government agreed that six representatives should be directly nominated by the TUC. With the proliferation of 'quangos' during the following two decades the principle was confirmed—by governments of both parties—that union appointments to public bodies should derive from the TUC (Martin, 1980).

Privileged access to the 'committee rooms of power'[4] helped the TUC to recruit several notable non-affiliates. A Conference of Professional and Public Service Organisations, formed in 1962 primarily as an alternative channel for non-TUC union representation, was refused any place on the NEDC; a rebuff which persuaded NALGO, its leading member, to apply to join the TUC (Spoor, 1967:551–9; Newman and Smythe, 1982). NALGO was followed by unions covering all levels of public education as well as professional and other senior civil servants. The TUC's almost exclusive coverage of all but the smallest British unions thus owes much to the growth of formal consultative machinery on macroeconomic policy.

TUC involvement with Labour Government economic planning, and in particular with incomes policy, brought two important internal developments in the 1960s. The first was the convening of frequent conferences of

---

[4] The phrase is from George Woodcock's presentation of the General Council's report on the NEDC to the 1963 Congress: 'We have sought, first of all, to formulate our view and formulate it in terms that could be put to the people in power. We left Trafalgar Square a long time ago. Second, we have to deal – we ourselves have sought to create the situation in which we do deal – with affairs of the moment in committee rooms, with people who have power; power given to them by the electorate of this country.'

executive committees of affiliated unions (a procedure utilised on occasion in the past, but only for exceptional purposes and not since 1950). The second was the publication from February 1968 of an annual Economic Review. Initially seen primarily as a statement of 'the General Council's views on the general level of increase in wages and salaries that would be appropriate in the ensuing year, and on the kinds of circumstances which would justify deviations from that general level', the report developed into a far broader manifesto of economic strategy. Appearing in the months preceding the government's budget decisions, it has consistently advocated expansionary and redistributive policies which with almost equal consistency have been ignored by Chancellors of both parties. In the 1970s increasing attention was also devoted to 'industrial strategy': an amorphous concept which came into vogue with the emergence of the 'social contract' and involved detailed proposals for planning and controls in the fields of investment, trade, and finance. It was taken far more seriously by the TUC than by the Labour Government, and during the late 1970s served as a more orthodox alternative to the 'alternative economic strategy' canvassed on the left of the unions and the Labour Party.

In September 1965 the General Council established an Incomes Policy Committee to monitor the wage claims submitted by member unions; even those 'opposed to the Government's incomes policy showed a surprising willingness to co-operate with the TUC' (Panitch, 1976:96). This essentially negative incursion in the collective bargaining activities of affiliates developed into more positive intervention. In 1967 Congress defined a minimum wage target of £15 for full-time workers, and this figure has been regularly revised upwards. Responsibility for pay bargaining targets was taken over in 1970 by a Collective Bargaining Committee and passed in 1973 to the full General Council (or its Economic Committee). Detailed co-ordination has also been undertaken by a series of Industry Committees (currently nine in number) which as well as providing a forum for formulating joint bargaining strategies also provide links with 'little Neddies' and with Sector Working Parties. Intervention in the pay disputes of the seamen in 1976, the train drivers in 1982, and the various health service unions in the same year, constitutes a trend without precedent since 1926.

The gradual accretion of the TUC's role as general representative of unions' economic interests has been accompanied by growing centralisation of decision-making. The annual Congress proceedings have become increasingly ritualised: key speeches are commonly directed outside the conference hall, policy conflicts are typically smothered in bland composites, and if unavoidable are decided by usually predetermined block votes; though the disposal of some unions' votes is less predictable than in the past, because of greater assertiveness by lay delegates. Policy initiatives come almost universally from the General Council, which itself for the most part merely endorses the detailed proposals generated within the TUC committee structure. The crucial decision in 1975 to support a £6 limit for pay increases was effectively taken by the 'NEDC six' in negotiation with government ministers. The diminishing significance of Congress itself helps to explain the growing criticism expressed at the method of election to the General Council; this culminated in the decision taken in principle in 1981 (and confirmed in 1982) for the automatic representation of all unions with over 100,000 members, despite General Council opposition.

Three other aspects of enhanced TUC authority may be briefly noted. Following the decision of the 1962 Congress in favour of a review of trade union structure—after a debate remembered for Woodcock's comment that 'structure, particularly in the trade union Movement, is a function of purpose'—a series of meetings was convened for unions with cognate industrial or occupational interests. In its role as 'honest broker' the TUC facilitated amalgamations and encouraged inter-union cooperation. Secondly, legislative intervention in industrial relations has led to increased status. The decision of the 1972 Congress, against General Council advice, to instruct non-cooperation with the institutions of the Industrial Relations Act was followed by the expulsion of twenty affiliates for non-compliance: an unprecedented exercise of disciplinary powers. The subsequent decision (taken virtually without debate, despite previous TUC policy) to pursue extensive positive statutory rights for workers and unions was implemented through detailed participation in the drafting of the Trade Union and Labour Relations Act and the Employment Protection Act. More recently, the TUC has coordinated relatively low-key opposition to the anti-union legislation of the Thatcher Government. Thirdly, its traditionally modest role in trade union education has expanded, following provision in the Employment Protection Act for paid time off work for union-approved training courses, and the introduction, also in 1975, of government subsidies for union education. If still very limited by international standards, the quantity and quality of TUC education services are nevertheless a substantial advance on a decade ago.

Overall, extensions to the powers and prerogatives of the TUC have occurred pragmatically, and primarily in response to external pressures. The elaboration of a common economic programme for the trade union movement—particularly as regards the public sector—is a significant development, but this remains largely symbolic, rather than a springboard for political mobilisation. Intervention in industrial disputes has appeared more decisive in curbing politically embarrassing initiatives by individual unions than in advancing common struggles. In any event, affiliated unions remain reluctant to contribute to enlarged resources or to concede further central authority. Symptomatically, the 'extensive review of the TUC's organisation, structure and services' initiated by the General Council in 1980 evoked little enthusiasm from unions whose individual financial problems reinforce traditional reluctance to fund central functions which might encroach upon their own autonomy.

Trade Unions and 'Labourism'

The political interests and activities of twentieth-century British unions have a unique institutional expression: the Labour Party, established by the 1899 TUC to advance the 'labour interest' in parliament and, in particular, to safeguard the legal status of the unions themselves. Broader social purposes were embraced only haltingly, and the 1918 constitution which registered an explicit commitment to the goals of Fabian socialism also consolidated the federal structure through which the unions, by virtue of their affiliated membership (far exceeding the individual members in the constituencies), numerically dominate the Party conference and its national executive committee.

But the relationship between numerical (and financial) dominance and real control has long been diffuse. The very existence of the Labour Party stems from the belief that 'politics' is external to unions' central functions and interests. 'Labourism' entails a definition of workers' interests within the framework of the existing social order, and an identification of 'politics' (as a sphere of social and economic aims and aspirations transcending the immediate agenda of collective bargaining) with the institutional arena of parliamentary government (Miliband, 1971; Saville, 1973). Unions have thus accepted both the impropriety of mobilising their industrial strength in pursuit of objectives external to the sphere of industrial relations, and the overriding jurisdiction of Labour's parliamentary representatives in formulating the political programme and priorities of the movement.

During its formative years the Parliamentary Labour Party (PLP) clearly established that it was not operationally accountable to the Party in the country, or more specifically to the unions; its primacy was symbolised by the evolution of the PLP chairman as leader of the Party as a whole. As Minkin put it (1974: 10, 14–5) 'the trade union leaders have neither sought to become the political leadership of the party nor generally have they sought close control over the process of policy-making'. But as a corollary, 'the internal policy-making and judicial affairs of trade unions could not be the subject of party policy, nor could the party attempt to support any policy that implied statutory interference with the process of free collective bargaining'.

This demarcation has broken down in the past two decades. During the early post-war years the traditional division of functions was strongly reinforced by a close understanding between the leaderships of the PLP and several major unions, united in hostility to radical social and economic ideas within the movement and in commitment to the developing bipartisan foreign policy centred upon NATO. In particular, the leaders of three unions—the TGWU, the GMWU and the NUM, together wielding roughly a third of total votes at the Party conference—became known as the 'praetorian guard' through their support for the parliamentary leadership against any variety of left-wing challenge. 'Loyalist' unions also dominated the conference arrangements committee, and elections to the national executive. Thus the platform won every conference vote (with one minor exception) between 1948 and 1960 (Minkin, 1980).

The shift in this pattern has in part reflected a more fluid balance within the major unions. The election of Cousins as general secretary of the TGWU heralded the collapse of the 'praetorian guard', and was reflected in that union's eventual support for unilateral nuclear disarmament, the issue on which the party leadership suffered a dramatic defeat at the 1960 conference. The subsequent attempt by AEU president Carron to assume the role of 'loyalist' leader provoked increasing opposition within his own union (Minkin, 1980:ch.7). The contrasting growth rates of different unions have also undermined the built-in 'loyalist' dominance: rising organisations such as ASTMS and NUPE have often opposed the party leadership.[5]

Such trends have been overlaid by a more general detachment between Party and unions. Shared identification with the record of 1945–51, once a symbolic reference point, had faded by the 1960s. The proportion of Labour MPs with a background as activists or officials in affiliated unions declined, with a corresponding increase in the proportion of 'professionals'; and the composition of the PLP leadership has altered even more markedly (Hindess, 1971: Minkin, 1978).[6] Other factors also weakened the traditional 'labour alliance'. Labour politicians blamed electoral defeats in the 1950s on their close association with the unions (often viewed as anachronistic and obstructive), and sought a more 'classless' image. Some trade unionists also saw the party connection as a liability. George Woodcock (who became TUC general secretary in 1960) was anxious to attract the expanding public sector unions into membership, and to consolidate the standing of Congress vis-à-vis governments irrespective of party; hence a 'non-political' stance was cultivated.

These tendencies were reinforced by the experience of Labour in government after 1964. Initial euphoria surrounding joint blueprints for economic expansion and a 'planned growth of incomes' gave way to the reality of economic crisis and stagnation, wage restraint and declining real net incomes. Statutory sanctions to back up the government's incomes policy (in which the TUC 'reluctantly acquiesced' in 1966, but which it overwhelmingly rejected two years later), gravely challenged the tradition that Labour would defend the unions' cherished principle of 'free collective bargaining'. Even more serious, and seemingly gratuitous, was the government's decision in 1969 to introduce new legislative restrictions on

---

[5] Many of the major 'white-collar' unions in the public sector are not affiliated to the Labour Party. The only significant (re-) affiliation in recent years is that of the POEU in 1964. NALGO held a ballot on the issue in 1982—an initiative scarcely conceivable a few years ago—but the proposal was heavily defeated.
[6] Paradoxically the proportion of MPs sponsored by unions, which had fallen since the 1930s, actually increased (Ellis and Johnson, 1973; Muller, 1979; Coates and Topham, 1980:ch.10); but this may be attributed to the 'opportunistic' sponsorship of politicians without solid union roots, as the significance of this status has become increasingly symbolic.

the 'right' to strike: the one occasion in recent history when the 'trade union group' of Labour MPs asserted its identity, insisting that it would not support the proposed legislation (Jenkins, 1970; Panitch, 1976). More generally, 'as some union leaders saw it in the late 1960s, the government at times appeared to be asserting a positive virtue of its unwillingness to court Labour popularity' (Minkin, 1978:464). The sharpening division was reflected in an unprecedented frequency of conference defeats for government policy, and in growing opposition within the Party's own national executive.

These breaks were temporarily healed during the 1970–74 Heath Government, with its abrasive challenge to many elements of the British post-war political consensus, and in particular its comprehensive assault on the unions' status and activities enacted in 1971. A Liaison Committee was created at the end of 1970 and formalised in January 1972, with equal representation from the TUC General Council, the PLP, and the Party's national executive. Regular meetings formulated policy proposals, notably the document *Economic Policy and the Cost of Living,* published in February 1973; as well as outlining an extensive programme of economic and social reform, this declared that the first task of a Labour government on taking office would be 'to conclude with the TUC . . . a wide-ranging agreement on the policies to be pursued in all these aspects of our economic life and to discuss with them the order of priorities of their fulfilment'.

Though analogous joint bodies had existed in the past, the Liaison Committee was unprecedented in its significance in that it was established when the authority of the General Council was far greater than in the past, and was envisaged from the outset as a key forum for policy formulation. In effect the direct participation of individual unions in the Labour Party was transcended by this new channel of collective representation, which gave the TUC 'for the first time in its history . . . a direct line into Labour Party policy-making and thus into general election manifestoes' (Elliott, 1978:31). The new accommodation was symbolised in the popular notion of the Social Contract.

The unions' relationship with the 1974–9 Labour Government had three main phases. Initially there was a close 'left' alliance between those on the Party executive and the General Council who opposed the EEC and demanded a radical interventionist and expansionist economic strategy. But the repeal and replacement of the Industrial Relations Act satisfied the unions' most urgent priority; and in mid-1975 the result of the EEC referendum, by undermining the credibility of the demand for withdrawal, destroyed a major foundation of union/party left unity. This allowed the government to remove Tony Benn from the Industry Ministry and gain TUC approval for the £6 pay limit. After 1975 a new leadership bloc emerged to link Government and General Council, vainly opposed by the left-dominated Party executive (Minkin, 1978:480). In particular, the erstwhile radical union leaders Jones and Scanlon were absorbed into a new orthodoxy, in which successive deflationary measures and mounting unemployment were deplored but not forcefully opposed. The Social Contract, a deceptive symbol of trade unions' power, had become a vehicle for their subordination (Clark et al., 1980; R. D. Coates, 1980; Taylor, 1980).

Renewed accommodation has in some respects been reinforced since 1979 by the shift to the right in such key unions as the AUEW-E. But in other respects new instabilities have emerged. Dissatisfaction with the experience of the 1964–70 Government gave rise to pressure for greater Party democracy, voiced among others by Jack Jones in 1970 (Taylor, 1980:129–30). This pressure developed a momentum which was sustained throughout the 1970s, culminating in constitutional changes agreed at a special conference in 1981: contested re-selection of MPs, and annual election of the Party leader and deputy (when contested) by a college equally representative of the unions, the constituencies, and the PLP. This procedure, applied in the election for deputy leader later the same year, forced unions to commit themselves directly in areas of party decision-making formerly the preserve of the PLP. Not only did the internal procedures of many unions—under the glare of media publicity—prove less than adequate for this task; political factions within the party had a novel incentive to intervene in internal union politics. The crisis in the Labour Party, symbolised both by the 1981 contest and by the emergence of the SDP,[7] may well intensify the pressures for greater union initiative within the party. The institutional framework for such a role is far less clear than it was a decade ago.

INTERPRETATIONS AND PROJECTIONS

'The trade union', insisted Gramsci (1977:265), 'is not a pre-determined phenomenon. It *becomes* a determinate institution, i.e. it takes on a definite historical form to the extent that the strength and will of the workers who are its members impress a policy and propose an aim that define it.' At the same time, it is a key characteristic of unions that they are secondary or intermediary organisations (Hyman and Fryer, 1975; Müller-Jentsch, 1981): they are associations of workers who are already 'organised' by those to whom they sell their labour power and whose actions they are designed to influence; and unions' policies are shaped by this pragmatic mediation between the members they represent and the external agencies with which they deal. Any adequate interpretation of trade union development must therefore link theoretically the active initiative of union members and representatives, the purposes and ideologies which inform their actions, and the external material forces which influence and constrain them.

---

[7] The latter has as yet won little support within the unions themselves; and its backing for Conservative anti-union legislation is unlikely to increase its appeal.

Academic analysis of trade unions has, however, typically resisted such integrated understanding. While the Webbs in their pioneering studies (1894, 1897) were concerned to link the changing material circumstances of workers, the organisational elaboration and internal politics of unions, their strategies for job control, and their place in the broader society, subsequent thinkers have adopted a more fragmented and particularistic focus. Contributions in the past two decades have, for the most part, merely elaborated these established particularisms.

An overwhelming empiricism has long been associated with a piecemeal approach to trade union analysis. Typical of this orientation was Roberts's lengthy descriptive study (1956) of union constitutional arrangements. A major break with tradition was Turner's attempt (1962) to generalise from the historical experience of the cotton unions, applying a dynamic focus on issues of union structure and government and proposing the categories of 'open' and 'closed' unions and of 'exclusive democracies', 'aristocracies' and 'popular bossdoms'. Subsequent criticism of the limitations of Turner's conceptualisation—e.g. Hughes (1967, 1968)—have, however, led to a return to essentially descriptive taxonomies, of which the major recent example is Undy et al. (1981).

The last two decades have seen increasing application of the concepts and perspectives of a range of social science disciplines. One approach has built on American attention to the electoral process in unions (e.g. Lipset et al., 1956). Thus Martin (1968) has made factional activity the central theme of an analysis of union democracy, while Edelstein and Warner (1975) have erected a grandiose interpretative model upon the computation of voting statistics. More recent 'behavioural science' approaches to organisational politics, outlined by Child et al. (1973), have analysed unions in terms of competition or conflict among 'elites' of activists and leaders (Banks, 1974; Moran, 1974; Hemingway, 1978).

The problem with these approaches is their tendency—which can be traced back to the early polemics of Michels (1915), and which has been shared by many of his critics—to over-emphasise the *internal* sources of politics and policy in trade unions. Unions are frequently treated as self-contained 'systems' on which an external 'environment' impinges only through a limited set of readily identifiable channels. Conversely, attention to the 'political' aspects of trade union activity (e.g. McKenzie, 1955; Allen, 1960; Harrison, 1960; Macdonald, 1960) has been largely detached from analysis of 'industrial' strategies and their refractions within unions' internal relationships.

In some respects, this traditional separation of union 'politics' from 'industrial relations' has been transcended in recent studies employing the notion of corporatism. This term has been applied with a variety of meanings, only rarely embedded within an explicit theoretical framework —as Panitch (1980) has argued in a recent critical discussion. Inherent in most usage is an emphasis on the growing interrelationship between the state and various 'interest' or 'producer' groups, supplementing or displacing the traditional parliamentary process. Much more contentious is the precise character of such relationships. Much popular discussion—reflected academically in the treatment of trade unions by Middlemas (1979:372) as 'governing institutions'—assumes that political involvement is in itself a reflection of political power.[8] Other approaches stress the formal concessions by government to the status of unions (or in particular their leaders) as part of an unequal exchange whereby material compliance with government economic strategy is secured. Such an exchange may indeed involve strengthening union officials' disciplinary powers over (or at least their independence from) their members, thus facilitating union cooperation with policies of wage restraint (Panitch, 1981; Sabel, 1981). Yet other writers—notably Crouch (1977, 1979) with his notion of 'bargained corporatism'—argue that the relationship is one in which both parties yield and obtain real concessions.

The imprecision, and often theoretical vacuity, of the notion of corporatism might be thought to undermine its utility. Most applications of the term merely emphasise, without elucidating, the changing relationship between workers, unions and the state in a context where state and economy themselves are unwontedly interlinked. Typically, discussion of corporatism represents a spurious short-cut to understanding.

The elements of unions' changing status must be adequately differentiated before they can be re-assembled theoretically. Three broad areas of analysis may be distinguished. Firstly, the role of unions within contemporary capitalism: no credible discussion of trade unions' internal relationships is possible without first establishing the antagonistic and oppositional characteristics inherent in their very existence. Manifestations of a system of production in which those who sell their labour power are forced into mutual competition while subject to the domination of those who direct their labour, trade unions were established to counter the inhuman priorities of capital accumulation. Yet unions also struggle to survive on the terrain defined by capitalist production relations: if their aims and actions threaten too frontally the profitability of those who employ their members, they may be faced with a terminal challenge to their very existence. Any general decline in capitalist profitability, by reducing the margin available for peaceful negotiation, necessarily narrows the agenda which unions may safely pursue. Increased overt involvement of governments in the realm of economic activity brings the resources of state power into sharper salience as an influence on union policy. In so far as particular patterns of internal relations are seen by these powerful external parties as more or less conducive to acceptable union goals and strategies, they will exert pressure on unions' internal affairs (see Hyman, 1975:ch.3). In such

---

[8] These views became widespread during the period of the Social Contract. But, as R. D. Coates has insisted (1980:203), 'publicity is never the most reliable index of influence'. While the unions' close consultative links had considerable (though not unqualified) effect in the framing of industrial relations legislation, their impact on broader industrial and economic policy was negligible.

ways unions can be subject to immense external constraints, both material and ideological; their character and structure can be profoundly conditioned by their opponents. (This is the essential starting point for assessing Flanders's insistence (1952, 1970a) on the central role of 'job regulation' in determining union policy and union development, and the more recent work by Clegg (1976b) linking union organisation and internal relations to the structure and character of collective bargaining.)

A second key focus must be the unions' actual and potential members. Unionism is an expression of workers' experience of shared interests and aspirations. But there are many possible forms of this expression: where boundaries of common interests are drawn, what aspirations are conceived as realistic and legitimate, what means are viewed as appropriate for their attainment. Workers are differentiated in both the labour market and the labour process: in the relative security of their employment and the remuneration they derive from it; in the degree of autonomy, of control over others, or of subordination to others which is inherent in their work itself. Such variations may be reflected in differential unionisation or in membership of different unions; or in differential involvement or influence within a single union. Dynamically, such factors will be significantly affected by changes in the structure of employment, in the organisation of production, in the conditions of the labour market, as well as in the general 'political climate' and in the broader social context of working-class life.

From within and without these two dimensions condition the third: the mediating role of policy formulation and more pervasive internal political processes in trade unions. Officials at different levels in the union hierarchy, and 'lay' activists with varying representative or 'bureaucratic' functions, pursue their intra-union activities in partial independence from both external pressures and from those of the membership. Often both officials and activists stem disproportionately from relatively advantaged sections of a union's constituency: white, male, higher-paid, higher-skilled, higher-status—a tendency sensitively explored, on the basis of American experience, by Herding (1972). Often they are differentiated in the nature and extent of the political sensitivity which informs even their routine union activities.

Because of the mediating strategies of those actively implicated in unions' organisational affairs, the terrain of union politics is not merely given. Trade unions 'simultaneously express and define the interests of the members' (Offe and Wiesenthal, 1981:79); unionism involves a continuous effort to collectivise workers' discrete experiences and aspirations, an effort which may be more or less vigorously and sensitively pursued in the face of powerful counter-pressures. This mobilisation of collectivity may sustain broader or narrower perceptions of community of interest, shaping the boundaries of alliance and division; it will influence the balance of concern with issues of wages, of work itself, and of broader social and political relations; and it can encourage or discourage membership activism, which should not be viewed as a fixed or invariable attribute (Batstone et al., 1977, 1978; Beynon, 1973:ch.8; Carpenter, 1983). The nature and extent of such mobilisation are correspondingly significant for the behaviour of employers and the state, affecting both the attractiveness and the feasibility of aggressive as against collaborative strategies. 'Governments', argued Cousins in the TUC debate over NEDC in 1963, 'are influenced by the power of the people I represent.' It is the members' 'willingness to act' (Offe and Wiesenthal, 1981) which makes union aspirations impracticable to suppress but difficult to 'incorporate', generating a weighty dilemma for both managerial and governmental policy. Conversely, forms of trade union practice which 'demobilise' the membership ease the task of external containment.

Union mediation between membership and external forces thus operates within an area of autonomous influence; but this autonomy is likely to vary according to material and historical context. This is a crucial question for both interpretation and prognosis. The key developments of the past two decades are clearly interlinked: union growth and structural consolidation, transcending some former divisions while perhaps reinforcing others (see, for example, the debate in Hobsbawm et al., 1981); economic crisis and decline creating a harsher environment for collective bargaining; the growing politicisation of industrial relations with the expanding economic role of the state. All are refracted in the broadening agenda of union policy debate, and the sharpening of internal conflicts and divisions.

There is little reason to doubt that the political and economic climate for trade unions in the 1980s will remain hostile, maintaining the contradictory pressures towards organisational consolidation and internal conflict. The key imponderable factor will be the ability of union activists and officials to mobilise wider membership support and engagement. There are, at present, few signs of advance in this task. Failure would render British unions more than ever before victims rather than initiators of societal developments.

3 Shop Steward Development and Managerial Strategies

Michael Terry

Shop stewards, representatives of trade union members at the place of work where they are themselves employed, are not unique to the United Kingdom, but the extent of their activity and influence certainly is. In no other country is this form of organised worker representation so well established and powerful, so central to an understanding of the pattern of industrial relations, and any account of the growth and development of shop steward organisation must take account of this fact. Such an account must also be sensitive both to the general historical development of shop stewards and their organisations and to variations within the overall pattern. The argument of this chapter is that the changing strategies both of the state and of employers towards workers and their trade union representatives are central to an understanding of the development of shop steward organisation. The chapter briefly sketches the changes in shop steward organisation in the last three or four decades, and goes on critically to consider various explanations of these observed changes. In particular, attention is focused on changes which took place over the decade following the publication of the report of the Donovan Commission in 1968.

THE GROWTH AND DEVELOPMENT OF STEWARD ORGANISATION

An estimate made in 1961 put the number of shop stewards in the United Kingdom at 90,000 (Clegg et al., 1961:153). The same research showed their distribution to vary widely: for example, most members in the then Electrical Trades Union and Amalgamated Engineering Union were represented by shop stewards but few, if any, were in unions organising in mines, shops, and white-collar occupations. The authors noted that the variation was best accounted for by differences between industries, although they also noted that 'stewards are rare when unions are relatively weak'.

This preponderance of shop stewards in engineering industries was still apparent seven years later when McCarthy and Parker (1968:15,94) put the number at 175,000, which they thought represented a growth of 14 per cent over the previous ten years. Of these, 45 per cent were in the metal handling industries, 13 per cent in the rest of manufacturing, and 36 per cent in non-manufacturing, including 12 per cent in transport and communication. Thus the picture in 1968 was one of selective growth over the previous decade. Engineering and associated industries still dominated, but there were significant increases in other areas, especially in distributive and service occupations.

This growth was small, however, compared to the following decade. Clegg (1979:51–3) estimated that the total number of stewards in 1978 was more than 250,000, and his estimate is supported by more recent work. The Warwick Survey suggested a total in 1978 of 119,000 manual shop stewards and 37,000 white-collar stewards in manufacturing industry alone (Brown, 1981:62). Similar recent increases have been reported for the private services sector (Hawes and Smith, 1981:268) and for the public sector, especially in services such as health and local government, where the growth may have been the most dramatic of all (see Somerton, 1977; Fryer et al., 1974; Terry, 1982). In 1981, for example, the National Union of Public Employees (NUPE) alone claimed to have 23,000 shop stewards (Eaton and Gill, 1981:248)

By the end of the 1970s, then, shop stewards were to be found well beyond the 'metal handling industries' and other earlier strongholds. In manufacturing industry they were all but universal among manual workforces with more than 100 workers (Brown, 1981:53). In both the public and the private service sectors, shop stewards, while less ubiquitous than their counterparts in manufacturing, were nevertheless widespread in both manual and white-collar areas. The Warwick Survey showed that in manufacturing industry the existence of shop stewards is virtually synonymous with the recognition of trade unions. Thus just under 76 per cent of establishments in the sample recognised at least one manual trade union, and just over 73 per cent had shop stewards. In plants employing more than 500 manual workers the two figures were identical. While size accounted for some of the variation—the larger the workforce the greater the probability of union recognition and shop stewards—there were also interesting inter-industry variations. Thus while industries such as vehicle building and metal manufacture, the industries traditionally associated with shop stewards, continued to show the highest incidence of steward organisation, other industries, such as food, drink and tobacco, and clothing, leather and footwear, had shop steward organisations in over 75 per cent of their establishments in 1978. In these industries there was no evidence of such organisation a decade earlier. As the Warwick Survey (Brown, 1981:79) concludes, there is 'considerable similarity between industries in the state of steward organisations, once the effect of workforce size is allowed for; there is still variability, but it has diminished substantially since the 1960s'.

The picture of growth over the decade is clear. More uncertain, however, is the question of what has been happening to shop steward organisations—the groupings formed by shop stewards within and between workplaces. The research done by Marsh and Coker (1963), Lerner and Bescoby (1966), and Turner et al. (1967) all points to inter- and intra-plant organisation of considerable sophistication within the engineering industry, and in particular within motor car companies and their component suppliers. Goodman and Whittingham (1973:132–3) also refer to significant unofficial committee structures in the docks, the building industry, and electricity supply. But the research done for the Donovan Commission tended to neglect this organisational aspect. Apart from noting some kind of meetings between stewards in 66 per cent of establishments, and some sort of senior steward system in almost exactly the same proportion (McCarthy and Parker, 1968:22, 24), nothing was said about the extent or significance of shop steward organisation. While this omission is intriguing in itself, given the central importance attached to shop stewards in the Commission's analysis of the 'two systems' of industrial relations in the United Kingdom, the present problem is to assess the extent to which the picture painted of shop steward organisation in more recent work represents a significant shift or development over the decade.

TABLE 3.1: INDICATORS OF SHOP STEWARD ORGANISATION

	Private Manufacturing Industry	Local Government
Manual		
Recognised senior steward	74·0	70·0
Full-time steward present	11·7	33·0
Regular steward meetings	36·8	50·0
Non-manual		
Recognised senior steward	61·4	73·0
Full-time steward present	2·3	17·0
Regular steward meetings	30·0	83·0

Sources: Brown (1981:64); Terry (1982:4, 8).
Note: Figures are expressed as a percentage of those establishments where a steward is present.

Before considering this point it is useful to look at details of the state of shop steward organisation at the end of the 1970s. Table 3.1 provides a picture of formal measures of shop steward organisation in private manufacturing and local government. Within the manufacturing sector these indicators varied with size, and, as with shop steward presence, there were considerable similarities between the traditional strongholds of stewards and those in which shop stewards have only emerged more recently. As Table 3.1 shows, similar patterns of organisation have emerged in local government, and there is evidence to show that this is typical of much of the public sector (see Brown et al., 1978:145; Clegg, 1979:35–8). Of all the changes noted, perhaps the increase in the number of stewards who spend all their working time on union duties (full-time stewards) is the most dramatic and the most frequently noted. Although precise estimates vary (Brown, 1981:65–7), most commentators accept that there has been an approximate quadrupling of their numbers across all unionised sectors in the decade since 1968, up to a figure possibly as high as 10,000.

Other changes have accompanied those detailed above. They include the increasing regularity and formality of shop steward election procedures (Parker et al., 1971:17; Brown et al., 1978: 146), and the increasing availability of a range of facilities (often provided by the employer) such as offices, secretaries, photocopiers, and telephones. At the same time shop stewards have become more professional and skilled in the discharge of their jobs. Helped by sympathetic legislation, the granting to stewards of time off work to attend courses has greatly increased since 1974. In 1979, 44,000 places were provided on TUC courses for shop stewards (WEA, 1980:1), and to this figure must be added the large number of courses provided by individual unions for their own stewards. This increasing expertise has been related to other developments in shop steward organisation, such as the growth of specialist committees to deal with particular topics on the steward agenda such as health and safety (Brown, 1981:75).

Thus by 1978 the presence of shop stewards in a workplace appeared to be virtually coterminous with the existence of shop steward organisation as identified by the indicators noted above. The straightforward inference is that the decade saw a growth of professional shop stewards organised in more formally complex groupings. In areas where steward organisation was not well-established before the late 1960s this picture is straightforward. But, as noted above, there are difficulties in identifying clear patterns of change in those industries, such as engineering, in which shop stewards have been a force since World War II. The problems here are clearly shown in the brief history of an engineering shop steward organisation (Batstone et al., 1977:281–9). This account shows a number of phases in the development of the organisation, but all show evidence of sophistication and complexity, at least since the achievement of near-complete trade union organisation in 1953. But this should not be taken as typical. As Brown (1973:136–57) demonstrated in his research in Midlands engineering plants in the late 1960s and early 1970s, the degree of organisational integration and complexity shown by shop steward bodies varies quite widely. Thus it is possible to conclude that in such industries the present picture of shop steward organisation reflects in some cases dramatic changes while in others the changes have been less noticeable (for a fuller discussion of these differences and the reasons for them see Terry, 1979).

By 1978, then, shop steward organisations appeared broadly similar wherever they were to be found, although the historical processes underlying this 'snapshot' have varied across and between industries. These variations, as well as the general trend, are the subject of the rest of this chapter, but before turning to them, it is important to identify some exceptions to the overall pattern. First, there remain substantial areas of industry with low rates of union recognition, and hence shop steward presence. Many of these are in the private service sector (Hawes and Smith, 1981). But there are also industries with dense union organisation and no shop stewards. Prominent among these is the boot and shoe industry where a combination of factors has kept shop steward development down (Goodman et al., 1977). Second, there are some groups of workers, women for example, whose representation in steward organisations is not proportional to their numbers in a given workforce (Brown et al., 1978:146–7; Aldred, 1981; Coote and Kellner, 1980). The same point can be made about organised black workers (Miles and Phizacklea, 1978:201). Finally, there are significant differences in the size of shop steward constituencies. Although this figure has been slowly coming down over the last decade to a median figure of thirty-nine unionists to each shop steward (Brown et al., 1978:141), there is some evidence that such a figure may conceal considerable variations (Terry, 1982:4). Thus not only is the coverage of shop stewards incomplete, but there are situations in which access by workers to a steward who is truly representative may at times be more difficult than the overall figures suggest. These are, however, fluctuations around a general trend which is the subject of the remainder of this chapter.

SHOP STEWARD ACTIVITY AND ORGANISATION: BEFORE DONOVAN

The Donovan Report provided the basis for a 'model' of shop steward behaviour that was amplified in other work produced around the same time (Donovan, 1968:25–9; Clegg, 1970:ch.1; Goodman and Whittingham, 1973). This model stressed a number of important features of shop steward activity, in particular the stewards' relationships with the work groups they represented, their independence from the official trade union movement, their relationships with the lower-level managers such as foremen and supervisors with whom they dealt, and their wage-bargaining activity. Each of these features will be briefly discussed and the overall picture they present will then be critically assessed.

First, shop stewards were closely identified with the work group they represented. They shared the working environment of those they represented, and were subject to membership control on a continuous and close basis. Such a view of shop stewards as being primarily workers who acted from time to time as representatives of small groups of which they themselves were members implied, in turn, that the shop stewards could unproblematically be seen as representing the interests of the workers who elected them. In the words of Kahn-Freund (1979:5), shopfloor organisation approximates to a model of 'direct democracy' in which decisions are taken in collective meetings by the electorate themselves, after which they may be handed over to a representative for implementation. This direct link was identified by Hyman (1971) as the most important basis of defence against any drift into forms of bureaucratic and oligarchic control as analysed by Michels (1915). It was perceived as the underpinning of British trade union democracy as opposed to more formal democratic structures such as ballots, elections, and systems of representation based on hierarchical structures. Kahn-Freund describes this latter system as 'representative democracy' in contrast to the 'direct' type described above. In a representative system, the electorate do not take decisions themselves, but choose those who are called upon to do so. This distinction will be returned to later.

Second, it was argued that the shop steward movement was largely autonomous from the official trade union movement (Donovan, 1968:30–1). Its unofficial, at times almost clandestine, existence combined with its multi-union character to make it unamenable to control by the official movement (Beynon, 1973:48). Turner et al. (1967:216–21) have described the system they found operating in the motor industry as one of 'parallel unionism', with the shop steward organisations undertaking virtually all the significant activity, often in the face of a degree of official trade union hostility. This development was part of the process underlying the increasing irrelevance of 'national' agreements at the industry level on pay and conditions to actual earnings in much of private industry (Donovan, 1968:16). Union leaders, and the employers and their associations with which they negotiated, came to find that there were no means of implementing the national agreements they signed.

Third, all this shopfloor activity was seen to happen without the formal approval of a senior manager. The bargaining process, if indeed bargaining was involved, took place between workers and their representatives and the lowest level of management organisation—foremen and ratefixers—often without the knowledge and approval of senior management. In other words, much was attributed to the loose or inadequate nature of management control systems that enabled informal deals to go unregistered and unchecked.

Finally, shop stewards' activity was primarily identified with the processes of shopfloor wage bargaining. As McCarthy noted (1966:30), shop stewards 'tend to be most prominent and influential where they can secure a measure of influence over earnings', although they are not without influence where they do not bargain over wages. Clegg (1970:33) identifies overtime distribution as another significant area, although he notes that this can be regulated internally by the work group without the need for a bargaining representative.

The ability of some workforces and their shop stewards to exert this independent strength derived from a particular basis of 'bargaining power': a power rooted in the tightness of the labour and product markets in which certain industries operated in the 1950s and 1960s, and was often exploited to best advantage in workplaces with assembly-line or batch production technologies and using piecework payment systems (see Clegg, 1970:31–2). This combination of internal and external circumstances in some industries and occupations enhanced both the feasibility and effectiveness of local-ised, brief forms of industrial action (extending right across the spectrum from 'irregular' working practices into strikes) in pursuit of pay and other claims. The association of shop stewards with unofficial, unconstitutional forms of industrial action seemed conclusively made (see Donovan, 1968: 104–8).

While all the features outlined above, and the notion of bargaining power that underlay them, contain much that is true and important, they also contain exaggerations and misstatements that must be noted in order to obtain a better understanding of shop steward activity and subsequent development. The picture painted above is one of a closed system involving workers, stewards, and low-level managers in a series of semi-legitimate negotiations removed from the scrutiny and control of senior managers and union officials. It will be argued below that this stereotype presents a partial picture, and that the crucial missing element is an understanding of the control systems and strategies adopted by managers in their dealings with their workforces.

There are two starting points for this argument. The first is in the considerable evidence that many managers above the level of foreman, especially works and personnel managers, were not only aware of the operation of the shop steward system, but were well satisfied with its operation, seeing it as an effective system of handling problems and grievances (McCarthy and Parker, 1968:27). The second is the evidence that workplace negotiation frequently extended well beyond pay into a wide range of 'job control' issues (McCarthy and Parker, 1968:50–2). These covered 'inefficient labour practices', the organisation and arrange-ment of work, the level of worker effort, and the extent of overtime working. These are identified by the Donovan Report (1968:79) as 'restrictive practices' and are held to be associated far more strongly with the behaviour of work groups than with shop stewards, but there is evidence to suggest that this is incorrect. Goodman and Whittingham, for example (1973:169, 176) provide several examples where stewards were closely involved in the negotiation of job control issues. Here it is sufficient to note that both workers and managers have an interest in exerting control over both wages and the intensity of work. It is against this wider view of workshop relations that the operation of shop stewards and management's noted preference for dealing with them must be evaluated.

Central to an understanding of the period is the fact that, through the 1950s and 1960s, managers confronted by the increasing power and authority of workplace trade unionism often tried to adapt it to their own advantage rather than to oppose and destroy it. This was not a universal response: many employers and managers did take a more oppositional course, and the timing and nature of more accommodatory behaviour varied greatly. Nevertheless, such accommodation was an important trend. It has, for example, been identified by Friedman (1977:78) in his analysis of post-war developments in Coventry motor car manufacture. Friedman calls the dominant managerial strategy in the period up to the late 1960s 'responsible autonomy'. In this period, he says, managers 'attempt to harness the adaptability of labour power by giving workers leeway and encouraging them to adapt to changing situations in a manner beneficial to the firm' by giving 'workers status, authority and responsibility'. Such a strategy included piecework bargaining and the procedural involvement of shop stewards in grievance handling.

This attitude on the part of managers might seem irrational were it to lead to a loss of managerial control over costs and effort. Several authors have noted that this need not be true. As Hyman and Elger (1981:116) have argued, job controls 'frequently . . . operated within limits acceptable to employers, and could often be viewed as elements in an accommodation which did not obstruct, and might even facilitate, the production and realisation of surplus value'. In other words, managers might, paradoxically, find their task of control made easier by the concession of a degree of their prerogative to workers. Burawoy (1979:ch.5) develops this argument still further by arguing that managers may actually devise forms of control that include a degree of scope for 'worker control' built in to operate in a manner pre-determined by, and hence advantageous to, management, while preserving the illusion that the workers are 'fiddling' the system. Treating job control as a 'zero-sum' phenomenon, with a gain for workers representing a corresponding loss for management, is over simple. 'Worker control' and its agents can further or hinder management aims.

This brings the argument back to management attitudes towards shop stewards. It follows from the points made so far that if management has an interest in accommodating to or even promoting certain forms of workplace job control, similar accommodations are likely to be made with the organisations that in some ways coordinate and 'preserve' that control—shop steward organisations. In fact, there has been considerable evidence of ambivalence and variation in managerial behaviour towards shop stewards for several decades. Management hostility to shop stewards, as to other aspects of union organisation, was found in industries, such as building, that were dominated by small firms. In the public sector, with its strongly centralised system of industrial relations, managements saw no place for local union negotiators. Even in well-organised industries some large companies, such as Ford (Beynon,1973:ch.2), persistently tried to undermine shop steward organisation through tactics of victimisation. One recent survey found that slightly over half the shop stewards questioned had experienced managerial resistance to shop stewards in the previous twenty years (Brown et al., 1978:148). Generally, however, despite exceptions such as Ford, management's reactions to the emerging strength of shop stewards was to develop a form of helpful accommodation with them. As Turner et al. noted (1967:214) 'the leading stewards are performing a managerial function, of grievance settlement, welfare arrangement and human adjustment, and the steward system's acceptance by management . . . has developed partly because of the increasing effectiveness—and certainly economy—with which this role is fulfilled'. Thus management views on shop stewards reflected their views on what shop stewards achieve. If those achievements were advantageous, or at least tolerable, to management, so were shop stewards.

It is therefore unsurprising to find evidence of longstanding relationships of mutual support between managers and shop stewards. Such 'bargaining relationships' as they have been termed (Brown, 1973: Batstone et al., 1977:ch.7) are central to an understanding of shop steward power and organisation. For not only do they constitute a power resource for both sides, to add to power derived from labour and product markets, but it is a power resource confined to the individual stewards and managers on each side. This is a crucial source of leadership both between stewards and those they represent and among shop stewards themselves, as Batstone and his colleagues argue at length. They note a strong managerial preference for dealing with stewards who act as 'leaders', shaping the opinions and preferences of their members, rather than being wholly directed by them. Thus management, by trying to choose the type of steward with whom they prefer to negotiate can, quite deliberately, contribute to the development of hierarchy and leadership within shop steward organisations.

The influence of managerial behaviour on steward organisation is confirmed by survey data. Brown et al. (1978:148) noted differences between shop steward organisations in companies pursuing hostile tactics towards stewards and those taking a more accommodating position. It is clear that the relationships between managers and shop stewards and their relationship to strategies of control is more complex than allowed for in the stereotype outlined above. This complexity underlies the partial nature of the earlier simple model. A more comprehensive view demonstrates a managerial interest in the regulation of job control as well as wages, and hence, in the steward organisations involved. The accommodations reached between stewards and management emphasised leadership tendencies within steward organisations and this means in turn that shop stewards must be differentiated from those they represent. Focusing attention on managerial behaviour thus helps to provide a more satisfactory picture of shop steward organisation. But it also helps in understanding the variations in organisation within and between industries noted earlier.

There is strong evidence that shop steward organisations developed after the war in some industries rather than others because of circumstances favourable to the effective deployment of local bargaining power. No other single explanation accounts for the evident concentration of stewards in engineering and a few other industries and for their absence from others. But this explanation of shopfloor power, rooted in labour and product market tightness, has difficulties in coping with, for example, significant differences between companies operating within similar markets. Consideration of managerial strategy again helps to account for this. Thus Turner et al. (1967:214–15) suggest that differences between Ford and other motor manufacturers' stewards' organisations owes much to personnel and industrial relations management practice, and in particular to the different methods of wage settlement. Friedman has developed this point by arguing that the piecework systems typical of much of the industry except Ford form part of the 'responsible autonomy' strategy, providing a degree of scope and discretion to workers. Shop stewards came to play a part in regulating the terms and extent of the use of that discretion, and although this was directed at securing a degree of continuity and stability in working and earning expectations in the interests of workers it also performed a 'smoothing' function for management. At Fords, on the other hand, the time-based payment system, combined with persistent managerial refusal to permit plant-based negotiations around manning and effort levels, left less scope for an accommodation between shop stewards and management. To argue this is not to suggest that stewards will not emerge under such conditions but that their organisation may be different. The inability of Ford management to break shop steward organisation, despite repeated attempts, is ample testimony to the independent strength of the steward organisations, and the preparedness of members to take action in support of their union representatives.

Management's interest in securing control over work can also account for occupational variations within industries. Thus, for example, skilled craftsmen have traditionally enjoyed considerable job autonomy or 'craft control'. Management accommodation to skilled workers' steward organisation reflects a strategy intended to direct that control along lines acceptable to management in the knowledge that an attempt to break such control could be very costly. The relatively less well represented labourers, in the same industry or company, for example, would not easily create similar control problems and possibilities of a negotiated accommodation. Managerial strategies can, therefore, vary between occupations within a company or plant and this may in turn be reflected in differences in shop steward organisation on an occupational basis.

Similarly, Hyman and Elger (1981:116) have pointed out that through the sexual division of labour, women traditionally work in occupations with a lower degree of job control than most men. The Commission for Racial Equality (1981b) has noted evidence of attempts to keep black workers out of skilled jobs. This is one factor helping to account for their under-representation by shop stewards noted earlier.

The argument so far implies that certain structural preconditions for the successful emergence of shop steward organisation existed in the post-war period, and that these provided an effective framework for understanding the broad industrial profile of steward coverage and organisation by 1968. Within that broad profile, however, variations reflected the control strategies adopted by management to deal with the particular problems presented by different groups of workers.

Managerial strategy is not determined by the constraints described, however, nor is it static. Within any set of parameters managements have a strategic choice to make; an example already mentioned is the contrast between Ford and other car manufacturers. When there is a choice, this can be changed. Therefore none of the arguments advanced should be taken to imply that management is the major determinant of the existence of shop steward organisation of the Donovan type, nor that, once established, forms of shop steward organisation can be 'read off' in a mechanical manner from the nature of management control systems. Related to this, there is no stability or permanence in the accommodations described. They reflect no more than temporary, and largely unstable, equilibria in the fluctuating pattern of relationships between management and workers. The sources of these fluctuations are complex and numerous. They include changes induced by changes in external product markets or internal technologies. Such changes can precipitate changing managerial strategies in such a way as to transform a previously 'acceptable', accommodatory working practice into a 'restrictive practice' unacceptable to management, with obvious consequences for the attitude of management to such customary practices and their guardians, the shop stewards (see Edwards and Scullion, 1982a). Further, fluctuations derive from the contradictions in both the conception and execution of management strategies and the problems created by attempting to change strategy. Such contradictions and weaknesses are consistently exploited and exacerbated by shop stewards in their constant push for improved wages and conditions (see Brown, 1973, and Terry, 1977 for examples of how this operates in wage and non-wage areas). The accommodations described above are therefore only comprehensible in the wider context of the continual struggle between workers and employers for control over the labour process—the transformation of the capacity for work into work itself—and the determination of both parties to secure the most favourable conditions for that transformation.

AFTER DONOVAN: MANAGEMENT AND THE STATE

The limitations of the managerial response described so far to the increasing bargaining strength of workers were first apparent during the late 1960s and early 1970s. Advances in control made by increasingly strong groups of workers were often consolidated through managerial concession as described above, thereby strengthening, rather than diluting, the challenge to managerial control.

There is evidence that the increasing shopfloor influence over wages and jobs came to constitute a serious problem for British industry. In 1975 the Central Policy Review Staff (CPRS, 1975:v) in its examination of the British motor car industry stated that 'several weaknesses are poor quality, bad labour relations, unsatisfactory delivery record, low productivity and too much manpower. With the same power at his elbow and doing the same job as his continental counterparts, a British car assembly worker produces only half as much output per shift'. Kilpatrick and Lawson (1980) have argued not only that these factors can be seen *post hoc* as significant explanations of the decline of British industry, but that they are important factors in understanding the persistently low rate of domestic investment in the post-war period and a preference for overseas investment. But if job control issues were central, wage costs played an important part as well. Thus Glyn and Sutcliffe have argued (1972:10) that the profitability crisis of British capitalism had developed as demands for faster growth in living standards by organised workers coincided with growing competition between capitalist countries.

Inevitably, these problems rapidly became matters of political, as well as industrial concern. It is not surprising that the search for answers to them revolved in large part around the role and activities of shop steward organisation, and it is in this context that the changes in shop steward organisation and coverage between 1968 and 1978 outlined above have to be understood. The decade was significant in that it saw a major shift in employer strategies towards shop steward organisation and their influence over wages and job controls. To note this is not to argue that such explicit strategies were either implemented or effective; it is merely to indicate that evidence exists of increasing preoccupation with the power and behaviour of shop stewards and a consciousness of the need for action. But the decade after 1968 was also important in that it saw a new force emerge, that of the state, which had previously abstained from direct entry into the battle over job and wage control. After the late 1960s, however, increasingly preoccupied with the declining competitiveness of British industry, the state attempted to influence the outcome of factory struggles over wages and manpower utilisation. Later, as political concern over the size and performance of the public sector grew, the state entered the arena in its role as employer of roughly a third of the working population, again looking for more efficient manpower utilisation and the reduction of government expenditure.

In the following section managerial and state action are discussed separately, although it will be clear that in many ways the two interacted in a significant manner. While management generally accepted the view stated in the Donovan Report that theirs was the primary responsibility for reform, the state also accepted a major role in influencing wage determination, labour productivity, and the role and activity of shop stewards. But the direction in which the state tried to exercise its influence varied dramatically during the decade.

Management Problems and Strategies of the 1970s

As argued earlier, management in the manufacturing sector came into the 1970s facing a considerable problem of profitability. To deal with this, they developed a number of strategies with both direct and indirect implications for shop stewards. The late 1960s and early 1970s witnessed a wave of mergers, takeovers and internal restructuring as firms sought to increase productivity through increased economies of scale and flexibility of production (see Utton, 1975:105–11; Beynon and Wainwright, 1979:30–3). Stewards in turn came to need new levels of organisation as management accompanied the processes of amalgamation with redundancies, closures, and transfers of production. As managements deployed their increasingly flexible powers, stewards found that their strategies and structures —developed around informal, often fragmented, bargaining over wages and job control—were inadequate to handle large-scale changes. Stewards within and between factories needed to exchange information and pool resources (Coates and Topham, 1980:150–2).

At the same time there was a development of single employer, multi-plant wage bargaining in private manufacturing industry (Brown, 1981:68). This put pressure on stewards to develop larger, more complex forms of organisation to enable them to negotiate within the changed managerial structure. Changes in company structure thus confronted shop stewards with the need to integrate and centralise their own organisations and, if multi-plant organisation were to succeed, to develop formal plant-based organisation on which they could be based.

Next, management extended the use of work study and job evaluation in both the public and private sectors of industry (Brown, 1981:110–14; Terry, 1982:7). The primary intention of these techniques was to formalise the link between the nature of work and the payment received, by breaking both the task and the effort of working into component units, each attracting an agreed reward. Management hoped to systematise the relationship between work and pay so that it could be regulated through a system of agreed rules, and not be subjected to frequent and troublesome renegotiation. By presenting work in abstract terms management hoped to remove work-related issues from individual shopfloor haggling, and to handle them in the committee room in bargaining designed to deal comprehensively with, for example, a company's entire manual workforce.

Such techniques added to the centralising pressures on shop stewards. In addition, they pushed shop stewards into becoming more professional in the use of these same techniques, as the burgeoning of shop steward education on these and other subjects testifies. But the impact has not been all in one direction. These techniques, by reducing all work to a common set of principles and by introducing common negotiations, can collectivise the workforce, weaken fragmented and sectional organisation that was fostered by previous more individualistic methods of wage payment, and encourage cooperative working between stewards in pursuit of common claims. While the reduction in fragmented bargaining may have been part of management strategy, (CBI, 1977a), its advantages have not fallen purely to management, as workers have formed wider, more effective coalitions.

Related to this, management have altered their techniques of wage payment. Both Lloyd (1976) and White (1981) have noted a decline in piecework and, interestingly, an increase in the numbers of group and plant bonus schemes. White confirms the rise in job measurement techniques and the abandonment of piecework in some areas where it was traditionally dominant, such as motor vehicle manufacture. This can remove responsibility for wage negotiation from the workers and their stewards on the shopfloor and transfer it to a smaller number of stewards at plant or company level. Under many of the newer schemes, the majority of stewards have little direct role in wage determination which is handled by a negotiating committee, or even by one person, whose authority with respect to other stewards may therefore be enhanced, especially given the importance generally attached to wage issues. Payment system reform can thus contribute further to the development of centralised shop steward organisation.

Finally, managements in many industries pursued quite explicit reform strategies with respect to shop stewards. These have been summarised elsewhere (see Purcell, 1979a; Terry, 1979). Taking their lead from the models of 'good' industrial relations espoused by the state and other agencies many managers set about encouraging the development of forms of steward organisation they considered appropriate to their needs. In some companies this process took the form of selective concessions to demands for improved facilities coming from the existing shop stewards themselves. Thus closed shop and checkoff agreements, and full-time shop steward status with much improved office and communications equipment, were all the more freely conceded by managements in the 1970s than in preceding decades. But certain facilities did not improve. There is, for example, little evidence of any increase in the use of mass or sectional meetings of workers and stewards as the normal forum of decision-taking. Managements have preferred to encourage the use of elections and ballots as the appropriate means of communicating approval or disapproval from members to stewards (Brown et al., 1978). In the terms used earlier, there has been a move from 'direct' to 'representative' forms of democracy. In such firms managements have tried to influence the shape and nature of shop steward organisations through selective intervention in their activities.

In other firms, with little or no previous history of shopfloor organisation, there is evidence that managements went further, and encouraged, or even deliberately fostered, the emergence and development of shop steward organisations. Without such encouragement the huge growth in coverage of shop steward organisation in private and public sector employment is hard to explain. But why should managers have done this? At a general level, the most straightforward explanation may be that shop steward organisation was seen as inevitable, and the preferred option was to control and structure its arrival rather than let it happen 'spontaneously'. But in addition, as has been argued above, managements were both embarking on a major restructuring exercise in many industries and increasing the use of 'collective' job measurement techniques. A strategy that tried to handle the former more smoothly and exploit the latter most advantageously through local plant bargaining was well developed and understood. The notion of 'orderly' industrial relations, based in part around the exercise of responsible authority by local union leaders, gained currency as is shown in management's concern to ensure the authority of union leaderships, whether at national or local levels (CBI, 1977a).

Once again, this is not to argue that managements pursued these strategies explicitly for the reasons suggested here, nor that the process was successful in its implementation on all occasions. On the one hand, there is evidence of instances in which steward organisations appear to act more as an extension of the personnel office, using the fiction of negotiation of pay and working agreements as a source of legitimation for the deal. On the other hand, it can be argued that there is a strong contradiction within such management strategies: supporting the emergence or development of representative organisation for a particular purpose carries with it the clear possibility that such organisation can come to represent a newly developed collective interest against management. In this respect this strategy echoes the pay system and work measurement changes in that they act to collectivise the workforce and to raise the possibility of its pursuing common interests.

Summing up, it has been argued that managements, confronted by problems of profitability stemming from a number of sources including decreasing control over the relationship between wage costs and output, adopted a range of related corporate and industrial relations strategies. Their cumulative effect was to contribute significantly to the spread and formalisation of shop steward organisation. By encouraging the development of independent steward organisations capable of operating without full-time officials, and by developing company-based measurement and payment systems, managements assisted in a process of increasing shop steward authority within a developing situation that could be seen as the first moves towards a form of 'company unionism'. At the same time, worker fragmentation, simultaneously a source of strength and weakness in bargaining, was reduced through the application of these same policies.

Management tried to shift the level of control in its dealings with steward organisations in industries where they existed prior to these changes. Moving away from concentration on individual worker performance which was, as noted, the focus of much earlier shopfloor bargaining, the basic bargaining 'unit' became much larger—an occupational group, or an entire factory or company manual workforce. In much of the rest of industry negotiations, if they existed, were decentralised to the same level. In both cases control relationships were to be structured into bargaining at this level through the application of job measurement techniques. Shop stewards would assist in the enforcement of individual norms through their commitment to agreements negotiated and signed with management. Thus managements hoped to resolve their problems of job control and profitability through the direct involvement of shop stewards themselves in the control process, through a simultaneous concession of centralised authority, and the use of less individual methods of controlling work and relating it to reward.

The discussion so far has concentrated on the private sector of manufacturing industry; developments leading to broadly similar forms of organisation were taking place during the same decade in the public sector. The political definition of the public sector was changing dramatically in the late 1960s and 1970s as governments became increasingly preoccupied with the size of the public expenditure budget. Given the labour intensity of much public employment it is not surprising that labour costs and manpower utilisation were central to the emergence in the 1970s of a more strictly commercial approach to the public service sector which was intended to provide proxies for the 'disciplines' normally imposed on private firms by the forces of competition. The public sector therefore was not only affected by the strictures of incomes policy, but also began to look seriously at forms of productivity bargaining often attached to job reductions. Preoccupation with resource allocation and utilisation led to the rapid introduction of work measurement and incentive payment schemes. Managements were persuaded that these changes could be most effectively pursued through local rather than the traditional national collective bargaining machinery, and to do this they had to develop more effective systems of local representation (Fowler, 1975). At the same time a succession of unofficial and official strikes across much of the public sector in the late 1960s and early 1970s demonstrated widespread dissatisfaction among workers with the levels of pay negotiated through the national system. This added to demands for effective local representation (Fryer et al., 1974), so that by the 1970s management, union officials, and workers were agreed on the need for a system of local representation. This consensus underlay the huge growth in shop steward organisation in the public sector noted above.

Thus it can be argued that during the 1970s the state as employer was faced with similar practical preoccupations to those of employers in the private sector. The similarity of the problem, combined with the state's espousal of a formal model of good industrial relations practice, underlies the apparent convergence of industrial relations practice, and forms of trade union organisation, including shop steward representation, between public and private sectors.

The State

It was noted above that the profitability crisis of British industry in the late 1960s also came to be defined as a political problem. Successive governments saw the control of incomes as a crucial policy in resolving this issue. The reasons for implementing incomes policies have been many and varied, but they can partly be viewed as responses to a perceived profitability crisis the resolution of which could be helped through a redistribution of income in favour of profits (Tarling and Wilkinson, 1977).

Clegg (1971:62–64) has suggested that the incomes policies of the late 1960s were in part frustrated by the autonomous strength of shop steward organisations, and subsequent government policies sought to rectify this. Thus the Industrial Relations Act 1971 tried to reduce the bargaining power of shop stewards. By contrast, the 1974 Labour Government attempted to contain wage militancy by agreeing its policies with a trade union movement that had increasingly integrated shop stewards into its official structure. Brown (1980) and Hyman (1979) have argued that the success of the Social Contract owed much to the involvement of powerful stewards and convenors in the official union movement. While England (1981) has challenged the view that the acceptance of the Social Contract was a result of the integration and 'incorporation' of shop stewards, there is no doubt that such acceptance, often formally reflected in union conference decisions, was an important factor in the years 1975–7.

But incomes policies frequently went beyond straightforward controls on wages. In the light of earlier observations about the relationship between wages and job control and their political and industrial implications, it is significant that several phases of the incomes policies themselves attempted to make a clear link between these issues. In particular, policies that granted a particular status to 'productivity bargains' made this link explicit. The evidence shows the complex effect of such policies. 'Productivity' bargaining encouraged the development and formalisation of shop steward organisation as statutory requirements stressed the need for explicit, written agreements which could be monitored, and for clear undertakings of joint commitment to implementation. Writers such as Cliff (1970) argued that the consequence of this would be the 'incorporation' of stewards into management and a loss of autonomy. Nightingale (1980:331) however, argues that this was by no means always true, as stewards and workers were able to use the new formal rules against management and to enhance their autonomy from management and union officials. The effect on job control was that on the one hand these policies enabled managements to make significant inroads into shopfloor controls by 'buying them out', while on the other the possibility of such a 'buy out' led inexorably to the proliferation of the very practices government was hoping to eliminate.

The point has already been made that the definition of 'restrictive' shopfloor practices as a 'problem' is not axiomatic; rather managerial perceptions vary according to changing circumstances. The effect of productivity-linked incomes policies was to suggest that all such practices constituted a problem for management and government, and to put an attractive price on them. They focused attention and a sharp divergence of interest around the subject, as well as providing a potential for shop steward activity in places where none might have hitherto existed.

If government incomes policies have been complex in their effects, legislation designed to affect the internal affairs of trade unions has been no less so. The failure of the Industrial Relations Act 1971 to achieve one of its many specific intentions, that of weakening shopfloor trade union organisation and circumscribing the activities of shop stewards, owes a great deal to the strength and determination of trade union resistance. It also owes something to the fact that it was by and large operating in the opposite direction to management's strategy of expanding the role of shop stewards and building a pattern of 'orderly' industrial relations. Managements saw it as a 'delicate' phase, when the last thing they wanted was the unsubtle intervention of the law.

The incoming Labour Government of 1974 faced no real opposition to its repeal of the 1971 Act, and proceeded to enact legislation that was more in line both with its own ideology and with the general tendencies of managerial and union strategies. Thus it tried to give both workers and shop stewards a minimum 'floor of rights'. In so doing it helped foster— unwittingly perhaps—the growth of the closed shop (with an increased degree of management agreement), and the overall 'security' of shopfloor organisation (Brown, 1981:58). Stewards were provided with statutory rights to time off for trade union activities, facilities for increased amounts of training, and an increased range of issues—health and safety, unfair dismissal—over which they could put their new-found expertise to the service of their members. While these changes certainly enhanced the role of the steward it can also be argued that they contributed to the 'distance' between the membership and their stewards, differentiating them into workers with individual rights and stewards upon whose expertise they depended to protect them should those rights be infringed.

There is little doubt that this round of legislation was responsible for an expansion in the number and coverage of shop stewards, perhaps most marked in the public sector where surveys (e.g. Terry, 1982) show that management overwhelmingly considered the legislation to have been the main spur to industrial relations reform. But it can, ironically, also be held to have contributed to a 'de-collectivisation' of some industrial relations issues. For example such matters as unfair dismissal, and other matters appropriate for reference to industrial tribunals, are increasingly seen as matters inappropriate for collective action—the traditional trade union response to management arbitrariness (see Dickens et al., 1981b). Thus the contradictory consequences of the legislation are both to collectivise and to individualise workplace relations.

Finally, for much of the post-Donovan period, the Government, both directly and through a number of agencies, proselytised a particular 'model' of what were held to be 'good' industrial relations practices. Through bodies such as the National Board for Prices and Incomes, the Commission on Industrial Relations and, to a lesser extent, ACAS, companies which encountered problems and requested advice were often recommended to adopt the model of formal plant or company trade union recognition advocated by the Donovan Commission (Purcell, 1979a; Parker et al., 1971). Certainly this model was crucial in much of the public sector (Terry, 1982). Its impact in the private sector was less straightforward, given its greater heterogeneity, but it undoubtedly made an impact.

MANAGEMENT AND STATE STRATEGY: 'INCORPORATION' AND COUNTER-TENDENCIES

This chapter has argued that the changes in shop steward organisation and coverage over the past decade can best be understood in the context of managerial and state responses to a crisis of profitability, seen in part as emanating from the shopfloor challenge to managerial control over labour costs and the labour process. These responses consisted in large part of a series of attempts not to destroy shop steward organisation but rather to 'mould' it into a particular form. Intentionally or not, these strategies combined to exaggerate certain tendencies, present in the earlier shop steward model, towards centralisation, formalisation, and professionalisation of shop stewards and their organisations. Certainly the impact has been considerable, as the comparison of the two stereotypes from either end of the decade confirms.

The combination of strategies has sought to resolve problems in several ways. Most important, it has tried to replace the individual by the large group as the basic 'unit' of management control. This has been accompanied by attempts by employers and the state to discredit the use of 'restrictive practices' as either anachronistic in a time of legal protections for workers, or as injurious to the interests of other workers. The combined effect was to remove negotiation from direct shopfloor control and to centralise it at a higher level within the plant or company. At the same time, stewards' formal rights to negotiate were agreed, provided, by and large, that they took place in the committee room and not on the shopfloor. The close and direct identification between stewards and individual members, often rooted in wage-related job controls, was under threat. To be effective, however, the increased authority conceded to stewards had to be matched by an increasing ability to control and discipline their own members (CBI, 1977a:36). To achieve this, managements adopted a strategy of encouraging the development of certain kinds of steward organisation to minimise the disruption of this process. With the help for much of the period since 1968 of governments and official agencies committed to a particular model of good industrial relations, managements have fostered the development of formal, company-level trade union organisation, usually around shop steward recognition. The impact of government intervention through incomes policies may also have contributed to this process.

These two sets of factors are important in understanding both the spread of shop steward organisation during the 1970s and the particular forms that it took. But once again general trends conceal individual variations that must be understood before general terms are deployed to analyse particular developments. Crucial to an understanding of the variations are two central points. First, the strategy described was only one, albeit a popular one, among many available to management and the state (see Storey, 1980). Others would include a stronger offensive against shopfloor organisation itself, or a preparedness to work within existing institutions rather than to press for reform. The second point is the independent strength of workers to resist or to capitalise upon management and state strategies, and to create and develop their own.

So far this chapter has treated management and their problems as a general phenomenon, and their responses as equally invariant. In fact, within and between industries, companies, and occupations, managements' perceptions of problems and the consequent pressure to reform vary greatly (Edwards and Scullion, 1982a). Thus, for example, the near-monopoly position of some large firms can significantly affect their preoccupations with labour costs and hence with industrial relations strategies more generally (see, e.g. Cowling, 1982:ch.5). The creation of internal labour markets within some large firms can also have a strong impact on their particular approaches to labour relations (Rubery et al., 1982), and, as Purcell and Sisson suggest in Chapter 4, it is possible to develop a typology of managerial strategy which shows the effect of a wide range of influences upon managerial choice.

While some features, such as size, appear to be sufficiently closely related to changes in steward organisation to suggest common problems and responses, they are not simple cause and effect. Size may best be seen as a shorthand for a set of organisational features that may, under certain circumstances, come to create control problems for management. The encouragement of bureaucratic forms of control—whether through a shop steward body or not—is a common form of response to such problems (Edwards, 1979). In the late 1960s and 1970s, moreover, it was a response for which a general set of helpful preconditions existed among all parties—management, the state, and the unions.

But almost all these groups, and academics, tended to ignore the central obstacle—trade union, and, in particular, shopfloor resistance. Goldthorpe's arguments (1974) against the Donovan assumption of general consensus on the need for reform seem to have proved well-founded. Not only were many organised workers deeply suspicious of management efforts, managements themselves, certainly outside the personnel field, were equally cynical about 'joint control' (Ogden, 1981). Thus, although reform was pursued in those companies diagnosed as suffering managerial problems as a consequence of strong shopfloor organisation, the impact of such reform was partial and limited (Ogden, 1981; Purcell, 1979a). In general it would appear that programmes for reform were least likely to satisfy managerial expectations in companies which already had strong shopfloor organisation and which were, according to the argument developed here about the concerns of management and the state, those most in need of reform. By contrast the sectors where it would seem to have had the most dramatic impact (in terms of changes over the decade) are those with only limited, if any, traditions of shopfloor organisation (e.g. large parts of the public sector, food, drink and tobacco). In engineering, print, and the docks, for example, there is some evidence that the traditional strength of sectional, multi-union organisation persisted, although it may have been masked, in part, by an appearance of greater formality.

Such differences are commented upon by Nichols and Beynon (1977:108–12) who discuss the considerable problems for collective organisation in a workforce which could draw on no historical traditions of such organisation and which was subject to the fragmentation and mobility of modern divisions of labour. Under these circumstances management had almost a 'clean sheet' from which to start its strategies of industrial relations reform, if it so wished. In the traditional areas of strong organisation the picture was very different. Managements had to confront organisations with well rooted practices and traditions. In these contexts the making of a new 'formal' agreement may do virtually nothing to affect the underlying pattern of relationships. For

> industrial relations 'problems', as perceived by management or workers, cannot be overcome in a once-and-for-all way, particularly without major changes in the structure of our society more generally. The making of a 'formal' agreement is merely a temporary affair . . . to believe that 'formal' agreements can overcome and remove a host of 'informal' understandings . . . is to misunderstand the very way in which some agreements come to have a day-to-day reality, *at least in strongly organised plants* (Batstone et al., 1977:264, emphasis added).

In other words, the 'convergence' in industrial relations practice across the manufacturing and public sectors may well have concealed important differences which reflect the ability of workers to defend existing arrangements against attempts at reform.

But the picture was not simply one of 'green' workforces at the mercy of 'reformist' managements, and 'traditional' workforces maintaining the *status quo*. In many industries changes in shopfloor organisation and strategy were occurring that owed little to managerial intervention of the kind described, but much to worker attempts to defend jobs and living standards. The extension of the use of the strike weapon into hitherto 'strike-free' areas, especially in the public sector, was one example of this trend. And as the state increasingly intervened into wage regulation and other aspects of work, the 'political' strike against incomes policies primarily, but also against pay beds in hospitals and reductions in educational services, began to appear, often coordinated around local shop steward organisation. Workers and their representatives capitalised on the institutional fillip given to their organisations by the processes described above. In other areas the creation of large multiplant, often multinational companies spurred the development of shop steward 'combine' committees, sometimes with the support of management in a desire to move towards multiplant collective bargaining, but equally often in the teeth of management (and official trade union) resistance. Although faced with internal problems of sectional organisations and 'factory consciousness', combine development has been accompanied in places by radical departures from workers' traditional collective bargaining goals. The 'workers' plans' and 'social audit' developments have in part been shaped through these developments as stewards and workers have come to experience the limitations of working and fighting with the traditional 'factory-based' organisation (see Coates, 1981).

These reactions and developments within workers' organisations call into question the appropriateness of the thesis of 'incorporation' as applied to the period 1968–79. Baldly stated, this argues that the state tried to develop forms of tripartite economic management so that the main agents of employers and organised labour became involved in the processes of policy-making and implementation (Panitch, 1977). To be effective on the labour side this required a centralised union authority capable of securing agreement to these policies which in turn required a degree of integration of workplace organisation into the formal structures of the union movement (Hyman, 1979). While the 1970–74 Conservative Government tried to achieve this through the legal requirements of the Industrial Relations Act, the succeeding Labour government adopted the different approach of a reform package designed to facilitate the development of joint consultative structures throughout the economy as well as within companies. Within this national context employers adopted strategies aimed at securing a degree of vertical structure and control within union organisations. These strategies were, in the incorporation thesis, designed to reduce shopfloor power and steward autonomy from management and unions. This would have the effect of countering their ability to oppose management and state strategies directed at controlling wages and increasing labour productivity.

Many of the strategies described above could be labelled 'incorporationist' in intent; here the more important question is their impact in practice. Viewed in this way the data suggest that strategies of incorporation are extremely varied and contradictory in their effects. At the most they may give rise to temporary coalitions operating to produce a desired management outcome under the legitimacy of joint, negotiated agreement. But such arrangements are unstable, and partial, whether at the level of the company or of the state (Panitch, 1977:81). Thus the 1975 Social Contract was accepted by the Biennial Delegate Conference of the Transport and General Workers' Union but heavily rejected by the same body two years later. Not only did 'incorporationist' strategies run up against worker resistance as they were thought to have a damaging impact on earnings and jobs, but they also contained their own contradictions. Both at the level of the state and that of the company, attempts to incorporate the union movement have necessarily involved the concession of a degree of power and authority to the unions that had hitherto been lacking. Governments and employers trying to increase their authority through agreements with unions faced a major challenge when unions considered that the agreements had been repudiated.

After a decade or more of at least sporadic attempts at incorporation, it is reasonable to look for criteria for evaluating its success or failure. As England (1981) has noted, most of the arguments hitherto have been based around observations, noted here, of management and state intentions and their overwhelmingly procedural or organisational, rather than substantive, consequences. Examining the latter, at least for the period 1968-79, the success of the strategy seems less apparent. Several authors have noted the persistence of multi-tiered, often fragmented, bargaining systems (Brown and Terry, 1978; Brown, 1980; Daniel, 1980b). Indeed, within the public sector the move has largely been away from centralised towards local wage bargaining. Furthermore for the same period there is little evidence of success on the fronts the strategy is held to have attacked. While the effects of incomes policies are always hard to determine, and there is some evidence that the Social Contract owed a degree of its success to incorporationist developments, the failures are also clear. More fundamentally, given the focus of this chapter, there is little evidence of an impact of the incorporation strategy on those features of industrial life it tried to effect. During the years 1973–8 the profitability of the private sector declined, and labour productivity increased at a much lower rate than it did in those countries which were Britain's main commercial rivals (Glyn and Harrison, 1980:130–2). During the same period, as Edwards argues in Chapter 9 below, there is no conclusive evidence of any impact of reform on levels of strike activity.

It is, of course, virtually impossible to isolate and analyse any of these factors outside the general, and possibly overriding, effects of recession and depression. But at least it is necessary to state that the incorporationist 'school' cannot realistically base a case only on formal, procedural change. As has been noted, at least some of that has been partial and superficial. Turning to more substantive indices, however, it might appear that the persistent and in some cases increased, strength and resources of shop steward organisation, was an important factor in the lack of success of the incorporationist strategy

One striking testimony to the failure of the incorporation strategy to solve the problems of employers and the state is the radically changed style of government and of some major employers since the 1979 general election, especially in their dealings with the trade unions. A combination of growing economic crisis and a government more hostile to the organised labour movement than any of its predecessors has made available to managements a strategy frequently contemplated but not often adopted since World War II—that of a major assault on union organisation in general and shopfloor organisation in particular. Helped by the debilitating effects of unemployment and recession on trade union power and organisation (and to some extent by law) a few employers, of whom British Leyland are often held to be the best example, have tried to undermine the traditional strengths of shopfloor organisation. Their strategies have made a combined attack on shopfloor organisation by reducing the numbers of full-time shop stewards and restricting the mobility of others, by attempts to 'by-pass' them by obtaining workforce opinions directly through ballots and referenda, and by the unilateral imposition of sets of working agreements designed to reduce or eliminate 'restrictive practices'.

The majority of employers have not adopted such tough tactics, but have exploited the weakening of trade union bargaining power within a framework of continued union rights. One interesting finding is the evidence of recent increase in the use of formal joint consultation procedures involving shop stewards in discussions with management about a range of company issues (Cressey et al., 1981; Dowling et al., 1981). Such bodies, which give shop stewards a degree of involvement without any formal rights to negotiation, were rejected as useless by stewards throughout the 1950s and 1960s (Donovan, 1968: 27). Employers adopting these strategies hope to be able to obtain radical change through agreement with a weakened labour force while at the same time preserving forms of union representation as the best guarantee of future order and stability should the balance of bargaining power shift again.

But such strategies are only part of a wide range of possibilities open to managements in the face of weakened opposition. The introduction of new technologies, and the increasing use by large firms of subcontracting, for example, can both significantly affect managerial controls over production and hence the role of trade union organisation. Indeed, Rubery et al.

(1982), have suggested that trade unions generally, and shop stewards in particular, may increasingly come to represent a decreasing 'primary' workforce, employed in large factories, and relatively sheltered from movements in the economic cycle. At the same time an increasingly large 'secondary' workforce, linked through contractors to the large firms, working in small firms, and subject to the vicissitudes of economic fluctuations, would be difficult to unionise, and hence would be outside this protection.

Whatever the case, the central argument of this chapter should still hold. The future development of shop stewards and their organisations—indeed much of the rest of labour relations—can best be understood only in the context of the continual struggle over wages and the control of work.

PART II
Management

4 Strategies and Practice in the Management of Industrial Relations

John Purcell and Keith Sisson

There has been little analysis of the role in industrial relations of those responsible for managing individual enterprises. It is true that there is a very considerable literature which is concerned with the techniques of personnel management. But 'this is overwhelmingly prescriptive or didactic; it deals with questions like manpower planning and recruitment at the firm or company level, the construction and effects of alternative payment systems and wage or salary hierarchies, the tactics and processes of negotiating with unions or consulting with workers' representatives, with welfare and safety arrangements, and a hundred and one subsidiary issues of labour management or labour relations, from selection systems to retirement arrangements' (Turner et al., 1977:1). There is also a growing body of literature inspired by Braverman (1974) which deals with the impact of 'scientific management' thinking on present-day approaches to the organisation and control of the labour process (Edwards, 1979; Littler and Salaman, 1982). But this is primarily concerned with the impact of management's design of technology and control systems on the degree of discretion which individual workers are able to exercise over the jobs they perform.

Both types of literature, in their very different ways, serve as a reminder that management can and does use a wide range of strategies to achieve its main industrial relations objectives: that is, in recruiting, in developing, and in maintaining control over its employees. Having said this, both types of literature tend to assume a sameness about the approach of management which makes little allowance for specific historical contexts. For that reason neither is very helpful in understanding how management in Britain has dealt with the challenge of trade unions and how, in particular, British management in recent years has tried to reconstruct workplace industrial relations in the light of this challenge.

It is with these and related questions that the present chapter is primarily concerned. It begins by considering why the importance of the industrial relations function in individual enterprises has increased in recent years. It goes on to discuss the strategies underpinning the reconstruction of workplace industrial relations in the 1960s and 1970s; in particular, it examines the type of reforms and the choice of bargaining levels. The third section identifies a number of approaches or styles which, more generally, influence strategies and practice in the management of industrial relations. The chapter concludes by speculating about future trends in the management of industrial relations.

THE INCREASING IMPORTANCE OF THE INDUSTRIAL RELATIONS FUNCTION

The context is set by the substantial increases in the size of workplaces and the corporations which control them. To illustrate the growth in the size of workplaces, Table 4.1 uses Census of Production data relating to *establishments* in manufacturing industry for the period 1951–78. Two-fifths of employees now work in establishments with 1,000 or more employees and over half in units with 500 or more employees. The industries where over

TABLE 4.1: ESTABLISHMENT SIZE IN MANUFACTURING INDUSTRIES, 1951–1978

| Industry Group | % OF EMPLOYEES WORKING IN ESTABLISHMENTS WITH: | | | |
| | 500 and More Employees | | 1,000 and More Employees | |
	1951	1978	1951	1978
Food, drink, and tobacco	28·6	62·6	17·3	46·5
Coal, petroleum products, chemical, and allied industries	51·7	68·5	33·4	53·7
Metal manufacturing	64·6	67·0	n.a.	55·8
Mechanical engineering	48·6	48·0	32·5	32·6
Electrical engineering	72·0	73·0	58·8	58·8
Shipbuilding and marine engineering	75·8	78·3	63·6	69·7
Vehicles	76·4	85·8	n.a.	80·7
Metal goods not elsewhere specified	n.a.	30·4	10·4	17·4
Textiles	25·0	44·7	12·8	31·8
Clothing and footwear	n.a.	32·1	5·7	16·5
Bricks, pottery, glass, and cement	28·1	51·1	15·0	36·1
Timber, furniture, etc.	n.a.	14·8	n.a.	3·4
Paper, printing, and publishing	32·8	36·0	16·9	24·1
All manufacturing	42·2	54·5	28·9	41·4

Sources: Business Statistics Office (1978: table 7; 1981: table 6).

60 per cent of employees work in establishments with 500 or more workers (food, drink, and tobacco; chemicals; metal manufacture; electrical engineering; shipbuilding and marine engineering; and vehicles) are identical to those industries where large enterprises are particularly dominant (Business Statistics Office, 1978: tables 7 and 12). In some industries, as Table 4.1 shows, the growth in large plants has been particularly marked even in those sectors where conglomerate companies are less common (clothing and footwear; bricks, pottery and glass).

The importance of the size effect in industrial relations has been noted in many surveys in the last fifteen years (Marsh et al., 1971; CIR, 1973; Parker, 1974, 1975; Brown, 1981). In particular, the Warwick Survey (Brown, 1981:32) indicated that there has been a substantial increase in general in the degree of specialisation of industrial relations management at the workplace, but that this was particularly noticeable in larger establishments. By 1977 it was almost universally true that establishments with more than 500 employees employed a specialist industrial relations manager.

One of the most notable developments since 1950 in Britain has been the evolution of giant corporations or *enterprises*, with an increasing trend for these industrial and financial conglomerates to be active in a large number of industries. Prais (1976:20) notes that in 1958 there were sixteen large enterprises active in ten or more industrial groups. By 1963 the number had doubled to thirty-two. At the same time the number of large enterprises whose activities were limited to a single industry fell from thirty-eight to nineteen. More up to date estimates are difficult to make because of a change in the recording of enterprises in the Census of Production but all the evidence points to a continuation of the trend. Both Prais (1976:164) and the Bullock Report (1977:4) note that the degree of concentration is greater in British industry than it is in either Europe or North America.

The extent of this concentration and its growth in the period 1958–78 is shown for manufacturing industries in Table 4.2. Enterprises with 10,000 or more employees employed a quarter of the working population of manufacturing industries in 1958. This had increased to just over a third in 1978, while the number of such firms grew from seventy-four to eighty-three. At the same time the average number of establishments owned by these conglomerates with over 10,000 employees grew from thirty to forty. This implies that the changing composition of British industries owes much more to increased merger and take-over activity than to the 'organic' growth in establishment size (Prais, 1976:59).

The degree of concentration varies between industries but much of the classic heartland of British industry is dominated by a small number of enterprises (chemicals, mechanical and electrical engineering, shipbuilding, and vehicles). In shipbuilding and marine engineering, for example, the five largest enterprises shared three-quarters of the employees in the industry, while in vehicles seven enterprises, each with over 20,000

TABLE 4.2: ENTERPRISE SIZE IN MANUFACTURING INDUSTRIES, 1958–1978

Enterprise Size *(Number of Employees)*		*2,000 and over*	*5,000 and over*	*10,000 and over*	*20,000 and over*	*50,000 and over*
Number of	1958	469	180	74	32	8
enterprises	1978	428	179	83	37	10
Number of establish-	1958	5805	3788	2224	1398	467
ments owned	1978	8108	5236	3476	2099	721
Proportion of employees	1958	45·8	34·3	24·8	17·3	7·3
working for these enterprises	1978	56·2	44·6	34·6	25·1	12·5

Sources: Business Statistics Office (1978: table 10; 1981: table 12).

workers employed over 57 per cent of the industry's employees in 1978. In electrical engineering six enterprises, each with over 20,000 workers, employed 37 per cent of the employees in the industry. A similar concentration is found in the food, drink, and tobacco industry where the rate of concentration has been growing rapidly. In this industry eight enterprises, each with over 20,000 workers, employed 35 per cent of the employees. The degree of concentration of ownership is below average in textiles (although even here eight companies employed 30 per cent of the workers); clothing and footwear; bricks, pottery and glass; timber and furniture; and paper and paper products. Outside manufacturing estimates are difficult to come by, but the Bullock Report (1977:4) gives some indication that large enterprises are prevalent in the service sector.

The nature of ownership and control within these enterprises has also changed. Instead of ownership being in the hands of the founding families or of a mass of private shareholders, it is increasingly a relatively small number of institutions—notably insurance companies and pension funds—that dominate. Between 1957 and 1975 the proportion of shares owned by institutional investors rose from 30 per cent to 50 per cent (Prais, 1976:135). It is a proportion which is likely to continue to grow, for this form of ownership tends to encourage further concentration. As Prais (1976:135–6) notes, 'a greater size of company leads to lower boardroom ownership, which leads to precarious control, which leads to takeovers, which lead to even larger companies'.

Foreign ownership has also increased. Although the rate is difficult to judge, in 1979 23 per cent of the largest private companies in Britain were owned by overseas interests and they employed just over a million people in their British establishments (Brown and Sisson, 1983). In manufacturing industry a little under one in five jobs were foreign-owned, the great majority by North American companies.

Finally, there have been significant changes in the internal organisation of these large enterprises. Twenty-five years ago the typical pattern was either one of highly centralised control of all functions or one of a holding company where the separate divisions had a high degree of autonomy. Since then there has been a general move towards the multidivisional pattern of organisation in which head office maintains close control over strategic matters while allowing divisions substantial day-to-day independence. For example, a recent study of 120 large enterprises suggests that the proportion organised on multidivisional lines increased from 42 per cent to 68 per cent between 1965 and 1971 (Steer and Cable, 1978:14). In its wake has come the development of 'management' as opposed to 'personal' or 'entrepreneurial' forms of control (Chandler, 1977). That is to say, a small group of senior managers at the heart of the enterprise plays the key role in developing corporate strategy, monitoring, and, where possible, influencing the external environment as well as discretely controlling the subsidiary companies by means of budgetary policy.

In themselves these changes in the size, ownership, and control of enterprises might have been expected to lead to much greater industrial relations activity. For example, size and the multidivisional pattern of organisation appear to encourage specialisation in most of the functional areas of management. Management specialisation, it seems, is necessary if the diverse activities of the subsidiaries are to be adequately controlled. Institutional investors, who tend to manage their equity holdings with a degree of professionalism, are likely to look for similar expertise in the management of the companies where they form the largest single block of shareholders. Foreign ownership, especially North American, appears to be particularly important. The managements of the parent companies tend to have had longer experience of both the multidivisional pattern of organisation and of dealing with trade unions directly rather than through an employers' organisation. The evidence suggests that under their influence the managements of British subsidiaries have been among the innovators so far as developments in corporate bargaining, pay systems, and personnel policies generally have been concerned (Gennard and Steuer, 1971).

Knowledge of the industrial relations activities of the senior managers involved is remarkably slight as they are as often hidden from researchers as they are from trade union negotiators. Nevertheless, the Warwick Survey gives some indication that multiplant enterprises paid greater attention to industrial relations than did single plant enterprises, to the extent that they had a director with industrial relations responsibilities and specialist industrial relations management. The probability of there being such a director was 'twice as great for establishments with 500 or more employees if they were part of multi-establishment firms than if they were single and independent' (Brown, 1981: 27–30). This trend was particularly noticeable in the larger enterprises. A large-scale survey by Marsh (1982:62) undertaken in 1980 gives further confirmation of the rapid growth especially since the mid 1970s of, as he terms them, 'employee relations' managers in multi-establishment companies: 'few major multi-establishment companies employing more than 5,000 employees are now likely to be without a main board director with head office responsibility for employee relations, together with a specialised staff, and, in many instances with divisional directors and staff also.'

How far this reflects an increase in the attention paid to industrial relations by the main board of the holding company is open to doubt. Even so it seems not unreasonable to suggest that the structural changes identified above have led to an increase in the specialisation of industrial relations management, the development of policies and initiatives, and a more lively debate within the ranks of senior management about the 'union question' which previously had often been delegated to management at plant level. In short, the strategic approach of the large corporations which tend to dominate the industries in which they operate is beginning to be the key factor in industrial relations developments.

However important these structural changes have been, they are not the only considerations which need to be taken into account. After World War I the great majority of managements in the larger enterprises in Britain, like their counterparts in Western Europe, dealt with trade unions through the agency of an employers' organisation. This was especially so in manufacturing industries. The exceptions among those managements which recognised trade unions, such as Imperial Chemical Industries and Ford, were extremely rare. Incidentally, this is perhaps the main reason for the neglect of the role of management in industrial relations: industrial relations was generally regarded as a matter external to the enterprise and its management (Clegg, 1979:124–5). As the following chapter will describe in more detail, employers' organisations periodically negotiated changes in the main substantive terms and conditions of employment with trade unions which covered all employers in a branch or industry; their officials intervened in the event of an issue being raised in the workplace under the disputes procedure, which in industries such as engineering formed the basis of the relationship with trade unions. The main advantage of these arrangements for management was that they more or less excluded trade union officials from the workplace or, at the very least, heavily circumscribed their role thus leaving individual managers a relatively free hand in the running of their departments. In brief, the effect was to protect or neutralise the workplace from trade union activity.

In the post-World War II period, however, this strategy of dealing with trade unions through the agency of an employers' organisation proved increasingly ineffective throughout much of British manufacturing industry. The 1920s and 1930s, it seems, had flattered to deceive. The institutional framework of multi-employer bargaining in Britain was very different from that in Western Europe. Essentially, it reflected the compromise struck in engineering in the 1890s with craft trade unions which already had a strong presence in the workplace. Multi-employer agreements were strong on procedure but very weak in their coverage of substantive issues. Not only were there very considerable gaps in the coverage of these issues which had to be filled in at the workplace; but managements' insistence on dealing with individual workers and stewards, rather than with trade union officials, provided considerable scope for workplace bargaining. Multi-employer agreements in Britain were also 'gentlemen's agreements'; they were not, as in other countries, legally enforceable contracts. Under the pressure of full employment and soft product markets, then, it is not surprising that managers in many workplaces increasingly found themselves drawn into workplace bargaining which often became 'largely informal, largely fragmented and largely autonomous' (Flanders, 1970a:169).

Initially, this workplace bargaining was predominantly the concern of individual managers such as supervisors, rate fixers, works managers, and personnel managers. Against the background of mounting international competition both at home and abroad, however, it began to assume a much wider significance. A growing number of commentators began to link the resulting shopfloor control over many aspects of production to the decline in competitiveness and profitability of manufacturing industry. The ability of groups of workers to veto management decisions proved a barrier to efficient production in many cases, while the developing pattern of unofficial and unconstitutional strikes and other forms of industrial action threatened delivery dates and undermined customer confidence. Or, at least, this is how the issues came to be interpreted. Increasingly from the late 1950s onwards, industrial relations became an issue which the senior managers could no longer ignore. How to regain control became a major concern, leading in many cases to the appointment of industrial relations specialists at board level.

Not all managements, even in engineering, experienced these kinds of pressures. Certainly, most managements in enterprises outside manufacturing did not. A further, and related, reason for the increasing importance of the industrial relations function was government policy. Increasingly preoccupied with Britain's declining economic performance, successive British governments—both Labour and Conservative—proceeded throughout the 1960s and 1970s to intervene in virtually every aspect of the employment relationship: in the labour market, in pay bargaining, in union recognition, in discipline and dismissal, in health and safety, in pensions and social security. The effect was both to intensify the pressure to appoint industrial relations specialists and to develop policies. Industrial relations specialists themselves seem in no doubt that government intervention was the main reason for the increase in importance of their function: in 1978 more than half of those in manufacturing establishments with over fifty employees cited government legislation as the main reason and another 12 per cent referred to the trend towards industrial democracy which had largely been triggered by the prospect of legislation (Brown, 1981:33). The next section is concerned with the major activities in which these specialists have been involved.

THE RECONSTRUCTION OF WORKPLACE INDUSTRIAL RELATIONS

As the introduction to this chapter observed, management has a wide range of strategies at its disposal to influence the conduct of industrial relations. Most of the so called context of industrial relations is not given. It is management who decides the location and size of the plant, and it is management who determines the technology and the organisation structure. Clearly, industrial relations is one of the considerations taken into account in making these decisions. This is not to suggest that management is a totally free agent, though it does have considerable discretion. For example, the tendency for managements, especially in large multinational enterprises, to standardise production in a number of centres while moving increasingly to multiple sourcing of material supplies is designed, among other things, to reduce vulnerability to industrial action. Similarly, the fact that new technology might provide a means of overcoming apparently intractable industrial relations problems has not been lost on management. National newspapers in Fleet Street are a good example (Martin, 1981; Turner, 1982). Nor should the battery of policies more usually associated with personnel management be ignored. The way in which people are recruited, selected, and trained can be highly significant in structuring attitudes. It only needs a moment's reflection to appreciate how different, in most cases, managements' treatment of white-collar workers has been from their treatment of manual workers in these respects, and the implications this has had (Institute of Personnel Management, 1977).

Important though these aspects are—and the final section of this chapter suggests that they are likely to become even more important in years to come—they will not be the main focus of attention here. The decline in the effectiveness of multi-employer bargaining, the impact of government policy, and the growth in the size of organisations posed problems which demanded immediate solutions. For many managements, especially in manufacturing where, in many cases, workplace trade union representatives effectively had the power of veto, the overriding need was to gain control of industrial relations in the workplace. Other managements which had control were anxious not to lose it. Neither group had any option but to embark on a reconstruction of workplace industrial relations.

As Chapter 3 indicates, discussions of the strategies involved in this reconstruction have paid considerable attention to the willingness of managements to recognise shop stewards and joint shop steward committees; to grant full-time status to some shop stewards; and to negotiate closed shop and check-off agreements. From managements' point of view, however, these measures were rarely ends in themselves; they were only one of a number of considerations. Managements were primarily concerned to legitimise their decision-making authority and to contain and as far as possible neutralise the impact of trade union activity. This involved, firstly, introducing a variety of procedures to institutionalise industrial conflict; and, secondly, restricting the scope of collective bargaining and avoiding it altogether, if possible, at the point of production. In some cases it also involved avoiding collective bargaining at corporate and divisional level. In this way key decision-making activities at the level of production and at the heart of the enterprise became protected from direct involvement in collective bargaining.

Needless to say this suggests a degree of conceptual thinking on the part of managements which bears little relationship to the day-to-day realities of industrial relations. Very rarely did a management set out with an explicit policy of restructuring workplace industrial relations. Most introduced reforms in a piecemeal and *ad hoc* fashion in response to events; sometimes the policies pursued appear to be contradictory. Nonetheless, it is possible to see many of their actions reflecting the considerations set out above. This is true both of the type of reforms introduced and of the decisions made about the levels of bargaining.

Type of Reforms

Throughout the 1970s managements in most enterprises introduced a wide range of procedures into the workplace: procedures for negotiations, for individual grievances and collective disputes, for consultation, for discipline and dismissal, for health and safety and so on (Brown, 1981:45,76–7; Hawes and D. Smith, 1981:268–70). Reforms in substantive arrangements, by contrast, have been relatively thin on the ground. Many managements engaged in some form of productivity bargaining in the late 1960s, but this was rarely comprehensive; in many cases it was simply a means of circumventing the Labour governments' incomes policies. It is also true that there have been significant reforms in payment systems and in the method of fixing pay differentials, but these reforms had far greater procedural than substantive implications.

A number of points can be made about the strategy underpinning the procedural bias of the reforms undertaken. First of all, most managements implicitly accepted the central core of the Donovan Commission's analysis. While managements had the appearance of control in the workplace the reality was very different or threatened to become very different. Increasingly, the legitimacy of the decisions taken by managements in key areas of industrial relations and personnel management was being questioned. Paradoxically as it may seem, the introduction of a variety of procedures, many of them jointly agreed with shop stewards, went a long way towards legitimising the decisions of management: the procedures enforced greater consistency on the part of individual managers at the same time as they offered opportunities to explain and to justify the decisions taken. The variety of the procedures is also significant. Objections to management decisions were no longer to be lumped together as 'disputes': 'issues' were to be dealt with separately and differentially, thereby lessening the impression of a conflict of interests.

In this connection the widespread introduction of joint consultation procedures is particularly interesting. Certainly, the introduction or, in some cases, the re-introduction of these procedures was a direct response to the industrial democracy debate which surrounded the work of the Bullock Committee; most managements were anxious to demonstrate, in conformity with CBI policy, that legislative moves in the direction of industrial democracy were unnecessary. But renewed support for joint consultation can also be seen as an attempt to emphasise the importance of 'cooperation' and 'problem-solving' and to minimise the amount of 'conflictual' or 'distributive' bargaining. Implicitly, too, most managements were rejecting the idea that the range of issues which were to be subject to joint regulation should be unrestricted. They were prepared to discuss their proposals with workers' representatives and to listen to the latter's views; but in the final analysis it was the management who would make the decision.

The widespread use of work study techniques—the Warwick Survey (Brown, 1981:113) suggests that their use has increased in a third of manufacturing establishments with over fifty employees over the years 1973–8—has also been important in legitimising management decision-making and reducing the scope for collective bargaining. The rate-fixing which was so prevalent, especially in engineering, invited challenge from individuals and their representatives. Indeed it is no exaggeration to say that rate-fixing was one of the mainstays of workplace bargaining. The systematic use of work study techniques by specialist industrial engineers who are removed from the day-to-day management of production has brought about a significant change. It is not that the times or allowances are necessarily accepted as scientific, but that the standards set tend to be more consistent as between jobs and over time. This is particularly true where 'synthetic' times are used; these are times which have been established and accepted in the past by workers on similar jobs or which are derived from such techniques as Predetermined Motion Time Study. In these cases there is no need for the industrial engineer to appear on the shopfloor with a stop-watch; the overall time for the job can be built up by an analysis of the operations involved and by reading-off the 'synthetic' times.

Clearly a major aim of the reforms was to put an end to, or to avoid, the fragmented workshop bargaining which had so bedevilled industrial relations in engineering. This meant making sure that negotiations did not take place at the point of production where management is at its most vulnerable. The introduction of a wide range of procedures played their part. Perhaps much more important in this regard, however, were the reforms in payment systems and the methods of fixing pay differentials.

Contrary to the impression that is sometimes given, there would appear to have been an increase in the number of workers whose pay is in some part dependent on productivity or performance (Lloyd, 1976; White, 1981). The significant trend, however, has been away from individual to group or plant-wide schemes. Managements, it seems, have been loath to abandon incentive payment systems; but they have become acutely aware of the industrial relations implications of individual schemes. The introduction of measured daywork, of group or plant bonus schemes such as value added, the modification of payment by results schemes where time is separated from price with the use of centrally-negotiated rates for converting times into payment—all these had the effect of placing the determination of actual earnings firmly in the hands of central negotiators. Significantly, too, where managements have reintroduced incentive payment systems after an interlude of flat-rate payments, as in British Leyland, Talbot and the National Coal Board, these have been on a group or plant basis.

No less important has been the widespread use of job evaluation as the method of fixing pay differentials (NBPI, 1968a; Daniel, 1976; Brown, 1981). Since job evaluation creates a structured set of differentials, it is extremely hard for section shop stewards or supervisors to influence pay levels themselves. Claims must be handled through the appropriate appeal machinery staffed by senior stewards and senior managers and the basis of the claim is, in theory, restricted to the 'rational' criterion of changes in job content. As the trade unions are often involved in the implementation and maintenance of job evaluation they are encouraged or forced to consider the impact of one sectional claim on the operation of the scheme as a whole. Thus unions can take on a quasi-managerial function of blocking or filtering claims which challenge the logic of the agreed pay differentials. The process of implementation, if undertaken by joint teams of management and unions, is a powerful means of encouraging joint problem solving techniques and a depolarisation of industrial relations. The domestic union leadership becomes, along with industrial relations management, the custodians of the scheme. Even if implemented unilaterally by management, job evaluation and the 'rational' ordering of differentials makes plant industrial relations more controllable. Taken with changes in the basis of bonus calculation the incidence of bargaining is reduced, the location of bargaining changed, and the bureaucratisation of union leadership encouraged.

The strategy underpinning these reforms can be seen in a different but complementary light. The rapid growth in fragmented workshop bargaining in engineering in the vacuum left by multi-employer agreements can be viewed as a failure of management to exercise control over itself (Maitland, 1980:357–62). With the introduction of the reforms a key role has been assumed by the industrial relations specialists: they assume the responsibility for ensuring that policies and procedures are enforced. The overall effect has been to reduce the amount of discretion available to individual supervisors and line managers to make the kind of concessions which were such a feature of the Donovan Commission's 'informal system'.

It also becomes difficult for them to indulge in arbitrary and inconsistent behaviour which can give rise to discontent. At the same time, the presence of the industrial relations specialist introduces a buffer between shop stewards and both junior and senior line managers, who are free to get on with the job of managing their functions.

One of the unintended consequences of these developments was their effect on the shop steward movement. As Brown (1973:136) makes clear, 'the control that management has over itself is a major factor determining the integration of the shop steward body', and 'in the long run, management itself is the most important influence shaping the behaviour of its shop stewards', a point more fully developed in the previous chapter. As power in management becomes more centralised the unions are virtually compelled to restructure their own domestic organisation. The process of negotiating revised bargaining and payment structures often leads management to sponsor the creation of hierarchical shop steward organisations, while removing the basis of shop floor negotiations. It is of considerable importance that such reforms can be welcomed by shop stewards since they accord with the principles of shop steward behaviour. Brown (1973:133–6) has listed these as 'the pursuit of unity and equity', 'maintaining a good bargaining relationship with management', and 'the reduction of uncertainty'. Since the reform of bargaining and wage payment systems encourages the creation of a unified shop steward body, the pursuit of unity is facilitated. As gross pay inequities are replaced by a structured set of pay differentials agreed with the unions, some form of equity is achieved. Uncertainty is reduced, both by the structured pay and negotiating arrangements and because the discretion of production and junior management has been reduced, thereby limiting arbitrary and inconsistent decisions. A good bargaining relationship depends on the development of trust which in turn requires power centralisation (Purcell, 1981:49–59). It is easier to develop such a relationship in a reformed and controllable bargaining arrangement.

The willingness of many managements to enter into closed shop and checkoff agreements can be interpreted in a similar light (Dunn, 1981). Few managements went out of their way to introduce a closed shop; there are a number of practical disadvantages in terms of recruitment and flexibility in dealing with completely unionised employees as well as in terms of an increase in trade union strength. But, equally, there are a number of advantages in agreeing to trade union requests for the closed shop. To paraphrase the responses of managements in the Warwick Survey (Brown, 1981:58), it means that trade unions and shop stewards represent all employees, it stabilises relationships between management and employees, and it ensures that procedures cover all employees. All these advantages contribute to a good bargaining relationship.

Described in this way the reassertion of management control initially over itself and then over industrial relations in the establishment is idealised. In practice, behaviour is less easily confined. For one thing it presupposes that the achievement of control is an end in itself, emphasised above other managerial objectives. Clegg (1979:146–7) noted, for example, that the consequences of implementing measured daywork, like productivity bargaining, involve a restructuring of managerial authority. If the agreement is to work 'its effective implementation has to take priority over most other objectives for line managers'. To the line manager this is to turn the organisation upside down with the pursuit of stable industrial relations given a higher priority than the achievements of production goals. As production goals are more immediate and more clearly linked to overall corporate aims, successful implementation of industrial relations control would appear to imply a change in the priorities of such managers and, in a different sense, of production workers. Terry (1977) found that this was unlikely to occur and the problems of the 'inevitable growth of informality' remain. More generally, Batstone et al. (1977:159) observed that 'particularly in the face of crises and uncertainty, managers will break certain rules and short-circuit various procedures in order to achieve what they believe to be their primary objectives'.

Ironically, the increasing power and professional status of the personnel manager in the 1970s and the associated use of management techniques has led to the emergence of new problems. If the fault with unfettered sectional bargaining was its lack of control and excessive flexibility, reformed bargaining and pay structures can be seen to be unduly inflexible, at odds with the dynamics of production. Power centralisation is unlikely to be willingly accepted by line managers or rank and file union members. The inflexibility associated with increased formalistion has been shown (Turner et al., 1977:35–9) to be linked with an increase in strike activity. White (1981:142–3) observed that 'the most disturbing aspect' of his survey's findings 'was the relatively high frequency of industrial disputes among establishments with collective incentives of one sort or another, especially with plant-wide bonus schemes based on output'. There is little evidence to suggest that the strategies of formalisation and the reform of wage payment systems have done much to encourage industrial peace, although it might be argued that conflict will arise during the transitional phase of reform. A further drawback has been that the rationalisation of pay differentials makes it harder to adjust the rates of pay of one occupational group in response to changes in the external labour market without influencing the pay of others. The reduction in pay differentials between skilled and semi-skilled workers is particularly notable in this context given the shortage of particular skills. Thus institutional linkages between occupational groups within the plant can lead to increased unit labour costs above that necessary for recruitment, while the ability to respond to relative falls in wages in the external labour market for some groups is restricted.

In short, increased formalisation and control reduce the organisation's capacity to respond to movements in both the internal and external environments. Given that environmental change has been so marked in the early years of the 1980s, especially in the labour and product markets, it is not surprising that there has recently been mounting criticism of the personnel function (Batstone, 1980:36–9; Thurley, 1981:24–9) and evidence that industrial relations specialist managers are losing their pre-eminent position. As a later section argues in more detail, the reformist strategies of the 1970s are now in doubt in some enterprises.

Choice of Bargaining Levels

A key element in management strategy, especially in the large multi-establishment enterprises, has been the choice of level for pay bargaining. As Chapter 6 demonstrates in more detail, the pattern of pay bargaining in Britain is highly complex. Categorising establishments by the *most important level* of pay bargaining, however, two major groups may be identified, depending on whether the bargaining covers one employer or more than one; that is, whether the bargaining is multi-employer or single-employer. Those in which single-employer bargaining is the predominant pattern—and this is very much the larger group of the two—may be further subdivided into those which bargain at the level of the individual establishment and those which bargain at the group, division or company level, which for simplicity's sake is here termed 'corporate bargaining'.

At first sight there are no obvious reasons to account for the diversity. For example a study using the statistical technique of discriminant analysis has suggested that in the case of manufacturing industry high regional concentration, high union density, and multi-unionism are associated with multi-employer bargaining whereas larger establishments, multiplant firms, foreign-owned firms, high concentration industries, and firms with specialist industrial relations management tend to have single-employer bargaining (Deaton and Beaumont, 1980:210). The authors were unable, however, to distinguish any clear features besides establishment size which might explain the choice between establishment and corporate bargaining.

Managements in roughly similar circumstances, it seems, can have markedly different approaches to this issue. The two big engineering firms which withdrew from membership of the Engineering Employers' Federation after the 1979 strike, the General Electric Company (GEC), and Philips, have moved in diametrically opposite directions. GEC have sought to decentralise bargaining as far as possible so that despite union opposition site negotiations as in the Old Trafford works in Manchester have been broken down to the level of the constituent profit centres. Philips have centralised bargaining at a national level, while drawing a distinction between negotiations over pay and conditions, with separate institutions for each. British Leyland has moved to central bargaining in line with other vehicle manufacturers like Ford, Vauxhall, Massey Fergusson, and International Harvester.

How is sense to be made of this diversity? The starting point is to recognise that the levels at which collective bargaining takes place both reflect the balance of power between managements and trade unions and are a major influence on it. For their part, managements use the levels at which collective bargaining takes place to control the activities of trade unions. Perhaps not surprisingly, then, their views about the appropriateness of these levels are conditioned first and foremost by what they perceive to be in their interests in the particular circumstances.

Take the example of those managements which continue to deal with industrial relations through the agency of an employers' organisation. The facts that the majority of establishments are small and that the industries tend to be highly competitive are very significant considerations. Clearly, for the small establishment there are economies of scale in dealing with trade unions collectively. More importantly, multi-employer bargaining is attractive because the impact of the trade union on the workplace is reduced. In highly competitive industries it also helps to achieve a measure of standardisation of terms and conditions (see, for example, Goodman et al., 1977). Even managements in larger organisations find multi-employer bargaining attractive in these circumstances. The clearing banks are a good example. Here too the joint operation of the clearing house where financial transactions between the banks are undertaken is an additional consideration: the temporary closure of one bank is likely to lead to the disruption of the activities of others.

In the case of the large multi-establishment enterprise, corporate bargaining has many of the advantages of multi-employer bargaining. It facilitates the possibility of the standardisation of conditions in each plant and separates the union negotiators from the workplace. The role of the shop stewards is much more restricted and the unity and power of the union movement more difficult to maintain. The success of this form of institutional separation is far from assured as witnessed by the periodic outbursts of unofficial industrial action directed against both full-time union negotiators and management (Friedman and Meredeen, 1980). However in a company with integrated production units, as in the motor industry, company-wide bargaining has particular attractions for the reasons just outlined. The 'roll-back' of the shop steward movement in British Leyland in 1981–2 could not have been done without the move from plant to company bargaining. Militant plants, such as Cowley in British Leyland or Halewood in Ford, can be outvoted in pay and strike ballots. They are isolated and power is diffused or neutralised through the separation of bargaining units from the source of union power at the workplace. Thus, while establishment bargaining isolates the union both from the powerholders in top management and from their colleagues in other plants, and also limits the impact of strikes, company level bargaining has the advantage of weakening union solidarity, making it more difficult to organise collective action, although once a strike begins it often lasts for longer than plant-based disputes.

If the advantages of corporate bargaining appear so strong, it might be asked, why do a majority of managements in large multi-establish-ment enterprises appear to prefer plant bargaining? A partial answer can be found by looking at the types of bargaining used in different industries. Significantly it is the engineering industry, the focus of attention in the Donovan Report, which shows the highest extent of coverage by establishment bargaining. In contrast corporate bargaining, although not dominant is much more extensive, especially when multi-employer bargaining is discounted, in industries like chemicals; food, drink, and tobacco; metal manufacturing; and clothing and footwear. As the Warwick Survey notes (Brown, 1981:11), the evidence on bargaining reforms suggests that many companies in these industries, which are generally characterised by little tradition of workplace bargaining, have moved straight to corporate bargaining from multi-employer arrangements without any intermediate phase at establishment level. This implies that one important factor in the choice of bargaining levels is the extent and strength of workplace union organisations. In engineering, particularly in those enterprises which were the result of merger and takeover, the patterns of workplace industrial relations which had developed under multi-employer bargaining were very different. The costs that would be involved in levelling up those plants with less favourable terms and conditions is in some cases prohibitive; it is also likely to result in a reaction from those plants which have received more favourable treatment in the past.

It would be wrong to infer from this, however, that most managements only bargain at plant level because of the problems associated with a move to corporate bargaining; or that, especially in engineering, plant bargaining is seen as an interim step between the end of multi-employer bargaining and the development of corporate bargaining. Plant bargaining has a number of considerable attractions for many managements. First and foremost, plant bargaining effectively denies the trade union any role in the determination of broad company policy such as investment or de-investment. It leaves divisional and corporate managements free to develop policy unbothered with the need to justify their decisions to trade unions, let alone bargain over them. It also enables managements to argue that each plant must stand on its own feet; that the ability to pay of each plant must be the main consideration in setting terms and conditions of employment; that, at best, comparability must be restricted to the local labour market. In this connection plant bargaining fits in with the formation of business and cost centres and the development of management by objectives.

The decision to bargain at plant level does not rule out the exercise of control over what happens by divisional or headquarters management. Far from it. It is not unreasonable to suggest that in the great majority of cases plant bargaining is an illusion. The bargaining itself may be decentralised but the key decisions are likely to be made at higher levels on the management side. Plant management, for example, may only be given freedom to negotiate within certain strict financial limits or may be expected—and in some cases required—to check with the divisional or headquarters management before coming to a final decision when certain specific issues are involved. For example, so far as pay is concerned, only one third of managements in subsidiary establishments in the Warwick Survey said that they had 'complete or almost complete discretion' (Brown, 1981:36). Even then, it is highly likely that such managements would check with divisional or headquarters management to make sure that what they intended to settle for would not embarrass other plants. On the basis of a more recent survey, Marsh (1982:161) concluded that 'it is evident that there can be few multi-establishment companies which have by this time failed to provide for coordination on pay and conditions claims of some kind . . . No doubt this is one reason why such negotiations and their possible consequences are likely to be discussed by main boards more frequently than most other employee relations issues.'

It is not that shop stewards are usually unaware of what goes on. Thomson and Hunter (1975:24), for example, quoted the experience of shop stewards in Shell where a combine committee had been set up after the stewards had 'found that agreements were virtually the same, despite having been negotiated at each plant in a theoretically free bargaining situation. Once they realised that the tune was called from the top and not at individual locations, they demanded to be able to go straight to the top'. Even so, the evidence suggests that it is extremely difficult for shop stewards to develop effective combine committees (Willman, 1981). The parochialism of the shop steward organisations in the more highly paid plants, which is encouraged by management, is often a major obstacle; while the refusal of management—and in some cases trade unions—to recognise such committees denies them crucial legitimacy.

The reaction of corporate management to threats of legislation over industrial democracy in the late 1970s is particularly instructive. Proposals in the Bullock Report (1977) and the later White Paper *Industrial Democracy* (Department of Employment, 1978a) were particularly threatening to multiplant companies with establishment bargaining, as they challenged the very centre of the strategy of institutional separation. The proposal that a Joint Representative Committee (JRC) composed of shop stewards should be established at company level was tantamount to compulsory recognition of a shop steward combine committee. The management response was particularly interesting in the light of the strategic considerations discussed here. The general approach favoured by the CBI (1977b) was to encourage the organic growth of industrial democracy at establishment level. A number of companies created consultative committees at both plant and company level (Hawes and Brookes, 1980:353–61), often distinct from the collective bargaining machinery. These maintained management's decision-making rights even if they were staffed by shop stewards. In Rolls Royce, for example, plant negotiations are encouraged on most items apart from hours and holidays (which are dealt with at multi-employer level) while a company consultative forum with over 100 shop stewards present meets from time to time, but any item of discussion which should be dealt with under the collective bargaining machinery is debarred.

As with the reforms discussed in the first part of this section, management strategies with regard to the levels of pay bargaining have not been without their contradictions. For example, bargaining which was introduced to overcome the problems of leapfrogging and parity claims is often less well received when memories fade: corporate bargaining, the critics argue, makes it more difficult to relate pay to performance and to close down unprofitable operations. At the other extreme, some managements which have opted for plant bargaining have experienced considerable problems in maintaining this position. This is especially so where other functions, such as production, are highly centralised. Kinnie (1982:34) has suggested that in these cases the inconsistencies and contradictions in management's arguments are very plain for the workforce to see; the success of the strategy of plant bargaining is precariously dependent on the shop stewards' inability to organise effectively between plants. A number of other managements who practise plant bargaining have come under pressure to explain the inconsistencies between this policy and that of emphasising the corporate image and identity. In some cases the addition of the company suffix or logogram to the name of the firm has been an important catalyst.

APPROACHES AND STYLES IN THE MANAGEMENT OF INDUSTRIAL RELATIONS

So far this chapter has dealt with the increase in the importance of the industrial relations function and with some of the strategies which managements have used. The impression which may have been given is that there is little difference, especially between the larger enterprises, in the approach or style of managing industrial relations. True, there are a number of common trends, but industrial relations is so central to the political debate about Britain's economic performance that values and beliefs, particularly with regard to the role of trade unions in society and within a given organisation, inevitably influence both policy and practice. Indeed, there may well be no consensus among top managers about many of the issues involved. It is one thing, for example, to introduce consultative machinery because it is a part of an overall approach designed to gain employee commitment to certain managerial decisions. It is quite a different matter if these arrangements are introduced to forestall the possibility of legislative compulsion.

In drawing attention to the crucial role of management ideology in determining policy and in interpreting events in industrial relations, Fox (1966) identified two major perspectives. The 'unitary' view of the enterprise emphasises the sense of togetherness, the achievement of common goals and organisational objectives, and the legitimacy of management. In this view trade unionists are seen as trouble makers, importing alien concepts and actions into the enterprise. Industrial relations problems are either the fault of the unions or the result of poor communication or both, with unions fermenting issues caused by a manager's failings. In the 'pluralist' view, the enterprise is recognised as being composed of a variety of interest groups, but predominantly two, labour and management, each with different aims and objectives, some of which conflict while others coincide, and each interest group has sufficient power at its disposal to hurt the other. Trade unions are seen as the legitimate representative of labour, and conflicts arising from the clash of interests are resolved if possible by bargaining and compromise, and, if not, by the application of overt power. The need for mutually agreed solutions to conflictual issues is thus elevated as the central function of industrial relations through the institutionalisation of conflict.

The academic debate over pluralism has raged since the publication of Fox's original paper (Fox, 1973; Clegg, 1975; Hyman, 1978). Clearly, the contrasts between the 'pluralist' and the 'unitary' views are not so stark as Fox suggested in 1966; pluralism can be a basis for managerial action to preserve the *status quo*. In the process of the debate, however, one thing has perhaps been lost sight of: many industrial relations specialists may be pluralist in their views, but the vast bulk of managers are more likely to incline to the unitary position. Indeed, there are good reasons for suggesting that this is the natural position for them to adopt. Unitary values have been strongly inculcated in their own training and development, they are uncomplicated in their implications, and they are self-reassuring.

Valuable though Fox's two frames of reference are in explaining differences in the attitudes of individual managers, they are of little help in themselves in drawing distinctions between the style or approach of managements in different organisations. Most large enterprises recognise trade unions and engage in collective bargaining; even the ones which do not are in important respects far less unitary than they may appear at first sight. Much more relevant to the task of distinguishing between organisations is Fox's later attempt (1974:297–313) to develop a number of ideal-typical patterns of industrial relations. These have been adapted here to suggest five ideal-typical styles of industrial relations management.

The first group are the 'traditionalists' whose approach to trade unions is aptly described as 'forceful opposition' (Bain, 1971:17–18) and whose treatment of employees is often overtly exploitive. While the image of this group is that of the nineteenth-century capitalist entrepreneur, it should not be discounted. From time to time disputes over union recognition, as at Grunwick in 1976, flare up out of all proportion to the numbers involved, capturing media attention and polarising public attitudes to trade unions into crude 'pro' and 'anti' camps (Rogaly, 1977:111–21). For directors and senior managers (and some politicians) with little or no direct contact with trade unions, such extreme disputes can become important influences helping to shape their own attitudes to trade unions (Winkler, 1974).

The second group might be described as the 'sophisticated paternalists'. Some of the large North American enterprises such as International Business Machines, Hewlett-Packard, and Kodak might be fitted into this category (Newman, 1980). So might some of the Japanese subsidiaries. An example of a British-owned enterprise of this type would be Marks and Spencer. Most of these enterprises, but not all of them, refuse to recognise trade unions. Their outward stance—certainly towards their employees—is essentially unitary. This is why they are often grouped together with the traditionalists. But there is a crucial difference. The sophisticated paternalists do not take it for granted that their employees accept the company's objectives or automatically legitimise management decision-making; they spend considerable time and resources in ensuring that their employees have the right approach. Recruitment, selection, training, counselling, high pay and fringe benefits—these and other personal policies are used to ensure that individual aspirations are mostly satisfied, that collective action is seen as unnecessary and inappropriate. As Lord Sieff (1981), chairman and chief executive of Marks and Spencer, put it recently:

> Human relations in industry should cover the problems of the individual at work, his or her health, well-being and progress, the working environment and profit sharing. Full and frank two-way communication and respect for the contribution people can make, given encouragement—these are the foundations of an effective policy and a major contribution to a successful operation . . . There is very little need for secrecy. At Marks & Spencer we try to ensure that all our staff are kept informed of proposed developments and that their views are taken into account . . . A policy of good human relations costs time, effort and money. Marks & Spencer's employees number 44,000 full and part-time, of whom over 1,000 are in personnel. Some 850 of the latter are in staff management spread throughout the stores. Their priority is the well-being and progress of, on average, the 50 to 60 people for whom each is responsible . . . We invest much time training our commercial managers in good human relations . . . Last year we spent £43 million on catering subsidies, medical and dental attention, non-contributory pensions and profit sharing for our staff. These benefits are for all, irrespective of position. Those who lead Marks & Spencer believe that money has been, and is, one of our best investments.

Fox's third type is the 'sophisticated moderns'. In this case, to quote Fox (1974:302), 'management legitimises the union role in certain areas of joint decision-making because it sees this role as conducive to its own interests as measured by stability, promotion of consent, bureaucratic regulation, effective communication, or the handling of change . . . It recognises that its discretion is being limited in certain areas of decision-making but it legitimises these limitations and therefore does not counter with low-trust behaviour and attitudes'. Purcell (1979b:29) has suggested that such a policy would have a number of elements: the encouragement of union membership and support for the closed shop where appropriate; the encouragement of membership participation in trade unions; the encouragement of inter-union cooperation and the development of joint shop steward committees; the institutionalisation of irreducible conflict; the minimisation of areas of avoidable conflict; the maximisation of areas of common interest; the reduction of the power of strategic groups; the development of effective control systems. The first three elements reflect the concern that the corporation has over the organisation and functioning of the trade unions as representatives of the employees. The next two deal with the institutions and procedures of industrial relations and the products of negotiations. The sixth, maximisation of areas of common interest, concerns the corporation's policy in handling consultative and participative structures to obtain the commitment of employees and legitimation of managerial decisions. The seventh and eighth can be seen as tactics to protect the corporation from the consequences of failure to achieve the objectives enunciated earlier, by establishing monitors of industrial relations performance and reducing or limiting the source and use of employee power.

In fact, the 'sophisticated moderns' comprise two groups. The first of these are the 'constitutionalists'. Examples in Britain are extremely rare—perhaps Ford (Beynon, 1973; Friedman and Meredeen, 1980) comes closest—but are much more common in North America. The limits on collective bargaining are clearly codified in the collective agreement. In those areas of decision-making where management is under challenge from the trade unions, or where it may be deemed expedient to concede joint regulation (in return for concessions from the union elsewhere), the frontier of control may be moved back but it is then firmly entrenched in a specific codified agreement. Clegg (1979:118) has described this as the 'statute law model' of collective bargaining where 'the formal assumption . . . is that managers are free to take their own decisions on matters which are not subject to collective agreements'. It would probably require collective agreements to be made legally enforceable before there was a significant increase in the number of constitutionalist managements.

Most of the 'sophisticated moderns'—examples would include ICI (Roeber, 1975; Nicholls and Beynon, 1977) and most of the large oil companies (Flanders, 1964; Gallie, 1978)—are to be found in the second sub-group. These might be described as the 'consultors'. Trade unions are recognised and collective bargaining is well-developed. But there is no desire on the part of management to codify everything in a collective agreement. On the contrary, every effort is made to minimise the amount of collective bargaining especially of a 'conflictual' or 'distributive' kind. Instead, great emphasis is placed on 'cooperative' or 'integrative' bargaining: 'problems' have to be solved rather than 'disputes' settled. To this end, the procedures for consultation are likely to be usually extremely detailed and wide-ranging, and individual managers will receive considerable training in communications and inter-personal skills.

The 'sophisticated paternalists' and both groups of 'sophisticated moderns' differ significantly in their approach. Nonetheless, they have two things in common. First of all, the approach tends to be fairly uniform throughout the organisation. Regardless of their personal views, individual managers in their day-to-day activities are expected to conform to the general approach; most come to accept and share the values which are implicit. Secondly, their approach has been fairly consistent and identifiable over many years. For example, ICI withdrew from the chemical employers' organisation in 1935 to negotiate a corporate agreement with the trade unions. Ford has never been a member of the Engineering Employers' Federation; it has negotiated at the corporate level since it first recognised trade unions in its British plants in 1941.

In these respects the fifth group, which is by far the largest and includes such engineering giants as the General Electric Company, Guest Keen and Nettlefolds and Tube Investments, is very different. These are referred to as the 'standard moderns'. Here the approach is essentially pragmatic or opportunistic. Trade unions are recognised and industrial relations specialists employed. But industrial relations tends to be viewed primarily as a 'fire-fighting' activity: it is something which is assumed to be non-problematic until events prove otherwise. Consequently, the significance of industrial relations considerations—and of the specialists who are nominally charged with responsibility for them—waxes and wanes in the light of changing circumstances. But it is not only that the approach can change from one period to another which is important. Unlike the 'sophisticated paternalists' and the 'sophisticated moderns', there does not appear to be a set of values or assumptions which is held in common. There can be marked differences of approach from one establishment to another; there can also be differences between various levels in the hierarchy within the same establishment. The result can be 'many confusions and uncertainties . . . caused by a mixture of unitary and pluralistic perspectives' (Fox, 1974:308).

How are these differences in approach or style to be explained? The nature of the business and the technology help to explain the differences between the 'sophisticated paternalists' and the 'sophisticated moderns'; inasmuch as the discretion which they allow individual workers is very different, so the personnel controls have to be different. But neither of these variables is of much help in explaining the differences between these groups and the 'standard modern' approach. Relative financial success is something which enterprises in the first three groups have in common. In as much as a particular approach or style becomes associated with success, it is re-inforced; it is also possible to meet the additional costs which tend to be involved. That said, many of the enterprises which have been labelled 'standard modern' are financially successful. There is certainly no one style of industrial relations which can be linked with financial success.

All things considered, the presence of key personalities at an early stage in the company's development appears to be the critical variable. In the case of Marks and Spencer, for example, the quotation from Lord Sieff speaks for itself. In the case of ICI the Mond family, especially Alfred and Henry, clearly played an important role. In the case of Ford, although the Ford family dominated the company's early approach to trade unions, a wider group of senior managers has been involved; and the main influence has been the North American practice of collective bargaining. In each case such individuals appear to have established a pattern which has influenced subsequent developments. Even the growth of the enterprise has been affected; most have grown 'organically' rather than by merger and takeover. In the case of the 'standard moderns' no such personalities can be identified. Key personalities may have emerged or been appointed subsequently, but their ability to impose an overriding approach or style is constrained by what has gone before. This is especially true where the enterprises have grown by merger and takeover. Faced with a wide variety of practices and approaches throughout the enterprise, then, it is not difficult to understand why most of them opt for pragmatism.

It is against this background that recent changes in approach—especially among the 'standard modern' type—is best explained. It is not simply a matter of 'macho' managements taking advantage of large-scale unemployment and a government which is hostile to trade unions to settle old scores, though there may well be some managers who think and act in this way. Rather it is the situation in the product market which is forcing change on management. Markets have declined; there has been an intensification of competition both at home and overseas; and there is great uncertainty. In such circumstances industrial relations which emphasise long-term stability achieved through cooperation can come to be challenged as corporations are compelled to adopt short-term actions to meet immediate product-market and financial demands. As such actions are often only needed at moments of crises, they frequently require a quick return in terms of cost reduction or productivity improvements. Consequently, the leeway for manoeuvre in negotiating the redundancies or restricted salary awards is often very limited, thereby placing considerable strain on the climate of industrial relations and on the preferred approach to problem solving adopted by 'pluralist' personnel managers. As the reduction in product markets or market share is linked in macro and micro terms to growing surpluses in the labour market which reduce the basis of union power, the pragmatic basis for the adoption of pluralist policies is weakened. The case for tough policies seems increasingly unanswerable as short-term benefits in productivity improvements and union acquiescence become widely reported. The shift towards unitary policies based more on coercion than cooperation is thus largely unchallenged in any meaningful sense. The unions lack the power and the members the will to mount a major campaign against policies, which are portrayed as 'common sense' and the 'economic facts of life'. And within management the loss of patronage brought about by the emergence of a new coalition of senior managers and the undermining of the rationale of earlier policies substantially reduces the power of specialist industrial relations managers.

The ebbs and flows in approaches to the management of industrial relations discussed in this section indicate that the search for definite statements is a hazardous exercise. The same is true of the strategies discussed in the previous section. It may be possible to discern certain patterns in management behaviour and, with some risk, ascribe motive and causation. But industrial relations is very much a subsidiary activity so far as management is concerned. In the words of Drucker (1951:81), 'the main function and purpose of the enterprise is the production of goods, not the governance of men. Its governmental authority over men must always be subordinated to its economic performance and responsibility'. When industrial relations managers complain that much of their time is spent in 'fire-fighting' with insufficient attention being given to policy, they are merely discovering that industrial relations, so far as most of their colleagues are concerned, is more to do with *ad hoc* responses to immediate problems than the pursuit of sophisticated strategies. This must be borne in mind in particular in considering possible developments in the management of industrial relations in the 1980s.

FUTURE TRENDS

It is not unreasonable to suggest that the management of industrial relations is in a state of transition. The era of reconstruction is largely over. The pressing need to come to terms with the trade union challenge in the workplace is receding. Trade unions are weak and likely to remain so for the foreseeable future because of high levels of unemployment. The present government is also hostile to them. This does not mean, however, that management will be able to relax its grip. Industrial relations managers may withdraw into the background but it is extremely unlikely that line managers will be allowed to exercise the discretion they had in the 1950s and 1960s. Short of major changes in government policy such as import controls, the international competition which provided the back-cloth to developments in the 1970s is likely to be even more intense in the 1980s; the pressure on British management to control labour costs will be greater than ever.

The more intense this pressure becomes, however, the more likely it is that there will be significant changes in management strategy. Already a number of managements are beginning to argue that compliance is not going to be enough if they are to match the international competition in terms of delivery, price, and quality; what is needed, it is suggested, is greater commitment on the part of employees. This suggests that much greater emphasis in future will be placed on individual personnel policies: on recruitment and selection, on training and development, on individual communications. This is likely to be linked Japanese-style with guarantees of greater security of employment for a smaller core of employees. There may also be developments in the harmonisation of the terms and conditions of blue- and white-collar employees and in job enrichment. The number of plantwide incentive and cost reduction schemes is likely to increase, the logic being not simply to relate some element in the pay packet to performance but also to encourage employees to identify more with the corporate objectives. There is also likely to be a considerable increase in joint consultation: in quality circles, briefing groups, business councils, and company councils. All this does not mean that recognition will be withdrawn from trade unions or that there will be an end to collective bargaining: both are far too entrenched. But it is likely that the strategy of restricting the scope of collective bargaining largely to pay and the conditions of employment will continue. Attempts are also likely to be made to involve shop stewards more and more in the process of joint consultation, though they will not be accepted as the only or, indeed, the main communications link with the shopfloor.

Underpinning this strategy, there is likely to be an increase in sub-contracting. This will not only enable management to concentrate its energies on the main activity of the business; by reducing many overhead costs it will also enable management to finance improvements in the terms and conditions of the remaining employees. Already, a number of companies have hived off such non-essential activities as catering and cleaning; in some cases employees have been encouraged to make them-selves voluntarily redundant and to set up small businesses to supply the parent company.

It goes without saying that the success of such strategies is by no means assured. To begin with there would have to be significant changes in management organisation and in the style of individual managers, and with ever-diminishing career prospects managers themselves are likely to become increasingly disaffected. Also the neo-human relations approach is likely to be viewed with some scepticism on the shopfloor in Britain. However much joint shop steward committees might appear to resemble company unions, their traditions are very different and they maintain strong links with the external trade unions (Clegg, 1979:61). Finally, the extensive use of subcontracting is bound to arouse opposition; depending on the government of the day, it is likely that there would be demands for legislation to control it.

One element in the strategy in particular may have unintended consequences. The logic of the overall strategy would seem to point to an increase in the number of company consultative councils. Indicative legislation supporting their formation is the most likely outcome of the current debate within the EEC over the Fifth Directive and the Vredeling and the Geursten proposals. Depending on the outcome of the next parliamentary election in Britain, such a development may take place irrespective of the debate within the EEC. But the formation of any company-wide institutions is at odds with the strategy of plant bargaining which most large enterprises are adopting. Quite clearly, management will try to maintain the institutional separation between joint consultation and collective bargaining, But, as many found in the workplace in the 1950s and 1960s, such separation is by no means easy to maintain. The formation of company consultative councils will significantly increase the opportunities for shop stewards to compare and discuss the pay and conditions in different plants; it is likely to give a considerable boost to the development of shop steward combine committees. The intensity with which comparisons are made between plants is likely to increase. Managements will find themselves under increasing pressure to bargain at corporate level. A possible compromise might be the negotiation of performance-related pay at plant level and non-pay issues at corporate level. Even so, trade unions would be much closer than ever before to policy-making and managements would be faced with a very different kind of challenge to the one they have experienced hitherto. How they face up to it is likely to be a major issue in British industrial relations throughout the rest of the 1980s.

5 Employers' Organisations

Keith Sisson

As the previous chapter has pointed out, the majority of managements in Britain for many years dealt with trade unions through the agency of employers' organisations. In some industries employers came together long before the emergence of trade unions—sometimes informally, sometimes within the framework of a trade organisation—to fix wages, to prevent the pirating of labour, or to formulate a response to proposals for legislation (Clegg, 1979:63). But it was nevertheless the challenge presented by trade unions which was the main impetus to this collaboration. In some cases—building, engineering, and printing are perhaps the best examples—the challenge was direct: the ability of craft unions, first on a local and then on a national basis, to pick off employers either one by one or by district. Employers might agree among themselves not to employ trade union members, to establish a strike fund, or to engage in a lock-out. Initially, the organisation needed for this type of action was often of a rudimentary or temporary nature; sooner or later, however, it was usual to establish a formal organisation or to expand the activities of an existing trade organisation. For example, Wigham (1973) suggests that a number of attempts were made to set up a national organisation before the forerunner of the Engineering Employers' Federation finally emerged in 1897. In other industries the challenge of trade unions was more indirect. For example, a number of national employers' organisations, notably in the chemical and in the iron and steel industries, were formed in response to the Ministry of Labour's attempt to introduce multi-employer bargaining machinery in the years immediately following the recommendations of the Whitley Committee in 1917.

In the years immediately following World War I many employers' organisations assumed the role of bargaining agent on behalf of their member firms. Perhaps not surprisingly, the very existence of employers' organisations came to be associated with the practice of multi-employer bargaining. For example, having considered a number of possible reasons why managements continued to belong to employers' organisations, the Donovan Commission (1968:22) concluded that 'above all, membership of employers' organisations is a consequence of an unquestioning commitment to maintain the "formal" system of industrial relations'. The implication seems to be that if British management ever abandoned the 'formal system' of multi-employer bargaining there would be little future for employers' organisations.

Fifteen years later, as the previous chapter has pointed out, there can be little doubt that the managements in most large enterprises have, in effect, abandoned the 'formal system'; there has been an increase in the importance of the industrial relations function, the development of domestic industrial relations policies and procedures, and a shift in emphasis to bargaining at establishment and corporate levels. Inevitably, these developments raise questions about the number and membership of employers' organisations, their functions, and their prospects for the future. These are the issues with which this chapter is concerned.

PATTERNS OF ORGANISATION

There has certainly been a reduction in recent years in the number of employers' organisations which fulfil the current legal definition laid down in the Trade Union and Labour Relations Act of 1974: namely, an organisation consisting 'wholly or mainly of employers or individual proprietors . . . whose principal purposes include the regulation of relations between employers . . . and workers or trade unions'. In 1968 the Donovan Commission (1968:7) quoted evidence from the Department of Employment to suggest that there were some 1,350 employers' organisations; in 1980 the Certification Office for Trade Unions and Employers' Associations (1981:4) suggested that the number was of the order of 300. For the most part, however, the reduction has resulted from the winding-up of small provincially based employers' organisations or from the amalgamation of the local primary organisations which make up some of the large national employers' organisations such as the Engineering Employers' Federation, the National Federation of Building Trade Employers, and the British Printing Industries Federation. There have been a few reductions in the number of national employers' organisations. Indeed, the only major casualties in recent years have been in iron and steel and in shipbuilding: both the British Iron and Steel Federation and the Shipbuilding and Repairers' Association were dissolved when the great majority of their members were nationalised in 1967 and 1977 respectively.

In the past employers' organisations have been associated with manufacturing industry. Perhaps the most interesting point to emerge from Table 5.1, which gives details of the larger national employers' organisations, is that thirteen of the twenty-one listed are to be found in the private service sector. It is also interesting to note that some of the employers' organisations in the sector are of relatively recent origin; the Federation of London Clearing Banks, for example, was formed in 1968.

The membership of national employers' organisations also appears to be holding up. True, there have been a number of significant withdrawals

TABLE 5.1: EMPLOYERS' ORGANISATIONS WITH ANNUAL INCOME
OF MORE THAN £500,000 IN 1979: SUMMARY OF STATISTICS

	GROSS INCOME				
Employers' Associations Each With Over £500,000 Total Income:	From Members[a] £000s	From Invest- ments £000s	Total Income £000s	Gross Expen- diture[b] £000s	Number of Members[c]
Engineering Employers' Federation	1,650	357	2,166	1,904	18
West Midlands Engineering Employers' Assoc.	664	38	984	984	1,210
Engineering Employers' London Association	665	61	846	809	850
Engineering Employers' West of England Assoc.	323	19	568	558	454
13 other Engineering Employers' Assocs. in Great Britain	1,913	160	2,481	2,303	3,369
*National Farmers Union	5,224	217	5,596	5,337	125,856
*General Council of British Shipping } British Shipping Federation	1,402	16	4,581	4,603	229
National Fed. of Building Trades Employers	3,321	280	3,799	3,766	10,146
*Freight Transport Association Limited	660	97	2,893	2,802	15,890
*Chemical Industries Association Limited	1,468	103	2,115	2,186	339
Test and County Cricket Board	—	27	2,044	2,044	19
British Printing Industries Federation	738	58	960	977	14
10 Constituent Associations of the BPIF in Great Britain	784	57	862	831	3,164
Electrical Contractors' Association	393	379	1,729	1,743	2,193
Federation of Civil Engineering Contractors	787	47	1,135	910	518
*Road Haulage Association Limited	736	73	1,089	1,047	15,045
British Paper and Board Industry Fed. Ltd	865	56	993	997	109
National Federation of Retail Newsagents	747	53	824	741	28,367
Newspaper Society	692	66	818	789	293
Heating and Ventilating Contractors Assoc.	432	115	756	756	1,185
*Incorporated National Association of British and Irish Millers Limited	587	22	669	731	46
Dairy Trade Federation	459	—	666	625	4,400
*British Jewellery and Giftware Federation Ltd	126	79	662	614	2,035
Federation of Master Builders	574	43	650	554	20,328
*Publishers' Association	462	24	584	554	257
Newspaper Publishers' Association Limited	539	1	540	534	10
Total of above employers' associations	26,211	2,448	41,010	39,699	236,344
Total of 128 other listed employers' associations	5,133	540	6,999	6,564	56,010
Total of 187 other unlisted employers' assocs	5,858	521	7,595	7,168	749
TOTAL of all employers' associations for 1979	37,202	3,509	55,604	53,431	293,103
TOTAL of all employers' associations for 1978	32,123	2,540	46,156	44,955	340,223

Source: Certification Office for Trade Unions and Employers' Associations (1981).

Notes:

* Employers' Organisations not listed by Certification Officer under section 28 of the Trade Union and Labour Relations Act 1974.

[a] The bulk of the income from members is in the form of subscriptions; these are related to the number of employees or the size of the wage bill or, in one or two cases, to capital employed. The amount of the subscription varies from organisation to organisation but rarely exceeds 0·5 per cent of the wage bill. In 1972, using a different formula, the report of the Inquiry into Industrial and Commercial Representation estimated that the total contribution of six large companies to all kinds of representative organisations, including Chambers of Commerce, varied between 0·014 per cent and 0·039 per cent of turnover (CBI, 1972:76).

[b] The main items of expenditure are staff and administration. In fact, many local organisations do not employ any full-time staff; they use the services of an accountant or solicitor. Some of the larger national organisations might have forty to fifty executive staff alone; whereas the NPA has no more than half a dozen.

[c] The government of employers' organisations is in the hands of the members. In the case of local employers' organisations there is usually an annual general meeting or general assembly which elects an executive council or management board. The executive council is responsible for the day-to-day government of the organisation and for the election of a chairman or president who is the chief office-holder. National employers' organisations also have annual general meetings and executive councils. In addition, a number—especially those which are federations—may have a general council which fits in between the two. Representation on these various bodies is normally determined by the amount of subscription, the number of employees, the size of the wage bill, or some combination of all three.

from membership in recent years: Esso withdrew from the Employers' Panel of the Oil Companies Conciliation Committee in 1964, Chrysler (now Talbot) from the Engineering Employers' Federation in 1971, Burton from the Clothing Manufacturers' Federation in 1975, and Daily Mirror Newspapers from the Newspaper Publishers' Association in 1974. More recently, British Leyland, the General Electric Company (GEC), and Philips have withdrawn from the Engineering Employers' Federation, the last two following the dispute in 1979 over the reduction in the working week. Also, a number of companies, such as Ford, have never been members of an employers' organisation; and others, such as Imperial Chemical Industries (ICI), have non-conforming status: that is, they do not follow the terms and conditions of the multi-employer agreement. Overall, however, there does not appear to have been anything approaching a mass exodus. In manufacturing, for example, where most of the losses have been experienced, the Warwick Survey (Brown, 1981:20) found that only 4 per cent of establishments said that they had withdrawn from membership of their employers' organisation in recent years; of these, a third had withdrawn before 1968. The density of membership may not be as high in some industries—especially in metalworking and chemicals—as in other Western European countries, but it is of the order of 70 to 75 per cent in most industries among establishments with 50 or more employees.

Perhaps the most significant developments concerning employers' organisations have been those involving the Confederation of British Industry (CBI). The CBI is an employers' confederation, the peak organisation of employers. It was formed in 1965 by the merger of the British Employers' Confederation with the Federation of British Industries and the National Association of British Manufacturers (see Grant and Marsh, 1977). Starting from its base in manufacturing, the CBI has made considerable gains in retailing and in banking and insurance. It now claims to have members in every part of the private sector. Overall it has more than 4,500 individual member companies with between 11,000 and 12,000 subsidiaries, and more than 200 employers' and trade organisations which, in turn, represent some 300,000 companies. Since 1969 the nationalised industries and public corporations have been eligible for full-member status and most are now members. The total number of people employed by companies affiliated to the CBI, either directly, or indirectly through an employers' or trade organisation, is of the order of 12 million. Significantly, too, these include the employees of most of the companies which are not members of the relevant national employers' organisation; Ford, for example, is an active member of the CBI.

Constitutionally, the CBI is very different from the local and national employers' organisations considered above. In effect, it inherited the constitution of the Federation of British Industries, which reflected its mixture of individual company and trade organisation membership. This means that it is governed by a council of no fewer than 400 people who are representative of the various categories of membership. In practice, however, a key role is played by the so called President's Committee. Formally, the President's Committee is one of the CBI's twenty-nine standing committees, but it has much wider terms of reference than other standing committees, its task being 'to advise the President on major policy issues, and to keep the CBI's public position and overall strategy under review'. Its twenty-six members include the chairmen of the most important standing committees such as Employment Policy and the Small Firms' Council.

THE FUNCTIONS OF EMPLOYERS' ORGANISATIONS: THEIR CHANGING SIGNIFICANCE

From the evidence, then, it would appear that British managements are not dispensing with their employers' organisations. Part of the explanation for this lies outside the scope of this chapter. The majority of employees' organisations, including the CBI, are also trade organisations; in other words, they reflect the interests of their members in their capacity as producers as well as employers. Indeed, of the national employers' organisations listed in Table 5.1, only the Engineering Employers' Federation is not a trade organisation. This means that most employers' organisations represent their members' interests across a broad front of trade and commercial issues. It also means that the range of activities in which they are involved is very wide; for example, credit facilities and joint marketing arrangements; research into new markets, products and technology; and the distribution of products.

Much of the explanation for the support which employers' organisations continue to enjoy, however, does lie within the scope of this chapter. In its evidence to the Donovan Commission the CBI (1965:8) suggested that employers' organisations strictly defined performed a number of industrial relations functions. As noted below, these may be grouped under four main headings: the negotiation of pay and conditions, the operation of disputes procedures, advisory and consultancy services, and representation. Contrary to the impression which may sometimes be given, employers' organisations continue to perform these functions. What has been changing is the relative significance which managements, especially in some manufacturing industries, attach to them. While this change in emphasis may well result in a major re-structuring in the longer term, there is every reason to believe that employers' organisations are unlikely to disappear for some considerable time.

Negotiation of Pay and Conditions

The main function with which employers' organisations have come to be associated is the negotiation of pay and conditions. But the significance of this function varies by industry, depending on the coverage of these issues in multi-employer agreements. Following the Commission on Industrial Relations (1972:21), three main types of agreement may be identified: minimum, comprehensive, and partial.

The first type, *minimum agreements*, is by far the largest in terms of number of workers involved and is found, for example, in engineering and chemicals. The rates of pay in the multi-employer agreement which the employers' organisation negotiates are minima; that is to say, management is free to pay more than these rates. In fact, in engineering and chemicals these rates have come to be regarded as 'safety-nets', and as Chapter 6 makes clear, only workers being paid between the old and the new rates actually benefit directly from increases in them. The multi-employer agreements which the employers' organisation negotiates also make little or no provision for relative levels of pay. In engineering, for example, the agreement provides only for rates of pay for labourers, fitters, and a small group of craft occupations. In other words, it does not provide for the rates of pay of the vast array of occupations which are likely to be found in an engineering firm. By definition, these rates have to be determined by management in the workplace. Finally, this type of agreement gives relatively little attention to conditions of employment other than pay. In most cases it covers only the length of the working week and holidays, the premia for overtime and shift-working, and holiday pay.

The second type, *comprehensive agreements*, which is at the other extreme, is to be found in industries such as electrical contracting, port transport, and shipping. Here the rates of pay in the multi-employer agreement which the employers' organisation negotiates are standard; the intention is that these should be the actual rates of pay which workers receive without supplements other than for overtime and shift-working. Multi-employer agreements of this type usually make detailed provision for relative levels of pay, and their coverage of conditions other than pay is also much more detailed than in minimum agreements. In electrical contracting, for example, the employers' organisation is responsible for negotiating a range of employment, training, and welfare issues.

The third type, *partial agreements,* falls in between the first two and is found in industries such as footwear, cotton textiles, construction, and printing. Here the rates of pay in the multi-employer agreement which the employers' organisation negotiates tend to be minima or basic, but they are often supplemented by standard piecework lists, as in footwear, or by extras or supplements for the performance of specific tasks or operations as in construction and printing. Also, multi-employer agreements of this type usually make detailed provision for relative levels of pay, although the individual management is likely to have more discretion in grading than in comprehensive agreements. Again, the coverage of conditions other than pay is likely to be fairly detailed.

In the light of this analysis it is perhaps not surprising that in industries such as engineering and chemicals single-employer bargaining over pay and conditions has developed to a point at which, in effect, it has replaced multi-employer bargaining. It was not so much that British management did not hold to the common regulation of its employers' organisations as the Donovan Commission (1968:22) implied, but that there was very little common regulation to which it could hold. By contrast, in those industries in which the comprehensive or partial types of agreements prevail the negotiation of pay and conditions continues to be regarded as an important function. The Warwick Survey (Brown, 1981:10), for example, suggests that in the printing and paper industries no less than 69 per cent of establishments with more than 50 employees regarded multi-employer bargaining as the most important level of pay bargaining; in construction the Department of Employment Survey (Hawes and D. Smith, 1981:267) suggests that more than four-fifths of establishments with more than fifty employees took that view.

How, then, are the different types of multi-employer agreement to be explained? The structure of the industries involved is very important. Industries such as engineering and chemicals are extremely heterogeneous; there are significant differences in the size of firms, in technology, and in products—all of which make the negotiation of the comprehensive type of agreement hardly practicable. In industries such as electrical contracting or shipping, on the other hand, the product or service is much more homogeneous: technology and jobs are very similar from one workplace to another and so lend themselves to standard rates of pay and conditions. Also, in many of these industries firms tend to be small, and hence there are significant economies of scale in using an employers' organisation as a bargaining agent.

Having said this, there is no obvious structural reason why engineering employers in Britain could not have negotiated multi-employer agreements of the partial kind. Moreover, their counterparts in Western European countries have done so in some cases across the entire range of metal working industries (Sisson, forthcoming). The explanation for the paucity of substantive issues in multi-employer agreements, it can be argued, is as much historical as it is structural and, in particular, turns on the accommodation which was reached by the engineering employers and the Amalgamated Society of Engineers in 1898. The very essence of the 'Provisions for the Avoidance of Disputes' which the employers imposed on the union was that settlements reached were not to have general application. In theory, unions were to be excluded from the establishment and individual managements were to determine most of the substantive terms and conditions unilaterally. In practice, everything depended on the balance of power. This was very firmly in managements' favour until the 1930s. Increasingly from then on, however, managements found it more and more difficult to avoid being drawn into workplace bargaining with shop stewards. But the more they engaged in workplace bargaining, the more difficult it became to develop common policies through their employers' organisations. This also helps to explain why, unlike their counterparts in Sweden and West Germany, it became virtually impossible to maintain the degree of solidarity necessary to engage in sympathetic lockouts.

Operation of Disputes Procedures

A second main function of employers' organisations has been the operation of a disputes procedure. Indeed, in a number of industries— engineering is the most notable example—the introduction of a national or industry-wide disputes procedure pre-dates, at least at national level, the negotiation of pay and conditions. The details of the procedure differ from industry to industry; see, for example, Commission on Industrial Relations, 1972; Hyman, 1972; and Marsh and McCarthy, 1968. Broadly speaking, however, they provide for three stages: the first takes place in the workplace, the second at the district or local level, and the third at the national level. Officials of the employers' organisation may be involved at each of these stages. Significantly, too, the procedures are designed to deal with any issue which arises; they do not simply deal with interpretations of the multi-employer agreement or a failure to reach agreement at this level. Implicitly, then, they recognise a strong trade union presence in the workplace and the likelihood of some form of workplace bargaining.

The evidence would appear to suggest that the help which employers' organisations give in the handling of disputes continues to be highly valued by the member-firms. In manufacturing, for example, the Warwick Survey (Brown, 1981:20) suggests that nearly half of the establishments reporting that their employers' organisation operated a disputes procedure had in fact made use of the procedure during the previous two years; on average, they had used it at least twice. Larger establishments made more use of the procedures than small ones: nearly three-quarters of those with more than 1,000 employees had used the procedure in the previous two years and, on average, had used it almost nine times. Contrary to what might have been expected, managers also reported an increase in their use of the procedure. Compared to five years previously, about one quarter estimated that their use of it had increased and only 8 per cent that it had declined. Table 5.2 gives the full details. Clearly, the industries in which the largest proportion of member-firms reported an increase in the use of the procedure are paper and printing; the largest number of firms reporting a decline are among members of the Engineering Employers' Federation (EEF).

When the respondents' replies were broken down by size of establishment there was not a great deal of difference between the categories so far as the number reporting an increase in their use of the procedure was concerned. Establishments in the 200–499 employee category seemed to have had the greatest increase, followed by those in the 100–199 category; there was hardly any difference at all between the very small and the very

TABLE 5.2: ESTABLISHMENTS IN MEMBERSHIP OF EMPLOYERS' ORGANISATIONS REPORTING A CHANGE IN THE USE OF DISPUTES PROCEDURE

Employers' Organistions	Used More %	Used Less %	About Same (Used) %	About Same (Not Used) %	Don't Know %
Engineering Employers' Federation	23	13	26	27	9
Other Engineering	32	1	7	55	3
Chemical Industries Association	33	3	12	41	
Any food etc.	34	3	2	19	40
Any textiles	35	1		55	8
Any clothing	2	2	6	77	4
Any paper/printing	50	8	15	23	2
All other	15	5	9	68	1
All organisations	23	8	15	44	7

Source: Unpublished data supplied by the Industrial Relations Research Unit, University of Warwick.

large establishments. Significantly, however, there was a marked difference between the categories in the number of establishments saying that they had used the procedure less. Here the numbers very definitely increased with size. There had been a decline in use of the procedure in less than 2 per cent of establishments in the 50–99 category, in 9 per cent of establishments in the 100–199 category, in 13 per cent of establishments in the 200–499 category, in 18 per cent of establishments in the 500–999 category, and in 21 per cent of establishments in the 1000+ category. The most plausible explanation for this state of affairs is that the smaller establishments have been experiencing greater industrial relations activity which has enhanced the value of the external disputes procedure, and that the larger ones have increasingly been developing procedures internal to the company.

Advisory and Consultancy Services

There seems little doubt that the major expansion in the work of most employers' organisations in recent years has been in the provision of advisory and consultancy services. Both the Commission on Industrial Relations (1972:ch. 7) and the Warwick Survey (Brown, 1981:21) confirm this trend. For example, the latter source suggests that not only do most employers' organisations provide a wide range of such services, but also that firms made considerable use of them. The full details are shown in

Table 5.3. It can be seen that nearly 60 per cent of firms had made use of the legal services provided by their employers' organisation, about half had used the information on local pay levels, and about 45 per cent had sought help in interpreting incomes policies. Significantly, too, these services are not simply used by the managements in the smaller firms. Table 5.3 suggests that in most areas the greater utilisation of services was by management in establishments with more than 1,000 employees. Overall, more than a third of the firms reporting that their employers' organisations provided advisory and consultancy services said that their usage of them had increased in recent years and only 2 per cent reported a decline. Those reporting an increase in utilisation were fairly evenly spread across the different size categories.

This expansion in the consultancy function of employers' organisations is not difficult to understand. The reconstruction of workplace industrial relations which was described in the previous chapter, coupled with the impact of a very considerable increase in employment legislation and government intervention generally, has placed considerable demands on the resources of individual firms. This is even true of the larger firms and it is particularly true of the smaller and independent firms. Clearly, there are considerable advantages in going for advice to employers' organisation officials who have been able to build up specialist knowledge of a particular industry. Compared to the cost of advice from other sources, such as independent consultants or solicitors, it is also very much cheaper; in most cases no more than the cost of the annual subscription which, as pointed out above, is rarely more than a fraction of 1 per cent of a firm's wage bill. Indeed, officials of many employers' organisations say that a number of small- and medium-sized firms have joined in recent years simply to get information and advice on the impact of employment legislation.

Representation

Employers' organisations are not only bargaining agents, dispute-handlers, and consultants; they are also one of the most important pressure groups in British society. Representation is one of their major functions. The interests represented may be individual or collective. The target of the representation may be central or local government, trade unions, or the public at large. The representation can also take many forms: a telephone call, lobbying, publicity campaigns, and financial support for individuals and groups willing to act on the members' behalf. Employers' organisations are also a major source of recruitment of employer representatives to the numerous permanent and *ad hoc* bodies which have proliferated in the post-World War II period due largely to government intervention in the management of the economy. The 'Little Neddies' and Sector Working Parties spawned by the National Economic Development Council are one example; industrial tribunals are another.

There can be little doubt that the performance of the representative

TABLE 5.3: THE UTILISATION OF EMPLOYERS' ASSOCIATION ADVISORY SERVICES BY INDUSTRY AND SIZE

	Recruitment Information	Education and Training	Labour Legislation	Work Study or Bonus Schemes	Job Evaluation	Redundancy Policy	Local Pay Levels	Incomes Policy
Engineering Employers' Federation	6	35	76	8	11	32	62	59
Other engineering	2	41	51	28	16	47	30	41
Chemical Industries Association	5	11	31	17	8	46	28	29
Any food etc.	1	16	37	9	10	24	33	33
Any textiles	21	26	79	10	10	14	82	72
Any clothing	12	45	65	48	36	43	52	52
Any paper/printing	24	45	72	32	23	36	62	64
All other	6	19	49	2	3	6	45	36
Number of full-time employees ⎡ 50–99	4	15	51	5	5	19	47	38
100–199	16	31	58	16	12	26	48	43
200–499	9	37	61	11	11	22	56	52
500–999	7	49	72	13	15	17	54	59
⎣ 1000+	14	42	75	13	15	24	62	68
ALL	9·0	27·1	57·4	9·9	9·2	21·6	50·4	44·8

Source: Brown (1981:22).
Note: Figures are expressed as a percentage of establishments in association membership.

function lies behind the very considerable increase in the membership of the CBI in recent years. Indeed, there is little else to explain it. Unlike employers' confederations in some other countries, the CBI is not a bargaining agent in its own right. Nor does it have any formal role in the coordination of the bargaining policies of its members, Again, the reasons are largely historical; employers' organisations such as the Engineering Employers' Federation have been as fiercely proud of their independence as have trade unions (Jackson and Sisson, 1976; Sisson, forthcoming). Of particular importance in the development of the CBI's representative role was the successful campaign which it waged against the proposals of the Bullock Committee of Inquiry into Industrial Democracy. If any management needed to be persuaded of the need for an effective employers' confederation as a counter-weight to the TUC, it was perhaps this episode which did it above all others.

PROSPECTS FOR THE FUTURE

The functions which employers' organisations perform in the future will depend, as in the past, on the needs of the individual firms which are their members. For example, in such industries as footwear, cotton textiles, construction, and electrical contracting, and, indeed, in many parts of the private service sector there is no reason to expect that the negotiation of pay and conditions by employers' organisations will decline in significance. Multi-employer bargaining continues to have a number of advantages from management's point of view. In particular, it both helps to reduce the impact of the trade union in the workplace and to take labour costs out of competition. Some of these advantages are also available to managements in the smaller firms in engineering and chemicals.

The prospect of long-term unemployment reminiscent of the 1920s and 1930s—at least in its scale—leads to speculation about the likelihood of a revival in multi-employer bargaining over pay and the conditions of employment in industries such as engineering and chemicals. Trade unions, in particular, might be expected to be more favourably inclined to negotiations at this level in order to give better protection to their members in the smaller and less profitable firms. In the light of the analysis in the previous chapter, however, it is difficult to avoid the conclusion that, far from there being a revival, multi-employer bargaining over pay and conditions is likely to assume less and less significance in these industries, primarily because the great majority of managements are actively pursuing a policy of ability to pay and this can best be achieved in the present context by bargaining at the establishment or corporate levels. Indeed, most managements are already non-conforming members of their employers' organisations in practice if not in name. Arguably the last opportunity to restructure collective bargaining along multi-employer lines was at the time of the Donovan Commission. But the Donovan

Commission does not appear to have seriously considered the possibility. Nor, perhaps, is this surprising. There was no indication then or since that most managements wanted such restructuring. By the 1960s the collective action which such restructuring would have required had ceased to be a serious proposition; it was largely a thing of the past.

Even so, this does not necessarily mean that employers' organisations in Britain will simply become the preserve of the small firm. Nor is it likely that representation will be the only function. There is evidence to suggest that the operation of a disputes procedure is a function which continues to be valued by managements even in many of the larger firms. The advisory and consultancy services which most employers' organisations have developed are also highly valued. Indeed, paradoxically as it may seem, in a number of cases employers' organisations probably exert more influence on workplace industrial relations through the performance of these functions than they did through multi-employer bargaining.

Pursuing this last point, it is also conceivable that in the future employers' organisations will come to assume a more important role in coordinating the collective bargaining of individual managements. Inevitably, the shift from multi-employer to single-employer bargaining raises the question of the relationship between firms. In theory, management tailors agreements to suit its circumstances, and ability to pay is of paramount importance. In practice, it is not as simple as this. Firms are not totally independent. Many jobs are similar from one firm to another and come under the jurisdiction of the same trade union. If the difference in earnings, for example, becomes too great, there is likely to be resentment leading to claims based on comparability. Clearly, the proposals contained in recent CBI publications (1977a and 1979) for a widening of bargaining units, the synchronisation of settlement dates, and the setting-up of a national economic forum suggest an increasing awareness of the problems, while the proposal to establish a strike fund recognises the greater vulnerability to industrial action of the individual firm under single-employer bargaining. It is true that with the deepening depression the CBI has been unable to persuade the majority of its members to take action on these proposals. Even so, the proposals have strong support among some powerful members and are likely to be resurrected if the problems they were intended to deal with ever return. In that event, there could be an important role for employers' organisations and, in particular, the CBI.

Perhaps the main imponderable is whether or not employers' organisations will remain in their present form. It is significant that one or two of the larger multi-establishment enterprises with interests in a number of industries are already beginning to question the effectiveness of the present patterns of organisations. With the decline in the significance of multi-employer bargaining, it is argued, subscribing to a number of single-industry national employers' organisations as well as the CBI makes increasingly less sense. The situation at the local level too is unsatisfactory: resources are spread far too thinly across a number of single-industry employers' organisations whereas their own enterprise structure is multi-industry. More positively, their thinking points to a restructuring of employers' organisation based on the CBI and a number of multi-industry regional organisations with internal committees to represent particular industries or sectors; these committees, in turn, might carry out the bargaining agency functions of the existing national employers' organisations. It remains to be seen whether these ideas result in a restructuring of employers' organisations. Alternatively, and perhaps more likely, the same result may be achieved by an evolutionary process as more of the larger enterprises withdraw from membership of the national employers' organisations. In any event, employers' organisations of some kind are likely to be around for many years to come.

PART III
Patterns of Industrial Relations

6 Industrial Relations in the Private Sector: Donovan Re-visited

Keith Sisson and William Brown

In 1968 the Donovan Commission produced its wide ranging analysis of industrial relations in Britain. Strictly speaking, the Commission was charged with the responsibility for looking at industrial relations in both the private and the public sector. In practice, however, the Commission's report concentrated almost exclusively on industrial relations in the private sector and, within that, on manufacturing industry. The report had a great deal to say about the parties to industrial relations: managements and employers' organisations, shop stewards and trade unions, and the government. Its treatment of the law was also exhaustive. For all that it had to say about these aspects, however, it was the Commission's analysis of collective bargaining which stood out and has subsequently dominated teaching and research in industrial relations.

The Commission's analysis of collective bargaining is the starting point for the present chapter. The central concern is with the nature and extent of the changes which have taken place in collective bargaining in the private sector since 1968. Following Fox (1966:6), the chapter distinguishes between collective bargaining over 'market relations', which basically means pay and hours of work, and collective bargaining over 'managerial relations', that is the deployment, organisation and discipline of the labour force. The conclusion is that there have been considerable changes in the conduct of bargaining over market relations, but that there has been surprisingly little change so far as managerial relations are concerned. In particular, the informality which characterised much of the bargaining in the 1960s continues to be a dominant feature twenty years later. The final section considers the implications for the future of collective bargaining.

THE DONOVAN ANALYSIS

The Donovan Commission (1968:12) argued that Britain had two systems of industrial relations: the formal and informal. In the private sector, especially in manufacturing, the formal system was based on multi-employer bargaining between employers' organisations and trade unions.

According to the Ministry of Labour's evidence, there were about 500 separate institutions, including the statutory wage councils, in which negotiations took place between employers' organisations and trade unions. In many industries—engineering is the largest example—this multi-employer bargaining had developed towards the end of the nineteenth century, first at district and then at national level. In others, such as chemicals, these arrangements were a direct result of Ministry of Labour intervention following the recommendations of the reports of the Whitley Committee in 1917. In the latter case the institutions usually bore the name of joint industrial councils.

As the previous chapter has pointed out, two types of collective agreement were involved in this multi-employer bargaining. The first dealt with substantive issues. Although the coverage was different from industry to industry, in most cases the agreements covered such issues as basic rates of pay, hours of work, overtime rates, and holidays. The second type was concerned with the procedures for negotiations and handling disputes which might arise between the parties at any level. In the case of dispute procedures three or four stages were usually involved, ending up with a national conference involving senior officials of the trade union and employers' organisation.

The informal system, the Commission suggested, arose out of the actual behaviour of the parties. In particular, the Commission focused on the developments in workplace bargaining which had taken place since World War II. Under the pressure of full employment, it suggested, many managements tended increasingly to settle matters in their own workplace by negotiating with shop stewards rather than through multi-employer bargaining involving their employers' organisation. The issue of pay was especially important. A decline had occurred in the extent to which the multi-employer agreements determined actual pay. Workplace negotiations over the amount of overtime, piecework payments, and workplace supplements had resulted in a substantial gap emerging between the basic rates of pay in the multi-employer agreements and actual earnings. But pay was not the only consideration. The arrangements for dealing with redundancies, sick pay, and such matters as the circumstances justifying discipline and dismissal were also increasingly becoming the subjects of workplace bargaining. So also were questions directly affecting the conduct of work such as flexibility, manning and effort. Overall, the Commission suggested, workplace bargaining was of equal or greater importance than multi-employer bargaining.

The nature of this workplace bargaining was important. The Commission, following Flanders (1970a:169), confirmed that it was 'largely informal, largely fragmented and largely autonomous'. It was informal because of the predominance of unwritten understandings and of custom and practice. It was fragmented because it involved individual shop stewards or relatively small groups of workers. It was autonomous because it rarely involved the employers' organisation or trade union officials and had little or no relationship with the terms and conditions of the multi-employer agreement.

The Commission (1968:37) summed up its analysis as follows:

> the extent to which at the moment industry-wide agreements both on pay and other issues are effective in the workplace cannot exactly be determined. What is of critical importance is that the practices of the formal system have become increasingly empty, while the practices of the informal system have come to exert an ever greater influence on the conduct of industrial relations throughout the country; that the two systems conflict and that the informal system cannot be forced to comply with the formal system.

Having reached the conclusion that the 'central defect is the disorder in factory and workshop relations' (1968:40), the Commission put the onus for undertaking reforms on the shoulders of individual managements. Multi-employer bargaining, it argued, could not deal effectively with such issues as 'the control of incentive schemes, the regulation of hours actually worked, the use of job evaluation, work practices and the linking of changes in pay to changes in performance, facilities for shop stewards and disciplinary rules and procedures'. What was needed was for individual managements to negotiate effective factory and company agreements covering the issues. Employers' organisations should support and assist their members in carrying out their tasks, 'confining industry-wide agreements to matters which they are capable of regulating, providing guide lines for satisfactory company and factory agreements, and where appropriate granting the agreements which follow these guide lines exemption from clauses of the industry-wide agreements' (1968:46).

In view of the argument developed later in this chapter, it is important to be clear about what the Donovan Commission was actually saying. As Clegg, who was a member of the Commission, has pointed out (1979: 232–40), he and his colleagues were not condemning informality out of hand. All collective bargaining arrangements are likely to involve a mixture of the formal and the informal; and informality can play an important role in expediting and supplementing the formal process. Nor was the Donovan Commission suggesting that the informality of workplace bargaining was necessarily resulting in breaches of the formal rules in multi-employer agreements; as the previous chapter has pointed out, there are few formal rules in most multi-employer agreements. The main concern was that so much was being determined informally in the work-place. Not only did this undermine the importance of multi-employer agreements, but the pretence that matters were being settled by multi-employer bargaining hindered the development of 'effective and orderly' workplace bargaining. To quote Clegg (1979:237),

> the Donovan Commission's objection to the state of plant bargaining at that time, therefore, was its doubtful legitimacy and furtive character. They proposed formalisation because they believed that open acknowledgement of the extent of joint regulation in the plant by all concerned would lead to a much-needed rationalisation of the whole process of collective bargaining.

The next two sections try to establish how far the Commission's objective has been realised.

THE CHANGING SYSTEMS OF PAY BARGAINING

The Donovan Commission's 'two-systems' analysis was mainly concerned with pay bargaining. At the time there were criticisms of the approach on the grounds that it did less than justice to the complexity of arrangements, especially in industries other than engineering (Feather, 1968). Whether or not this was an over-simplification at the time, fifteen years later the analysis is certainly inappropriate. It is true that at a superficial level the institutions of multi-employer bargaining do remain largely unchanged in most industries; employers' organisations and trade unions continue to negotiate multi-employer agreements which deal with such issues as rates of pay and hours of work. But the operation of these agreements at the workplace has for the most part changed fundamentally. As Chapter 4 has pointed out, managements have made considerable alterations to their methods of payment. There has also been a considerable increase in bargaining over pay in the private services. The result, so far as the great majority of workers in the private sector is concerned, is that multi-employer bargaining can no longer be described as the formal system.

Operation of Multi-Employer Agreements

The previous chapter followed the Commission on Industrial Relations (1972:21) in identifying three main types of multi-employer agreements: minimum, comprehensive, partial. In recent years there have been significant changes in the operation of the 'minimum' type of agreement so far as rates of pay are concerned. The most significant of these took place in rubber in 1967 and in engineering and chemicals in 1968. Previously, to use the analogy drawn by Brown and Terry (1978), the rates of pay in the multi-employer agreement operated as 'floors'; that is to say, when the rates of pay were increased everyone covered by the agreement benefited. Anxious to avoid the compounding of increases in their paybills from both national and workplace negotiations, employers in these industries insisted that henceforth the rates of pay arising from multi-employer agreements should be treated as no more than minimum earnings levels. In effect, the multi-employer agreements became 'safety nets' so far as pay was concerned, and only workers earning between the old and the new rate benefited from an increase in it. The result is that, for the vast majority of workers in these industries, increases in the rates of pay of multi-employer agreements now have no direct impact because they already earn in excess of them.

Another important change in the operation of many multi-employer agreements concerns the date of implementation of settlements. Increasingly, managements in the industries in which the 'minimum type' of agreement prevails have tended not to implement the provisions of the multi-employer agreement from the date of the national settlement, preferring instead to wait until the outcome of their workplace negotiations is known so as to be able to absorb the national settlement in it. This practice was formally recognised by the engineering agreement in 1979. Managements which follow more than one multi-employer agreement for different parts of their workforce have been particularly prone to do this in order to prevent the emergence of pay anomalies. Again, the effect has been to diminish the significance of the multi-employer agreement.

The subjects on which multi-employer bargaining continues to have an important impact, even in the industries with the 'minimum' type of agreement, are the premia for overtime and shift-working, holidays and holiday pay, and, above all, the basic working week. Indeed, in 1979 it was the attempt of the Confederation of Shipbuilding and Engineering Unions to secure a reduction in the forty-hour week which led to a series of stoppages involving the largest number of striker days in one dispute since the General Strike of 1926; altogether sixteen million days were lost due to the strike (Rice, 1981). Managements, it seems, are extremely reluctant to abandon a common line at least so far as the length of the basic working week is concerned. Their anxieties about the difficulty of resisting demands for reductions at single-employer level have been confirmed by the widespread collapse of the forty-hour week since 1979.

Methods of Payment

Accompanying the alteration in multi-employer agreements has been an increase in the number of workers whose pay, in some part, is dependent on productivity or performance (Lloyd, 1976; White, 1981). Much more important, however, have been developments in the type of incentive schemes used. There has been a substantial decline in the use of traditional payment by the piece and its replacement by schemes with standards set in terms of time. Secondly, there has been a tendency to reduce the variable bonus element in the overall make-up of pay. Thirdly, and most importantly, there appears to have been a trend away from individual to group and plant-wide incentive schemes. In the late 1960s and early 1970s time-rate payment systems with work-studied output standards and no variable bonus (sometimes called measured daywork) became popular as a remedy for the inadequacies of payment by results (NBPI, 1968b; OME, 1973), but more recently these have declined in popularity. There have been moves instead towards target schemes which link bonuses to specified levels of productivity or to value-added schemes in which bonus is related to differences between the cost of raw materials and sales revenue. It has also become normal to have these schemes based upon relatively rigorous work study techniques rather than the traditional and largely intuitive rate-fixing or estimating. Overall, the effect of these changes has been to reduce considerably the scope for the informal and fragmented pay bargaining which featured so prominently in the Donovan analysis.

A development that has had particularly far-reaching implications for pay bargaining is the increased use of job evaluation techniques; that is to say, the use of systematic methods of comparing jobs, such as grading or points rating, as the basis for establishing the relative levels of pay within a bargaining unit. In 1968 the NBPI concluded that nearly a quarter of all employees in manufacturing were covered by some form of job evaluation; in 1978 the Warwick Survey (Brown, 1981:111) suggested a figure of 55 per cent, which implies a rate of growth consistent with intervening research (Daniel,1976). Both for manual and for non-manual workers, the likelihood of an establishment using job evaluation increases with its size (Brown, 1981:111), and is substantially greater if it is covered by a single-employer rather than a multi-employer agreement. The technique has also spread beyond manufacturing; it is both widespread and developing in the distributive trades, in miscellaneous services, and in banking and finance (Thakur and Gill, 1976).

The increased use of job evaluation has had a three-fold effect on pay bargaining. First, it tends to reduce considerably the number of pay grades. To take one example, the scheme which British Leyland introduced in 1980 reduced a myriad of manual pay grades to just five. Second, it centralises pay bargaining. Although there are as yet few examples of single-status or integrated schemes covering both manual and non-manual workers (IPM, 1977), it is normal for most manual workers to be covered by one scheme, most non-manual workers by another, and most managers by a third. Consequently it is difficult to continue with fragmented pay bargaining once a job evaluation scheme has been introduced without jeopardising the whole scheme. Third, although the combination of job evaluation and multi-employer bargaining is not in principle incompatible, managements have found it difficult to maintain the integrity of their newly-established pay structures if they have to accommodate subsequent increases in the rates of pay arising from multi-employer agreements. Thus the spread of job evaluation has been a stimulus behind the change in the operation of multi-employer agreements.

Most Important Level of Pay Bargaining

Coupled with the growth in trade union membership in the 1960s and 1970s, especially among workers in non-manual jobs and in service industries, these developments have transformed the pattern of pay bargaining in the private sector. The present picture is best described in terms of the most important level of pay bargaining. If establishments are categorised in this way, four main types may be identified: these will be referred to as the 'wage councillors', the 'association bargainers', the 'plant bargainers', and the 'corporate bargainers'. Each type is described and an attempt is then made to establish their coverage by industry, by size of establishment, and by group of workers.

In the case of the 'wage councillors' and the 'association bargainers' the most important pay agreement covers other employers in the same industry or branch of activity; that is, the arrangements are multi-employer. The 'wage councillors' rely on the statutory wages councils or boards to settle rates of pay and other basic conditions of employment. Further details of these institutions are given in Chapter 8. For the 'association bargainers' the most important pay agreement is that negotiated by an employers' organisation and one or more trade unions in some form of joint industrial council. These agreements may be national or regional in scope; for example, in construction and printing they are national but in road haulage and certain parts of textiles they are regional.

The Donovan analysis has never been wholly appropriate to those arrangements where multi-employer bargaining is not only the main source of increases in pay but also stipulates occupational differentials and many of the other substantive conditions of employment. It is true that any workplace bargaining which takes place is likely to be informal, and likely to be fragmented inasmuch as it more often than not involves individual shop stewards rather than a joint shop steward committee. Yet this workplace bargaining is not generally in conflict with multi-employer bargaining and is not as autonomous as the Donovan Commission implied. Instead it is more likely to be concerned with the administration of the terms and conditions contained in the multi-employer agreement or with the negotiation of supplements. It is also likely to involve both employers' organisations and trade union officials when major issues are raised.

The third and fourth types, the 'plant bargainers' and 'corporate bargainers', are more complex. Between two-thirds and three-quarters of them belong to employers' organisations and observe some of the conditions in the multi-employer agreements which they negotiate, the basic working week being the most general. So far as pay is concerned, however, multi-employer bargaining is no longer the most important source of increases. In the case of the 'plant bargainers' the most important level of bargaining is located within the individual establishment. The bargaining may take place at one or more of a number of possible levels—it may, for example, involve a gang or a department—but is increasingly likely to do so at the level of the whole establishment. It is also likely to involve joint shop steward committees; full-time trade union officials may or may not be involved.

'Corporate bargainers' are, by definition, only to be found among multi-establishment enterprises. Their most important pay agreement is negotiated at a level in the enterprise higher than the individual establishment which may be a division within the overall enterprise or the enterprise itself. Here the negotiating committee is likely to involve convenors and senior shop stewards drawn from individual establishments together with full-time trade union officials.

The only survey that provides information on the coverage of these arrangements for the whole of the private sector is that carried out in 1980 by the DE/PSI/SSRC consortium, which has been based on a representative sampling of establishments with twenty-five or more employees. These cover approximately three-quarters of the private sector workforce, the coverage being just over 90 per cent for manufacturing industry and some two-thirds for services.

The figures in Table 6.1 express the percentage of all employees, manual and non-manual combined, which the survey suggests are covered by the particular arrangements in each industry. The results should be interpreted with considerable caution. The managers responsible for industrial relations at each establishment were asked about the level of negotiation which had been most important, directly or indirectly, on the occasion of the last pay increase for their largest groups of manual and non-manual workers. Where unions were not recognised they were asked whether the increase was determined by a wages council or by some other method. There are a

TABLE 6.1: THE MOST IMPORTANT LEVEL OF PAY BARGAINING BY INDUSTRY

		MULTI-EMPLOYER		*SINGLE EMPLOYER*		
				Corporate		*Mana-*
		Associ-	*Wages*	*(Multi-*	*Single*	*gerially*
SIC	*Industry*	*ation*	*Council*	*Plant)*	*Plant*	*Determined*
3	Food, drink, and tobacco	18	1	25	42	14
4+5	Chemicals etc.	11	0	19	15	54
6	Metal manufacture	8	0	7	76	9
7	Mechanical engineering	4	0	9	64	22
8	Instrument engineering	0	0	34	32	30
9	Electrical engineering	5	0	30	53	11
10	Shipbuilding	0	0	5	64	31
11	Vehicles	7	2	28	52	11
12	Metal goods n.e.s.	11	1	10	65	13
13+14	Textiles and leather	38	9	18	13	22
15	Clothing and footwear	46	14	22	2	13
16	Bricks, pottery, glass, and cement	62	0	16	15	7
17	Timber and furniture	42	4	16	14	23
18	Paper and printing	54	1	15	17	13
19	Other manufacturing	8	3	31	35	22
2+20	Quarrying and construction	52	7	4	7	30
22	Transport and communication	22	4	39	18	17
23	Distribution	16	10	21	15	37
24	Banking and insurance	19	2	31	0	47
25	Education and professional services	42	4	4	2	47
26	Hotels and misc. services	8	24	13	7	48
	Total private industry	21	5	18	30	26

Source: Unpublished data from DE/PSI/SSRC Workplace Industrial Relations Survey, 1980.
Notes: The figures are the percentage of employees covered in each industry. Each row totals 100 per cent.

number of definitional problems in these questions, but the principal difficulty is that the more distant the level of settlement from the workplace, the more inaccurate the reply is likely to be. The inconsistency of replies about multi-employer agreements and awards suggests that, especially in non-manufacturing employment, local managers at, say, pubs and petrol stations may know little of the origin of the pay scales sent down to them from head office. It is thus likely that the results in Table 6.1 significantly understate the multi-employer categories and overstate the 'managerially determined' category. Certainly they do so in comparison with previous attempts to map the structure of pay bargaining (Brown, 1980:132–3; Brown, 1981:7–19).

Table 6.1 demonstrates the considerable extent to which the incidence of the four different types of bargaining arrangement differs between industries. If the 1980 survey had covered agricultural employment it would have been seen to be dominated by 'wages councillors'. In Table 6.1 the influence of wages councils is, as noted, probably substantially understated. Despite this, it is apparent in retail distribution, hotels, and miscellaneous services, and, in manufacturing, in clothing and textiles.

The 'association bargainers' stand out in the construction industry and in much of manufacturing, including textiles, leather, clothing, footwear, bricks, pottery, glass, cement, timber, furniture, paper and printing. Only a small minority of these are covered by regional arrangements; the normal practice is one of nation-wide industry agreements. In the service sector of the economy, 'association bargainers' have some strong pockets, probably heavily understated in the table, such as those covered by the Motor Agents' Association, where nearly half a million workers are involved (ACAS, 1980:275).

It is in the metalworking industries that 'plant bargainers' are to be found in large numbers, although a substantial proportion are also in the food and the drink industries. The fact that bargaining is conducted at plant level does not mean that these industries are necessarily characterised by independent establishments; far from it, the 'plant bargainers' include engineering giants such as the General Electric Company, Guest Keen and Nettlefold, and Tube Investments.

Single-employer bargaining is important in non-manufacturing, but here 'plant bargainers' are the exception and 'corporate bargainers' more normal. In banking, insurance, transport and distribution the dispersion and mobility of workforces make any arrangements that are not company-wide unpractical. The relatively recent development of corporate bargaining (often at a divisional level) within the food, drink and tobacco industries is notable. So also is the use of corporate bargaining by the four big motor vehicle assembly firms—British Leyland, Ford, Talbot, and Vauxhall—and by the largest of the chemical firms, ICI.

A major influence on the type of bargaining arrangement is the size of an establishment's workforce. Table 6.2 analyses the most important level of bargaining reported in the 1980 survey by successive size bands.

It separates manufacturing from non-manufacturing industries and, within these, manual from non-manual workers. In each size band the percentage distributions are in terms of numbers of establishments and not numbers of employees.

TABLE 6.2: THE MOST IMPORTANT LEVEL OF PAY BARGAINING BY ESTABLISHMENT SIZE

| | Size of Establishment by Number of Full-Time Employees | | | | | | |
	25–49	50–99	100–199	200–499	500–999	1000+	Total
MANUFACTURING							
MANUAL							
Multi-employer							
Association	22	34	37	30	21	16	29
Wages council	2	3	2	2	1	0	2
Single employer							
Corporate (multi-plant)	4	10	13	16	25	32	11
Single plant	26	20	28	39	46	53	28
Managerially determined	46	33	20	12	5	0	30
Total	100	100	100	99	98	101	100
NON-MANUAL							
Multi-employer							
Association	3	6	8	10	6	5	6
Wages council	0	3	2	2	1	0	1
Single employer							
Corporate (multi-plant)	1	7	13	14	28	37	9
Single plant	10	9	18	30	45	47	17
Managerially determined	86	76	60	44	21	11	67
Total	100	101	101	100	101	100	100
NON-MANUFACTURING							
MANUAL							
Multi-employer							
Association	19	16	22	27	14	33	19
Wages council	15	11	12	4	0	0	13
Single employer							
Corporate (multi-plant)	7	12	20	22	26	33	11
Single plant	4	5	10	5	21	17	5
Managerially determined	55	56	36	42	39	17	52
Total	100	100	100	100	100	100	100
NON-MANUAL							
Multi-employer							
Association	11	12	13	15	11	0	12
Wages council	12	8	6	4	2	0	9
Single employer							
Corporate (multi-plant)	8	12	15	24	32	50	11
Single plant	1	3	7	4	9	25	3
Managerially determined	68	66	59	53	46	25	65
Total	100	101	100	100	100	100	100

Source: Unpublished data from DE/PSI/SSRC Workplace Industrial Relations Survey, 1980.
Note: The figures are the percentage of establishments in each size band.

It is clear from Table 6.2 that the probability of pay being determined by management alone diminishes sharply with increased establishment size and does so, for both manual and non-manual employees, particularly strongly in manufacturing industry. By contrast, reliance upon wages councils is very sensitive to establishment size in non-manufacturing industry, but not in manufacturing; the difference may be greater than shown because understatement of the influence of wages councils is probably heavier in small non-manufacturing establishments.

The incidence of single-employer bargaining increases very substantially with increasing establishment size for both manual and non-manual employees in both manufacturing and non-manufacturing. Furthermore, both single-plant and multi-plant bargaining share in this; they both become more common in larger establishments. For multi-plant or corporate bargaining this is assisted by the fact that the probability of being a part of a multi-plant enterprise rises with establishment size.

The relationship between association bargaining and establishment size suggested by the table reflects the fact that it is to some extent a residual bargaining arrangement. It is the smaller establishments where workforces lack the strength to engage management in collective bargaining. It is the larger ones that have the independence to cope for themselves. Consequently it is disproportionately the middle-sized establishments which still rely upon association bargaining.

The long-term decline in the proportion of manual jobs in the economy adds particular interest to the differences between manual and non-manual bargaining arrangements. If those employees for whom some sort of bargaining takes place are considered, then for both manufacturing and non-manufacturing industry, non-manual employees differ from manual employees in having less reliance on association bargaining and, within single-employer bargaining, a greater use of corporate arrangements. The first characteristic reflects the historical fact that there is little recognition of non-manual trade unions on an industry basis; even in the case of the major exception of engineering, the agreements were of a 'minimum' type and thus had limited effect. The second, the greater use of corporate agreements, reflects not only the greater inter-plant mobility of non-manual workers, but also the fact that their terms and conditions were often fixed by management on a corporate basis before the question of recognising and negotiating with their unions ever arose. On this reckoning, both association and plant bargaining are likely to diminish as a consequence of the increasingly non-manual character of employment.

These findings suggest that pay bargaining is not only less informal and fragmented than it was when the Donovan Commission reported, but that the distinction which it drew between a formal system of multi-employer bargaining and an informal system of workplace bargaining is no longer apposite. Britain has developed a dual structure of pay bargaining which in some respects is similar to that in North America. In industries with a large number of small establishments, and with relatively low capital requirements and ease of entry, multi-employer bargaining continues to be of primary importance. Nor is there any reason to believe that this situation will change, for, as the previous chapter argued, multi-employer bargaining helps both to neutralise the impact of trade unions on the workplace and also to take labour costs out of competition. Elsewhere, and more generally, among the larger establishments, single-employer pay bargaining has now become a formal system. Whether it takes place in the individual establishment or at a corporate level depends in part on the size of the establishment and the type of workers involved. Above all, to return to the arguments of Chapter 4, it depends on the strategies and tactics of management.

COLLECTIVE BARGAINING AND MANAGERIAL RELATIONS

When the Donovan Commission reported, there were signs that substantial changes were taking place in bargaining over 'managerial' as well as 'market relations'. These changes had a major influence on the direction of reform pointed to by the Commission. Increasingly concerned by the relatively poor productivity records of some of their British plants, a number of multinational companies, including Alcan, Esso, ICI and Mobil, began to embark on a novel type of collective bargaining (Flanders, 1964; NBPI, 1966, 1967). Not only did the agreements they subsequently negotiated explicitly involve shop stewards and deal with actual pay levels, they also covered such issues as the deployment of mates, the demarcation between crafts, time allowances, manning arrangements, and a wide range of work practices. Sometimes these issues were covered by very general statements of intent, but often they were the subject of detailed clauses which itemised the new working practices. These were supposed to be issues over which management already had control. In reality, however, the practices which management wished to change were customary or, more likely, had been imposed unilaterally by workers. Either way, they became the subject of explicit agreements for the very first time.

But productivity bargaining, as it became known, proved to be a temporary phenomenon. First of all, the spread of productivity agreements under the pressure of the Labour Governments' incomes policy devalued the coinage considerably. Few of those agreements reached in this second phase were as well-thought out or as comprehensive as those of the pioneers; most were designed to get round the constraints of the policy (McKersie and Hunter, 1973). Perhaps more significantly, the spread of productivity agreements confirmed some of the earlier criticisms of the pioneering agreements. The inherent danger of productivity bargaining from management's point of view is that workers are encouraged to develop work practices which may then have to be bought out (NBPI, 1969). Many managements also found that there were other, and less risky, ways of securing the benefits of productivity bargaining. For example, the reforms in the methods of payment discussed above often proved the key to greater flexibility in the use of labour; group incentive schemes and simplified pay structures usually make it possible for individual workers to be moved from task to task without loss of earnings. The principal procedural novelty of productivity bargaining, that it provided unprecedented status to hitherto formally unrecognised shop stewards, quickly faded, a process hastened by the message of the Donovan Commission itself.

In important respects, then, bargaining over managerial relations is not so very different from what it was when the Commission reported. It is generally agreed that one of the distinctive features of collective bargaining in Britain, especially in manufacturing, is the 'considerable control that many workplace organisations exercise over the arrangement and conduct of work' (Clegg, 1979:59). Indeed, this is explicitly recognised in the spread of *status quo* clauses in collective agreements. The most important of these is the engineering agreement of 1976 which states that 'in the event of any difference arising which cannot immediately be disposed of, then whatever practice or agreement existed prior to the difference shall continue to operate pending a settlement or until the procedure has been exhausted'.

The long debate from which this form of words emerged reflected the awareness of both management and union negotiators that the 'practices and agreements' in question were rarely written down, so that arguments over *status quo* generally revolved around the legitimacy of oral 'custom and practice' and that this, in turn, was strongly influenced by the relative strength of management and workers at the workplace (Brown, 1972). The lack of codification was a fundamental source of volatility. Yet, despite this, there is little evidence to suggest that there has been any substantial effort to codify these practices and settlements in collective agreements in the years following Donovan. The early productivity agreements are still outstanding for the precision of their description of working practices.

The minimal change in the scope and form of bargaining over managerial relations is particularly notable when the substantial increase in statutory intervention that occurred in the 1970s is considered. The provisions for further recognition under Section 11 of the Employment Protection Act of 1975 illustrate this; strange as it may seem in the light of trade union demands for the extension of collective bargaining, hardly any claims for further recognition appear to have been raised. Many of the procedures which were discussed in Chapter 4, were not jointly agreed; management may have submitted proposals for a disciplinary code and procedure to shop stewards for their comments, but very rarely were they the subject of formal agreements (Singleton, 1975:39; Weekes et al., 1975:21–2). In short, the scope of collective bargaining over managerial relations appears as hazy as it ever was. It is massively variable from industry to industry and from workplace to workplace, heavily dependent upon the form of management controls and the relative power of the protagonists.

Another way of putting this is to say that there are few signs that collective bargaining in the private sector is moving in the direction of the 'statute law' model which is associated with most other countries (Kahn–Freund, 1972:56–61). To quote Clegg (1979:116), such a model

> starts with a substantive agreement on all matters currently subject to joint regulation. This agreement governs relations between the parties until it reaches the end of its term when a new agreement is negotiated. In the meantime it is the job of the procedure laid down in the agreement to settle disputes about its interpretation. Disputes about matters outside the agreement cannot be settled by the procedure but must await termination of the agreement when they may be resolved by amendments or extensions to the agreement if the parties are willing. Industrial action is permitted only at the end of the agreement as a means of reaching a new agreement. Managers are therefore free to make their own decisions on matters outside the agreement for the unions cannot appeal to the procedure on such issues with any hope of success, and they are debarred from taking industrial action.

Much of the collective bargaining in the private sector might be said to conform to a 'common law' model. To quote Clegg again (1979:117), this model

> starts with an agreed disputes procedure to resolve differences between the parties. Any dispute may be referred to the procedure, which resolves it by reference to any relevant substantive rule there may be between the parties, or to a custom which appears to be generally accepted by the parties, or by finding a compromise which is acceptable to the parties. For the model recognises no sharp distinction between disputes of right under existing agreements and disputes of interest concerning the terms of a new agreement. Industrial action is allowed whenever the procedure has failed to resolve a dispute, or whenever one party has given notice to terminate an existing substantive agreement and the notice has expired. In this model, agreements have no fixed term, and there is no need for a single comprehensive agreement. Substantive matters can be regulated by as many agreements as the parties choose to make. The procedure may experience considerable difficulty in resolving disputes over managerial rights unless the matter is specifically regulated by agreement. Once procedure has failed to resolve the issue, however, the union is free to take industrial action against a managerial decision.

In the light of this 'common law' model it is useful to characterise the post-Donovan developments as ones in which the ambiguity of procedures has decreased and in which their location has shifted from national to company or workplace level. But little else has changed and the practice of collective bargaining continues to be one that does not lend itself to detailed written agreements.

As Clegg points out, however, there are substantial areas of collective bargaining in the private sector in Britain which do not conform to the 'statute law' or the 'common law' models. Here the negotiation and administration of agreements which have come to be associated with collective bargaining (Flanders, 1970a:220–26) are noticeable by their absence. For example, trade unions are rarely involved in drawing up disciplinary codes, and most disciplinary procedures lack their consent. A second area is that of redundancy arrangements which, in the private sector, are rarely the subject of agreements. Even though management may seek to reach an *ad hoc* settlement, the initial reaction of the trade unions is likely to be one of opposition. A third example is the organisation of work. Few aspects of the organisation of work are the subject of formal or informal agreements. A *status quo* agreement may be in force which implies that management will honour the existing practice pending negotiations with shop stewards. But defining existing practices is often open to a great deal of argument. In these and other cases, then, one or other of the parties may refuse to enter into either a formal or an informal agreement or to recognise custom and practice. Usually, one of the parties seeks to impose a settlement on the other; it is left to the other party to react.

Clegg suggests that this method of dealing is very similar to the primitive forms of industrial relations which prevailed before the development of more formal collective bargaining. The historical comparison is apt. Yet this method continues to be widespread. Moreover, the power relationship which is so transparent in this activity also underpins the practice of collective bargaining in the case of both the 'statute law' and the 'common law' models. For these reasons, then, it can perhaps best be described as the 'basic' model of collective bargaining.

How is the informality which continues to be so dominant a characteristic of collective bargaining over 'managerial relations' to be explained? There is a technical problem. Issues such as pay and hours of work are measurable quantities, and it is not only easy to make them explicit but important to do so to avoid misunderstanding (Flanders, 1970a:235); by contrast issues such as disciplinary rules are much more difficult to define with the same exactness. But it is more complicated than this.

As Chapter 4 observed, the willingness of management to recognise trade unions is not unqualified; nor does it mean that management is any less anxious to minimise their impact. From management's point of view there are advantages in not making managerial relations the subject of formal agreements. The reasons which McCarthy (1966:27–8) gave to the Donovan Commission for management's reluctance to legitimise informal procedures have a general validity: firstly, it would mean that concessions could not be withdrawn; secondly, even if the present generation of stewards would not take advantage of legitimation, the next generation might; thirdly, if present concessions were legitimised, the stewards might seek a further set of even more advantageous formal concessions; and, 'finally, some *de facto* concessions could not be written down because management, particularly at board level, would not be prepared to admit publicly that they had been forced to accept such modifications in their managerial prerogatives and formal chain of commands'.

Informality also has a number of advantages for shop stewards. The public posture adopted by many managements means that an insistence on making issues the subject of formal agreements might have the effect of limiting the scope of bargaining; a concession which has been made informally can always be used as a precedent in future arguments. Also many of the issues involved, such as discipline and redundancy, are perishable. Shop stewards, in particular, wish to remain free to take action which is appropriate in the circumstances. By putting their signature to a disciplinary procedure or to a redundancy agreement, they would be tacitly legitimising management's right to discipline workers or to make them redundant. By refusing to commit themselves in advance, they may be better able to defend the individual in the specific case or to postpone a decision on redundancy in the hope that there may be a change in circumstances.

There is also an important historical dimension to the question. It is often forgotten that in Britain collective bargaining was not foisted on management by trade unions (Clegg, 1979:25–6). In such industries as building, engineering, and printing there was a long tradition of unilateral regulation by workers which preceded the development of formal collective bargaining. Custom was also extremely important. Indeed, it was unilateral regulation and custom over which the battle was fought in engineering in the 1890s. Management insisted on their right to run things as they saw fit, subject only to individual workers or their representatives being able to raise grievances under the provisions for avoiding disputes. But, as the previous chapter has pointed out, any settlements were not to have wider application. The outcome of this compromise was to have a profound effect on the subsequent development of collective bargaining in Britain. It not only set a seal of legitimacy on workplace bargaining and guaranteed that it would be largely autonomous of external trade unions; it also ensured that workplace bargaining would be informal and fragmented. This, in turn, meant that a contractual or 'statute law' system of collective bargaining, especially so far as substantive issues were concerned, was hardly feasible.

Many of the problems which are encountered in analysing collective bargaining stem from seeing its essential character as a process of joint regulation: the joint negotiation and administration of agreements between management and worker representatives. Clearly, the negotiation and administration of agreements are important aspects of collective bargaining. But to see it solely in these terms is both too restrictive and too idealised. In its basic form collective bargaining is a pressure group activity in which management and workers struggle to impose their views without any rules or agreements emerging. Management and governments may try to institutionalise the process in order to avoid anarchy and uncertainty, and this, in turn, may give rise to the types of situation described by the 'statute law' and 'common law' models of collective bargaining. But the 'basic' model is always likely to remain an important feature. Underlying it there is a tacit agreement to disagree, an acceptance that there are areas where joint regulation is unwelcome. But that does not mean that it can be described as unilateral regulation. Management's actions are shaped by its expectations of what workers' reactions will be. It is a form of bargaining more commonly found in France where both management and unions engage in vigorous 'attitudinal structuring', to borrow a term from Walton and McKersie (1965), and the union representatives carefully avoid commitment to the outcome.

THE PROSPECTS FOR COLLECTIVE BARGAINING

There is no reason to believe that collective bargaining over managerial relations will become more formal in the future. As well as the historical background, there are also the implications of the prospect of sustained high levels of unemployment to consider. Although some management opinion may still argue for the legal enforceability of collective agreements, the absence of formal agreements covering the deployment and organisation of labour works to management's advantage when workers' bargaining power is weak. The absence of codification makes it easier to force through changes in work practices. In line with the argument of Chapter 4, there are already signs that managements are trying to shift the emphasis away from collective bargaining towards joint consultation. A clear consequence of this would be diminished willingness of management to codify matters in written agreements.

For their part, shop stewards are in no position at present to insist on greater formality. Nor are they likely to see it in their interests to do so in a period of high unemployment. By agreeing to changes in work practices or by entering into redundancy agreements they effectively legitimise management's right to introduce such changes or to make redundancies. By not entering into agreements on these issues, they leave themselves free to challenge management at some stage in the future when the balance of power may change. In short, the 'basic' form of bargaining is in the ascendancy with the unemployment statistics.

There is another consideration. The current recession has tended to mask longer-term trends in the decline of employment in manufacturing in Britain. Thirlwall (1982:22) suggests that there has been an 'almost runaway decline of industrial jobs—a four million or 34 per cent loss since 1966 . . . [which] is unparalleled anywhere in the world'. Nor are there reasons to believe that this decline in the private sector will cease. This suggests that the future of collective bargaining will increasingly rest in the hands of workers in services and of non-manual workers more generally. But collective bargaining is a relatively recent experience so far as many of these workers are concerned, and large numbers remain unorganised.

Certainly few have the tradition of workplace bargaining of manual workers in, say, engineering. No doubt some groups will find themselves in a strong bargaining position. Others may be able to develop their own forms of work control much in the way that some of the older professions have; that is, by establishing a corpus of occupational rules within which the individual enjoys a measure of autonomy. But it remains to be seen whether they are capable of developing that collective response which has been such a distinctive feature of British workplace industrial relations for manual workers.

So far as bargaining over market relations is concerned, there is little reason to expect major changes in the pattern which has been described earlier in this chapter. The private sector in Britain is likely to be characterised by a dual structure of pay bargaining; a mixture of association and single-employer arrangements. The main imponderable is whether, in the case of the multi-establishment enterprise, the bargaining will take place in the establishment or at a higher level. Chapter 4 argued that most managements are likely to want to avoid bargaining at levels higher than the establishment in the present economic climate. It remains to be seen how successful they are.

7 Industrial Relations in the Public Sector

David Winchester

A substantial shift in the focus of public policy debate in British industrial relations has occurred over the past decade. In the latter half of the 1960s the Donovan Commission centred its analysis on the alleged disorder in workplace industrial relations in manufacturing industries. Its recommendations for the institutional reconstruction of collective bargaining—to deal with unconstitutional strikes, inefficient working practices, decaying payment systems, and wages drift—seemed to have little relevance for most of the public sector. At this time the relatively centralised and rather formal collective bargaining machinery seemed to facilitate a high degree of stability in public sector industrial relations and the growth of public expenditure provided a more sheltered bargaining context than the cost pressures arising from the increasing international competition which lay at the root of the criticism of private sector industrial relations practices.

In sharp contrast, by 1980 it had become commonplace to consider the major source of instability in British industrial relations as lying in the relationships between governments and public sector trade unions. In one of the first systematic attempts to analyse industrial relations in the public sector as a whole Thomson and Beaumont (1978:2) identified three closely related factors that help to explain this change. First, there was a widespread assumption that public sector pay had been increasing faster than private sector earnings and that the public sector was playing a significant role in wage inflation. Second, a variety of incomes policies introduced by governments to control public sector pay had led to a quite new pattern of industrial conflict in which highly publicised national disputes in the public sector had given rise to unprecedented political consequences. The confrontation between the coalminers and the Conservative Government in 1974, and the public services disputes in 1979, were undoubtedly central issues in the general elections of those years. The third, closely-linked argument, centred on the scale of public expenditure; by the mid-1970s it was widely believed that reductions in the planned growth of public expenditure, in which pay comprises the most substantial element, was essential to reduce levels of inflation and improve Britain's economic performance. Indeed, Bacon and Eltis (1976) had popularised the 'crowding out' thesis in a series of influential publications, arguing that Britain had too many employees providing non-marketed public services and 'too few producers'.

Industrial relations research and analysis has scarcely adjusted to this recent shift in policy preoccupations. The public sector has not of course been ignored in the industrial relations literature. Studies of union growth, incomes policies, wage determination, strikes and so on, as other chapters in this book illustrate, have included as part of their analysis, a consideration of distinctive features of public sector employment and industrial relations. In addition there have been numerous studies of individual parts of the public sector, with far more interest in nationalised industries than in the public services and a tendency towards descriptive accounts of the development of collective bargaining machinery or the history of individual unions. There have been very few attempts, however, to develop a more comprehensive analytical approach to industrial relations in the public sector as a whole.

Two main reasons can be suggested to explain this lacuna in the literature. First, trade unionism, collective bargaining, and the 'right' to strike have been long-established in most parts of the public sector in Britain and, for the last sixty years, rarely subject to the distinctive and often controversial legal regulation found in many other countries (Rehmus, 1975; Hepple and O'Higgins, 1971). Thus the rapid growth in public sector employment and trade unionism in the 1960s and 1970s presented no legal or constitutional dilemmas and gave rise to few institutional innovations. It was accommodated in procedural arrangements largely based on the earlier Whitley model, which shared many features in common with private sector collective bargaining and seemed to regulate industrial relations problems more effectively. Until recently, therefore, there seemed to be no pressing policy interest in developing a more comprehensive framework for analysing the public sector as a whole.

A second and more fundamental problem arises from the nature and scope of the public sector in Britain. As it comprises a large, complex, and diversified set of industries and services it may be doubted whether it is possible to develop an integrative analytical approach, or, more modestly, to make generalisations about public sector industrial relations that are accurate across the whole sector. It is a matter for empirical investigation and analytical judgment whether recent political and economic developments (for example, the imposition of cash limits on public expenditure) or trade union initiatives (for example, the attempts within the TUC to coordinate public sector pay claims) have increased the degree of unity or differentiation within the sector as a whole.

The scope and diversity of the public sector can be better understood by identifying the major sub-groupings of industries and services. It is usual to differentiate between three main groups. First, central government, consisting of the industrial and non-industrial civil service and other organisations which are responsible to government departments and funded through taxation, such as the National Health Service. The second group consists of the local authorities which are responsible for a range of services, including education, housing, social services, police and fire services, and are financed mainly through a combination of central government grants and local taxation (rates). Third, there are the public corporations, mainly the nationalised industries with statutory responsibilities for the supply of energy, transport and communication services, and the recently nationalised aircraft and shipbuilding industries. These are trading companies with a significant nominal degree of financial independence of central government.

Considerable diversity can be found within each of these three broad categories, but especially between different nationalised industries. For example, variations in the labour and capital intensity of the postal services compared with telecommunications, the nature of competition or degrees of monopoly of the gas and steel industries, and the 'profitability' of the railways compared with that of air transport might all be expected to influence significantly industrial relations behaviour. In addition to the impact of these economic variables, the contrasting industrial relations traditions and workplace conditions and practices that pre-dated and often survived nationalisation suggest that generalisations based solely on state ownership and ultimate government control have only limited validity. There are also important differences between central government, the National Health Service, and the various local government services in their industrial relations procedures and problems, but it can be argued that this group of public services exhibits a degree of similarity, and faces a number of common problems, that allow more useful generalisations to be made.

The aim of this chapter is to explore the transformation in public sector industrial relations that has occurred over the last ten to fifteen years. It begins with a brief consideration of the traditional pattern of industrial relations that was sustained by the favourable political and economic context of the 1950s and 1960s. The second part traces the impact of different kinds of government intervention in pay bargaining that was largely responsible for the crisis in public sector industrial relations in the 1970s. The chapter ends with some observations on the need to ground an analysis of the institutional problems of public sector pay bargaining in a wider framework that includes a more explicit treatment of the nature of state intervention in economic activity and a more sensitive analysis of trade union bargaining power.

TRADITIONAL PATTERNS OF PUBLIC SECTOR INDUSTRIAL RELATIONS

Public Expenditure Growth

For most of the post-war period, as Table 7.1 indicates, there has been a sustained expansion in the demand for public goods (especially health, education, and personal social services), a dramatic rise in public expenditure in absolute terms and as a proportion of gross national product, and a substantial increase in public sector employment. The broad political consensus that supported the development of the welfare state, the balance

TABLE 7.1: GROWTH IN PUBLIC EXPENDITURE AND EMPLOYMENT, 1950–1975

	PUBLIC EXPENDITURE		PUBLIC SECTOR EMPLOYMENT (000s)				Public Sector as %
	£m	% GNP	Central Government	Local Government	Public Corporations	Total	Labour Force
1950	4,680	39	3485	1422	2383	5597	24·3
1960	9,451	41	1639	1821	1865	5834	24·2
1965	14,142	44	1370	2154	2028	5975	23·7
1970	21,880	50	1533	2559	2016	6480	26·2
1975	54,465	58	1910	2993	2003	7242	29·0

Source: Thomson and Beaumont (1978:107, 115)

of the mixed economy and the commitment to full employment, economic growth, and the Keynesian techniques of demand management, which were believed to be the means by which these policy objectives could be realised, provides the core of the political and economic context that is essential for an understanding of public sector industrial relations. The failure to achieve planned rates of economic growth increased, rather than diminished, the political incentive to sustain higher levels of public expenditure and the growth of public sector employment.

By the mid-1970s, public sector employment accounted for nearly one third of the labour force although important changes had occurred in its composition. The most rapid expansion had taken place in central and local government, while the relative stability of employment in the public corporations' aggregate concealed the major contractions of the labour force in coal mining and the railways, and the transfer of Post Office and steel industry employment to this subsector. Furthermore, most of the growth in employment in central and local government had been in non-manual rather than manual occupations and among female rather than male employees, many of whom work part-time (Elliott and Fallick, 1981:21–4).

The political economy of public sector growth had important consequences for industrial relations in the sector. It inevitably influenced management organisation and policies, the growth and character of trade unionism, and the structure and outcome of collective bargaining. For most of the 1950s and 1960s, this favourable political and economic environment protected the interests of management and unions and supported their formal industrial relations procedures. Towards the end of the period, however, government intervention in collective bargaining became more frequent and its consequences more disruptive. The increasing intensity of conflict, combined with a deepening economic crisis, led to the emergence of a quite different economic orthodoxy by the end of the 1970s. Successive governments replaced their previous commitments to growth and full employment with the overriding policy objective of reducing the rate of inflation, and attempted to control the supply and circulation of money through high interest rates and to reduce the Public Sector Borrowing Requirement by the restraint of public expenditure (Wright, 1981).

Trade Union Organisation and Character

High levels of trade union density have existed in most parts of the British public sector for many years. Given that similarly high figures, compared with the private sector, can be found in many other countries, it has been argued that they can be largely explained by characteristics of public sector employment that are widespread, if not universal. These include employment concentration, bureaucratic organisation and the standardisation of terms and conditions of employment, and government willingness to recognise trade unions and encourage membership (Bain, 1970; Clegg, 1976b). The upsurge of trade union membership in the public sector in the

TABLE 7.2: SELECTED PUBLIC SECTOR UNION MEMBERSHIP (000s)

	1960	*1965*	*1975*	*1980*
National and Local Government Officers' Association (NALGO)	274	349	625	782
National Union of Public Employees (NUPE)	200	248	584	699
National Union of Teachers (NUT)	245	265	290	232
National Union of Mineworkers (NUM)	586	446	262	257
Civil and Public Services' Association (CPSA)	140	146	225	216
Confederation of Health Service Employees (COHSE)	54	68	167	216
Union of Communication Workers (UCW)	166	175	185	202
National Union of Railwaymen (NUR)	334	255	180	170
Post Office Engineering Union (POEU)	73	92	125	131
Iron and Steel Trades Confederation (ISTC)	117	120	104	100

Source: TUC Annual Reports or individual unions.

post-war years, as shown in Table 7.2, reflects both an increase in density (especially in central and local government and the NHS) and an expansion in overall employment.

The public sector provides the major examples of managerial trade unionism and the potential conflict between trade unions and professional associations in their claims to recruit and represent membership at higher levels of the occupational structure. Membership is organised in all forms of open and closed unions: the largest general and ex-craft unions have extensive public sector interests, the National Union of Mineworkers (NUM) can claim to be an industrial union, the civil service unions organise by grade of staff, teachers are in occupational unions, and the National Union of Public Employees (NUPE) and the National and Local Government Officers' Association (NALGO) have achieved remarkable growth as sectoral unions organising manual and non-manual workers respectively across the public service sector. Clegg (1979:165–94) indicates some of the distinctive forms of inter-union competition and conflict that have arisen from this complex structure of public sector trade unionism.

Workplace trade union organisation has a long history in most of the nationalised industries, but in the public services sector, it has developed significantly only in the last decade or so. The absence of effective shop stewards or staff representatives obviously reflected the limited opportunities for negotiation at the local level and contributed to a widespread assumption that public sector trade unionism was characterised by a greater passivity than was generally found in manufacturing industries. Several elements in this stereotype can be identified. Large, bureaucratically administered branches tended to be organised along the lines of the civil service department, local authority, or health district and were often dominated by members from higher levels of the occupational structure—their hierarchic or managerial status being transferred from their employment to their trade union activities. Many unions were not affiliated to the TUC or the Labour Party and seemed more concerned to sustain professional standards and their members' beliefs about public service than to pursue more narrowly defined collective bargaining objectives. Strikes were often prohibited by union rules or avoided in union practice. In Blackburn's terms (1967), public service trade unionism was not very 'unionate', although from the mid-1960s onwards, significant changes occurred in the majority of public service unions along all of the dimensions of union behaviour and affiliation that he identified.

Employers' Organisation and Management Policies

It can be argued that management decision-making in the public sector involves complex, hierarchic administrative structures, a tendency towards centralised intervention to achieve consistency and uniformity of rules and standards and, in the absence of easily identifiable performance criteria, the need to reconcile political commitments and expectations with professional judgments and operational demands. Unfortunately, this generalisation obscures major variations within the public sector and significant changes within particular parts of it which emerged at different times. It is probably more useful to identify three developments that have shaped management policies and to be content with the more limited initial observation that, outside the nationalised industries at least, specialist industrial relations and personnel management was largely absent until the last decade.

The first development is the changing nature of central government influence on public sector management policies. This influence ranges from the direct Treasury control of the civil service, and the pervasive influence of the Department of Health and Social Security (DHSS) on health authorities, to the more diffuse and complex relationships between government ministers and the boards of nationalised industries and individual local authorities and their political associations. The degree of government intervention, and the financial control mechanisms through which it is operated, have changed since the crisis in public expenditure in the mid-1970s, but ministerial edicts and guidelines still have to pass through various spheres of discretion embodied in the management structures of the direct public sector employers.

Second, the major re-organisations of the civil service in 1969, local government in 1972, and the NHS in 1974 only took place after sustained and widespread criticism of the previous pattern of management organisation and practice. Administrative decisions, made by remote committees and often implemented in fragmented and sheltered operational departments, were more likely to be defended in the name of 'public service' than any quantifiable definition of efficiency. With relatively few challenges to management prerogative from workplace trade union organisation, traditional bureaucratic structures and untrained managers survived until a decade ago, when numerous reports from the National Board for Prices and Incomes (Liddle and McCarthy, 1972) and other inquiries, castigated most parts of the public sector for their inertia, inflexibility, ambiguous lines of management authority, and inefficiency. In many areas these criticisms preceded major reorganisations and severe financial constraints; taken together, these pressures were to produce major problems of adjustment and charges of excessive managerialism in the late 1970s.

Third, the nature of the work and the service provided in parts of the public sector has encouraged distinctive managerial ideologies. Unitary assumptions in management are most clearly seen in the administration of the 'caring professions' and the provision of essential or emergency services. For example, the emphasis on 'patients first' in the National Health Service, transmitted through the professional authority of consultants, the vocational commitments of senior nursing staff, and the general or functional authority of administrators, produced a distinctive managerial environment and value system that had important implications for industrial relations (Trainor, 1982). More generally, the absence of market definitions of success, difficulties in measuring output and productivity, career expectations associated with often lengthy incremental grading structures and unquestioned job security, and the obligation to be a 'good employer' combined to sustain a widespread unitary perspective among public sector managers for much of the post-war period. This was reinforced by and largely embodied in the collective bargaining arrangements with trade unions that can now be examined.

Collective Bargaining

The origins and essential features of public sector collective bargaining are well-known (Clegg, 1979:104–15). Following the reports of the Whitley Committee in 1917–18, the government eventually agreed to the establishment of national negotiating machinery and local consultative committees for civil servants in 1919. Within a few years national negotiating machinery had been established for local authority manual workers, teachers and railwaymen, and the Whitley model was widely adopted in the late 1940s for the newly-created National Health Service and nationalised industries. Herein lay the origins of the centralised and rather bureaucratic collective bargaining machinery that is assumed to characterise public sector industrial relations and pay bargaining. While broadly accurate, this sketch ignores important variations in the institutional machinery throughout the public sector and the often tortuous processes that were necessary to establish or enforce nationally agreed terms and conditions of employment in parts of it.

National negotiating committees often consist of large numbers of representatives. There are numerous examples of inter-union conflict over representational rights and bargaining objectives and tactics, many of which originate in earlier periods of breakaway unionism or the exclusion of particular unions from the machinery (Lerner, 1961). Similar problems exist in the private sector, but conflict over union recognition and bargaining rights assumes a distinct character in the nationalised industries where there are statutory obligations on employers to recognise, consult, and negotiate with appropriate organisations (see, for example, the Pearson Report (1968) on the steel industry). Inter-union conflict between teachers' unions is deeply rooted in differing conceptions of status, professionalism, and the legitimacy of industrial action, but ministerial power to alter trade union side representation in collective bargaining has undoubtedly exacerbated the problem (Coates, 1972). The exclusion of the National Association of Schoolmasters from the national negotiating machinery was only ended in 1962 after forty years, while inter-union conflict and rivalry was further encouraged in 1981 by the decision of the Secretary of State for Education to grant a seat on the negotiating committee to the non-TUC Professional Association of Teachers.

Representation on the employers' sides of some public sector negotiating machinery also reflects a dispersion of power and potential conflict that has no obvious counterpart in the private sector. Considerable variation exists in the relative influence of central government (expressed in statutory powers or less formally), the direct employers, and intermediary associations and levels of organisation. In the NHS, for example,

McCarthy (1976:11) noted that the management side consisted of 'employers who do not pay and paymasters who do not employ'; while in local government, the employers' side is further complicated by the existence of party political divisions between the local authority associations. Such divisions have played an important part in collective bargaining conflicts in recent years.

The importance of nationally negotiated rates of pay, salary structures, and a wide range of other conditions of service remained the central feature of public sector bargaining throughout the 1950s and 1960s. To express the point negatively, at district, local or departmental levels, managers and union representatives had little opportunity to negotiate additional wages and salaries. Outside the nationalised industries, the distinction, derived from the Whitley Reports, between the national negotiation of pay and local consultation over non-pay issues was generally sustained, although consultative machinery in most of the NHS, local government, and the civil service could be viewed as a relatively unimportant prop for management's unitary conceptions of common interest and public service.

Two crucial features of public sector collective bargaining need be noted only briefly here, as they will provide an important focus for the discussion of the major changes in the 1970s. The first concerns the central importance attached to the principle of comparability in pay determination and the machinery and conventions designed to implement it. After the Priestley Commission (1955) had recommended that 'the primary principle for determining the pay of civil servants should be fair comparison with the current remuneration of outside staffs employed on broadly comparable work, taking account of differences in other conditions of service', comparability arguments, already legitimised by the Fair Wages Resolutions of Parliament, dominated collective bargaining throughout the public services. In a political and economic environment where counter-arguments based on 'ability to pay' did not yet seem vital, and the professional skills of management necessary to relate pay to productivity or efficiency were not yet developed, comparability arguments sustained relatively stable pay relationships and industrial peace throughout most of the public sector. The final feature of collective bargaining to be noted here—the extensive provision of arbitration machinery throughout the public sector—provided further support for the peaceful settlement of conflicts that characterised so much of the first two decades following World War II.

THE CRISIS IN PUBLIC SECTOR INDUSTRIAL RELATIONS IN THE 1970s

The control of public expenditure and its most substantial component—public sector pay—was one of the most important issues in British economic policy in the 1970s. In a context of high inflation and deepening economic recession, traditional patterns of public sector industrial relations were transformed by a series of changes in government, management, and trade union policies. The most visible evidence of a substantial breakdown in the system of public sector collective bargaining can be seen in the series of major pay disputes that destroyed a succession of incomes policies and injected a new dimension of instability into British politics. The most obvious explanation of these dramatic developments can be found in an analysis of the impact of different kinds of incomes policy on the established methods, principles, and outcomes of pay determination in the public sector.

The complexity of the changes that have occurred, however, present formidable problems of description and analysis. Different phases of a series of incomes policies, developed in quite different political and economic circumstances, had an uneven impact on different groups of public sector workers. The discussion will therefore be divided into two main sections: the first, focusing on the way in which incomes policies led to the emergence of widespread industrial unrest in the early 1970s and the second, exploring the connections between pay restraint and the crisis in public expenditure since the mid-1970s. Throughout the whole period the impact of government intervention on pay relativities and the operation of comparability principles in public sector collective bargaining will be emphasised as part of a wider consideration of changing patterns of conflict.

The emergence of actual or perceived pay grievances, however, provides only a starting point for an analysis of public sector conflict over the last decade. The discontent had to be organised by trade unions with a changing membership composition, developing shop steward organisations, and new leadership strategies and political perspectives. It was often expressed in new and distinctive forms of industrial conflict that, in turn, led to changing political calculations, further government intervention, and important shifts in the policies of public sector employers. It will be possible to note only a few of the most significant developments that have taken place since 1970. Even so, this should facilitate a more interesting interpretation of the cumulative changes of the last decade that goes beyond the oversimple proposition that incomes policies discriminate against public sector employees and that this unfair treatment leads inevitably to widespread disruption in the sector.

Emergence of Wage Militancy: 1960–1974

The first clear example of government discrimination against the public sector occurred during Selwyn Lloyd's pay pause of 1961–2. The government delayed the implementation of pay settlements in the public sector while putting its faith in exhortation to modify private sector agreements. The policy was a temporary and modest success and no major disputes took place during the eight months' standstill. However it encouraged the start of a process of more explicit political engagement on the part of union leaders in many white-collar public sector unions that would lead to eventual TUC affiliation and major revisions in their attitudes to industrial action (see, e.g. Undy et al., 1981). In addition, the sequence of events leading to the demise of the policy, as Fallick and Elliott (1981b:111–12) have argued, would be repeated in many later periods; one key pay settlement, for electricity supply workers, negotiated under the threat of industrial action, led to many other comparability claims elsewhere in the public sector.

The impact of the Wilson Government's incomes policy (1965–9) on the public sector was more substantial. Even though reliable data on pay movements in the public sector relative to the private sector do not exist before 1970, the evidence suggests that by 1968–9 there had been a general deterioration in the pay of public sector employees and a sharper relative decline in the pay of non-manual workers in the sector (Elliott and Fallick, 1981:140). This can be partly explained by the characteristics of public sector collective bargaining outlined earlier. Centralised negotiations covering whole industries or services and setting rates of pay that comprised a very large proportion of actual earnings were obviously more amenable to scrutiny, not least by the government acting as paymaster, than the more decentralised negotiations in most parts of the private sector. In addition, the emphasis on productivity bargaining in this incomes policy increased the scope for pay discrimination against the public sector and had other, longer-lasting effects.

Throughout the whole of the period, the central argument of government White Papers and the reports of the National Board for Prices and Incomes (NBPI) was that pay increases should be more directly linked with improvements in productivity. In the short term, by allowing pay increases above the 'norm' where employees could demonstrate a direct contribution towards increasing productivity, the policy inevitably discriminated against public service workers, especially those in non-manual occupations whose output was not easily measured. The impact on manual workers was quite different. In a series of reports on government industrial workers, railwaymen, busmen, and manual workers in gas, water, electricity supply, local authorities and the NHS, the NBPI argued that the introduction of incentive bonus schemes could simultaneously improve manpower utilisation and deal with the problem of low pay (Liddle and McCarthy, 1972; Balfour, 1972). Though the introduction of incentive bonus schemes took place only slowly in some sectors and was invariably subject to nationally negotiated guidelines, it provided the first significant focus for the development of workplace trade union organisation and local bargaining in most parts of the National Health Service and local government. It also provided an important stimulus to greater managerial specialisation and the emergence of work study and personnel management skills in these sectors (Terry, 1982).

In the nationalised industries, there were apparently contrary developments, each usually justified in the name of efficiency. By 1966 face workers in coal mining had agreed to abandon their position as the largest group of pieceworkers in the public sector and the National Power-Loading Agreement, the culmination of a decade of bargaining reforms, was to have a significant effect on earnings movements and the pattern of industrial conflict in coalmining. Meanwhile, traditional standard-rate industries such as the railways, electricity supply, and gas were introducing incentive bonus schemes—in the case of electricity supply, largely in an attempt to reverse the decline in relative earnings that followed from the implementation of the innovative and widely-praised 'status and productivity agreements' in 1964 (Edwards and Roberts, 1971; Bell, 1975).

The 1965–9 incomes policy created anomalies, disturbed customary pay relativities, and ended with a wage and strike explosion that affected all groups of workers. However, its attack on the principle of comparability in wage determination, and its advocacy of productivity bargaining and incentive schemes, presented distinctive problems for different parts of the public sector. If pay grievances were the immediate cause, the dramatic form and consequences of the public sector disputes in the early 1970s can only be explained by examining the changing political and economic context of government intervention in collective bargaining and the equally rapid developments in trade union leadership strategies and organisation during this period.

Public sector wage militancy against the policies of the Conservative Government developed in two phases. For the first two years following its election in June 1970, the government chose to respond to sharply rising cost inflation through its so called 'n-1 policy'; it attempted to reduce successive public sector pay settlements below the level of preceding ones in the expectation that this example would influence collective bargaining in the private sector. The policy was both ambiguous and arbitrary. Government ministers consistently denied direct intervention in public sector negotiations, but they limited negotiators' access to the conciliation and arbitration services of the Department of Employment, and their public statements about the fairness of pay offers ignored the merits of individual claims, emphasising the need to reduce settlements below the current levels. The sense of injustice aroused by this policy was predictable, but the scale of disruption that occurred can be explained only in terms of a series of government miscalculations about the support or acquiescence of public sector employers, the impact of public opinion, and the nature of trade union leadership and militancy.

Within eighteen months lengthy official strikes involving manual workers in local authorities, postal services, and coal mining took place and widespread disruption was caused by an overtime ban and a work-to-rule in electricity supply and the railways industry. These disputes involved 1.5 million workers, many of whom had no previous experience of collective industrial action, and all except the 1971 postal strike led to exceptionally large pay increases. All the disputes had a direct and visible impact on public safety or convenience, yet the government was unable to achieve widespread public support for its policies. It was also apparent that the various forms of government influence on senior public sector managers were insufficient to encourage their active commitment to the strategy. Having refused to sanction management concessions during negotiations to avoid strikes, the government was forced to accept much larger concessions to end protracted disputes, usually after a committee of inquiry had been set up. This was demonstrated most vividly in the seven-week coal mining strike in early 1972; the widespread power cuts, industrial disruption, and three-day working week were followed by a pay settlement of more than 20 per cent after the pre-strike offer of less than 8 per cent.

The coal mining strike led to a complete reversal in government policy. Abandoning its earlier opposition to formal incomes policies, the government introduced a statutory pay freeze followed by two periods of pay restraint based on codes and monitored by a Pay Board and a separate Price Commission. Thus traditional public sector pay comparisons and relativities, already distorted by the uneven impact of the 'n-1' policy, were further affected by the November 1972 pay standstill. Disputes in the gas industry, the National Health Service, and the non-industrial civil service took place as a result of such anomalies, again involving large groups of workers with little previous experience of industrial militancy. And even though the third stage of the policy was designed to anticipate and accommodate the claims of stronger unions—with its provisions for payment for 'unsocial hours' and for reducing anomalies and obstacles to efficiency—it did not prevent a second coal miners' strike that, in contrast to the one in 1972, at once involved the government as primary participant. Largely because of the oil crisis in the autumn of 1973, the government declared a state of emergency on the second day of the miners' overtime ban, and within a few months, had called a general election as a means of resolving the dispute (Allen, 1981:240–58).

The scale, intensity, and consequences of public sector disputes between 1970 and 1974 cannot be adequately understood simply by reference to strike data, although Clegg (1976c:55) estimated that 43 per cent of the 70 million working days lost in this period occurred in the public sector. The political context was obviously important; trade union opposition to pay policies was viewed by some leaders and activists as merely one part of a wider struggle that was being fought against the Industrial Relations Act, rising unemployment, the government's industrial policies, and Britain's entry in to the European Economic Community. While this heightened level of ideological conflict between the government and the trade union movement did not lead to a more sustained or effective coordination of collective bargaining by union negotiators, it encouraged and partly legitimised important changes in individual union policies. The emergence of new leadership strategies and the relationship between full-time officers, activists, and members took a variety of forms, reflecting the different characteristics of public sector employment, trade union organisation, and membership discontent. A few general observations about changes in trade union policies in the 1970–74 period can, however, be made.

First, several of the disputes were based on sustained, national wage campaigns that official union leadership developed in response to earlier unofficial and localised industrial action. In coal mining, the 1972 dispute followed extensive unofficial stoppages in 1969 and 1970 and a major shift in the internal politics of the NUM, while the 1970 strike of local government manual workers was planned by NUPE's leadership after the successful unofficial strike of London refuse collectors, mainly members of the Transport and General Workers' Union, a year earlier. This latter dispute illustrates a second important point: in several sectors, inter-union rivalry and competition for the recruitment of an expanding labour force provided additional encouragement for leaders to abandon the traditional 'moderation' of public service trade unionism. The antagonism between the NUT and the NAS had previously played a significant part in the first major teachers' strikes of the late 1960s and inter-union competition later influenced the emergence of conflict in hospitals.

Third, the disputes in this period often involved innovative strike tactics that provided flexible models of industrial action that could be adapted by other public sector unions later in the decade. The nationally coordinated selective stoppages employed by NUPE had several obvious advantages: they mobilised the relatively few pockets of strong workplace organisation that existed in 1970, protected union strike funds, and avoided the politically damaging consequences of public hostility that would have followed the withdrawal of the most essential public services. The undoubted success of the coal miners' picketing in 1972 had other longer-term consequences, namely the development of legal restrictions on the number and location of pickets.

Control of Pay and Public Expenditure: 1974–1982

It can be argued that many of the sources and consequences of public sector unrest in the early 1970s have remained important since then. There is a continuity in the development of trade union workplace organisation and management reorganisation and specialisation in many parts of the sector. Furthermore, a similar cycle of relative pay decline, increasing conflict, and large pay awards seems to have occurred and contributed to the outcome of a general election in 1979 as in 1974. However, important changes in the political and economic context that have led to the decline in public expenditure and new mechanisms of control have resulted in significant developments in pay bargaining, patterns of conflict, and job security.

The Labour Government's election in March 1974 provided a basis for a period of relative stability in public sector industrial relations. The government's Social Contract with the unions—at this time, an implicit assumption that unions would exercise some degree of pay restraint in return for a more extensive influence on economic and social policy—involved no intervention in collective bargaining. On the contrary, the average increase in the growth of earnings doubled to nearly 30 per cent between 1974 and 1975 and the pay of public sector workers relative to the private sector improved dramatically. Public sector pay benefited in part from the unanticipated level of cost-of-living threshold payments introduced by the previous government's incomes policy, but substantial increases accrued from the more favourable reception of comparability claims and from the reports of *ad hoc* committees of inquiry. The very large coal miners' settlement influenced agreements in other nationalised industries, and the restoration of the Pay Research Unit's work for non-industrial civil servants and inquiries on teachers' and nurses' pay (Houghton and Halsbury Reports, 1974) recommended very substantial settlements to reverse the decline in relative pay over previous years.

The two years of pay restraint agreed between the TUC and the government after the economic crisis of mid-1975 caused few immediate problems in the public sector. The pay limits did not discriminate against public sector employees and, as will be seen later, union opposition to government policies was directed against the public expenditure cuts that were introduced in 1976. However the third year of pay restraint received only tacit support, rather than formal endorsement, from the TUC. The suspension of civil service comparability exercises and the more generally strict enforcement of pay limits in the public sector had already undermined the relative gains, or 'catching-up' settlements of 1974–5, and real disposable income was declining. Widespread industrial unrest was avoided for a time by isolating the more obviously powerful public sector groups from the majority of public service employees; for example, coal miners and electricity supply workers achieved higher pay settlements on the basis of productivity agreements from 1978. Firemen, after a prolonged strike, and policemen, as a result of an inquiry that was set up to avert threatened industrial action (Edmund-Davies Report, 1978), achieved large pay increases and an indexation formula to sustain their more favourable pay relativities in the future.

The attempt to sustain a fourth year of restraint, however, with a pay limit set at only 5 per cent, led to widespread industrial action in the 'winter of discontent'. Industrial action involving local government workers, teachers, hospital workers, and civil servants in early 1979, followed major private sector disputes and, it is widely assumed, contributed significantly to the Labour Government's electoral defeat in May 1979. Public service union leaders varied in their degree of loyalty to the Labour Government, in their confidence that plans for a comparability commission would resolve their members' pay grievances, and in their ability to control their executive committees and workplace activists. Conflict and uncertainty within and between unions added to the public hostility aroused by extensive picketing of hospitals and schools, inevitably highlighted by politicians and the mass media already preparing for a general election.

It has been argued that the experience of the mid-1970s had been repeated five years later (Dean, 1981:61). Public sector workers had been unfairly treated by incomes policies and had eventually responded with extensive industrial action. This militancy and the pre-election political commitments it invited from the major parties would lead to a sudden surge in public sector pay and a consequential crisis of public expenditure control. This argument is broadly accurate, though in contrast to the earlier period, the Labour Government's policy was sufficiently flexible to accommodate the pay demands of the more powerful public sector unions and thus isolate the nationalised industries from the growing unrest in the public services sector. In addition, two potentially important mechanisms for regulating public sector pay were inherited by the Conservative Government—the Standing Commission on Pay Comparability and cash limits on public expenditure.

The Clegg Comparability Commission seemed to offer the prospect of a more rational and consistent application of the principle of comparability in public service collective bargaining. In March 1979 when the Commission was established, separate machinery existed for industrial and non-industrial civil servants, three review bodies dealt with the pay of the armed forces, 'top salaries', and doctors and dentists and, as noted above, the pay of police and firemen was adjusted annually by an indexation formula related to the movements of average earnings. Different bodies, using a variety of conventions and data sources, produced inconsistent recommendations that had an important influence on the pay of other public service workers. These systems had been introduced, suspended, modified, or renewed on the basis of successive governments' short-term political calculations and had led to the irregular fluctuations in relative pay movements that had generated periodic industrial unrest. The longer-term task for the Standing Commission was, therefore, 'to report on the possibility of establishing acceptable bases of comparison' for most of the public services sector. Its more urgent function was to resolve a number of disputes, to act as an arbitration body with an undefined comparability principle built into its terms of reference (Clegg, 1982).

In its two years' existence, the Commission made recommendations on the pay grievances of twenty-five groups of public service workers—2.5 million employees—but it made only limited progress in achieving the time-consuming longer term objective. The Commission's examination of different methods of comparison (indexation, job-for-job, and factor comparison), the technical problems involved in the choice and remuneration of comparators and the maintenance of comparability, and the organisational problems of collecting and analysing data had to be linked to the more pressing demands of negotiators trying to resolve pay disputes. More important, the limited commitment of the Conservative Government to the principle of comparability had been indicated in its evidence to the Commission as early as September 1979. Its emphasis on linking pay to improvements in efficiency, labour market considerations, and the alleged advantages of public employees' pensions, job security, and other conditions of service was a thinly-veiled attack on comparability (Clegg, 1980:49–51). Within six months, and following the report on teachers' pay that was found to have based its recommendations on inaccurate information, the government announced that the Commission would be abolished when it completed its existing references. The eloquent defence of the role of comparability in public sector pay determination contained in the Commission's General Report (Clegg, 1980:32-5) contrasted sharply with the government's plans to cut public expenditure and, in particular, with its stress on labour market forces and the use of cash limits to restrict the 'ability to pay' of public sector employers.

The introduction of cash limits in 1976 grew out of the crisis in public expenditure planning and control of 1974–5 (Thomson and Beaumont, 1978:122–6). The previous system involved a planning process, coordinated by the Treasury Public Expenditure Survey Committee (PESC), in which the Cabinet determined the volume of resources and their distribution between spending departments for the current and three succeeding years. Volume planning involved no pre-determined limit on cash expenditure; estimates were based on current pay and price levels and unanticipated costs were met through supplementary votes in Parliament. At times of rapid inflation, such a system was unlikely to control expenditure effectively and, in 1974–5, large wage settlements, the reorganisation of local government and the NHS, and other escalating costs resulted in overspending the original estimates by around 30 per cent. Since 1976 cash limits have been set on civil service and NHS expenditure, on government grants to local authorities, and External Financing Limits have been set on loans and grants to the nationalised industries. Thus, cash limits operate differently upon the three major parts of the public sector (Bevan et al., 1981:384; TUC, 1981).

Initially, cash limits simply provided an administrative support for the existing incomes policy of the Labour Government. When the Conservative Government inherited the problems of the public sector pay explosion of 1979–80, however, it tried to retain the planned cash limits and required the additional expenditure on pay to be financed by staff cuts and administrative savings. The policy seemed to envisage an income-employment trade-off in which public sector negotiators reached settlements without any overt government interference and in the absence of any announced pay norms. This approach resulted in considerable difficulties in negotiations and wide variations in the level of settlements. Large salary increases—for example, in the civil service—were staged or deferred so as to remain nominally within the cash limits and they disturbed customary relativities within the public sector and set unwelcome precedents for private sector negotiations. From 1980–81, therefore, the government has included a pay assumption in its cash limits and attempted to reduce management discretion in negotiations by various other forms of administrative and financial control. In doing so, the operation of cash limits seems to have taken on a similar function to earlier incomes policy norms. There are, however, a number of important differences.

At first sight cash limits seem to provide the government with a more flexible method of controlling public sector pay than by means of more formal incomes policies. Discrimination between the tax-dependent public services and the nationalised industries and variations within the two broad groups are built into the policy, as the Treasury statement of 15 September 1981 indicates: 'the pay factor does not imply that all public service pay increases will be 4%, some may be less, and some may be more. There is no automatic entitlement to any particular pay increase; each must be justified on its own merits'. In practice, settlements within the public services have shown a marked degree of uniformity for the last two years, partly because of the stress on comparability arguments by both union and management side negotiators and partly because the government made strenuous efforts to keep pay settlements fairly close to the cash limit pay assumption. This was illustrated most clearly in the case of the 1981 civil service dispute.

The government terminated its agreement with the National Staff Side without giving the six months' notice required—abandoning the principle of comparability and the report of the Pay Research Unit—and was prepared to sustain a twenty-week strike to keep the pay settlement around 7½ per cent. The strike was remarkable in a number of ways. It demonstrated an unprecedented degree of unity and cooperation between civil service unions that allowed selective strike action which imposed very heavy costs and inconvenience on the government by delaying the collection of tax revenue and interfering with the collection and analysis of economic and financial data. The settlement, which included a government undertaking to consult with the unions before deciding on cash limits for the next pay round, a willingness to accept arbitration and the establishment of the Megaw Inquiry into civil service pay, could undoubtedly have been reached ten weeks earlier, saving the government an estimated £500 million in interest payments on borrowing and lost revenue.

Pay settlements in the nationalised industries, though significantly higher than in the public services generally, have also shown the way in which cash limits allow selective discrimination. For example, the different treatment of the British Steel Corporation and the National Coal Board negotiations over the last two years, and the government's response to the lengthy national steel strike in 1980, can be only partly explained by the different trading conditions of the industries and their 'ability to pay'. It is clear that ministers have built into cash limits—and their willingness to revise them subsequently—pay assumptions that are partly based on their calculation of the prospects of successful industrial action. As Pliatzky (1982:20) has pointed out, cash limits have thus provided a flexibility which allows for exceptional treatment more easily than formal incomes policies: 'you cannot write industrial muscle into a White Paper or a piece of legislation as grounds for special treatment'.

It is too early to reach any firm conclusions about the impact of cash limits on public sector pay bargaining, and as is known from studies of other forms of incomes policy, an evaluation has to overcome formidable methodological problems. A few tentative points can be made. First, the system of cash limits is unlikely to be abandoned and, therefore, it can be assumed that a more or less permanent pay policy for the public services is in prospect. However, in isolation, cash limits provide little indication of the details and possible consequences of pay policies. These will depend on other expenditure decisions and financial controls and the government's attitude towards the avoidance or resolution of industrial conflict in particular sectors. Recently, for example, the Conservative Government has indicated its intention to remove the right of unions to unilateral arbitration, where it still exists, and to ensure that arbitrators take proper account of what the employer can afford to pay. Similarly, in contrast to the attitude of governments throughout most of the 1970s, the current administration seems to have made calculations about the political costs of industrial conflict that imply benefits or gains from intransigence and an unwillingness to sanction concessions. Such strategic calculations have more impact on public sector bargaining than the administrative system of cash limits.

Second, the impact of government pay restraint policies based on cash limits depends more directly than formal incomes policies on the decisions and choices of public sector employers. In the 1981–2 pay round, several examples of conflict between the government and public sector employers emerged. In the teachers' negotiations, the wider conflict between central and local government, party political conflict between local authority associations, and interest group conflict within individual associations all influenced the bargaining process and its outcome. In the NHS, six chairmen of regional health authorities who had publicly criticised the government's pay policy were replaced when their contracts expired. More generally, the separation of national negotiations on pay and local discretion on manpower decisions presents obstacles to an effective income-employment trade-off in most public service negotiations.

Third, the dispersion of power between government and public sector employers that has led to fragmentation and disunity on the employers' side in some public service negotiations, contrasts sharply with the recent emergence of more effective trade union coordination in the civil service, local government, and the NHS. In the 1981–2 pay round the TUC successfully encouraged a more extensive exchange of bargaining information, the development of common core elements in union wage claims and, in the case of the NHS negotiations, a widespread response to the commitment to give 'practical, moral and financial support' to unions involved in disputes. This development contrasts with the much less successful attempts at coordination earlier in the 1970s and while it has coexisted with continuing expressions of separatism, sectionalism, and antagonism between unions within some negotiating committees, it may have a significant development on future public service pay bargaining.

The introduction of cash limits at a time of public expenditure restraint has projected the relationship between pay bargaining and manpower decisions into the centre of political controversy and stimulated important changes in public sector industrial relations. However, there are major problems in deciphering the ambiguous meanings of public expenditure 'cuts', analysing the political and managerial processes through which they have been implemented, identifying the employment impact on different services, functions and grades of staff, and evaluating the response of trade unions to the new threat to their members' job security. A few points can be made about each of these related issues.

Considerable confusion has arisen from discussions of public expenditure cuts that fail to distinguish between capital and current expenditure, reduction in planned growth and real reductions in resources, changes in the volume of services and their costs, reductions in the scale of spending programmes and reallocation of resources within them, and planned and unplanned changes in expenditure (Wright, 1981:11–13). This confusion is intrinsic to the recent debate on the control of public expenditure. The complexity of the data provides almost unlimited opportunities for the government, management, and trade unions to develop arguments in defence of their interests that contradict the others' assessment of the impact of public expenditure changes. In very general terms it can be noted that cuts in expenditure on public services, introduced from 1975, were initially concentrated on capital expenditure and were usually marginal cuts in planned growth. From 1979 the position changed; the Conservative Government was committed to reducing the size of the public sector in absolute terms and while it is too early to assess whether this objective will be realised, the intention to plan a medium-term reduction in public expenditure marked a significant turning-point in post-war British politics.

The evolution of cash limits has involved a substantial revision of the political processes of public expenditure planning and control and in the administrative and budgetary practices that, until recently, embodied a presumption of continuous growth. Different kinds of cuts have been perceived in different ways by different groups and interests that comprise public service management: civil servants, national and local politicians, competing professional groups, and the various groups of functional managers. In major areas of employment—social services and education, for example—there are 'long institutional linkages in the creation and delivery of policy' (Kogan, 1981:153). Managerial discretion coexists with statutory duties to provide certain services and it is therefore extremely difficult to generalise about organisational responses to different phases of cuts in public expenditure. As indicated above, large-scale reorganisation, centralisation, increased capital investment, and greater managerial specialisation (incuding the rapid spread of work study and work measurement) largely pre-dated cuts in expenditure in most of the public services, though the impact of such developments on industrial relations is inevitably conflated with recent financial constraints.

In most of the public services inadequate employment statistics and the obscure processes involved in setting establishment figures have made it difficult to analyse the impact of public expenditure cuts on manpower. From the mid-1970s, the implementation of 'soft cuts'—in planned growth and in capital expenditure—had little impact on overall employment in the public services, though it may have added to the increasing level of unemployment in manufacturing industries and construction. More generally, expenditure cuts have tended to reduce the quality of provisions and standards of service and when this has led to job losses, they have often been achieved by 'natural wastage' and an increase in the number of unfilled vacancies. In the last two years the scale of expenditure cuts has raised the prospect of substantial redundancy in many parts of the public services and large-scale dismissals are now expected in several sectors. Undoubtedly, the most severe impact will be on ancillary and clerical workers, rather than the technical and professional grades, although the compulsory redundancy of teachers in all parts of the education sector seems inevitable in the light of recent expenditure decisions. For example in the two years up to September 1981 while the number of teachers and lecturers declined by 3·8 per cent the number of manual workers employed by local authorities decreased by nearly 14 per cent. Part-time women's employment—in the school meals service and as home helps—has been most affected.

The response of public service trade unions to public expenditure cuts and the threats they have posed to job security can be divided into two phases. The first, between 1975 and 1978, involved national demonstrations and publicity organised by eleven unions under the loose organisation of the National Steering Committee Against the Cuts. It signified a remarkable development in the national leadership strategies of civil service and local government unions and in the political involvement of workplace activists compared with the character of these unions a decade earlier. The achievements of the campaign—new forms of organisation involving inter-union cooperation, links with community and pressure groups, and a political perspective that integrated traditional union interests with a broader defence of public services and the social wage—have to be set against its limitations. The principal general unions and the more powerful unions in the nationalised industries were not involved; indeed, the campaign contrasted sharply with the muted criticism of the TUC against public expenditure cuts, arising from its relationship with the Labour Government and the partial acceptance of the view that public expenditure restraint was desirable to pursue the industrial policies of the TUC that focused on the collapse of manufacturing (Fryer, 1979).

The second phase of trade union resistance to the impact of expenditure cuts on their members' jobs has only recently begun. It seems unlikely that public service trade unions will face the scale of problems found in some of the nationalised industries; for example, the decisive defeat of the steel unions' resistance to the loss of 50,000 jobs in 1980 alone and the equally decisive, but successful, action of the NUM in preventing an escalation in the pace of pit closures in 1981. Public service unions, however, are now confronted by the prospect of continuing real cuts in expenditure and very limited opportunities to adjust to them via 'natural wastage'. Most have responded by developing firm policies of resistance to redundancy, backed by the creation of action committees and the commitment to various forms of industrial action in the event of compulsory redundancy. The effectiveness of such policies will undoubtedly vary between services, occupational groups and geographical areas, but the strike action already undertaken in some areas, (for example, a successful six-week all-out strike of teachers in Barking in early 1982) suggests that the traditionally weaker public service unions, when supported by local community groups and when able to mobilise professional interests and political alliances, may achieve greater success than their counterparts in nationalised industries and the private sector.

CONCLUSIONS

This chapter has explored the recent transformation in public sector industrial relations in a relatively descriptive and chronological manner in an attempt to reflect the complexity and diversity of the most important changes, and to emphasise the sequential and cumulative impact of many of them. The overall direction and magnitude of the changes cannot be in doubt. For two decades after World War II, the stability of public sector industrial relations was based on an implicit understanding that as long as government and senior management discharged their responsibility to be 'good' employers, then employees and their union representatives would accept a reciprocal obligation to avoid industrial conflict. The central institutional expression of this tacit agreement was the system of 'fair comparison' for civil service pay, which also offered the major point of reference for salary adjustments for other staff throughout the public sector, and the existence of consultative machinery and the widespread use of arbitration provided further methods of minimising conflict. Generally favourable conditions of work, job security, and status also provided a material basis for the less tangible commitment to the values of 'public service' that many groups of public sector employees shared with their employers, and this, in turn, was sustained by the rapid expansion of public expenditure and employment (Thomson and Beaumont, 1978:155–8).

This portrait of harmony, stability, and consensus needs qualification; it characterised industrial relations in the public services more accurately than in the nationalised industries, and it applied to non-manual employees more clearly than to many groups of manual workers. It also ignores latent sources of conflicts and occasional expressions of overt antagonism, but in contrast to both the development of industrial relations in manufacturing industries in the 1950s and 1960s, and the changing character of public sector industrial relations since then, the portrait is broadly accurate. Moreover, the argument in this chapter is not that all elements in the traditional pattern of industrial relations have disappeared in every part of the public sector. In the absence of satisfactory empirical research, the impressionistic evidence suggests that developments in workplace trade union organisation, local bargaining, and management policy-making, for example, have been partial, uneven, and contradictory. They have been stimulated, of course, by the central unresolved problem of public sector pay determination that emerged in the deepening economic crisis, high inflation and volatile political environment of the period since the late 1960s.

It has been argued that most of the unrest in public sector industrial relations has arisen from government intervention in collective bargaining; in particular, from the way in which different forms of incomes policy have disturbed customary pay relativities and undermined the principle of comparability that for a long time was the foremost influence on public sector pay determination. Explanations of recent conflict have usually emphasised the institutional and technical deficiencies of existing bargaining arrangements and led to recommendations for procedural reform. The Megaw Report (1982), for example, advocated a number of changes in the way in which the pay of non-industrial civil servants should be determined. Detailed proposals on the type of comparisons that should be made and the way in which the data should be collected and analysed by a new civil service Pay Information Board were developed within a more general recommendation that pay comparisons 'should have a much less decisive influence than in the past'; a greater emphasis in the system of 'informed collective bargaining' should be placed on market forces and financial constraints, and more priority should be given to sustaining coherent internal relativities and linking pay to performance.

The analysis and policy prescriptions of the Megaw Inquiry are yet another reminder of the complex relationship between institutional forms and the political and economic conflict that they are designed to regulate. The recommendation that 'informed collective bargaining' should somehow place equal emphasis on comparability, labour market forces, and ability to pay is not a solution, but simply a respecification of the problem of public sector pay bargaining. It obscures two crucial questions that arise from the transformation in public sector industrial relations over the last fifteen years. The first requires a much clearer understanding of the direction and forms of state intervention in economic activity and, in particular, in the political processes of public expenditure planning and control. This analysis must go beyond a ritual genuflection towards 'the political and economic context' of public sector industrial relations, not least because recent government plans for expenditure cuts, disengagement and privatisation, however ambiguous in practice, have presented an ideological challenge to the earlier political consensus on the shape and function of the public sector.

The second, largely unexplored, question arising from the conflict in public sector industrial relations in the 1970s, concerns the nature of the bargaining process and the various dimensions of trade union bargaining power. If the capacity and willingness of trade unions to impose sanctions on management is assumed to be an essential feature of collective bargaining, then it can be argued that in many parts of the public services sector, the recent conflict has signalled the arrival, and not the breakdown, of collective bargaining (Thomson and Beaumont, 1978:157). Industrial relations research in Britain, in contrast to the United States, has rarely analysed the distinctive processes involved in collective bargaining and the variations in the political constraints placed on management negotiators in different parts of the public sector (Lewin et al., 1977). Similarly, little progress has been made in specifying the diverse sources and expressions of union bargaining power. Public policy debate has concentrated on proposals for institutional and legal restrictions on the exercise of trade union 'monopoly power' and attention has been diverted away from a more sensitive analysis of different kinds of latent power, the organisational and ideological preconditions for its effective mobilisation, and the changing strategies of management and government in calculating the political and economic costs of different responses and initiatives. It can be concluded that until a more systematic analysis of the forms of state economic intervention and the nature of power in collective bargaining is combined with an institutional analysis of public sector industrial relations, future developments will appear as unpredictable as many of the changes of the last fifteen years have seemed to observers and participants.

8 Wages Councils, the Unorganised, and the Low Paid

Chris Pond

Partly as a result of the economic recession, low pay has once again become a matter of central importance in industrial relations. This chapter is concerned with the extent, nature and causes of low pay, and in particular with its concentration in the largely unorganised wages council sector.

The persistence of low pay has a number of adverse consequences. The National Board for Prices and Incomes (NBPI, 1971:39) referred to the economic effects in terms of 'the misuse or underutilisation of resources'. The Commission on Industrial Relations (CIR, 1971) found an association between low pay and high staff turnover, representing a further loss in efficiency. However, most attention has been focused on the social policy implications, and in particular on the extent to which low pay results in the creation of poverty and hardship. Independent studies (Townsend, 1979; Field, 1979), as well as official analyses, suggest that an increasing proportion of those in poverty (having incomes below the supplementary benefit level) are in families dependent on low wages: in 1979 almost one quarter (22.7 per cent) of those with an income below the supplementary benefit level were living in families where the head of household was employed full-time or self-employed (DHSS, 1982). The aggregation of earnings within households tends to disguise the link between low pay and poverty, but official estimates suggest that the numbers in poverty would increase fourfold were it not for married women's earnings. (McNay and Pond, 1980; CPRS, 1980).

Low pay can also have substantial indirect effects in generating poverty throughout the life cycle. The association between low earnings when in work and a high incidence of unemployment is now well established (see Pond, 1980a). So too is the link between low-wage employment, ill health, and an absence of fringe benefits. As Atkinson (1973) has argued 'low pay must be seen more generally as disadvantage in the labour market'. Low paid workers are more vulnerable to the interruption or loss of earnings and, because they are less able to accumulate savings, pension or property rights, are more likely to experience poverty during periods outside the labour market.

Without a proper understanding of the causes of low pay, an assessment of its importance and of possible remedies is impossible. The emphasis throughout this chapter is therefore on the causes and explanations of low pay. Before dealing with this the next two sections of the chapter discuss possible definitions of the problem and assess its extent and incidence. They examine the characteristics of the low paid and of the jobs and industries in which they work. The chapter then considers the explanations for low pay offered by economic theory, including the orthodox neo-classical approaches and those which emphasise the role of structural divisions within the labour market. The fifth section of the chapter is concerned with the wages council sector in which low wage and un-organised employment is heavily concentrated. Finally, the appropriate policies to tackle low pay are considered. The problem is complex and there are no simple answers, but the conclusion tries at least to identify the direction in which policy should move in the years ahead if low wages are to be effectively challenged.

DEFINITIONS OF LOW PAY

Low pay is inevitably a relative and subjective concept, and a search for a value-free and objective measure is likely to end in disappointment. Nevertheless, if the extent and nature of low pay is to be assessed, and the groups most affected identified, a benchmark is necessary which most people might accept as a broad definition of the problem. The most appropriate approach to arriving at such a benchmark is to examine a number of different criteria, reflecting different conceptions of poverty and low pay.

In its report on the general problems of low pay, the NBPI (1971:6) considered the possibility of relating earnings to official criteria of need:

> the fixing of the minimum standard of need cannot be exact. The only yardstick which we can appropriately use is that laid down in practice by Parliament, in that Parliament has approved scales of supplementary benefit and made other provision with the result that it has *de facto* expressed a view as to the level of income below which families are in need.

In 1981–2 a family of conventional size—consisting, say, of a man with a wife not herself earning and two dependent children—living in accommodation for which a conventional amount of rent and rates are paid and in otherwise 'typical' circumstances required gross earnings of £87 a week to be left with a net income at the supplementary benefit level. An alternative measure of officially defined need is the Family Income Supplement (FIS) eligibility limit. FIS was introduced in 1971 as an income-related benefit payable only to families with children in which the main breadwinner was employed full-time (Stanton, 1977). In 1981 a two-child family was eligible to claim FIS if its earnings were less than £82 a week.

The disadvantage of this approach is that the choice of family unit to be used as a calculation of the appropriate level of earnings is inevitably arbitrary. The family unit which the NBPI considered 'typical' in 1971, a married man with two children and a non-earning wife, now represents only 5 per cent of the labour force (Rimmer and Popay, 1982). Moreover, while this model of a 'typical' family is still widely used both in policy discussions of low pay and in trade union wage submissions, the 'family wage' concept which it embodies is coming under increasing criticism because it undermines the bargaining position of wage earners who are not themselves the sole breadwinners, a group which includes the majority of young workers and married women (see, for example, Bennett, 1981).

Because of the difficulties in deciding on the appropriate family unit to be adopted in any subsistence-based definition, the NBPI preferred instead to take an explicitly relative definition of low pay. It included in this category those whose earnings fell 'into the bottom tenth of the earnings league taking men and women separately'. A similar approach was adopted by the Royal Commission on the Distribution of Income and Wealth (Diamond, 1978) in its report on lower incomes, except that it applied the same definition of low pay (the lowest decile of male manual workers) to both men and women. To apply a different definition to women's earnings would be to reinforce the existing inequality in pay between the sexes. The same argument may be used against adopting a target based on manual earnings alone, since the majority of low paid men are manual workers. For this reason the Low Pay Unit (LPU), an independent research organisation, has considered it more appropriate to define low pay as that falling below the lowest decile of male earnings, manual and non-manual together (Pond, 1981). In 1981 this definition suggested a figure of £82.90 a week.

The lowest decile approach is valuable in that it allows an assessment of the changes which are taking place over time in the relative position of the low paid. While it is a useful measure to be used in analysing the existing situation, however, it offers little scope as a target in collective bargaining, since the numbers and proportion of low paid are effectively pre-determined. In recent years, the TUC has adopted various 'minimum wage targets' based on two-thirds of average earnings. Unless this is to represent an unattainable goal, the target must of course be specified as a proportion of median earnings (at the mid-point of the earnings distribution) rather than as a proportion of the simple average of earnings (the mean) which will itself move in step with increases in earnings at the lower end. In April 1981, two-thirds of median earnings of full-time adult men gave a figure of £84.33 a week. Of course the choice of a cut off at two-thirds average earnings is itself arbitrary. In his major survey of poverty, however, Townsend (1979:629) found that 'employees with earnings of less than 60 per cent of the mean for their sex are much more liable to be deprived than those of higher earnings both at work and outside work, according to a fairly generous spread of indicators'. His results showed that of those with earnings of less than 60 per cent of the mean, 67 per cent of men and 61 per cent of women suffered substantial or severe 'work deprivation' (having for instance unsocial hours, poor working conditions, and few fringe benefits) and 38 per cent of men and 32 per cent of women experienced severe social deprivation. Because the distribution of earnings is weighted towards high earners the mean is consistently higher than median earnings, so that a definition based on 60 per cent of the mean is close to the figure of two-thirds (66 per cent) of median earnings.

Each of the definitions discussed above has drawbacks, and each contains a considerable measure of subjective judgment. Yet when expressed in cash terms there is a remarkable consistency between the different definitions. The various methods yield weekly figures ranging from £82 to £87 a week. Thus a figure of £85 a week would seem an appropriate definition for 1981–2 and one likely to command general acceptance. This measure of low pay relates to full-time adult workers aged eighteen years and over, whether male or female; a lower definition might be adopted for younger workers. It is also necessary to convert the weekly figures to an hourly basis when considering the incidence of low pay among part-time workers: a standard working week of forty hours implies an appropriate hourly definition of £2.10. Equipped with a definition of low pay which might be considered generally acceptable, the extent and nature of the problem can now be assessed and the groups most affected can be identified.

THE PATTERN OF LOW PAY

Extent

The estimated numbers of individuals falling below the definitions of low pay (£85 a week for adult full-timers and £2.10 an hour for adult part-timers) described in the previous section are set out in Table 8.1. The figures relate only to employees aged eighteen and over whose pay during the survey period was not affected by absence for any reason.

It can be seen that in April 1981 there were almost one and a half million adult men (most of them manual workers), together with almost two and a half million adult women (most of them non-manual employees), who worked a full week plus overtime but who were still low paid. These four million low paid represented more than a quarter of the full-time adult workforce at that time. Overtime is of relatively little significance to women workers or to non-manual males, but overtime earnings have a significant effect on the total pay of male manual workers. The effect of excluding overtime earnings is to increase the numbers classified as low paid among this group by about half, adding an extra 500,000 to the total. Whereas less than a fifth of manual men are registered as low paid when

TABLE 8.1: NUMBERS AND PROPORTION OF LOW PAID WORKERS
IN BRITAIN, 1981

	FULL-TIME WORKERS EARNING LESS THAN £85 PER WEEK[a]					
	Including Overtime Pay			*Excluding Overtime Pay*		
	No. (millions)	*Proportion Who Are Low Paid (%)*	*Proportion of All Full-Time Low Paid (%)*	*No. (millions)*	*Proportion Who Are Low Paid (%)*	*Proportion of All Full-Time Low Paid (%)*
MEN						
Manual	1.0	18.3	27.0	1.5	27.3	34.1
Non-manual	0.4	9.7	10.8	0.5	10.7	11.4
Total	1.4	14.4	38.0	2.0	19.9	45.5
WOMEN						
Manual	0.8	80.0	21.6	0.8	80.0	18.2
Non-manual	1.6	48.5	43.2	1.6	48.5	36.4
Total	2.3	53.5	62.2	2.4	55.8	54.5
TOTAL FULL-TIME	3.7	27.4	100.0	4.4	32.6	100.0

Part-Time Females Aged 18 and Over Earning Less Than £2.10 Per Hour[b]		
	No. (millions)[c]	*Proportion (%) Who are Low Paid*
Manual	1.0	88.8
Non-manual	0.7	61.5
Total	1.7	75.4

Source: Unpublished data supplied by Department of Employment.
Notes:
[a] The analysis is for men and women aged 18 and over whose pay during the survey period was not affected by absence. The Department of Employment defines 'adult' males as those aged 21 and over. Substantial numbers of males aged 18–21 receive low earnings.
[b] Figures are not available on the hourly earnings of part-time males for 1981. An estimate for 1980 suggested 300,000 low paid part-time male workers (Pond, 1981).
[c] In estimating the number of low paid females, the sample size has been grossed up by a standard factor of 115. The figures are almost certainly an underestimate.

overtime is included, the figures demonstrate that the proportion would rise to more than a quarter (from 18 to 27 per cent) if overtime earnings were not available. The continuing recession is also likely to increase the problem of low pay among this group as the opportunities for overtime are reduced and the social pressures to restrict overtime working in an attempt to alleviate the increase in unemployment are increased. At the moment one-third (32.6 per cent) of the full-time adult workforce is low paid if overtime is excluded.

The largest group among the low paid are women, more than half of whom had earnings below £85 a week in 1981. Among manual women four out of five fell into the low pay category. Of the total number of low paid adult workers, almost two-thirds (62.2 per cent) are women, although this proportion falls slightly (to 55 per cent) when overtime pay is excluded.

The concentration of low pay among the female workforce is further emphasised when part-time workers are included in the overall analysis. Britain has the largest part-time labour force in the European Economic Community (EEC), with almost half the Community's part-time workers living in the United Kingdom. The majority of these are women and are poorly rewarded (Robinson, 1979; Hurstfield, 1978, 1980). As Table 8.1 shows, the earnings of three-quarters of all adult part-time females (an estimated one and three-quarter million) fell below the level of £2.10 an hour. Hourly earnings of part-time males were not available for 1981, but the previous year's analysis suggests that at least a quarter of a million were low paid. The New Earnings Survey (NES), from which the above earnings data are derived, is based on national insurance records, and the sample 'excludes significant numbers of part-time employees' whose weekly earnings are below the national insurance exemption limits because their hourly rate of pay, or their working hours, or both, are low. A recent official estimate suggested that as many as a third of all part-timers had earnings below the national insurance exemption (Hansard, 1980). It is therefore likely that the NES estimate of 2 million adult low paid part-timers understates considerably the size of the problem among this group.

Taking the total numbers of low paid, full-time and part-time together, it appears that 5½ million adult employees received low wages in April 1981, a figure which would increase to at least 6½ million if the overtime earnings of full-time employees were excluded. Thus official estimates suggest that almost a third of the adult workforce are low paid. This figure is probably an underestimate because, as noted above, the use of national insurance records excludes many part-time employees and probably also a considerable number of young workers. Moreover those industries known to have a high concentration of low paid workers are under-represented in the NES (LPU, 1980). There also appears to be differential coverage by size of firm, and the Office of Manpower Economics (1976) has suggested that the NES 'is deficient in response from small employers'. Since the incidence of low pay is known to be higher in the small firms sector, this too will lead to an underrepresentation of the low paid in the NES.

These shortcomings in the NES data encouraged Atkinson et al. (1982) to look again at the evidence on low pay contained in the Family Expenditure Survey (FES). Although based on a smaller sample and having a higher non-response rate than the NES, the FES is not subject to such a marked differential response by place and type of employment. Comparing the two surveys for 1977, the authors concluded that 'the extent of low pay appears to be greater than indicated by the usual analysis of the NES'. Even adjusting for the fact that the FES includes Northern Ireland, which has a very much higher incidence of low pay than Britain, to which the NES applies, and for the fact that the FES figures include teenagers (aged sixteen and over) a large proportion of whom receive low earnings, the FES estimates suggest a figure for the number of low-paid men one-fifth higher than that recorded in the NES; the proportion of low-paid women was found to be 9 per cent higher. If it is assumed that the NES for 1981 understated the extent of low pay among adult men and women by the same magnitude, this would suggest an increase in the numbers of full-time adult low paid of almost half a million (divided equally between men and women) in addition to those given in Table 8.1. This would bring the estimated total of full-time low paid to over 5 million, in addition to at least 2¾ million part-timers.

An alternative measure of the extent of low pay has been suggested by Metcalf (1981:9–10):

> mere head counting is a popular, but inadequate, way of describing the extent of low pay. It is useful to supplement numbers by a measure of what we might call the wage gap. This is the estimate of the total money amount by which the workforce falls short of the chosen bench mark for low pay, expressed as a percentage of the total wage bill for the workforce.

Using the 1979 NES data Metcalf calculated that the wage gap for full-time adult men represented only 0.68 per cent of the corresponding wage bill. For females, he calculated a wage gap of 10.13 per cent, giving a figure for the total labour force of 2.83 per cent. Having access to data on individual earnings from the FES, Atkinson and his colleagues (1982:10) were able to undertake a more precise calculation of the size of the wage gap. Their estimates suggest that the wage gap for men aged eighteen and over stood at 1.7 per cent (compared with Metcalf's figure of 0.68 per cent); for men aged eighteen and over the FES suggested a wage gap of 14.6 per cent (compared with the NES estimate of 10.13 per cent).

Distribution of Low Pay

Low pay is heavily concentrated within certain groups. It was noted above that the great majority of the low paid are women who, despite the Equal Pay Act, still earn on average less than three-quarters as much as men for each hour they work (Glucklich and Snell, 1982; Sloane, 1980a). There is also a close association between earnings and age. In 1981 males aged under eighteen earned less than 40 per cent of the average for adult men; females aged under eighteen received an average wage which represented slightly more than half (53.0 per cent) of adult earnings. Contrary to suggestions that the rise in youth unemployment is largely attributable to increases in the relative earnings of young people, the earnings of those aged under eighteen have declined slightly since the mid-1970s (Makeham, 1980; Pond, 1982).

The observed increase in earnings with age may partly be associated with the accumulation of additional years of work experience. Manual and non-manual men have very different age-earnings profiles, however, with the former reaching a peak before middle age and then declining. Male non-manual workers often reach their peak earnings at retirement age (and sometimes later, for those enjoying index-linked occupational pension schemes). Older manual workers are therefore particularly vulnerable to low pay. As Layard, Piachaud and Stewart (1978:51) concluded: 'broadly speaking no manual jobs offer much prospect of real wage increases (other than from economic growth) after the first ten years. So in a sense more than half the labour force are in jobs without prospects'.

Racial differences also appear to be associated with differences in earnings as Chapter 13 shows. Layard, Piachaud and Stewart (1978:38) found that, holding other factors constant, those born in the West Indies could expect to earn on average 13 per cent less than a white person with the same characteristics, while non-whites born elsewhere earned 22 per cent less. Irish born whites earned on average 7 per cent less. Similar conclusions emerged from a more detailed analysis carried out by PEP in 1974. This suggested that differences in earnings between whites and racial minorities increased with level of education and job status. In the lowest grade jobs, differences in gross earnings were not so marked, but the study concluded that even this reflected the much greater amount of shift work undertaken by non-whites. In part the lower earnings of those from racial minorities may reflect labour market discrimination or employer preferences (see Chapter 13) but it also largely reflects the industrial and occupational concentration of non-whites.

Low pay is also heavily concentrated in certain industries. Just two industrial sectors—the distributive trades and miscellaneous services (which includes hotels and catering, hairdressing, laundries, and private domestic service) account for one-third of all low paid men and women, even though these two sectors employ less than one-sixth of the total workforce. A disproportionate number of low-paid manual men and women work in professional and scientific services (which includes education and the NHS). Public administration (the armed forces, civil service, police and fire services, and local authorities) also accounts for a larger number of low paid than would be expected given its total employment. The industrial distribution of low pay is shown in Table 8.2 which, being based on published NES data, uses £80 a week as a benchmark, rather than the figure of £85 referred to above.

It is important to draw a distinction between concentrations of low pay within industrial sectors and the contribution of each industry to the total number of low paid. For instance, 35 per cent of manual men working in agriculture are low paid. But agriculture is now a relatively small sector employing only 2.6 per cent of the workforce. Its contribution to the total low pay problem is still remarkable (with almost 9 per cent of low paid manual men working in this industry). But more low paid workers are employed in the giant construction industry even though the proportion of low paid in that industry is below the national average. A similar example may be observed for manual women working in the clothing trades. This distinction is important in framing appropriate policies. If policies intended to tackle the problem are focused on the sectors in which low pay is most heavily concentrated (as is the case with the selective, industry-based minimum wage systems of the United Kingdom and Eire), significant pockets of low pay in generally high paying sectors will remain unaffected.

Low pay is also unequally distributed geographically. The south-west of England and East Anglia have relatively high concentrations of both men and women on low earnings. The Midlands has a high proportion of low paid women, but an average or below average incidence among men. While Wales has a greater low pay problem among men the proportion of low paid women is no higher than the national average. The highest incidence of low pay is to be found in Northern Ireland, where one third of the workforce is recorded as receiving low wages (Black et al., 1980; Richard Steele, 1982).

These regional differences in the incidence of low pay, as the Diamond Commission noted (1978: para 6.12), are attributable chiefly to differences in their industrial and occupational structures. East Anglia has proportionately four times as many male manual workers employed in agriculture, forestry, and fishing as is the case in Great Britain as a whole. The top ten industries, ranked according to proportions of low paid men, accounted for 30 per cent of male manual workers in East Anglia and the south west compared with a quarter nationally (LPU, 1980). Evidence of earnings and employment in the inner cities, or the declining urban areas more generally, suggest that the higher concentration of low wages in these areas is also largely explained by their industrial and occupational structure (Playford, 1980).

LOW PAY AND ECONOMIC THEORY

Short-term fluctuations apart, the distribution of earnings in Britain appears to have changed remarkably little over a period of almost a century. As the Department of Employment (1981c:446) was moved to point out in its introduction to the New Earnings Survey of 1981, 'the distribution of manual men's earnings has remained stable since 1970, and indeed the results of early surveys show that this distribution has changed little, particularly at the lower end, over the period from 1886 to the present day.' The figures are given in Table 8.3.

This long run stability in the distribution of earnings has sometimes been regarded as inevitable. Looking at the movements in the different components of the pay structure, however, Routh (1980b) has concluded that the stability is something of a statistical illusion. Although differentials *between* linked occupations have narrowed, as Chapter 11 shows, the dispersion *within* occupations has widened. The end result is an apparent stability which disguises the ever present, but contradictory, movements. A further illusion arises from the variability of individual earnings from year to year. Department of Employment analysis

TABLE 8.2: INDUSTRIAL DISTRIBUTION OF LOW PAY, 1981

Industrial Sector	*MANUAL MEN*			*NON-MAN*	
	Proportion of All Employees	*Proportion Earning Below £80*	*Proportion of All Those Earning Below £80*	*Proportion of All Employees*	*Proportion Earning Below £80*
Agriculture, forestry, and fishing	2.6	34.9	8.9	0.4	10.7
Mining and quarrying	3.9	0.6	0.2	1.0	1.1
Food, drink, and tobacco	4.3	6.1	2.6	2.2	3.1
Coal and petroleum	0.4	0.6	0.02		
Chemicals	3.2	3.0	0.9	2.7	1.6
Metal manufacture	3.2	3.9	1.2	1.3	1.9
Mechanical engineering	6.2	6.5	4.0	4.2	2.3
Instrument engineering	0.7	7.8	0.6	0.9	2.9
Electrical engineering	3.5	7.0	2.4	4.3	2.3
Shipbuilding	1.1	2.4	0.3	0.5	1.7
Vehicles	6.4	1.6	1.0	3.0	1.7
Metal goods	3.1	9.9	3.0	1.4	3.2
Textiles	1.9	16.6	3.1	0.8	6.2
Clothing and footwear	0.6	21.8	1.4		
Bricks, pottery, etc.	1.7	6.2	1.0	0.7	3.7
Timber and furniture	1.8	13.5	2.4	0.7	2.8
Paper, printing, and publishing	3.2	5.0	1.6	2.5	3.2
Other manufacturing	1.6	9.8	1.6	0.9	3.2
Construction	12.0	7.8	9.2	4.7	3.6
Gas, electricity, and water	3.0	0.2	0.1	2.6	0.6
Transport and communication	13.5	5.3	7.0	7.7	2.2
Distributive trades	6.6	23.7	15.2	10.9	14.4
Insurance, banking, finance	1.2	13.9	1.7	10.2	4.7
Professional and scientific services	3.7	21.9	7.9	17.6	4.5
Miscellaneous services	6.3	27.5	17.0	6.3	11.2
Public administration	4.1	14.5	5.8	12.6	3.5
All industries	100	10.2	100	100	5.1

Source: Department of Employment, *New Earnings Survey 1981*, pt. C.
Note: Figures relate to full-time males (aged 21 and over) and full-time adult females (aged 18 and c whose pay during the survey pay period was not affected by absence.

ortion Those ning low 80	MANUAL WOMEN			NON-MANUAL WOMEN		
	Proportion of All Employees	Proportion Earning Below £80	Proportion of All Those Earning Below £80	Proportion of All Employees	Proportion Earning Below £80	Proportion of All Those Earning Below £80
0.9						
0.2						
1.4	7.1	54.4	5.8	1.6	44.3	1.7
0.9	3.5	51.5	2.8	1.5	30.6	1.1
0.5	0.9	64.2	0.9	0.5	46.4	0.6
1.9	2.3	48.2	1.7	1.7	56.6	2.3
0.5	1.4	56.9	1.2	0.5	51.0	0.6
2.0	7.5	56.8	6.4	2.1	45.1	2.3
0.2						
1.0	2.2	29.1	1.0	1.0	32.8	0.8
0.9	2.9	67.7	3.0	0.8	58.3	1.2
0.9	5.9	76.8	6.9	0.6	73.6	1.0
	8.9	80.0	10.8			
0.5	1.6	61.7	1.5	0.4	52.8	0.6
0.4	1.0	60.7	0.9	0.4	65.8	0.7
1.6	4.0	53.3	3.2	1.8	36.3	1.6
0.5	2.7	73.5	3.0	0.5	56.1	0.7
3.4				1.5	64.0	2.4
0.3				1.6	15.7	0.6
3.4	4.1	29.1	1.8	5.2	30.4	3.9
1.0	6.3	77.1	7.3	15.3	74.3	27.8
9.5				12.5	39.6	12.2
15.7	16.9	72.7	18.5	32.0	25.9	20.3
13.9	17.1	78.1	20.2	6.9	44.3	7.5
8.7	3.5	59.0	3.1	11.5	35.6	10.0
100	100	65.9	100	100	40.9	100

TABLE 8.3: DISPERSION OF WEEKLY EARNINGS OF FULL-TIME MANUAL MEN, 1886–1981

Year	Lowest Decile (as % of median)	Lower Quartile (as % of median)	Median Weekly Earnings £	Upper Quartile (as % of median)	Highest Decile (as % of median)
1886	68.6	82.8	1.21	121.7	143.1
1906	66.5	79.5	1.47	126.7	156.8
1938	67.7	82.1	3.40	118.5	139.9
1960	70.6	82.6	14.17	121.7	145.2
1968	67.3	81.0	22.40	122.3	147.8
1970	67.3	81.1	25.60	122.3	147.2
1971	68.2	81.8	28.10	122.1	146.5
1972	67.6	81.3	31.30	122.3	146.6
1973	67.3	81.4	36.60	121.6	145.3
1974	68.6	82.2	41.80	121.0	144.1
1975	69.2	82.8	53.20	121.3	144.4
1976	70.2	83.4	62.10	120.8	144.9
1977	70.6	83.1	68.20	120.3	144.4
1978	69.4	82.4	76.80	121.2	146.0
1979	68.3	81.7	88.20	122.2	148.5
1980	68.4	82.2	105.00	122.9	149.2
1981	69.7	82.8	114.20	122.5	150.6

Source: Employment Gazette (October 1980), p. 1090, table 2; (October 1981), p. 447, table 5.

of a matched sample of individuals in the NES over a period of years has demonstrated the considerable movement that takes place within the pay structure. The analysis shows that less than 3 per cent of manual men remained in the lowest decile of the earnings distribution throughout the period 1970 to 1974, whereas over a fifth of the male manual workforce found itself among the low paid for at least one of the five years. The Department of Employment (1977) concluded that the low paid 'are a continually changing group'.

Orthodox Economic Theory

The apparent stability in the earnings distribution lends itself to a number of very different interpretations. Neo-classical wage theorists have tended to emphasise the role of individual characteristics in determining the quality of the labour supply. Implicit in this approach is an assumption that differences in reward reflect differences in productivity, in contribution to total output, and in 'marketable' skills. As Chapter 12 indicates, the theory assumes that with the unhindered operation of competitive markets, the wage will be equivalent to the amount that the last worker employed contributes to total output, the marginal product. At this point earnings and the level of employment will be stable; beyond this point, assuming diminishing returns, employers will begin to pay more in wages than they gain in revenue if they employ extra workers. It follows that workers who have lower productivity will only be employed at lower wages. This in turn is taken to be sufficient explanation for the persistence of wage inequalities. As Thurow (1969:26) has explained: 'the distribution of marginal product is identical with the distribution of earned income . . . If an individual's income is too low, his productivity is too low. His income can be increased only if his productivity can be raised'.

The theory accords with popular conceptions about the causes of inequality: 'if you are paid a lot it must be because you are worth a lot' (Routh, 1980b:10). Since 'the marginal product of labour' is a concept which defies precise measurement, however, economists have tended to use wages as a proxy measure of marginal product itself. The concept can thus become no more than a tautology devoid of analytic or prescriptive value (Thurow, 1970:29). The concept can only have any meaning if it is accepted that there will be circumstances in which the wage does not equate with marginal product. And for the wages exactly to equal the marginal product market mechanisms must be working perfectly, without restriction, and without the intervention of social or institutional factors. These circumstances are more likely to be the exception than the norm. There will therefore be many cases in which the wage is below the marginal product of labour; others in which it is above. Marginal productivity theory, even if accepted as an explanation of wage determination, cannot be taken to justify the existing wage distribution, or prove its inevitability.

In spite of these difficulties with marginal productivity theory, recent years have seen attempts to develop the general proposition that wages are determined by the productivity of labour through the 'human capital' approach to earnings described in Chapter 11. The emphasis of the approach is on the role of education and training, which are seen as an investment in an individual's stock of human capital and for which a higher return is required in terms of future earnings. In Chapter 11 Marsden shows that there is a strong link between educational qualifications and earnings levels. But it is also true that there is 'an enormous spread of earnings' even among those with the same educational qualifications. Hence, Layard, Piachaud and Stewart were led to the conclusion that 'if all educational disparities were eliminated the remaining inequality would still be over 93 per cent of what it is now' (1978:41). Moreover the effects of educational qualification—the meritocractic escape route from low pay— can easily be swamped, as Chapter 13 demonstrates, by other more powerful factors such as sex and race.

For most jobs formal educational qualifications are of less relevance than more specific skills. The NBPI (1971:table 6) drew attention to the high proportion of people doing relatively unskilled jobs in low paying industries as a possible explanation for low wages. However, the Board's own survey data showed that at least half the skilled and supervisory staff in these industries were also low paid. The earnings of skilled workers appear to vary in accordance with the general level of earnings in the industries in which they work. The NBPI assumed that the link between skill levels and pay would be through the value to the employer of the work performed, as indicated by the level of skill. In many industries, however, especially in the service sector, the level of skills required is low, and the employer would gain little or nothing by employing a more qualified worker. In general skills are specific to the jobs that people do rather than to the individuals themselves. A simple equation between earnings and level of skills or qualifications is therefore misleading.

The concepts of marginal productivity and human capital are the theoretical underpinnings for the notion, particularly popular with the post-1979 Conservative Government, that wages are determined by the market forces of supply and demand. Employers' demand for labour will depend on workers' productivity; meanwhile workers are free to decide how much labour they will supply and, subject to the constraints of their own innate abilities, to improve the quality of the labour they offer through education and training. But in his examination of changes in occupation and pay between 1906 and 1979, Routh (1980a:183) concluded that 'some of the obvious movements in supply and demand have not been reflected in the expected changes in relative pay'. And when applied to important policy questions, such as the effects of the Equal Pay Act, the theory has proved unhelpful. Before the implementation of the Act economists anticipated a significant increase in female unemployment. Yet despite a substantial increase in women's relative pay between 1970 and 1975 their level of employment increased.

This lack of empirical evidence in support of the 'market forces' model is partly explained by what Routh (1980a:183) describes as 'the socio-economic complexity of the determinants of pay' which economists are too often prone to ignore. Demand and supply undoubtedly do have a part to play. But the question remains 'what shapes supply and demand?' Drawing on evidence submitted to the Diamond Commission, Dorothy Wedderburn (1980:13) showed that top management salaries were often determined according to the 'image' the company wished to portray. High salaries denoted prosperity and success; lower salaries were seen as the mark of corporate responsibility. The Commission found little correlation between the level of salary of top managers and the profitability of their company, its rate of growth, or its size. Although economic factors are important in helping to determine both the level and the distribution of wages, they do not operate in a vacuum. Economic, social, and institutional factors interact together in a complex matrix which helps to produce the wage structure. It is not sufficient to appeal to 'market forces' alone for an explanation of the existing wage inequalities or for proof of their inevitability. As Wootton (1955:163) has warned, 'the main effect of classical wage theories has been to justify an existing situation by explaining an imaginary one'.

Labour Market Duality and Segmentation

The orthodox wage theories described above include the implicit assumption that, in fully competitive market conditions, wages (or at least the 'net advantage' of different jobs) will tend towards equality. Remaining inequalities are considered to be 'exogenous', or external to the economic system, reflecting differences in individual abilities or stocks of human capital, or barriers to mobility. But competitive pressures have not resulted in a reduction of wage inequalities between groups in the labour market. Recent years, therefore, have seen the development of theories which suggest that labour market inequalities are generated within the economic system itself. These theories shift the emphasis away from the supply-side of the labour market and focus instead on the structure of demand and on the factors which help to explain the industrial concentration of low pay. And while analysing the economic and industrial factors at work, this approach also acknowledges the institutional determinants of pay.

One such approach—the 'dual labour market theory'—developed out of studies of local labour markets and shares many of the assumptions of orthodox economic analysis. But its focus is on the development of structural divisions in the labour market. The theorists distinguish between 'the external labour market of conventional economic theory' and 'the internal labour market, governed by administrative rules'. The explanation offered for the development of an internal labour market is the increasingly job-specific nature of skills. Employers need to invest in the training of workers in these specific skills and are reluctant to lose their return on this training investment through high labour turnover. This requires that conditions of employment are adequate and that jobs provide reasonable prospects. Entry to this internal labour market is only possible at the bottom of the hierarchy, where applicants compete in the open market for jobs, and at other specified 'ports of entry' for suitably qualified applicants. Once inside, however, external market conditions become largely irrelevant. Labour has become a 'quasi-fixed factor of production' which needs to be retained despite short-run fluctuations in economic conditions. But firms and industries still need some element of flexibility in their labour costs in order to adjust to changes in product market conditions. Hence some element of the labour force is required to remain more easily 'disposable'. Little training is provided and staff turnover is not discouraged among this group. They are, in effect, excluded from the internal labour market.

Interwoven with this concept of 'internal' and 'external' labour markets, although not completely overlapping, is that of 'primary' and 'secondary' sectors of the labour market. The features of the two sectors were described by Piore (1971:91):

the primary market offers jobs which possess several of the following traits: high wages, good working conditions, employment stability and job security, equity and due process in the administration of work rules, and chances for advancement. The . . . secondary market has jobs which, relative to those in the primary sector, are decidedly less attractive. They tend to involve low wages, poor working conditions, considerable variability in employment, harsh and often arbitrary discipline, and little opportunity to advance. The poor are confined to the secondary labour market.

Secondary sectors need not engulf whole industries; industries, or even individual firms or organisations, may provide both primary and secondary employment conditions for different groups of workers.

The theory of structured or segmented labour markets moves the emphasis in explaining wage inequalities from the characteristics of labour supply towards industrial, economic, and institutional factors. The approach suggests a strong relationship between employment conditions (including low pay) and industrial characteristics. A recent study of six sectors in which wages councils had once operated (Craig et al., 1982) adopted a labour market segmentation approach and concluded that 'the causes of low pay, bad working conditions and the difficulties of establishing effective organisation on one or both sides of industry result mainly from the technical conditions of production, the structure of the product market and the existence of vulnerable minorities in the labour market available at low rates of pay'. They argue that these conditions ensure the development and persistence of secondary employment conditions which, although to be found in all industries, are most prominent in low paying sectors, and especially those covered by wages councils. Primary and secondary sectors might be identified in terms of the employment conditions they provide, but these are closely linked to the structural features of each sector. Firms and industries in the primary sector are large, modern, capital intensive, and use up-to-date technology. They are able to exert some control, and therefore stability, over their product market. The firms in this sector are usually unionised and wages and other conditions are determined by company or plant level bargaining. By contrast, the secondary sector is characterised by small firms using traditional and labour intensive technology. Operating in declining and unstable product markets over which they have no control, the firms in this sector are under considerable competitive pressure. They are poorly unionised and wages are therefore determined at a national or industry level, with little local bargaining. Each of these different characteristics interact one with another to perpetuate the divisions between primary and secondary employment sectors. Secondary employment conditions are to be found to some extent in all industries, but such conditions are particularly prominent in sectors covered by wages councils. And an examination of wages council sectors is a valuable means of explaining the forces which help to perpetuate low pay.

SECONDARY EMPLOYMENT IN THE WAGES COUNCIL SECTOR

Wages councils are independent tripartite bodies, made up of representatives of both sides of industry together with a number of independent members whose function is to conciliate between the two sides and, where agreement cannot be reached, to vote in favour of one side or the other. Once the councils have decided on the level of minimum rates and other conditions these have the force of law. The councils therefore represent a selective industry-based system of legal minimum wages.

Twenty-seven wages councils were in operation in Britain in mid-1982 covering an estimated two and three quarter million employees in about 400,000 establishments. A similar system operates in Northern Ireland where eleven councils set minimum wages, holidays and holiday pay for 40,000 workers in about six thousand establishments. The number of employees and establishments covered may be greater than this, since firms are not required to inform the Department of Employment's Wages Inspectorate, whose job it is to police the system, when they establish themselves in business. Winyard (1976) suggests the number of firms covered may exceed official estimates by up to 20 per cent. The most important sectors covered in Britain are retailing, in which two councils set minimum rates for over a million workers, and catering, in which three councils have responsibility for up to a million employees in cafés, public houses, restaurants, and hotels. A third of a million clothing workers are also covered (by three councils), together with 140,000 hairdressing employees. In addition to the twenty-seven wages councils, there are two wages boards, one for England and Wales and one for Scotland, to regulate the wages and holiday entitlements of 275,000 farmworkers. The Agricultural Wages Boards are administered, not by the Department of Employment, but by the Ministry of Agriculture.

The foundations of this selective minimum wage system were laid in 1909 with the passing of the Trades Board Act, which provided for the fixing of minimum wages where 'the rate of wages prevailing in any branch of the trade was exceptionally low, as compared with that in other employments' (Starr, 1981:19). In spite of the Act's objectives, Table 8.2 demonstrates that low wage employment is still heavily concentrated in the wages council sector. The industries in which wages councils are the main form of wage determination (the distributive trades, miscellaneous services, and clothing) account for only 18 per cent of full-time adult workers but for 36 per cent of the full-time adult low paid. Agriculture acounts for almost a tenth of low paid adult male manual workers.

Institutional Constraints

Much of the explanation for the failure of the wages councils to fulfil the objective of overcoming low pay has been attributed to the institutional failure of the wages council mechanism itself. Trade unions in particular have been critical of the level of rates traditionally established by the wages councils. In mid-1982 most minimum rates in the wages council sector stood at between £57 and £62 a week for the safety-net 'all other workers' grades, while the lowest paying wages council—that covering hairdressing undertakings—set a minimum rate of only £43 a week for its lowest grade adult workers. Young workers are entitled to significantly lower rates than this. Hairdressing, for example, sets a minimum of £27.50 for a first year apprentice. Moreover, it appears that in many wages council industries earnings have moved closer to the minimum rates themselves in recent years. This is particularly the case for women workers who represent the majority of the labour force in the wages council sector and for whom total earnings exceed the minimum rates by a relatively small margin (MacLennan, 1980).

In addition to the generally low level of minimum rates, the system is subject to an increasingly serious problem of underpayment. In 1971 15 per cent of employers inspected were found to be illegally underpaying some or all of their employees. By 1981 this proportion had increased to 41.3 per cent (LPU 1982b). A number of explanations have been given for this high level of underpayment. In the view of the Department of Employment (1978b), 'many employers are breaking the law because they cannot understand the orders or because the effort to understand them is too great'.

Part of this misunderstanding results from the complexity of the wages council system itself, which has adapted poorly to changes in the industrial structure. Catering is subject to the provisions of three separate councils. Until recently there were nine separate wages councils for retailing and ten in the clothing industry. Each of the councils establish separate rates for age, area, type of occupation and so on. The retailing councils have recently been amalgamated into two and clothing into three with a considerable improvement in the comprehensibility of the system. Nevertheless, coverage of the system is patchy. People working in grocers, bakers, newsagents, outfitters, furnishers, and booksellers are covered by the retail wages councils, but those working in butchers, florists, pharmacists, and photographic shops are not; those working in public houses, cafes, hotels, and restaurants are covered by the catering wages councils, but those working in boarding houses and in contract or industrial catering are not.

This complexity in the structure of wages councils is reflected in the wages orders which explain their provisions. The Commission on Industrial Relations (1975) described the orders as 'complex, turgid, and legalistic documents' and ACAS's investigation of the Button Manufacturing Wages Council (1978) indicated that half the sample of workers claimed never to have heard of the wages council. Most of the remainder said that they did not bother to read the notices on display, partly because they found wages council orders difficult to understand. The Department of Employment has in recent years been encouraging wages councils to simplify their provisions, and has itself prepared simplified guides to the orders in an attempt to reduce underpayment.

Misunderstandings of the system are no doubt part of the explanation for the high level of underpayment, but they are less than satisfactory as an explanation for the increase in the problem. Despite the amalgamations in wages councils and measures to improve general understanding of their provisions in recent years, infringement has increased. An alternative explanation is that the system of enforcement of the minimum rates is ineffective and has become more so over time. A reduction of the number of inspectors by one third between 1979 and 1981 was associated with an increase in recorded underpayments from 31.5 per cent of establishments to 41.3 per cent (LPU, 1982b). With only 119 'outdoor' inspectors in 1981, the wages inspectorate was able to maintain contact with only 7.5 per cent of establishments on its lists in addition to the 2.5 per cent visited following a complaint. This implied that an employer might expect to hear from the inspectorate on a routine basis on average only once every thirteen or fourteen years. Given the high turnover of both staff and establishments in the wages council sector, many firms and individuals might never come across an inspector. Moreover, some of these 'routine' contacts are now made by postal questionnaire or by telephone rather than through a personal visit. As the Department of Employment has candidly admitted, 'the infrequency of the inspector's visits encourages employers to underpay since the risk of a second inspection followed by prosecution is so limited' (quoted in Metcalf, 1981:70).

The level of resources made available to the wages inspectorate compares unfavourably with that allocated to social security abuse. While the number of civil servants deployed to tackle minimum wage abuse was cut from 177 to 119 in 1979–81, those deployed on social security abuse were increased by 1000 to 5500. The risk of prosecution is reduced further by a policy of prosecuting only those employers found guilty of underpayment on a second or subsequent inspection. First offenders are rarely prosecuted. As Metcalf (1981) points out, combined with a policy of trying to visit every employer once before visiting any employer more than once, this means that very few prosecution cases are likely to emerge. In 1981, of almost 12,000 establishments in which underpayment or other infringement of the wages council orders was uncovered, only eight prosecutions were brought to bear. The maximum penalties are, in any case, low and the courts, generally unaccustomed to hearing such cases, have tended to impose penalties well below the maximum level permitted (Crine, 1981).

The Abolition Debate

The Wages Council Act of 1945 established the wages councils in their present form. The provisions of the Act were intended primarily to protect an orderly system of voluntary collective bargaining against the rigours of a further anticipated downturn in the business cycle. However, the next fifteen years witnessed instead economic growth and full employment, conditions which were said to have made the councils redundant in their objective of providing minimum protection against low pay. As Bayliss (1962:74) reported in the early 1960s,

> under full employment it is no longer the prime function of wages councils to provide a legally enforced level of wages and conditions markedly above that which would otherwise prevail. The protection with which the Councils are historically associated—protection against the tendency of the free market in labour to settle the price of some workers' labour below what society would accept as 'reasonable remuneration'—has become unnecessary for all but a small proportion of workers. The main protection which workers have against being compelled to accept socially 'unreasonable' pay has been the state of the labour market itself . . . If statutory wage regulation were abolished overnight only a small proportion of those who are at present provided with legal minimum wages and conditions would find themselves receiving unreasonably low wages.

Bayliss believed that the main weakness in the wages council system was the absence of effective provision for the abolition of councils now that the protection against low wages was no longer necessary. The established wisdom of industrial relations at this time was that if wages councils had a role it was to help further the establishment of voluntary collective bargaining rather than to provide protection against exploitation. By the end of the 1960s even this rationale for the continued existence of the wages council system was considered dubious. The weight of opinion within the trade union movement was that the wages councils had acted to inhibit, rather than to stimulate, the development of voluntary collective bargaining arrangements. This view was echoed by the Royal Commission on Trade Unions and Employers' Associations (Donovan, 1968:66) and by the National Board for Prices and Incomes. Examining the operation of the laundry wages council the NBPI (1971: para 124) reported that 'once more we are led to conclude that it affords inadequate protection to the low paid and that its existence inhibits the development of voluntary arrangements which could be more effective'. The Board noted with approval that the Industrial Relations Act of 1971 would 'make it easier to abolish wages councils which have outlived their usefulness'.

On coming to office in 1974 the Labour Government extended this strategy still further by encouraging the abolition of wages councils, although permitting their transformation into Statutory Joint Industrial Councils (SJICs), bodies with similar regulatory functions but without independent members. In the ten years from 1969 to 1979 no fewer than fourteen wages councils were abolished (although no new SJICs were established in their place). Few dissenting voices (Greenwood, 1972; LPU, 1975) were to be heard opposing this approach. The only real opposition appeared to come from employers' associations which 'feared that without legal enforcement of the rates of pay and hours of work some of the smaller firms might resort to undercutting in both wages and prices, and their organisation would not be able to put a stop to it' (Clegg, 1976a:358). As the decade wore on, however, industrial relations opinion became more cautious. The Commission on Industrial Relations, and later ACAS, found that in many industrial sectors covered by the councils there were significant minorities of workers who would be vulnerable if statutory protection were withdrawn. Somewhat belatedly perhaps, the Department of Employment commissioned the research cited above (Craig et al., 1982) into the effects of abolition. The researchers found that in the six sectors studied voluntary collective bargaining had not in general developed following abolition and in all but one sector low pay and underpayment of national agreements remained a problem. In industrial catering, for example, the researchers were strongly critical of the decision to abolish the Industrial and Staff Canteens Wages Council: 'there have been no benefits resulting from the abolition of the wages council to justify the removal of protection for a large number of vulnerable workers, and it is hard to see how any benefits could have been expected'. Indeed, the researchers found that many of the workers were 'probably in a worse position than they were before abolition' (Craig et al., 1980d:108). Similarly, in the cutlery industry the researchers concluded that retention of the wages council and effective enforcement of its rates would have resulted in wages being higher than they now were 'for significant numbers of vulnerable workers' (Craig et al., 1980a).

In the light of such evidence, much industrial relations and trade union opinion is moving back to a position of acceptance of the wages councils as a necessary form of safety-net protection. In its 1980 annual report, ACAS (1981:58) noted that 'the retention of the councils has been necessary partly as a result of lack of progress in the development of collective bargaining, and partly because surveys of pay in wages council industries have indicated that there remain significant numbers of low paid workers who would be vulnerable if statutory protection was to be removed'. Moreover the report noted that the councils did not cover all sectors in which low pay was prevalent. In contrast to the earlier report on the laundry and contract cleaning industries by the NBPI, ACAS suggested a possible extension of the wages council sector. In contract cleaning ACAS recommended the establishment of a new wages council, the first such official recommendation since 1956, and proposed that unless voluntary arrangements developed in the foreseeable future the Laundry Wages Council might be extended to cover workers in laundrettes.

But the weight of government opinion following the election of a market-orientated Conservative administration in 1979 has begun to move in the opposite direction. Now, as during the inter-war depression, pressures for real (and sometimes money) wage cuts have developed. Considerable opposition is directed towards the wages councils which, it is said, are contributing to the rise in unemployment by preventing wages from falling as an adjustment to the deteriorating economic conditions.

In particular, the councils were said to be 'pricing young people out of jobs' (see for example NFSE, 1981). The Secretary of State for Employment has made it clear that he would seriously consider abolition of the entire wages council system in 1985 on the expiry of ILO Convention No. 26 which 'requires the creation and maintenance of machinery for fixing minimum wages in manufacturing and commercial trades (and in particular home-working trades) when no arrangements exist for the effective regulation of wages by collective agreements or otherwise and wages are exceptionally low' (Starr, 1981:v).

In the meantime, other policies are having the effect of weakening the wages councils. The Young Workers' Scheme, introduced in 1982, offers a weekly subsidy of £15 a week to firms who pay employees aged under eighteen a wage of less than £40 a week (or a subsidy of £7.50 for those paying less than £45). Since some wages councils have established minimum wages for seventeen-year-olds in excess of this figure, there is the possibility that employers may receive a government subsidy for illegally underpaying their young workers. No special safeguards are built into the scheme to prevent this happening. Similarly, although the government has had no direct control over the activities of wages councils since they were rendered independent bodies by the Employment Protection Act, it has nevertheless applied pressure to each of the councils to reduce the level of increases awarded. This is despite the fact that, as noted by ACAS (1982:62–3) 'the minimum rates set by wages councils had been relatively very low and have often increased at a slower rate than pay rates in industry generally'.

In response to this threat to the wages councils, trade unions are beginning to reassess their own position. A number of unions, including those with membership within the wages council sector and those representing wages inspectors themselves, have started to campaign for an improvement in the effectiveness of the councils. The TUC has made official representations to the Secretary of State for Employment opposing suggestions that wages councils might be abolished altogether or that young people might be removed from their scope.

Industrial Constraints

But strong feelings remain, within sections of the trade union movement, that wages councils have acted, not as an incubator for voluntary nego-tiating machinery, but as its replacement and that they have prevented the achievement of the only effective long-term solution to low pay: full unionisation of the workforce and collective action to raise wages. As Chapter 1 has indicated, the 'wages council industries' are characterised by a low level of unionisation. In agriculture and forestry union density in 1979 was only 22·7 per cent; in miscellaneous services it was 7·3 per cent; and in the distributive trades it was 14·9 per cent. The CIR pointed out in its report on retail distribution (1975) that there are a number of characteristics of wages council industries which tend to frustrate attempts to increase the level of organisation of the workforce. These include the industrial structure and the characteristics of the workforce.

Perhaps the most important feature of the structure of wages council industries is the prevalence of small firms. In 1980, for instance, the wages inspectorate records suggest that each establishment in the wages council sector had an average of fewer than seven employees. Clothing and catering were marked by a larger establishment size (twenty-eight and ten employees per establishment respectively) but in retailing only five employees were recorded for each establishment and in hairdressing only four. The generally lower level of pay enjoyed by workers in small firms is well established. The Bolton Committee on Small Firms (1971: para 2.40) found that holding skill levels and hours of work constant, the difference in earnings between small and large firms was of the order of 20 per cent. The CIR investigation into the clothing industry (1974a: para 33) found that the incidence of low pay in small establishments (twenty-five and fewer employees) was twice that recorded in establishments employing more than 500 people.

Part of the explanation for the higher incidence of low pay in the small firms sector is undoubtedly the level of unionisation. The Bolton Committee found that only 8 per cent of small firms were fully unionised and almost two thirds had no union membership at all. As Chapter 1 indicated, where workers are employed in small, scattered establishments, this presents practical difficulties for unions in their recruitment attempts, and unions naturally tend to concentrate their efforts and resources on the larger establishments. These difficulties are compounded by the fact that perceptions of common interest and solidarity are weakened where workers do not share the same workplace. And where people work in close proximity with their employer, personal relationships develop which inhibit workers from asserting their own interests. Although the popular caricature of the small firm is of an organisation in which paternalism and the development of personal relationships have rendered redundant the formality of negotiation by an outside body such as a trade union, the CIR (1974b: paras 68–9) found this vision of employment in the small firm questionable. It noted 'the exposed position of the individual employee which discourages him from taking any action. Unwillingness to upset his relationship with his employer and fear of jeopardising his job are both powerful deterrants'. The Commission found that 'the owner manager tends to be an individual who sets great store by his independence and resents any interference in the running of his business . . . our own enquiries produced evidence of some overt hostility to the principle of trade unionism'.

Employers' resistance to unionisation, or to any mechanism which might raise wage levels, is increased further by other elements of the economic environment. As noted above, firms in the secondary employment sector tend to use traditional technology and to be labour intensive. Hence labour costs represent a large proportion of total costs and the acute competitive conditions in which firms operate increases the incentive to hold wage costs down. In contrast to large firms, small employers have little or no control over their product market, largely because, where trade unions exist they are too weak to be able to offer employers a market regulating function. They are therefore continually constrained by the competitive need to reduce costs.

Competition also reduces the resources available for investment in capital or improved techniques resulting in 'the apparently inferior return of small firms in terms of labour employed . . . attributable (to an unknown extent) to the smaller amount of capital used per worker' (Bolton, 1971; Duncan, 1982:29–33). The NBPI's belief that low pay could be largely explained by a low level of labour productivity (a belief underpinned by the neo-classical wage theories described above) rested on the assumption that this low productivity reflected individual skills and poor labour utilisation. A more plausible explanation might be the more labour-intensive technology used by low wage firms.

Labour Force Constraints

The low pay problem, although concentrated in the small firms sector, and often in industries with declining markets, is not confined to this sector. Nor is low wage employment synonyomous with non-unionised employment. Many of the low paid, for instance, are to be found in the public sector where unionisation is generally very high. Trade union density in footwear is also well above average and firms tend to be relatively large in comparison to the rest of the wages council sector. In such circumstances it is necessary to look for explanations other than those associated with the structure of the industries concerned and the economic environment in which they operate. As Craig et al. (1980e:49) concluded:

> low pay exists both within industries where the general level of pay is low, and low wages are an important factor allowing firms to compete, and in isolated cases within firms or industries where the general level of pay is reasonable. In these latter cases, low pay reflects the weak bargaining position of 'vulnerable workers' and not the weak competitive position of the firm or industry. Low pay is therefore not confined to the industries where the general level of pay is low.

This is the real relevance of the association between low pay and certain groups within the labour force—women, juveniles, part-timers, and those from ethnic minorities—that was noted earlier. The increased incidence of low pay among these groups is explained, not by their individual characteristics or productivity, but by their vulnerability to exploitation, using the term in its neo-classical sense of wages paid below marginal product. This vulnerability springs largely from an imbalance in the labour market between employers and workers.

The vulnerability of women to secondary sector employment may be explained in part by the need to reconcile their domestic and employment roles, given the division of labour within the family and the home. This is especially the case for married women, who are encouraged to work part-time or at home, or in industries where high staff turnover provides the flexibility to move in or out of employment. This helps to ensure that married women often represent an available supply of cheap labour with few alternative employment opportunities. Secondary employment conditions may therefore persist, even if other economic and industrial factors make this unnecessary, simply because labour is readily available at low cost. From the point of view of the employer, even those operating mainly in the primary sector, this supply of low wage and largely unorganised labour may represent an important element of flexibility in adjusting labour costs to general market conditions. Hence ACAS (1978) found that homeworkers were often employed by firms as a buffer against changes in demand. Craig et al. (1980e:46) found that certain occupations, such as cleaning and catering services, were almost always confined to the secondary employment sector, even where these activities took place within primary sector organisations. 'Here, the availability of labour at low rates of pay, rather than constraints on the ability of the firm to pay must be the major determinant of low wages.' A prime example of this type of employment is that of civil service cleaners. Although the civil service may be considered a classic example of an internal labour market, and therefore firmly in the primary sector, directly employed cleaners receive exceptionally low rates of pay. A survey undertaken in 1980 showed that most civil service cleaners worked between eighteen and twenty hours a week and had take home pay of between £23 and £26 a week. The majority of the cleaners were found to have family responsibilities (80 per cent were married and 40 per cent had at least one dependent child) and most had spouses who were themselves low paid or not working at all: 'the picture that emerges is of a workforce with few choices of alternative employment working unsocial hours for very little reward'. Directly employed civil service cleaners are, of course, fully unionised (Beardwell et al., 1981). A very similar picture emerged from the ACAS (1981b:18) study of contract cleaners which found that a high proportion of the cleaners were married women with children: 'very few of them were the sole earners in the family but most saw their earnings as a necessary contribution to the family income. By far the most widely held reason for choosing cleaning was the need to have a job compatible with family responsibilities.'

Women are not the only groups of workers trapped into the secondary labour market through absence of alternative employment opportunities. Those from ethnic minorities often find themselves in a similar situation. Bosanquet and Doeringer (1973), for instance, have described how the Yorkshire clothing industry relies heavily on immigrant workers, drawn into the industry during prosperous times and expelled during periods of downturn in the market. Young people may also find themselves as part of a reserve labour force, especially during times of high youth unemployment. Industries such as retailing rely heavily on an annual intake of school leavers.

A higher level of unionisation and collective negotiations among some of these groups of workers might help to reduce the degree of exploitation by improving the balance between employers and workers in the labour market. But the characteristics of this workforce inhibit the development of unionisation. As the CIR (1974d:22) noted, 'part-timers may be difficult to contact on an occasional visit to a store; women and part-timers may have less experience of union organisation or they may see their interests as distinct from other groups of employees and not be convinced that the union can or will adequately represent their point of view'. Family commitments may also preclude full participation by women in union activities, especially if these involve commitments outside working hours. The problems of recruitment are compounded by the fact that these groups are also characterised by high rates of staff turnover. During 1981, for instance, USDAW enrolled more than 100,000 new members, equivalent to almost a quarter of the union's total membership. But at the end of the year the overall membership figure was more than 12,000 lower than in the previous year (USDAW, 1982:3).

LOW PAY: THE POLICY OPTIONS

Recent policies in Britain have been influenced by two important assumptions about the nature and causes of low pay. First there has been a belief that low wages are not a major contributor to the wider problem of poverty. Where hardship arose this was thought to be primarily the effect not of low wages, but of exceptional family commitments which could best be dealt with through the social security system. Hence the NBPI (1971: para. 123) felt that 'the use of appropriate redistribution measures through the tax and social security system has been the most effective means up to now of improving the relative position of the low paid, and will probably continue to be in future'. This approach is also consistent with the second dominant assumption that the main causes of low pay are to be found on the supply-side of the labour market. Thus attempts to influence wages directly through institutional, non-market mechanisms are thought to be ill-advised. The underlying inequalities, generated by differences in individual abilities and market forces, are always likely to reassert themselves. The only lasting effect may be distortions in market relationships which lead to problems such as unemployment and wage inflation. If this interpretation is correct, it would be more appropriate to try and improve labour supply through measures such as training and education, perhaps also increasing the demand for certain types of low-skilled labour through regional policy. Meanwhile, the effects of low wages are best tackled through social and fiscal policy rather than through wages or employment policy. Cash transfers such as family income supplement, negative income tax, or tax credits are means whereby hardship can be alleviated without resorting to direct intervention in the wage determination process.

This chapter has challenged both the assumptions on which these policies are based. Low wages are themselves an important direct and indirect cause of poverty. But the policy of extending the social security system to the 'working poor' has been less than successful (Stanton, 1977). Benefits such as Family Income Supplement, housing rebates and allowances, and free school meals are subject to low take-up and have tended to create a 'poverty trap' which sometimes conflicts with the wage bargaining process (Pond et al., 1976). Measures to improve the workings of the social security system (including a move away from means-tested benefits such as FIS and an improvement in universal child benefit), combined with a reduction in the tax burden on the low paid, would help alleviate the effects of low wages. But they would not tackle the problem itself.

The scope for improving individual earnings through additional education and training is limited. The evidence does not appear to support the assumptions of neo-classical wage theory, built on the role of human capital and individual characteristics in determining earnings. Institutional, industrial, and economic factors appear to offer a more plausible explanation for the persistence of low wages. This interpretation offers greater scope for intervention by the state or trade unions in influencing the overall distribution of earnings. Such intervention can take a number of forms, including incomes policies, general or selective minimum wage legislation, equal pay and discrimination laws, an extension of collective bargaining, and the adoption by trade unions of minimum wage targets.

This chapter has focused on the wages council sector where the persistence of low wages is partly attributable to the institutional failure of the system and the absence of voluntary collective bargaining machinery. Better coordination between the councils, a rationalisation of their structure, and the provision of better research and information facilities would therefore help to ensure the establishment of minimum rates at a more acceptable level. Simplification of the wages orders, better publicity, a substantial injection of resources to the wages inspectorate, and more determined enforcement would result in a lower level of infringement (see Pond, 1980b). Similarly, the option under the Employment Protection Act 1975 for councils to transform themselves into Statutory Joint Industrial Councils (SJICs), approximating more closely normal collective bargaining, would also have improved the effectiveness of industry-based minimum wage machinery. But no councils have yet taken this opportunity. Measures to extend trade union collective action in this sector, perhaps through the proposal for a trade union development fund (through which trade unions might pool funds to assist recruitment in the most difficult areas), would also help. An effective 'fair wages law'—perhaps combining elements of both Schedule 11 of the Employment Protection Act (abolished in 1980) and the Fair Wages Resolution (abolished in 1982)—would provide a means of extending the benefits of collective bargaining to less well-organised groups of workers, including those in the wages council sector.

But, as pointed out above, the secondary employment conditions of wages council industries can not be overcome by the removal of institutional constraints alone. The industrial structure and the economic conditions prevailing in low-paying industries are likely to ensure the persistence of secondary-employment conditions. And as economic conditions change, new secondary employment sectors may develop so that selective minimum wage machinery is unlikely to provide sufficient protection over time. Moreover, so long as there is a supply of cheap and easily available labour, exploitation is likely to continue, even in industries in which wages generally are adequate. Wages councils can, to some extent, provide minimum protection in these circumstances, but they do not cover all vulnerable workers. Hence Craig et al. (1982) concluded that the policy of abolishing wages councils was misguided. Minimum protection should be extended by the introduction of a national minimum wage rather than reduced through the abolition of wages councils. A national minimum wage could provide 'much needed protection for both workers and employers against the worst abuses of low pay produced by an unregulated industrial system' (Craig et al., 1980e: 54).

Proposals for a national minimum wage were at the centre of industrial relations debate in the late 1960s and early 1970s, although enthusiasm for this approach subsequently evaporated among trade unions as part of their more general opposition to the wages policies of the Heath and Wilson Governments. For the next few years the trade unions resisted any proposals for state intervention in wage determination. By the early 1980s, however, there were signs that the climate was beginning to change once more in favour of an approach which combined collective action with legal measures to tackle low wages including a national minimum wage. David Basnett, General Secretary of the GMWU and Chairman of the TUC Economic Committee, argued for the extension of legal minimum standards on pay, hours of work, job security, holidays, sick pay, and pensions. 'We need such legislation because we have to face the fact that in too many of these areas free collective bargaining has failed adequately to protect the most vulnerable of workers' (Basnett, 1982). This willingness to consider a wider role for legislation on minimum wages and other conditions to underpin (but not to replace) collective bargaining was echoed in other sections of the trade union movement (see, for example, LPU, 1982a). The reports of ACAS also indicate increased acceptance of the arguments for minimum wage regulation.

A minimum wage would not by itself eradicate low pay, but it would provide a floor on which other elements of wages policy might be built. It might, for example, have a disproportionate effect in raising the relative earnings of women, who represent the majority of the low paid. In this respect it might have a more significant impact on women's earnings than the Equal Pay Act, which appeared by the mid-1970s to have exhausted its effectiveness in closing the gap between men's and women's earnings. But improvements in the operation of the Equal Pay Act itself would remain necessary (Glucklich and Snell, 1982; MacLennan, 1980). In the public sector, where low pay persists despite the absence of the industrial and economic conditions traditionally associated with secondary sector employment, a minimum wage would also help. However, it would need to be accompanied by mechanisms which allowed appropriate comparisons of public sector rewards with those available in private sector employment.

Some have argued that an annual incomes policy is a necessary prerequisite to tackling low pay. Low pay criteria were built into the pay policies of the late 1960s and mid 1970s but the experience of such policies in this respect was disappointing, having little effect on relative earnings. This is largely because the policies were designed with broader macro-economic objectives in mind; the low pay criteria were often added to render the policies fairer in their effects, but they could not have been expected to make significant inroads into the problem itself (see Playford, 1980).

Although general minimum wages have been adopted in an increasing number of countries in recent years (Starr, 1981), proposals for a national minimum wage in Britain have been opposed, principally in the belief that the unemployment consequences would be unacceptable. The belief that an increase in wages will result automatically in a decline in employment rests precariously, as noted above, on the neo-classical assumption that wages—in all circumstances—already equal the marginal product of labour. As the ILO has noted, however:

> as exceptionally low wages are raised, there may be increases in productivity either because of induced management improvements or because of greater labour efficiency due to a decrease in wasteful labour turnover and industrial disputes . . . if higher wages, at least over a certain range, are accompanied by significant improvements in labour productivity, it is conceivable that labour costs could decrease rather than increase and to such an extent employment would not fall. There would also be no need to expect a decline in employment as a result of minimum wage increases, at least within a specified range, if some wages previously had been maintained at an exceptionally low level because of weaknesses in the bargaining position of individual workers (Starr, 1981:157).

In addition to improvements in productivity, the employment effects of a minimum wage might be mitigated by other factors. At the industry level, the existence of minimum wage regulation, by preventing competition based on wage undercutting, can protect employers who might otherwise go out of business. This need not imply a loss of efficiency, but rather competition based on factors other than wage costs, such as quality, design, and reliability. At the macro-economic level, in circumstances of unemployment and under-utilisation of resources, the introduction of a minimum wage might increase the overall level of employment in the same way as a fiscal stimulus. Indeed, this form of reflation might be expected to be more effective than some types of fiscal measure because of the low savings and low import-propensity of the low-income households which would benefit most. The employment effects resulting from a minimum wage will depend on the balance of forces acting in opposite directions, on the circumstances in which the minimum is introduced, and on the level at which it is set. The evidence from general inquiries, special surveys and econometric analysis in a number of advanced and developing countries is inconclusive in indicating whether minimum wages result in an increase or a decrease in overall employment (Starr, 1981).

Other objections relate to the inflationary impact of increasing wages at the lower end of the distribution and on the compression of differentials that might result. It was noted earlier that the increase in the total wage bill resulting from a raising of the wages of the low paid to a level equivalent to two-thirds the median was small. Metcalf (1981) assessed the increase to be less than 3 per cent; the estimates by Atkinson et al. (1982) implied a cost which was slightly higher, but no more than 5 per cent. Hence, even though these additional wage costs would be concentrated in particular industries, the direct effect on inflation would be small.

Unless differentials were compressed, however, there might be indirect effects resulting from increased earnings for workers who were not themselves low paid. Some have argued that pressures to restore differentials following the introduction of a minimum wage would 'jack up' the entire wage structure, leaving the low paid no better off in relative terms. This is a legitimate concern, but it needs to be placed in its proper perspective. Since low pay is concentrated in (but not confined to) industries in which earnings generally are below average, an increase in the earnings of all workers in these sectors, without disturbance of traditional differentials, would still leave the low paid generally better off. A narrowing of relativities between industries or occupations, however, may be necessary, and as Chapter 13 warns attempts to reduce relativities may be met with considerable resistance.

It is largely because social and institutional factors are so important in determining wage inequalities that the economic effects of trying to tackle low pay directly are difficult to assess. The impact on employment and inflation of introducing a minimum wage will depend on the balance between forces operating in opposite directions. Although the available evidence is inconclusive, the prospect of detrimental effects on employment, inflation, or differentials arising from the introduction of a minimum wage cannot be dismissed. But these effects might be associated with any measure which effectively increased the relative wages of the low paid, and not with a minimum wage alone. Such problems must be tackled as they arise. Unless low wages are accepted as a permanent feature of the British economy, with the hardship and industrial inefficiency with which they are associated, decisive policies are now necessary.

9   The Pattern of Collective Industrial Action

P. K. Edwards

The purpose of this chapter is to analyse recent trends in industrial action and to relate them to other aspects of British industrial relations. Its title indicates its scope. First, it is not about industrial conflict in the broad sense in which that term is used to refer to the basic clash of interests between employers and workers. It is specifically about industrial action, that is the use of sanctions in the course of bargaining. Second, it is about collective action. As is frequently pointed out, conflict can occur in a wide variety of forms including absenteeism, labour turnover, and sabotage. It is not possible to cover this great range of behaviour here. Third, however, the chapter goes beyond the usual concern with patterns of strikes as revealed in official figures. Given the enormous attention which strikes receive in popular discussions, it is important to indicate what the figures show and what conclusions can be drawn from them. But, in addition, the chapter uses survey and case study material to put the official figures in the context of workplace action more generally. After examining strike trends and the distribution of strike activity it therefore considers industrial action other than strikes before assessing the place of strikes in the pattern of British industrial relations.

STRIKE TRENDS

Measuring Strikes

The only comprehensive national data on strikes come from the Department of Employment, which regularly produces figures on the three main dimensions of strike activity (the number of strikes, the number of workers involved, and the number of working days 'lost'), as well as a variety of classifications of the figures such as the distribution of strikes by their size and length. The accuracy of these official data has been the subject of much debate (for example, Turner, 1969a; Fisher, 1973; Shalev, 1978), and only a few aspects of that debate will be touched here.

The Department does not attempt to count every strike that occurs. All stoppages for 'political' reasons are excluded from the published figures.

And no strike involving fewer than ten workers or lasting less than a day is included unless it involves the 'loss' of at least 100 working days. Since the reporting of strikes is not obligatory, it is also possible that stoppages which meet the Department's criteria are not included in its figures. The only systematic analysis of these problems suggests, on the basis of a survey of manufacturing industry, that about 62 per cent of strikes that meet the criteria are in fact included in the figures. There is also a very large number of short, small strikes which fall outside the Department's definitions; the survey estimated that there are one and a half times as many strikes lasting less than a day as there are strikes of a day or more, and hence that the official figures represent only about a quarter of the total number of strikes (Brown, 1981:98–100). The significance of very short strikes, which are often seen as among the key characteristics of British workplace relations, will be considered later in the chapter. While the widespread nature of these strikes means that the published figures do not measure the true number of strikes, these figures can be used to examine broad trends. Since recording practices have remained largely the same the figures should pick up the same sort of strikes from one year to the next, so that changes in the number recorded reflect real changes in the number of strikes coming within the Department's criteria. More detailed breakdowns must, however, be treated with more caution. For example it is often said that short strikes are particularly prevalent in sectors such as the car industry, which will mean that the official figures on the industrial distribution of strikes will underestimate the relative strike proneness of these sectors.

The figures for workers involved and days 'lost' tend to be more accurate measures than the estimate of the number of strikes. This is because workers involved and days lost are concentrated in a few large stoppages. But there are difficulties in interpreting these figures. Both sets of figures are based on estimates of the number of workers who are on strike, or are laid off as a result, in plants where a strike is taking place; workers laid off in other plants as a result of a strike are not included. This may underestimate the effects of a strike, even assuming that, in a situation in which employers and workers have differing interests in estimating the effectiveness of a strike, accurate numbers can be obtained within the struck plants. Figures for days 'lost', on the other hand, may exaggerate the costs of strikes. There are cases in which management have encouraged strikes at times when their order books are empty, so that no production was 'lost'. And estimates of losses often assume that, in the absence of a strike, production would have carried on at full capacity and that no 'lost' output is made up after the strike. In other cases, as in the transport or service industries, a strike may cause inconvenience without meaning that the level of production in the economy as a whole is reduced in proportion to the number of days 'lost'.

In the following discussion figures for worker involvement and days lost will be used as rough indicators of the extent of strike action. In many ways, however, it is the trend in the number of strikes which is most important, for this shows, albeit imperfectly, how often workers have been prepared to stop work in disputes with management.

The Number and Length of Strikes

The main indices of strike activity for the years between 1960 and 1981 are shown in Table 9.1. The table gives figures for all industries and for all industries apart from coal mining; the trend in coal was very different from that elsewhere and the aggregate figures thus obscure the picture in most of the economy. As will be seen in more detail later, at the start of the 1960s coal mining dominated the strike picture, with the industry accounting for 59 per cent of all strikes in 1960. By 1970 this proportion had fallen to 4 per cent. Hence, while the overall number of strikes showed a modest increase

TABLE 9.1: STRIKE TRENDS, 1960–1981

| | ALL INDUSTRIES | | | | % Strikes Lasting Less Than 3 Days | EXCLUDING COAL MINING | | | |
	S	W	D	D/W		S	W	D	D/W
1960	2832	819	3024	3·7	76·7	1166	582	2530	4·3
1961	2686	779	3016	3·9	73·7	1228	530	2279	4·3
1962	2449	4423	5798	1·3	72·6	1244	4268	5490	1·3
1963	2068	593	1755	3·0	75·2	1081	441	1429	3·2
1964	2524	883	2277	2·6	75·3	1466	711	1975	2·8
1965	2354	874	2925	3·3	68·8	1614	756	2513	3·3
1966	1937	544	2398	4·4	68·0	1384	494	2280	4·6
1967	2116	734	2787	3·8	65·6	1722	693	2682	3·9
1968	2378	2258	4690	2·1	61·0	2157	2228	4636	2·1
1969	3116	1665	6846	4·1	62·3	2930	1520	5807	3·8
1970	3906	1801	10980	6·1	54·9	3746	1683	9890	5·9
1971	2228	1178	13551	11·5	50·7	2093	1155	13488	11·7
1972	2497	1734	23909	13·8	48·5	2273	1392	13111	9·4
1973	2873	1528	7197	4·7	49·0	2572	1481	7107	4·8
1974	2922	1626	14750	9·1	42·8	2736	1319	9125	6·9
1975	2282	809	6012	7·4	40·7	2070	781	5960	7·6
1976	2016	668	3284	4·9	46·7	1740	630	3214	5·1
1977	2703	1166	10142	8·7	41·0	2441	1113	10054	9·0
1978	2471	1042	9405	9·0	42·4	2133	938	9210	9·8
1979	2080	4608	29474	6·4	42·0	1782	4555	29361	6·4
1980	1330	834	11964	14·3	51·4	1028	748	11812	15·8
1981	1338	1513	4266	2·8	55·5	1036	1415	4031	2.8

Source: Derived from the *Employment Gazette*, published by the Department of Employment and its predecessors, annual articles on stoppages of work due to industrial disputes.
Note: S is number of strikes beginning in year. W and D are, respectively, numbers of workers involved and days lost (in thousands) in strikes in progress during year. Hence D/W is the number of days lost per worker involved.

of about one third between 1960 and 1970, the number outside coal more than trebled. The upsurge in the number of strikes, however, halted after 1970: during the 1970s the number fluctuated around a level well below the peak of 1970 although above the average level of the 1960s. This was followed by a dramatic fall in 1980: the number of strikes was the smallest recorded since 1942, and the low level of strike activity continued during the early 1980s.

How can this remarkable series of fluctuations be explained? Commentators differ in their emphases, but there is remarkable agreement on the main factors to be taken into account: the changing structure of collective bargaining and the impact of incomes policies, price inflation, and unemployment are commonly mentioned (Hyman, 1977:180–89; Clegg, 1979:278; Coates and Topham, 1980:222). The problem, however, is to explain why these influences have had an effect on strike activity. It is one thing to provide a list of possible influences on strike patterns and another to explain how these influences have come together to affect particular aspects of strikes. The debate about strikes tends to take place, moreover, at several levels ranging from specific questions about the frequency or length of stoppages, through arguments about Britain's relative strike-proneness and the damage caused by disputes, to general issues of the cause and nature of industrial conflict. The present discussion concentrates on the most immediate level of assessing the different factors which have been identified as influences on strike patterns.

Collective bargaining. During the 1960s changes in workplace bargaining created an increasingly fertile environment for strikes. The Donovan Commission (1968) argued that the rise in the number of strikes was due to the progressive breakdown of the 'formal' system of industrial relations and the rise of the 'informal' system. Clegg (1979:277) has elaborated what he dubs the Donovan theory of postwar strikes: rising wage drift encouraged the fragmentation of bargaining while the growing number of shop stewards and the increasing volume of workplace bargaining contributed to the ability of workers to exploit the possibilities that this presented. This is, of course, far from a complete theory. As Clegg goes on to note, it was 'not grounded in any detailed investigation of the evidence', being little more than a plausible linking together of observed strike trends with presumed trends in workplace bargaining. There was little evidence, such as would be provided by studies of companies with a growing volume of shopfloor bargaining and with severe wage drift, with which to back up the argument. There was, moreover, no real explanation of the trends which were observed. As Crossley (1968) pointed out at the time, Donovan tended to assume that the trends were immutable and that describing them served to explain why they were taking place, the implication being that they would necessarily continue. One dramatic illustration of the dangers of treating trends as inevitable was provided by the prediction by McCarthy (1970:233) that the increase in strike frequency to 1970 showed no sign of abating, a prediction made when the increase was about to be reversed.

The analysis was, however, correct in so far as it identified a key development in the nature of workplace relations. British industrial relations have long been characterised by strong organisation at workplace level. But it was only during the 1970s, with the unprecedented period of sustained full employment after 1945, that the power of workplace organisations become firmly enough established to challenge management strenuously and frequently. One consequence was the emergence of the small unofficial strike which so concerned governments and analysts during the late 1960s.

The Donovan Commission laid particular emphasis on the growth during the 1960s of the short workplace-based strike. The data in Table 9.1 apparently contradict this argument, for the proportion of all strikes lasting less than three days fell from 77 per cent in 1960 to 55 per cent in 1970. There are, however, no publicly-available figures on the length of strikes outside coal mining. Since most coal strikes were very short and since the number of strikes in the industry was falling rapidly, it is likely that the decline in the importance of the short strike was due to trends peculiar to the coal industry. It is possible to assess what was happening in the rest of industry by making various assumptions about the distribution of coal strikes by length and subtracting these estimated figures from the aggregate totals. As Edwards (1982:11–12) shows, if it is assumed that all coal strikes lasted less than three days, the proportion of short strikes in the rest of industry rose: the proportion lasting less than three days, for example, would have increased from 20 per cent in 1957 to 43 per cent in 1960 and 60 per cent in 1969. The most plausible interpretation is certainly that there was some increase in the number of short strikes during the 1960s.

Since 1970 matters have been less straightforward, for the expected impact on strikes of the various trends that have taken place has been less clear than was the case during the 1960s. As previous chapters have shown, workplace bargaining has changed considerably, with a rapid growth in the number of shop stewards and with these stewards playing an increasingly important role in bargaining as negotiation at plant and company level has become more significant. According to the Donovan model the increasing volume of bargaining, together with the presence of more shop stewards, would be expected to be associated with more strikes. At the same time, however, the nature of bargaining has changed, with a growth in the prevalence of disputes procedures and with a formalised structure replacing the informality of the 1960s. Some reformers expected these developments to reduce the number of strikes, at least in those parts of private industry where the 'informal system' had become most firmly established. The evidence here is far from conclusive. One study of 45 manufacturing plants in six industries found that, as against 'reformist' expectations, 'labour unrest' tended to be higher in those plants with formal collective agreements and conciliation procedures than in other plants. It suggested that, since it was implausible to suppose that a plant's strike record caused management to standardise and formalise its operations, it was reasonable to infer that formalisation tended to encourage unrest (Turner et al., 1977:36–9). The measure of unrest was, however, the number of days lost per worker. Since institutional reform was meant to prevent small strikes this measure, which is heavily influenced by one or two big disputes, does not provide the most relevant test. And a survey of plants at one time cannot show whether firms which reformed their bargaining arrangements were able, over time, to reduce their incidence of strikes.

One recent study provides some illustrative material on this question. In one large engineering factory management had tried to reduce shopfloor 'disorder' by centralising its bargaining arrangements and by replacing the piecework wage payment system with measured day work. These reforms might be expected to reduce the number of pay and other disputes at shopfloor level. Yet managerial records, which included any stoppage lasting over an hour and which were thus very sensitive to the small disputes allegedly characteristic of unreformed systems, showed that the number of strikes was unchanged (Edwards and Scullion, 1982a:235–7). This plant exemplifies one type of reform: management attempted to change the form of bargaining without altering the substance of shopfloor industrial relations, and the number of strikes was unchanged. In other cases reform may have been more successful, although there is little hard evidence to support such an argument. More generally, as Hyman (1977:183–4) has argued, reform was a complex and often contradictory process: the introduction of new procedures could be a source of conflict, and in the longer-term the centralisation of bargaining could encourage lengthy plant-wide strikes in place of short and relatively painless shopfloor stoppages (Durcan and McCarthy, 1972). Far from resolving the 'problem' of strikes, reform may reduce one aspect of the problem only to replace it with another, possibly more intractable, aspect.

The tendency of 'reform' to shift disputes away from the shopfloor may, then, have contributed to the lengthening of strikes noted above. In other respects, however, the relationship between strike patterns and the structure of bargaining became increasingly uncertain during the 1970s. As well as the ambiguities of the process of reform itself broader economic and political factors meant that bargaining was far from being the only influence at work.

Economic and political conditions. There is a long tradition of correlating fluctuations in the number of strikes with the state of the economy, the usual argument being that strikes will be concentrated in booms when workers' bargaining power is greatest. Before examining these economic models it will be useful to continue the discussion of the changing length of strikes.

Although the lengthening of strikes is one of the more dramatic features of strike statistics, and although a broad influence on this can be identified in bargaining reform, there has been little detailed work on the relationship between economic conditions and the length of strikes. Much of the discussion must therefore be speculative. A close link between strike length and the state of the economy should not be expected. As Skeels (1971) argues in assessing data from the United States, the decision to call a strike is likely to be made in the light of the chances of success, so that fluctuations in the number of stoppages will reflect economic factors, whereas how long a strike lasts will depend on a wide range of influences and will not be so directly related to economic conditions. A broader association may, however, be present. The 1970s were characterised by rising rates of unemployment and a very high rate of inflation. On the former, it is often argued that recessions will be associated with long strikes because employers can afford to take a long stoppage and because they will try to recoup the concessions made to workers during the previous boom; strikes then become bitter battles (Hill and Thurley, 1974). On the latter, inflation in the context of slow economic growth meant that workers faced substantial problems of maintaining real wages while employers suffered a squeeze on profits. Hence, in contrast to the 1960s, strikes became lengthier battles, with employers feeling that they could not afford to give way and with workers having to fight hard even to maintain their living standards. This tendency may have been further encouraged by the reform of bargaining structures noted above.

The large number of econometric studies of strike frequency (Pencavel, 1970; Shorey, 1977; Davies, 1979) may suggest that the causes of trends in the number of strikes can be identified with more confidence. But these studies must be treated with caution. As Smith et al. (1978:67) note in their review of economists' models, different studies have produced very different estimates of the effect of the state of the labour market on the number of strikes. Moreover, as suggested above, the theoretical rationale for the expectation of an inverse relationship between the unemployment rate, which is the usual measure of the state of the labour market, and the number of strikes is far from obvious: workers may have more reason to strike in a recession than in a boom if they have to defend themselves against an employer's attack, and, in a boom, employers may be willing to grant workers' demands without a strike (for elaboration of this point see Mayhew, 1979). The empirical evidence for a precise and stable link between a variable such as the unemployment rate and the number of strikes is far from convincing, and the theoretical bases of the models are less firm than might at first appear. The question of the stability of relationships is particularly important. There may be a tendency for rising unemployment to reduce the number of strikes but, between one cycle of economic activity and the next, a given level of unemployment may be associated with different numbers of strikes. Hence the study by Davies (1979) showed that the level of unemployment did not explain variations in strike activity, although the rate of change of unemployment was important. More generally, all the relationships considered by the models relate only to the specific periods under investigation: one consequence is, as Davies remarks, that models specified for one period may not work for another, so that, for example, the great upsurge of strike activity at the end of the 1960s could not be explained by models based on relationships in other periods.

What conclusions can, then, be drawn from these models? One influential explanation of the experience of the late 1960s was that inflation, together with the effects of the tax system, was eroding workers' real take-home pay: the association between real wage trends and the number of strikes and working days lost was seen as 'pretty conclusive evidence that the sharp increase in the British strike-incidence was a response to the stagnation of net real wages' (Jackson et al., 1972:88). Davies' results for the period from 1966 to 1975 confirm the association between price changes (or, to be exact, a variable proxying expectations of future price increases) and the number of strikes. As just noted, Davies also found that the rate of change of unemployment was significant. In view of the dramatic growth of unemployment since 1975 this point needs considering further. It is certainly likely that the very rapid rise in unemployment which occurred during the late 1970s and early 1980s was a prime cause of the dramatic fall in the number of strikes. Case study material indicates some of the processes at work. A study cited earlier (Edwards and Scullion, 1982a), in which the fieldwork was carried out between 1978 and 1980, found that managements in several of the factories studied were explicitly linking wage offers to the number of jobs: the recession was reducing profits and creating spare capacity, and workers were told that the only way to save their jobs was to accept low wage increases. Evidence such as this suggests that a qualitative shift may have occurred in the link between strikes and unemployment. During periods of relative prosperity workers and employers may not have had to concern themselves directly with the overall rate of unemployment, and any relation between changes in unemployment and strikes may have reflected the impact of business activity more generally on workers' bargaining power. By the late 1970s there was a more direct association between jobs and strikes, for many employers were making it clear that militancy would endanger workers' own jobs. Unemployment, then, can be used to explain strike trends, but the meaning of the relationship between it and strikes has altered as the recession has deepened.

Finally, the role of incomes policies must be considered. The impact of incomes policies on strikes has been as controversial as that on any aspect of industrial relations. Early econometric work focused on the contrast between 'policy on' and 'policy off' periods. This simple dichotomy was expanded by Hunter (1973), who distinguished between periods of 'hard' incomes policy (characterised by strict government enforcement of the policy, sometimes backed up by statutory provisions) and 'soft' policies. This was taken further by Davies (1979) who identified the period of a year at the end of each phase of incomes policies as one of 're-entry' to free collective bargaining. Davies noted the common argument that the breakdown of incomes policies tends to create an upsurge of strikes, but there had been no work which estimated the strength of the 're-entry' effect once other factors were taken into account. Davies showed that, even allowing for the effects of the other variables, there was a strong tendency for re-entry to increase the number of strikes. He also showed that the period of incomes policy itself had no significant effect on the total number of strikes. This was because they reduced the number of strikes over pay issues while increasing the number over other matters.

Even the distinction between hard, soft, and re-entry phases, together with that between pay and non-pay strikes, may however be insufficient to capture the complexities of incomes policies. As Hyman (1977:189) points out, the Social Contract was associated, in its early days at least (1975–6), with low levels of strike activity; this could be attributed to official trade union acceptance of the policy and to the ability of union leaders to persuade their members to accept it. Are these events to be summed up as examples of 'hard' policy, in that the government was fairly firmly committed to it and union leaders were willing to try to impose it on the rank and file, or a 'soft' policy, in that there was none of the rigid statutory enforcement which characterised earlier policies? If it is accepted that the social contract policy was a very different animal from earlier incomes policies then trying to find relationships which are the same for all norms, guidelines and understandings which come under the rubric of incomes policies becomes futile.

Some general conclusions are, however, warranted. First, in certain circumstances and for a limited period, the combination of coercion and persuasion can reduce the number of strikes. Second, however, the work of Davies provides clear evidence that, even when other factors have been taken into account, the operation of incomes policies need not reduce the total number of strikes, and that the breakdown of an incomes policy is associated with a rise in the number. It is widely accepted, for example, that the dramatic rise in the number of strikes during 1969 and 1970 was due in part to collapse of the the incomes policy which had been instituted in 1966. It is true that, as Table 9.1 shows, the demise of the Social Contract was not marked by a similar rise. But, as noted, above, rapidly rising unemployment meant that the economic context was very different. It is quite possible that, when influences such as unemployment have been taken into account, the period of 're-entry' would still tend to increase the number of strikes. Third, the institutional, as well as the economic, context of incomes policies must be taken into account. Hence Hyman argues that the institutional reforms of the 1970s enabled union leaders to exert a more direct control over their members than had been possible during the 1960s when the gap between the 'formal' and 'informal' systems of industrial relations had been so marked. Put in this way, the argument is too simple, for unions differed in the extent to which the rank and file was 'incorporated' into the official hierarchy, and it is questionable how far leaders were able directly to impose agreements on an unwilling membership (England, 1981). But there certainly have been circumstances in which acquiescence in incomes policies has been achieved and in which the degree of union acceptance of the policies has been an important factor.

Conclusions. The most general conclusion to be drawn is that attempts to explain strike trends which rely exclusively on changes in the structure of collective bargaining or on economic trends are equally unsatisfactory. During the 1960s and 1970s collective bargaining was increasingly affected by broader economic and political developments, so that, although the rise in the number of strikes during the 1960s is consistent with trends in workplace bargaining, subsequent developments have owed a great deal to other influences. These external influences, however, have operated in particular institutional contexts. The 'success' of econometric models of strike frequency does not imply, contrary to the claims of some users of such models, that explanations can ignore institutional factors. As noted above, even in their own terms the models have several important limitations. In addition, there are structural shifts in the relationships between the variables included in the model which have to be explained by factors external to them.

In summary, a rough-and-ready distinction may be made between the 1960s and the 1970s and early 1980s. During the former the rise of shopfloor bargaining power gave workers the organisational resources to engage in large numbers of strikes. The volume of workplace bargaining, together with pressures on workers' real wages associated with inflation and characteristics of the tax system, provided ample opportunities for the use of this power. Relatively low levels of unemployment meant that the use of bargaining power was less constrained than it was later. The main constraint was provided by incomes policies between 1966 and 1968, but their overall effect seems to have been slight, while their breakdown during 1969 and 1970 gave the upward trend in the number of strikes a powerful push.

All of this argument is directed at the question of strikes. It does not imply that the growth of workplace bargaining was universal. As many critics (e.g. Hawkins, 1976:71–5) have argued, the Donovan report tended to generalise from a few industries, notably cars and engineering, to the rest of the economy whereas in fact many industries did not experience any dramatic disjuncture between the formal and informal systems. But if the problem is to explain the rise in the number of strikes this point is less relevant: the rise reflected trends in particular industries to which the Donovan theory of strikes, suitably amended to take account of other influences, is applicable. During the 1970s post-Donovan reform may have tended to reduce the number of strikes, although the evidence here is not strong. It may be put forward more confidently as an explanation of the rise in the length of stoppages. Although the pressures of inflation became greater than they were during the 1960s rising unemployment and a succession of incomes policies tended to counteract these pressures. Hence the number of strikes fluctuated according to the precise state of the labour market and the form of incomes policy being employed. There was no general upward or downward trend until the end of the decade when rapidly rising unemployment was associated with a steep fall in the number of strikes.

Worker Involvement and Days Lost

Perhaps the most obvious feature of strikes in the recent past has been the re-emergence of the large official strike. It is this type of strike which has the greatest impact on worker involvement and days lost: between 1960 and 1979, 46 per cent of all days lost occurred in just sixty-four big disputes (Department of Employment, 1980a). Many, although certainly not all, of these strikes have been in the public sector and have involved hitherto generally strike-free groups such as civil servants and health service and local authority workers. As several commentators have pointed out this pattern can be related fairly directly to incomes policies and other attempts to control inflation. Although the overall relationship between wages in the public and private sectors may not have moved against the former, specific groups have felt unfairly treated and existing agreements have been disrupted (Dean, 1981:58–62). Workers have been forced into industrial action in the face of attempts to use the public sector to hold down wages. The civil servants' dispute of 1979, for example, involved a group of workers for whom only a few years previously such a long battle would have been unthinkable. The dispute was occasioned by the government's offer of a wage increase which was not only lower than many offers elsewhere but was also based on a refusal to use existing agreements for settling civil servants' pay.

Given the importance of the public sector to the government in persuading private employers to follow pay guidelines it is not surprising that public sector workers have increasingly engaged in strikes. And the prevalence of national agreements means that the strikes have been conducted at the national level and thus that they have involved large numbers of workers. But it must not be forgotten that national strikes have often been preceded or accompanied by local action. This neglected aspect of public sector strikes requires some consideration here.

In sectors such as local authorities and the health service traditional bargaining arrangements have been changing rapidly. As Chapter 7 and Terry (1982) have shown, the growth of personnel management and formal disputes procedures, together with the use of job evaluation and incentive schemes, indicates a dramatic change in management's approach, away from the traditional cosy way of doing things towards a stress on the efficient use of manpower. This managerially-induced disruption of traditional relationships made overt conflict more likely. Although itself a reaction to the initial wave of unofficial action during the late 1960s the 'reform', like that in the private sector, was double-edged: it put relationships on a formal basis but also strengthened the position of the growing number of shopfloor activists and made levels of effort and reward topics for explicit bargaining. As Terry (1982:7–8) found in his survey of thirty local authorities carried out during 1979, managers in every authority surveyed reported some form of industrial action over a two-year period, with 60 per cent reporting a strike lasting a day or more. As will be seen below, the figures are much higher than those reported in surveys of manufacturing industry. This is at first sight very surprising, but one is not really comparing like with like. Terry's local authorities were much larger than the average manufacturing plant, and proneness to industrial action increases sharply with size; when manufacturing plants and local authorities of similar size are compared the difference disappears. Moreover, even units of the same size are not directly comparable, for a local authority employing, say, a thousand workers will be composed of many different groups of workers, each of which may be involved in its own disputes; a manufacturing plant is more likely to operate as a unit.

Local authority and other public sector workers probably remain less strike-prone than workers elsewhere. The official figures give an average of 5·2 strikes per 100,000 workers in local authorities in the period 1970–75, as against 22·9 in manufacturing and 12·4 in all industries (Smith et al., 1978:104). But the emergence of new forms of local action remains a significant development which shares several features of the rise of strikes in the private sector earlier. In addition, local organisation has provided a crucial basis for the effective mobilisation of action at national level.

The overall pattern of strikes in the public sector is hard to assess since the published figures on the distribution of strikes by industry do not allow the public and private sectors to be clearly separated. A simple comparison between the two sectors is, moreover, affected by the character of the industries which make them up: an average for the public sector that includes the coal industry will give a misleading impression of strike activity in the sector as a whole. Some broad trends can, however, be identified. Clegg (1976c) estimates that predominantly public sector industries other than coal and steel accounted for between 1 and 8 per cent of strikes, but for 20 per cent of total employment, between 1949 and 1974. More detailed figures for 1966–76 permit a finer separation between the two sectors and generally confirm that the non-coal public sector has had a lower proneness to strikes than the private sector (Smith et al., 1978:25). There appears to have been no marked change in the relative strike-proneness of the two sectors.

Large strikes have, of course, occurred outside the public sector, but they have reflected a wide variety of influences which cannot be summarised within a few neat patterns. For example, by far the largest strike in the period since 1960, the national engineering stoppage of 1979, was the product of very specific forces which have little in common with those lying behind other large strikes. Thus, although writers such as Hyman (1977:187) stress the role of rank and file pressure in forcing union leaders into militant postures, this strike at least was characterised by considerable scepticism at the base both about the initial decision to call a stoppage and about the subsequent conduct of the dispute (Edwards and Scullion, 1982b).

The re-emergence of the large national strike has, then, reflected a variety of forces, although the large confrontations in the public sector around incomes policies have been perhaps the most notable. These developments must not, however, be seen in isolation. Incomes policies should not be separated from the increased stress on efficiency in the public sector, for both reflected the growing pressures on the sector: the series of crises which affected the economy as a whole were felt particularly acutely here, with successive governments stressing the need to reduce deficits and fight inflation. The strikes cannot be understood outside this context. They provide one of the sharpest of illustrations of the way in which strike patterns have reflected broad economic and political pressures and not just the structure of bargaining. It must not be forgotten, however, that the great majority of strikes remained small and short. Consideration of dramatic confrontations should not divert attention from this fact.

THE DISTRIBUTION OF STRIKE ACTIVITY

Distribution between Industries

An immediate question which arises from an analysis of overall trends is whether these trends have been uniform across all industries or whether they have been concentrated in particular sectors. A further question is how the marked differences between the strike records of different industries can be explained.

As already indicated, trends in the coal industry were very different from those elsewhere. The decline in the number of coal strikes after 1957 is usually explained by declining levels of employment in the industry and by the changes in its bargaining structure which were associated with mechanisation and the replacement of fragmented piecework bargaining with a system of day work payment and which culminated in the national power loading agreement of 1966 (Clegg, 1979:273–4; Hyman, 1977:29). The possibility of sectional disputes was thus reduced, although it is never clear how much of a reduction would be predicted from arguments about bargaining structure: does the change in bargaining structure explain all the fall in the number of strikes or, alternatively, was the fall less marked than might have been expected? As Table 9.2 shows, the industry has continued to have more strikes per 100,000 workers than most parts of the economy. More generally, the distribution of strike activity has remained fairly stable, with the ranking of industries displaying little change (Silver,

1973). The rise in strike activity during the 1960s, in other words, was broadly based.

Illustrative strike figures for eleven industries are given in Table 9.2. The industries include the main strike-prone sectors, namely coal, the docks, iron and steel, shipbuilding, and motor vehicles, together with a range of sectors which tend to be relatively strike-free. Not too much weight should

TABLE 9.2: STRIKE INDICES, SELECTED INDUSTRIES, 1970–1980 (ANNUAL AVERAGES)

	Number of Strikes per 100,000 Employees		Number of Days Lost per 1000 Employees	
	1970–75	*1976–80*	*1970–75*	*1976–80*
Coal mining	63·2	100·2	9199	421
Docks	168·4	115·9	4187	1065
Iron and steel	41·1	28·4	1117	6938
Motor vehicles	49·2	37·4	3422	4494
Shipbuilding	43·3	22·1	2876	1023
Footwear	6·2	14·1	69	146
Furniture	10·3	8·4	70	68
Printing & publishing	6·3	9·3	178	757
Gas, electricity, water	4·2	5·7	202	130
Railways	5·0	4·4	130	267
Distribution	2·2	1·9	17	20
All industries	12·4	9·4	569	567

Source: Calculated from *Employment Gazette,* various issues. Where industrial definitions in the *Gazette* and in the more detailed analysis by Minimum List Heading are the same, data for 1970–75 are taken from Smith et al. (1978: tables 6 and 7).

be placed on the precise figures; the data on days lost will be affected by a few large stoppages and by differences between industries in the significance of counting as 'involved' only workers in plants actually on strike; and figures for the number of strikes will be affected by differences in recording practices. Other limitations will become apparent in the course of the following discussion.

Attempts to explain the distribution of activity have been carried out at a number of levels, with some writers assessing statistical patterns across a range of industries, others identifying the common features of strike-prone or strike-free sectors, and yet others analysing patterns in individual industries. The statistical analyses use measures such as average wage rates, plant sizes, and levels of unionisation to explain differences in strike measures (Shorey, 1975 and 1976; Holden, 1978). The analyses have been limited, however, by being restricted to fairly small numbers of industries, particularly those in the manufacturing sector, for which comparable data are available. More fundamentally, the meaning of observed patterns of association is often unclear. It is generally found, for example, that strike activity is directly related to the average size of plant in an industry. But it is unclear what these industry averages reveal about the causes of differences in strike rates. Most of the strikes recorded in official figures are concentrated in a few plants, and it has not been shown that the average plant size of an industry reflects the size of the minority of plants which account for the major part of its strikes. More generally, knowing that strike-prone industries share certain features such as a high average level of wages seems to contribute little directly to an understanding of the differences reflected in Table 9.2.

There is a further problem with statistical analyses which raises some issues of more general significance. It is common to employ a measure of union strength such as density, the general expectation being that such a measure will be positively associated with strike rates. But what is required is not a measure of whether workers belong to unions but the extent of the challenge which they make to managerial authority. Footwear, for example, has had a density of over 70 per cent since 1948 but it has not had the kind of union organisation which has challenged management on the shopfloor. Survey data make available a more sophisticated range of indices such as the number of shop stewards and the presence of full-time stewards, but even these do not directly measure the power of shopfloor organisations: Edwards and Scullion (1982a:271) found that most of their plants 'had full-time stewards and other characteristics that are often associated with union strength, but patterns of shopfloor relations were very different'. Two implications follow. First, union strength is unlikely to be accurately measured by even relatively sophisticated plant-level indices of union presence. Second, the link between strength and strike rates is uncertain; as is often pointed out, strong unions may not need to strike to attain their ends. There is, in any event, unlikely to be a stable relationship between 'union strength' and the number of strikes. What is required is an assessment of the characteristics of the strike-prone sectors and an explanation of how they have interacted to produce a high strike rate.

Clegg (1979:274–7) has provided an important step in this direction. He does not rely on such broad and unsatisfactory explanatory variables as plant size or technology but on specific features of the four most strike-prone industries of the late 1950s and the 1960s, namely coal, docks, cars, and shipbuilding. These industries shared two characteristics, fragmented bargaining and fluctuating earnings, which marked them off from other industries. Fragmented bargaining for Clegg creates the possibility of frequent bargaining pressure, while the uncertainty of earnings provides the impetus to exploit this possibility: 'there can be few more frustrating experiences for wage-earners than to suffer wide fluctuations in their earnings' (Clegg, 1979:273). It should be noted, however, that these sectors had a third common characteristic: well-developed union organis-ations with the ability to turn such frustrations into collective action. Although strong unions do not mean that strikes will necessarily occur, their presence is necessary if frustrations are to lead to collective protest.

This theory is consistent with various aspects of strikes such as the fall during the 1960s in the number of coal strikes, for the fragmentation of bargaining and the variability of earnings were both being reduced. It also fits the recent rise in the number of strikes in the industry reflected in Tables 9.1 and 9.2; after 1977 there was a move back to local bargaining with the introduction of an incentive payment system. Yet, as Clegg admits, several things remain unexplained. In particular, docks and cars remained very strike-prone during the 1970s despite changes in bargaining structures (associated, respectively, with de-casualisation and the shift to measured day work) which should have reduced strike activity. Clegg's explanation of this is that, as mentioned earlier, the process of reform was a considerable source of friction and that new bargaining arrangements created the possibility of new types of dispute over matters such as job re-grading. Yet this leaves the status of the original explanation in doubt: the strike-prone industries shared certain characteristics but changes in these characteristics were not sufficient to reduce the number of strikes. Moreover, as Goodman et al. (1977:60) point out, industries such as footwear have been characterised by fluctuating earnings and widespread use of piecework but have had very low levels of strike activity. Footwear has not, of course, had fragmented bargaining, which implies that for Clegg's theory to work fluctuating earnings and fragmented bargaining must both be present.

The presence of these factors is not sufficient to explain strike rates, as the qualifications about union organisation and the effects of changes in bargaining structures show. Clegg (1979:286) later adds a third qualification. He notes that the car and printing industries have both been characterised by the strength of their workplace organisations and that printing has had a low, and not a high, strike rate. The anomaly is explained by the technologies of the two industries: craft methods in printing provided a 'relatively high degree of job satisfaction' compared with the 'frustrations of assembly-line production' in the car industry. The argument that technological differences are the sole, or even the major, cause of differences in strike rates has fallen into disrepute. Many studies have shown that technology does not determine workers' attitudes and behaviour, for the same technology can be associated with markedly different responses (Gallie, 1978). As a well-known study of the car industry (Turner et al., 1967) showed, car workers do not see the boredom of the assembly line as a central problem, and the industry's strike experience had to be explained by features other than technology. It remains possible, of course, that technological differences between the car and printing industries can be used as part of an overall explanation. But, in view of the weight of evidence that car firms employing identical technologies have very different strike rates, to mention technology raises more questions than it answers. In particular there is no evidence that it is the 'frustrations' of assembly line work, and not the tactical advantages to be gained from stopping the track, which contributes to car workers' strike behaviour. Similarly, the rarity of strikes in printing may be due in part to the ability of print workers to wrest concessions from employers, who are anxious not to lose an extremely perishable commodity, without needing to strike.

There is, then, no all-embracing explanation of differences in the strike rates of various industries. Many explanatory factors, including, in addition to those mentioned above, the community integration of workers, skill levels, the proportion of the labour force accounted for by women, the concentration of ownership, and the characteristics of product markets, have been suggested. But once monocausal explanations have been rejected there remains little but an *ad hoc* listing of factors which can be multiplied endlessly. Multivariate analysis is in itself little help, for it is possible for several models to perform equally well statistically without there being any theoretical reason for choosing between them. And, since specific characteristics of industries tend to go together, it may be impossible to separate the effects of various 'influences'.

The solution is not to give up attempts at explanation but to consider the interactions between the characteristics of particular industries and the traditions and expectations which they develop. For example, the well-known thesis of Kerr and Siegel (1954), that the high strike rates of industries such as mining can be explained by the presence of 'isolated masses' of workers who are cut off from the rest of society, can be rejected as a total explanation: it does not explain, for example, why strike rates in industries such as mining vary between regions and countries and over time, and it has several logical and methodological weaknesses (Edwards, 1977). But one aspect of miners' strikes is the very high degree of solidarity displayed by the workers, and the determination with which strikes have been fought may have something to do with the community and work situations of miners. Strong historical traditions have meant that other features of the industry such as fluctuating earnings have taken on a quite different character from their role in other industries.

As Clegg (1979:280) rather despairingly puts it in explaining why reform on the docks and in the car industry did not reduce the number of strikes, 'striking can become something of a habit'. By this he means that 'the effect will come only when the workers have learned the lesson that sectional strikes do not pay off; and, if concessions are made despite centralised bargaining, the lesson may never be learned'. But there is a much wider sense in which striking becomes a habit. If workers find that the existing way of settling disputes serves their interests they may resist managerial attempts to teach them new lessons: it may not simply be a matter of management failing to implement reform but of direct resistance to it. Striking may then be far more than an outworn carry-over from past behaviour. It may be part of a tradition which is actively defended. In industries such as the docks the tradition of settling disputes by immediate action at the point of production is unlikely to disappear simply because pay bargaining has been 'reformed'. There are many other aspects of work relations which are sources of conflict and the resolution of these is likely to depend on long-estabished traditions.

Yet this is simply to suggest that the 'habit' of striking may be more firmly rooted than Clegg might imply. There is also a more fundamental point about the basis of his theory of strikes. Miners and dockers strike frequently not simply bcause their earnings have tended to fluctuate or because bargaining arrangements have allowed them to exploit the tactic of sectional stoppages. Industrial relations in their industries have been characterised by the presumption that disputes will be settled through immediate action at the point of production. The fragmentation of bargaining exacerbates this tendency. But it may itself be the product of a wider struggle between employers and workers: as argued above, reform may not work if workers find it in their interests to resist it and, similarly, the failure of employers to impose their own definition of order may be the product of resistance. In other words, factors which are used to explain relative strike-proneness are themselves the product of continuing struggles between workers and employers.

Some of these points will be developed in the final section. Their present purpose is to stress the earlier note of caution about the dangers of isolating factors which cause differences between industries. Time-series analysis can, by assuming that broad historical and institutional forces remain more or less constant, analyse fluctuations in strike activity in terms of the impact of a relatively small number of factors. In cross-sectional analysis, however, differences of history and tradition cannot be assumed away for they are central to the emergence of distinct strike patterns. Discussions such as this can merely point to the complexities involved and the dangers of simple explanations. There are several more detailed studies (in the case of the car industry, for example, those of Turner et al., 1967 and Friedman, 1977) which provide more developed accounts of the strike characteristics of specific sectors.

Distribution between Plants

Perhaps it is the characteristics of individual plants which account for the record of different 'industries'. This is, indeed, the logic of the study of official statistics mentioned earlier. It was found that, in any one year, only two per cent of manufacturing plants will experience an officially-recorded strike; over a three-year period only five per cent of plants had experienced stoppages, and this five per cent, representing 0·25 per cent of all manufacturing plants, accounted for a quarter of all strikes and two-thirds of all days lost (Smith et al., 1978:55). The study uses this finding to criticise 'generalised remedies for what are specific problems'; the Donovan Commission, for example, was wrong to stress general procedural reform when the strike problem was concentrated in a few plants with most of the economy being 'entirely strike-free' (Smith et al., 1978:90). This is, however, to miss the point of the Donovan analysis, which was that strikes were a symptom of an underlying malaise which was also expressed in restrictive practices, wage drift, the uncontrolled use of overtime, and so on. Hence Donovan rejected legalistic solutions to the 'strike problem' in the abstract and stressed that the symptoms would disappear only when the underlying cause was eradicated. And Donovan was, of course, concerned with precisely those strikes which never reach the official figures, namely short unofficial stoppages. The Commission concluded that 'industrial disharmony manifests itself in overt action on the shop floor more frequently than the official statistics imply' (1968:100). This conclusion is amply supported by subsequent surveys: in one comprehensive survey of manufacturing industry 33 per cent of plants reported having had at least one strike during a two-year period, and 29 per cent reported action short of a strike so that, in all, 46 per cent had experienced some form of industrial action (Brown, 1981:81). Industrial action of some form is remarkably widespread, although much of it is very short-lived: two-thirds of strikes in the survey were reported as lasting less than a day, and, depending on assumptions about the precise duration of these very short strikes, it appears that the average length of all strikes is between two and two-and-a-half days.

It has long been recognised that some plants are far more strike-prone than others (for example, McCarthy, 1966:22), and the survey found that 4 per cent of plants accounted for 49 per cent of all incidents of action. Yet the reasons for this have been little investigated. Further analysis of the survey showed that there was a clear tendency for large plants to be more strike-prone than small ones but that a variety of other influences which the studies cited earlier have been found to be important in explaining differences between industries, such as the proportion of total costs accounted for by wages and salaries and the proportion of the work force who were women, were unimportant (Edwards, 1981). It might also be expected from industry-level studies, and from general discussions of strikes which assume that strike-proneness is a characteristic of whole industries, that the industry in which a plant was located would have a powerful effect on its strike record. Only a very small part of the variance in the number of strikes could, however, be explained in this way (Edwards, 1981:148).

There are two important implications. First, although some models may perform well when tested against industry-level data, they break down when the focus is shifted to the most appropriate level for testing the effects of such things as establishment size, technology, and the type of payment system in operation, namely the individual plant itself. Second, the results strengthen the earlier argument that the cross-sectional analysis of strikes depends on detailed investigations of concrete cases and not on the identification of a few strike-inducing characteristics. The same survey data can be used to produce generally satisfactory statistical analyses of such things as union density (Bain and Elsheikh, 1980): on the effect of the proportion of women in the labour force, for example, if women tend not to join unions then plants with a female labour force will tend to have low levels of unionisation. But there is no such direct link in the case of strike rates since many questions of the nature of grievances, feelings of militancy, mobilisation, and managerial and union strategy intervene (Edwards, 1981:145).

The conclusion is negative but nonetheless important. The strike-proneness of industries or plants cannot be seen as the result of the operation of a few distinct 'independent variables'. Time-series analyses of strikes, and cross-sectional analyses of such things as union density, can abstract from the complexities of the real world to produce estimates of the relationships between the dependent variable and a set of independent variables. But in the case of differences in strike rates structural influences have highly changeable effects. This is not to suggest that none of the possible determinants mentioned above has any effect: payments systems which create uncertainty, for example, can plainly be a source of discontent. But, given the large number of theories and purported theories of differences in strike rates, it is important to be wary of easy explanations. Historical traditions, which are often used in accounts of other aspects of industrial relations, are the essential factor through which various influences are mediated.

INDUSTRIAL ACTION SHORT OF STRIKES

Given the lack of systematic information on actions other than strikes, trends in the use of such action are hard to identify. Writing in 1965 Flanders (1970d:112) suggested that there was an 'increasing use of "cut price" industrial action such as overtime bans, working to rule or going slow'. It is certainly likely that increasingly self-confident shopfloor organisations were employing a range of sanctions against management that disrupted production without causing their members to lose money. And the more recent survey evidence (Brown, 1981:81) suggests that, while it was slightly less common for plants to have experienced non-strike sanctions than to have had a strike, the total number of non-strike sanctions was greater than the number of strikes, so that 57 per cent of all incidents of industrial action took forms other than the total stoppage of work. Since previous surveys have not asked comparable questions, it is difficult to estimate trends. But there has been a consistent tendency for the proportion of plants reporting non-strike sanctions to fall relative to the proportion reporting strikes. One explanation advanced for this trend was that, with increasing unemployment, employers have been increasingly willing to resist limited sanctions so that the strike has become relatively more popular (Brown, 1981:85). But the comparison refers only to the proportion of plants experiencing certain types of action. Over the period under consideration (1968 to 1978) shop steward organisations were growing rapidly across a whole range of manufacturing industries. As suggested below, the sustained use of sanctions seems to depend on an established shopfloor organisation. Relatively youthful organisations will not have developed such an established position and may thus have relied more on the weapon of the strike. The use of non-strike sanctions, being confined to a limited range of plants, became (relatively) less prevalent.

Much of this can, however, be no more than guess-work. But several things can be said with more confidence. First, of course, non-strike sanctions are a popular form of pressure, for their deployment can be varied to meet tactical needs and can put pressure on management while involving few costs for workers. But, second, their use is far from universal. The deployment of sanctions on a regular basis in manufacturing industry depends on the presence of strong shopfloor organisation. The survey evidence shows that 48 per cent of plants in the well-organised vehicles industry had experienced action short of strikes, whereas the figure for clothing was only 5 per cent; and, while union density was not strongly related to proneness to have strikes, experience of non-strike sanctions was much higher in plants with high levels of density than it was elsewhere (Brown, 1981: 84, 89–90). And, in line with an earlier argument, case study material suggests that a high level of union membership may be necessary but not sufficient for the deployment of sanctions: a shopfloor organisation needs to have wrested from management considerable control over the planning of work before the withdrawal of cooperation in such planning, on which a successful deployment of sanctions depends, becomes possible. As Batstone et al. (1978:41) discovered in a well-organised vehicles plant, 'since many aspects of this day-to-day cooperation were negotiated continually between stewards and foremen or other members of management', withdrawing cooperation was a readily available sanction. But in plants where shopfloor control is less developed sanctions do not emerge naturally from the day-to-day process of bargaining. In plants where there is little collective awareness the notion of working to rule may be completely inapplicable because the rules are determined by management and are accepted unquestioningly by workers (Armstrong et al., 1981:107–12; Edwards and Scullion, 1982a:169–75).

This is a neglected but crucial point. In explaining why strikes, as well as non-strike sanctions, emerge in some situations and not others it is essential to have some understanding of the broad pattern of workplace relations. Theories based on the bargaining structure or the economic structure of the industry or firm are apparently more specific than theories which discuss strikes in the context of the general conflict between capital and labour because they identify particular factors which affect how this general conflict is expressed instead of treating all strikes as simply reflections of it. Yet they gain this precision at considerable cost. They treat the strike as the phenomenon to be explained, ignoring the relationship between strikes and other forms of action within the workplace. And they limit the range of explanatory variables to the proximate influences on strike rates, ignoring the context in which these influences operate. This is not to suggest that these approaches are simply wrong or inadequate: they point to a range of important factors which must be taken into account in explaining strike patterns; for certain purposes they can be perfectly adequate; and they are infinitely preferable to approaches which ignore variations and complexities to stress the conflictual nature of capitalism. The point is simply that these approaches do not mark the end of inquiry. The workplace studies mentioned above show that the ability to deploy collective sanctions rests on the nature of shopfloor organisation, which is itself the product of struggle between workers and employers. This context determines whether influences such as fluctuating earnings will encourage strikes or will be submerged within the overall managerial control system. To understand the significance of collective action it is necessary to go beyond the bargaining structure to investigate the context of which it is part.

Non-strike sanctions are not, however, limited to the pursuit of specific factory-level objectives. A notable feature of many recent national pay disputes has been the use of overtime bans and forms of non-cooperation either instead of or alongside strike action. And this action has been sustained, often for considerable periods, by groups such as teachers and civil servants who lack strong shopfloor organisation. This appears to contradict the previous argument. But this argument was deliberately expressed in terms of 'the deployment of sanctions on a regular basis in manufacturing industry'. Workers in manufacturing are given little discretion, with even skilled workers being required to attend work at specified times and to carry out tasks according to managerial instructions. Professional groups have more freedom, and hence withdrawing cooperation can be done relatively easily, as when teachers refuse to supervise meals or to attend meetings outside school hours. Such action is, moreover, not carried out on a regular basis but is part of a specific campaign: its relationship to the immediate effort bargain is more remote than is the activity of workers in manufacturing, for which strong shopfloor organisation is essential.

The use of non-strike sanctions in national disputes, particularly those in the public sector, is still a significant development. Together with the increasingly sophisticated use of strikes, as in withdrawing the labour of only key personnel or holding a series of one- or two-day stoppages in place of the all-out strike, it reflects careful planning by the leadership and a willingness among the members to confront the employer that was largely absent a few years ago. This can in turn be related to the way in which successive governments have attempted to control pay increases and to the consequent need for unions to take explicit action in response. It is hard to know whether this pattern, and indeed the pattern of non-strike sanctions generally, will continue. It certainly seems likely that the control of pay settlements in the public sector will be part of any government's policy. And once workers have learned the tactics of industrial action they will not easily forget them. In other words, while workers may in certain circumstances accept pay offers, in the long term the possibility of militant and sophisticated action remains likely. But non-strike sanctions have limits, the most important being the willingness of employers to play by the existing rules: employers always have the option of declaring such sanctions to be a breach of contract, thus forcing a stoppage which is effectively a lock-out. In addition, if those employers who are seeking a thorough reorganisation of workplace relations are successful, then shopfloor organisations will be weakened and their ability to deploy sanctions will be impaired. The outcome of these conflicting tendencies remains to be seen.

CONCLUSION: INDUSTRIAL ACTION AND SHOPFLOOR RELATIONS

It is conventional in commentaries on British strikes to point out, for example, that Britain is far from being uniquely strike-prone (Creigh et al., 1980) and that the 'damage' caused by strikes is often exaggerated. Yet this does not advance very far an understanding of the nature of industrial action. There is a need not only to destroy the many simplistic myths about the 'problem' of strikes but also to examine the origins and significance of the use of strikes and to relate strikes to other forms of collective action and to the context of workplace relations more generally. This chapter has given some indications of how such an approach can build on existing accounts of strikes. It has been suggested, for example, that analysis based on structures of bargaining is limited to the extent that such structures are not themselves seen in terms of the wider set of relations between workers and employers. One consequence is that strikes tend to be divorced from other aspects of workplace relations; in particular, strikes and other collective sanctions deployed in pursuit of a bargaining objective tend to be treated in isolation from the many individual and collective ways in which workers adapt to, and struggle against, their employment conditions. One study mentioned above (Edwards and Scullion, 1982a) has considered some of these points in more detail, in particular the need to give industrial conflict a broader definition than is common within 'industrial relations' by examining 'individual' forms of behaviour such as absenteeism and by relating them, and the use of collective action, to the broad pattern of workplace relations. Strikes and sanctions are not then seen simply as the weapons which organised groups of workers deploy when there is a dispute with management; they are instead seen as part of a wider relationship which encompasses the organised pursuit of interests through collective bargaining. Some implications may be briefly outlined.

As Batstone et al. (1978:218) argue, 'strike action is a continuous possibility in our system of industrial relations and merges into other forms of collective action and work behaviour', going on to note that when 'collective opposition to management has developed, the strike is simply a further tactical extension' to this organised opposition. There are several points here. First, the possibility of strikes is ever-present; Batstone et al. do not elaborate on why this is so, but the answer plainly lies in the opposition of interests between workers and employers. Second, in well-organised workplaces the strike is merely one form of sanction that may be deployed against management; since it merges with other actions it cannot sensibly be discussed apart from them. Third, however, collective opposition to management does not always exist. In weakly organised plants it has not been established that the terms of the daily bargain over effort are explicitly negotiable, and hence the possibility of strikes and collective sanctions is not realised. It is only in factories with well-established shopfloor organisations which have gained a considerable say in the day-to-day conduct of operations that sanctions are an understood part of industrial relations. This is not to suggest that they are a frequent aspect of relations; as noted earlier, if shopfloor organisations have established the right to control various aspects of workplace relations, they may not need to apply sanctions, and, more generally, their struggle with employers is institutionalised in various ways which mean that overt conflicts are far from being daily occurrences. But it does mean that, in this type of workplace, the possibility of sanctions being applied is taken for granted. Elsewhere, sanctions are not such an established aspect of relations, and strikes do not merge with other types of action. As various disputes involving supposedly quiescent workers have shown, the absence of a strong organisation does not rule out the possibility of strikes. But, as the very fact that these disputes have been seen as worthy of special comment suggests, they have breached normal expectations and have challenged the existing order, often dramatically. Hence, although strikes are always a possibility, the significance of the realisation of that possibility will vary considerably. The meaning to be attached to a strike depends on the context in which it occurs. This apparently simple point can easily be overlooked by studies which see all strikes as the direct product of the conflictual relations between workers and employers, and which thus ignore the crucial role of the form which these relations take, as well as by studies which concentrate on the structural aspects of bargaining and which similarly give insufficient attention to the context of workplace relations.

Disputes at workplace level, which, as noted above, account for the great majority of British strikes, can thus be seen as part of a continuing struggle in which the nature of shopfloor organisation is crucial. They are thus political as well as economic weapons. Since there seems to be some confusion about their political role, this aspect requires careful consideration. The official information on the 'cause' of strikes show that one 'economic' issue, pay, has dominated the strike figures, accounting for half the stoppages and three-quarters of the working days lost over the period 1925–74 (Smith et al., 1978:43–4). Yet it does not follow that strikes have simply been about 'economic' matters. First, as Turner (1963:18) pointed out twenty years ago, up to the early 1960s there was a marked rise in the number of wage disputes other than those for increases. Turner suggested that these new strikes over working arrangements and the way in which wages were negotiated represented a substantial challenge to managerial authority; this can properly be described as a political challenge within the workplace. There has subsequently been an upsurge in the number of 'pure' wage strikes (Edwards, 1982:15), but this can be attributed to the impact of inflation, for workers have increasingly faced cuts in real wages and it is not surprising that the stated issues in strikes have shifted to pay. This leads to the second point, namely that pay strikes can reflect political pressures and have political consequences; various public sector strikes illustrate both sides of this argument. Third, pay cannot necessarily be divorced from other matters. As Batstone et al. (1978:47) found, in the strikes which they observed in one factory the reasons most commonly advanced by workers referred to managerial actions such as breaking agreements, taking a 'hard line', or generally ignoring the views and interests of the workers themselves. There is more to this than the familiar point that the causes of strikes go much deeper than the articulated issues, although that is important. The implication of the finding is that workers in well-organised factories see strikes as part of the political processes within the plant, with managerial actions that cut across workers' interests having to be resisted.

To argue that strikes have political elements is not to suggest that unions have exceeded their proper authority by challenging the democratic process (as some critics on the right would suggest) or that wage strikes demonstrate an incipient class consciousness (as some on the left, for example, Gill, 1981, claim). Part of the above argument relates to the politics of the factory, that is the distribution of power and control as between managers and workers, and not to national politics. However, a large number of pay demands in the context of an economy which cannot meet those demands is certainly significant for national politics. But it does not follow that workers are driven by concerted political aims. It is the failure to appreciate that strikes have political implications without being consciously directed at political matters which vitiates simplistic analyses from both left and right. Strike activity reflects part of workers' attempts to gain control over their working lives, but such attempts are often limited and sectional.

The 1960s and early 1970s seemed to some to indicate a dramatic upsurge of militancy, while by the late 1970s and early 1980s others pointed to the emergence of the 'new realism' and the solution of the strike problem. Both perceptions are inadequate, for they are based on very simple understandings of the significance of strikes in British factories. But they illustrate the dangers of prediction; strike patterns have altered in many ways which have confounded expectations about new trends towards militancy or the withering away of conflict. What can safely be said, however, is that the character of British strikes is firmly embedded in traditions of workplace organisation, that the growth of workplace unionism during the 1960s strengthened this position, and that it will take a major upheaval to destroy the practice of solving disputes at the point of production and the pattern of short workplace-based actions which goes with it.

PART IV
The Labour Market

10 Unemployment

David Deaton

In the first twenty-five years after World War II, Britain experienced a period of low unemployment, but during the last twelve years unemployment has risen dramatically until in early 1982 it exceeded three million. This chapter attempts to explain this increase in unemployment, to demonstrate how different groups in the economy have been affected, and to consider the prospects for unemployment in the future.

TRENDS IN UNEMPLOYMENT

Figure 10.1 shows that the rise in unemployment took place in three distinct phases: in 1971; between 1974 and 1977, with the sharpest rise being in 1975; and in 1980–81. But the reasons for the rise in unemployment do not lie in these periods alone. There is an inherent tendency for employment and unemployment to fluctuate over a four- to five-year business cycle. In the 1950s and 1960s these fluctuations took place around a static unemployment trend, but during the 1970s they occurred around a rising trend. It may be fruitful therefore to look at trends in the labour force in order to explain rising unemployment.

To gain an accurate picture of these trends it is important to compare points in time which represent similar phases in the business cycle. In Table 10.1 the comparison is made between 1966 and 1979, years in which unemployment was at a low point in the cycle. In the period 1966–79 unemployment rose by about one million, two-thirds of this being attributable to a rise in the size of the labour force and one-third to a fall in the level of employment. The population of working age grew by roughly the same amount as the labour force, but there was a substantial increase in the proportion of women in the labour force. This increase reflects a rise in the proportion of women working or seeking work (the participation rate) and, to a lesser extent, a fall in the participation rate of men. The latter trend is due partly to more early retirement but mainly to a rise in non-compulsory education. There has also been a trend towards more education among young women and hence their participation rate has also fallen. This means that the rise in the participation rate of women over the age of twenty-five is much greater than the overall increase suggests.

During the period 1966–79 the level of employment fell by what in retrospect seems a modest amount. But within that overall trend employment in manufacturing industries fell considerably and it was only the growth in public service employment, concentrated in the health and education sectors, which restrained the decline in aggregate employment.

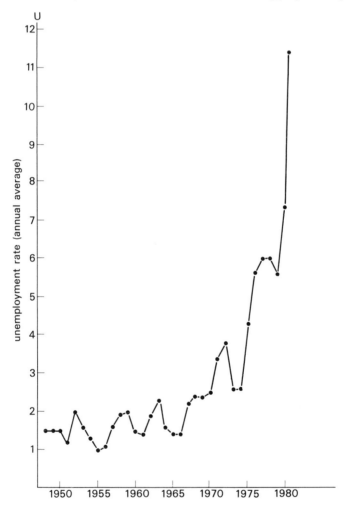

FIGURE 10.1:   Unemployment in Great Britain, 1948–1981
Source: See, for example, *Employment Gazette,* May 1982, table 2.2.

Employment in the remainder of the economy was almost static overall in this period though there were major changes in individual industries.

Since 1979 the major increase in unemployment has undoubtedly been due to the sharp fall in manufacturing employment which was considerably in excess of the declining trend in employment. In addition there was a

TABLE 10.1: TRENDS IN EMPLOYMENT IN GREAT BRITAIN, 1966–1981

	June 1966	June 1979	December 1981	Changes 1966–79	Changes 1979–81
Population of Working Age (000s)[a]	32429	33252	33651	+823	+399
Working Population (000s)	25071	25796	25338	+725	−458
Males	16405	15666	15474	−739	−192
Females	8667	10130	9864	+1463	−266
Employed Labour Force (000s)	24818	24515	22506	−303	−2009
Manufacturing	8408	7036	5772	−1372	−1264
Public Services[b]	3955	5020	4958	+1065	−62
Others (including self-employed)	12455	12459	11776	+4	−683
Unemployed (000s)	253	1281	2832	+1028	+1551
Participation Rates (%)[c]					
Male	97·7	90·4	87·8		
Female	55·4	63·6	61·5		
Overall	77·3	77·6	75·3		

Sources: Department of Employment Gazette (March 1975), 193–205 (1966 employment data); (November 1973), 1087 (1966 population); *Employment Gazette* (May 1982), tables 1.1 and 1.2 (1979 and 1981 employment data); *OPCS Monitors*, PP1 79/8 and PP2 no. 11.
Notes:
[a] 'Working Age' is defined as fifteen to fifty-nine for women and fifteen to sixty-four for men although the school leaving age was raised to sixteen in 1972–3.
[b] Public services included central and local government, both private and public health and education, and the armed forces. Nationalised industries are excluded.
[c] Participation rates are the working population as a percentage of the population of working age. The working population will include some people over retirement age and the population of working age will include (in 1979 and 1981) those aged 15 in compulsory education.

significant fall in employment in the residual sector and the growth in public service employment has stopped. Indeed, it is the present government's policy to reduce the size of the public sector. Table 10.1 also shows a decline in the size of the labour force between 1979 and 1981 due not to a decline in the population of working age but to a fall in the participation rate; indeed, the population of working age grew more rapidly in this period than previously, due mainly to a low birth rate during World War I and hence a low retirement rate of men in the years 1979–83. The fall in participation rates is almost certainly a consequence of the recession itself as people withdraw from the labour force because of the lack of job opportunities. This suggests that there is considerable hidden unemployment in addition to the registered unemployment recorded in the statistics (see Garside, 1980).

This examination of the trends in employment and the size of the labour force provides some clues in the search for an explanation of the rise in unemployment, but it would be wrong to rely on this approach exclusively.

For instance, the conclusion might be drawn that the increased participation rate of women was the cause of rising unemployment up to 1979 or that the failure of the government to compensate for the fall in manufacturing employment was responsible for the surge in unemployment after 1979. But many other interpretations are compatible with these data, including the view that the growth of the public sector was the cause of the decline in manufacturing (Bacon and Eltis, 1976). To evaluate these competing explanations requires a consideration of the wider question of how the economy and the labour market work.

There is another danger in looking only at the overall trend in unemployment. It tends to conjure up what Daniel (1981c:495) has called the 'rubbish-dump image of unemployment'. To think of rising unemployment as simply adding more people to the dole queue is misleading. Closer inspection of the unemployment figures reveals that the number of people registering in any one year is high relative to the stock of unemployment. For instance, in 1979 when the unemployment stock averaged 1·4 million (5·8 per cent) there were some 4·5 million registrations and 4·5 million cases of people leaving the register. These were not necessarily 4·5 million different people since some would have experienced more than one spell of unemployment. But on average a completed spell of unemployment must have been sixteen weeks long (1·4/4·5×52 weeks).

As unemployment has risen, the numbers becoming unemployed in any period have remained fairly constant while the average duration of unemployment has increased. Thus in 1955 when unemployment was 1.1 per cent, the average duration of a spell of unemployment was only three and a half weeks (Cripps and Tarling, 1974:306). The flow into unemployment tends to be relatively constant for two reasons. First, certain flows are relatively independent of the state of the labour market: for example, the number of school leavers and graduates entering the labour market, those coming to the end of fixed-term contracts, and those dismissed for disciplinary reasons. Second, of the flows into unemployment which do depend on the state of the labour market, redundancies will be positively related to unemployment and quits to search for another job will be negatively related to unemployment, and these tend to offset one another.

The picture of unemployment that emerges is one of a large number of people joining the register, with the state of demand affecting their probability of re-employment and hence their duration of unemployment. But unemployment duration also varies considerably between individuals. The way in which unemployment statistics are collected makes it difficult to say anything directly about completed spells of unemployment. But by tracing a cohort of unemployed workers through a succession of registers something can be inferred about how quickly they are re-employed (Bowers and Harkess, 1979).

The following tabulation (Manpower Services Commission, 1981b) shows that the probability of re-employment declines as unemployment duration increases:

Year of Unemployment	Number Unemployed in October 1980	Percentage Still Unemployed One Year Later
1st year	1,594,000	31
2nd year	191,000	59
3rd or subsequent years	188,000	76

One interpretation of these data is that people start with a high probability of finding employment and that this probability declines as they remain unemployed: either they get discouraged or employers become more reluctant to hire them. While there is some truth in this view, it is not the major part of the explanation. When workers become unemployed, their probability of re-employment within a certain period depends on their skills, age, personal characteristics, and the area in which they are seeking work. Some people have a high probability of re-employment and are therefore likely to find a job quickly; others have a low probability and remain unemployed longer. The observed declining probability of an unemployed person getting a job thus reflects the changing composition of the cohort.

The finding that increased unemployment occurs through increased duration is reflected in Table 10.2 which shows the extent to which a doubling of unemployment between 1979 and 1981 affected its distribution. The unemployment rate in the West Midlands rose to a much greater extent than in other regions; and certain occupations, particularly those associated with engineering, showed a larger proportional increase than the average. But despite considerable variation in the rate of unemployment by region, occupation, and age group, there was a general tendency for it to double in each of the groups. The uniformity of the increase by age group is particularly striking, especially if the smaller increase in the over sixty age group is explained by an increase in early retirement.

The uneven distribution of unemployment is not only interesting in itself, it is also crucial to an understanding of the nature of aggregate unemployment. At lower levels of unemployment there will be certain occupations and regions in which the number of unfilled vacancies exceed the number unemployed. This is illustrated for the regional dimension in Table 10.3 which shows the unemployed and vacancies in December 1972. In four of the regions—South East, East Anglia, South West, and East Midlands—vacancies exceeded the level of unemployment, whereas in the other six regions unemployment exceeded vacancies. On the basis of this imbalance between unemployment and vacancies, unemployment can in principle be broken down into three components. First, there are 430,200 unemployed workers for whom there are vacancies in the same region (for the moment ignoring that they may be in the wrong occupation); this figure is made up of the total number of unemployed workers in the four regions where vacancies exceed unemployment plus the total number of vacancies

TABLE 10.2: DISTRIBUTION OF UNEMPLOYMENT, 1979 AND 1981 (%)

	1979	1981	1981÷1979
REGION			
South East	3·6	7·1	2·0
East Anglia	4·4	8·2	1·9
South West	5·6	9·0	1·6
West Midlands	5·2	12·1	2·3
East Midlands	4·5	9·2	2·0
Yorkshire & Humberside	5·4	10·7	2·0
North West	6·7	12·1	1·8
North	8·0	13·4	1·7
Wales	7·5	13·0	1·7
Scotland	7·4	12·0	1·6
Northern Ireland	10·3	16·4	1·6
SEX			
Male	6·6	12·6	1·9
Female	3·7	7·0	1·9
AGE			
Under 18	8·9	17·4	2·0
18–19	9·3	17·9	1·9
20–24	7·9	15·9	2·0
25–34	5·3	10·4	2·0
35–44	3·6	7·0	1·9
45–54	3·6	6·5	1·8
55–59	4·4	7·7	1·8
60+ (men only)	11·7	17·4	1·5
OCCUPATION			
Managers	1·1	2·5	2·3
Education professions	1·2	2·1	1·8
Health professions	1·5	2·5	1·7
Other professions	2·4	6·0	2·5
Literary, artistic, sports	2·3	4·0	1·7
Engineers & scientists	1·5	3·8	2·5
Technical & draughtsmen	1·4	3·4	2·4
Clerical	4·0	7·0	1·8
Sales	4·4	9·1	2·1
Supervisors	1·9	5·7	3·0
Engineering craftsmen	2·2	7·4	3·4
Other transferable craftsmen	4·4	13·0	3·0
Non transferable craftsmen	0·6	1·5	2·5
Skilled operatives	3·3	8·8	2·7
Other operatives	4·1	10·2	2·5
Security occupations	1·4	3·1	2·2
Personal service, labourers and others	11·6	20·7	1·8
Non-manual	2·7	5·2	1·9
Manual	5·8	12·3	2·1

Sources: Employment Gazette (January 1982), table 2.3 (regions 1981), table 2.15 (age and sex); (January 1980), table 106 (regions 1979). The occupational rates are calculated from unpublished data supplied by the Institute for Employment Research, University of Warwick. Non-manual workers are those in the first nine occupations in the table.
Note: Sex, age, and occupational rates are unadjusted; regional rates are seasonally adjusted. Regional and occupational rates exclude school leavers. All rates exclude adult students. All rates are for April except the occupational rates which are for June.

in the six regions where unemployment exceeds vacancies. Second, there are 136,500 unemployed workers for whom there are vacancies in other regions; this figure is made up of the surplus vacancies in the first four regions which are less than the surplus unemployment in the remaining six

TABLE 10.3: UNEMPLOYMENT AND VACANCIES BY REGION, DECEMBER 1972 (000s)

Region	Vacancies (V)	Unemployment (U)	Minimum of V and U	Residual V	U−V
South East	264·0	140·8	140·8	123·2	−123·2
East Anglia	20·4	15·6	15·6	4·8	− 4·8
South West	48·6	40·4	40·4	8·2	− 8·2
East Midlands	37·2	36·9	36·9	0·3	− 0·3
West Midlands	40·8	66·3	40·8		25·5
Yorkshire & Humberside	41·7	69·6	41·7		27·9
North West	42·0	123.9	42·0		81·9
North	24·9	72·0	24·9		47·1
Wales	17·1	43·3	17·1		26·2
Scotland	30·0	121·2	30·0		91·2
Total	566·7	730·0	430·2	136·5	163·3

Source: Employment Gazette (January 1977), table 119; (October 1975), table 110.
Note: Data are seasonally adjusted. Unemployment excludes school leavers and adult students. Vacancies are three times the notified level to take account of under-recording; see Department of Employment (1978: 655).

regions. Third, there are 163,300 unemployed workers for whom there are no vacancies; this figure is simply the residual unemployment and represents the aggregate difference between unemployment and vacancies. Such a breakdown has important implications for the analysis of unemployment and forms the basis of the unemployment classification discussed in the next section.

UNEMPLOYMENT CLASSIFICATION AND THEORY

Frictional and Structural Unemployment

To carry out fully the classification of unemployment it is necessary to consider both the regional and occupational distribution of unemployment and vacancies. The procedure is illustrated by a hypothetical example in which an economy has two regions, north and south, and two occupations, technicians and operatives. The basic data for this example are given in Table 10.4. Each occupation in each region constitutes a separate labour market.

In each of the four labour markets there are both unfilled vacancies and unemployed workers. If all jobs within an occupation are similar, and if the regions are small enough to comprise a reasonable travel-to-work area, it is clear that much of the unemployment could be relieved simply by some unemployed workers finding the vacancies for which they are

TABLE 10.4: UNEMPLOYMENT AND VACANCIES IN TWO OCCUPATIONS AND TWO REGIONS

| | UNEMPLOYMENT | | | VACANCIES | | |
	Technicians	*Operatives*	*Total*	*Technicians*	*Operatives*	*Total*
North	102	160	262	53	27	80
South	92	72	164	204	102	306
Total	194	232	426	257	129	386

qualified in their own area. In the technician-north labour market there are 102 unemployed workers and fifty-three vacancies and so unemployment could be reduced by fifty-three without much difficulty. In the operative-south labour market all seventy-two unemployed workers could find work among the 102 vacancies. Such unemployment is called frictional. All that is required to remove it is that unemployed workers and firms with unfilled vacancies become aware of each other's existence. It may be that the government can assist the process by improving communication in the labour market. It is by no means certain, however, that the government has to do anything at all. Since unemployment and vacancies have been measured at a fixed point in time, it is quite possible that those vacancies in the technician-north labour market and those unemployed in the operative-south labour market were removed from the employment exchange's lists within a matter of days. They may have been replaced by new vacancies and more short-term unemployment which in turn vanishes very quickly. Frictional unemployment represents a process of continuous movement within the labour market and may present no problems.

The lefthand side of Table 10.5 shows the amount of frictional unemployment in this economy. In each labour market frictional unemployment is equal to whichever is the smaller of unemployment or vacancies. Thus there is a total frictional unemployment of 244. The righthand side of Table 10.5 shows the difference between unemployment and vacancies in each labour market. In the northern labour markets the positive figures indicate that a certain amount of unemployment remains after frictional unemployment has been removed. In the southern labour markets the negative figures indicate that some vacancies remain after frictional unemployment has been removed. This mismatch between unemployment and vacancies implies a second type of unemployment, namely structural. Part of this problem could be relieved by either encouraging labour mobility from north to south or by regional policy designed to shift jobs from south to north. But neither policy is sufficient to eliminate structural unemployment because there is an occupation mismatch as well; the overall number of technician vacancies exceeds the

TABLE 10.5: FRICTIONAL UNEMPLOYMENT AND STRUCTURAL IMBALANCE

	FRICTIONAL UNEMPLOYMENT			*UNEMPLOYMENT – VACANCIES*		
	Technicians	*Operatives*	*Total*	*Technicians*	*Operatives*	*Total*
North	53	27	80	49	133	182
South	92	72	164	−112	−30	−142
Total	145	99	244	−63	103	40

unemployment of technicians so some degree of retraining of operatives is also required.

The total amount of structural unemployment is the amount by which unemployment could be reduced if all vacancies were filled, apart from those filled through the elimination of frictional unemployment. There is therefore structural employment of 142 in this economy, but the removal of this would require 142 regional moves (of either jobs or workers) and sixty-three occupation moves. It may be feasible to carry out both at the same time if, for instance, a technician's job is moved from the south to the north and is filled by an unemployed operative being taken on as a trainee technician. But while this may reduce the total volume of mobility, it may be more difficult to achieve than two separate moves.

Even if the matching problem is solved, however, there remains an aggregate excess of unemployment over vacancies of forty. The removal of this aggregate unemployment requires some macroeconomic policy such as an expansion of aggregate demand. Indeed, such unemployment is usually termed 'demand-deficient' unemployment. But a general expansion of demand sufficient to generate forty extra jobs is unlikely to create them all in the operative-north labour market where the surplus unemployment is located. Such a policy is more likely to create jobs in all four labour markets (say, ten extra jobs in each labour market) and this would increase the amount of labour mobility required by a further thirty. In this example the difference is trivial, but it raises a problem which is crucial in estimating the level of structural unemployment when aggregate unemployment is very high.

The exercise of separating unemployment into these three categories is useful in that it suggests the extent to which different sorts of unemployment policy might be appropriate. There are, however, several problems to be overcome in applying it to real rather than hypothetical data. First, it is by no means true that all the vacancies in the labour market are recorded in the Department of Employment's lists. Employers are under no obligation to report vacancies and they may have little incentive to do so, particularly if they are seeking to attract workers who are currently employed elsewhere. A survey by the Manpower Services Commission suggested that only one-third of vacancies are reported (Department of Employment, 1978d). A factor of three has been used to 'correct' the vacancy figures in Table 10.3, but there is no justification for assuming that the proportion of vacancies notified is constant across occupations, regions, or even over time. Nor does registered unemployment measure the true level of unemployment since many workers, particularly married women, have little incentive to register.

Second, the structural problem is much more complicated than the above example suggests. The Department of Employment's definition of a travel-to-work area gives rise to 380 separate geographical labour markets and its unemployment and vacancy data is collected for 396 occupational categories. Even within such occupations not all jobs could be performed by those registered without substantial retraining costs. The effect of computing the three types of unemployment, using broader categories such as the ten regions, is to overestimate frictional unemployment and underestimate structural unemployment.

Third, at high levels of aggregate unemployment the measurement of structural and frictional unemployment is distorted. For instance, the classification of unemployment for September 1981 (using the correction factor of three for vacancies and using ten regions and eighteen occupations) shows that out of a total of 2,533,733 unemployed, there was frictional unemployment of 312,459, no structural unemployment, and the rest was demand deficient. The finding of no structural unemployment arises because in none of the 180 labour markets did vacancies exceed unemployment.

Now it would be nonsense to say that the problem of structural unemployment had been eliminated from the British economy. It is almost certain that if demand expanded there would be substantial areas of excess vacancies before unemployment was eliminated. What the calculation does indicate, however, is that an attempt to remove structural unemployment at the present time would have no effect on the overall level of unemployment. It may produce a more even distribution of unemployment, or it may put the labour market in a better position when the economy does expand, but it would not by itself reduce aggregate unemployment. To identify the true extent of the structural problem, Cheshire (1973) suggests that it must be asked what the level of unemployment would be if there were an expansion of aggregate labour demand up to the point at which total unemployment equals total unfilled vacancies. This would show the amount of frictional plus structural unemployment. Then how much of this unemployment is matched by vacancies in the same occupational and local areas? The answer to this question would be the amount of frictional unemployment. This procedure would indicate which combinations of policies to adopt to solve the unemployment problem.

Aggregate Unemployment

It is now useful to abstract from the problems of structural and frictional unemployment and deal simply with the category which has been called demand-deficient unemployment. In the simplest version of the Keynesian model, aggregate demand (D) has three components: consumers' expenditure (C), investment expenditure by firms (I), and government expenditure (G), all expressed in real terms:

$$D=C+I+G \tag{1}$$

Since it is a short-run model, prices, wages, and labour productivity are taken as given and are assumed to be sufficiently attractive for firms to produce at any level of output that is demanded subject only to the maximum available force (L). The level of output (Y) is therefore given by

$$Y=\text{minimum of } [D,\ eL] \tag{2}$$

where e is the level of labour productivity. The level of employment (E) depends on output and labour productivity:

$$E=Y/e \tag{3}$$

The model distinguishes between two types of consumer: those employed and those unemployed. The unemployed consumer's expenditure is a per period and the employed worker consumes an additional b per period. Total consumer expenditure can therefore be written as

$$C=aL+bE \tag{4}$$

Although no time lags are specified in the equations, in practice neither the impact of demand on output and hence employment, nor the impact of employment on consumption will be instantaneous. However, this model is concerned only with the ultimate effect of changes in government expenditure and investment on employment, and this is given by the solution to these four equations. The equilibrium level of employment is therefore

$$E=\frac{I+G+aL}{e-b} \tag{5}$$

unless, of course, this is greater than the size of the labour force. Equation (5) implies that the level of employment depends on two sets of factors:

first, those components of demand which are independent of the level of employment: investment, government expenditure, and the basic consumption of all consumers (aL); and, second, what Keynes calls the multiplier, which in this case depends on labour productivity (e) and the additional consumption of employed workers (b).

According to this model, the government can eliminate unemployment fairly easily by increasing its expenditure until the whole labour force is employed. In the real world things are not as simple as that. First, the concept of full employment is ambiguous. Because of frictional and structural problems, unemployment and vacancies are bound to coexist. The government may have to expand the economy and at the same time provide assistance for re-training and mobility of labour to remove all non-frictional unemployment. But what are the consequences of expanding the economy and allowing serious skill shortages to develop in certain areas? They may cause bottlenecks which hinder the expansion in other sectors, they may be inflationary, or they may cause a sharp rise in imports. All these possible consequences require the building of a more elaborate model.

Second, the government faces the problem of how to finance its extra expenditure. If it does so through an increase in taxation, this may simply offset the effect of the increased expenditure. If it finances the expenditure by borrowing, it may force up interest rates and cause a reduction in investment. This effect is known as 'crowding out'. Keynesians usually argue that the higher level of income results in greater savings which permits the government to borrow without crowding out private investment (see Trevithick, 1977).

Third, the present model assumes that private industry is willing and able to meet extra demand by increasing output. It may be that the economy does not have the capacity to produce at full employment or that private industry does not find it sufficiently profitable to expand production at the current levels of wages and prices.

The model can be made less restrictive if, following Malinvaud (1977 and 1980a), the level of output is limited not only by the level of demand and the available labour supply, but also by the level of productive capacity (K) which can be used profitably at existing wages and prices. This means that equation (2) determining the level of output is now

$$Y=\text{minimum of } [D, eL, K] \tag{6}$$

Thus rather than the simple dichotomy of being at or below full employment, there are three possibilities depending on which factor is limiting output. First, if aggregate demand, D, is the smallest of the three quantities, the Keynesian theory outlined above applies. There is an excess supply of labour and potentially an excess supply of goods because firms would produce at full capacity if there were sufficient demand. Unemployment in this situation can be called 'Keynesian'. Second, if eL, the full employment level of output, is the smallest of the three, there will be excess demand for labour and excess demand for goods since firms would be willing to produce the minimum of D and K if they could find sufficient labour. There is a situation of generalised excess demand which is likely to be inflationary. Since the model is one of fixed wages and prices, however, this situation is usually referred to as repressed inflation. Third, if productive capacity, K, is the smallest, there will be an excess demand for goods and an excess supply of labour. There will be unemployment but, unlike the Keynesian case, it arises because of a lack of profitable productive capacity. Such a deficiency may arise from an insufficient rate of capital accumulation in the past, or because at current wages and prices some of the existing capital stock cannot be used profitably. In this situation unemployment is referred to as 'classical'. Between these three types of situation there will be intermediate cases. One which is of particular interest is where the three quantities are all equal and where both labour and goods markets are in equilibrium. This situation is normally referred to as 'Walrasian equilibrium'.

The quantities, D, K, e, and L which determine the state of the economy are not, of course, fixed numbers but depend on other variables. The level of aggregate demand (D) depends on government demand (G) and on the purchasing power of income and wealth which, in turn, depend on the level of output (Y), the real wage rate (w), and the price level (P). This can be represented by the equation

$$D=D(Y,\ w,\ P,\ G) \qquad (7)$$

where D increases with Y, w and G, and decreases with P. Labour supply depends positively on the real wage rate and negatively on the real wealth of consumers. A rise in the price level, in addition to any effect on the real wage, reduces real wealth. This means that labour supply is an increasing function of the price level. So

$$L=L(w,\ P) \qquad (8)$$

The level of productive capacity (K) is the output which it is most profitable for firms to produce from their existing capital stock. There is some degree of flexibility in that old equipment will be used or left idle depending on the level of real wages. This means that in the short-run capacity varies inversely with the real wage:

$$K=K(w) \qquad (9)$$

Equations (6) to (9) can be used to show how three sorts of macro-disequilibrium arise from various combinations of money wages (W), the price level, and government expenditure (see Malinvaud, 1977). Figure 10.2 shows this for a given level of government expenditure. The point Z

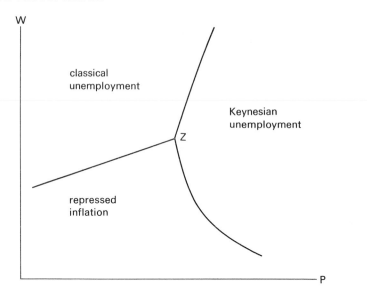

FIGURE 10.2:   Three Sorts of Macroeconomic Disequilibrium

represents the combination of wage and price levels consistent with Walrasian equilibrium, where $D=K=eL$. In the region to the north-west of Z the real wage is higher than its equilibrium value, the main effect being to reduce the level of productive capacity (K) and create classical unemployment. In the region to the south-west of Z both the money wage and the price level are below their equilibrium values. This has the effect of reducing labour supply and increasing demand. The supply of labour is the constraint on output and the economy is in a situation of repressed inflation. In the region to the east of Z the price level is higher than its equilibrium level. This reduces the level of demand and the economy experiences Keynesian unemployment.

Figure 10.3 shows the effect of an increase in the level of government expenditure. This is represented by a shift from the solid to the broken curves. Since an increase in government expenditure raises the level of demand, it has the effect of reducing the region of Keynesian unemployment and increasing the region of classical unemployment and repressed inflation. The higher level of demand means that the Walrasian equilibrium occurs at a higher level of wages and prices (Z').

Figures 10.2 and 10.3 indicate how the two types of unemployment can be eliminated. Where unemployment is classical the real wage $(w=W/P)$ is too high and has to be reduced to achieve Walrasian equilibrium. A reduction in the real wage works mainly through increasing the productive capacity which in this region is the factor limiting output. Where, however, unemployment is Keynesian, a reduction in the real wage does not reduce unemployment. Indeed, it will probably increase unemployment because a reduction in the real wage will tend to reduce demand. Figure 10.2 suggests

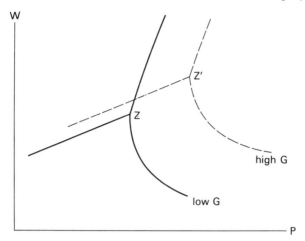

FIGURE 10.3:   The Effects of an Increase in Government Expenditure

that the appropriate policy in the region of Keynesian unemployment is a reduction in the price level. It is doubtful, however, that such a policy is feasible. In theory it works through the real balance effect: as prices fall the real value of people's wealth increases and they spend more. The flaw in this argument is that the real value of debts will also increase and lead to bankruptcies (see Keynes, 1936:264; Tobin, 1980). This suggests that in the above model productive capacity (K) should depend on the price level as well as on the real wage. Figure 10.3 shows that the alternative policy for Keynesian unemployment is an increase in government expenditure which shifts the equilibrium point Z to the right. The effect of this is to increase demand which is the factor limiting output.

The model outlined is a useful conceptual device for distinguishing between two quite different sorts of unemployment. As it stands, however, it abstracts from a number of important aspects of unemployment. In particular, it neglects the dispersion of unemployment across sectors, it ignores international trade, and it assumes wages and prices have already been determined.

The earlier discussion of structural unemployment showed that at any moment some sectors of the economy exhibit an excess of unemployment over vacancies and others an excess of vacancies. The Malinvaud model suggests that any particular sector can be in one of three situations: excess demand for both labour and goods, deficient demand implying Keynesian unemployment, or a lack of profitable productive capacity causing classical unemployment. Some of the implications of the mixture of Keynesian and classical unemployment are considered in Malinvaud (1980b), but the main one is that macroeconomic policy alone cannot eliminate unemployment.

The simplest way of incorporating international trade into the model is to postulate a demand for the country's exports which is dependent on the price level. This means that a reduction in the price level would increase demand not through the controversial real balance effect but through increased demand for exports and reduced demand for imports. But, in addition to this, opening the economy to international trade means that the extent to which Keynesian unemployment can be reduced by increased government expenditure is limited by the balance of payments constraint. Dixit (1978) has extended the model to incorporate international trade in a different way. The main additional assumptions in his model are that the domestic price level is determined by the world price level times the exchange rate, that firms can sell as much as they wish at these prices, and that consumers can buy as much as they wish. This means that the goods market is always in equilibrium with any discrepancy between domestic demand and output showing up as an imbalance between exports and imports. The implication, then, is that all unemployment is classical, and arises because real wages are too high. Malinvaud (1980a:95) has disputed this conclusion on the grounds that it relies on the assumption that the world goods market is always in excess demand. He argues that the state of the world market can also lead to Keynesian unemployment in the domestic economy.

So far wages and prices have been taken as fixed or subject to adjustment by government policy. Such an assumption is reasonable in a short-run model where imbalances between supply and demand do not affect wages and prices. But since the extent and nature of unemployment depend on the degree to which wages and prices differ from their equilibrium values, it is necessary to consider next what determines them.

Wage and Price Movements

In the short-run model outlined above, wages and prices were taken as given and unemployment arose when demand or productive capacity fell short of the level of output associated with full employment. But such unemployment can only persist beyond the short-run if wages and prices continue to differ from their new equilibrium levels. This means that the behaviour of wages and prices is central to an analysis of unemployment. Indeed, many of the differences between economists over the nature of unemployment come down to disagreements as to the appropriate models of wage and price determination.

Most models of wage and price setting behaviour are based to some degree on the Phillips curve: an observed relationship between the rate of change of money wage rates and the level of unemployment. Modern versions of the Phillips curve treat it as a short-run theoretical relationship augmented by price expectations. In this form it can conveniently be summarised as:

$$\dot{W}=f(u)+\dot{p}^e \tag{11}$$

That is, the rate of change of wages ($\dot{W}$) is equal to some function of unemployment plus the expected rate of change of prices. When there is no expectation of prices increasing, the curve is thought to take the form depicted in Figure 10.4 At positive rates of expected price increase the curve retains the same shape but is shifted up by the level of price expectations.

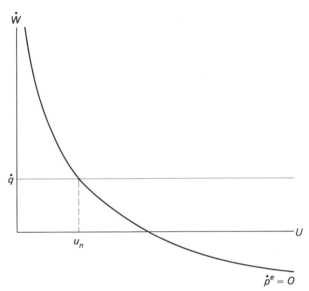

FIGURE 10.4:   Augmented Phillips Curve with Zero-Expectations

The simplest form of the price equation is based on the idea that firms mark-up on their labour costs by a constant margin. Thus price increases ($\dot{p}$) reflect the rate of change of money wages ($\dot{W}$) less the rate of growth of labour productivity ($\dot{q}$):

$$\dot{p}=\dot{W}-\dot{q} \tag{12}$$

Equations (11) and (12) suggest that there will be a single rate of unemployment at which prices will rise by the expected amount. Thus if no price increases are expected ($\dot{p}^e=O$), price stability is only maintained if money wages rise in line with the rate of growth of labour productivity ($\dot{W}=\dot{q}$). The level of unemployment at which this is achieved is often called the *natural rate of unemployment*. But, because this term is associated with monetarism and carries the implication that unemployment has a tendency to return to the natural rate, a more neutral term such as the 'non-accelerating inflation rate of unemployment' (NAIRU) is often preferred.

It is sometimes suggested that NAIRU is equivalent to the sum of frictional and structural unemployment and thus if total unemployment were equal to total vacancies, there would be no tendency for price increases to accelerate. But to substantiate this claim requires rather special assumptions; for example, that money wages rise faster than the average rate of productivity growth in labour markets with excess demand and correspondingly slower in markets with excess supply. Such an heroic assumption is difficult to justify. Indeed, the whole notion of a short-run trade-off between inflation and unemployment requires some theoretical justification.

One explanation of the short-run Phillips curve is Phelps's (1971) model in which wages are set by employers so as to ensure an adequate supply of labour. Each firm adjusts wages periodically bearing in mind the wages that it expects other firms to be paying. Where a firm has particular difficulty in recruiting and retaining labour it will pay more than the expected market rate, and where there is little labour turnover it will increase wages by less than the expected increase in the market rate. If the majority of firms are experiencing difficulty in retaining and recruiting workers, wage increases are likely to exceed the expected increase in the market rate; conversely, wage increases will be less than expected if the majority of firms have no difficulty recruiting labour. The rate at which money wages increase relative to expectations depends on the state of the labour market and hence on the level of unemployment. But the relationship between unemployment and wage increases is indirect and dependent on the relationship between unemployment and labour turnover. There is certainly no implication that wage stability is achieved when unemployment and vacancies are equal.

But even if the natural rate does not imply equilibrium in the sense of unemployment equal to vacancies, it does imply equilibrium unemployment in another sense. In a labour market characterised by heterogeneous workers and jobs it makes sense for the unemployed workers not to take the first job offered but to conduct job search until they feel that the chances of obtaining a better offer would be outweighed by the cost of remaining unemployed to continue searching. Thus there is a level of optimal search unemployment and this in many analyses has been equated with the natural rate of unemployment. In this sense the labour market is in equilibrium at the natural rate. Job searchers choose the level of unemployment in response to the structure of wage offers. The natural rate of unemployment will be higher in a market where job search can be carried out more effectively while unemployed than on the job. Similarly unemployment will be higher the greater is the dispersion of wages.

The alternative model of inflation and unemployment brings collective bargaining to the centre of the analysis. In Rowthorn's (1977) version of this model, wage and price setting are the consequences of conflict between employers and workers over the distribution of income. Trade unions aspire to a certain share of national income and seek to negotiate a wage which will achieve that share. Similarly, employers aspire to a certain share of national income and aim to set prices to achieve it. If the aspirations of both sides are compatible, wage and price stability can be achieved. But if the sum of the shares to which they aspire exceed what is left over after the government has taken its share, a spiral of wage-price inflation results. However, aspiring to a certain share does not mean that it is achieved even immediately after a wage or price increase. Labour's ability to achieve its desired share depends on its bargaining power which is, in turn, dependent to some degree on the level of unemployment. Similarly, firms may not be in a secure enough product market position to increase prices in accordance with the level of profits they seek. Hence distributional conflict will be damped if the level of demand is reduced.

This model, like Phelps's natural rate model, predicts that inflation depends on past inflation rates and the level of unemployment, and that there will be a rate of unemployment at which inflation does not accelerate. There are, however, two major differences between these two models. The first difference is that in the collective bargaining model wage increases will be influenced not only by the state of demand and price expectations but also by past changes in post-tax real earnings. This means that an increase in the tax rate will increase wage claims and that any failure to achieve real wage increases will lead to inflationary pressure in the future.

The second difference is the nature of NAIRU in the two models. In the first model the natural rate of unemployment implies equilibrium in the labour market and represents efficient job search. The natural rate will depend on those factors which influence job search such as the level of unemployment benefit. In the collective bargaining model NAIRU represents the level of unemployment at which distributional conflict is contained. Here the link between unemployment and inflation is indirect. As Rowthorn (1977:203) argues:

> consider the example of a severe crisis in which unemployment remains at a high level for a long period of time . . . Both workers and capitalists are subject to severe market discipline . . . and inflationary pressures are effectively contained. In time, however, structural changes occur which lead to a reappearance of inflationary pressures, even though unemployment remains as high as ever: capitalists may reorganize their production methods and scrap equipment, eliminating excess capacity . . . the labour market may break up into non-competing segments, so that local shortages develop despite the overall high level of unemployment.

Hence in this model, NAIRU can be both unacceptably high and subject to major variations.

In both of these areas the disagreement could, in principle, be resolved by an appeal to empirical evidence. There has been no shortage of empirical work on wage inflation, but the literature is dominated by two main approaches which reflect the two models discussed above: the 'augmented Phillips curve' and the 'real wage hypothesis'. The augmented Phillips curve suggests that wage inflation is inversely related to some measure of the excess supply of labour (usually unemployment) plus expectations of price inflation. Unless workers and employers are subject to money illusion price expectations are fully reflected in wage increases. The basic equation is then:

$$\dot{W}=f(u)+\dot{p}^e \tag{13}$$

with price expectations modelled as some function of past inflation rates.

The real wage hypothesis is based on the assumption that money wage inflation is related to the discrepancy between workers' target real wage and the actual real wage. One difficulty with this approach is how to specify the target real wage. In practice this is normally done by representing it by a time trend. If unemployment and incomes policy are thought to modify the rate at which the discrepancy between target and actual real wages work into money wage increases, the basic equation is

$$\dot{W}_t=a+bt+cw_{t-1}+dI_t+eu_t \tag{14}$$

where t is the time period, w_{t-1} is the lagged real wage, and I_t captures the effect of incomes policies.

While there is evidence in the studies of wage inflation to suggest that unemployment has an inverse relationship with wage inflation, and that price expectations, lagged real wages, and incomes policies also have an important impact, they do not provide a sufficiently consistent picture to resolve the policy differences which depend on them. In reviewing the evidence, Artis and Miller (1979:61) conclude that 'neither the collection of equations representing various attempts to implement the augmented Phillips curve approach nor the collection of real wage equations could be said to contain estimates which are particularly robust with respect to what might appear to be minor modifications of the specifications used, and it cannot be said that there are as yet well-established results in this area'.

There are sufficient difficulties in estimating such equations that anyone convinced of their own theory of wage inflation is unlikely to be swayed by any empirical results. The main problem is that it is often impossible to measure many of the things thought to be important in the determination of wages. Price expectations are an obvious example. With no direct measure, investigators have relied either on some mechanistic formulation in terms of past inflation rates or rather crude survey results (Carlson and Parkin, 1975). The effects of incomes policy are never as neat as the above equation supposes. Apart from the conceptual problems of what constitutes an incomes policy, the after-effects and the anticipation of a policy confuse the picture considerably. Even the unemployment variable itself is often regarded as an inadequate measure of the state of the labour market. In this area, where many of the disagreements about unemployment and the appropriate macroeconomical policy hinge, the chances of resolving the difference by empirical evidence remain rather slim.

The second difference between the two models concerns the relationship between NAIRU and the level of unemployment benefit. One indication that NAIRU has increased in Britain over the post-war period is the change in the relationship between unemployment and vacancies. It is apparent that for a given level of vacancies, unemployment was considerably higher in the 1970s than it was in the early 1960s. One explanation of this is the rise in the ratio of unemployment benefits to earnings, due, in particular, to the introduction of the earnings-related supplement (ERS) in 1966. The effect of a high benefit ratio may be to induce unemployed workers to take longer searching for work which means that unemployment in aggregate is higher for the same level of vacancies. A time-series analysis by Maki and Spindler (1975) seems to confirm this argument and suggests that unemployment in Britain was 30 per cent higher than it would be in the absence of ERS. But this study has been heavily criticised (see Atkinson, 1981), particularly because of the difficulties of separating the effect of unemployment benefit from other trended variables.

An alternative approach is to use cross-section evidence on the individual probabilities of re-employment. Nickell (1979), for example, using the General Household Survey, concluded that ERS had increased the expected duration of recipients by about 25 per cent. This does not mean that ERS has increased unemployment in aggregate by a quarter; only a minority of claimants receive ERS, and by reducing the probability of re-employment of some unemployed workers, the probability of re-employment of others is increased. Although not immune from criticism, the cross-section evidence leads Atkinson (1981:146) to conclude that there is 'little ground to suppose that the introduction of ERS led to an "avalanche" of claims or that its abolition [in 1982] will dramatically reduce the level of unemployment'.

Of the two models of inflation and unemployment presented, the collective bargaining model would seem to provide the more convincing account for Britain in the post-war period. Its underlying assumptions are more plausible, the failure of investigators to find stable wage equations is entirely consistent with the model, and the lack of convincing evidence that the increase in NAIRU reflects an increase in unemployment benefit suggests that NAIRU is influenced by factors other than the behaviour of job searchers.

THE CURRENT UNEMPLOYMENT

How far do these various models help to explain the current high levels of unemployment? Despite their differences the common thread running through them is the distinction between some level of unemployment representing macroeconomic equilibrium (NAIRU) and the deviations in unemployment from that level. Indeed, there would be a high degree of consensus with the view that the increase in unemployment between the 1960s and 1982 has two parts to it: an increase in NAIRU and current unemployment in excess of NAIRU.

Economists would differ, however, over the nature of NAIRU, the degree to which it has increased, whether it is stable in the face of deviations from it, and the most appropriate ways of reducing it. There would, moreover, be disagreement about the movements around NAIRU:

whether they represent demand deficiency, the effects of poor information and surprises, or movements in classical unemployment. Also, different factors are identified as disturbing the actual level of unemployment from NAIRU: external factors such as the increase in oil prices or the world recession; errors in government policy such as an attempt to use Keynesian policies to reduce structural unemployment; struggles over the distribution of incomes; and changes in the overall performance of the economy.

Meade (1982) agues that there has been an increase in NAIRU for two reasons: first, trade union bargaining power has increased over the post-war period, and, second, there has been a fall in the rate of growth of labour productivity. The increase in bargaining power of trade unions means that for a given level of unemployment, unions seek a higher rate of growth of real earnings. But the fall in the rate of growth of productivity implies a lower rate of real wage growth if the share of profits remains constant. These two changes taken together mean either accelerating inflation or an increase in unemployment to reduce trade union bargaining power to a level compatible with non-accelerating inflation. In addition to these factors, the increase in oil prices in the mid-1970s threatened to reduce real incomes and led to an inflationary struggle to maintain them. The major impact of these forces has only recently been felt on unemployment since the government has bought time by expanding the economy in an attempt to achieve an unemployment level below the new NAIRU.

The monetarist account of high unemployment resembles Meade's in many ways. NAIRU is replaced by the natural rate to which the economy has a natural tendency to return. Inflation is attributed to past attempts by the government to reduce unemployment below the natural rate by allowing too rapid a growth in the money supply. Government plans to reduce inflation by a gradual reduction in the rate of growth of the money supply involved a transitory increase in unemployment above the natural rate. But much of the unemployment increase is attributed to increases in the natural rate. Monetarists normally emphasise increases in the level of unemployment benefit and legislation which places restrictions on redundancy and dismissal as factors pushing the natural rate upwards.

But the monetarist strategy for the British economy aims to achieve more than simply a return to zero inflation at the natural rate. It is based on the view that there is something seriously wrong with the British economy and that fundamental changes are required. Spurred by a vision of the neo-classical model of the competitive economy as a self-regulating mechanism, the aim is to reduce the size of the public sector which is seen as a burden on the private sector. The function of the present recession is not simply to reduce inflation but to promote competition between both firms and workers. Inefficient firms will be compelled to change their production methods or be driven out of business. At the same time workers will be forced to cooperate with employers in the elimination of restrictive practices and the introduction of new technology.

For Keynesians the level of unemployment is governed largely by aggregate demand. Aggregate demand depends on government fiscal policy, investment by private industry which will depend on business confidence and profitability, and on the savings decisions of consumers. But what is mainly responsible for disturbing the British economy is the demand for exports and imports. Typical of the Keynesian position is Thirlwall (1981:26) who argues that

> the rise in commodity prices in the early 1970s, and particularly the continuous increase in the price of oil since December 1973, has done two things to deflate aggregate demand. It has redistributed world income to a group of oil producing countries which lack the capacity to spend their incomes on goods produced by those countries which use oil . . . This situation has made it impossible for industrialised countries to grow at the same rate as hitherto without the willingness and ability to finance massive balance of payments deficits. Secondly, the rising cost of commodities and oil in the first half of the 1970s led to domestic inflation, and also caused a contraction in demand for domestically produced goods. The increased expenditure on necessary imports itself diverted monetary expenditure from domestic goods.

More recent increases in unemployment are attributed to a high exchange rate—due to the combination of North Sea Oil and restrictive monetary policy—and to the world recession.

For Keynesians, therefore, the balance of payments rather than the possibility of accelerating inflation is the main constraint on the government expanding demand. But in so far as the alternative to a balance of payments deficit is a deterioration in the exchange rate which would accelerate inflation, there is an implicit NAIRU in the Keynesian model. But such a NAIRU is then subject to considerable variation: it is influenced by developments in the world economy and it can be reduced through a successful incomes policy, or, as some Keynesians would argue, through import controls (Ward, 1981). As such it can be influenced by the main macroeconomic movements which would normally be associated with deviations from it. For this reason many Keynesians would not find NAIRU a particularly useful concept.

All three accounts of the current unemployment merit serious consideration because each highlights some important aspect of the problem. But none of them can be said to provide a complete answer: in each case only the proximate cause of unemployment is identified. Meade's account of the increase in NAIRU in terms of conflict over the distribution of income attributes much of the current unemployment to the system of wage bargaining in Britain. The implication is that what needs to be done is to devise a system of wage fixing which forces trade unions to take account of the employment consequences of their wage claims. But, as Tarling and Wilkinson (1982) have argued, the basis of this proposal fails to appreciate the realities of the British labour market. The monetarist account is appealing in so far as it points to the limitations of macroeconomic policy instruments in providing full employment and identifies fundamental problems with the British economy. But it is difficult to take seriously a view which assumes that the economy can never suffer from a deficiency of demand. The Keynesians by contrast are so obsessed by the level of demand that they incline to the view that sufficient demand will always cure unemployment without creating insuperable problems.

Only when these different views are brought together does a complete picture of Britain's economic problems emerge. The British economy has become locked in a vicious circle of cumulative decline, the origins of which can be traced back to the nineteenth century (Eatwell, 1982). Low demand has meant low investment and a slow rate of productivity growth, but low investment and low productivity have restrained the government's ability to expand demand without inflationary consequences. By the end of the 1970s the low productivity of its capital stock left the economy in a very vulnerable position. The recession has turned this into high unemployment but at the same time led to the scrapping of out-dated equipment which will hinder any attempt to reduce unemployment in the short-term.

THE PROSPECTS FOR UNEMPLOYMENT

Despite the considerable differences between economists over the nature and causes of the current unemployment, there does seem to be a surprising degree of agreement over the medium term prospects for unemployment. Some forecast a modest fall, others a further rise; but virtually all forecasts of predictions are for unemployment in Britain to remain in the region of three to four million for the next five years. What lies behind this pessimistic prediction?

Many of these predictions are based, of course, on the premise that the government will maintain its present monetary policy designed to reduce inflation and that this policy inevitably means continued high unemployment. But even those who argue that the rise in unemployment over the last three years could have been avoided if a different policy had been pursued, do not believe that a simple reversal of the policy could reduce unemployment to its 1979 level of one million. The reason for this is that the industrial base of the economy is now very weak.

Apart from the low level of training and investment over the last three years, the recession and the high value of sterling have resulted in the closure of plants and the scrapping of equipment which is unlikely to be re-usable however high demand is pushed up or sterling devalued. There are some signs of increased efficiency in those sectors of industry which have weathered the recession but there is not sufficient capital to employ much more labour, particularly if the level of labour productivity is as high as is often supposed. Such a sector of the economy may form the basis of a long-term recovery towards full employment but it is unlikely to provide many more jobs in the immediate future.

There remains the possibility of reducing unemployment in the shorter run by increasing employment in the less capital-intensive service and public sectors. Attempts to achieve this through general expansionary policies runs the risk of over-expansion in the manufacturing sector. But a policy of direct job creation in the public sector, or a policy of subsidising jobs generally through reductions in employers' national insurance contributions, might avoid these problems. The attractiveness of direct job creation is that it might be done at little net cost to the Exchequer: against the cost of wages paid must be offset the reduction in unemployment benefit and the increase in income tax. The task then is to design a job creation scheme or subsidy which is, as far as possible, paid in respect of extra jobs. This means that across-the-board subsidies, such as a reduction in national insurance contributions, are not as effective as direct job creation in the public sector. But the prospects of drastically reducing unemployment by these means are poor. It is often argued that short-term job creation hinders the long-run recovery by directing labour and expenditure to tasks which do little to improve the country's economic performance, and even the most enthusiastic supporters of such a policy would not expect to create more than half a million jobs in the next five years (Barker, 1982).

The main policy debate now centres on how to generate a long-term recovery to restore unemployment: should the government pursue a tight policy together with measures to promote competition, should it expand demand as much as possible to promote expansion, or should it intervene more directly in the process of investing in industry? Most forecasters agree that whatever policy is pursued it will not have any substantial effect on unemployment over the next three to four years, but they do predict major differences in the effects of the various policies by the end of the decade. But against this must be set the argument that new developments in microelectronics will have a considerable effect on employment over the next decade.

In classifying unemployment no separate category called 'technological unemployment' was identified. This is perhaps not surprising since unemployment classification tends to distinguish between different explanations of why equilibrium in the labour market is not reached rather than between the factors which disturb labour market equilibrium in the first place. To ask whether technological unemployment exists is to ask whether there are any factors associated with the introduction of new techniques which will prevent a restoration of full employment. One possibility is that technical change creates demand-deficient unemployment. Technical change implies increasing labour productivity and if there is no change in aggregate demand this would mean a reduction in labour demand. Unless there is insufficient capital to employ more workers the government should be able to stimulate demand and so reduce unemployment to NAIRU.

Technical change may have an impact on NAIRU in two ways. First, it may create structural unemployment. Technical progress will mean an increase in the demand for labour for some occupations and a reduction in demand for other occupations. Unless the allocative mechanism of the labour market is very efficient the transfer of labour is unlikely to be achieved without some structural unemployment. Second, NAIRU is determined not simply by the level of structural unemployment but by the position the Phillips curve and the rate of growth of labour productivity. Meade attributes much of the current unemployment to the low rate of productivity growth. If he is correct, the increase in labour productivity associated with the introduction of new technology ought to lower NAIRU. This assumes that the position of the Phillips curve remains the same. In terms of Rowthorn's analysis what matters is whether technical progress exacerbates distributional conflict. If employers and workers together seek to capture a proportion of the gains from technical progress which add up to more than is available, technical progress will lead to a higher rate of unemployment.

Thus if technical change does have an impact on unemployment, it can be analysed within the usual classification of unemployment without creating a new category of technological unemployment. This is not to say that the relationship between technical change is straightforward or that the impact of microelectronics on unemployment can be easily predicted. But the factors which will determine whether new technology will mean high unemployment or economic recovery are precisely those which were found to be important in explaining current unemployment. What has mattered in the past and what will matter in the future are the level of investment, the constraints imposed by the world economy on the government's ability to stimulate demand, and the extent to which unemployment is used to contain the rate of inflation.

11 Wage Structure

David Marsden

Pay relativities are a major source of contention in industrial relations, giving rise to problems at the plant and company level in collective bargaining and at the national level in the management of incomes policies. Economists and managers point out that wages are the price of labour, and that differences in wage levels play an important part in directing labour to those jobs in which it is most needed and will be most productive. But workers have strong views on fairness, the importance of which is also stressed by many sociologists and industrial relations specialists. Many believe that pay should be commensurate with the status and the usefulness of a person's job, or that because the ability to earn one's living is a badge of citizenship, all jobs should provide a living wage which does not require supplementing from public funds. At a more concrete level, comparability with the pay levels of other groups of workers is a common argument used in pay negotiations. Sometimes all these views coincide, but often they do not, and the difficult problem arises as to how far the achievement of one objective, for example, economic efficiency, may prejudice the achievement of another, for example, social justice. To tackle this problem it is necessary to have some idea of the factors which determine wage structures and how they interact.

This chapter begins with a discussion of pay differentials between industries, and an analysis of some of the evidence relating to the extent to which the inter-industry wage structure serves to allocate labour between industries. Clearly, if differences in pay levels play a major part in this process, then there is a price to be paid if differentials are altered to achieve some other objective. The second part of the chapter deals with occupational differentials, including skill differentials. The main focus is on the secular decline in occupational differentials over the century, and, in particular, on the compression of such differentials during the 1970s. The factors that account for these changes are analysed in order to shed some light on the processes governing occupational pay structures. The conclusion attempts to bring together these various strands and to see how far the explanations of pay structures and of changes in them can illuminate the difficult choice of balancing economic efficiency and people's beliefs about fair differentials.

INDUSTRIAL WAGE STRUCTURE

One of the interesting features of the industrial wage structure is its broad stability over time, combined with periodic and sometimes dramatic changes in the position of individual industries. This has given rise to two broad competing views. One is that the industrial wage structure is largely determined by customary pay relativities which grow out of the widespread use of arguments based on comparability by union bargainers. The other is that differences in average pay levels between industries reflect certain underlying economic factors which change fairly slowly, such as differences in the relative level of skill required in different industries or differences in the pleasantness of working conditions. These two views are not mutually exclusive, but individual economists differ greatly in the weight which they attach to one or other view.

This section of the chapter begins with an account of which are the highest and lowest paid industries, and of some of the reasons put forward to explain differences in pay levels. The following section examines some of the changes that have occurred in recent years and why they took place. It also considers evidence on the extent to which industry wage differentials promote the flow of labour to those industries in which it is most needed.

Current Industrial Wage Structure

In April 1981 workers in newspaper printing and publishing stood at the top of the industrial earnings league for manual men, followed by those in mineral oil refining, and then by coal miners. Coming about seventieth, at the bottom of the earnings ladder, were agricultural workers, who were trailing some way behind manual men in catering who, in turn, were behind those in educational services, textile industries, and retail distribution. The full details of the ten highest paid, and the ten lowest paid industries for manual men are shown in Table 11.1.

Many writers have observed that the position of workers in different industries on the inter-industry earnings ladder does not change greatly even over fairly long periods. Indeed, despite the almost five-fold increase in hourly earnings between 1970 and 1981, seven of the top ten industries and eight of the bottom ten industries in 1970 were still in their respective group in 1981. Marsden (1980) and Saunders and Marsden (1981) showed that there was a similar overall stability of inter-industry ranking in other West European countries, and Crossley (1966) and Phelps Brown and Browne (1962) brought together evidence for earlier periods for the United Kingdom and the United States. Before discussing some of the exceptions to this pattern, it is necessary to look at the reasons for inter-industry wage differentials. Simple inspection of the industries themselves will reveal a number of fairly obvious factors, but their equally obvious

TABLE 11.1: THE TEN HIGHEST AND LOWEST PAID INDUSTRIES FOR
MANUAL MEN, APRIL 1981

Ten Highest Paid Industries			*Ten Lowest Paid Industries*		
MLH		*Pay*	*MLH*		*Pay*
485	Newspaper printing	157·8	812	Other wholesale distribu-	
262	Mineral oil refining	143·2		tion (exc. food and drink)	86·7
101	Coal mining*	133·6	XIII	Textiles (exc. synthetic	
	(underground)	(145·9)		fibres)*	86·2
707	Air transport	130·8	894	Motor repairs &	
601–2	Electricity & gas*	122·9		distribution	85·5
489	Other printing &		831–2	Dealing in industrial	
	publishing	120·7		materials	85·3
706	Port and inland water		441–9	Clothing*	84·0
	transport	119·8	820–1	Retail distribution	83·6
271	General chemicals	117·5	414	Woollen worsted	82·3
383	Aerospace equipment		872	Educational services	80·6
	manufacturing*	117·3	884–8	Catering	77·9
311	Iron and steel (general)	113·9	001	Agriculture	72·4

Source: Department of Employment, *New Earnings Survey 1981*, pt. C.
Note: Adult manual men, average gross hourly earnings, including overtime. Earnings as per cent of all industries and services (manual men).
* Not in top or bottom ten in 1970.

diversity will also suggest that there is no single factor which accounts for pay levels in all industries.

Whether an industry employs a relatively highly skilled or an unskilled labour force is one reason for differences in average earnings between industries. Among the top ten industries a number employ a very skilled labour force: for example, coal mining, printing, and aerospace manufacture. Among the low paid industries, a number rely to a great extent upon casual and relatively unskilled labour: for example, catering, educational services, and retail distribution. But most process workers in mineral oil refining, chemicals, and iron and steel, as well as most baggage handlers in air transport, are considerably less skilled than engineering craftsmen who make up the larger part of the labour force in a number of industries not even represented in the top ten either in 1981 or in 1970. Moreover, agricultural and horticultural workers often undergo quite long periods of training and have to work with a far greater variety of equipment than most semi-skilled workers. Hence differences in relative skill levels are not the only factor explaining differences in average earnings between industries.

Working conditions are another factor affecting earnings, as people expect to be compensated for unsocial, unpleasant, and dangerous working conditions. According to Marshall (1920), workers judge jobs by their 'net advantages'. Thus industries in which such conditions predominate might be expected to be more highly paid. This is certainly borne out in industries such as newspaper printing and air transport, which involve unsocial hours, and in industries such as coal mining and iron and steel, which involve a significant amount of shift working or danger. On these criteria, however, agriculture again should be one of the higher paid industries in view of the long hours in certain seasons and of the relatively high incidence of pulmonary disease among farm workers. Hence the overall correlation between relative earnings and working conditions in different industries appears to be fairly weak but this may result from the diversity of occupational groups found in such diverse industries as agriculture and oil refining. A stronger relationship might be found among a more homogeneous group of industries and between people in the same occupation. This is because workers in different occupations often constitute non-competing groups. For example, electrical work to be carried out in particularly unpleasant or dangerous working conditions would require special payment in order to attract suitably qualified electricians from other electrician jobs. However, precise testing of the impact of conditions upon relative earnings is hard because of the difficulty of measuring working conditions.

Inspection of the highest and lowest paid industries points to two other possible influences on pay structure. First, most of the highest paid industries are fairly concentrated, dominated by a few large firms, whereas the lowest paid industries, except for educational services, are characterised by small and medium-sized firms. Moreover, data on unionisation presented in Chapter 1 indicate (in so far as differences of industrial classification permit comparison) a higher level of union density on the whole among the highest paid group of industries. One possibility, therefore, is that concentrated industries can obtain higher profits through their greater power in product markets, and that the high degree of unionisation enables workers to obtain a share of these monopoly gains. A good deal of research (Weiss, 1966) indicates that there is a definite tendency for industrial concentration to lead to higher earnings, but the nature of the link is uncertain. Weiss found that workers in the more concentrated industries also tended to be more skilled and better endowed with a number of other productive traits so that, once account was taken of these factors, the effect of concentration on earnings was much reduced.

A number of studies in Britain and the United States have found that unionisation has a positive effect upon earnings. This is usually thought to occur because unions are able to push the price of labour above the level indicated by long-run supply conditions—that is above the level required to call forth an adequate number of suitably trained workers—with the result that employers take on rather fewer such workers. Those not taken on are left to increase the supply of non-union labour which increases competition in that section of the labour market, and may often depress the wage there. Pencavel (1974), looking at the differential between union members and non-members, estimated the differential for those unionised to be about

14 per cent. Mulvey (1976) estimated that those covered by local (as distinct from national) agreements earned between 46 and 48 per cent more than those not covered by collective agreements, while Nickell (1977) put the differential between those covered by collective agreements and those not covered at between 20 and 28 per cent for men and between 44 and 49 per cent for women. Thus there is some evidence that workers in the higher paid industries may benefit from a greater degree of unionisation and in particular from a higher degree of coverage by collective agreements, but the higher of the results appear rather extreme.

A futher important difference between the higher and the lower paid industries, particularly among those in manufacturing, lies in the age and sex composition of their labour forces. The textile industries, in common with a number of other lower paid manufacturing industries, employ a relatively high proportion of young workers, and an even greater proportion of women. Marsden (1980) found a similar pattern in production industries in the six original member countries of the EEC. The number of young people in such industries with stable or declining employment suggests that they only remain there a short time before seeking jobs in other industries, and this gives rise to high rates of labour turnover, although it is also likely that the work experience of these young workers will be of little help to them in obtaining access to the more skilled jobs in the better paid industries. This difference in the pattern of employment between some of the lower paid and the higher paid industries may be an indication of labour market segmentation. In these conditions, some industries are low paid because the firms in them either choose, or are forced, to operate with a low wage section of the labour force consisting of women, young workers, or other poorly organised groups. For some of the low paid manufacturing industries, for example textiles, this may be the only way to survive against competition from producers in the Third World.

Changes in Industrial Pay Structure in the 1970s

The main changes which occurred in the ten highest and lowest paid industries between 1970 and 1981 have been in the rise into the top ten of coal mining, aerospace equipment manufacture, and electricity and gas; and the fall of the car industry from fourth position in 1970, just behind mineral oil refining, to a position in the middle of the distribution, with earnings falling from 31 per cent above the average for all manual men in 1970 to less than 5 per cent by 1981. Some of these changes are the result of the oil crisis which gave rise to the sharp increase in the bargaining power of workers in the energy sector, particularly in coal mining, and of the collapse in the bargaining power of car workers as British car producers struggled against greatly intensified competition. At the lower end the main changes have been the arrival of textiles and clothing in the bottom ten, and the movement of manual men in national and local government to positions just above the bottom ten.

Although it may be possible to find plausible reasons for the pay movements of specific industries, evidence of more general influences upon changes in industry ranking is much more uncertain. Indeed Turner (1957) tried to reconcile the broad stability of the inter-industry ranking of pay levels over the time with occasional dramatic movements from individual industries by arguing that the ranking was based largely upon custom, and that only from time to time were economic pressures so great as to break the mould and bring about such readjustments as happened in the coal and the car industries in the 1970s.

It is often said that wage differentials play an important role in the allocation of labour between firms and industries. Thus one of the chief options open to a firm wanting to expand its labour force is to raise its wages; firms which are either unable or unwilling to respond will experience a corresponding fall in job applicants and possibly an increase in labour wastage. The OECD (1965) carried out a major review of the evidence, did some statistical work of its own, and found that there did not appear to be any convincing relationship between increases in an industry's relative wages and changes in its share of employment. Such evidence as did appear to support the view that movements in relative wages served an allocative function equally supported the view that industries with expanding markets, and thus with increasing employment needs, could afford to bargain away some of their increased profits. Thus employment and relative wages could rise together in response to some third factor without relative wages playing much part in attracting new job applicants. In some countries the OECD noted that there was a correlation between changes in relative wage levels and employment changes at the broad industry level, but that this disappeared when a more disaggregated industrial classification was used. Reddaway (1959), who observed this pattern for Britain, suggested that at the more aggregated level the bargaining arrangements of larger industries prevailed, and that it was their employment needs which dominated wage movements. At the more disaggregated level the relationship disappeared because there were many smaller industries whose wage movements did not reflect their changing employment needs but were determined by the wage settlements reached in larger industries. This argument is not very convincing, however, since it was put forward at the very time when plant bargaining, which could be expected to increase the possibility for independent wage movements among the more disaggregated industries, was growing rapidly.

The OECD was criticised for relying too heavily upon the use of correlations between two variables which precluded detailed analysis of the effect of third variables such as those related to changes in an industry's prosperity. Pissarides (1978) postulated a different model in which firms could signal their need for labour to the market by announcing vacancies and by increasing relative wages. Using quarterly series on wages, employment, and vacancies for fourteen broad sectors, he found that changes in both relative wages and vacancies helped increase employment in an industry, although much smaller increases in relative wages were needed in order to produce the same percentage increase in employment as compared with increases in vacancies. Thus Pissarides's work suggests that changes in relative wages may well have the allocative effect stressed by economic theory.

These results have to be qualified by the findings of a number of local labour market studies, notably by Robinson (1970) and by MacKay et al. (1971). These show that wide disparities in earnings levels for the same occupation can persist even between firms in close proximity to each other, and that there is a good deal of ignorance among workers about the wages paid for similar jobs in other firms. These findings are not necessarily inconsistent with those of Pissarides, but they cast doubt on the quality of the labour mobility induced by changes in industry relative earnings. It is quite possible, but requires further investigation, that the mobility picked up by the highly aggregated statistics used by Pissarides is mainly among young workers, the unskilled, and only to a lesser extent among skilled workers. Another reason for these wage disparities for similar jobs may be that access to many of the better paid jobs, with the notable exception perhaps of craft jobs, is through the firm's internal labour market. In many cases access to skilled jobs is by upgrading within the firm, with the result that higher paid semi-skilled and non-craft skilled workers from other firms cannot compete directly for these jobs but must first accept an initial period in a less skilled and lower paid job.

Finally, although changes in industry-relative pay might be expected to be related to changes in productivity, very little long-term evidence has been found to support this (see Phelps Brown and Browne, 1962; and Salter, 1966). But Phelps Brown and Browne point out that only in certain extreme cases was there a relationship between increases in an industry's productivity and increases in its relative wages. This they suggested was because in most industries productivity gains were passed on to the consumer in the form of lower prices because of competitive product market conditions. It is also possible that normative pressures in pay differentials are such that industries which do not experience such productivity increases have to pay the wage levels set in more prosperous industries, and that this hastens their decline in employment.

To conclude, the problem with analysing the industrial wage structure is that theory and policy ask questions about the functions of wage structure, and the possible consequences of changing it, to which the data provide only faint and ambiguous answers. Over fairly long periods the industrial wage structure displays a high degree of stability, although there have been a number of notable changes affecting specific industries. This might be seen as a partial vindication of the forces of custom and comparability over market forces, but it has also to be remembered that such stability in the industrial wage structure is not unique to Britain. It can be found in most other industrial countries, with widely differing institutional arrangements for pay determination. Comparability is an argument very frequently used in British wage bargaining because of its highly decentralised and fragmented structure, but it is less commonly invoked in many other countries where different bargaining structures prevail. A similar set of problems can be found concerning the occupational wage structure.

OCCUPATIONAL WAGE STRUCTURE

The measurement of occupational differentials is more complicated than that betweeen industries. There is an element of arbitrariness in the delineation of the highest paid occupational groups, and a more disaggregated view of these groups is likely to show bigger differentials between the highest and the lowest paid occupations because of the skewed nature of the distribution of earnings. Fringe benefits also pose difficult problems, particularly for the measurement of the earnings of the highest paid groups. Hence the following discussion will focus upon gross earnings. It does not deal with fringe benefits and non-cash payments; an analysis of managerial fringe benefits in Britain and abroad can be found in HAY-MSL (1976). The discussion begins by examining the range of occupational differentials and some of the factors which underlie them; it goes on to look at long-term changes and their causes, followed by short-term changes in structure and their causes.

Structure of Occupational Differentials

An overall picture of occupational differentials and their long-term changes this century is given in Table 11.2 which is based on Routh (1980a). In 1978 the average earnings of the higher professional group were about 73 per cent above the average for all workers, while those of the unskilled were about 30 per cent below this figure. Thus differences in pay between occupations are markedly bigger than those between industries. In Britain, as compared with other countries, differentials between higher management and other occupations are somewhat smaller than in France and Italy, but somewhat larger than in West Germany, and roughly similar to those in the United States (see HAY-MSL, 1976; Saunders and Marsden, 1979).

There is considerable controversy concerning the explanation of occupational differentials and about the policy implications of changes in them. The first explanation to be examined is the 'human capital' approach, the view that the differentials reflect the rate of return on investment in education and training. The second, the 'non-competing group' approach, accepts that training is important, but stresses that it also serves to restrict access to occupations, so that differentials often may include an element of monopoly rent. The third, the 'hierarchy' approach, stresses that the pay hierarchy is a reflection of the social hierarchy so that social status and the structure of authority in different societies are as important determinants of occupational differentials as is investment in education. Empirically, it is very difficult to choose between these explanations because of the close relationship between all the variables

TABLE 11.2: OCCUPATIONAL DIFFERENTIALS FOR MEN, 1913–1978

Occupational Class	1913–14	1922–4	1935–6	1955–6	1960	1970	1978
1. Higher professional (a)	348·9	323·3	340·9	243·1	239·9	171·5	173·1
(b)	(348·9)	(328·8)	(342·7)	(261·2)	(272·7)	(202·6)	(195·4)
2. Lower professional	164·9	177·8	165·6	96·2	99·9	110·4	113·6
3. Managers	212·8	266·7	236·6	233·4	218·2	199·2	168·2
4. Clerks	105·3	101·1	103·2	82·5	80·4	78·3	77·3
5. Foremen	130·9	148·9	146·8	123·7	119·7	97·8	97·9
6. Skilled manual	112·8	100·0	104·8	98·1	93·9	84·4	91·0
7. Semi-skilled manual	73·4	70·0	72·0	74·0	68·5	75·5	80·0
8. Unskilled manual (a)	67·0	71·1	69·4	68·6	63·1	67·6	70·8
(b)	(67·0)	(72·3)	(69·7)	(73·7)	(71·7)	(79·9)	(79·9)
All classes (current weights)	100·0	100·0	100·0	100·0	100·0	100·0	100·0

Source: Derived from Routh (1980: table 2.27).
Note: The figures show the average earnings of men in seven occupational classes as a percentage of the weighted average of all groups. Figures (a) show differentials using current weights and thus reflect the effect of changes in occupational structure on the average for all groups, while figures (b) shows the differential that would apply had there been no change in occupational structure since 1913.

involved, but an assessment is important because of the different consequences each would predict for a reduction or an increase in occupational differentials.

'Human Capital' and Earnings

Human capital theory (see, for example, Becker, 1975; Mincer, 1962, 1974) tries to account for both the size of occupational differentials and their function in allocating labour between different occupations. The basic idea underlying this approach is very simple: the earnings differentials between occupations, after allowing for compensation for differences in such factors as working conditions and risk, embody the return earned by different levels of investment by the employee in education and training. Differences in the rate of return earned by the investment in the training required to enter different occupations serve to allocate labour between these occupations; those with the higher rate of return attracting investment by additional people, and those with a lower rate discouraging it. As additional people enter a particular occupation the rate of return will fall, and, under conditions of competitive equilibrium, the rate of return on investments in all forms of training should be the same, except in so far as they reflect compensation for other aspects of the work involved, such as risk or working conditions.

Because of the time required to undertake additional training, changes in occupational differentials can only bring about gradual adjustments in the supply of labour to different occupations. Thus many employers may be reluctant to raise or lower the relative pay of a particular occupation as a means of short-term adjustment, particularly in view of the amount of negotiation that would probably be required. Hence they may prefer to increase overtime or to spend more themselves on training. To assess the effectiveness of the allocative function of occupational differentials it is necessary to examine some of the evidence bearing on the relationship between education and training (as the prime means of access to many occupations) and earnings.

The relationship between education and earnings is best illustrated in Table 11.3. The bottom row of the table shows that men with a degree or equivalent diploma earned about 70 per cent more and that the unskilled earned about 10 per cent less than the median for all men. The table also shows another important aspect of differentials which applies equally to

TABLE 11.3: EARNINGS OF MALES BY AGE AND BY HIGHEST QUALIFICATION LEVEL ATTAINED, GREAT BRITAIN, 1975–1976

	Degree or Equivalent	Below Degree Higher Education	GCE 'A' Level or Equivalent	GCE 'O' Level or Equivalent or CSE Grade 1	CSE Other Grades/ Commercial or Apprenticeship	No Qualification	All Males
16–19	. .[a]	. .[a]	. .[a]	42	37	45	42
20–24		86	81	84	85	80	82
25–34	144	121	116	111	104	94	107
35–44	200	150	130	120	105	99	111
45–59	217	155	128	124	101	94	103
60–64	. .[a]	. .[a]	. .[a]	. .[a]	92	84	87
All aged 16–64	168	131	107	100	97	91	100

Source: General Household Survey (1976).
Notes: Median annual earnings of males aged 16–64 in full-time employment (i.e. working 31 hours or more per week including overtime) as per cent of the median for all men (£2790).
[a] Too few observations.

educational levels and occupations: earnings inequality increases with age. Between the ages of twenty and twenty-four, those in full-time employment with a degree earned about the same as those whose highest qualifications were the General Certificate of Education at Ordinary levels, the Certificate of Secondary Education or apprenticeship. By their late forties, however, they were earning twice as much as those with the CSEs or an apprenticeship.

In the case of the formal education shown in Table 11.3, the investment made by employees consists of direct costs such as course fees, and indirect costs in the form of the income that could have been earned had the employees worked with their existing level of qualification instead of studying. In Britain, a high proportion of the direct costs are borne out of general taxation and so represent an investment by the community as a whole, but the indirect costs can be considerable. If the difference between a student grant and alternative annual earnings were £4,000, the foregone earnings from a three-year degree course could be as much as £12,000. The human capital theorist argues that people will approach each additional stage in their training in the same way as they would investment in capital equipment or stocks and shares. Hence they will only undertake additional training if the differential represents an adequate return on their investment.

A different type of training underlies the tendency of earnings to increase with age. It is argued that this is related to the accumulation of experience and training on the job. If this is the major factor, it is clear that opportunities for on the job training vary greatly between occupations, and must be greatest for people who have a university degree, since their earnings increase most with age, and least for those requiring no qualifications. Investment in on-the-job training involves the employer to a considerable extent, but the nature of the involvement depends upon the type of qualification. In the case of transferable skills, such as those obtained in most apprenticeships, employers may be reluctant to incur the full cost of the investment because they will lose all benefit from it if workers leave after completing their training. Where this is likely to happen, the employer is likely to share the cost of the investment with the employee, and this is usually done by the payment of a special trainee rate which is below both what the worker could earn elsewhere (compare the earnings of sixteen-to-nineteen-year-olds with CSE or an apprenticeship with those with no qualifications in Table 11.3) and the worker's marginal product. This gives rise to an indirect investment by the employee in the acquisition of transferable skills, and this in turn gives rise to an earnings profile which increases with age until the full skill level is attained.

In the case of non-transferable skills—that is, skills which have only a limited market outside the employee's present firm—the likelihood of leaving is lower. Hence the employer will be willing to bear more of the cost of training, thus requiring a smaller investment by the employee. In theory then, the employer will recoup the greater part of the return on training, and the employee's age-earnings profile will be flatter. For people with a degree, the extra time and effort spent on the job early in their careers, competing for their first promotion, may represent the additional source of investment needed to account for the greater increases of their earnings with age.

It is exceedingly difficult to measure investment in on-the-job training because much of it is highly informal and unlikely to figure in company accounts. Mincer (1962, 1974) estimated the extent of on-the-job training (including apprenticeships) compared with formal education for the United States. To do this he had to use the age-earnings profiles for different levels of formal education. He had to assume a sufficiently close approximation to competitive equilibrium in labour and other markets in order to be able to link the earnings profiles to employees' increasing marginal productivity through investment in training; perfect capital markets so that funds for investment in training were equally available to equally suitable candidates; and perfect information about alternative investment opportunities. On this basis Mincer estimated that at each level of education (primary, secondary, and higher) the marginal cost of on-the-job training (the cost of each additional stage of training) was greater than for formal education, and that the amount invested in on-the-job training was greater the higher the initial level of formal education. In this way Mincer was able to highlight the great economic importance of on-the-job training.

He estimated that the total amount of the variation in earnings explained statistically for the United States by investment in formal education and in on-the-job training was about two thirds. Psacharopoulos and Layard (1979) argued that, because of certain technical estimation problems, Mincer's estimate was probably too high, and on their own analysis found that in Britain human capital explained about one third of the variation in earnings. The ideal test of the allocative function of occupational differentials would be to study changes in the rates of return on the investment in education and training required for entry into different occupations. Those offering the highest rates of return would attract investment by additional workers, whose entry into these occupations would cause the rate of return to decline back towards the average. Similarly, occupations for which demand was in decline would offer lower rates of return and so discourage investment. Thus the working of the market for human capital would bring rates of return on different qualifications into rough equality. But such a test would be extremely difficult. Hence empirical support for the allocative function depends upon empirical support for the theory as a whole, and thus on the ability of the theory to account for differentials between people with different qualifications.

A good deal of the controversy about the contribution of human capital theory arises because many of the simplifying assumptions made in order to proceed to econometric testing beg fundamental questions raised by other approaches. First, the assumption of equal availability of funds for investment in education for people with equal potential (perfect capital markets) begs the question of the effect of inter-generational inequality and of social stratification upon the occupational pay structures. Second, the assumption that earnings differentials reflect the marginal product of different employee investments in education and training requires competitive labour markets with a high degree of labour mobility. This is hard to justify in non-competitive labour markets, and particularly in the wage structures of internal labour markets. Third, the assumption that rising age-earnings profiles reflect investment in on-the-job training makes the bold assumption that the hierarchy of authority within organisations is simply a hierarchy of marginal productivity, and that it only requires technical or social skills developed on the job.

Finally, it should also be said that Saunders and Marsden (1981) found that differentials between as few as eight occupations explained about 30 per cent of the total variation in earnings in production industries in Britain, and more in several other West European countries. This finding may indicate that the direction of causality between education and occupational earnings can be reversed, and it is consistent also with the theories to be discussed in the next two sections.

Non-Competing Groups and Occupational Differentials

The theory of non-competing groups tends now to be invoked more often to account for certain specific aspects of the occupational pay structure than as a fully blown theory in its own right, although the theory, as expounded by Cairnes (1887) and Taussig (1927), was intended to stand alone. The basic idea, as it has survived, is that the labour market is fragmented into a large number of occupational sub-markets, and that the forces of labour market competition and labour mobility are effective only within these. Each skill or professional group tries to regulate entry into its own occupational sub-market in order to restrict the supply of its own type of skill and thus push its income above the competitive level, thereby earning a monopoly rent.

Restrictive rules on access to training are among the commonest devices used, and were cited by the Webbs (1920) as one of the 'economic devices' used by craft unions in the nineteenth century. The use of the apprenticeship system today to control access to craft-work occupations remains one of the most sensitive issues facing the reform of Britain's system of industrial training. But such rules are also common in the professions. According to human capital theorists, the low pay and poor status and conditions experienced by young people entering such occupations represents an investment by trainees in acquiring training which will enhance their marginal product. But it could equally be argued that such conditions in fact represent barriers to entry, and discriminate against people from families which are unable to afford the economic burden, thus reducing the numbers that could enter the occupation. The financial burden might still be treated by the individual families as an investment, but it would be made under very different conditions to those assumed by the human capital approach.

The market power of such non-competing groups is limited by the factors affecting the elasticity of demand for the services which they provide, which in most cases is a derived demand, that is, one greatly influenced by the demand for the goods or services in which their labour is used. The less elastic the derived demand for their labour, the greater the extent to which they are able to raise their relative earnings by restricting access. The following four conditions determining this elasticity, known as the 'Marshall Rules', enable occupational groups to extract monopoly rents: a lack of available substitutes for their labour, an elastic supply of capital or of other groups of workers with which they work, an inelastic demand for the final product (consumers not being able to switch to other products), and their representing a small proportion of the total labour costs (the 'importance of being unimportant'). Hicks (1963:241–6, 375–8) has shown that the last condition holds only if the elasticity of demand for the product is greater than the elasticity of substitution between the occupational group in question and other groups. Indeed, he shows that if, for example, the demand for the product is inelastic while technical change enables easy substitution by other occupations for the group in question, the elasticity of demand is in fact greater the smaller the fraction of labour costs represented by the group.

Hence among the important factors limiting the market power of non-competing groups, and thus the extent to which they can raise their relative earnings, are the extent to which employers can find substitutes in production, and consumers can switch to alternative products. Collective bargaining may make it harder for employers to substitute other occupational groups, but it is unlikely to have much influence over consumer preferences. The existence of such pressures leads many economists to expect the position of any particular non-competing group to be undermined in the long run. It could be argued that the great increase in access to public education this century has reduced the ability of many occupational groups to restrict the supply of their labour and increased the possibilities of substitution, and hence is a reason for the long-term decline in occupational differentials to be observed in Table 11.2 and to be discussed shortly.

One of the most important forms of non-competing group in labour markets today arises out of the development of internal labour markets. An internal labour market may be said to exist when an employer regularly fills certain vacancies by upgrading or redeploying existing staff, while reserving certain positions as entry grades. Doeringer and Piore (1971) have argued that one reason for the development of such practices lies in the importance of on-the-job training in technical environments which do not give rise to transferable skills, but this is unlikely to be the whole explanation. One important consequence of this development is that once workers have developed such non-transferable skills they cannot leave to go to another firm and expect to earn the same income, and employers cannot recruit people for such vacancies from their local labour markets. Hence normal labour market competition cannot apply, and relationships of bilateral monopoly predominate in which bargaining plays a major role involving employers and many small groups of workers within each firm.

The non-competing groups associated with internal labour markets differ markedly from those on which the earlier theory was based as their existence is largely confined to individual firms, and entry into the group is usually governed by the employer rather than by a union or professional body. Moreover, the extent to which they can earn a monopoly rent depends on the countervailing power of the employer.

Pay structure within internal labour markets is governed by many complex processes. Internal differentials have to be adequate to persuade workers to accept and even seek upgrading, but pay levels must also be adequate relative to other firms in order to reduce wastage among workers, such as craftsmen, whose skills are transferable. A study by Marsden (1982) illustrates some of the difficulties of combining these two objectives in the mining industry, where face workers traditionally have the strongest position in their union and have the highest status and basic rates of pay. As a result craftsmen, now about one third of the skilled labour force in mining, have lower basic rates, but transferability of their skill has made their wastage rate fairly sensitive to earnings and employment opportunities, notably in the engineering and construction industries. In the event the solution adopted was to train more apprentices and to boost craftsmen's earnings with overtime and bonus payments. After the major increase in miners' pay in the early 1970s, shown in Table 11.1, wastage among craftsmen, though still a problem, became less serious.

The development of internal labour markets poses a number of difficult problems to conventional economic theories of pay structure, because these markets represent a major departure from the traditional model of the competitive labour market and place a much greater emphasis on the internal workings of the firm as opposed to those of local labour markets. Within the firm it is to be expected that workplace custom and organisational factors will exert a much stronger influence on pay.

Organisational Hierarchies and Earnings

A third explanation of occupational differentials, and particularly those related to managerial and related occupations, is that they are generated by the hierarchical structure of organisations. Education and training may help individuals gain access to certain jobs and may even develop certain skills that are required, but there is no straightforward link between earnings and the marginal productivity of investments in human capital. Earnings differentials may be related to a number of intra-organisational factors such as the level of responsibility required at different points in the managerial hierarchy, or the scale of operations in terms of output or the number of employees, or to more 'sociological' processes such as the functioning of the hierarchy of authority itself.

The distribution of individuals' earnings is approximately log-normal, except at the top end which conforms to the Pareto distribution. That is to say, when individuals' earnings are measured in proportionate terms by their logarithm, instead of in absolute terms, they are spread evenly on either side of the median, except for those of the highest paid among whom a progressively smaller percentage earn an amount progressively higher above the median. It has been suggested that the great spread of higher levels of earnings at the top end of the distribution can be explained by the hierarchical structure of organisations. Lydall (1968) proposed a simple hierarchical model which he fitted to the distribution of top earnings. In his model he assumes that employees within the firm are arranged hierarchically into discrete grades, that each manager supervises a constant number of people, and that at each level the manager receives a constant proportion of the earnings of those in the grade below. In this way, Lydall was able to account for the observed skewness in the distribution of higher earnings. An argument in the same vein is put forward by Thurow (1975) who proposed that the earnings levels associated with each level of the managerial hierarchy are determined by organisational rather than market forces, and that the prime form of labour market competition lies in competition for jobs whose earnings levels are fixed in accordance with organisational norms rather than in competition over the price to be paid for labour doing certain jobs.

Phelps Brown (1977) examined the relationship between occupational pay and the status or social prestige of certain jobs using the scale devised by Goldthorpe and Hope (1974). The scale was derived by asking a random sample of about 600 people to rank a selection of occupations by their status, and the rankings were then converted into a cardinal scale. Phelps Brown was able to show that the rankings of occupations by status and by average weekly earnings were in fairly close agreement, although the size of the dispersion about these averages was such as to give rise to a high degree of overlap between the earnings of large numbers of individuals in occupations with different levels of status. The evidence reviewed by Phelps Brown provides no conclusive answer as to whether status determines pay, or pay status, although it is probable that they are mutually reinforcing.

Some additional light is cast on this question by a series of multi-disciplinary research projects carried out at the Laboratoire d'Economie et de Sociologie du Travail (LEST). Daubigney and Silvestre (1972) and Maurice et al. (1978) compared a matched sample of French and West German manufacturing establishments. Their findings raise many important questions about the relationship between organisation structure, status, and relative earnings. First, the detailed matching of jobs and functions in the French and German firms revealed major differences in the organisation of the managerial hierarchy between the two countries (see Brossard and Maurice, 1974) which casts doubt on the extent to which hierarchical models of the type proposed by Lydall can be generalised to all countries. The main differences between the two countries to emerge in the studies were that the French firms had steeper hierarchies with a greater number of levels and, at each level, a smaller amount of autonomy from the level above. The contrast was particularly striking for foremen who were employed in greater number, and with less autonomy, in the French than in the German firms. They, in turn, left less autonomy to skilled workers whose skills were acquired to a much greater extent by company organised schemes and informal training. The authors argued that the resulting greater dependence of managerial and workers' skills upon the enterprise meant that managerial authority was not legitimated by an externally certified technical competence as in Germany and that this was why bigger occupational differentials within the French firms were required to reinforce managerial authority. Thus the authors were able by their comparative approach to give more substantive content to the 'status' factors affecting pay structure. The studies also have important implications for economic explanations of the occupational pay structure. The LEST found that the French firms not only paid their managerial and technical staff relatively more than manual staff as compared with their German counterparts, but that they also employed them in greater proportion, which is very difficult to account for in terms of conventional labour market theory and, in particular, of human capital theory.

This micro-level work has subsequently received some confirmation from aggregate statistical analyses of earnings structures in industry by Saunders and Marsden (1981), and has been extended, at this level, to include Britain and Italy. The authors found evidence of a greater reliance upon on-the-job training and of upgrading as a means of reaching skilled and higher white-collar occupations in France and Italy as compared with Germany and Great Britain. This lends further support to the observation of differences between countries in the pattern of hierarchical organisation within firms, and in the organisation of internal labour markets and their influence upon occupational pay structure.

Finally, occupational differentials as shown in Table 11.2 differ between countries not just in their overall spread, but also in their rank order. In Britain male clerks earn less than semi-skilled manual workers of the same sex. This is also true for West Germany, and would seem to bear out Marshall's (1920) prediction that as literacy spread, the earnings of copy clerks, which had once placed them among the highest paid artisans, would fall to the level for unskilled work. This is not true of either France or Italy, however, where literacy has spread to a broadly similar degree, but where clerical staff continue to earn more than skilled manual workers. The reason for this may lie in the organisation of the authority hierarchy in French and Italian firms, and in the greater dependence of the skills of manual workers in France and Italy upon the enterprise, owing to the absence of the highly developed apprenticeship systems found in Britain and Germany which provide skilled manual workers with a good deal of their independence and bargaining power. This poses a further problem for the human capital and other universalistic approaches, and suggests the need to look more closely at the way social structure interacts with such factors to shape pay structures.

Long-Term Trends in Occupational Differentials

The discussion so far has focused upon differences in pay between occupations at a particular time, but Table 11.2 shows that there have been marked changes in the course of this century. The following discussion begins with an analysis of some of the longer-term changes, and then turns to changes in the 1970s and the reasons behind some of these.

Table 11.2 shows that since the beginning of the century there has been a major reduction in the spread of occupational earnings between the professional and managerial occupations on the one hand, and the semi-skilled and unskilled on the other. The decline has not been steady, however, and the pattern has varied between occupations. The relative pay of the higher professional group fell during World War I, during World War II, and again during the 1960s, but the pay of managers and foremen followed a rather different course.

One of the chief factors believed to underly these long-term changes, although it does not fit very precisely with any particular change in the sub-periods in Table 11.2, has been the secular expansion of education. This has reduced the scarcity element which may have enabled the more highly paid groups to exact higher earnings earlier in the century. Similar trends have been observed in France, West Germany, and the Netherlands since about 1960 at least (Saunders and Marsden, 1981). The increase in education has also been associated with an increase in the proportion of workers in the higher paid occupations. This raises the level of average earnings for all workers combined, and so has tended to reduce the difference between the higher paid occupations and the average. The figures in Table 11.2 show occupational earnings compared with the average for all occupations based on the numbers in each occupation in the year to which the earnings figures relate; that is including the effect of the growth of the higher paid occupations. For the sake of comparison it also shows the earnings of the higher professional and the unskilled as a percentage of the average had there been no change in the proportion of workers in each occupation over the whole period (using 1911 weights). Comparison between these two sets of figures shows the extent to which the increase in the proportion of workers in the higher paid white-collar occupations has reduced the gap between these and the average level for all workers.

Routh (1980a) pointed out that the dispersion of earnings between individual manual workers has declined very little over the century. In so far as this represents the pattern for the dispersion of earnings between all workers (manual and non-manual), it can be shown that the reduction in differentials between occupations has been accompanied by an increase in the spread of earnings within occupations. Routh argued that one of the reasons for this has been the increasing importance of wage structures within internal labour markets, and that consequently the occupational groups listed in Table 11.2 correspond less closely now than at the beginning of the century to social groups with which individual workers might identify.

Changes in differentials in wage rates (as distinct from earnings) between skilled and unskilled workers over the century are brought out more clearly in Figure 11.1 which relates to the engineering and construction industries. Knowles and Robertson (1951) showed that the skill differential remained fairly stable up to World War I. It was then reduced drastically to about one-third of the pre-war level by 1919, and partially re-established in the early 1920s before beginning a further long decline from the mid-1930s to the early 1950s.

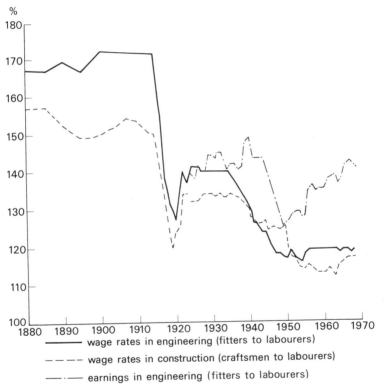

FIGURE 11.1: Skill Differentials in Wage Rates in Engineering and Construction, 1880–1968 and in Earnings in Engineering, 1920–1968
Source: Knowles and Robertson (1951); Department of Employment and Productivity, *British Labour Statistics: Historical Abstract* (1971: table 10); Hart and MacKay (1975).

Changes in earnings differentials, which include the effect of local bargaining excluded in the data on wage rates, as shown in Hart and MacKay's series (1975) which stretches from 1920, were broadly similar to those in wage rates in the 1920s and early 1930s, but the second period of decline in earnings differentials did not begin until about 1940 and was of shorter duration. From 1947 differentials in earnings began to increase and continued to do so until the late 1960s, compared with no change in differentials in nationally negotiated wage rates. Marked similarities in long-term trends in skill differentials can also be found in Germany, France, and the United States (see Saunders and Marsden, 1981: ch. 4).

There has been considerable debate about the causes of the secular reduction in skill differentials. Writing about the period up to the middle 1920s during which there had been a big reduction followed by a partial recovery in differentials, Rowe (1928) stressed two key factors. The first was technical change and the effect of changes in work practices during World War I brought about by 'dilution', through which semi-skilled and female workers were trained very quickly to undertake certain elements of craft work to help with the war effort. Rowe argued that whereas fitters had been a fairly homogeneous group up to World War I, by the end of the war their work had become much more specialised so that forty different specialisations could be identified. Although evidence is hard to come by it is likely that, despite the skilled workers' attempts to restore pre-war conditions after the war, they did not fully succeed in re-establishing their former degree of control over the supply of labour for skilled work.

The second factor, which was not unrelated and which was also stressed by Knowles and Robertson (1951), was the practice of compensating for increases or decreases in the cost of living by means of flat-rate rather than percentage increases in pay. Under normal conditions in which prices rise and subsequently fall, these sliding-scale agreements should not have any long-term effect upon differentials, but after World War I prices did not return fully to pre-war levels, so the flat-rate increases produced a permanent narrowing of differentials. Knowles and Robertson suggested that this was an unintended consequence of the system, but the point remains that skilled workers would not have allowed such a reduction to persist if they had had the organisational or market power to resist.

Turner (1952) suggested that skilled workers had indeed lost a good deal of their market power for the reasons already suggested by Rowe, and that the sliding-scale agreements, and the consequent reduction of differentials, was the price the skilled workers paid for integrating the unskilled and semi-skilled into their unions. By organising these groups, the skilled workers sought to prevent management from using them to undercut skilled work, and to keep control over any further dilution. They thus adopted a bargaining strategy designed to reinforce solidarity by demanding the same money increases for all grades. Turner strengthened his argument by pointing out that such changes had been strongest in the engineering and construction industries, in which unskilled and semi-skilled workers are prevented from attaining skilled status by the apprenticeship system, but that they had been much weaker in industries such as textiles, in which skilled status was much less exclusive and could be reached by upgrading. Moreover, in the latter industries workers of all skilled grades were organised into the same industrial unions. The main difficulty with Turner's argument is that while it is very persuasive for Britain, there is no reason to believe that it would apply to France, Germany, and particularly the United States, in which similar reductions in differentials occurred, since they all had very different trade union structures. Thus Turner's argument is probably best interpreted as illustrating one of the institutional processes through which the effect of technical change on skill differentials worked.

Reder (1955) sought to explain the pattern of change in skill differentials in the United States resting most of his evidence upon the fluctuations and decline in skill differentials in construction, which followed those of Britain fairly closely, plus more limited data on manufacturing. He suggested that changes in differentials were caused by changes in the elasticity of supply of skilled and unskilled workers over the economic cycle. In the upswing differentials are reduced because employers can upgrade unskilled and semi-skilled workers, thus increasing the supply of skilled workers, but the supply of unskilled labour is squeezed both by upgrading and by the fall in unemployment. Conversely, differentials increase in the downswing because the supply of unskilled workers increases faster. Reder's argument depends, however, upon the ability of employers to upgrade and downgrade workers over the cycle. This may be fairly common in American manufacturing industry as access to skilled jobs is commonly through seniority and upgrading (see Doeringer and Piore, 1971), but this is less true of either Britain or Germany, where apprenticeship plays a major role in skill training. Moreover, although Reder's argument is presented in general terms, the data to which he referred in his article are similar to those in Figure 11.1, and provide only tentative evidence of cyclicality in differentials. A further qualification of Reder's hypothesis is that in those industries in Britain in which Turner suggested that upgrading was the main route to skilled status the reductions in skill differentials in the war periods had been smaller than in engineering. Finally, Knowles and Robertson point out that for Britain there was relatively little connection between the periods of reduction in skill differentials and the level of unemployment, which indicates a further absence of support from British data for Reder's hypothesis.

The evidence on the secular decline in occupational and skill differentials suggests a mixture of certain economic changes, particularly through changes in long-term supply conditions as a result of the increase in general education, and technical change which affects the organisation of skilled work and the ability of skilled workers to control access to skilled status. The comparative evidence on the reduction in skill differentials from other European countries and the United States suggests that the institutional changes which occurred in Britain were mainly the channel through which were transmitted the effects of changes in production methods, work organisation, and education. But, as Turner's comparison between the engineering and textile industries showed, institutional factors can also exercise their own independent influence. Finally, the fluctuations about the long-term trend in skill differentials up to the 1970s do not appear to be the result of cyclical influences, nor to be closely related to variations in the level of unemployment.

Occupational Differentials in the 1970s

The 1970s were a very interesting period for pay structure. They saw both inflation and provisions in incomes policies designed to give greater protection to the low paid, both of which have been associated in the past with a narrowing of differentials. The decade also saw a marked rise in unemployment, which by virtue of its greater impact upon the unskilled, might have been expected to increase skill differentials.

In Table 11.4 the experience of eighteen occupations found mostly in production industries is followed from 1973 through to 1981. Year-to-year variations in relative pay may be the result of sampling errors or of the timing of major collective agreements and should be treated with caution. The period covered by the table spans the second stage of Mr Heath's incomes policy (April to November 1973—maximum increases of £1 plus 4 per cent) which had a mildly egalitarian leaning, and his fall from power in 1974 over the miners' strike. It also spans the rapid inflation of 1974–5 before the introduction of the Labour Government's and the TUC's Social Contract, which gave greater protection to the lower paid between mid-1975 and mid-1977, the subsequent relaxation and breakdown of this policy, and from mid-1979 the abandonment of incomes policy for the private sector under Mrs Thatcher's Government.

Although there were exceptions, many of the managerial and higher level white-collar occupations experienced a reduction of their relative pay in the mid-1970s. But in several cases the sharpest fall came between April 1974 and April 1975 before the special provisions of the Social Contract favouring the lower paid were introduced. This suggests that many groups of non-manual workers may have reacted less quickly to the increase in inflation which followed the oil crisis and the collapse of Mr Heath's incomes policy, and that the subsequent restrictions on the higher paid, while having some equalising pressure, exerted their main influence by preventing these groups from obtaining the bigger increases necessary to restore their relative pay levels.

There was some recovery of the differentials of higher paid non-manual workers towards the end of the last Labour Government, but the main changes came in 1980 and 1981. This probably reflects both the effect of the rise of unemployment on the bargaining position of less skilled manual workers, and of the pressures building up for a 'restoration of differentials' in the later phases of the Social Contract. One important factor is that the recession has led to a fall in overtime working, which is the main reason for the recent very sharp fall in the relative pay of engineering foremen, electricians, maintenance fitters, toolmakers, repetitive assemblers, and general labourers. This decline would also contribute to the increase in the

TABLE 11.4: RELATIVE EARNINGS OF SELECTED OCCUPATIONS, 1973–1981

Rank of Pay in 1981	1973	1974	1975	1976	1977	1978	1979	1980	1981
1 Finance etc. specialists	191·6	183·4	163·8	172·0	162·7	172·1	160·5	168·4	174·2
2 Personnel and industrial relations managers	157·0	151·6	146·9	146·0	142·9	142·2	134·8	149·0	155·3
3 Company secretaries	n.a.	n.a.	n.a.	138·2	143·4	147·4	144·5	143·7	152·4
4 Marketing & sales managers	155·1	154·1	139·6	135·5	146·3	147·5	142·6	147·1	144·9
5 Mechanical engineers	132·7	127·5	132·1	137·7	132·7	129·6	134·6	128·6	136·9
6 Production managers	129·4	124·9	119·7	125·2	125·1	124·0	123·3	131·2	127·3
7 Systems analysts and computer programmers	120·3	122·6	119·9	124·4	124·4	123·5	122·6	126·3	125·8
8 Accountants	128·4	125·2	121·4	120·5	121·6	120·5	118·1	126·2	124·1
9 Production engineers	123·9	116·8	120·9	119·6	119·7	118·3	118·2	118·1	111·4
10 Electricians (plant installation & maintenance)	106·9	108·0	106·7	105·8	105·2	106·7	112·2	107·3	102·4
11 Foremen (engineering machining)	111·7	109·4	109·4	106·3	106·5	112·0	112·3	106·7	102·1
12 Engineering draughtsmen	100·0	98·7	98·5	99·3	99·9	103·3	103·3	103·1	101·2
13 Clerical supervisors	99·8	104·8	99·0	101·7	98·1	95·4	95·3	100·2	101·1
14 Maintenance fitters	101·2	102·3	103·3	101·5	102·2	102·5	104·7	103·4	99·9
15 Toolmakers	103·6	105·0	99·5	98·2	98·6	100·8	102·7	98·4	90·4
16 Clerical (production etc.)	81·4	82·2	79·3	80·8	80·2	79·7	80·2	77·6	76·4
17 Repetitive assemblers	91·9	91·6	87·3	87·3	88·2	87·9	88·6	81·4	75·4
18 General labourers	77·1	77·1	78·5	78·4	76·5	77·0	78·1	75·5	73·2
All adult men	100·0	100·0	100·0	100·0	100·0	100·0	100·0	100·0	100·0

Source: Department of Employment, *New Earnings Survey*, D, 1973–81.
Note: Occupations arranged by level of pay in 1981. Average gross weekly earnings of adult men as per cent of all men. Pay is not affected by absence and includes overtime.

pay of managerial occupations as a percentage of the average for all workers. In contrast, some occupations experienced a steady improvement in their relative pay over the period as a whole, for example, systems analysts and computer programmers. Over the same period the numbers in these occupations roughly doubled indicating a strong demand for their skills. Hence, despite the rather negative evidence discussed earlier on the impact of supply and demand pressures on differentials, there are nevertheless individual cases in which their effect is apparent.

A more detailed picture of skill differentials in engineering and related industries in the 1970s is provided by a different survey by the Department of Employment which is given in Table 11.5. In the engineering industry, a small increase in skill differentials in the mid-1960s was followed by a sharp compression in the early to mid-1970s, and a subsequent 'restoration' of differentials in the late 1970s. The compression of the early 1970s was also noted by Brown (1976) using data obtained from another sample of engineering firms.

TABLE 11.5: SKILL DIFFERENTIALS IN ENGINEERING AND RELATED INDUSTRIES

	1963	1968	1971	1976	1979	1980
Skilled						
Maintenance	112·5	113·3	116·4	114·3	115·7	117·4
Toolroom	111·6	113·3	109·5	107·0	110·2	110·4
Other skilled	105·2	106·3	105·5	102·8	104·7	106·7
Semi-skilled	97·6	96·1	96·9	97·7	95·6	93·5
Unskilled	76·3	76·4	76·9	81·9	82·7	82·3
All grades	100·0	100·0	100·0	100·0	100·0	100·0

Source: Derived by Marsden (1981) from a Department of Employment survey of earnings in engineering and related industries.
Note: Average gross weekly earnings as a percentage of the mean for all grades, adult manual men; June of each year.

The impact of Mr Heath's Stage 2 between April and November 1973, and of the special provisions for the lower paid of the Social Contract between 1975 and 1977, clearly do not account for the whole reduction of skill differentials in engineering between 1971 and 1976. A number of other factors were also involved. First, the rise of the relative pay of the unskilled, although accelerated by incomes policy, predates the periods of special provision for the low paid, and had not been significantly reversed by 1980 (after which the survey was discontinued). The unskilled have been a declining proportion of the engineering workforce, and it is possible that the lowest paid and least skilled jobs are gradually being replaced by mechanisation.

Second, Eyraud (1981) has argued that the improvement in unskilled relative pay may also have been helped by changes in bargaining policy by the engineering unions at the close of the 1960s. He suggested that the decision to decentralise bargaining to the enterprise level (or to recognise officially what had already happened in reality) was accompanied by a decision to focus bargaining at the national level on minimum rates designed to improve the position of the lowest paid. However, the data indicate that if indeed this factor did cause a reduction in differentials, its effect was not felt until some time later.

The third factor was the change from payment by results to measured daywork payment systems in the car industry (except at Ford which had always used time payments), which led to the collapse of the toolroom workers' differential in the early 1970s. This eventually led to the long and bitter strike for separate bargaining arrangements by the toolroom workers in 1976. The change came about because payment-by-result systems were more widespread among the semi-skilled than among the skilled workers, and, as the negotiations were concerned with management's desire to 'buy back' control over the payment system, it was perhaps inevitable that the semi-skilled should benefit most from the changeover and that differentials should suffer (see Saunders et al., 1977).

Despite these changes skilled maintenance workers survived with only a very small reduction in their relative pay in the mid-1970s, and by the close of the decade they had even improved their position on 1970. One reason may lie in the amount of overtime worked by maintenance workers. While some of this may be the result of genuine need for extra hours of work, it is probably also used by employers as a way of increasing the earnings of this group in order to retain them because, unlike toolroom workers and a number of other groups whose skills are fairly specific to the engineering industry, the skills of maintenance workers are highly transferable to other firms or sectors. Preliminary results from a study of internal labour markets by Marsden (1982) indicate that wastage among maintenance craftsmen, compared with other groups of skilled workers, is quite sensitive to relative earnings and employment opportunities elsewhere.

Finally, what of the effects of variations in labour demand upon short-term variations in occupational differentials? The predominant influences in the 1970s appear to have been those of incomes policies and bargaining, but there is some indication that the strong demand for certain occupations (notably systems analysts and computer programmers) may have contributed to an increase in their relative pay. More generally, it has been suggested that variations in unemployment may cause fluctuations in differentials. Reder's (1955) theory of shifts in the relative supply of skilled and unskilled workers over the economic cycle has already been discussed in the context of the long-term changes in skill differentials, but his theory could, in principle, be applied equally well to short-term as to long-term changes. An alternative demand-side explanation has been put forward by Oi (1962) who suggests that in recession the demand for unskilled workers will fall off more rapidly than that for skilled workers because employers wish to retain their skilled labour, partly because they have invested more in its training, especially for those skilled workers integrated into internal labour markets, and partly because they fear greater recruitment problems for skilled labour in the upswing. Both Reder's and Oi's theories imply that skill differentials should increase as unemployment rises and decrease as it falls. This does not appear to have been a factor in the compression of differentials in the early to mid-1970s. Although male unemployment fell between 1972 and 1974, it rose sharply during the period in which differentials were most strongly reduced. Only at the close of the decade did unemployment and differentials rise together, when one major factor behind the increase in differentials was the earlier build-up of pressure for their restoration.

In the light of the secular decline in occupational differentials and the failure of the higher paid and skilled fully to restore their differentials after a period of compression, it may appear puzzling that the restoration of differentials, after the sharp reduction in the mid-1970s, should have been so complete. If the restoration of differentials in 1978–80 represents the reassertion of market forces after a period of control, why did they not lead to a restoration of differentials in the past? Likewise, if the restoration was caused by institutional pressures and social norms, why did these not lead to a restoration in the past? Four main factors may explain this. First, the period of the sharp reduction in differentials was fairly short even if pay controls subsequently prevented an immediate restoration of differentials. Second, the source of the compression was identified with a single and central policy—the Social Contract. Third, changes in union structure mostly concerned extension into the public services and white-collar sectors rather than extension from more to less skilled workers. Finally, the technical changes of the 1970s probably affected all workers from the skilled to the unskilled, and while they may have caused reductions in such skilled groups as toolroom workers, they led to a compensating increase in the demand for other skilled groups such as maintenance workers.

CONCLUSIONS

The fundamental point made by economic theory about wage differentials is that they serve to allocate labour between different jobs and different occupations. Apart from questioning this contention other theories of wage structure, such as those which suggest that it is determined by status or by the hierarchical structure of organisations, are much less clear in their policy implications. This is not a reason for rejecting them, but it does make discussion of their consequences rather abstract. Before developing these implications it is necessary to pull together some of the strands of evidence for the allocative function of wage differentials and for the alternative theories.

For industry differentials, the study by Pissarides (1978) has given new support to the allocative function as between industries after the rather inconclusive evidence reviewed by the OECD (1965) fifteen years earlier. However, his findings do not necessarily contradict those of Robinson (1970) and MacKay et al. (1971) which showed a good deal of variation in wage levels for the same job in the same locality, a high degree of ignorance among workers about alternative pay levels, and that many workers had obtained access to their present jobs through internal labour markets and so could not easily obtain similar jobs in another firm. Even if Pissarides's evidence finds further support in other studies, it is still important to know which categories of worker are moving. Whether the mobility is produced by job changes among young workers, the unskilled, and casual labourers, and the degree of mobility of skilled and highly qualified workers are also central considerations if the 'quality' of the adjustments is to be assessed.

Human capital theory provides a theory of occupational choice, and thus suggests an allocative function for occupational differentials, although because of the length of time needed to acquire new skills, adjustments for most occupations have to be fairly slow. Thus, in most cases, short-term fluctuations in occupational differentials are unlikely to induce significant shifts from one occupation to another. It is difficult to evaluate longer-term changes in occupational differentials because the work content of occupations itself evolves. The success of human capital theories in explaining differences in earnings provides some evidence for this allocative function, although a stronger test would be provided by a study of movements in the rates of return over time. Several difficulties remain, not least in the assumptions required in order to measure the effect of human capital on earnings, and the fact that these assumptions are contested by other theoretical approaches. Moreover, the lack of any clear relationship between changes in skill differentials and variations in unemployment, which could affect differentials either according to the supply-side mechanisms suggested by Reder (1955) or the demand-side ones suggested by Oi (1962), must be taken as evidence of considerable imperfection in any short-run allocative mechanism based on price changes.

The non-competing group approach to occupational differentials suggests that part of the earnings of the higher paid occupations is the result of monopoly rents obtained by the restriction of access to these occupations. Although the extra competition for entry may confine access to the most highly qualified, the additional qualification is only made necessary by the restrictions, and not by the technical requirements of the work involved. Hence in such cases differentials could be reduced without any adverse effect upon the community as a whole. It would gain, moreover, from the lower price of the service provided, and the saving of the resources devoted to the obtaining of unnecessarily high qualifications. However, the most effective way of reducing such differentials would be to remove the restrictions on access, since direct attempts to reduce the occupation's earnings could be frustrated by employers bidding against each other for the limited number of workers in that occupation.

Internal labour markets represent a new departure within the theory of non-competing groups, although their origins go back many years and lead to a much heavier emphasis upon the importance of pay structures within the firm. The processes governing these are as yet poorly understood, except that they represent a major departure from the traditional model of competitive labour markets. There is some evidence that within the firm internal pay structures have the same sort of allocative function as those postulated by competitive labour market theory, and that restrictions in the periods of incomes policy did create difficulties for management in persuading workers to accept upgrading or redeployment. Hence sudden changes in occupational differentials could be expected to affect the flows of workers within internal labour markets. In view of the importance of local bargaining norms, it is also likely that such changes could lead to strong pressures for a restoration of differentials.

The hierarchical theories of occupational differentials are sometimes cited as though to suggest that these differentials are arbitrary and so can be changed at will. Although Lydall's model fits the upper tail of the observed distribution of individuals' earnings, it says little about the reasons for the size of the differential between different levels within an organisation, and thus it appears somewhat arbitrary. This is not the case, however, with the hierarchical models developed in the research at the LEST. If the wage structure within the enterprise plays an important role in reinforcing the hierarchy of authority, then a major reduction in differentials could be expected to lead to difficulties in maintaining the existence of current authority patterns, and ultimately in maintaining managerial control within the enterprise. This is not to say that the authority hierarchy is in any way sacrosanct. Indeed, major changes in the style of authority have accompanied the secular decline in occupational differentials shown in Table 11.2.

Scientific theories are usually presented as though each had the sole claim to truth and all the others were wrong. But in view of the incompleteness and ambiguity of the evidence for each of the main approaches discussed in this chapter it is unlikely that any one of them contains all the truth, and equally unlikely that any one of them is completely wrong. This puts practitioners dealing with problems of pay structure in a very difficult position, be they employers designing a salary structure, union officials deciding on their bargaining objectives, or governments weighing up the arguments for and against a particular exception to their incomes policy norms. Although it is of little immediate help to the practitioner, the answer probably lies in multidisciplinary research designed to probe the areas of overlap and disagreement between these different approaches with a view to discovering more about the relationships between market forces, the processes governing the internal workings of the firm, the functioning of bargaining institutions, and the social norms of fairness.

12 The Firm and Labour Market Behaviour

Peter Nolan

The operation of labour markets has always been regarded as an important area of study for students of industrial relations. It is generally assumed, for example, that the state of the labour market—whether it is near or substantially below full employment—is an important factor determining the relative bargaining strength of different groups within a firm. In this chapter the relationship between the firm, the social relations of production, and the labour market is examined in the light of recent contributions to the debate on labour market structure. Thus it considers the dynamic relationship between the organisation of work, processes of management control, and the segmentation of labour markets. Specifically, it looks at the observable effects in the labour market of variations in employers' wage setting behaviour.

The analysis is developed against the backcloth of orthodox economic analysis. There are two reasons for this. First, neo-classical theory remains the dominant approach within this subject. Second, and more important, the most refined and rigorous versions of orthodox theory assume away problems of industrial relations. In order to understand why this is so it is necessary to examine the orthodox analysis of production and its articulation with the theory of exchange. This is all the more important since many of the recent contributions to the debate on labour market structure have emphasised the central role of industrial relations in an explanation of the diversity of employers' behaviour and its implications for the structure of employment.

PRODUCTION AND EXCHANGE: THE NEO-CLASSICAL APPROACH

Production

In neo-classical theory the analysis of the production process is organised around the concept of the production function. This concept describes the set of technical possibilities available to the firm at a particular moment; hence it is defined for a given state of technology. Specifically, the production function expresses an engineering relationship between different combinations of factor inputs—for example, physical plant and equipment (capital) and human labour—and the maximum obtainable flow of output from these alternative production techniques. The analysis is usually extended to allow for the effects of technological progress. Changes in the state of technology are assumed to occur at an exogenous rate, automatically and independently of any economic processes; their effect is to transform the input-output relationship so that a greater quantity of output can be produced by each combination of inputs.

An important characteristic of this approach is the very narrow, technological conception of the production process. The fact that production is a social process, organised within a specific institutional and social framework, is ignored. Instead, human and non-human factors of production are treated symmetrically, distinguished in the production function only by a different letter or subscript (see, for example, Henderson and Quandt, 1980: ch.4). Not surprisingly, the organisation of the work process is considered to be unproblematic. Inside the firm an entrepreneur transforms inputs into outputs, subject to the rules specified by the production function. It is thus axiomatic for this theory that the firm is technologically efficient, that the maximum quantity of output is always produced from any feasible combination of inputs.

Added to these technical considerations is one simple behavioural rule: the firm is in business to maximise profits. This means, given the prevailing set of relative prices, that it will always adopt the least-cost technique of production from those currently available. Assuming, then, that inputs are both divisible and interchangeable, the firm will respond to an increase in the relative price of labour (for example, in the event of a decline in the flow of labour services) by substituting capital for labour in the production process. In this way the firm is said to be both economically and technically efficient.

Given these assumptions the neo-classical theory of the firm reduces to a simple problem of constrained optimisation. Firms pursue the objective of profit maximisation within the constraints set by an exogenously determined level of technology and input and output prices. This objective is achieved when the difference between total revenue and the total costs arising from the purchase of inputs is greatest. The theory is then used to predict movements in equilibrium prices and quantities following a change in one of the conditions of the economic environment (for example, technology, wage rates, or the level of product demand). Significantly, these predictions are generated by a theory which takes as its object the hypothetical behaviour of 'numerous anonymous . . . symbolic firms'. It is not, in other words, attempting to explain the observable behaviour of real firms. On the contrary, in attempting to predict market outcomes as effects of changes in the economic environment, the firm is simply a 'mental construct' which provides a 'theoretical link' in the movement from one equilibrium state to another (Machlup, 1967:8–9).

It follows that a necessary condition for the application of this theory is the existence of competitive markets, since the firm, or any economic agent for that matter, cannot be allowed to influence the market pricing process. It is assumed then that firms are price takers in all markets, including the labour market, where wages are determined by the competitive forces of supply and demand. Each firm is constrained to pay the going market rate for different grades of labour. But having purchased the services of labour the analysis immediately proceeds to the stage where commodities have been produced and are ready to be exchanged on the market, again at prices which are beyond the control of any individual buyer or seller. The economic process is thus reduced to an analysis of the exchange process without any serious examination of the intervening process of production. Accordingly, the relevance of workplace industrial relations to economics is denied together with important questions of work organisation and the origins of conflict inside the firm. Exactly why these issues have been ignored is the subject of the next section of the chapter where the orthodox analysis of exchange is considered.

Exchange

The exchange process is typically identified within neo-classical theory by the following sequence of events:

$$C_i \rightarrow M \rightarrow C_j$$

Individuals exchange goods and services (C_i) on the market in return for money (M) in order to facilitate the purchase of other commodities (C_j). Although the object is to exchange different goods, C_i for C_j, it is assumed that they are value equivalents. This analysis takes as its theoretical point of departure the initial distribution of resources or factor endowments among individuals and their preferences. On this basis it assumes that individuals, guided by the pursuit of self-interest, enter into the exchange process voluntarily, confronting one another as equals in the market place. Consequently, goods and services are exchanged only when each party is satisfied that better terms of trade could not otherwise be secured. Now this condition holds when individual traders are in possession of reliable and comprehensive information on the terms of trade ruling in other parts of the market and, indeed, in other markets. Following the French economist Léon Walras, this strict assumption of full information is met within the theory by assuming the existence of a central coordinator or, as it is often known, an auctioneer (see Arrow and Hahn, 1971; Nell, 1980). The auctioneer's job is to coordinate the potentially inconsistent trading plans of innumerable individuals. It does this in two ways: first, by disseminating price information costlessly to all transactors and, second, by ensuring that no trade is effected until the set of market-clearing prices has been identified. Thus a tâtonnement process, in which the auctioneer gropes towards the set of equilibrium relative prices, always precedes the act of exchange. In each particular market the auctioneer adjusts relative prices in the light of individuals' notional trading plans. Where offers to supply exceed demands, the price is revised downwards until a point is finally reached where the two sets of plans are mutually consistent. Only then is trade made effective.

So far as the exchange of labour services is concerned, the theory assumes that a market clearing price (in this case a wage rate) is identified for each homogeneous grade of labour. These prices reflect the interaction of individual labour supply decisions with the demands of profit-maximising firms. On the demand side, firms will be willing to hire labour (assuming other factors are held constant) as long as each additional unit contributes more to total revenue than to total costs. In equilibrium, then, the value of the marginal product of the last unit of labour employed is equated with the exogenously determined wage rate. Labour supply decisions, on the other hand, are governed by individual tastes and the desire to maximise utility (satisfaction). In this case, the relevant choice variable is time and how it should be allocated between work and leisure. Generally, it is argued that work is substituted for leisure as the wage rate increases, a relationship described by the familiar (positively sloping) aggregate labour supply curve. Put another way, this relationship suggests that as the proportion of time devoted to work increases relative to leisure, each additional sacrifice of leisure must be compensated for by a higher wage rate if the level of individual utility is to remain constant. Once again equilibrium can be characterised by a set of equalities; at the margin of choice, the wage rate is just equal to the marginal disutility of work for all individuals.

The main outcome of this analysis of exchange is clear and simple: so long as markets are characterised by atomistic competition, with no individual buyer or seller influencing the structure of relative prices, the conflicting objectives of myriad self-seeking individuals can be reconciled through the market. Not only is conflict banished from this world but the resulting allocation of resources is considered to be highly efficient in the sense that no single individual can be made better off without someone else being made slightly worse off. Competitive equilibrium is the term reserved in the economic literature for this extremely desirable (if unlikely) state of affairs. Most importantly, it is characterised by the exchange of equivalent values, where each good or service is evaluated by the competitive forces of supply and demand in the relevant markets.

On the basis of this analysis of exchange a theory of distribution is developed relating the origin of different incomes (wages, profit, and rent) to the exchange of initial endowments (labour, capital, and land). Labour services, for example, are exchanged for wages so that utility maximising individuals can consume other goods of their choice. The performance of work is simply a means of achieving maximum satisfaction with a given set of initial endowments. The rate at which labour services can be exchanged for wages is governed by the simultaneous determination of prices in factor markets under conditions of perfect competition. The argument is generalised for all factors of production so that in equilibrium each is paid the value of its contribution to output at the margin, as determined by the technical conditions of production together with the structure of individual preferences. An obvious corollary of this theory of distribution is that where the conditions of exchange are characterised by perfect competition 'it really does not matter who hires whom; so have labour hire capital' (Samuelson, 1957:894).

This last point, which certainly captures the spirit of the orthodox approach, helps to shed some light on the question: why does orthodox economic analysis only consider the conditions in which labour is exchanged while ignoring the conditions in which labour is performed? Or to restate the problem slightly: why is the production process treated as though it is governed by technological considerations alone? The above discussion has implied that at least part of the answer lies in the orthodox analysis of exchange which is dominated by the concept of perfect competition. Where this condition exists, self-seeking individuals confront one another as equals within the market place. Questions of economic power simply do not arise. Furthermore, so long as exchange is voluntary the conflicting interests of individuals can be resolved in the market. Finally, it was noted that whenever individual income is derived from the sale of initial factor endowments under competitive conditions, the owners of factor services are rewarded according to their respective contributions to output. It is thus possible to maintain that factors combine harmoniously in the production process, united by the common goal of maximising income within the constraints of technology. It is but a short step to treating all factors symmetrically within production, ignoring the fact that labour services are qualitatively different from land or physical plant and equipment.

It is argued below that this particular conception of the economy, which in essence reduces to a theory of the exchange process, is unable to provide an adequate account of firms' behaviour in the labour market precisely because it abstracts from the socially specific nature of capitalist production. But these arguments can be developed more effectively after a brief examination of some empirical characteristics of the labour market. In the next section wage data derived from a local labour market study is considered alongside some recent developments within orthodox analysis.

THE LABOUR MARKET

Some Empirical Characteristics

The basic elements of neo-classical exchange theory have been sketched above. It was noted that the concept of perfect competition is fundamental to this approach and that it provides a basis for a theory of prices and resource allocation. In the context of the labour market this analysis suggests that the level of wages for a particular occupation will tend to be equalised across firms within geographically well defined labour markets.

This basic prediction, generated at a relatively high level of theoretical abstraction, is usually qualified to allow for the effects of non-pecuniary job advantages on supply-side behaviour. Thus it is 'net advantages' and not just wage rates that are equalised by the competitive process. The limited evidence that exists on this issue, however, suggests that wage and non-wage benefits tend to be positively correlated (MacKay et al., 1971; Robinson, 1970); that is, better wages tend to be associated with better jobs. In the discussion that follows, therefore, the effects of non-pecuniary benefits are ignored.

More fundamentally, the conventional model of perfect competition requires that all individual buyers and sellers are price and wage 'takers'. This raises the obvious question of how prices and wages are set in the real world where the convenient fiction of an auctioneer cannot be maintained. Surprisingly, this question has only recently been addressed in the theoretical literature (a useful survey can be found in Weintraub, 1979). The implications for the conventional analysis of wage determination are considered below. At this stage it is sufficient to note that even without an auctioneer, a long-run competitive outcome is predicted by orthodox analysis so long as the forces of supply and demand remain unfettered. This requires, on the demand side, that firms are small in relation to the size of the labour market and that they are trying to minimise costs, subject to the constraints of their production functions. On the supply side, individuals must be free to move from one establishment to another in response to any short-term differentials in pay.

Several studies have examined the external wage structure in the context of different local labour markets (e.g. MacKay et al., 1971; Robinson, 1970; Nolan and Brown, 1983). In general, the evidence has not been very encouraging for the proponents of competitive analysis. In particular the equalising effects of competition on both the demand and supply sides have been variously described as weak to almost non-existent. Pointing to evidence of the very considerable degree of intra-occupational wage dispersion that characterises local labour markets, one study concluded that 'the limits set to wage differentials by market forces are not . . . very narrow' (MacKay et al., 1971:98). A more recent study of the engineering industry carried out in a West Midlands local labour market has reinforced this conclusion (Nolan and Brown, 1983). It examined the wage experience of seven well defined occupations in twenty-five factories over a period of ten years. The seven occupations were chosen to minimise variance in job content and skill requirements, and were: from the skilled grade, toolmakers, maintenance electricians and machinists; from the semi-skilled grade, storekeepers, internal and external truck drivers; and an unskilled grade of labourers. All the workers were members of trade unions.

Table 12.1 gives some indication of the range of settlements that were observed over the ten-year period. In the top row the highest paying factory in the district is compared with the lowest paying factory over the period. Average earnings in the former are expressed as a percentage differential of average earnings in the latter. The average earnings figure in each factory is derived from the seven occupational earnings figures. Thus in 1971 the average wage in the highest paying firm is 56 per cent higher than average earnings in the lowest paying factory. The differential is lowest in 1978 at 35 per cent.

TABLE 12.1: DISPERSION AND RANK STABILITY OF EARNINGS
LEVELS

	1971	1972	1973	1974	1975	1976	1977	1978	1979	1980
Highest Paying Firm as a Percentage of Lowest Paying Firm	155·5	155·0	168·3	165·5	155·9	147·6	154·4	134·6	143·5	160·5
Coefficient of Variation of Average Wages	10·4	11·2	11·1	10·6	9·7	9·2	9·6	7·5	9·5	11·8
Rank Coefficient of Average Wages (Annual Change)		·87	·95	·89	·64	·94	·91	·88	·75	·82

Source: Data based on Nolan and Brown (1983).

The second row of Table 12.1 provides a measure of relative dispersion for all twenty-five factories. Again, it is the variance in factory average earnings that is being examined. The coefficient of variation identifies changes in the spread of average plant earnings over time. The statistics reveal that there was some narrowing in the spread of plant earnings between 1975 and 1979, with the sharpest compression occurring in 1978. This tendency can be partially ascribed to the constraining influence of incomes policies at this time (Brown, 1979). Since 1978, however, firms appear to have pulled further apart.

The third row provides some evidence of the stability of the local labour market's wage hierarchy. Specifically, the rank correlation coefficient indicates the extent to which firms change their position in the district wage 'league table' from one year to the next. A correlation coefficient equal to unity would suggest that there had been no change in the rank ordering in that particular year. A coefficient closer to zero would reflect a substantial amount of annual disordering. In fact, Table 12.1 suggests that individual factories generally make very minor changes in their league table position, not only between years but also over periods of several years. Only the year 1974–5 shows any major upheaval, and this is largely explained by the dramatic decline of three factories within the same company. Apart from these, however, the rank order of the remaining twenty-two factories is remarkably stable over the whole period, with the correlation coefficient being as high as 0·92.

These results clearly suggest that firms possess (and exercise) a considerable degree of discretion in the wage setting process. Even over a period of ten years there is little sign that individual firms are bound to acquiesce in the dictates of the market. In fact, the evidence points in the opposite direction: firms are often remarkably unresponsive to conditions in the external labour market. At the same time a particular firm may choose or be compelled by circumstances to change its wage setting behaviour. For example a sharp decline in profitability, internal reorganisation, or a more aggressive pricing strategy designed to increase market share are all factors that might precipitate a change of policy. The important point to emphasise is that wage setting behaviour is not uniquely determined by developments in the external labour market or any other single set of forces for that matter—a point that is discussed in greater detail below. But first, it is important to examine the response by orthodox theorists to these well known empirical findings.

'New' Microeconomics: A Generalisation of Orthodox Analysis

A different rationalisation of the empirical characteristics of local labour markets has been advanced by proponents of the so-called 'new' microeconomics (e.g. Addison and Burton, 1978; Addison and Siebert, 1979). It differs from the basic analysis of exchange outlined above in one crucial respect. The presence of an auctioneer is no longer taken for granted. This change in the conditions of exchange has a number of important consequences in the short term. In particular, the costs of producing or acquiring reliable and reasonably comprehensive wage and price information can no longer be considered insignificant. Consequently, transactions will generally be carried out on the basis of sketchy and incomplete information. This raises the possibility that goods and services will be exchanged at non-equilibrium prices and that markets may not clear in the short run.

So far as the labour market is concerned, this departure from the theoretical terrain of perfect markets eases the problem of accounting for the existence of wage dispersion within well defined occupational labour markets. If exchange is a strictly 'do-it-yourself' affair, individuals must carry out their own search for acceptable terms of trade. Generally, it is assumed that information on the existing distribution of wage offers can be produced more efficiently by specialising in 'off-the-job' search. Individuals will only be prepared to forego wages from current employment, however, if a net gain from additional job search is anticipated. In practice this means that search will be terminated before the entire set of alternative wage offers has been identified. As a result occupational labour markets will be characterised by some degree of wage dispersion. Thus predictions which are consistent with the empirical evidence can be generated by the theory once the strict Walrasian postulate of perfect information has been relaxed.

Apart from this one concession to the empirical anomolies of the exchange process, however, the new microeconomics remains firmly anchored within the tradition of orthodox competitive analysis. The assumption of continuous market clearing, previously guaranteed by the auctioneer, is now replaced by the concept of long-run competitive equilibrium. In the presence of uncertainty, atomistic firms are able to exercise some discretion over the wage setting process; but this monopsony power is always limited by the potential mobility of agents on the supply side. In the longer run, it is assumed that wage-making behaviour gives way to wage-taking behaviour as the labour market approximates the conditions of perfect competition. Thus the essential force of long-run adjustment is provided by the search behaviour of those seeking jobs.

This particular development within the literature provides a clear illustration of the criterion of adequacy that guides orthodox theoretical analysis. The overriding priority is to achieve consistency with the empirical evidence. That is to say, the theory must be capable of generating predictions which are consistent with the 'facts'. In this particular example, theoretical consistency is achieved simply by assuming a change in the conditions of exchange; specifically, the strict Walrasian postulate of perfect information is abandoned. The rest of the theory, however, remains firmly intact. Most importantly, atomistic firms are assumed to respond passively in the long run to pressures generated on the side of labour supply. Economic power thus appears, but only as a temporary phenomenon attributable to all economic agents in the presence of uncertainty. Eventually it is bound to disappear as the impersonal forces of the market reassert themselves. Of course this is more an act of faith than a statement based upon close examination of the behaviour of social institutions within the market. But it is an act of faith that is required in order to preserve the coherence of a theory which predicts a tendency towards long-run competitive equilibrium.

In the remaining parts of this chapter, an alternative framework of analysis is presented which attempts to explain structural change in the labour market in terms of the dynamic behaviour of firms and not simply as effects of the conditions of exchange. The analysis emphasises the link between the organisation of work, industrial relations, and the behaviour of employers in the labour market.

INDUSTRIAL RELATIONS AND THE ECONOMY

Social Relations of Production

The orthodox analysis of production abstracts from basic problems of industrial relations and work organisation by reducing the labour process to a set of technical relations as summarised by the production function. In so far as human beings are recognised at all, it is assumed that they share a common interest in maximising income within the existing technical constraints. This picture of mutual cooperation and harmony is reinforced by an idealised account of the exchange process under conditions of long-run perfect competition. Since workers' cooperation is assured through the act of exchange, technical efficiency can simply be assumed. The problem of how to get work out of the worker does not even arise. But this analysis is unsatisfactory in a number of respects.

Most importantly, the symmetrical treatment of factor inputs within the production process conceals the fact that what is actually purchased in the labour market is an individual's capacity to work for a given period of time (labour power) rather than a specified quantity of performed labour. Having purchased this unique commodity, labour power, it is management's job to ensure that it is used effectively within the production process. In other words, contrary to the orthodox analysis of production, technical efficiency cannot simply be assumed; the path from technology to output is mediated by a framework of social relations which, in the capitalist firm, take the specific form of an opposition of interests between workers and employers. Consequently, the total value which is generated within production, on which the firm's profits ultimately rest, will depend upon the conditions in which labour is performed and on management's ability to secure and maintain the cooperation of the workforce.

By taking the distinction between labour and labour power as a starting point, it is possible to develop an analysis of production which does not assume away problems of industrial relations and struggles over the performance of work. To consider this it is helpful to abstract from the complex effects of competition within the exchange process, between different firms and between different groups of workers and trade unions. Even at this very simple level, however, it is necessary to comprehend the basic unity of the spheres of production and exchange. Before production can be carried out money capital must be advanced within the exchange process in return for those basic commodities necessary to carry out production. Thus the firm buys raw materials, physical plant and equipment, and labour power, and sets them to work in production. At the end of this process the commodities that have been produced are exchanged on the market in return for money. This process, which begins and ends with money (M), can be represented in the following terms:

$$M \rightarrow C \rightarrow M$$

where C refers to the means of production and labour power. Clearly, production is not undertaken for its own sake; nor is the object merely to recoup the amount of money capital advanced in the first place. The firm is in business to make profits and this means that the value created within production must exceed the money initially advanced. Additional value is generated within production as a result of the expenditure of human effort. The value that is created there is embodied within commodities which are then exchanged on the market in order to realise a profit. The whole process can be represented thus:

$$M \rightarrow C \ldots . . P \ldots . . C' \rightarrow M'$$

where P refers to the process of production, C' the commodities produced there, and M' the money realised from the sale of C'. In commodity form, the additional value created within production is equal to the difference between C and C'. Once this has been converted into money and realised as profit, denoted by the movement from C' to M', the entire process can begin again; only this time the process can be expanded if the profits generated during the previous circuit, $\triangle M$, are advanced as capital along with the original money, M. The circuit of capital is thus a process of self-expanding value.

Several points are highlighted by this analysis. Firstly, a necessary pre-condition for the circuit of capital is the existence of a class of people who are bound to sell their capacity to work. Secondly, and crucially, the amount of additional value generated within production cannot be specified in advance. The difference between C and C', $\triangle C$, will vary according to the social and technical conditions in which labour power is exercised as labour. Specifically, $\triangle C$ will be determined by two conflicting sets of forces: employers' organisation and control of the work process, and workers' ability to modify and displace these controls. In general employers will endeavour to organise production in such a way that tensions and discontinuities within this process are minimised. Nevertheless conflict remains inherent within the situation and production rarely proceeds smoothly as assumed within orthodox analysis. Instead, the social and technical conditions of production are subject to continuous change as the struggle for control is carried on.

Two further points need to be mentioned at this stage. First, although additional value, $\triangle C$, is created within the sphere of production it may not be realised as profit within the sphere of exchange. Firms may fail to exchange commodities on the market because an adequate demand for their output does not exist. This particular problem and its economy-wide implications has been the preoccupation of the Keynesian school of economics for many years. In terms of the circuit of capital outlined above, it implies that there is a break, or discontinuity, in the circuit between C'→M'; generally, this will have further consequences for that part of the circuit denoted by the movement M→C. It is possible, for example, that some firms will withdraw from industrial production or, perhaps more likely, that existing resources will be channelled into another sector of the economy. It is also possible, however, that firms will choose to realise the additional value created in production, not as profit, but as cheaper inputs for other parts of the company. This is often the case within vertically integrated multinational companies, where some plants are engaged in producing inputs to be worked-up into finished commodities by other plants within the company. Profits can then be realised where the conditions (e.g. corporation tax structure) are most favourable. One final possibility is that some firms, by acquiring monopoly power in their respective product markets, may be able to appropriate a greater share of profit than they themselves produced within production. Through their pricing strategies they are able to exert a claim on the aggregate surplus produced within the economy. For any particular firm this implies that $\triangle M$, the total amount of profit realised, is greater than $\triangle C$, the amount of additional value created within production. Indeed, for some economists, these 'monopoly profits' are the most important source of profits within contemporary capitalism (see, for example, Baran and Sweezy, 1968; Cowling, 1982).

The second point is concerned with the question of income distribution. Unlike orthodox economic analysis, the analysis presented above does not imply that distributive shares are determined by the respective contributions of factor services to output. On the contrary, labour power is exchanged for wages before the process of production has been carried out. The additional value created within production belongs to the firm and not to the direct producers. In terms of the circuit this is clearly illustrated by the separation of M→C, the payment for labour power and other commodities, and C', the output resulting from production. It is possible, of course, that wage payments may be varied in order to induce a greater expenditure of effort within the process of production. But this is always a tactical decision, taken by management in the light of a number of competing considerations (Nolan and Brown, 1983). The point remains, however, that distributional relations are governed by the specific framework of social relationships within production, and not, as assumed in orthodox theory, the other way round.

Competition, Control, and the Process of Labour Market Segmentation

The circuit of industrial capital has been characterised as a process involving the expansion of value. It is a process which depends upon a satisfactory outcome both in production and in the exchange process. Similarly, the firm can be treated as a representative block of industrial capital, undertaking production in order to secure expansion. When viewed in this light it is clear that firms confront one another as rivals; each firm views the existence of others as a potential barrier to its own expansionary activities. Competition, then, is the form in which each firm experiences the expansionary thrusts of other blocks of capital (cf. Aaronovitch and Smith, 1981; Shapiro, 1976). In the competitive battle over markets, some firms will emerge as victors while others face extinction or take-over by the more successful companies. The rising level of concentration, both at the aggregate level and within particular industries, may be seen as an inevitable outcome of the competitive process (see Aaronovitch and Sawyer, 1975). Furthermore, as firms extend their right of disposition over economic resources, their capacity to invade new economic territory is increased. As Clifton (1977:147) has observed:

the fixed capital of the firm has become increasingly mobile as the firm has grown, by industrial and geographical diversification, out of its original sphere of production. Such a firm may be called a 'unit of general production', because it organises production across a wider spectrum of the full range of production possibilities than the single product firm in one locale.

Another aspect of this process of economic development is the rise of the multinational corporation, a development associated with the extension of firms' productive activities across several nation states. With this development capital mobility is raised to a new level, involving the transmission of investment funds between different sectors, at the level not only of the national but also of the world economy. Strategic investment decisions within the multinational companies are taken by top-level executives separated from the routine activities of the constituent parts of the company (Chandler, 1977; Williamson, 1981). Thus questions of where to produce, and what to produce, are tactical decisions governed only by the search for profitable opportunities.

These developments, associated with the evolution of the firm as a 'unit of general production', have simultaneously transformed and intensified the nature of competition. From an orthodox perspective, the overall degree of competition is expected to decline as product markets become increasingly concentrated; competition appears in its most developed form when firms are small in relation to the size of the market and are unable to affect the structure of relative prices. In contrast, it has been suggested that as firms develop their organisations and increase their control over economic resources they are able to compete more effectively.

From the point of view of any particular firm, the competitive process is experienced as an external force of coercion. A failure to organise production effectively will mean relatively high unit costs and a declining market share, a situation ultimately punishable by bankruptcy and elimination from the competitive arena. For the employer, the ownership and control of the means of production does not, by itself, guarantee a successful outcome within the sphere of production. The problem of how to get work out of the worker remains. At the root of this problem is the need to extract sufficient effort to ensure the eventual realisation of profits. It is the attempt by employers to reconcile these two problems—of securing workers' cooperation and a surplus product—that distinguishes the employment relationship from other types of exchange. Specifically, it is different in the sense that the parties continue to stand in a contradictory relationship after the exchange has been consummated. Consequently, employers have sought to develop systems of labour control which both minimise tensions and conflict and facilitate profitable production (Burawoy, 1979; Edwards, 1979; Marglin, 1974; Lazonick, 1983; Friedman, 1977). These strategies, moreover, give rise to distinct but changing patterns of behaviour within the external labour market.

A clear example is provided by the local labour market wage structure described earlier in the chapter. It was shown that well defined labour markets tend to be characterised by a significant degree of pay dispersion, even for occupations where potential mobility is high (e.g. external truck drivers). This widely reported market outcome has been the subject of considerable controversy. It has already been noted that orthodox theorists point to the imperfect conditions of exchange: workers do not possess complete information on the set of alternative wage offers. Other economists have argued that even if complete information were available some inter-firm pay dispersion would persist because internal labour market considerations take priority over external labour market factors. But why should this be so?

One explanation (Doeringer and Piore, 1971; Berger and Piore, 1980) suggests that with the advance of technology, many firms have come to depend increasingly upon a highly skilled and reliable workforce. These skills are usually job specific and can only be acquired after a period of 'in-service' training. From the employers' point of view, these workers represent an important investment which has to be looked after. Consequently, employment stability is encouraged by the provision of high wages and good career prospects. These benefits are further consolidated by restricting the flow of new entrants into the firm to pre-specified 'ports of entry'. These relatively favourable conditions of employment are facilitated, within the corporate (or primary) sector, by stable product markets and a high level of demand.

In contrast, the secondary sector of the economy is made up of small, technologically backward firms. Product market conditions are generally unstable and certainly not conducive to employment stability. Workers experience these inferior structural conditions in the form of routine and relatively unskilled work, low pay, and poor career prospects. This fundamental duality within the labour market tends to be reinforced by organised workers within the primary sector who are trying to minimise the effects of competition from external sources of labour supply. In this way the labour market has become increasingly segmented into non-competing groups. The persistence of significant intra-occupational wage differentials is just one manifestation of this tendency (Robinson, 1970; MacKay et al., 1971).

These important observations have been given a different emphasis in the work of a number of American economists (see, for example, Gordon, 1972; Edwards, 1975, 1979; Gintis, 1976). Although there is broad agreement about the observable effects of the process of labour market segmentation, these writers downgrade the crucial role previously assigned to technology and skill specificity. Instead, the issue of labour control is placed at the centre of their analysis. Specifically, it is argued that the progressive compartmentalisation of the workforce—the process of labour market segmentation—is the market expression of more fundamental changes taking place within the production process. Underlying each of the market segments is a distinct system of labour control inside the firm. Thus the institution of internal labour markets is located historically in terms of the evolution of 'bureaucratic' forms of control within the giant corporations. Internal rules and institutions have been developed in order to carry out the traditional functions of the external labour market: job placements, promotions, and wage structures are administered from within the corporation, thereby increasing the sphere of management control. At the same time the detailed organisational structure has been in large part contrived and consciously designed to fragment the workforce. As Edwards (1975:92) explains:

> each job appeared more unique and individualized by its particular position in the finely-graded hierarchical order, by the job criteria which specified work activities, and by distinct status, power, responsibilities, and so on. Elements of the social organisation of the firm which differentiated between jobs were emphasised, while those which created commonality diminished.

Within the work process an elaborate set of rules and job criteria has served to minimise uncertainty and arbitrary forms of control. Similarly, the development of complex, hierarchical reward and incentive structures biased towards tenure and seniority inside the firm have encouraged a greater degree of commitment and employment stability. At the same time these desirable patterns of behaviour have been reinforced by a selection process designed to elicit modes of behaviour 'consonant with the form of control in the firm' and 'not with the actual work tasks themselves' (Edwards, 1975). In other words the selection process gives far more weight to personal characteristics and attitudes than to skill attributes. A similar tendency has been observed in a recent study of firms' recruitment practices in a British local labour market: individuals are segmented within the labour market according to their personal characteristics (Blackburn and Mann, 1979).

In the same way secondary employment conditions are produced (and reproduced) by 'simple hierarchical' forms of control which have tended to persist within small enterprises. Typically these firms face adverse economic conditions both in the form of intense market competition and unstable product demand. Survival is secured by minimising unit costs (especially wages) and by extracting maximum effort within the production process. Inside the firm the system of labour control relies heavily on close personal supervision and strict discipline enforced by the threat of redundancy. These conditions have in turn engendered high levels of absenteeism and labour turnover, characteristics which can provide the employer with a welcome degree of flexibility in the face of volatile market conditions. In orthodox theory these behavioural patterns would be rationalised in terms of factors which lie outside the market process, such as individual tastes and personal qualities. Here it is being argued that workers' behavioural characteristics are in large part produced by the organisational context in which labour is performed.

By highlighting the issue of social control at the point of production these writers have transcended the a-historical framework that character-ised the earlier, largely taxonomic, studies of labour market structure. Furthermore the simple unilinear chain of causality—from technology to work organisation to labour market structure—postulated by Doeringer and Piore (1971) is firmly rejected. Instead, developments in technology are located within a specific historical and social context. As Gordon (1976) notes: 'there are no universally efficient forces and relations of production for all societies. Capitalism has developed a production process which not only delivers the goods but also controls its workers . . . Other [technical and social] relations of production—less degrading and routin-ised—might conceivably match or outstrip the productiveness of capitalist relations.' In short, the particular method of work organisation, the choice of production techniques and the implications for the employment structure cannot be assumed to flow automatically and uniquely from exogenous changes in technology; on the contrary, developments in technology both reflect and reinforce the existing structure of social relations inside the firm and in society more generally.

At the same time, however, American economists have largely ignored the diversity of behaviour observable at the level of individual firms. To some extent this is unavoidable given the level of abstraction at which their analysis is developed. Furthermore, by assuming that different control systems coincide with structural change in the economy, their analysis implies that industrial relations develop in a simple unilinear fashion. Thus with the rise of large oligopolistic corporations simple hierarchical forms of control are gradually broken down and replaced by bureaucratic systems. Secondary employment conditions are thus viewed as 'the continuation of the employment practices of an earlier competitive capitalism' (Edwards, 1975).

Other contributors to the debate, however, have been quick to point out that the correspondence between structural conditions and employment practices often breaks down on closer examination. Many firms, typically identified with the primary or core sector of the economy, continue to offer terms and conditions of employment more closely associated with second-ary sector employers. Similarly, the institution of bureaucratic control is by no means universal within the primary sector (see, for example, Lawson, 1981). The diversity of employment conditions is perhaps most clearly demonstrated by local labour market wage studies. These suggest that although product market conditions limit the set of choices available to the employer the scope for tactical decision making within these limits is still considerable (Nolan and Brown, 1983; Windolf, 1981). Consequently, different groups of workers often experience very different terms and conditions of employment even within the same firm.

Indeed, this last point highlights a further problem with this work. The role of trade unions has been left largely unexplored. Not surprisingly, this has led to a rather one-sided account of the development of industrial relations, with employees being cast in a more or less passive role. Others, such as Rubery (1978), have emphasised the role of trade unions in the development of internal labour markets and the establishment of stable and relatively favourable conditions of employment. These significant gains achieved by organised labour should not, according to this view, be lightly dismissed. One important effect has been to deny certain groups of workers access to primary sector jobs; in particular, women and racial minorities, underrepresented within the stronger manual trade unions, have been seriously disadvantaged (Rubery, 1978; Beechey, 1978; Armstrong, 1982). Thus, on this interpretation, the process of labour market segmentation cannot be explained by the activities of management alone; the role of organised labour, particularly in maintaining some control over the supply of labour, is an important factor shaping the structure of employment and the distribution of job opportunities.

Forces of Change

In the preceding analysis changes in the production process, specifically in the organisation and control of work, were discussed in terms of two sets of relations. First, by abstracting from the effects of competition between firms, the basic antagonism between workers and employers was identified as a fundamental source of tension and change. Second, it was argued that firms, confronting one another as rivals in the exchange process, experience competition as an external force of coercion. The interaction of these two sets of relations provides the basic dynamic of the economic system and achieves concrete expression in the form of changing industrial and employment structures.

In Britain these changes can be observed in the form of the dramatic collapse in its core manufacturing industries. Some measure of the problem is given by the decline in the share of manufacturing employment in total civilian employment—from 35 per cent in 1965 to 30 per cent in 1976, a reduction of 14 per cent in just over ten years and a trend that shows every sign of continuing (see, for example, Barker, 1982). For some writers, notably Kilpatrick and Lawson (1980:87), the process of de-industrialisation in Britain can be explained in terms of the unique, highly decentralised industrial relations system that has evolved in this country. The early acceptance of trade unionism in Britain facilitated the 'growth of real power by workers to resist changes and to defend standards' established 'before the introduction of mass production techniques'. Subsequently, this system of plant-by-plant bargaining has resulted in higher manning levels and a lower growth in productivity than in most other advanced countries. Organised labour in Britain has, according to this view, been far more successful in resisting change, both in working practices and production techniques, than its counterparts elsewhere. This has resulted in a serious loss of competitiveness, a declining share of world markets, and a generally low level of profitability for British firms. Thus, unlike other explanations of Britain's long-term relative decline, these writers take as their theoretical starting point the opposition of interests at the point of production. The comparatively unimpressive performance of British firms in world markets is explained by the failure of employers to transform the social and institutional constraints within their immediate business environment—the workplace. Instead these firms sought profits in the relatively protected markets afforded by the British Empire, a situation that persisted until after World War II when foreign competitors were eventually able to penetrate these markets.

Although an important strength of this analysis is the attention that it gives to the social relations of production, it can and has been criticised for presenting an over romanticised view of the achievements of the British labour movement (see, for example, Hyman and Elger, 1981). Even more worrying, however, is Kilpatrick and Lawson's failure to identify any dynamic tendencies within the British economy. Apparently British employers were unwilling to look for fundamental change within production as long as profits could be secured from the protected markets of the Empire. With this option removed a more dynamic response might be anticipated. Yet the effect of increased competition in these markets works in the opposite direction in their analysis. British manufacturers have continued to experience decline and have failed to transform the technical and social relations of production in an attempt to reverse this situation. Thus the conclusion emerges that the forces of competition are irrelevant to their analysis which ultimately reduces to a simple inverse relationship between trade union strength and economic performance (Fine and Harris, 1983).

Certainly the weakness of manufacturing industry in Britain is not in question, although there are some notable exceptions. But it would be a mistake to overlook the important changes in the organisation and location of production that have taken place within Britain and in the wider international context. Indeed, it was noted above that the rise of the multinational corporation has greatly increased the fluidity of capital, allowing production to be carried out wherever the conditions are most favourable. In fact British-owned multinational companies are second only to those of the United States in terms of the growth of their international operations. Together these two countries have been responsible in the early 1970s for more than 60 per cent of the operations of all multinational companies in the mature capitalist countries (Fine, 1982). Thus it is clear that not all British owned companies have been inactive in recent years, despite the fact that manufacturing production in Britain has continued to decline.

For these companies, or more exactly their top-level management, the strategic decision of where to produce will no doubt be affected by industrial relations considerations. To some extent, this will account for the large amount of investment that has been channelled into the newly developing countries (Fröbel, et al., 1980) and those developed nations where trade unionism is weak and industrial militancy low. At the same time, however, the development of industrial relations within particular countries will be shaped by the international reorganisation of production. Once again, Britain provides a good example of traditionally strong union organisation, oriented towards the workplace, which can be swiftly undermined by large companies reorganising themselves by, for example, relocating production either at the national or international level. Industrial relocation at the national level not only effects change in the spatial distribution of employment but also facilitates the introduction of new techniques of production and working practices (Massey, 1978). Moreover, firms can seize the opportunity provided by a new environment to restyle their pay structures. Relocation at the international level provides similar opportunities for fundamental change only on a wider scale. From the point of view of a particular country, however, the effects on aggregate employment can be quite dramatic as the experience of Britain demonstrates.

A further aspect of the process of change is the development of new forms of work organisation. For the employer this involves a renewal of the circuit of industrial capital and a basic change in the institutional arrangements governing the performance of work. New technologies, for example, provide the potential for decentralising and fragmenting production processes, a potentiality that has clearly been exploited with the re-emergence of 'outwork' (Rubery and Wilkinson, 1981). As these authors point out, this particular development has been common in, though not exclusively confined to, industries where product demand is volatile. The use of subcontracting arrangements has also been widely identified (Friedman, 1977; Rubery and Wilkinson, 1981). The significance of these new forms of work organisation, however, is that they represent a challenge to existing structures of employment, work organisation, and industrial relations practices. Indeed, this applies as much to the larger and more successful firms, usually identified with primary sector employment conditions, as it does to the smaller and generally less secure firms. All of these are, to a greater or lesser extent, subject to the discipline of competition and this means, from the employees' point of view, changes within the process of production that both undermine and displace existing patterns of behaviour and positions of bargaining strength. For the employer, however, a failure to respond to these forces of change—specifically, a failure to establish the conditions necessary for profitable production—will precipitate its decline and eventual elimination from the competitive process.

These forces of change, then, ultimately shape and underpin the existing structure of employment, the job opportunities available to particular groups within the labour market, and the path of development of industrial relations within particular companies. The processes of change, identified above, demonstrate that these structures can develop in complex ways. In the case of British firms a great deal of reorganisation has taken the form of relocation abroad. Those firms that continue to manufacture in Britain, however, remain under considerable pressure to restructure their production processes, to introduce new methods of production and terms and conditions of employment, in order to avoid further decline. These changes, moreover, will form the basis of new struggles within the sphere of production, ensuring the centrality of industrial relations to the process of economic development. It is thus essential that economists respond to the challenge of history by developing an analysis which does not assume away the social character of production.

13 Discrimination in the Labour Market

Ken Mayhew and John Addison

This chapter is concerned with discrimination against racial minorities and against women. Racial minorities comprise 4 per cent of the population and 3·3 per cent of the economically active. The corresponding figures for women are 52 per cent and 40 per cent. In terms of numbers, therefore, the scales of the two problems are very different; but in terms of their potential social and political consequences, both are important.

Both groups are poorly paid relative to white males. This could be the result either of receiving low earnings within occupations or of being crowded into a narrow subset of badly paid occupations. Either form of disadvantage might be the consequence of discrimination in the labour market. The term 'wage discrimination' is often used to refer to low pay within occupations and the term 'job discrimination' to refer to occupational crowding. These disadvantages, however, may also result from the possession of inferior productive characteristics. The potential role of discrimination is not exhausted, since these may in turn be the consequence of what is often called 'discrimination before the labour market', in such areas as access to education or housing.

Although economists have placed most stress on earnings, other aspects of the labour market experience of minority groups also merit attention. Racial minorities as a whole exhibit many of the characteristics of the inhabitants of a secondary labour market. They quit jobs more frequently than the average and yet achieve less upward mobility. Their unemployment rates are also higher (Smith, 1980). Women do not exhibit higher unemployment rates, as officially recorded, but their labour force attachment is weaker and correspondingly their activity rates are lower. This undoubtedly means that their unemployment rates are underestimated. They too exhibit less upward mobility than men.

Although there are many reasons for these peculiarities, they are undoubtedly partly the result of discrimination. To give two examples. Whatever effect job discrimination has in crowding blacks into a narrow range of occupations, it is also a contributory factor to their higher unemployment rates. Whatever the role of discrimination in promotion decisions which cause women both to have lower earnings within occupations and to be under-represented in the higher level occupations, it also contributes to their low activity rates. Frustration in their career aspirations may cause many women to leave the labour market and devote themselves to rearing children.

The chapter begins by reviewing the economic theories of discrimination, and goes on to evaluate the evidence on sexual and racial discrimination respectively. In particular, the impact of anti-discrimination policies is discussed. The chapter concludes by briefly assessing the extent and form of discrimination, its importance in explaining the disadvantaged position of racial minorities and of women, and implications for policy.

ECONOMIC THEORIES OF DISCRIMINATION IN THE LABOUR MARKET

Economic models of discrimination can conveniently be divided into three groups: those which assume a perfect labour market, those which allow for imperfections of market structure, and those which allow for imperfections of information. The first approach, often classified as the 'neoclassical' theory of discrimination, was first developed by Becker (1971) and Arrow (1972a). This approach is chiefly, though not exclusively, concerned with situations of perfect competition in labour markets. It is based on the notion that a 'taste' for discrimination is analogous to any other kind of preference: the individual who has such a taste will be prepared to sacrifice money income to indulge that taste. A distinction can be made in principle, though not necessarily in practice, between the tastes of employers, employees, and consumers.

Beginning with a uniform employer taste for discrimination, and assuming for the present an absence of employee discrimination, each employer will act as though the wage rate payable to blacks (female) workers is not the actual wage, say W_B, but rather W_B+d, where d is the discrimination coefficient. This coefficient can be interpreted as the money equivalent of the psychic costs which the employer incurs in employing blacks rather than whites. As usual, the employer equates the wage rate with the value of marginal product, but in the case of blacks the wage rate will be inflated by d. In equilibrium,

$$W_W = VMP$$
$$W_B + d = VMP$$

where W_W is the wage rate payable to whites. This implies that $W_B = W_W - d$. Accordingly, there will be a racial (sexual) differential in wages, the magnitude of which will depend on the discrimination coefficient. Becker argues that employers will have to sacrifice money profits in order to indulge their taste for discrimination. One implication of the model is that blacks (or females) will have to accept lower wages to ensure their employment, providing there is a shortage of white (or male) workers.

Thus far the argument has been confined to the short run, with the scale of operations of each producer taken as given. As Becker suggests, assuming different discrimination coefficients and identical production functions, those employers with a lower *d* value will have lower costs so that in the long run under competitive equilibrium, there may be employment segregation but little or no wage discrimination. Within monopolistic industries, however, the median coefficient will not be subject to erosion. And even where there is competition in the product market, wage discrimination may still be an equilibrium phenomenon where there are limits to the expansion of firms with low or negligible discrimination coefficients. This outcome would simply reflect diseconomies of scale.

Next consider employee discrimination. By analogy with the previous example, employees may be said to have a taste for discrimination if, when offered employment in a mixed group, they act as though the wage rate offered is $W-d$; the magnitude of *d* indicating the intensity of their dislike for working with members of the relevant minority group. In a perfect labour market with no employer discrimination, it follows that this discriminatory attitude will lead to segregation of the workforce but not to a wage differential. No employer will employ a white worker if he has to pay that worker a premium to work with a black labour force. So all-white or all-black labour forces will be cheaper than racially mixed ones. Workers will receive a wage equal to the value of the marginal product.

But if blacks are underrepresented in the skilled grades and whites in the unskilled grades for example, the two groups will be complementary. Here blacks will be employed alongside whites and will have to accept lower wages for a given job. If the objections of whites are more strident the greater the number of blacks employed, the model will lead to a direct relation between wage discrimination and the proportion of blacks employed. Also if white workers do indeed discriminate, the variance of white earnings for given levels of education and experience should increase with the proportion of blacks in the labour force—the higher that proportion, the more likely are whites to be working with blacks, and thus the higher the wage premium.

What of consumer discrimination? The basic proposition is that white consumers are willing to pay more for goods sold by whites. This directly lowers the value of the marginal product of non-whites in the same way as would reduced motivation. Discrimination of this type is likely to prevail in service jobs which will consequently tend to be populated by individuals who possess the same colour characteristics as their clients; the preponderance of females in such jobs would rule out customer discrimination in their case. A wage differential will result given the maintained hypothesis that whites can afford to pay more than blacks. Unfortunately, many of the jobs which offer opportunities for self-employment, and which therefore permit workers to evade employer (or employee) discrimination, are in the service trades and are thus likely to encounter consumer discrimination.

Is the taste to discriminate to be taken as an independent determinant of rational economic behaviour or is it a consequence of such behaviour? If the problem is put in terms of white unions limiting, via restrictions on training and promotion, the amount of capital invested in blacks by firms, the result is an explanation of discrimination based on power. It is likely to be to the recurring economic advantage of whites (or males in trade unions) to restrict the access of blacks to education (or females to apprenticeships). In so doing, whites (or males) are improving their job opportunities and hence their incomes. Such behaviour follows from economic motives and not dislike or prejudice. Much hinges on the question of whether the motive for discrimination is 'economic' or reflects a taste for discrimination. Clearly they each figure in both sexual and racial discrimination, but the 'taste' elements probably differ as between women and blacks. Clearly physical distaste or dislike of physical proximity are unusual in male attitudes to women, whereas male resentment concerning relative status may be more deep-seated in the case of women than blacks.

The problem of assessing employment discrimination against women is not just a matter of estimating the benefit obtained by men from its application but also one of judging the impact of supply-side differences in motivation and/or job preference. Without knowledge of job preference, only a loose assessment can be made of the extent of employment discrimination. The problem is of major importance with respect to married women whose labour force participation over the life cycle differs markedly from that of men.

Research in human capital theory is currently developing hypotheses which assist understanding of the impact of supply-side differences. One such hypothesis is that withdrawal from the labour force for extended periods results in an accelerated depreciation of schooling and postschooling investments (Mincer and Polachek, 1974). An implication of this analysis is that women who expect to be absent from the labour force for either long or frequent intervals will elect to invest less than males in on-the-job training. They will present themselves for occupations in which the penalty for intermittent participation is lowest. This human capital reasoning leads to the expectation that women will be less well represented in, say, managerial and professional jobs for reasons of income maximising choice, quite apart from possible discrimination in hiring or promotion practices. Another implication of this hypothesis is that the job opportunities of single women, while similar to those of men, will differ markedly from those of married women because the supply-side difference is assumed to be the differential family care commitment of married women. Wage discrimination may itself of course discourage investment in education and training by females (and blacks).

Next relax the competitive assumption further and consider monopsonistic influences—that is, where there is a single buyer of labour. Differences in group supply functions have already been mentioned. Married women's job choices in particular will tend to be more constrained than those of their husbands, which might reflect the tendency for wives to search for jobs close to home. Also, of course, family income maximisation may require the wife to make a larger career sacrifice than her husband, who typically will possess a greater stock of human capital. As a result of these forces, married women may occupy less favourable jobs for given productivity characteristics. Also, married women may receive lower pay for the job, because of their implied lower responsiveness to economic signals. This is a case of deliberate discrimination or exploitation.

Another type of market imperfection is imperfect knowledge, although discussion will be widened to include the dual labour market hypothesis. The application of an 'economics of information' theory to labour market problems has led a number of economists to develop models based on the notion that easily observable indices such as race or sex may be used as a cheap screening device in the hiring process (Arrow, 1973; Phelps, 1972; McCall, 1973). The basic approach is relatively straightforward: it derives from the fact that employers have very imperfect information about the potential productivity of job applicants. They will nevertheless have some idea from past experience of the probability distribution of productivity characteristics across individuals with given indices such as colour, sex, and marital status. If colour, sex, or marital status is well enough correlated with attributes that have a direct bearing on production, such as absentee-ism, it will pay the employer to guard against the greater risk associated with the employment of a coloured or female worker by offering employment at a reduced wage. Indeed, the worker may be screened out altogether, especially if there is some restriction on the payment of lower wages. In this latter case women or blacks will tend to be hired only for jobs in which their 'inferior' characteristics are relatively unimportant. There may then be a crowding effect which will lower the wage in women's occupations below that in men's occupations.

Once allowance is made for imperfect information, equilibrium may be consistent with some women earning less than the actual value of their marginal product. Then if the probability distributions of, say, absenteeism overlap for men and women, a minority of female workers at the lower end of the distribution will actually have a rate of absenteeism which is less than the male average. *Ex post* a minority of women will receive the female wage, even though the value of their marginal product is greater than the male wage; or alternatively, they may be passed over for employment in favour of men who are in fact less productive. This situation is referred to as 'statistical' discrimination, where some women or blacks will earn less simply because of their sex, not because of their productivity. Note, however, that the use of sex or race as a cheap screening method may be an efficient way of taking hiring decisions given the costs of obtaining full information about individual workers.

The above discussion has assumed that employers know the probability distribution of the workforce in terms of the relevant characteristic, while ignorant of any single individual's place in that distribution. In practice, their knowledge of the distribution may be imperfect. The stereotypes developed by employers need continual updating in the light of changes in the labour market. Because information about these changes is costly to obtain, the process of updating will never be complete. Consequently it is quite likely that the empirical rules developed will become outdated and that incorrect or biased decisions will tend on average to be made. Translated into terms of probability distribution of the workforce by relevant characteristics, the actual distribution of, say, absenteeism, may be the same for both male and female workers, but employers although correctly informed about the male distribution incorrectly believe female distribution to be inferior and base their offers on the 'imagined' distribution. An employer might be expected to learn, however, and it has been claimed that tight labour markets favour minorities via the induced experimentation and revision of employer stereotypes (McCall, 1973). The empirical implications of the information theory is that hiring and promotion policies are likely to be suboptimal over a much wider range than unionised (see below) and monopolistic firms, particularly with respect to married women whose labour market participation has greatly increased over time.

Unfortunately there is a more pessimistic view which reinforces rather than erodes the basis of statistical discrimination. In one sense informational theories of discrimination, as developed in the models of Spence (1973) and Stiglitz (1973), point to 'self-selection' and different investments by individuals in their own training and education. If the stereotype is not challenged it will persist. Having said that, where behaviour is based on misconceptions, such as a mistaken belief that women are less productive than men, once the process of exclusion is broken (say, by a minimum quota stipulation) there should be a fairly rapid change, known as the 'tipping' phenomenon (Spence, 1973.)

But this is not necessarily the end of the story once institutional models of labour market duality are introduced (Doeringer and Piore, 1971). The essence of dual labour market theory is that the labour market consists of two sectors: primary and secondary. The former offers good wages and conditions, job stability and security, together with opportunities for advancement. The latter offers none of these benefits. The essence of the dualist thesis is that segmentation eliminates opportunities for workers in the secondary sector as opposed to limiting them either through discrimination or market imperfections. Once a pattern of exclusion is established there is no turning back as there is in informationally-based theories, because men and women (whites and blacks) will be slotted into different training opportunities which will lead their actual as opposed to their innate ability to diverge rapidly over time. Indeed, it is argued that assignment to the secondary sector will reinforce, or even create, the undesirable characteristics associated with that market; even if they did not possess these characteristics initially, workers would acquire them. For example, if their terms and conditions of employment are based on the assumption that they will be absent frequently, workers will have little incentive to keep up a regular rate of attendance. In other words, disadvantage produces self-confirming behaviour and produces the shift in the actual distribution to the 'imagined' position noted above. Though elements of segmentation exist, there is little evidence that it occurs in a systematic manner (Mayhew and Rosewell, 1979).

SEXUAL DISCRIMINATION

The theoretical discussion suggests that employee discrimination will be reflected in considerable employee segregation; that employer discrimination will yield wage differentiation by sex; that a 'taste' model will be of greater relevance in non-competitive product market environments, with the event of wage discrimination being positively associated with the relative size of the female labour force; and that a crowding model points to segregation as the direct cause of low wages.

It is difficult in principle to distinguish between the various models of discrimination. Moreover, there is the added difficulty of disentangling discriminatory forces from other non-discriminatory elements in wage and employment determination. This latter difficulty is of course pronounced in the case of women because of their potentially very different tastes and motivations. Faced with such difficulties the modern approach has been to estimate discrimination as a residual and to forego direct testing of individual models of discrimination. But first the aggregative evidence is examined.

According to Edgeworth (1922), the pressure of male unions was primarily responsible for the crowding of women into comparatively few occupations and for depressing female wages. There are of course other possible sources of crowding of which mention will be made later. What is the actual extent of crowding? Three principal hypotheses are relevant: first, the greater the percentage of women in the labour force, the lower the level of female earnings; second, the higher the pay of men, the lower the percentage of women in the labour force; and third, the greater the percentage of women in the labour force, the greater the male/female earnings ratio.

The most recent empirical estimates are those of Sloane and Siebert (1980). They conclude that females are not unduly concentrated in low paying occupations, excluded from high paying male occupations, or concentrated in occupations where the male earnings differential is particularly high. Unfortunately, the data base employed in this study does not permit the authors to standardise for labour quality and other variables. The authors' parallel industrial analysis yields a set of similarly insignificant coefficients. Their finding that there is limited crowding implies that low pay within occupations is the prime cause of female earnings disadvantage. Computations by Chiplin and Sloane (1976a), using New Earnings Survey (NES) data for 1971, 1973 and 1974, suggest that inequality of pay is roughly twice as important as inequality of occupational distribution. Much the same results were obtained by Addison (1975) for a sample of four other European countries. Such conclusions, however, have occasioned considerable controversy.

The dispute has centred on the occupational categories employed in analyses of this type. Clearly one major difficulty is in assuming that the same job is being compared, it being argued that the classification selected is too broad. Certainly an analysis at a much lower level of occupational disaggregation yields a stronger impression of occupational crowding (see Mayhew and Rosewell, 1978: app. C). Even within occupations, women may be concentrated in low-paying firms. This, coupled with the use of incremental pay systems, could explain the importance of pay inequalities. Accordingly, it may be wrong to argue that equal pay legislation is the crucial corrective: a major source of pay inequality may well be inter-firm rather than intra-firm. Small firms tend to pay lower wages than large firms, and it is possible that females are concentrated in small establishments. There is little direct evidence on this question, though Nickell (1977) shows that average plant size has a significant positive effect on female earnings. Here, as will be seen, the effect of plant size is not unrelated to unionism.

Crowding may be the consequence of monopoly power and reflect the ability of employers to indulge their 'taste' for discrimination. Chiplin and Sloane (1974) attempt to relate the percentage of female industry employment and the female-male earnings ratio to the extent of industrial concentration. While a statistically significant negative coefficient on concentration is obtained in the case of the female equation, the explanatory power of the regression is negligible. Nickell's (1977) analysis also fails to detect any significant impact of the degree of industrial concentration. Thus it would appear that there is no real evidence to favour the proposition that women's wage and employment disadvantage is related to monopoly in the product market.

Trade unions may have an unfavourable effect on the occupational/industrial representation of women via the erection of entry barriers. Unions may thus widen the male-female wage differential at the same time as narrowing that differential within the firms in which they operate. Some evidence on craft unionism's deleterious effect on the relative earnings of blacks in the United States is supplied by Ashenfelter (1973). Unfortunately, there is no comparable evidence in the case of women for Britain. There is *ad hoc* evidence of British unions restricting access to a number of occupations and industries on the basis of sex; the classic example being printers (McCarthy, 1964). The overall underrepresentation of women in skilled manual work and in the professions is marked, as shown in table 13.1. Moreover, only 8 per cent of girls aged fifteen to seventeen entered apprenticeships in Great Britain in 1972, as compared with 39 per cent of boys, and the vast majority of girl apprenticeships were in hairdressing. Yet it is difficult to evaluate the extent to which women's relatively unfavourable occupational composition reflects exclusion by craft and professional organisations. The principal difficulty, here as elsewhere, is one of ascertaining the weight to be put on differences in male and female employment preferences and ways of life (see below). This issue transcends the problem of inadequate standardisation for human capital variation in the table. The general point is that unions (and professional

TABLE 13.1: OCCUPATIONAL DISTRIBUTION OF EMPLOYMENT BY SEX, GREAT BRITAIN, 1961 AND 1971

Occupation	Numbers (000s), 1971 Male	Female	Index[a] of Female Occupational Representation 1961	1971
Employers and managers	1936	419	·49	·48
Professional	790	85	·29	·26
Intermediate non-manual	875	985	1·66	1·44
Junior non-manual	1858	3397	1·81	1·75
Personal service	147	1125	2·69	2·40
Foremen and supervisors	549	51	·22	·23
Skilled manual	4601	533	·35	·28
Semi-skilled manual	1968	1109	1·07	·98
Unskilled manual	1071	698	·91	1·07
Agricultural workers	243	63	·38	·54
Armed forces	238	11	·11	·12
Own account	786	190	·70	·53

Source: Department of Employment, *The Changing Structure of the Labour Force* (London: HMSO, 1977).
Note:
[a] Computed from $[L_{if}/(L_{if}+L_{im})]/(L_f/L)$; where L_{if} (L_{im}) is the number of women (men) in the ith occupation, L_f is the total number of women, and L is the size of the labour force. Hence a value of unity in any occupational classification means that female representation equals that to be expected on the basis of their representation in the workforce as a whole. Values less (more) than unity indicate under (over) female representation.

associations) do provide an institutional framework for collusion against women for solid income maximising reasons, and there is an urgent need for research in this area, underwritten by the revelation of unionism's often passive and even negative role in implementing equal pay (Snell, Glucklich and Povall, 1981).

The limited British research of a systematic nature focuses upon union relative wage effects by sex, usually using aggregate (industry) data. An analysis of specially-prepared data from the 1973 NES by Thomson, Mulvey and Farbman (1977) reveals that 28·3 per cent of manual women are not covered by a collective agreement, compared with only 16·8 per cent of male manuals; for non-manual males and females the position is reversed, with respectively 39·6 per cent and 35·2 per cent uncovered. The authors report that manual females covered by one of three types of agreement—national agreement only, national plus supplementary agreements, and company/district/local agreements—earn 18·6 per cent more than women who are not subject to a collective agreement. The equivalent figure for female non-manuals is 28·1 per cent. In both cases the union/non-union differential is higher for females than for males.

Sloane and Siebert (1980), again using NES data for 1973, attempt to explain low earnings, specifically the percentage of manual (non-manual) women earning less than £40 per week, by extent of coverage by collective agreements, years of service, hours of work, and the female share in employment. In the case of manuals, they find that all three types of coverage yield a negative sign and that 'national and local agreements' and 'national agreements only' are highly significant. For non-manual women, however, collective bargaining coverage does not appear to be related to the incidence of low pay.

Finally, Nickell (1977) is able to test for the relationship between levels of earnings and degree of unionisation. The coefficient on the percentage unionisation in the female wage equation indicates that in 1966 the union mark-up on female wages was 13 per cent, whereas in the male equation the coefficient was 5 per cent and insignificant. In 1972 strong mark-ups emerged for both groups. The data suggest that individuals covered by 'local agreements only' do better than the rest. More importantly, the average level of the mark-up appears slightly higher for females than for males. This pattern holds true for most of the period 1970–75, with the exception of 1974–5 when it would appear that women lost ground in the post-Heath wages explosion. Metcalf (1977) has used Nickell's results on mark-ups together with coverage rates to infer that unions have narrowed the sex differential by over 1 percentage point. As Metcalf himself cautions, however, the argument rests on the assumption that either the extent of unionisation is not a determinant of the non-union wage or that if unionisation does affect the latter it does so uniformly for men and women. Until more is known about the extent to which crowding effects are caused by trade unions, the only safe conclusion is that men covered by collective agreements do not appear to be better off than women in similar circumstances. This less ambitious statement is consistent with the possibility that unions have widened the overall female-male differential even though they may narrow it within their jurisdictions.

Turning now to monopsony, women are more likely to be subject to this influence than men. And because monopsony applies more to married women than to single women this provides a further reason for wage differentiation within the ranks of female labour. The monopsony model also predicts a higher female-male earnings ratio where employers are bunched, as for example in urban areas, because here the more geographically limited job search of females will be of less deleterious consequence. Unfortunately, there is little direct evidence on which to draw in this area. Nickell (1977) reports that the percentage employed in conurbations has a positive effect on female earnings. This is supportive of the model to the extent that women's job search may be constrained by the location of the husband's job and its subsequent effect on the place of residence: the constraint is likely to be smaller where the husband locates in a conurbation, reflecting the greater job opportunities for the wife. From the perspective of equal pay policy, it is urgent that further analysis of monopsony be undertaken, focusing on such variables as size of town and time taken for journey to work. In the simple unorganised case the imposition of equal pay will increase female employment. In the partially organised case (males being unionised), however, firms with a preference for male employees might seek to recruit a wholly male labour force. As so often in this area, the effects of legislation are ambiguous.

In the preceding discussion mention was made of differences in male and female preferences and ways of life. It is now appropriate to consider such differences explicitly, for supply-side differences between the sexes may be expected to explain a further component of the wage gap. Because it is impossible to proxy differences in female preferences and ways of life, it becomes especially important to control for all other measurable differences between the sexes that might be expected to affect differential productivity. It was noted earlier that aggregative studies are handicapped in general by lack of data on human capital variables. A common approach to estimating the role of sex in earnings differences has been to run a single earnings equation which, in addition to standard human capital variables, includes sex as a dichotomous variable (1 for women and 0 for men). If the coefficient on the sex variable is negative and significant, this indicates that women earn less than males even after the effects of other characteristics are accounted for. This measure may then be interpreted as a composite measure of sex discrimination. But this general approach is unsatisfactory. The problem quite simply is that the earnings structure is not the same for men and women; significant interactions may exist between sex and the various other characteristics and may be tested for.

One way to deal with this problem is to estimate separate earnings functions for men and women. However, this is to assume that married and single women have similar preferences and ways of life. In the context of sex discrimination an attempt must be made to differentiate between these two groups of women on the grounds that the latter are very much more likely than the former to resemble males in their attitude towards work and career orientation; this procedure is justified given the inability to model tastes and preferences directly. Of major relevance here is the typical role specialisation between married men and women. The measure of sex discrimination should therefore be taken from a comparison of single men with single women (though the omission of a motivation variable implies that the comparison will measure a lower bound to sex discrimination), while differences between married and single men and between married and single women might be identified with family role differences. On the other hand, differences between the two latter groups might affect marital status discrimination.

The necessary distinction between married and single women imposes a further data requirement. Yet the key problem in the British case has been inadequate data which until very recently mandated crude analyses of the aggregate type discussed earlier. Fortunately, two recent British studies have gone some way to redress the chronic imbalance between British and American research by estimating separate-earnings functions for males and females by marital status. A third study has compared males and females at a level at which the provisions of both equal pay and equal opportunity legislation are meant to apply, while a fourth has reported modest advances in identifying techniques for analysing offers made to different groups by employers.

The study by Greenhalgh (1980) is the first British analysis to employ an economy-wide earnings function for females using individual data. Greenhalgh uses General Household Survey data for 1971 and 1975 to derive samples approximate to the relevant comparison groups discussed earlier. In common with two of the three other studies, she employs an earnings function test in which discrimination is obtained as a residual. Greenhalgh's method is as follows. Earnings functions are first estimated separately for each group, defined by sex and marital status. Next, a hypothetical earnings ratio is computed as though both groups under comparison (say single males and females) had the same earnings function and differed only in measured productivity characteristics. In this index-number method, if all relevant productivity characteristics are included in the earnings function, the residual difference between the actual and hypothetical earnings ratio will reflect different treatment of those with the same productivity; that is, economic discrimination. Greenhalgh's results suggest a large reduction in discrimination against single women between 1971 and 1975. No improvement is recorded in the position of married women over the same period. Greenhalgh attributes this development to a differential impact of the Equal Pay Act, reflecting the likely concentration of married women in sex segregated employment. Single younger women (aged less than thirty) failed to record parity with their male counterparts in 1975. Although Greenhalgh terms the residual unexplained 10 per cent 'discrimination', it is not altogether clear whether this refers to sex or (potential) marital status discrimination.

Siebert and Sloane (1981) conducted an analysis of sex and marital status discrimination in a sample of five establishments in light engineering, finance, the public sector, food processing, and clothing. Reflecting the personnel records data base of study, the quality of the educational variable is inferior to that employed by Greenhalgh and hence the earnings function is less appropriately specified. But the experience variable is correspondingly better defined. Familiarly, Siebert and Sloane express the wage rate as a function of education, experience both within and outside the firm, and a set of additional productivity-standardising variables. They, too, present index number comparisons of earnings using the four sex and marital status groups. Siebert and Sloane detect clear evidence of sex discrimination—that is, comparing single males with single females—in only one of three firms for which a comparison is possible. Here (the light engineering company) females were paid up to 16 per cent less than similar men with similar characteristics. As for the effect of marital status on pay, the authors detect that in two cases both marital status discrimination and family role factors can be ruled out. In other cases, the authors find evidence of discrimination in favour of married females in the public sector establishment and against married females (in favour of single females) in the financial institution. Siebert and Sloane, then, find that sex discrimination exists in some establishments but not others (at least subsequent to the hiring decision). This is an important result and suggests that few general conclusions can be drawn from more aggregative data. Against this it is questionable whether the sort of organisations willing to participate in such a study are fully representative.

The importance of the third and earlier study considered here (Chiplin and Sloane, 1976b) is that it examines the promotional aspects of discrimination. The authors investigate a professional two-grade occupation within a particular organisation. Promotion from the lower to the higher grade is postulated to be a function of experience within the company and, in the wider model, also of mobility and marital status. Two equations are run for both sexes, and produce some limited evidence of discrimination in promotion.

There are many deficiencies in the earnings function approach, whereby discrimination is measured as a residual. The results of such studies are as reliable as the earnings functions on which they are based – not a reassuring thought. The residual may overestimate discrimination to the extent that the equation is mis-specified, and that it fails to include characteristics which determine earnings. It may underestimate it in the sense that discrimination before the labour market may cause women to possess lesser educational qualifications and the like. In other words, it is clear that correct specification of the wage equation is crucial. Although some specification problems are avoided or minimised by distinguishing between individuals by marital status, a number of difficulties still attach to the British estimates. The use of a single equation approach in particular is flawed to the extent that earnings and labour supply are simultaneously determined. The implication is that an appropriate technique should be employed to estimate the determinants of earnings and labour supply simultaneously. Without such an approach there is no way to be sure that the unexplained earnings differential stems from the demand side of the market, and reflects discrimination, rather than from the supply side as a result of tastes and preferences of individual employees and potential employees influenced by, among other things, the division of labour within the household. Clearly, there is also a problem of selectivity bias implicit in the use of observed outcomes. Gronau (1974) for example, has argued that wage comparisons ignore the fact that at any given moment something like 50 per cent of women are not working and that the bias thereby introduced means that the size of the wage gap to be explained is a considerable understatement of true wage differentials. However, Gregg Lewis (1974) has cogently argued that the direction and magnitude of the selectivity bias cannot be determined *a priori* but will depend on certain assumptions regarding the nature of the distributions and the characteristics of groups.

A further difficulty attaches to the validity or otherwise of the arguments included in the earnings function. This is a problem wider than the standard econometric specification problem and, as Chiplin (1979) points out, raises two main issues. The first concerns different treatment of the same characteristics, and the second the reasonableness of the criteria adopted by the firm in determining hiring and promotion. Different treatment of the same characteristics does not inevitably imply discrimination. As Polachek (1975) has noted, structural differences in the male-female earnings function can be interpreted as being consistent with non-discriminatory behaviour. Thus the quantity of human capital investment embodied in one year's labour market experience may be less for a woman than for a man and the quantity of human capital investment per working year (i.e., its intensity) may also be less. Different treatment of the same measured characteristic in different functional relationships does not necessarily amount to discriminatory behaviour if the characteristics are unreliable in the sense that their measurement is sexually biased.

Consideration of the reasonableness of the criteria adopted by the firm in hiring and promotion decisions leads directly to the fourth study, Chiplin (1981), and subsequently to a discussion of signalling and self-confirming behaviour. Chiplin's attempt to deal with the various problems considered above takes the form of estimating a 'wage offer' rather than an earnings function. His data relate to offers of university places made to potential students in one department of a British university in which the same conditional offer is made to all candidates irrespective of sex. The question raised is: do females have a lower probability of receiving an offer for given characteristics. The latter are taken as given, and so wider issues concerning the acquisition of characteristics are perforce ignored. Interestingly, Chiplin is unable to detect evidence of discrimination against females. Again, it is recognised that academic achievement could reflect discrimination within the schooling system and school references could relay sexual prejudice. But taking these factors as given, there is little evidence of any sex discrimination in admissions either against or in favour of women. This is an important result in itself but the principal significance of the study is that it represents a potentially important step forward in analytical techniques which could be useful in assessing the extent of discrimination within firms.

Thus far attention has been focused on direct discrimination, especially on the measurement of pure discrimination as a residual after allowance for various other factors or personal characteristics. The residual may be thought of as a measure of ignorance, and even so little faith can be placed in the reported magnitudes themselves because of specification error.

These British studies which distinguish individuals by marital status have avoided some of the pitfalls, but do not overcome all the problems associated with wage equations. Personal characteristics emerge as highly significant determinants of wages although controversy rages over the interpretation of that part of the residual which can also be explained by them.

This is not the end of the story because the acquisition of characteristics may itself reflect discrimination. A process of discrimination may occur in the socialisation and educational process and may influence the kind of market choices that women and men make. Supply-side differences, then, will reflect elements of discrimination. This has a number of dimensions. Thus young women's choices about education, marriage, children and career may be affected by the experience of older women who have been victims of direct market discrimination. But equally, women may self-select themselves into particular occupations for reasons unassociated with past market discrimination. Again, it is very difficult in practice to assess the importance of self-selection arising from 'free choice'. However, Chiplin and Sloane (1976a) have offered an interesting procedure. They argue that women's participation in criminal activities, which may be viewed as reasonably free from demand-side influences, evinces clear evidence of self-selection. Female crime is apparently concentrated (unlike that of males) in three particular areas: namely, shoplifting, the handling of stolen goods, and other theft or unauthorised taking. Two-thirds of female offenders were found guilty of these offences in 1973. So there is evidence of sex-stereotyping in areas where there are low barriers to entry and free choice. Since self-selection involves occupational segregation there are obvious difficulties confronting equal opportunities legislation.

Yet it is likely that the perpetuation of discrimination in the long run is linked to some feedback relationship between an original prejudice or misconception and female-male productivity. In Spence's (1973) signalling model, for example, where the markets for male and female labour are regarded by the employer as separate, the requirements in terms of educational qualifications may be different between the two groups despite the lack of objective differences between them. In other words, sex alone signals to prospective employers that a woman is less productive than a man with similar qualifications. Women will thus receive different returns for the same educational investment. If it has been the case in the past that women have on average accumulated less job experience than men, then highly productive women may have to spend more on education than comparable men to convince employers that they are in the 'high productivity' group. Thus the return to education is lowered and fewer women than men will find it pays to make the investment. So the argument that women earn less because they have less investment in human capital has a certain circularity, and may reflect the informational structure of the market. Indeed, if signalling costs (access to education) differ for equally productive individuals then equal treatment will imply wage discrimination against women.

If behaviour is self-confirming, as in the Spence case, then beliefs about women's productivity, correct or incorrect, will not be challenged. Such a situation can arise from an original employer misconception based on prejudice or inadequate information, and may continue undisturbed. But once the pattern of exclusion based on misconception is broken, employers' market experience changes and the vicious circle is broken. If the barrier is based on prejudice, however, such a change may not take place. Much hinges, therefore, on the optimality or otherwise of employer hiring standards, and it is a fact that knowledge in this area is sketchy. An altogether more pathological scenario is painted by the dual labour market hypothesis, wherein the barriers facing women are not primarily informationally based. What evidence there is suggests that this particular labour market dichotomisation and its associated feedback on the attitudes and tastes of workers is unlikely to characterise female employment in Britain (Sloane, 1980).

Finally, what of the impact of equal pay and equal opportunities legislation? Greenhalgh (1980) pointed to some improvement in the single female-male earnings ratio over the period 1971–5. This development was ascribed to equal pay legislation. However, Chiplin, Curran and Parsley (1980) reach a somewhat different conclusion, arguing that some of the improved female-male hourly earnings ratio might be accounted for by flat-rate increases under successive stages of incomes policy. Certainly it seems fair to argue that equal pay legislation would not have worked as well as it did but for the fact that it was treated as an exception in a period of incomes policy. The continued improvement in women's relative earnings for the two years after 1975 also owes something to incomes policy and possibly to the growing unionisation of women in some sectors. Between 1977 and 1979 the improvement faltered only to resume slowly in 1980 and 1981.

Despite the importance of intra-occupational differences in earnings, occupational segregation and differences in characteristics 'explain' much of the wage gap and this fact coupled with a likely concentration of women in small, lower paying firms and the use of incremental pay scales to reward service would suggest that the impact of equal pay legislation is likely to have been modest. Indeed, if it is also argued that much of the wage gap between the sexes is accounted for by factors arising prior to labour market entry, the legislation has little direct relevance. Again, knowledge of the overall extent of discrimination is rather rudimentary, and there is little information as to the importance of the various discriminatory mechanisms. Both less and more might be expected of equal opportunities legislation. Less, because occupational segregation, the concentration of women into lower paying firms and the use of incremental pay scales based on length of service are untouched by the 1975 Act. More, in that the legislation may be expected in the long term to feed back on the acquisition by females of education, experience, and training. Whether there is any marked change in the signals between the sexes may depend to a large extent on whether the division of labour within the family undergoes substantial alteration. It is possible that the equal pay legislation had a perverse effect, and caused increased unemployment among women. Like all minimum wage legislation, this happens if the low-paid individual had been receiving pay in line with the value of her contribution to output. There is no convincing evidence on the likely magnitude of this effect.

Thus far much mention has been made of the inferior productive characteristics of women and of the role that discrimination might play. This issue is now considered in more detail – for reasons of space the same aspect of racial disadvantage is also discussed in advance of the next section which is specifically concerned with racial minorities. In Britain women (and blacks) would appear to be considerably less well educated than males. For example, the proportion of men in the workforce with a degree is almost three times that of women, and there is a similar relative under-representation of women with 'A' level qualifications. Given the high correlation between education and earnings, educational endowments can be shown to be an important factor in women's and black's low average pay.

Different groups can have unequal levels of schooling for a variety of reasons. On the demand side, a group may face a lower return to given amounts of schooling and thus decide to invest less. This, for blacks, might reflect expectations of future discrimination once in the market and, for women, expectations of future family commitments. There is also the supply side to consider, namely the terms on which funds are available for education. For both demand and supply reasons, therefore, the equilibrium rate of return to education for women (blacks) could differ from that of men (whites). It is by no means clear that the terms on which educational funds are made available differ as between groups, given the important role of government. In the United States, however, the exclusion from political representation of blacks has historically (prior to the Voting Rights Act of 1965) been associated with discrimination in the provision of central government funds (Myrdal, 1964). Nevertheless there might well be 'cultural traditions' reducing the access of women (and blacks) to education. This issue can be investigated by estimating schooling functions by race and sex, and comparing the coefficients on the various variables: ability, taste, information factors, availability of family funds, and so on.

Unfortunately, there has been no systematic analysis of the determinants of schooling level in Britain. What British work there has been has focused on males, with the contribution of family background factors to the level of schooling being 'measured' by cross-tabulation of socio-economic status of fathers and the schooling level of their offspring. Overt discrimination in the educational field is more likely to occur against blacks than against women, and indeed complaints are made every year. In 1980, for example, the Commission for Racial Equality received twenty-five applications for assistance on individual complaints – eight against local authorities, ten against schools and seven against colleges, polytechnics and universities. Beyond that, there is concern that some groups 'under-achieve'. Part of this is put down to the inadequate steps taken by educational authorities in the case of immigrant children, and more generally to a failure to take adequate steps to allow for special difficulties—for example, different cultural background. Environment may also influence earnings potential, and in this context discrimination in housing may be important.

Racial minorities tend to occupy lower quality housing than the population as a whole. This to a large extent reflects their lower socioeconomic status rather than being specially attributable to their colour. However, judging from tests carried out by PEP (Political and Economic Planning), from complaints, and from investigations carried out by the Commission for Racial Equality, direct and indirect discrimination still occurs despite the race relations legislation. Many pressure groups also criticise housing authorities for not taking the more positive steps required by the Race Relations Act 1976.

RACIAL DISCRIMINATION

In 1974 PEP conducted a survey of a sample of 3,292 Asians and West Indians (Smith, 1977). Less than 1 per cent of the sample were not immigrants. Data collected at this period refer primarily to immigrants, since few British-born blacks had reached the labour force. PEP also had a control group of 1,239 whites. Table 13.2 gives median gross weekly earnings. Its figures are uncorrected for the job level. Table 13.3 makes a crude correction for this.

TABLE 13.2: GROSS WEEKLY EARNINGS OF DIFFERENT RACIAL GROUPS (£)

White men	40·20
Minority men, total	36·70
Of whom: West Indians	37·10
Pakistanis/Bangladeshis	35·40
Indians	38·10
African Asians	34·10

Source: Smith (1977:table A25).

The data in Table 13.3 make it appear that at lower job levels minority men earned more than whites. However this fails to take account of differences between the age structures of the two populations. Earnings are at their highest in the twenty-five to forty-four age groups, and the minorities had a higher proportion of their total in this age range than did whites.

Correcting for this, at the higher job levels the difference was substantial; at the middle job levels, it was less but still substantial; at the lower job levels, minority and white men earned the same. To achieve this, however, minority men had to work more shiftwork.

Turning to the impact of education, for white males education was strongly related to earnings. Those who had completed their full-time education by the age of fifteen had median earnings of £37.30 per week compared with £46.70 for those whose education continued beyond that point. By contrast there was very little difference for minority men. At the same time, PEP found that minority men tended to be at lower job levels than whites with equivalent qualifications. Minority women did not suffer any particular earnings disadvantage relative to white women.

TABLE 13.3: EARNINGS ANALYSED BY JOB LEVEL—WHITE AND MINORITY MEN (£)

Median Gross Weekly Earnings	Professional/ Management	White-Collar	Skilled Manual	Semi-Skilled Manual	Unskilled Manual
White men	53·50	41·70	38·10	34·40	29·70
Minority men	46·20	36·10	37·50	35·90	33·70

Source: Smith (1977: table A26).

The PEP data, therefore, clearly establish that minority males are paid less than white males. Even after a crude correction for education this seems to remain the case. Chiswick (1980) did a slightly more detailed correction for environmental and educational differences. Using the General Household Survey of 1972 to examine the earnings of white and coloured foreign born adult men in Britain, he corrected for the following variables: years of schooling, labour market experience, weeks worked during the year, whether or not the man worked in an urban area, whether or not he was married. He found that there was little difference in the earnings of native-born and foreign-born white men, whether or not human capital and demographic variables were held constant. Coloured immigrants had about 25 per cent lower earnings than either native or foreign-born white men, other things being equal. This relative earnings disadvantage increased with years of schooling. It did not result from recent entry, since the length of time in the country had the same impact on earnings as pre-immigration experience. There was a very small sample of native-born coloured, but they appeared to be at a much smaller earnings disadvantage than foreign-born coloured men. McNabb and Psacharopoulos (1981), again in a regression analysis of the General Household Survey for 1972, found that particularly important explanations of earnings disadvantage were low returns to secondary modern education and to experience in the labour market.

This work by PEP and Chiswick leaves two major questions largely unanswered. The first is the extent to which this earnings disadvantage results from low pay within occupations rather than occupational crowding. PEP make some comparisons within job types, but only at a very high level of aggregation. The second question is the role of discrimination.

The Unit for Manpower Studies (Department of Employment, 1976), using the 1971 Census which has detail on occupation but no information on earnings, found that a much higher proportion of economically active immigrants than of all workers were labourers, and that the percentages of immigrants who were administrators and managers, clerical and sales workers were below the corresponding percentages for all economically active persons. The Unit also visited establishments during the course of its study, and found that the majority of immigrants employed in these establishments were in unskilled or semi-skilled jobs, and that in the manufacturing establishments they were usually employed directly on production or on related activities such as packing (see also Barber, 1980).

Mayhew and Rosewell (1978) conducted a more detailed analysis using the 1971 Census. They showed that immigrants were more occupationally crowded than the population as a whole, but that the extent and type of crowding varied greatly from one group to another. Some, such as the Irish, Pakistanis and West Indians, were unequivocally crowded into undesirable, low-paying occupations. These occupations reflect a lower class, lower pay, and more unskilled jobs than the ten most common occupations for the population as a whole. The 'New Commonwealth Europeans' (from Malta and Gozo) were in an intermediate position: the relative pay of the jobs into which they were crowded being low, and having fewer non-manual jobs than in Great Britain as a whole. But their class position was not so unfavourable. The other three groups studied were in a rather different category. For example, the group from the rest of the New Commonwealth (mainly of Chinese extraction) was the most crowded of all, but this was to a large extent into non-manual and professional jobs whose status is high. New Commonwealth Africans and Indians, who were less crowded than this, were also often in reasonably good jobs with high levels of pay. There are thus two elements in these groups' experience of crowding: its extent and the kinds of occupations that it involves. How far does disadvantage reflect productivity differences? Levels of education are one proxy for this, the more so as the PEP survey found that better education was associated with fluency in English. The most disadvantaged groups were also the least well educated, while the groups who did least badly were better educated than the population as a whole. Length of time in the country might also be a proxy for experience, but there was no relationship between the degree or type of crowding and this factor.

What emerges from these results? The experience of different minority groups varies. Clearly for some occupational crowding is a major source of poor earnings whatever further disadvantages are suffered within occupations. It is at present impossible to make a precise split between the two sources. For other groups occupational crowding is not such a source of disadvantage. Unfortunately, the available work on earnings does not allow firm conclusions as to whether or not this is carried to lack of earnings disadvantage. However, it is possibly misleading to treat racial minorities as a homogenous group.

All the work mentioned suggests that where a discrepancy exists some of it remains even when correction is made for quality differences or differences in endowments. It would be easy to attribute this to discrimination, but this would be misleading. For the corrections made are very rough and ready, and it may be that some of the remaining discrepancy reflects uncorrected-for quality differences. It is necessary, therefore, to look for more direct evidence of discrimination in the labour market. At the same time many of the quality differences may be the result of discrimination before the market, and again direct evidence must be looked for.

Certain types of discrimination are illegal. British legislation, unlike American, does not generally permit 'reverse discrimination'. The Race Relations Act of 1965 set up conciliation machinery to deal with complaints of discrimination, and made unlawful discrimination on the grounds of 'race, colour, ethnic or national origin' in such places as hotels, restaurants, places of entertainment or on public transport. The Race Relations Act of 1968 dealt with discrimination in employment, housing, the provision of goods, facilities or service to the public, and the publication or display of discriminatory advertisements or notices. The 1976 Act set up the Commission for Racial Equality to replace both the Race Relations Board and the Community Relations Commission. It also defined two kinds of racial discrimination: direct and indirect. Indirect discrimination refers to behaviour such as where an employer requires applicants to pass a test before obtaining employment and that test has the effect of excluding black applicants and cannot be shown to be significantly related to the performance of the job.

The Commission for Racial Equality was empowered to carry out investigations without complaint being made. At the same time a number of criticisms of the previous complaints-based system were met. In particular, unlike the Race Relations Board, the Commission was not to process individual complaints. Instead individuals had direct access to the courts, although the Commission might help them to prepare their case. The new strategy focused on the policies and practices of organisations rather than on the actions or complaints of individuals. There was also greater stress not on discrimination *positively* in favour of blacks, but on employers' acting more positively to prevent discrimination, to act against it, and to recognise and, as far as possible, allow for any particular difficulties or disadvantages employees or applicants might have by virtue of their race.

By the nature of things it is impossible to document the precise extent of discrimination, but that such discrimination exists, and on a substantial scale, seems clear. The PEP, among other organisations, has conducted situation tests—either actor tests or correspondence tests, where individuals of obviously different races apply either in person or in writing for the same job (Smith, 1976, 1977). These showed a substantial incidence of discrimination in recruitment—in just under half of all cases. The two alternative measures of discrimination are the actual number of such acts and claims from aggrieved parties. The former is impossible to measure. The latter is bound to be a personal and, therefore, potentially unreliable judgement. (See Department of Employment, 1980b, 1981d.) Vexatious litigants may complain without cause. At the other extreme just complaint may not be made by individuals who are too cowed, too gentle, or too ignorant. Since the preferred test (i.e. situation) is difficult, if not impossible, to conduct at anything other than the recruitment level, evidence on the other forms of discrimination in employment is bound to be less convincing, based, as it is, on complaint and on the occasional case study. In its case studies, the PEP found instances of discrimination in redundancy practice and in promotion. Further evidence of the latter appears in several questionnaire studies of minorities. That discrimination exists is, therefore, undeniable. The important question is the extent to which it has increased or diminished, and, in particular, the extent to which legislation has had an impact. The PEP surveys of 1966–7 and 1974 can be compared. There was a very substantial drop in the proportion claiming personal experience of discrimination, and indeed it seems clear that the 1968 Act had largely eliminated overt discrimination. It is doubtful, PEP argued, whether the actual level of discrimination had been reduced to the same extent.

The Commission for Racial Equality is less sanguine. The Commission funded a study in Nottingham, similar to that done by PEP in 1973–4, where correspondence tests were employed. It found that one in two black applicants was discriminated against. This compares with the one in three figure from the PEP study. When asked to comment, the Deputy Director of the Nottingham Chamber of Commerce said that employers might have been influenced not by colour prejudice, but by the fact that blacks had failed to do a good job in the past. In other words, blacks are 'screened' out, regardless of individual merit, by stereotyped views about their race. This is an example of statistical discrimination. The Commission also reported cases of several companies who had refused to employ blacks under pressure from unions who claimed that their men would not work with blacks. A tendency towards indirect discrimination because of the practice of relying on word-of-mouth recruitment was also stressed, as was language testing, whether formal or informal, being applied without any proper assessment of the language requirements of the jobs concerned or any proper consideration of the most appropriate means of testing.

While overt discrimination has probably been reduced, and while the legislation has had an impact, discrimination is still common. Though managers do not, by and large, view the legislation with hostility, they have taken probably insufficient positive steps to ensure compliance and even less so to take a constructive approach to helping racial minorities. In the same way more could be done by trade unions. TUC policy is unequivocal, but few positive initiatives have been taken from the centre. Moreover, the unions have sometimes done little to combat discrimination that is known to occur. An important reason for this is the reluctance of union leaders to move too far ahead of their membership. Indeed, both the PEP and the Commission found instances where rank-and-file unionists were central instigators of particular acts of discrimination.

Strangely, another set of legislative measures has had a more definable impact on the pattern of racial disadvantage – that is immigration legislation. The Aliens Restriction (Amendment) Act of 1919 and the 1920 Aliens Order introduced a system of work permits. Foreigners could enter Britain to take employment only if they had 'a permit in writing for their engagement issued to their employers'. Permits were issued only if suitable labour could not be found among residents. Such arrangements still regulate the entry of foreigners. There were no restrictions on immigrants from the Empire and Commonwealth or after 1923 from Eire. The 1962 Commonwealth Immigrants Act restricted the entry of Commonwealth immigrants for the first time. Category A vouchers were issued for those with definite jobs to come to, B vouchers for those with a specially needed skill or qualification, C vouchers for the rest. Demand for A and B vouchers was so high that in 1965 Category C vouchers were abolished. In 1968 controls were extended to holders of United Kingdom passports. In other words, Commonwealth immigrants since 1962 have either to have a special skill or to fill a gap which cannot be filled by local manpower. They have thus fallen into two sorts. The first and smaller category are those with professional skills. The occupational mobility of such people, whether immigrant or not, is likely to be slight. In so far, then, as such professionals are a high proportion of an immigrant group, this is likely to be reflected in occupational crowding for some time. The second and larger category are those who come in with definite jobs to go to. In most years over half of them came into four types of jobs: shop assistants, domestic workers, waiters and kitchen workers, and unskilled factory workers. While discrimination may clearly play a role in preventing occupational diffusion after entry, it is equally clear that the immigration legislation has played an important role in causing occupational crowding. Further it also helps to explain the relatively fortunate position of a minority of immigrant groups.

How does the sort of discrimination observed square with the various distinctions made by the discrimination theorists? Is it wage discrimination or job discrimination? At first sight the evidence on recruitment would seem to point to the latter. But it is possible that people who suffer in this way get jobs in the same occupations as white workers but at different plants. In the same way promotion discrimination could be a bar to earnings advancement *within* an occupation, but might also prevent occupational mobility within the firm.

As for motives for discrimination, most of the types outlined in the first section of this chapter can be discerned. The tastes for discrimination model seems to be relevant with regard to the behaviour of employees, but not so much of employers. The screening (or statistical) approach also rears its head. Like the more neo-classical theories, the internal labour market approach stresses the role of coalitions. The motives that such coalitions have for discriminating vary from straightforward physical distaste to the wish to extract economic advantage. However, it is hard to see economic advantage as a systematic force. Where it might appear to have a role, in denial of promotion for instance, it may just as easily reflect white individuals resenting doing less well than a member of a group thought to be inferior.

While all the various theories seem to find some real world correlation, none of them provides the whole answer. This is hardly surprising. What is more disconcerting is that none of them provides more than a blunt tool for analysing the problem. This reflects partly the inadequacy of the data on which to conduct tests, but mainly the poverty of their analysis of the motives for discrimination. Interestingly, PEP found fairly widespread support among the white population for strengthened legislation. But, it might be argued, if there is widespread discrimination there must be widespread prejudice whatever people say in answer to survey questions. As PEP put it, however, 'widespread discrimination springs not from widespread racial prejudice but from a widespread acquiescence in the consequences of the prejudices of the few, from a widespread lack of alertness to the possibility and importance of discrimination, and from a widespread failure to prevent the prejudices of the few from expressing themselves in action'. If this is correct, there is cause for optimism about the role of the law, its function being to control behaviour not attitudes. But the attitude—particularly of employers—towards the law needs to change if the law is to have a more significant impact. There is a common feeling that more direct steps need to be taken by employers and unions towards its implementation and towards monitoring whether or not it is implemented.

CONCLUSIONS

Clearly discrimination exists against women and against blacks, and it affects both their earnings within occupations and their occupational attainment. Its precise extent and type and its precise impact are difficult to pin down. Direct evidence through complaints or situation tests can only give a partial picture of the extent of the problem. This is also true of the econometric work. Such work is more concerned with the specific problem of measuring the impact of discrimination on earnings disadvantage. So many are the assumptions made and so flawed are the econometric techniques used that these measures are unreliable. While it may be difficult to paint a precise picture at any given moment, it is safe to say that discrimination today is less than it was ten or twenty years ago.

It seems that the direct impact of anti-discrimination legislation in this respect is easily over-estimated. Much more of the improvement is to do with the climate of opinion which is both the child and father (or perhaps, more appropriately, the mother) of the legislation. Certain improvements in the earnings position of women are also the consequence of specific factors such as incomes policies and possibly changing power groups within trade unions.

The motives for and types of discrimination are equally hard to catalogue. The econometric work makes little or no attempt at this. Case studies and other direct investigations can uncover some types (e.g. at recruitment) more easily than others. While the pursuit of economic advantage is a factor, much discrimination would appear to stem from deep-rooted prejudice. This prejudice may be widely shared, in a weak form, but most people wish to control their feelings and are reluctant to translate their prejudice into specific action. At the same time they do not take enough positive action against the minority with a stronger prejudice. Thus the role of the government, employers, and unions should be to encourage such positive attitudes. In the long term the position of racial minorities may be more easily ameliorated than that of women, for whom labour market disadvantage is so inextricably bound up with slowly changing attitudes to sex roles.

PART V
The State and its Agencies

14 Active Manpower Policy

Robert M. Lindley

Britain's relative performance on industrial training has been disappointing. The achievements of other countries, especially France, Germany, and Sweden, have frequently been cited as examples of the kind of government commitment required in a modern economy in order to promote adequate investment in human capital. There have, however, been substantial changes since it began to be accepted in the 1950s that the government should have a training policy, if only to lead the antiquated British system of apprenticeship out of the nineteenth century. How and why the broad lines of policy developed as they have done and what may happen in the future is the main subject of this chapter.

While the debate over industrial training has dominated the field of so-called 'active manpower policy', other elements of policy have also been evolving in the last two decades. Three main areas in which significant policy changes have taken place can be discerned in the period since 1960. The first deals with the creation of an industrial training system to cater for the long-term needs of the economy and it received most of the attention devoted to manpower policy during the 1960s and early 1970s when the credibility of the threat of major skill bottlenecks to industrial expansion was at its peak. The second covers job search, recruitment, and placement activities and experienced a major boost during the 1970s through the reorganisation of the public employment service and the creation of the modern jobcentres. The third area of policy emerged in response to acute difficulties of a different kind from those envisaged when the training and employment services were reformed. The world recession in 1975 was felt very severely in the United Kingdom and domestic economic policy explored new avenues for ameliorating unemployment without undermining attempts to restrain the growth of public expenditure. Very broadly speaking these attempts fell into two areas: those which aimed to provide temporary employment outside conventional labour market arrangements, with some opportunity for training where possible; and those which worked more through the market system by subsidising the retention of existing employees, or their early retirement from the labour force, and the recruitment of new people. Of course job creation (in the form of bringing forward plans for public works during recession) and employment subsidies (as part of regional policy) were already quite familiar elements of post-war policy long before the emergence of the plethora of 'special employment and training measures' in 1975 and thereafter. However, the special programmes, which contained to varying degrees elements of temporary employment, training, and employment subsidy, have formed an integral part of the 'manpower scene' since 1975 and have provided examples of alternative programmes against which to judge more conventional approaches to industrial training and further education.

The chapter is therefore concerned primarily with industrial investment in human capital and the ramifications of the relevant 'special measures'. The development of the employment service is given only incidental attention. The analytical perspective adopted is that of economics and, as a preliminary, the next section reviews the economic case for intervention in the labour market, with particular reference to training. Mainstream industrial training policy since 1960 is then examined, followed by a brief discussion of the significance of the 'special measures', the conflicting interests of the main groups involved in the manpower policy field, and the links between manpower policy and other areas of policy. The chapter concludes with some views on potential future developments.

THE ECONOMICS OF LABOUR MARKET INTERVENTION

The main reasons for intervening in the labour market are to increase efficiency and to promote greater equity. The efficiency of any market will be impaired if participants are poorly informed, operate under great uncertainty, are slow to make decisions, are subject to restrictive contracts, or encounter high barriers to entry; it will also be impaired if the market interacts with other markets which are themselves inefficient.

There are two parts to the general efficiency case for labour market intervention: one draws upon the contribution that manpower policy might make to the unemployment-inflation trade-off under normal conditions and the other stresses its contribution to dealing with shocks to the labour market environment which require significant adjustment to the structure of employment. The 1970s provide examples of both worsening unemployment-inflation trade-offs and serious shocks to the structure of world trade and the pattern of industrial output resulting from dramatic changes in oil prices. During the decade there also arose an increasing concern with the potentially disruptive structural change which might follow the development of revolutionary new technologies. But although the co-existence of high rates of inflation and high unemployment, the impact of price shocks, and major technical change can be distinguished as separate problems for which manpower policy has been advocated as a partial solution, the treatment offered is basically designed to reduce the non-accelerating inflation rate of unemployment (NAIRU) (see Chapter 10) by reducing sources of frictional and structural unemployment. Monetarists need not write off manpower policy as 'weak-minded fiscal policy' provided they believe that high rates of registered unemployment are indicative of a malfunctioning labour market. If past increases in NAIRU reflect improvements in social welfare (for example, through increased unemployment benefit), however, this is a consequence which should be recognised. Manpower policies aiming to reduce unemployment partly by reducing NAIRU could fail to do so in these circumstances and instead slow down the decline in unemployment. Equally, though, manpower policy could be designed to speed up the reduction of unemployment without aiming to lower NAIRU itself. Some loss of microeconomic efficiency might result but the considerable loss of output from a longer period of adjustment could be saved.

Three particular issues have received most attention in respect of training (Ziderman, 1978). The first relates to individuals' wanting to invest in themselves. Their willingness to swap current for future consumption will tend to decline with income and there will be a reluctance to accept a major reduction in current standards of living in order to acquire skills capable of generating higher income and consumption levels in the future. Moreover, potentially profitable investments in education and training will be missed because of difficulties in borrowing to finance such investments. Wealth inequalities mean that most individuals cannot offer enough security to warrant substantial loans in cases where the capital assets created are not themselves accessible to the lender in the event of default. The individual's human capital cannot be used as collateral. In addition, a lack of good information and great uncertainty about the job prospects attached to the available training opportunities will also tend to encourage sub-optimal investment.

Becker (1975), however, stresses the importance of distinguishing between general and specific training. He argues that individuals will only invest in the former as this provides them with skills which raise their potential productivity and income-earning capacity in many firms. In the case of specific training which raises the productivity of individuals in jobs specific to only one or relatively few employers, the employer has the prime incentive to invest but may propose arrangements in which the individual will share in both the costs and the benefits. Although the general-specific distinction is important, its significance in practice is reduced by the fact that training is rarely completely general or completely specific. Moreover, the attitude of the employer will depend not only upon how training affects relative productivity in different firms but also upon the factors determining the risk of the employee leaving the firm during or after training. To the extent that workers are immobile, general training will amount to specific training and firms may find it a profitable investment (Oatey, 1970). Similarly, individuals may be willing to share the cost of specific training to the extent that they are confident that they will not be made redundant before collecting enough of the benefits to make it worthwhile (for the training will provide no return if they are employed elsewhere).

The second and third issues relate to the position of the employer in circumstances where there is no satisfactory solution to the capital-market deficiency faced by the individual. In this case employers must step in to finance general training as well as specific training. If they all enter into the spirit of enhancing the nation's stock of human capital, then they must tackle one particular problem: that of predicting their collective skill requirements far enough ahead. Training takes time and it is quite possible that demand conditions will have changed by the time the new skills are available. Fluctuating demand will tend to increase uncertainty and lower investment in training. Coping with irregular trade cycles and increasing international competition may invite some employers to break ranks in order to cut costs during recessions and the training budget will suffer accordingly. This may, of course, happen in the absence of demand fluctuations but the consequence will be the same: those firms that continue to train will generate benefits or 'externalities' which will be shared by firms not contributing to the costs.

This gives rise to the third problem, namely that these externalities will be on a sufficient scale to encourage large numbers of firms to adopt a systematic policy of training fewer people on average than they would hope to employ subsequently. Becker's analysis suggests that completely general training would not be financed by an employer except as an activity profitable in itself and, once some employers break the agreement on training, this is the limiting case to which the situation will tend even though there are other considerations which will come into play to prevent this ultimate outcome.

Remedial action by the government could, in principle, concentrate upon tackling the first issue: that of inadequate access to finance by potential trainees. Various options from loans to outright grants could be considered and the trainee would be under contract with the state. Employers would then compete for trainees and run their training programmes so as to make a normal return on investment in the training activity itself. Some employers may drop out entirely, relying on those with a comparative advantage in providing training. The number of trainees supported by the state would depend on the prospects for demand and the expected supply position (Lindley, 1982). Alternatively, employers may be subsidised to the extent that they train in line with conditions agreed with the government. In this case the employment contract between employer and employee, which accompanies most industrial training in Britain, may or may not be retained. The employer would now be under contract to the state to supply a service to the trainees. Between these two schemes there are many variants according to the scale and type of government financial involvement.

On the face of it there seems to be no good reason why the government should itself provide general training any more than specific training (except, in the latter case, for its own employees). If it believes that there is insufficient training, then it can stimulate individual demand for training or the supply of training opportunities by the methods outlined above. It can pay for, but why should it provide, training? The most compelling reasons are to do with extending access to training in circumstances where the institutional barriers to the flexible use of training capacity in industry or private training schools are just too great to surmount. Given these labour market imperfections, it could well be a good economic investment to provide government training centres. The aim may also be to promote new training methods or introduce programmes to help disadvantaged groups in society. This does presume, however, that reform of the industrially based system is not possible and may shift the difficulty from that of access to training to that of the acceptability to employers and trade unions of government-trained people once they begin to seek jobs.

The burden of financing the training system could fall upon general taxation or upon those groups that benefit directly from increased levels of training. The latter might take the form of a 'training tax' on the individual's subsequent earnings or might involve a system of loans. An alternative device would be a payroll tax on employers which, in principle, could vary according to the type of employer (size and skill structure of the organisation, industry, region, etc.). The choice between these options or combinations of them will depend partly on how much the government wishes to create a 'market for training opportunities' rather than a bureaucratic adjunct to the labour market which deals with 'the problem of training'.

DEVELOPMENTS IN TRAINING POLICY SINCE 1960

In the course of the late 1950s and early 1960s there was much discussion about the inadequacies of both the quality and quantity of industrial training (see, for example, Williams, 1957, 1963; Ministry of Labour and National Service, 1958; Wellens, 1963). In so far as this contributed to shortages of manpower and low productivity, it was considered to be an important factor in the poor growth of British industry. The pace of technological change was expected to require the continual development of new skills. Existing facilities for, and the organisation of, training and retraining were thought to be increasingly inadequate both in terms of securing an appropriate skill mix in the supply of labour to industry and in providing individuals with opportunities to adapt to changing employment conditions. The imminent increase in school-leavers requiring first jobs in the early 1960s, despite the mitigating effects of the expansion of full-time educational opportunities, was a further spur to action.

This groundswell of concern led to the passing of the Industrial Training Act of 1964, the main aims of which, as enunciated in the White Paper *Industrial Training: Government Proposals* (Ministry of Labour, 1962:4), were: '(i) to enable decisions on the scale of training to be better related to economic needs and technological developments; (ii) to improve the overall quality of industrial training and to establish minimum standards;

and (iii) to enable the cost to be more fairly spread.' The main vehicle for reform was the establishment of an industrial training board (ITB) system. Boards were to operate a levy-grant scheme in their respective industries by which a levy or payroll tax was imposed on all firms and grants would be paid out so that those firms achieving acceptable training standards and maintaining adequate numbers of trainees would gain relative to those which neglected training. Power was given, however, to exclude firms below a certain size.

The Rise of the Industrial Training Boards

A decade after the publication of the White Paper and at the time of a major review of the training board system, there were twenty-seven ITBs covering industries employing 15 million workers. The ITBs varied greatly in the initiatives they took to stimulate sufficient training courses or to provide facilities themselves and to set standards of training and related further education. By 1972 there were almost 12 million employees in establishments subject to levy and levies ranged from 0·04 per cent for the Electricity Supply ITB to 3·8 per cent for parts of the Air Transport and Travel ITB. In the main, though, levies were of the order of 1 or 2 per cent. Total income for 1970–71 amounted to £208 million and included grants of £5 million from the Department of Employment. The training board initiative thus resulted largely in the collection and redistribution of money from firms with only modest supplementary financial assistance from the state.

In contrast to a certain amount of general agreement before the introduction of the Industrial Training Act, there was subsequently considerable criticism from industries saddled with poorly organised training boards, by firms (especially small ones) feeling that the levy-grant system affected them unfairly, and by educationalists who saw the influence of industrial training upon technical colleges and colleges of further education as tending to undermine their broader educational purpose. Some economists also took a particularly jaundiced view. For example, McCormick and Manley (1967) and Lees and Chiplin (1970) argued that the Industrial Training Act ignored the important economic distinction between specific and general training made by Becker (1975) and the implications it has for the financing of training and particularly for the sharing of costs between firms and individuals.

In support of the setting up of the training boards was the argument that the appropriate decision-making environment could not have been created merely by propaganda revealing to firms wherein their best interests lay. The experience of the 1950s was an adequate testimony to that. There was a need for shock therapy. But the intention was not to impose yet another arbitrary burden upon management. The system should try to offer rough justice at least. Justice was to be administered in the 'national interest', and hence in that of the nation's business enterprises, to those who trained badly and above all to those who simply 'poached'. Although this concept can be shown to be largely devoid of economic content, it became extremely influential because the natural reaction to the question of how to make industry train more was to make those who trained very little or not at all do their 'fair share'.

While the notion of making the poacher pay has provided a resilient justification for the industrial training board system, in practice the redistribution of levy income to achieve this objective for the main groups of skilled occupations had become a secondary consideration by the time of the Department of Employment's review of the ITB system in 1971–2. As the training boards developed they became much more generally concerned with the training and manpower planning activities of their constituent firms. Although for boards in the production industries the training of craftsmen continued to be the main single reason for expenditure, a marked diversification of the activities of ITBs took place to include particularly the training of managers, technologists, technicians, and operatives. Grant schemes moved towards those which rewarded 'the introduction and operation of a sound system of training in firms related to each firm's particular training needs' (Department of Employment, 1972:59). Firms with sound training schemes were exempt from the levy-grant systems of certain boards (for example, Petroleum) on condition that they paid a much smaller levy in order to contribute to the board's general costs and maintained regular contact with the board staff so that their progress could be monitored. The more the training boards moved towards awarding a 'good training seal of approval', the less the labour market circumstances for certain skilled occupations were able to influence the distribution of grant relative to levy.

In its first review of ITBs the Department of Employment evidently approved of such a pragmatic approach to tackling the question of redistributing costs. As far as the limited statistical evidence permitted, the Department (1972:52) concluded that increases in the volume of training had been achieved notwithstanding the weakening of financial penalties. The institutional evidence for a positive impact upon the quality of training was clear enough, however. It is nonetheless unsatisfactory that there seem to be no cost-benefit studies of ITB schemes which compare them directly with previous less formal arrangements. Indeed, reputable studies of training costs under the new schemes were not published until the 1970s and the only cost-benefit studies proper are concerned with courses run by Government Training Centres (for example, Ziderman, 1975). These showed favourable rates of return at least for the late 1960s.

Three broad options for reform presented themselves at the beginning of the 1970s. First, to increase the sophistication of the monitoring process and the sensitivity of the levy-grant system to the genuinely different circumstances of firms, so as to achieve greater fairness while preserving the aim of redistributing costs. Second, to concede that equating contributions to training among firms was too difficult and wind up the boards once it was established that the shock treatment had created a permanent change in attitudes to training as well as having improved quantity and quality. Or, third, to accept the practical problems of redistribution but recognise the risks of returning to the bad habits of the past and retain the levy-grant system, with boards having scope for influencing the level of training (especially counter-cyclically), safeguarding and enhancing training standards, and disengaging from firms which continued to show good practice in this field or whose circumstances could not reasonably be catered for.

In 1973 the government chose the third option. In 1982 a major shift towards the second option took place as all but six boards were disbanded (though one new board was created). But the adoption of a levy-grant-exemption scheme in 1973 marked the second rather than the first phase of modifying the commitment to redistribution. The first occurred quite soon after the establishment of the ITB system when attempts to set levies at rates sufficient to cover the total costs of training (which were then to be recouped as grants by firms undertaking the training) were abandoned. The reason for this was mainly a fear of escalating levy rates to pay for the training stimulated by full cost reimbursement at a time when disparities in the treatment of firms were already beginning to arise for reasons, as mentioned above, unconnected with the adequacy of training provision in any real sense.

As the cause of the equitable sharing of training costs withered away it was replaced quite explicitly by the notion of employers training properly for their own needs. By this means firms could be exempt from paying the full levy. The 1973 Act went further, however, by providing for central government financial support of the general operating costs of boards so that suitable firms could be exempt entirely from the levy-grant system. This was more than a concession to the realities of labour market life. It was a decision not to pursue the possibility of paying firms to train more than they required for their own purposes and charging the cost to other firms. In order to maintain the overall training effort the focus then had to be upon making sure that all firms trained sufficiently. Yet the levy penalty was also to be reduced with a maximum of 1 per cent allowed. The government subsidy did mean that grants did not suffer particularly, but behind the cuts in levy rates lay the view that though firms may not be perfect at least they were not as bad as they used to be.

So the ITB system did survive the review at the beginning of the 1970s. However, the Employment and Training Act of 1973 introduced a major reorganisation of the public employment and training services which led to the establishment of the Manpower Services Commission (MSC) with responsibility to the Secretary of State for Employment for the activities of two executive agencies: the Employment Services Agency and the Training Services Agency. The latter supervised the ITB system and exerted a strong influence upon it through grants to the boards for both general running costs and expenditure under specific programmes initiated by the MSC.

Since the creation of the MSC the evolution of active manpower policy has largely reflected a gradual realisation that the underlying unemployment problem was getting worse not better and that the institutional framework created by the 1973 Act was at its weakest in dealing with the type of skill shortages likely to persist in those circumstances—shortages which were highly skill-specific and geographically localised. The interaction between the mainstream industrial training system and other major programmes aimed at ameliorating the effects of high unemployment began to create serious problems for the overall rationale of policy and its implementation (Lindley, 1978).

The last Labour Government's Industrial Strategy eventually dealt two particular blows to conventional notions of manpower policy. In the first place it raised expectations unduly high, by generating a lot of excitement about the need to make sure that skill bottlenecks would not impede recovery. This invited misplaced emphasis upon the long-term training effort as the appropriate way of providing enough skilled labour in the 1980s at the same time as reducing the extent of skill shortages which seemed to be persisting during the recession. In the second place, as the problematical medium and long-term future of the economy was beginning to attract attention, the micro-economic orientation of the strategy led to the rediscovery of better utilisation of existing skills as the remedy for many alleged shortages and a much more flexible training system as the remedy for those shortages which appeared to be 'genuine'. Moreover, a further problem with relying upon the ITB system as the centrepiece of the nation's training effort became apparent, the position of the individual seeking to be trained.

Training and the Individual

The inequity of most significance to training boards has been that arising between firms in respect of their different levy-grant positions, not that which occurs when the individual's access to training for working life is controlled by the coincidence of reaching school-leaving age at a low point in the economic cycle. Not until 1973 did the notion of meeting the needs of the individual acquire a meaningful status of its own in legislation on industrial training.

While the general debate from which the ITB system emerged did show a concern for the opportunities available to the individual, the provision of more and better opportunities for individuals was largely a by-product of pursuing a strategy geared to the needs of employers (Central Training Council, 1969: app. VIII, 41). The significance of this by-product should not be underrated but before being able to take advantage of it, the trainee had to become an employee of the firm and, moreover, the main training schemes were usually restricted to young people. Once there occurred a major recession in which ITBs had great difficulty in maintaining a stable training activity, the initial ITB system was seen to have a further weakness: its inability to secure enough training for young people in skilled occupations requiring substantial periods of preparation.

In *Training for the Future,* the Department of Employment (1972:6) emphasised the 'dual aspect of training', noting 'the economic gains which can result to individual enterprises and to the community, and the social importance of wider opportunities for individuals. Future policies must provide for both.' There is a very strong tendency to associate policies which directly affect employers with economic objectives and those which directly affect individuals with social objectives. This asymmetric treatment of action to influence the decision of participants on the demand and supply sides of the labour market tends to cloud the debate even though the social (individual) benefits of the former and the economic gains from the latter (e.g. the increase in 'the capacity for real labour mobility in the economy') are sometimes mentioned. It creates a presumption that the primary route to achieving labour market efficiency is by ironing out or circumventing the market imperfections as seen from the demand-side point of view.

Though the provision of training by government has periodically been attached to specific economic objectives, as during World War II and the aftermath of the resettlement of servicemen and the regeneration of the economy, for most of its history it has been concerned more with helping the unemployed, the disabled, and ex-regular servicemen. An expansion in the number of trainees under the Vocational Training Scheme was undertaken after 1962 in order to 'enhance their economic role' and the proportion of disabled and unemployed fell substantially while the proportion joining courses (averaging six months' duration) direct from employment rose. The resulting scale of provision was still low, however, amounting to about 18,400 and in 1972 the Conservative Government embarked upon a major expansion of what was re-named the Training Opportunities Scheme (TOPS). Operated by the newly formed Training Services Agency, TOPS was set a target of 100,000 course completions 'as soon as possible'. This figure was all but reached in 1977–8, though it included about 20,000 young people (under nineteen years) in special programmes.

The major reassessment of TOPS in 1978 was provoked by a number of factors, not least the need to examine its performance after a spectacular expansion. Difficulties were arising with the perceived economic role of TOPS, especially the fact that, even for skilled trades apparently in short supply, the proportions of TOPS completers finding work in their new skills were disappointing. The *TOPS Review* (MSC, 1978a:49) recommended that 'TOPS occupational training should be more closely related to employers' actual or prospective needs, and trainees' success in securing subsequent employment should be taken as a major indicator of the effectiveness of TOPS training.' The review of TOPS concluded that the role of dealing with labour shortages in the short term should be given greater emphasis, involving concerted action in local labour markets coordinated with the activities of employers, ITBs, and educational establishments. Crucial to the success of the great variety of initiatives envisaged, however, would be removal of the limitations placed upon the effectiveness of TOPS by the institutional arrangements for entry to different occupations settled between employers and trade unions. In the years following the review, whatever the long-term stance, TOPS, like many other public expenditure programmes, was eventually required to share in the cuts imposed by the Conservative Government. By 1980–81 there were 66,400 adult completers compared with 80,000 in 1977–8. Thus, in terms of the false dichotomy between pursuing 'economic' and 'social' objectives it might seem that from 1978 TOPS was steered in the former direction. In fact, the dangers of TOPS (together with the MSC's direct training services) becoming a social welfare programme for ineffective employers, as opposed to disadvantaged individuals, needed to be recognised and it was argued that such assistance should be conditional upon radical reform of the employer's approach to training (Lindley 1980:365). The MSC was already trying to achieve this but on a much wider canvass than covered by TOPS.

The System under Strain

The notion of a national training scheme based on the achievement of agreed standards rather than forms of time-serving has been under serious discussion for many years. Such a scheme would aim to provide opportunities for training suited to the abilities and circumstances of the individual and designed to prepare people efficiently for the tasks performed in relevant jobs. It would seek to offer access unrestricted by such factors as sex, age, and length of service, and to provide training which is widely recognised by employers and trade unions. These objectives—which may be summarised as 'certification, flexibility, access, and acceptability'—can be further linked to three others: first, the desire for broadly based initial training for young people, including elements of further education and industrial training which would be mutually reinforcing; second, the need for correspondence between the standards of competence achieved by young people and adults beyond the stage of initial training; and, third, the provision of opportunities for training and further education throughout the working lives of people to enable them to adapt to changes in employment patterns.

From about 1975 onwards a particular sense of frustration was beginning to develop among those seeking to pursue these various objectives in the light of the experience of the 1973 Act. By 1976 there was sufficient concern, fuelled by the fear of the effects of manpower shortages upon the Labour Government's Industrial Strategy, for a joint DE/MSC consultative document to be published. *Training for Vital Skills* marked a significant change in the official analysis of industrial training policy. It distinguished quite clearly between general and specific training though not precisely in those terms. It saw the main problem as the securing of a sufficient supply of general or 'transferable' skills and argued (DE and MSC, 1976:11) that the provisions of the 1973 Act tended more to foster sensible behaviour by the employer in respect of specific skills: 'submission of ITBs' forward plans to the MSC, and MSC approval of levy, grant and exemption proposals—provide potentially powerful tools for promoting adequate internal labour market training.' While the notion of 'poaching' put in an inevitable appearance, the consultative document proceeded to examine two main funding alternatives which were designed to tackle the problem of transferable skills. The first amounted to the creation of a permanent system of marginal funding to replace intervention on an *ad hoc* basis but nonetheless akin to that exercised in 1971–2 and 1975–6 in which government award schemes acting mainly through the ITBs were used to reduce the extent of cut-backs in apprentice recruitment. The second was a more ambitious scheme of collective funding confined to certain transferable skills with the levy and training grants covering the whole employed population: proposals which, for the first time, began to look like those which might conform to some economic model of intervention. Lest this be thought to be a dubious recommendation it should be stressed that the consultative document was couched in cautious, not to say diplomatic, terms. Attention was drawn to the practical difficulties of deciding upon the types of training to be covered, the volume of training to be achieved, the method of raising the fund, and how employers should be reimbursed from it.

From 1976 until the emergence of the New Training Initiative five years later, roughly four stages of discussion and decision may be discerned. First, the collective funding proposal was abandoned through lack of agreement not only about the scheme itself but also about the problem to which it was supposed to be addressed. The consultative document was criticised for not providing enough evidence that skill shortages (as opposed, for example, to poor manpower utilisation) really were a significant brake on economic growth. As a result the Vital Skills Task Group was set up to look at skill shortages in a wider context and then consider the appropriate policy response, especially regarding the recruitment of young people.

The second stage began with the publication (MSC, 1978b) of the Task Group's report *Training for Skills: A Programme for Action* (TSPA). This emphasised the importance of reforms which would increase the efficiency of the labour market, remove some inequities in the provision of training and make more sense of the state's involvement in training. Adopting the recommendations of the Group the MSC established certain criteria by which it proposed to operate a new long-term Training for Skills programme, set up to 'maintain a consistent and permanent means to deal with training in important skills'. Since the new proposals kept the problem of transferable skills, identified in *Training for Vital Skills*, at the centre of the stage, this aspect of the 1976 initiative was not lost. From the financial year 1979–80 TSPA replaced the selective annual assistance provided under special measures and other *ad hoc* programmes by what amounted to a 'permanent' system of marginal funding. While the counter-cyclical leanings of the new arrangements were clear enough, there was also an implied intention to remedy the problem of under-training in general notwithstanding the doubts about the evidence for this which affected the reception of *Training for Vital Skills*. It was not, however, clear how the levy-grant-exemption scheme would be affected in the long term.

The third stage of policy development after 1975 concerned 'RETA'—Review of the Employment and Training Act 1973. This gave rise to the publication of *Outlook on Training* (MSC, 1980). It is not possible to do justice here to its many conclusions and recommendations, nor is it necessary in the present context. The report concluded that major problems remained to be solved and their solution did not lie in a radical dismantling of the whole organisational apparatus in the belief that industry had learnt the error of its ways and could be relied upon to adopt forward-looking training strategies. Nor was it thought that the solution lay in a radical re-organisation of the system: other ways could be found of 'combining cross-sector, local and voluntary initiatives with the existing industry-focused structure' (MSC, 1980:32). But it was recognised that some principles needed to be established more firmly in guiding future developments and the ramifications of their acceptance went beyond the traditional confines of active manpower policy.

In this last respect *Outlook on Training* was disappointing, neither coming to grips with the economic issues involved in a way which related the general arguments for intervention to the basic questions of style and structure discussed earlier in this chapter, nor stepping in with specific proposals for reform which matched up to the scale of the problem described. The training system was in for a further round of consultation. The review did, however, give rise to certain specific proposals which indicated the direction in which the ITB system was likely to move. It was recommended that the funding of ITB operating costs should once again be the responsibility of industry, that Boards should continue to have power to raise levy (but that this should now be allowed to cover operating costs and should not be subject to an upper limit) and that boards should have discretion as to whether or not to introduce exemption for other than small firms. These recommendations and many others which are discussed in detail in *Outlook on Training* were intended to clarify and strengthen the relative roles of the MSC, ITBs, and non-ITB training organisations. Though the motives for changing the financial responsibilities of Boards were mixed, the effect would be to allow the MSC to fund an ITB only when it was 'acting in effect as an agent of the MSC in pursuance of a priority national objective' (MSC, 1980:34).

But the MSC also recommended that the training board system should remain in existence (i.e. with statutory powers but subject to a review of each sector of the economy), supervised by the MSC and the Department of Employment. The economic philosophy of the Conservative Government clearly predisposed it to closing them down altogether, leaving those industries which wished to retain their boards on a voluntary basis to make what arrangements they could. The Employment and Training Act of 1981, among other things, cleared the ground for the abolition of the boards after consultation with, but no longer on the recommendation of, the MSC. Nonetheless, in its review of training provision in each sector, the MSC (1981a) concluded that statutory arrangements should continue for a large part of seven industrial sectors covered by seven ITBs. No firm recommendation was made for or against the continuation of the sixteen other boards but, after a further round of consultation, a narrow majority of the Commission concluded that no board should be abolished. It was, however, less difficult than it might have been for the Secretary of State to proceed with the abolition of those boards receiving no very positive support from the MSC.

The birth of *A New Training Initiative* and the subsequent Employment and Training Act of 1981 mark the fourth stage of policy development mentioned earlier. Their implications are considered in the concluding section of this chapter.

FURTHER PERSPECTIVES ON POLICY

Special Employment and Training Measures

While active manpower policy has been dominated by the debate about industrial training for most of its two decades of existence, its diversification during the 1970s took place rapidly, and by the financial year 1980–81 the scale of expenditure on special programmes funded by the MSC approached £250 million. In 1976–7 about 70 per cent of MSC-funded expenditure was devoted to training services and a negligible amount to special programmes. By 1980–81 the corresponding figures were 45 per cent and 30 per cent respectively. Expenditure expanded rapidly in real terms during the early years of the MSC, doubling between 1974–5 and 1976–7, then rose (at a declining annual rate) by roughly a third between 1976–7 and 1980–81.

In addition to those schemes supported by a grant-in-aid to the MSC, job creation programmes applicable mainly to adults were also launched, funded by the Department of Employment but administered by the MSC. Finally, there were the various employment subsidies and the job release (early retirement) scheme operated directly by the Department of Employment. Starting with the Temporary Employment Subsidy in 1975, these built up more quickly than the special training and job creation measures, reaching a peak in 1977–8 and then declined until 1980–81 when the Short-Time Working Scheme briefly took the numbers supported through subsidies back to the earlier peak of about 200,000.

Changes in the overall level and broad pattern of special programmes are summarised in Figure 14.1 which distinguishes the numbers of people supported by special measures devoted to boosting training within industry; the variety of programmes concerned with the young unemployed; job creation for adults; employment subsidies; and the Job Release Scheme. The main features are the gradual build-up of measures to help the young unemployed and the marked change in the impact of employment subsidies. The total number supported reached a peak of 330,000 in autumn 1977, declined to about 230,000 in spring 1980, then rose again to

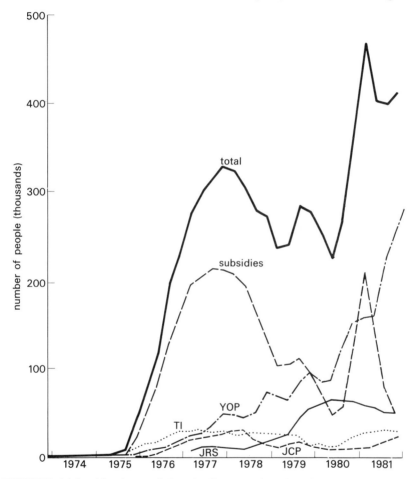

FIGURE 14.1: Numbers of People Supported under the Special Measures, 1974–1981

JCP   Job Creation Programme (and later variants excluding participants under eighteen)

JRS   Job Release Scheme

TI   Training in Industry

YOP   Youth Opportunities Programme plus Community Industry plus JCP under eighteen

Source: Unpublished data from Manpower Services Commission (point observations are quarterly averages).

about 410,000 in autumn 1981 after recording a peak of 470,000 at the beginning of 1981 due to the temporarily high take-up of the Short-Time Working Subsidy. At the 1977 peak, two-thirds of all those supported were covered by the Temporary Employment Subsidy and 15 per cent by programmes for unemployed young people. By the end of 1981, two-thirds, or 260,000, were covered by YOP (plus Community Industry); the employment subsidies and, equally important, the Job Release Scheme together accounted for about 25 per cent, or 50,000 each. The earlier Job Creation Programme and its subsequent variants, the Special Temporary Employment Programme and the more recent Community Enterprise Programme, have never exceeded quarterly average placements of much more than 30,000 adults. The same is true of the placements of young people under Training in Industry (mainly the Training for Skills programme).

The striking aspect of this experience of special programmes is the supplanting of market-related measures which are designed to reduce the level of unemployment through altering the costs of employing, recruiting, training, or retiring by a broad programme creating opportunities for the young unemployed outside the conventional labour market. An alternative strategy entirely would have been to devote the same resources to maintaining employment subsidies at high levels, perhaps attaching them to the employment of certain disadvantaged groups and young people, and to funding more training in industry through training grants or subsidies. The much-publicised Young Workers' Scheme, introduced in 1981, is a variant which attempts to promote the recruitment of young people to jobs with relatively low pay and, at the same time, to induce employers to keep pay low enough to be able to obtain the subsidy. This reflects the view that youth unemployment is higher than it might be because in the United Kingdom the wages of young people are relatively high proportions of the adult rates (but see Makeham, 1980). The development of YOP and its further expansion under the New Training Initiative suggest a very substantial government scepticism of the ability of employment and training subsidies to employers plus recession-induced increases in educational participation rates to provide the required reductions in the unemployment of young people (Lindley, 1981).

The Pursuit of Equity and Clashes of Interest

With mass unemployment of 3 million or more, Britain evidently has a labour surplus economy. If the training system were to be governed entirely by the state of labour demand, this would imply a major reduction in opportunities for training, unless the surplus is a temporary one. Suppose, however, that the labour surplus is not expected to be temporary but is likely to last for about a decade and, in addition, will undoubtedly affect skilled as well as unskilled workers. The case against reductions in the economy's investment in industrial training is then largely one of equity rather than efficiency. In so far as the training provided by industry is general, any marked cut-back could have a significance for the individual's 'life chances'.

This notwithstanding, however, there are two particular elements in the situation which contrive to keep training in its place. The first is a view within the education lobby that training is a bastard form of education which embodies both a narrow and short-sighted vision of the interests of the individual. New delivery systems for vocational training combined with further education are then viewed with scepticism, if not hostility. The second element tending to undermine any radical training contribution to what might be called the 'management of high unemployment' is the implicit collusion between employers and trade unions. Employers may be attracted by the notion of a larger pool of skilled manpower for this should make recruitment easier and raise the average quality of the labour force. But there are disadvantages: in particular, under the present training system, part of the cost of even general training in industry normally falls on the employer and industrial relations would probably deteriorate if companies maintained high levels of trainee recruitment while laying off large numbers of skilled workers. Trade unions may put up with continuing recruitment of young trainees as a clear-cut counter-cyclical strategy but, as uncertainty clouds the economic situation and the 'cycle' becomes much less visible, union members are likely to develop more critical attitudes to the training policies of their respective companies and industrial training boards.

While the commitment of 'industry' can be stretched to some degree to promote supplementary apprentice training, there are other areas of manpower policy where problems are increasingly difficult to contain as unemployment remains at very high levels and where the natural suspicions of both sides of industry are aroused more quickly. The most important are the training of adults through TOPS and the participation of young people in what has become YOP. It is to be expected that TOPS trainees will find it more difficult to gain access to skilled employment when unemployment is high (MacKay et al., 1971, and Hall and Miller, 1971). As for YOP, its uncertain status between further education, industrial training, and work experience invites as much criticism from industry as it receives from the education lobby. Greater effort has been devoted to strengthening the training element of the programme and to placing young people in positive working environments from which they will benefit during work experience. While these allay one set of fears, concerned more with benefits to the individual, they excite another set, connected with the impact a large-scale YOP might have upon the existing training effort by employers and patterns of conventional employment. While the prejudices of employers could be bought off, in principle, by suitable subsidies, it is clear that YOP could be seen as a prime threat to the influence of the trade unions. But the trade unions have understandably not stressed this particular aspect. Their reservations about YOP have been linked increasingly to the accusation that the work experience component amounts to 'cheap labour' compared with those job-creation schemes which pay the local rate for the job. Indeed, according to some, the element of training involved in work experience has not often warranted treating YOP as a special case where normal collective bargaining should be suspended. These potential clashes of interest would remain even if the costs of extending training opportunities, as a matter of equity rather than in order to meet labour demand, were borne fully by the state.

Manpower Policy and Other Areas of Economic Policy

Manpower policy has generally been seen as a worthwhile but secondary part of the overall policy package, expected to contribute to the growth of the economy but not to initiate measures which would create difficulties for the practice of industrial relations, prices and incomes control, industrial and regional policy, and the evolution of the public sector (Lindley, 1980). Yet the approaches adopted in these other areas of policy constrain the potential gain from manpower policy. It is reasonable to speculate, for example, that the very symbiotic relationship between training boards and their industries, combined with implicit instructions from government amounting to 'do not rock the boat, just train the crew', have produced slower training reform than might have otherwise been possible.

Across the economy as a whole the scope for reform is enormous and after almost two decades of government involvement there must be grounds for asking whether a training policy with more 'teeth' is now called for. That would mean allowing the pursuit of national training objectives to put considerable direct pressure on the industrial relations system, something successive governments have tried to avoid because of the need to obtain management and trade union cooperation over more important things such as pay restraint. However, this would seem a more worthwhile reform affecting industrial relations than much of that enacted during the 1970s and early 1980s in order to reduce the powers of the trade unions. For example it would be likely to improve the flexibility and productivity of the labour force far more than will the legislation on the closed shop introduced by the Conservative Government elected in 1979. If a government must sour the bargaining environment, it might at least do it for higher stakes.

There are also grounds for ensuring that those firms hoping to take advantage of financial support through government industrial and regional policy should agree to implement progressive reform of their training systems in order to meet the criteria of certification, flexibility, access, and acceptability embodied in a national policy. In the public services and public corporations (which cover roughly 30 per cent of the employed labour force and 60 per cent of TUC membership) the government could exert similar though more direct pressure.

CONCLUSIONS

In reviewing the economic arguments for state intervention in training, three problems have been identified: capital market failure, the difficulties of coping with fluctuating demand, and the presence of externalities. Policy developments over the last two decades have tended to ignore the first of these and to deal with the second and third in a way which failed to come to terms with the distinctions between 'general' and 'specific' training and between the government 'paying for' and 'providing' training. From about 1976, however, the policy debate did become more sophisticated.

By the beginning of the 1980s when doubts about the likelihood of continuing high levels of unemployment were no longer being expressed even by the government, three main training strategies presented themselves. The first option was to muddle through by extending the scope of YOP, hoping that the trade unions would acquiesce, that somewhat higher quality training places would be forthcoming from employers, and that YOP would become an accepted part of the employment scene. This strategy would have been the 'minimalist' approach because something substantial, at least in scale if not conception, was evidently required to help to tackle the problem of youth unemployment.

The second strategy was to transform YOP quite considerably, moving towards a common scheme for all young people under eighteen years of age, in which the MSC would reach agreements with training boards, employers, local authorities, voluntary organisations, and a variety of training and educational institutions to provide places of work experience, training, and further education. Combined these would offer suitable opportunities, lasting for at least a year after leaving school, to join the 'labour force'. *Training for Skills* would then have to be re-designed to cope with the fact that young entrants to industrial training would have to pass through the new youth programme. Subject to certain controls on the quality of training given during the first year and some special arrangements for skills involving lengthy training periods, such a programme would probably have been acceptable to the trade unions and (with suitable arrangements for finance) to most groups of employers. A general concern for young people could have carried industry along with what may be termed the 'radical youth-orientated strategy'.

The third strategy would have been to contain the youth unemployment problem but not to allow concern with training young people to dominate. A continuing YOP and an extensive application of youth employment subsidies might have done that, though great pressure upon employers and trade unions would still have been required. The preoccupation of this strategy would have been not with young people as such but with the need to implement to the hilt the ideas developed in *Training for Skills*. That would have meant radical reform of industrial training, concerned as much with the opportunities for adults as with those for young people and focused firmly on the broad economic case for state intervention combined with a strong push to achieve greater equity. It would involve creating a market for training opportunities largely independent of the labour market *per se* in order to break the constraint on the supply of training that arises when training is mainly available through obtaining an employment contract and jobs are hard to get. Decisions about the balance between financing the individual (i.e. tackling the capital market imperfection) and financing the supplier of training would depend on the circumstances of different industries and the type of training capacity already available. The government would need to deal with the question of transferable skills as a priority. This 'market-orientated strategy' as a whole would not alone guarantee a satisfactory reduction in youth employment for that would not be its main objective. Nor can a training policy be a substitute for an employment policy. Nonetheless, it is quite likely that beginning in this way would eventually lead to the introduction of a new youth programme. Whether or not the second strategy could evolve into the third one is another matter, however. But to the extent that the vested interests tending to block the third strategy could be overcome directly, it is probably the case that, if pursued relentlessly by the government, the establishment of a new youth training programme would be a step to more extensive introduction of certification, flexibility, access, and acceptability. So if the third strategy is politically feasible, this should also be true of the second.

The details of these alternative strategies need not be examined here. Nor is it necessary to follow the various stages of the debate over the new training initiative (MSC, 1981c, 1981d: Dutton, 1982) leading to the publication of the White Paper *A New Training Initiative: A Programme for Action* (Department of Employment, 1981a). Essentially the government proposed to adopt a compromise between the first and second strategies, by replacing YOP with a £1,000 million Youth Training Scheme (YTS) as from September 1983. This comprised an increase in the numbers catered for at any one time from about 250,000 to 300,000, a doubling of the average training cost per participant but almost a halving of the personal training allowance compared with that paid to those in YOP. The higher training cost reflected the increased inducement to employers to provide places. Since 'the new scheme is first and last a training scheme', the government felt that young people should receive training allowances in keeping with their learning role: 'that is how they will make their contribution to the cost of a foundation training which improves their prospects of employment' (Department of Employment, 1981a:9).

The scheme's proposals for lowering the allowance and introducing supplementary benefit conditions equivalent to those applying to young students in further education attracted much hostility. Doubts about the ability of the MSC to create the required number of really good training opportunities under YTS led to suggestions that the scheme amounted to providing even cheaper labour than was the case with YOP. The proposal that young people who refused suitable training places would, like unemployed adults, have their supplementary benefit reduced also appeared to introduce an element of coercion if not compulsion into the operation of the scheme.

But the White Paper proposed more than a restructuring and upgrading of the preparation of young people for employment in which the young person, while still being guaranteed a place on the scheme, was invited to take a cut in allowance in return for an improvement in the quality of training. Particular importance is attached to setting a target date of 1985 for the establishment of recognised training standards and the need for an 'examination of longer-term possibilities for more effective, rational and equitable sharing of the costs of training between trainees themselves, employers of trained people and the general tax payer' (Department of Employment, 1981a:3).

Finally, there are the two aspects which disqualify the proposals in the White Paper from amounting to either the complete second or partial third strategy outlined above. First, YTS is not proposed as a scheme to cover employed as well as unemployed young people. At the same time, though, the government welcomes the MSC proposal to establish a working group to investigate the possibilities of setting up a general scheme of foundation training for all young people, whether employed or unemployed, and is willing to consider re-allocating resources in the light of that report. This opens up chances of adopting the radical youth-orientated strategy but it must be stressed that the government seems to have in mind a re-allocation of 'resources available for young people' rather than a topping-up of the planned YTS to cover the employed as well as the unemployed.

The second limitation of the latest training initiative is the way in which it endorses the commitment to adult training as one of the 'three major national objectives for the future of industrial training' and its subsequent blithe disregard for the implications of this objective. The White Paper in this respect turns the clock back a decade or more, failing to appreciate the significance for both efficiency and equity of a flexible training system, the heart of which must be the effective training and retraining of adults as much as the initial training of young people. The government appears then to have decided to leave the subject of adult training well alone, not as a matter of industrial tactics in order to make progress with youth training, but because it does not really believe it has much more of a role to play than by redirecting TOPS and funding an 'Open Tech' programme. As far as the third strategy is concerned, therefore, the Young Workers' Scheme introduced in July 1981 would seem to be compatible with it, the YTS is altogether too ambitious, while the resolve to reform adult training is non-existent. Yet elsewhere in the White Paper the language and comment does reflect the market orientation essential to the third strategy.

Overall the initiative may be new but the mixture is not unfamiliar: part reassertion of the need for selective state involvement that does not undermine the autonomous response of industry; part reaction to specific inadequacies in the present system; to some degree decisive but in other respects temporising; laced with a reference or two to the practices of other countries; and skating round the central economic and industrial relations issue of adult training. As a basis for the future, however, the fact that the economic situation has forced the government's hand as far as young people are concerned cannot be ignored even if, in respect of adults, it has restored the old epitaph for industrial training: 'this is primarily a matter for industry' (Department of Employment, 1981b:11). The New Training Initiative does contain within it the potential for a radical youth-orientated training strategy. It might even be a step towards the creation of a market for youth training opportunities which will work to the advantage of both young people and employers. There is also the feeling that a major diversification of provision for the education and training of young people is desirable as an end in itself. If only unemployment were not so high, the whole development could have been presented and received as perhaps one of the most creative policy initiatives yet in the field of post-compulsory education and training. It will take some time, and possibly a new government, however, for the Youth Training Scheme to shake off the suggestion of making a virtue of necessity.

15 Collective Labour Law

Roy Lewis

Labour law is an aspect of industrial relations which interacts with the institutions, processes, and behaviour analysed in other chapters of this book. An appreciation of industrial relations is essential for any lawyer who wishes to understand labour law as something more than a set of technicalities, and the student or practitioner of industrial relations has to acquire some knowledge of the relevant law. The importance of the law as part of industrial relations has long been recognised, though it has been underlined by the rapid increase in legal intervention over the last two decades.

Collective labour law is the legal framework of collective labour relations. It is concerned with such matters as collective bargaining and agreements, workplace union organisation, the closed shop, inter- and intra-union relations, and manifestations of collective industrial conflict such as strikes and picketing. Collective labour law may be distinguished from individual labour law, that is, the law governing the relation between individual workers and their employers. The distinction, which is a useful analytical device, is reflected to some extent in actual legal provisions and institutions, but there is considerable overlap between the two categories.

This chapter is an essay on the policy aims and development of collective labour law. Legal policy is a short-hand term for the law's expression of the national interest. It inevitably raises some difficult questions about the state and the state's relation with employers and workers. In a strictly formal sense the state determines legal policy. But the state is not a monolithic entity: it includes the cabinet, parliament, judges, the civil service, the military, and the police. The different organs of the state may pursue different strategies; for example, judge-made 'common law' may be at variance with legislative policy, or the civil service may have its own plans irrespective of the party label of the government. The state moreover interacts with the rest of society. Legal policy cannot be divorced from the interests and ideologies of the law-makers and from wider political and industrial conflict. The nature and extent of legal regulation have been determined not by some abstract rule-making force but by the interplay of judicial innovation, public policy controversy, the relative power of management and labour interests, and party politics with a view to electoral advantage.

The first theme of this chapter is the historical development of Britain's unique 'non-interventionist' framework of labour law, and how this fostered the growth of a voluntary system of collective industrial relations in which legal regulation was accorded a secondary role. The chapter then discusses the many recent developments in labour law. These are explained in terms of a fundamental conflict of strategic policy aims. There is the Donovan Commission's strategy of 'reform' which underpinned some of the provisions in the Industrial Relations Act 1971 and several of the measures enacted during the subsequent period of the Social Contract. But there is also the strategy of 'ultra-restriction', which was a stronger current than reform in the 1971 Act, and which pervades the Employment Acts of 1980 and 1982. The two strategies, it will be argued, are indicative of the conflict between collectivist and individualist values.

LEGAL POLICY: HISTORICAL DEVELOPMENT

'The principal purpose of labour law', according to Kahn-Freund (1977a:4), 'is to regulate, to support and to restrain the power of management and the power of organised labour'.[1] The need to restrain the power of management arose from the nature of the individual employment relationship, which has been characterised as 'typically a relation between a bearer of power and one who is not a bearer of power. In its inception it is an act of submission, in its operation it is a condition of subordination, however much the submission and the subordination may be concealed by that indispensable figment of the legal mind known as the "contract of employment" ' (Kahn-Freund, 1977a:6). Indeed the historic function of the contract of employment was to reinforce and legitimate the employer's power. In the face of this social and legal inequality the primary task of labour legislation was to mitigate and regulate the employee's subordination and the employer's domination. The inequality of the individual employment relation was also, on this theory, the justification for trade unionism itself. However, the course of trade union history indicated that labour law had a major purpose besides mitigating inequality. At the very time when the basic pattern of workers' legislative protection on safety, health, and welfare was emerging (as described in Chapter 16), the other and no less

[1] Many of the themes in this chapter were influenced by discussions with Professor Lord Wedderburn and Dr. Jon Clark preparatory to Wedderburn et al. (eds.), *Labour Law and Industrial Relations: Building on Kahn-Freund* (1983). The chapter also draws heavily on Kahn-Freund's writings, several of which are listed in the bibliography. For critiques of his work, see Lewis 1979a, 1979b; Lewis and Clark, 1981; and Wedderburn et al., 1983.

important aim of both the legislature and the judges was the suppression of the trade unions.[2]

Only after several generations of industrial and political struggle did Parliament adopt a more sympathetic attitude towards the unions. The main landmarks were the repeal of the Combination Acts in 1824, which gave industrial workers the possibility of organising in unions without fear of criminal prosecution (though the extent of this liberty was reduced by an amending Act in 1825); the Trade Union Act of 1871, which gave immunity from the common law doctrine of restraint of trade; the Conspiracy and Protection of Property Act of 1875, which gave immunity from simple criminal conspiracy where persons acted 'in contemplation or furtherance of a trade dispute'; and, above all, the Trade Disputes Act of 1906. The last statute was passed in the aftermath of the *Taff Vale* case[3] in which the defendant union was held liable for damages and legal costs totalling £42,000, an enormous sum at the time. It entrenched a structure of union legal freedoms based on statutory immunities from judge-made liabilities. It was of course difficult for lawyers and for middle-class opinion at large to conceive of the immunities as anything other than anomalous privileges, which excused unions from legal and social responsibility for their actions. But without the immunities the unions could not lawfully have fulfilled their basic function of counter-balancing the employer's dominance over the individual employee. The immunities were in essence the British legal form of basic democratic liberties, the equivalent of what in other countries took the form of positive rights to strike guaranteed by legislation or by the constitution (Wedderburn, 1980). Furthermore, the immunities did not place unions above the law. If outright legal repression was abandoned, the law retained a restrictive function: the freedom to take industrial action was always qualified by the possibility of legal remedies to restrain the unlawful consquences of such action. Thus under the 1906 Act unions as such (and employers' associations) were granted immunity from liability for civil wrongs (torts), but individual persons including union officials were not automatically immune. Persons escaped liability only if their acts were protected by immunities covering specific torts (conspiracy, inducing breach of employment contract, and interference with a person's freedom to use his capital or labour), and if they acted 'in contemplation or furtherance of a trade dispute', which was defined in industrial rather than political terms. Moreover, the judges could widen the common law liabilities and narrow the statutory immunities through the process of judicial interpretation.

Unions were legally restricted not only in their conflicts with employers but also in their dealings with members. Despite a provision in the Trade

---

[2] For accounts of the historical development of labour law, see Kahn-Freund, 1959, 1968, 1977a; Wedderburn 1971, 1978, 1980, 1983; Lewis, 1976; Lewis and Simpson, 1981; Clark and Wedderburn, 1983.

[3] *Taff Vale Railway Co.* v. *Amalgamated Society of Railway Servants* [1901] A.C. 426.

Union Act of 1871 which excluded the direct legal enforceability of domestic trade union agreements, legal principles based mainly on the contract of membership contained in the union rule book were developed in order to safeguard the position of individual members. The judges interpreted union rules very strictly and subjected the exercise of powers under the rules to the requirements of 'natural justice'. This was a difficult area because individual legal rights, to which the judges were acutely sensitive, might be asserted at the expense of the industrial and political solidarity of the collective organisation. *Osborne's* case was a classic example.[4] It invalidated union financial support for the Labour Party and led to the Trade Union Act of 1913 which permitted union political expenditure, provided that the money was drawn from a separate political fund and that the rights of members who chose to 'contract out' of political contributions were safeguarded. But ultimately legal protection from union power was arguably, from the point of view of the individual, an essential complement to protection from employer power (Kahn-Freund, 1970).

In any event the law's restrictive role did not appear to impede the long-term growth of trade union membership and of the collective system of industrial relations. Despite the costs of strikes, collective bargaining was seen to provide a practical method of securing industrial peace and of regulating terms and conditions of employment without legalistic rigidity. As these advantages came to be appreciated by employers and the state, labour law assumed the additional function of supporting voluntary collective industrial relations through various measures which Kahn-Freund (1954b:66) described as 'a gloss or footnote to collective bargaining'. Public policy in favour of collective bargaining can be traced back at least as far as the final report of the Royal Commission of Labour in 1894, which led to the Conciliation Act of 1896, and the Reports of the Whitley Committee in 1917–18, which stimulated various developments including the Industrial Courts Act of 1919. Legal support was unobtrusive and indirect. Thus the framework of state-sponsored conciliation and arbitration embodied in the Acts of 1896 and 1919 was designed to assist the process of voluntary conflict resolution. The use of the state's facilities was at the option of the collective parties, priority was given to agreed disputes procedures, and there was no question of using legal sanctions. While the civil servants were themselves responsible for conciliation, their role in arbitration was to arrange for the task to be undertaken by outside persons or panels or by the Industrial Court, a standing arbitration body (Sharp, 1950; Wedderburn and Davies, 1969). The Fair Wages Resolution, the modern version of which was passed in 1946 but which dates back to 1891, encouraged collective bargaining by stipulating labour relations standards for public contractors (Bercusson, 1978). But the Resolution was not 'law' save where the fair wages clause was inserted into certain highly exceptional statutes as

---

[4] *Amalgamated Society of Railway Servants* v. *Osborne* [1910] A.C. 87.

a condition for the grant of a licence or subsidy. The statutory wages councils, which originated in the Trade Boards Act of 1909 dealing with 'sweated' trades, laid down minimum wages in selected industries, an apparently strong form of state intervention. But the councils came to be established only where voluntary collective bargaining was inadequate, and whenever practicable they were dismantled in favour of voluntary bargaining machinery (Bayliss, 1962).

Deviations from Non-Intervention

There were, however, two major attempts before the 1960s to subject collective industrial relations to more extensive forms of state regulation. The first arose from the need to maintain production during wartime. The Munitions of War Act of 1915 banned strikes and lockouts and established a system of compulsory arbitration. It ceased to operate in 1919, but comparable prohibitions on industrial action in the context of compulsory arbitration were enacted in 1940 by Order 1305. This Order, in combination with other wartime policies, had the effect of reinforcing the recognition of official trade unionism by employers and by the state (Bullock, 1967; Middlemas, 1979:266–303). In 1951 Order 1305 was replaced by Order 1376, which jettisoned the illegality of strikes and narrowed the scope of compulsory arbitration. On employer insistence, Order 1376 was itself withdrawn and, after a brief gap, replaced by s.8 of the Terms and Conditions of Employment Act 1959, which provided for limited compulsory arbitration in order to assist both unions and management in extending collectively bargained 'recognised' terms and conditions to employers who were not observing them. This line of intervention, therefore, eventually conformed to the policy of unobtrusive support for collective bargaining.

The other major development which appeared to deviate from the non-interventionist norm was the response of the state to the threat of large-scale industrial action in the decade after World War I. The resurrection of the Triple Alliance of miners, railwaymen and transport workers led to the Emergency Powers Act 1920. Under the statute (which is still in force and is supplemented by an Act of 1964), the government is empowered to declare a 'state of emergency', to take emergency powers where 'essential supplies' are threatened, and to make regulatations to secure 'the essentials of life to the community'. Though the armed forces may be used and criminal offences created, the introduction of any form of industrial conscription is prohibited; nor may it be made an offence to take part in a strike or peacefully persuade others to do so. Thus the 1920 Act is concerned with safeguarding the community in national emergencies without prejudice to the separate question, placed at the top of the political agenda by the general strike of 1926, of the legal liabilities of strikers. At the time it was debated whether the general strike was a sympathetic action in furtherance of the miners' trade dispute with the coalowners, and therefore protected by the immunities of the 1906 Act, or whether it was an unlawful political strike to challenge the government (Goodhart, 1927). In any event the Trade Disputes and Trade Unions Act of 1927, the legal punishment for the strike, imposed criminal sanctions on industrial action calculated to 'coerce' the government, protected persons who refused to participate in such strikes from union disciplinary action, and restricted the ambit of lawful picketing. The Act's practical impact on strikes was negligible if only because their scale declined dramatically with the onset of the depression. But it was of great significance as an example of state intervention in industrial relations, or so it seems today when the issue of political strikes is again to the fore. The 1927 Act contained other provisions which are also relevant to contemporary public policy: it forbade public authorities to demand union membership of their employees or the employees of their contractors, it segregated civil servants into separate non-political trade unions, and it substituted 'contracting-in' for 'contracting-out' in respect of union political fund contributions. Although this Act has sometimes been dismissed as an intemperate measure, it fell short of the demands of the employers' lobbies which pressed for the repeal of the 1906 Act and the prohibition of strikes in essential services, and of the Conservative constituency organisations which wanted compulsory strike ballots (Anderson, 1971; Phillips, 1976:274–9).

Collective Laissez-Faire

The 1927 Act was repealed in 1946 and by the 1950s, when Order 1305 had been replaced by Order 1376, it seemed that British collective labour law had assumed its dominant characteristic: it set a framework for bargaining and conflict but it abstained from regulating the core of collective industrial relations. Legislation regulating the individual employment relationship— apart from statutory protections in respect of industrial safety, welfare and the payment of wages—was conspicuous largely by its absence. This left great scope for regulation through collective bargaining. The immunities, which provided the legal freedom to strike, might not have eliminated but certainly limited the role of the courts in industrial conflict. The laws 'auxiliary' to collective bargaining tended to be supported by indirect sanctions or by none at all. Employers had no general legal duty to recognise or bargain with unions (though the nationalised corporations were placed under a more or less unenforceable duty to consult with appropriate unions), there was no legally protected right to organise in unions and, it must be emphasised, collective agreements were not enforceable as legal contracts. Kahn-Freund was the first labour lawyer to argue that British collective agreements were 'gentlemen's agreements' based on social rather than legal sanctions. They were not contracts in the legal sense because normally the collective parties lacked the intention to create legal relations (1954b:56–58).[5] Non-contractual arrangements fitted in with the characteristically informal style of collective bargaining: the emphasis on the procedural relationship rather than on detailed substantive terms, agreements of indefinite duration, the variety of custom and practice based on each factory or workshop, and the general absence in collective agreements of the lawyer's distinction between conflicts of 'rights' (the meaning and application of existing terms) and conflicts of 'interests' (matters outside the existing terms) (Kahn-Freund, 1954a). Nevertheless, as explained in Chapter 16, collective agreements had a legal effect at the level of the contract of employment into which suitable collectively agreed terms could be incorporated; Kahn-Freund (1954b:56) could therefore justly describe collective negotiators as 'lawmakers'.

The absence of positive organisational rights was also a distinguishing characteristic of British industrial relations. There were a few historical indications that the law was not necessarily hostile to union organisation, notably, the repeal of the Combination Acts in 1824 and the granting of immunity from restraint of trade in 1871 (the equivalent modern protection is embodied in s.2(5) of the Trade Union and Labour Relations Act of 1974). Nor did the law seriously impede the methods of consolidating organisational strength. The practice of the 'check-off' of union subscriptions was not restricted by the truck legislation provided that the individual authorised the deduction,[6] and industrial action in support of the closed shop was held not to be a civil conspiracy.[7] There was also the Fair Wages Resolution, clause 4 of which provided that 'the contractor shall recognise the freedom of his workpeople to be members of trade unions'. But there was no positive legal right. Even though in 1949 and 1950 Britain ratified ILO Conventions No. 87 on Freedom of Association and the Right to Organise and No. 98 on the Application of the Right to Organise and to Bargain Collectively, the appropriate measures and machinery were not considered to involve legislation. As Kahn-Freund (1943:143) explained:

> British collective labour law is in one respect unique among the legal systems of the larger industrial countries. Trade union recognition was achieved in this country by purely industrial as distinct from political and legislative action. No Wagner Act, no Weimar Constitution, no Front Populaire legislation has imposed upon British employers the duty to enter into negotiations with trade union representatives. The proud edifice of collective labour regulation was built up without the assistance of the law.

The non-interventionist framework of labour law came to be regarded as part of the natural order of British industrial relations. It was a singular fact

---

[5] His analysis was adopted by the Donovan Report (1968: ch. 8), the High Court (*Ford Motor Company Limited* v. *AEF* [1969] 2 Q.B. 303), and was the basis of subsequent legislation described below.

[6] *Hewlett* v. *Allen* [1894] A.C. 383; *Williams* v. *Butlers Ltd.* [1975] I.C.R. 208; [1975] I.R.L.R. 120.

[7] *Crofter Hand Woven Harris Tweed Co.* v. *Veitch* [1942] A.C. 435; *Reynolds* v. *Shipping Federation Ltd.* [1924] 1 Ch. 28.

that the unions, although they had numerous other political and legislative objectives, did not press for positive rights in respect of agreements, organisation, recognition, bargaining, and strikes. In these vital areas they preferred to rely not on state support but on industrial self-help. The absence of positive legal rights and obligations was consistent with the spirit of laissez-faire which pervaded even trade unionism for much of the last century. In this century the principle of industrial self-government with minimal state regulation was steadily entrenched as part of a wider pluralistic democracy. The nineteenth-century doctrine of individual laissez-faire eventually gave way to what Kahn-Freund described as 'collective laissez-faire' (1959:224).

FROM DONOVAN TO THE INDUSTRIAL RELATIONS ACT

Twenty years ago the analysis would have stopped at this point. Since then legal policy has been transformed by a rapid succession of reports, statutes, and case law. The background to this frenetic activity was the British economy's persistent decline, which was thought to be connected with failures in industrial relations: inefficient labour practices, inflationary wage settlements and a costly incidence of industrial conflict, which in the 1960s tended to be both unofficial (not sanctioned by the union) and unconstitutional (in breach of agreed procedure). Broadly speaking, governments have pursued two remedial strategies both of which have had major implications for labour law—reform, combined with greater or lesser degrees of restriction, and ultra-restriction.[8]

Strategy of Reform

Reform was the strategy of the Donovan Commission (1968). The problem addressed by Donovan was how to preserve the voluntary institutions of industrial relations and yet to restore order, peace, and efficiency. The solution was voluntary reform whereby management and trade union officials would regain control over the workplace through detailed and comprehensive agreements. (The detailed implications of 'reform' for shop stewards, managers, and collective bargaining arrangements are discussed in Chapters 3, 4 and 6). The reform of industrial relations was to be encouraged by a new legal framework, including unfair dismissal rights, a procedure for employers' recognition of unions for collective bargaining, the registration of collective agreements, and a public agency with special responsibility for promoting reform. While the encouragement and extension of collective bargaining were public policy objectives of long-standing, its reform was a departure. The idea of using the law to promote more efficient industrial relations as part of a drive towards better economic performance was no part of collective laissez-faire.

---

[8] For a more extensive and somewhat different elaboration of these two strategies, see Clark and Wedderburn, 1983. Cf. Lewis and Simpson, 1981:10–22.

Donovan's legal policy to some extent reflected developments which were already discernible in the mid-1960s. In the sphere of individual labour law, the Redundancy Payments Act of 1965 was designed, among other things, to encourage labour mobility and productivity (see Chapter 16). In the sphere of collective labour law, incomes policies to restrain and rationalise the growth of money incomes were given statutory backing under the Prices and Incomes Acts of 1966 to 1968 (Wedderburn, 1971: 211–18). The 1966 Act's legal orders to delay the implementation of pay awards, though not often invoked, and the criminal sanctions aimed at those who engaged in direct industrial action to contravene the orders, though never used, were still the 'deepest inroad ever made into . . . the freedom of collective bargaining in Britain' (Kahn-Freund, 1968:19). Although the references in the Donovan Report to incomes policy were arguably 'brief and superficial' (Turner, 1969b:9), there was nevertheless a 'logical connection' (McCarthy and Ellis, 1973:26) between its reform strategy and the problems of wage drift and inflation. The projected changes in collective bargaining practices were intended to 'assist an incomes policy to work effectively' (Donovan, 1968: para. 207), and it was even proposed that arbitrators should be placed under a legal duty to take incomes policy into account when making their awards (para. 285). Incomes policy and the reform of industrial relations could therefore be regarded as two sides of the same coin.

Reform and Restriction

Reform then was not a simple 'pro-trade union' or 'pro-management' proposition. It saw virtue in the autonomous collective system and wished to expand both its scope and coverage. The Donovan Commission's commitment to collective values was expressed in its opinion that 'properly conducted, collective bargaining is the most effective means of giving workers the right to representation in decisions affecting their working lives, a right which is or should be the prerogative of every worker in a democratic society' (para. 212). But it wanted collective bargaining to be 'properly conducted', that is, consistent with what it saw as the national interest in reducing strikes, inefficient practices, and inflation. The reform strategy was also compatible with the restrictive function of labour law. While the Donovan Commission rejected most of the proposals put to it for the direct legal suppression of industrial conflict, it did make a majority recommendation to confine the 1906 Act's immunity from liability for inducing breach of contract to registered unions only (para. 801), a blow aimed at unofficial militancy. Moreover, while the Commission advocated the general continuance of the non-contractual status of collective agreements, it recommended a scheme for the selective legal enforceability of disputes procedures after their reform in cases where strike proneness was 'due to irresponsibility or to agitation by eccentrics or by subversives' (para. 508). This proposal showed that the law's restrictive function could be adapted to promoting specific changes in the pattern of industrial conflict as part of the reform of industrial relations.

Reform and restriction were the dual aims of Labour's White Paper *In Place of Strife* (1969), though its 'penalty clauses' with their criminal sanctions against employers, unions and unconstitutional strikers were at variance with the proposals of the Donovan Commission (Simpson, 1969; Jenkins, 1970). The Conservatives' Industrial Relations Act of 1971 also attempted to combine these two aims.[9] But whereas the Donovan Report insisted that reform should be 'accomplished, if possible, without destroying the British tradition of keeping industrial relations out of the courts' (para. 190), the architects of the 1971 Act and the accompanying Industrial Relations Code of Practice (1972) saw the law as the 'main instrument' in achieving reform (Department of Employment, 1970: para. 8).

The Industrial Relations Act set out to reform collective agreements and bargaining structures. According to *Fair Deal at Work,* the Conservative Party policy document published in 1968 in advance of Donovan, the non-legal enforceability of collective agreements fostered the informality, vagueness, and pervasive disorder of much collective bargaining. If breach of agreement could lead to damages and injunctions, there would be a strong incentive for bargainers to negotiate precise fixed-term agreements with clearly defined rights and obligations, which would in turn be conducive to a relatively predictable and less costly pattern of industrial conflict (Lewis, 1970). It was also thought that the lack of a North American-style procedure for establishing bargaining units encouraged overlapping and illogical patterns of union recognition and membership. The Industrial Relations Act therefore provided that written collective agreements would be presumed to create legal relations in the absence of an express clause to the contrary, and for a legal procedure for determining 'bargaining units' and 'sole bargaining agents'.

The Act's attempt to promote legally enforceable collective agreements failed because the optional clause disclaiming the intention to create legal relations became a universal feature of agreements. The requirement that the parties to a legally enforceable collective agreement 'take all such steps as are reasonably practicable' to prevent members and persons acting and purporting to act on their behalf from breaking agreements was therefore a dead letter. As for the bargaining unit procedure, it had little impact on bargaining structures in general, though it did feature somewhat unhelpfully in certain multi-union problems involving unrecognised staff and professional associations and breakaway unions. In fact there was little chance of reform under the Act if only because TUC-affiliated unions boycotted the new procedures. They refused to register as 'trade unions' with the Registrar of Trade Unions thus avoiding his powers to oversee their

---

[9] See Kahn-Freund, 1972; Wedderburn, 1972; McCarthy and Ellis, 1973; Simpson and Wood, 1973; Weekes et al., 1975; Thomson and Engleman, 1975; Moran, 1977; Crouch, 1977. This chapter relies on Weekes et al. for the industrial relations effects of the 1971 Act.

internal affairs in the interests of 'responsible' trade unionism. Other provisions relevant to reform (apart from the unfair dismissal provisions discussed in Chapter 16) included the registration of procedure agreements, which was in practice unimportant; a duty on employers to disclose information for collective bargaining, which was not brought into effect; and a mechanism to impose legally enforceable procedure agreements, which was never used. But if the Industrial Relations Act failed to reform industrial relations, how did it fare in its other objective of restricting trade unions?

The Act created a National Industrial Relations Court (NIRC) which adjudicated on a new range of civil liabilities known as 'unfair industrial practices'. Organisations as well as individuals could be legally liable as the Act restored the principle of *Taff Vale,* under which it was possible to sue trade unions as such. Unregistered organisations were particularly vulnerable. In *Heaton's* case the House of Lords held that the unregistered Transport and General Workers' Union was vicariously liable for the apparently unofficial acts of its shop stewards in the docks.[10] The judgment was part of a remarkable sequence of events in which the courts resorted to unorthodox methods in order to release a group of dockers' shop stewards— the 'Pentonville Five'—whose imprisonment for contempt after deliberately flouting court orders was becoming the focus of a major industrial and constitutional confrontation. There were other embarrassments under the Act. A dispute in the railway industry in 1972 prompted the government's single attempt to avail itself of its right to apply to the NIRC for restraining orders under 'national emergency' procedures for a cooling off period and a ballot. The railwaymen voted in favour of their claim by six to one, which had the effect of strengthening the unions' bargaining position.[11] At a later point the Amalgamated Union of Engineering Workers called off a national strike only after the NIRC had accepted an offer from a group of anonymous donors to pay the fines and compensation owed by the union.[12]

Ultra-Restriction

The Act's practical impact on strikes was negligible but its restrictions on unions were so extensive that they represented a new development in legal policy. This was 'ultra-restriction' as distinct from the less drastic forms of legal restriction which were part and parcel of collective laissez-faire and the reform strategy. Although unions might have limited their liabilities to some extent by registering, which they chose not to do, the myriad of unfair industrial practices, which included the basic liability for inducing breach of employment contract, came close to obliterating any legal

---

[10] *Heaton's Transport Ltd.* v. *TGWU* [1973] A.C. 15; [1972] I.C.R. 308; [1972] I.R.L.R. 25.
[11] *Secretary of State for Employment* v. *ASLEF* [1972] I.C.R. 7; (No. 2) [1972] I.C.R. 19.
[12] *Con-Mech Ltd.* v. *AUEW* [1973] I.C.R. 620; (No. 2) [1974] I.C.R. 332.

freedom to take industrial action. The Industrial Relations Act was the most restrictive legislative intervention since the 1927 Act. The usual role of the legislature from the 1870s onwards at least had been to provide relief from the rigours of judge-made liabilities. In the 1960s Parliament was still performing this function: the Trade Disputes Act 1965 was enacted to grant immunity from the obscure tort of 'intimidation' which the Law Lords had discovered in *Rookes v. Barnard*.[13] That was the traditional way in which a balance had been achieved between immunities and liabilities, allowing some degree of legal freedom to strike, which one distinguished judge over forty years ago had recognised as 'an essential element in the principle of collective bargaining'.[14] While this point was taken on board in Donovan's prescription for reform, the 1971 Act appeared to aim at weakening trade unions to the point of undermining the collective system of industrial relations. Reform was hardly compatible with a form of restriction which discarded the collectivist ethic.

Collectivism, whether laissez-faire or reformist, assumed that the only viable way in which workers could protect themselves from the inequality of the individual employment relation was through trade union organisation, and further that collectively regulated industrial relations benefited society as well as trade unionists. In contrast the 1971 Act's individualist philosophy saw unions as an illegitimate distortion of the market relations between the employer and the individual employee. Furthermore, unions interfered with individual liberty not only in the economic sense but also in terms of personal freedom. This was threatened by the union aspiration for collective solidarity, discipline, and 100 per cent organisation.

In conformity with this philosophy the Act introduced individual legal rights which might be asserted at the expense of the organisational strength of trade unions. These included: the right to belong to and to participate in the activities of a registered trade union and the right not to belong to any organisation of workers whether registered or not, as qualified for registered unions only by the possibilities of an 'agency' or 'approved closed shop'; the right to be admitted to a union if appropriately qualified; and the right to request the withdrawal of recognition, which constituted a potential challenge to the continuance of most collective bargaining arrangements. As in the celebrated cases of *Goad* and *Langston*, a few individuals attempted to rock the collective boat, but with little impact on industrial relations at large.[15] The right not to belong, together with the specific prohibition of pre-entry closed shops, clashed with the widespread reality of union security arrangements, though managerial connivance permitted the vast majority of existing practices to continue.

Management indifference and union hostility towards the Industrial Relations Act severely limited its effect. In fact the individualist free

---

[13] [1964] A.C. 1129.
[14] *Crofter Hand Woven Harris Tweed Co.* v. *Veitch* [1942] A.C. 435, 463 (Lord Wright).
[15] The sagas of 'Goad' and 'Langston' rank in the annals of industrial relations folklore. See *Goad* v. *AUEW* [1972] I.C.R. 429; (No. 2) [1973] I.C.R. 42; (No. 3) [1973] I.C.R. 108;

market economics with which it was associated had soon been abandoned; after an abortive attempt to achieve voluntary restraint on pay and prices, the government adopted a statutory incomes policy under the Counter-Inflation Acts of 1972 and 1973. Nevertheless, the 1971 Act laid the foundation for a line of individualistic legal policy which was to be revived by the Employment Acts of 1980 and 1982. The contemporary structure of labour law is, however, full of contradictory elements. Collectivist values survive mainly in the unrepealed parts of the legislation introduced in the mid seventies, the era of the Social Contract.

LABOUR LAW AND THE SOCIAL CONTRACT

This legislation was planned in three stages. First, the Trade Union and Labour Relations Act of 1974 repealed the Industrial Relations Act. It restored the presumption that collective agreements were not intended to be legally enforceable and specified conditions which had to be satisfied before collectively agreed restrictions on strike action could be incorporated into individual contracts of employment (s.18). It also restored the 1906 Act's traditional immunity for inducing breach of employment contract (s.13). As there was only a minority Labour government between February and October 1974 the opposition was able to insist on this relatively narrow form of immunity. For its part the government had intended to widen the immunity to meet the new developments in judge-made civil liabilities, namely, inducing breach of commercial contract and interference with commercial relations short of breach.[16] Such liabilities had not been foreseen by the architects of the 1906 Act (Wedderburn, 1980:88–9). An amending Bill was therefore brought forward to deal with the provisions in the 1974 Act which had been inserted by the opposition. This became the Trade Union and Labour Relations (Amendment) Act of 1976. It extended the immunity for inducing breach of contract to cover commercial contracts and repealed the statutory remedy against being unreasonably excluded from a union, in return for which the TUC set up its own Independent Review Committee to hear appeals from those excluded from membership in closed shops. The Act also confined to religious belief the ground on which an individual employee could claim unfair dismissal if dismissed for refusing to join a closed shop union. (The 1974 and 1976 Acts are abbreviated as TULRA.)

The second stage was the Employment Protection Act of 1975 (EPA). This reshaped the institutional framework of collective labour law. The Advisory, Conciliation and Arbitration Service (ACAS), which had begun

---

Langston v. *AUEW* [1973] I.C.R. 211; [1974] I.C.R. 180 and 510. But some litigation had serious implications for inter-union conflict; e.g. *Post Office* v. *UPW* [1974] I.C.R. 378; [1974] I.R.L.R. 22.

[16] The leading cases were *Stratford and Son Ltd.* v. *Lindley* [1965] A.C. 269 and *Torquay Hotel Co. Ltd.* v. *Cousins* [1969] 2 Ch. 106. See Wedderburn, 1971: 304–409.

its work in 1974, was given a statutory constitution and powers described in detail below. ACAS was provided with a Central Arbitration Committee (CAC) composed of a chairman and lay members from both sides of industry. In addition to new compulsory arbitration functions, the CAC assumed the voluntary arbitration role of the old Industrial Court. The EPA also established the Certification Officer to maintain a list of trade unions and to determine whether unions satisfied the new statutory criterion of independence on which many legal rights depended. The Certification Officer took over the functions previously discharged by the Registrar of Friendly Societies in respect of internal union administration, including political fund and merger procedures.

The EPA introduced many new legal rights for both individual employees and trade unions. The individual rights, which were enforceable in the industrial tribunals, were later consolidated in the Employment Protection (Consolidation) Act 1978 (EPCA) and were supplemented by separate statutes on sex and race discrimination (see Chapters 13 and 16). But some of these rights, though individual in form, were designed to protect and support trade union membership and activity at the workplace. British law was in effect 'building a collective "right to associate" out of the bricks of certain "individual" employment rights' (Wedderburn, 1976:169). Employees unfairly dismissed by reason of membership of, or activity at an appropriate time in, an independent union were provided with the expeditious remedy of 'interim relief', whereby the continuation of the employment contract could be ordered pending a full hearing (EPCA s.77). Employees were also given the right not to be penalised for, or deterred or prevented from, joining an independent union, or taking part in its activities at an appropriate time, by employers' actions short of dismissal (EPCA s.23). Further, employees who were officials of independent recognised unions were given the right to take paid time off during working hours for duties concerned with industrial relations with their employers or any associated employer, and also for relevant training approved by their union or by the TUC (EPCA s.27). (Safety representatives of recognised unions were given similar rights.)[17] In addition, employers were required to permit employees who were members of independent and recognised unions to take time off during working hours—but without the obligation to pay wages—for trade union activities, excluding activities which constituted industrial action (EPCA s.28).

These individual rights complemented the collective rights introduced by the EPA. Independent unions were given the right to refer a recognition issue to ACAS, either a claim for fresh recognition or for 'further recognition' to extend the scope of collective bargaining. ACAS was given what were thought to be wide discretionary powers to investigate, report,

---

[17] Safety Representatives and Safety Committee Regulations, S.I. 1977 No. 500, and Health and Safety Commission Code of Practice *Time Off for the Training of Safety Representatives*, 1978.

and to make recommendations. Failure on the part of an employer to implement an ACAS recommendation led to the possibility of an arbitration award by the CAC (EPA ss.11–16). Independent unions were also given the right to claim arbitration on 'recognised' terms and conditions of employment (the equivalent of s.8 of the Terms and Conditions of Employment Act 1959) or, in the absence of such terms, the 'general level' for comparable workers in the district (EPA Schedule 11). In this context it is also worth noting the arbitration procedure to ensure that collective agreements conformed with the principle of equal pay (Equal Pay Act 1970 s.3.) Employers were placed under a legal duty to disclose information for collective bargaining to recognised, independent trade unions (EPA ss.17–21). Employers were further required to consult with independent recognised trade unions on proposed redundancies (EPA Part IV). Consultation rights were also enacted to cover industrial safety (Health and Safety at Work Act 1974 s.2) and occupational pensions (Social Security Pensions Act 1975 s.31(5)). Finally, in provisions which were later incorporated in the Wages Council Act of 1979 the EPA strengthened the wages council system by allowing the councils to make their own orders instead of referring back to a minister, and by expanding the potential scope of the orders to cover all terms and conditions of employment, not just pay and holidays. Also, as a way of encouraging the extension of collective bargaining in wages council industries, the EPA provided for the conversion of wages councils into 'statutory joint industrial councils'.

The third stage was to be legislation on industrial democracy. To that end a committee of inquiry was appointed to suggest how union representation might best be exercised at boardroom level in the private sector, though the Bullock Report (1977) yielded not a statute but only a White Paper *Industrial Democracy* (Department of Employment, 1978a).

Even without legislation on industrial democracy, the Social Contract labour laws were a formidable legal initiative. In some respects they reaffirmed the traditional legal structure, for example, the restoration of the immunities and of the presumption about non-enforceable collective agreements. Moreover the extension of individual legal rights entrenched an interventionist trend in individual labour law which by the mid 1970s was already advanced and having major implications for collective industrial relations (a point which is argued in Chapter 16). But the real novelty of the legislation was the injection of positive legal rights into the hitherto virgin areas of trade union organisation and collective bargaining.

Intended and Unintended Limitations

There was however no intention to destroy or threaten the tradition of collective autonomy. The collective legal rights in particular were seen as 'statutory "props" to collective bargaining' (Wedderburn, 1976:174). This had a limiting effect on the nature of the relevant legal sanctions. In the case of the recognition procedure, the sanction against an employer who did not observe an ACAS recommendation was not an injunction or a fine but an arbitration award by the CAC. The award was statutorily incorporated into the individual contracts of employment of those covered by the claim. If the employer failed to perform his contractual obligation, the individual employee could in principle have sued him for breach of contract. Furthermore, the CAC could only make awards on terms and conditions of employment and would not award collective procedural terms obliging the employer to negotiate (Doyle, 1980). The arbitration award operated in a similar way under Schedule 11 (as it did under the predecessor measures: s.8 of the Terms and Conditions of Employment Act 1959 and Order 1376). Arbitration was also the final sanction under the disclosure of information duty. Breach of the obligation to consult over redundancies led to an indirect sanction of a different kind. A trade union was empowered to complain to an industrial tribunal, which could make a modest 'protective award' for the benefit of individual employees, who then would have to make their own claim in the tribunal if the employer failed to pay up. In legal theory the duty to consult over industrial safety could have been enforced by the Health and Safety Executive through 'improvement' notices and criminal prosecutions. In practice the Executive would not as a matter of policy use its legal powers to enforce industrial relations procedures, and consequently there was (and is) no legal enforcement at all, except for contravention of a recognised safety representative's right to paid time off, which may be referred to an industrial tribunal.

Apart from indirect sanctions, there were many other limitations inherent in the legislation, though it was perhaps less clear whether they resulted from the intention to preserve voluntarism or simply from defects in drafting (Clegg, 1979:436–8). For example, the duty on employers to deal with unions on proposed redundancies necessitated not negotiation but consultation, a process involving only the disclosure of certain information and minimum periods of advance notice, and even these requirements could be diluted if the employer experienced 'special circumstances' (EPA s.99(8)). The parallel duty to notify the Department of Employment did not empower the state authorities to block, postpone, or even question the need for redundancies. The duty to disclose information for collective bargaining was limited by extremely wide exceptions covering information communicated to the employer in 'confidence' or disclosure of which would cause 'substantial injury' to the employer's undertaking (EPA s.18), and generally it has had an insignificant impact on collective industrial relations (Gospel and Willman, 1981:22).

Another very important limitation was the effect of judicial interpretation. It is not suggested that every judicial decision ignored the intent of the legislation. In the leading case on paid time off, for example, the Court of Appeal recently took a broad view of the scope of industrial relations duties with the employer which constitute the pre-condition for the exercise of the right: they were not restricted to questions of collective bargaining or to matters in respect of which the employer recognised the union.[18] However, the overall trend of judicial interpretation was to limit the new positive rights. Thus the organisational rights apart from time off—not to be unfairly dismissed or subject to action short of dismissal because of union membership and activity—have on the whole been narrowly construed.[19] The judicial interpretation of Schedule 11 was also mixed. On the one hand, the Lord Chief Justice correctly inferred from the absence of a right of appeal from CAC decisions that 'Parliament intended these matter to be dealt with without too much assistance from the lawyers'.[20] On the other hand, the courts interpreted 'recognised' terms, the existence of which barred a claim to the more advantageous 'general' level, as minimum rates however unrealistically low.[21]

Several of the statutory rights applied (and still apply) only if a union was recognised by an employer for collective bargaining: time off, disclosure of information, and consultation on safety and redundancy. In many circumstances it has become unclear whether the judges will accept a union as being recognised for these purposes.[22] The importance of recognition in the overall framework of labour law was a good reason in itself for having a recognition procedure which would be operated by industrial relations experts and kept away from the courts. But the EPA's recognition procedure gave the judges unforeseen opportunities for intervention. Despite the absence of a formal right of appeal from the decisions of ACAS, there was a series of cases (including the famous one of *Grunwick*[23]) based on the allegation that ACAS had exceeded its statutory powers. In a remarkable demonstration of individualist values—some of the judges equated a union's right to bargain collectively with compulsory purchase orders against individual employees—ACAS was denied its discretionary powers to resolve recognition problems. Though the House of Lords belatedly overruled the Court of Appeal in two major cases,[24] this kind of decision remains a classic illustration of the judicial inability to comprehend let alone support the realities and values of collective industrial relations (Simpson, 1979; Lewis and Simpson, 1981:140–47).

[18] *Beal* v. *Beecham Group Ltd.* [1982] I.R.L.R. 192 (attendance at a union's national advisory committee for a corporate group held to be an industrial relations duty for purposes of paid time off).

[19] E.g. *Birmingham District Council* v. *Beyer* [1977] I.R.L.R. 210 (denial of unfair dismissal relief to blacklisted union activist in construction industry). *Chant* v. *Aquaboats Ltd.* [1978] I.C.R. 643 (organising a safety petition held not to be union activities). *Marley Tile Co. Ltd.* v. *Shaw* [1980] I.C.R. 72; [1980] I.R.L.R. 25 (steward dismissed for convening meeting not agreed to by employer held not to be engaged in union activities at the appropriate time). But cf. other cases, especially EAT decisions with Phillips J. presiding: *Lyon* v. *St. James Press Ltd.* [1976] I.C.R. 413; *Dixon* v. *West Ella Developments Ltd.* [1978] I.C.R. 856; [1978] I.R.L.R. 151. See Davies and Freedland, 1979: 40–60.

[20] *R* v. *CAC, Ex parte TI Tubes Ltd.* [1978] I.R.L.R. 183, 184.

[21] *R* v. *CAC, Ex parte Deltaflow Ltd.* [1978] I.C.R. 534.

[22] See Davies and Freedland, 1979: 168–72.

[23] *Grunwick Processing Laboratories Ltd.* v. *ACAS* [1978] A.C. 655; [1978] I.C.R. 231; [1978] I.R.L.R. 38.

[24] *UKAPE* v. *ACAS* [1980] I.C.R. 201; [1980] I.R.L.R. 124; *EMA* v. *ACAS* [1980] I.C.R. 215; [1980] I.R.L.R. 164.

Rationale of the Legislation

The problems of weak enforcement, drafting defects, and narrow judicial interpretation raise the issue of what the legislative programme was supposed to achieve. Surprisingly, it was part of a broader strategy which was intended, according to the Labour Party Manifesto of October 1974, to bring about 'a fundamental and irreversible shift in the balance of wealth and power in favour of working people and their families'. The radical purpose of the legislation was assailed in the 1979 Conservative Manifesto: 'between 1974 and 1976 Labour enacted a "militants' charter" of trade union legislation. It tilted the balance of power in bargaining throughout industry away from responsible management and towards unions, and sometimes towards unofficial groups acting in defiance of their official union leadership.' While the purpose and effect of legislation are not to be accurately gauged from the rhetoric of election manifestos, it would be true to say that the Social Contract initiative as a whole did signify a new aspiration in public policy. It was designed to achieve both social justice and economic recovery through interventionist state policies which included the National Enterprise Board, public ownership, planning agreements, other measures to encourage investment in British industry, and an extension of industrial democracy. The vision of a transformation towards a more planned and egalitarian society was detectable in the early phases of the Social Contract, when the unions were most involved in determining government strategy, and perhaps also in the proposals of the Bullock Report.[25]

The Social Contract was however a variant of a reformist rather than a revolutionary strategy, and it was significant that from 1975 onwards it involved voluntary restraint on pay increases. Such was the importance attached to incomes policy that there was an understandable tendency to equate the Social Contract exclusively with pay restraint. This aspect eventually led to the politically traumatic strikes during the 1978–9 'winter of discontent', which was a reaction to an over-rigid 5 per cent pay policy. Conscious of their respective precarious situations, the unions and the government made a final and, in electoral terms, doomed attempt at a 'Social Concordat', which included annual pay assessments and the TUC's own voluntary guides on the conduct of industrial relations.[26] Incomes

---

[25] On the development of the Social Contract, see Clark, Hartman, Lau and Winchester, 1980. On the policy of the Social Contract employment legislation, see Clark and Wedderburn, 1983. For different interpretations of the Bullock Report, see Kahn-Freund, 1977c; Davies and Wedderburn, 1977; Lewis and Clark, 1977; Coates and Topham, 1977. On the record of the 1974–9 governments, see Coates, 1979 and Hobsbawm et al., 1981.

[26] *The Economy, the Government and Trade Union Responsibilities: Joint Statement by the TUC and the Government*, 1979, which included the TUC's guides *Negotiating and Disputes Procedures, Conduct of Industrial Disputes*, and *Union Organisation and the Closed Shop*.

policy was, as argued above, an integral part of the reform strategy associated with the Donovan Commission. To what extent did the Social Contract employment legislation also reflect Donovan principles?

The nearest the legislation came to giving an explicit answer to this question was in the EPA's provisions on ACAS. ACAS inherited two different traditions. First, it took over the Department of Employment's peace-keeping functions of conciliation, arbitration, and mediation (EPA ss.2, 3). This move was intended to insulate third-party intervention from incomes policies. It was thought that a tripartite body with a governing council of employers, trade unionists, and independent experts would be relatively immune to direct government pressure. This background was perhaps one of the reasons why the EPA expressly provided that ACAS was not to be subject 'to directions of any kind from any Minister of the Crown as to the manner in which it is to exercise its functions under any enactment' (Schedule 1, para.11(1)).

Second, ACAS was the successor to the Commission on Industrial Relations, which had been set up in 1969 in order to encourage the reform of industrial relations along Donovan lines. The concentration of peace-keeping and reform in a single service would, it was argued, have the effect of strengthening both functions (McCarthy and Ellis, 1973:121-9). ACAS was 'charged with the general duty of promoting the improvement of industrial relations and in particular of encouraging the extension of collective bargaining and the development and, where necessary, reform of collective bargaining machinery' (EPA s.1(2)). ACAS's role in the EPA's recognition procedure was accordingly designed to reform as well as extend collective bargaining. The option of 'further recognition', though in practice hardly used, was supposed to help in eliminating the poverty of content in collective agreements which the Donovan Report had identified as a major inadequacy. The procedure, moreover, applied only to single or associated employers and not to employers' associations. This exclusion of multi-employer bargaining units was supposed to encourage the Donovan ideal of orderly and comprehensive arrangements in the middle levels of bargaining below the decaying industry-wide structures (Kahn-Freund, 1977a:75-6).

The object of reform was no less apparent in ACAS's other functions. ACAS was authorised to provide a free advisory service covering the whole field of industrial relations and personnel management including pay structures, job evaluation, manpower planning, discipline, employee communications, and, in so far as it affected collective bargaining, the internal organisation of management and trade unions (EPA s.4). This function was particularly conducive to what Kahn-Freund (1977a:112) described as the 'so urgently necessary modernisation' of British industrial relations. ACAS was further empowered to publish its inquiries into industrial relations problems if that was 'desirable for the improvement of industrial relations' (s.5). Its powers to issue codes of practice were couched in similar terms (s.6). So far ACAS has issued three codes which must, if relevant, be taken into account by the industrial tribunals and the CAC: *Disciplinary Practice and Procedures in Employment* (1977), *Disclosure of Information to Trade Unions for Collective Bargaining Purposes* (1977), and *Time Off for Trade Union Duties and Activities* (1978). ACAS's codes, annual reports, and other publications such as the post-Social Contract document *Improving Industrial Relations—A Joint Responsibility* (1981) revealed the main elements in its conception of improved industrial relations: the efficient use of manpower, orderly pay structures and disputes procedures, and detailed, joint control over the activities of shop stewards. For example, ACAS's code on time-off stated that voluntary agreements on time-off and other facilities 'should be consistent with wider arrangements which should deal with such matters of workplace representation as constituencies, number of representatives, and the form of any joint credentials' (para. 12). (See Chapter 3 for an analysis of the impact of public policy on the role of shop stewards.) Only one major aspect of reform was missing: the need to restrain the results of collective bargaining in so far as they contributed to inflation. ACAS could not have remedied this omission without prejudicing its independence, though in the period of Social Contract the gap was filled by a voluntary incomes policy.

ACAS was thus assigned the task of reforming industrial relations. It was not too difficult to see a similar rationale for the recognition procedure and (though Donovan did not make recommendations in these areas) for the legal duties on employers to disclose information, not to dismiss or take other action against their employees because of their union activities, and to allow them time off for industrial relations purposes. Furthermore, the stimulus for many of the important developments in individual labour law was not the demands of the trade union movement but the need to make British law conform with international and, from 1973 onwards, Common Market standards. This was another important dimension to the reform and modernisation of British industrial relations (Kahn-Freund, 1977a: 42–3; Hepple and O'Higgins, 1981:335–49). Even one of the major provisions in collective labour law—the recognised trade union's right to be consulted over redundancy—was based on an EEC Directive (Freedland, 1976).

A continuation of something akin to the Donovan reform strategy was clearly less radical than an irreversible transfer of wealth and power. But the factors which most severely circumscribed the potential effect of the Social Contract legislation between 1974 and 1979 were the deteriorating economic conditions and the overall direction of government policy. Mounting unemployment, persistent inflation, public expenditure cuts, fluctuating living standards, and the basic failure of Labour in office to implement the economic and industrial strategy of the Social Contract were the background to the fairly modest legislation which was offered to the unions as consideration for their active involvement in pay restraint. 'In this situation the new laws were indicative not of a transfer of power but rather of the encouragement which the government offered to trade union leaders to assist in the maintenance of social and economic stability' (Lewis and Simpson, 1981:18).[27]

THE EMPLOYMENT ACTS 1980 AND 1982

During the winter of discontent and the election campaign which culminated in the Conservative victory of May 1979, political controversy focused on picketing, secondary action, and the closed shop. The Conservative Party promised legislation to redress the balance of power between employers and trade unions and between individual liberty and collective organisation. The principal measures to date have been the Employment Acts of 1980 and 1982. Unlike the Industrial Relations Act, this legislation does not establish a comprehensive framework administered by a new set of institutions: its technique in the main is the 'step by step' amendment of earlier statutes and case law. However, its critics maintain that the overall legislative objective is to undermine trade unionism and the whole collective system of industrial relations in accordance with an ultra-restrictive strategy (Lewis and Simpson, 1981, 1982; Wedderburn, 1982b; Ewing, 1982; Clark and Wedderburn, 1983).

The 1980 Act sweeps away several of the laws which supported the development of collective industrial relations. The EPA's recognition procedure is repealed, a move which sparked only minimal protest as the procedure had already been emasculated by the judges. Also destroyed are Schedule 11 of the EPA and the Road Haulage Wages Act of 1938. The repeal of the 'recognised' terms and conditions provision in Schedule 11 was criticised by some employers' organisations as well as unions for reasons explained by the CAC in its 1979 Annual Report: 'the application of recognised terms and conditions has been a feature of our industrial relations for many decades, serving as it does to protect the worker who may be exploited and the good employer who may be undercut. Support should continue to be given to established negotiating machinery'. The case for the repeal of the 'general level' provision was that it was inflationary, did nothing for the low paid, and weakened voluntary procedures, though each of these arguments was open to serious doubt (Dickens et al., 1979:50–52; Jones, 1980). The Road Haulage Wages Act 1938 provided that, in return for the grant of a licence to employers, the remuneration paid to workers who drove vehicles used by the employers for their own purposes should be 'fair'. It is difficult to see the point of this repeal except as a step towards the dismantling of fair wages clauses in other similar

---

[27] For analyses of incomes policies, Donovan reformism, and the Social Contract in terms of a corporatist strategy of control under contemporary British capitalism, see Panitch, 1976; Crouch, 1977; and Schmitter and Lehmbruch, 1979. For the classic discussion of corporatist (and pluralist) ideas with reference to earlier epochs of British industrial relations, see Milne-Bailey, 1934.

statutes (the Civil Aviation Act 1949, Films Act 1960, Independent Broadcasting Authority Act 1973, and Public Passenger Vehicles Act 1981) and of the Fair Wages Resolution. Despite ILO Convention 94, which requires clauses similar to those in the Fair Wages Resolution to be inserted in public contracts, the government has in fact declared its intention to rescind the Resolution. The one apparent exception to its negative attitude towards collective bargaining law is contained in a measure quite separate from the Employment Acts. The Transfer of Undertakings (Protection of Employment) Regulations 1981 require, in the case of certain transfers of commercial ventures, automatic transfers of contracts of employment, collective agreements and union recognition, and impose a duty to inform and consult the representatives of recognised trade unions. However, the Regulations were introduced only after the EEC Commission threatened proceedings against the United Kingdom for failing to implement the EEC Directive on Acquired Rights (1977); in any case, the information and consultation duties fall short of those in the Directive and the sanctions for breach are 'derisory' (Hepple, 1982:38).

Rights to Disorganise

The erosion of collective relations is the clear aim of a new series of individual legal rights enforceable against employers and unions. Requirements that work should be performed only by union members or only by the employees of firms who at least recognise unions are extremely common in all branches of industry. Unions insist on them as a method of upholding and extending collectively agreed conditions and of restraining 'cowboy' sub-contractors. As the Green Paper *Trade Union Immunities* (Department of Employment, 1981b) acknowledged, 'there are practical limitations on the extent to which such long-standing practices can be eradicated by law and there is inevitably some uncertainty as to what would be the effects of trying to do so' (para. 304). Nevertheless, a legal onslaught on these practices was foreshadowed by the 1980 Act's withdrawal of immunity from persons organising industrial action in order to compel into unions workers employed by a different employer and at different premises from those taking the action. This was aimed at a specific form of union recruitment in the printing industry (Leggatt, 1979). The 1982 Act goes much further. It renders void requirements in contracts that work is to be done by union members only and that a party to the contract must recognise, negotiate, or consult with a trade union; also there are parallel statutory duties not to exclude persons from approved lists of suppliers or to terminate or refuse to enter contracts for these reasons. Acts inducing the enforcement of such agreements and practices are deprived of statutory immunity (Employment Act 1982 ss.12–14).

Orderly collective relations are endangered by other measures which, even in the absence of a formal right not to belong to a union, are tantamount to a right to dissociate. The 1980 Act amends EPCA s.23(1)(c) to give individual employees a right not to be compelled into a union by employer action short of dismissal. This is drafted in the form of a correlative to the rights not to be subject to such action to deter union membership or activity. In addition, the 1982 Act redrafts EPCA s.58 so that a right not to be unfairly dismissed for non-membership of any or a particular union appears side by side with the rights not to be unfairly dismissed because of union membership or activity. The equation of a right not to belong to a union with the legal support for trade unionism represents a fundamental shift in public policy. The Donovan Commission was adamant that there was no case for the enactment of a non-membership right as a correlative to its proposed ban on employment contracts debarring union membership because 'the former condition is designed to frustrate the development of collective bargaining, which it is public policy to promote, whereas no such objection applies to the latter' (para. 599). In a collective bargaining system based on the single channel of trade union representation, the legal right to dissociate may be regarded as the equivalent of a right to disorganise the union.

The remedies available for breach of the rights to non-membership are broadly similar to those for the rights to organise. However, the compensation principles for dismissal on these grounds have been radically amended to provide a minimum 'special' award of £10,000 to £20,000, a 'basic' award with a minimum of £2,000, plus a 'compensatory' award if the individual suffers any actual loss. These amounts are in stark contrast to the normal run of unfair dismissal awards: in 1980 the median was £598. Although the awards are subject to the tribunal's discretion to make reductions to take account of the complainant's behaviour, the policy is clearly to deter employers from unfair dismissal. Deterrence, however, depends on management having to pay. If the employer dismisses the non-unionist without inducement from industrial pressure, the employer alone is liable. But if inducement is shown there may be 'joinder' of the trade union or other persons exercising the pressure, who may in turn be ordered to pay all or part of the compensation. The complainant as well as the employer may join those persons and furthermore the award can be made directly against them.

The non-membership rights are applicable whether or not there is a union membership agreement (UMA). But if there is a UMA special rules apply which are particularly important when considering unfair dismissal. The circumstances in which the dismissal of a non-unionist might be regarded as fair have been curtailed. The 1980 Act defined three specially protected categories of employees whose dismissal for non-membership of a specified union is unfair: genuine objectors 'on grounds of conscience or other deeply held personal conviction' to membership of any union whatsoever or of a particular union; employees who at the time of the UMA's introduction were not members and who subsequently stay out of membership; and non-members where the UMA took effect after 14 August 1980 without the approval of 80 per cent of those entitled to vote in a secret ballot (although even if the ballot does have this majority, those who remain non-members are still protected). In addition, since most existing UMAs pre-date the 1980 Act, the 1982 statute goes further and makes it unfair to dismiss an employee for non-membership of any or a particular union unless there has been a secret ballot in favour of continuing these existing UMAs. The necessary majority in favour is 80 per cent of those entitled to vote or 85 per cent of those voting. Some rather inadequate guidance on balloting procedures is contained in the Secretary of State's Code of Practice *Closed Shop Agreements and Arrangements,* which is mainly concerned to confine and progressively eliminate closed shops. But in the light of numerous objections raised by the Engineering Employers' Federation and other employers' organisations to balloting on such a large scale (an estimated half of all union members—a quarter of the working population—are employed in closed shops), the government has announced that the requirement to ballot on existing UMAs will not be brought into force until a year or more after the commencement of the 1982 Act.

The architects of the legislation were, however, impervious to other objections, many of which focused on the danger that inter-union conflicts could be exacerbated if individuals were to assert their rights to disorganise on behalf of unions which are neither parties to closed shops nor recognised by the employer. That is also one of the implications of the right, embodied in sections 4 and 5 of the 1980 Act, not to be unreasonably excluded or expelled from a trade union where there is a practice of a UMA. This statutory right, as augmented by the closed shop code, is intended to have a dampening effect on unions' freedom (already circumscribed by the common law) to regulate and discipline their memberships in general and in trade disputes. This potentially cuts across the operation of the TUC's Independent Review Committee and its 'Bridlington' procedure for containing inter-union conflict.[28] Ignoring or perhaps welcoming such possibilities, the government's attitude is symbolised by the retrospective scheme introduced by the 1982 Act giving the Secretary of State discretion to make £2 million worth of ex gratia payments to individuals dismissed for non-membership in a closed shop between 1974 and 1980. This scheme was justified in part by reference to the former railwaymen who successfully appealed to the European Court of Human Rights alleging that their dismissal by British Rail after the introduction of its closed shop contravened the European Convention on Human Rights (Forde, 1982).

Such an individualist legal policy is difficult to reconcile with the realities of collective industrial relations. Research indicates that UMAs normally

---

[28] TUC *Disputes Principles and Procedures,* 1979. In addition to the new statutory rights, Bridlington decisions may be challenged indirectly at common law in actions brought by individuals against affiliated organisations e.g. *Rothwell* v. *APEX* [1976] I.C.R. 211. In 1982 a majority of the Court of Appeal held that where a union had admitted a member in conscious violation of Bridlington it was not entitled to expel him to comply with a decision of a TUC disputes committee: *Cheall* v. *APEX* [1982] I.R.L.R. 362.

develop out of high levels of voluntary membership and contain exceptions for categories such as existing employees. There is, moreover, no general link between the closed shop in its usual post-entry form and restrictive practices or union bargaining power. The closed shop contributes to smooth inter- and intra-union relations and, though it may not significantly reduce unconstitutional strikes, consolidates the whole system of joint regulation. The growth of the formal UMA has been an integral part of the management-initiated reform of industrial relations (Gennard et al. 1979, 1980; Dunn, 1981; Brown, 1981: 54–8).

Reduction of the Immunities

The attack on the legal freedom to take industrial action extends beyond labour law into social security law, where the entitlement of strikers' families to supplementary benefit has been cut (Partington, 1980). The position of individual employees engaged in industrial action is also undermined by an amendment to the principle embodied in EPCA s.62 that, in the case of someone who has been dismissed while on strike, a tribunal may determine the fairness of the dismissal only if there has been victimisation. The 1982 Act makes it more difficult to show victimisation and, even if it can be shown in the form of selective re-engagements, the Act blocks unfair dismissal claims if the industrial action persists for over three months. But the main thrust has been to narrow the TULRA immunities. This has been done with such enthusiasm that in some instances there is serious doubt as to the legal consequences. For example, the 1980 Act repeals TULRA s.13(3) which 'for the avoidance of doubt' declared that an act which by reason of TULRA immunities was itself not actionable or a breach of contract in contemplation or furtherance of a trade dispute would not be regarded as unlawful means or an unlawful act for the purposes of liability in tort. The Court of Appeal and the House of Lords have already taken diametrically opposed views on the meaning of this repeal, which remains one of the mysteries of the 1980 Act.[29] The 1982 Act also repeals TULRA s.13(2) which 'for the avoidance of doubt' restored the historic immunity against liability for interference with a person's freedom to use his capital or labour. Whether or not this tort really exists is debatable (Wedderburn, 1971:358–68; Simpson, 1982; Miller, 1982), but litigation on the point might now ensue. But the main lines of the statutory offensive against industrial action point towards picketing, secondary action, the definition of trade dispute, and the legal liability of trade unions as such.

Picketing has become a progressively more controversial subject over the last two decades (Kahn-Freund, 1977a:261–5). Mass and flying picketing in the strikes by miners and construction workers in 1972 created an atmosphere of public condemnation in which deterrent sentences were

---

[29] *Hadmor Productions Ltd.* v. *Hamilton* [1982] I.C.R. 114; [1982] I.R.L.R. 102.

handed down to the 'Shrewsbury' pickets (Arnison, 1974). This affair was one of the reasons for the Criminal Law Act of 1977, which redefined both the offence of and the immunity for criminal conspiracy and provided that the maximum penalty for conspiracy was the maximum for the substantive offence. Subsequently, secondary picketing during the winter of discontent inspired the 1980 Act's restriction of lawful picketing as defined in TULRA s.15. This provision, which was similar to s.2 of the 1906 Trade Disputes Act, permitted attendance for the purpose only of peacefully obtaining or communicating information or peacefully persuading a person to work or abstain from working, provided it was done in contemplation or furtherance of a trade dispute. Physically stopping persons or vehicles was always unlawful. The effect of s.16 of the 1980 Act is broadly that the only lawful pickets are those who attend at or near their own place of work, or are union officials at or near the place of work of members whom they accompany and represent. 'Own place of work' is not defined, but according to the Secretary of State's Code *Picketing*, 'lawful picketing normally involves attendance at an entrance to or exit from the factory, site or office at which the picket works' (para. 12). All the other entrances within a plant, factory, industrial complex, multi-plant company or multi-national group are out of bounds. The Code advises further that 'in general the number of pickets [should] not exceed six at any entrance to a workplace; frequently a smaller number will be appropriate' (para. 31). It also specifies the functions of the 'picket organiser' who must get his 'directions' from the police and, among other things, 'ensure that employees from other places of work do not join the picket line and that any offers of support on the picket line from outsiders are refused' (para. 34). The Code is, if relevant, taken into account not only by the tribunals but also by the courts, both criminal and civil. As regards civil liabilities, the 1980 Act provides that unlawful picketing is afforded no protection against liability in tort by the immunities in TULRA s.13. Employers in dispute, their customers and suppliers, and perhaps others who are adversely affected may therefore sue for injunctions and damages.

The immediate pretext for the statutory restriction of secondary action was the House of Lords decision in *MacShane's* case.[30] The Lords overruled a line of earlier decisions (in which Lord Denning had played a prominent role) to the effect that where unions inflicted loss on innocent third parties their acts might be so remote from the original dispute as not to be a 'furtherance' of it within the formula 'in contemplation or furtherance of a trade dispute'. According to the majority of Law Lords, the test of furtherance is subjective, that is, a person acts in furtherance of a trade dispute if he honestly and genuinely believes that his actions will further the interests of one of the parties to the dispute. The steel strike of 1980, in which action was taken against private steel producers in support of a wage

---

[30] *Express Newspapers Ltd.* v. *MacShane* [1980] A.C. 672; [1980] I.C.R. 42; [1980] I.R.L.R. 35.

claim to the nationalised British Steel Corporation, led to another appeal to the House of Lords. The subjective test of furtherance was reaffirmed but, as in *MacShane* and the earlier *NWL* case,[31] several of the Law Lords condemned the TULRA immunities as giving the unions a legal licence to bring 'the nation to its knees' by the exercise of 'industrial muscle'.[32] This was the judicial invitation to legislate which the government accepted with alacrity in s.17 of the 1980 Act. The meaning of this exceedingly complex section is far from clear (Wedderburn, 1981; Lewis and Simpson, 1981: 202–9), but in broad outline it removes the immunity provided by TULRA s.13(1) against liability for interfering with commercial contracts where there is secondary action, unless the action is able to pass through a gateway to legality as specified in the statute. Secondary action is defined in terms of interfering with employment contracts where the employer under those contracts is not a party to the trade dispute. The main gateway to legality requires the principal purpose of the action to be directly to prevent or disrupt, during the dispute, the supply (under a contract subsisting at the time of the secondary action) of goods or services between an employer party to the dispute and the employer party to the contracts of employment to which the secondary action relates, and further that the action is 'likely' to achieve that purpose. The difficulties of squeezing through this gateway are already apparent.[33] Where there is secondary action the immunity for interfering with commercial relations, which was first introduced in 1976, has been effectively removed.

The 1982 Act narrows the definition of 'trade dispute' in TULRA s.29(1) and thereby restricts the application of the immunities. The Act requires that a dispute 'relates wholly or mainly to' the list of trade dispute topics in s.29 rather than be merely 'connected with' them as in the original definition. The main aim of this amendment is to expose political strikes to legal liability after the House of Lords ruling in the *NWL* case. The Lords decided that although a purely political strike having no connection with the list of subjects in TULRA s.29 was outside the definition of a trade dispute, so long as there was a genuine connection with the list then a dispute however political came within the definition and therefore within the ambit of lawfulness.[34] However, the Green Paper *Trade Union Immunities* was unenthusiastic about reverting to the 'wholly or mainly' formulation first used in the Industrial Relations Act's definition of 'industrial dispute'. It was concerned that the judges would be placed in an 'invidious' position (para. 191) if they had to undertake the task of separating and measuring the political element in a dispute, given that strikes over terms and conditions frequently involve a political dimension

---

[31] *NWL Ltd.* v. *Woods* [1979] I.C.R. 867; [1979] I.R.L.R. 478.

[32] *Duport Steels Ltd.* v. *Sirs* [1980] I.C.R. 161, 184 (Lord Diplock).

[33] *Marina Shipping Ltd.* v. *Laughton* [1982] I.C.R. 215; [1982] I.R.L.R. 20. See Wedderburn, 1982a.

[34] Cf. *Universe Tankships Inc. of Monrovia* v. *International Transport Workers' Federation* [1982] I.C.R. 262; [1982] I.R.L.R. 200.

especially in the public sector. Also excluded from the definition are disputes 'between workers and workers'. Such disputes were in effect removed from the scope of statutory immunity by the secondary action formulation in s.17 of the 1980 Act, though their explicit removal from the trade dispute definition underlines the legislative policy, which again harks back to the 1971 Act. It is now doubtful (as it was under the Industrial Relations Act) whether employers are legally parties to disputes between unions over recognition, demarcation and recruitment, and disputes between unions and individuals over the maintenance of closed shops.[35] Other amendments narrow the range of international industrial action which may fall within the definition of trade dispute, and confine the parties to a trade dispute to workers and *their* employers. The intention is to limit union solidarity and sympathetic action at a time when employers are increasingly organised on a multi-plant and multinational basis.

Trade unions and employers' associations as such lose their wide immunity from liability in tort (Employment Act 1982 ss.15–17). The restoration of the *Taff Vale* principle exposes trade unions in particular to actions for injunctions and damages. In order to avoid the possibility of bankrupting unions, the Act insulates their provident and political funds from awards of damages and imposes ceilings on awards which vary according to the size of the union. Nevertheless the ceilings, which anyway would not apply to fines for contempt, are quite high: a quarter of a million pounds in each set of proceedings for a union with more than 100,000 members. The removal of this immunity revives a legal policy issue which was of great importance during the currency of the Industrial Relations Act, namely, the 'vicarious' responsibility of unions for the acts of their officials and members. Although two cases turning on this issue were appealed to the House of Lords,[36] 'by the time the 1971 Act was repealed there was considerable uncertainty about when a trade union might or might not be held responsible for the actions of its officials' (*Trade Union Immunities,* para. 116). Difficulties centred on the application of agency law principles to the determination of the scope of shop stewards' authority, which could be derived not only from union rules but also from custom and practice and the facts and circumstances of the case (Hepple 1972; Davies, 1973). Research indicated that rule books tended to provide only minimal guidance on this question (Weekes et al., 1975:98–100), and that even within the same union the relationship between stewards and full-time officers varied greatly, often according to such factors as the structure of management and collective bargaining arrangements (Boraston et al., 1975). Similar problems may reappear under the 1982 Act, though it does attempt to provide express guidance on the authority of full-time officers and committees to which they report. The rationale of vicarious liability was explained in *Trade Union Immunities:* to 'induce

[35] See e.g. *Cory Lighterage Ltd.* v. *TGWU* [1973] I.C.R. 197 and 339.
[36] *Heaton's Transport Ltd.* v. *TGWU* [1973] A.C. 15; [1972] I.C.R. 308; [1972] I.R.L.R. 25; *General Aviation Services Ltd.* v. *TGWU* [1976] I.R.L.R. 214.

unions to reform their structures and rule books and to turn themselves into more authoritarian organisations, reversing the trend towards the increasing authority of the shop steward and power of the working group at the expense of the authority of branch and national officials' (para. 125). However, the assumption that there is or ought to be some kind·of chain of command in trade unions is misconceived for, as the Donovan Commission said, 'trade union leaders do exercise discipline from time to time, but they cannot be industry's policemen. They are democratic leaders in organisations in which the seat of power has almost always been close to the members' (para. 122).

The legislation of 1980 and 1982 invites comparison with the Industrial Relations Act 1971. Under the earlier statute, the legality of industrial action was subject to a comprehensive set of 'unfair industrial practices' administered by a special court. Although the Employment Acts preserve the traditional form of the law of industrial conflict, the legal freedom to strike has been drastically curtailed by the reduction of immunities for those engaged in picketing, secondary action, and acts in support of union- and recognition-only practices, the narrowing of the definition of trade dispute, and the reintroduction of the liabilities of unions as such. Even the basic immunity for inducing breach of employment contract is lost to the picket who attends at the wrong location. The new legal rights for individuals enforceable against employers and unions both in and outside closed shops may also take a different legal form from the Industrial Relations Act's right not to belong, but the policy implications are similar. In fact, the Acts of 1980–82 are in some respects more individualist and restrictive than the 1971 Act. Various provisions on union recognition and arbitration which supported collective industrial relations have been repealed. Even the laws on unfair dismissal (first introduced by the 1971 Act) and maternity, which protect individual employees irrespective of whether they are trade union members, have been eroded as they interfere with the individual employment relation to the supposed detriment of employers (see Chapter 16). At a time when unions are severely weakened by mass unemployment, the legal policy of the present government has the straightforward aim of cutting down still further the organisational strength of trade unions.

CONFLICTING LEGAL POLICIES

The momentum of ultra-restriction has yet to reach its peak. As a prelude to further legislation, the government has promised a consultative paper on mandatory trade union ballots. Apart from the legal requirement to ballot on mergers and on the establishment of political funds, the issue of balloting has traditionally been left to each union to decide for itself in accordance with its rules. The 1980 Act, however, attempted to encourage ballots: s.1 enables the Certification Officer to administer a financial subsidy to unions to cover their expenditure on secret ballots, and s.2 gives a legal right to hold workplace ballots on employers' premises. The financial subsidy is at present confined to postal ballots over the calling and ending of industrial action, wage offers, rules amendments, mergers, and elections for executive committees and full-time officers. The closed shop code states that a union should not take disciplinary action against a member who has refused to participate in industrial action which has 'not been affirmed in a secret ballot' (para. 54). Such disciplinary action could be unreasonable and therefore unlawful by virtue of s.4 of the 1980 Act. There are also the balloting requirements in respect of union membership agreements described above.

The government's favourable view of balloting is based on the individualist assumptions that ballots of members are the best expression of internal union participation and democracy; that there should be no differentiation between those who are active in union affairs and those who rarely, if ever, attend a meeting; and that the minority of union activists and leaders are more militant than the majority of non-active individual members who, in the privacy of a secret ballot, would be inclined to vote for moderate policies and leaders. The general validity of the third point at least may be regarded as extremely doubtful in the light of historical experience (Clegg, 1979:226–7), the arguments in the Donovan Report (paras. 426–30), and the classic example of the railwaymen's ballot under the 1971 Act's national emergency procedures. But more legislation is planned and, furthermore, it may not be confined to ballots. Union political affiliation could be subjected to new legal restrictions and there could also be a narrowing of what is left of the legal freedom to take industrial action. A major strike might stimulate renewed demands for legal limitations on industrial action in breach of procedure agreements, or in the 'essential' and public services, or even for the replacement of the immunities with a system of positive rights and duties which would be applied by the judges.

The strategy of ultra-restriction reflects the breakdown of consensus in the law and politics of industrial relations. The Green Paper *Trade Union Immunities* referred to 'a widespread public feeling' that unions 'have too few obligations and too much power' (para. 12). It is clear that influential groups within the Conservative Party and the business world regard the legislation of 1980 and 1982 as insufficient. But the trade union and labour movement sees it as a massive and intolerable onslaught. The Labour Party is pledged to repeal it and, despite unfavourable conditions in the labour market, the TUC has adopted a policy of opposition and confrontation reminiscent of its campaign against the 1971 Act. The policy involves refusal to accept financial subsidies for ballots, boycott of ballots on union membership agreements, maintenance of Bridlington principles if need be in defiance of the law, withdrawal of union members from the tribunals and the Employment Appeal Tribunal in cases arising from union membership agreements, a special levy for a defence fund, and financial assistance to unions in legal difficulties. But the most militant point is the power vested in the TUC's General Council to coordinate, at the request of a union experiencing litigation, 'action by other affiliated unions in support of the union in difficulties, including, if necessary, calling for industrial action against the employer concerned, or more widely' (TUC, 1982:21). At its 1982 Congress the TUC endorsed a resolution that 'militant resistance to the application of anti-trade union laws, including the use of industrial action, is imperative'.

The prospect of confrontation underlines the need for alternative labour law strategies linked with economic alternatives to monetarism and mass unemployment. An incomes policy designed to reduce unemployment and inflation has become a central feature in the approach of the Alliance of the Liberal and the Social Democratic Parties (SDP, 1982c). The policy could be reinforced by an inflation tax, that is, a tax on wage increases levied on employers in proportion to the increase in their workers' earnings above a prescribed norm (Layard, 1982). The tax would stiffen employers' resistance to wage demands, which might of course lead to industrial conflict. As regards the law of industrial conflict, it would seem that the Alliance is more in favour than against the reduction of the immunities by the Employment Acts of 1980 and 1982. The policy might also be under-pinned by arbitration: where bargainers fail to agree, a national arbitration board or pay commission would make a non-inflationary award to encourage job creation. According to a leading economist identified with the SDP, industrial action in breach of an arbitration award might be deterred by various sanctions: supplementary benefits to strikers' families would take the form of loans, tax refunds would not be paid until the end of a strike, strikers would be regarded as having terminated their contracts of employment, the TULRA immunities for persons organising the action would be lost, and unions as such would be legally liable for official action (Meade, 1982:115–17). Moreover, the Alliance is favourably disposed towards works councils and other forms of industrial participation apart from the single channel of trade union representation, and towards various systems of secret balloting on such issues as the election of officials, strikes and political affiliation (SDP, 1982 a, b). Alliance pressure was largely responsible for the section in the 1982 Employment Act which inserts certain aspects of employee involvement into the subject matter of directors' reports under the Companies Acts.

A different strategy is advocated by the TUC-Labour Party Liaison Committee in a document entitled *Economic Planning and Industrial Democracy: The Framework for Full Employment* (1982). This argues that full employment, industrial revival, and social justice could be achieved through a comprehensive system of economic planning explicitly linked to the development of industrial democracy through trade union representation. An Economic Planning and Industrial Democracy Act would be introduced to strengthen the machinery of state economic planning and provide for new positive legal rights for unions and their active members.

The laws buttressing workplace organisation would be strengthened, employers would be placed under legal duties to disclose information and consult with recognised unions over the whole range of corporate strategy, and 'joint union committees' would have representational rights at all levels of the enterprise up to and including the board. These principles would apply without exception to multinational corporations, and this would facilitate the full application of the various international attempts at codes of conduct for multinationals. The projected Act would also involve the reform of company law and its integration with the legal framework of employment rights and economic planning, something that was not attempted at the time of the 1975 Industry Act and the Employment Protection Act. This ambitious programme builds on the more radical ideas developed within the labour movement in the aftermath of the Social Contract and the Bullock Report. It is, however, a left-wing variant of the strategy of reform. Industrial democracy is desirable not only for its own sake but for the sake of achieving better economic performance. The unions are to have responsibilities as well as rights, and a proposed 'national economic assessment' could be interpreted as involving an understanding on pay, though some unions have indicated that they would not support that interpretation. But the fundamental question for this type of strategy is whether it could succeed in the face of determined opposition from those who control industrial and finance capital.

Against a background of continuous economic crises, successive governments representing different interests and ideologies have turned the legal framework of industrial relations into a political football. However, it would perhaps be mistaken even now to underestimate the residual capacity in British society for compromise or at least acquiescence. Managers and trade unionists are becoming weary of frequent and bewildering changes. The chairman of ACAS was surely expressing a general sentiment when in April 1981 he told the Secretary of State that legal changes 'are bound to be disruptive if they are made too frequently or if they do not command a wide measure of agreement in industry' (ACAS, 1982:64). Unfortunately 'a wide measure of agreement' is unlikely since the conflicts in society as a whole are reflected in industrial relations. There would seem to be little prospect for long-term stability in this field. The consensus and supposed equilibrium of social forces which once sustained collective laissez-faire have vanished.

16 Individual Labour Law

Bob Hepple

THE INDIVIDUALIST TRADITION

Expansion of Individual Rights

The language and philosophy of individual legal rights have become increasingly pervasive in British industrial relations. This has been one of the most significant developments of the years since the mid-1960s. One indication of the trend is the sheer volume of legislation, much of it conferring rights upon employees. Compared with some five general Acts of Parliament regulating employment passed from 1950 to 1959, and sixteen from 1960 to 1969, there were thirty from 1970 to 1979 and a further eight from 1980 to 1982. To these must be added dozens of statutes applying to specific sectors of employment and hundreds of supporting pieces of delegated legislation made by ministers and others. Another indication is the growth of case law. Most of the new legal rights are enforced through the industrial tribunals which were first set up in 1964 (Hepple and O'Higgins, 1981:362) to hear appeals against industrial training levies and since then have gradually acquired over thirty other statutory jurisdictions. The most important of these is in respect of the right not to be unfairly dismissed. In 1971, before the Industrial Relations Act had introduced this right, there were 6,641 applications to the tribunals. By 1976 the number had risen to 43,066. In 1981, despite the removal of several million workers from the coverage of the legislation by measures of the Conservative Government,[1] there were 40,042 applications. To some extent the high figure is a reflection of the growing number of redundancies, but there are no signs of a change in the underlying trend towards the juridification of individual disputes.

The characteristic features of these rights are that they are legal and that they belong to individuals rather than to collective groups. When employers claim the 'right to manage' or workers demand the 'right to work' or the 'right to job security' they are usually asserting social rights

---

[1] Unfair Dismissal (Variation of Qualifying Period) Order 1979, S.I. 1979 No. 959 (qualifying period for complaints of unfair dismissal raised from 6 months to one year from 1 October 1979); Employment Act 1980 (hereafter EA 1980), s.8(1) (extended qualifying period of two years where 20 or fewer employees).

which they expect to be settled by collective bargaining or achieved by the policies of governments. But legal rights can, in the event of violation, 'be enforced by some compulsory mechanism provided by the state' (Kahn-Freund, 1954b:43). Legal sanctions may be criminal (e.g. fines or imprisonment), or civil (e.g. an award of compensation), or administrative (e.g. withdrawal of a licence or subsidy by government). Unlike the autonomous sanctions of the strike and lockout, these legal sanctions involve the active participation of the state for their enforcement. The individual nature of most of the legal rights in the British system means that, even where collective bargaining is well-established, individual workers are free to assert and enforce their rights without the assistance of a trade union or, what is more, even against its wishes.

The implications of the growth of rights of this kind are enormous. Matters which were once entirely within the sphere of managerial prerogatives, or left to collective bargaining, are now directly regulated by positive legal rights and duties. For example, in 1963, an astute American observer (Meyers, 1964:28) found that discipline was regarded by British employers as a managerial prerogative and he commented: 'surprisingly to the American observer, with the exception of victimisation for union activity, this attitude . . . was generally shared by union officials.' He found that unofficial strikes by groups of workers were a common method of securing reinstatement for dismissed workers. Indeed, some 20 per cent of all strikes in Britain in 1960 were in protest against disciplinary dismissals, and in the period 1964–6 an average of 267 unofficial strikes took place over dismissals each year and 203 of these arose out of dismissals other than redundancies (Donovan, 1968: para. 528). The Donovan Commission argued 'that the right to secure a speedy and impartial decision on the justification for a dismissal might have averted many of these stoppages'. Since the introduction of unfair dismissals legislation there does seem to have been some decline in the number of working days lost due to strikes over dismissal and there has been a decline in the proportion of all strikes attributable to disputes over dismissals, but it would be unsafe to draw any firm conclusion from these statistics because so many factors other than legislation influenced the strike wave of the 1970s (Sweet and Jackson, 1977:35).

What can be said with confidence is that legislation and codes of practice have given a tremendous stimulus to the introduction of individual grievance and disciplinary procedures, which 'are now part of the normal fabric of industrial relations in manufacturing industry' (Brown, 1981:41). The professionalisation of industrial relations management has been a direct response to the new demand for an expert grasp of the complexities of legislation and case law. This has not, however, been matched on the trade union side. Although trade union legal services have grown, and officials undoubtedly spend more time than before exploiting specific statutory rights for the benefit of members, it is significant that only about 16 per cent of applicants are represented at industrial tribunal hearings by trade union officials. The field has largely been left to barristers and solicitors: according to statistics collected in 1980, 35 per cent of employees and 51 per cent of employers are legally represented at hearings (COIT, 1981), and a study by Hawes and G. Smith (1981:16–21) indicated that such representation is also increasingly common at the conciliation stage.

Critical Issues

This intrusion of the legal profession has been explained as an inevitable byproduct of the creation of a statutory system of tribunals with a hierarchy of appeals on points of law under complex legislation (Munday, 1981:146). This is certainly not what the Donovan Commission (1968: para. 572) foresaw when it advocated the development of 'labour tribunals' as an 'easily accessible, speedy and inexpensive' means of resolving individual disputes where voluntary machinery did not exist, although earlier, in a perceptive report, a committee of the National Joint Advisory Council of the Ministry of Labour (1967:47) had recognised that statutory machinery 'might have the effect of importing a legalistic element into industrial relations in the place of work'.

The same Ministry of Labour committee (1967:47) arguing against the early introduction of legislation on unfair dismissals feared that statutory machinery 'could lessen the incentive to develop satisfactory voluntary procedures, both internal and external, where these do not already exist'. In practice, most of the grievance and disciplinary procedures which have been introduced under the influence of the legislation have been management-inspired and designed, and only in relatively few establishments has this involved any extension of joint participation. This perspective of legislation and codes of practice as a means of improving personnel management (Ashdown and Baker, 1973) has been reinforced by the conservative tendency of formalised procedures to act as a brake upon informal shop floor pressures (Mellish and Collis-Squires, 1976:167). Trade unions have generally seen individual employment legislation, in Wedderburn's classic phrase (1971:8,16; 1980:83), as a 'floor of rights' and 'a set of norms already achieved by collective bargaining'. As such they have mainly been relevant in the absence of collective bargaining. It is debatable whether trade unions have generally been willing to use these rights to protect trade union members in a relatively weak bargaining position. As indicated later, the design of the legislation is an expressed preference for collective bargaining, and the content of the statutory rights is generally below that of the best results of collective bargaining from the workers' viewpoint. The General Secretary of the TUC said in 1980:

> there can be no doubt that because of the law, unions are now able to offer better services in some respects to members in small and dispersed groups on whose behalf it had proved difficult to negotiate collectively. At the end of the day they can represent their members in cases before industrial tribunals and perhaps win compensation where previously they could, in practice, do

nothing. In short our view is that the industrial tribunal system has been valuable insofar as it has provided workers with some protection against abuse in areas where trade union organisation is non-existent or ineffective.[2]

However in comparison with a country such as Sweden, where individual rights are more extensively defined than in Britain, trade unions have shown relatively little willingness to use a combination of individual rights and collective procedures (Anderman, 1981:198).

Underlying trade union ambivalence about these rights is the feeling, expressed by Mellish and Collis-Squires (1976:167) 'firstly that individuals do not get—in the tribunal machinery—a sort of legal substitute for collective bargaining and, secondly, that the principles enumerated by tribunals are not always seen as appropriate in collective bargaining situations'. From this perspective, 'law which promotes collective bargaining directly may improve individual rights in employment more than law which gives employees individual rights against the employer'. An even more radical critique (Fryer, 1973a:1; 1973b) sees the treatment as individual rights of issues such as redundancy, discipline, and dismissal as weakening workers' protective attitudes by putting a monetary price on their jobs which many are willing to accept rather than engage in defensive collective action.

The criticisms of the expansion of individual rights most frequently heard from the employers' side are that these rights discourage recruitment, especially in small businesses, and that they actually prevent the creation of jobs by employers. The empirical evidence—such as a study commissioned by the Department of Employment (Daniel and Stilgoe, 1978) and another by Department of Employment staff (Clifton and Tatton-Brown, 1979)—does not support this view and indicates that only a relatively insignificant number of small employers regard employment legislation as a factor inhibiting recruitment.

Indeed legislation is often more of a symbolic focus for emerging ideological and political conflicts than an expression of rational cost-benefit preferences. For example, in his study of the impact of the legislation giving women the right to return to work after pregnancy and confinement, Daniel (1981b:74) found that there had been no general impact upon the rates of return to work, nor had there been any great burden on employers in the first three years' operation; instead the issues had been symbolic ones of principle. The right of reinstatement symbolises trade union power and the decline of property rights as a basis of managerial prerogatives. It also symbolises official approval of women returning to work after childbearing. In earlier generations the factories legislation provided a similar focus for emerging interests and values. Marx and Engels (1848:76) hailed the Ten Hours Act as 'a legislative recognition of particular interests of the workers, by taking advantage of the divisions among the bourgeoisie

---

[2] Trades Union Congress, transcript of speech by Lionel Murray C.B.E., Birmingham, April 1980.

itself'. At the same time many of the larger employers were anxious to show their own humanitarian concern to eradicate a minority of employers who abused child and female labour. This served to legitimise the new factory system and, in the course of time, to remove the stigma attaching to the profit-orientated activities which endangered life and limb (Carson, 1974:121; 1979:37; 1980:187; cf. Bartrip and Fenn, 1980:175).

In order to understand and evaluate these issues of legalism, of the relationship between individual rights and collective bargaining, and of the general nature and impact of protective legislation, it is necessary first to deal with a conceptual issue. Why is the notion of the individual contract of employment central to the legal analysis of industrial relations and what are the implications of this? This question is discussed in the remainder of this section. In the second section of this chapter the functions of aspects of the legislation are considered. The final section returns to the general issues and looks ahead to possible future trends.

Contract of Employment

The fragmentation of industrial relations into millions of individual relationships is not an accidental or modern phenomenon. It is deeply rooted in social and legal tradition. The lawyer's reinterpretation of the reality of industrial relations is through the model of the individual contract of employment. This is, in Wedderburn's words (1971:51), 'the fundamental institution to which he is forced to return again and again'. It is the 'cornerstone of the edifice of labour law' (Kahn-Freund, 1954b:45), because it is an indispensable tool of thought for distinguishing the purposive exchange, of a promise to work or to be available for work in return for a promise of wages, from the older forms of status relationship. It presupposes an element of freedom of choice to enter into or terminate the relationship which is incompatible with compulsory labour (Kahn-Freund, 1959:31; 1967:635).

This conception of the reciprocal rights and duties of the parties flowing from their free exchange of promises arrived relatively late on the legal scene in Britain (Kahn-Freund, 1977b:508) in comparison with the continental countries influenced by Roman law. The reason was the tradition of the Statute of Labourers passed by Edward III in 1351, following an Ordinance of 1349, later reinforced by the Elizabethan Statute of Artificers of 1563, and the tradition of the Poor Law Act 1601. Under these laws the 'servant's' status determined the obligation to work at wages arbitrarily fixed by justices of the peace, usually themselves masters. Servants were liable to punishment for not accepting the work, for not doing it according to directions, or for deserting the master. As late as 1850 Blackstone's definition of the master-servant relationship was still in vogue among lawyers, and, according to that definition the relationship need not be based on contract: for example, a labourer could be compelled to serve by justices of the peace; a parish apprentice indentured under the

Poor Law had to serve a master with whom he had no contract; and the mere condition of 'having no visible effects' could give rise to a direction to compulsory work (Kahn-Freund, 1977b:511). The sanctions were criminal. When the Elizabethan Statute fell into disuse, the legal basis for prosecutions against workers were the nineteenth-century Master and Servant Acts.

It was the trade unions which were largely responsible for the modification and repeal of these penals laws by the Master and Servant Act 1867 and the Conspiracy and Protection of Property Act 1875 respectively. Trade union agitation arose primarily because of the effect of the laws on the freedom to strike: 'it was a recognised tactic of the employers, particularly in dealing with smaller strikes, to cause all the strikers to be arrested for breach of contract and then to confront them with the alternatives of returning to work on the employer's terms or suffering up to 3 months' imprisonment. Furthermore, as the law stood, a troublemaker might be silenced not just once but repeatedly' (Bagwell, 1974:30). Between 1858 and 1875 an average of 10,000 prosecutions of workmen for breach of contract took place each year in England and Wales (Simon, 1954:160).

The repeal of the Master and Servant Acts removed a major impediment to the development of the notion of freedom of contract between equal contracting parties protected by civil sanctions alone. However, the intellectual backwardness of the legal analysis of 'master and servant' relationships has had a lasting impact on the modern law. One consequence has been the patchy and inadequate coverage of labour law. The old law determined rights and obligations not according to the kind of contract under which persons were employed, but by the nature of their work, for example, as a 'servant in husbandry', an 'artificer' or 'labourer'. As new employments developed in the course of the industrial revolution, the courts struggled to develop a general notion of a 'contract of service'. In the twentieth century the master's power of command, and the servant's subordination, became a test. After 1950 the emphasis on the command power of the master was increasingly criticised in its application to modern relationships between managers, who themselves have a contract of service with their corporate employer, and skilled employees, but despite the emergence of more flexible and pragmatic tests, the employer's power of 'control' is still regarded as a necessary, even if insufficient, hallmark of a contract of service. There is no uniform or consistent judicial definition of a contract of service, and legislation is often confined to specific employments (e.g. merchant seamen, teachers, agricultural workers) or to certain types of contract of service, with complex exclusions in particular statutes of different categories such as some part-time workers, casuals and domestic servants in private households. Moreover, quite apart from the nearly two million persons classified as 'self-employed', and hence outside the scope of labour law, there are many who in reality fall within the category of dependent labour, such as civil servants and those on the 'lump' in the building industry, who are not always regarded as working under contracts of service. There is ample scope for avoidance of labour legislation.

Another consequence of the late development of the legal concept of the contract of employment is the inordinate complexity of labour law. The bulk of labour legislation has developed outside the frame of the contract of employment. This 'atrophy' of the contract of employment, as Kahn-Freund called it (1977b:524), is largely attributable to the absence of an explicit and flexible contract model in the formative period of individual labour law. For example, the Truck Acts—the principal Act of 1831, as amended, is still in force—which make the employer liable to pay wages in cash and without deductions, do not operate on the contract but create a statutory obligation outside the contract and are currently enforceable by the small Wages Inspectorate through the criminal courts; small wonder that prosecutions are extremely rare and the law is widely disregarded in practice. A breach of an employer's statutory safety duties may be the subject of criminal prosection, or administrative enforcement (e.g. an improvement or prohibition notice served by the Health and Safety Executive) under the Health and Safety at Work Act 1974 or, in some cases, a civil action for damages by an injured employee in tort (i.e. a civil wrong other than breach of contract) but not in contract. The practical effect of this can be seen in the case of *Davie* v. *New Merton Board Mills Ltd.*[3] in which the House of Lords decided that an employer who supplies a defective tool to an employee, who is injured as a result, discharges his duty of care in tort so long as the supplier from whom the employer obtained the tool was reputable. Had the duty been classified as arising in contract, the employer would have been liable for breach of a warranty that the tool was safe. It was necessary for Parliament to provide the injured worker with a remedy by the Employer's Liability (Defective Equipment) Act 1969.

Although some recent legislation (e.g. the Equal Pay Act 1970) expressly provides that the duties they impose are to take effect as terms of the individual contract, others create rights which are distinct from the contractual ones with the result that there have to be complex provisions either for the set-off of amounts awarded under the statute against amounts due under the contract or vice versa, or for the creation of 'composite' rights enabling the employee to claim those features of the contractual and statutory rights which are most favourable (e.g. the complex provisions of EPCA s.16, regarding guarantee payments). Some statutes are silent on the relationship with the contract of employment, thus leaving the courts and tribunals free to decide whether or not the rights arise under the contract, sometimes with the result that the employee is deprived of statutory protection (e.g the protection against unfair dismissal is lost if the contract is illegal because of an agreement to defraud the Revenue of PAYE tax).

The most important consequence of the heritage of ideas evolved over

---

[3] [1959] A.C. 604.

centuries under the influence of the Statute of Labourers, the Statute of Artificers, and the Poor Law is that the form of contract which emerged in the nineteenth century effectively guaranteed the rule-making power of the employer. When the worker at the factory gate accepts an offer of employment, neither he nor the employer may be conscious that they have concluded a binding contract of service. In law they have done so although nothing was said about wages or hours of work, let alone such matters as holidays, sick pay, pensions or what is to happen if there is a stoppage of work due to a power failure. If there is no legislation in point, and no express agreement, it is left to the courts and tribunals to make sense of the contract by implying terms as to these matters. As indicated later, where there is collective bargaining the courts may be prepared to fill in the gaps by incorporating the relevant terms of the collective agreement as implied terms of the individual contract. The great success of collective bargaining in many industries has meant that the courts have rarely been called upon to imply terms. In reality, where there is no collective agreement or arbitration award or legislation, the superior economic power of employers enables them to dictate the terms of the contract which the individual employees are in no position to contest through the courts, least of all when they are still working for the employer. It is this fact upon which the Austrian and German sociologists of law seized when they tried to expose the function of the contract of employment as a support for the property rights of the capitalist employer (Renner, 1949:105) and as a fiction which reinforces the employer's domination and the worker's subordination (Sinzheimer, 1927). Kahn-Freund (1977a:7) synthesised these ideas in his characterisation of the contract of employment, in both capitalist and non-capitalist forms of society, as a power relationship of command and subordination. From this pluralist perspective, labour law is seen as a means either of supporting or limiting the employer's power of command.

These universal features of the contract of employment acquired particular features in English common law. The law of contract was developed by the courts, and the principal conceptual instrument they use to fill the gaps left by the parties is the implied intention of the parties. In a few extreme cases (such as contracts in restraint of trade) public policy is used to nullify a contract, but never to mould it. This means that the idea of positive legal regulation of the contract by imperative norms is alien to the common law approach: parties are even free to 'contract out' of protective legislation unless and until Parliament says they cannot do so. This is quite different from the continental legal systems which for two centuries have applied general imperative norms to all contracts and special norms to the contract of employment. Moreover, when British judges have sought to imply terms they have relied heavily on custom and practice. The task of discovering the custom is greatly simplified, as indicated later, when there is a collective agreement. Where none exists everyday obligations, such as the speed of work, the conditions of labour, and the subjection to discipline, are implied from what the parties do in practice, and that means in effect what the employer has laid down and applied in works rules, even informally. Some obligations, such as fidelity, the maintenance of mutual trust and confidence, and obedience to the employer's reasonable commands, are regarded as fundamental. They are implied as a matter of law from judicial precedents which have been influenced from the traditions of the law of 'master and servant'. The judicial perspective, even in recent times, has been unitary rather than pluralist, although under the impact of modern legislation there are signs of change (Napier, 1977:1).

Collective Bargaining and the Individual

The way in which the law has developed has given it the three features that have been described: patchy and inadequate coverage, inordinate complexity, and, above all, an almost infinite capacity to support the rule-making power of the employer. On the face of things the legal model of the contract of employment also conflicts with reality because the main terms and conditions of over two-thirds of the working population are resolved not by individual bargaining but by collective bargaining between employers and trade unions. The legal model has its roots in a conception of society before collective bargaining had helped to redress the economic inequality between the employer and individual worker.

The logical counterpart of a system of collective bargaining is the complete replacement of the individual contract by a collective contract enforceable between the collective parties. This is the solution adopted, for example, in the United States where if employment is in a unit that has a collective bargaining representative, the contract of employment 'does little more than establish that the worker will work for the enterprise and, perhaps, the initial job classification assigned to the worker' (Goldman, 1979:43). Everything else will probably be governed by the collective agreement. This solution is not without its problems, however, because individuals who are in opposition to the majority union, or otherwise vulnerable because they belong to an ethnic, political or other minority, are exposed to unfavourable discrimination by the union which is designated as bargaining agent for that unit. Labour law in the United States has struggled to provide protection for the individual through devices such as the duty of the union fairly to represent all members of the bargaining unit, and the right of the individual in some circumstances to enforce a collective agreement if the union unfairly declines to do so.

This is not the way in which British labour law has dealt with the problem. For reasons discussed above in Chapter 15, collective agreements are generally not regarded as legally enforceable between the collective parties. However these agreements are clearly intended to have a kind of legislative function, laying down the terms and conditions of employment of individuals covered by the agreement. In giving effect to that function the very source of weakness of the common law as a means of protecting the worker has proved to be its strength. By use of the flexible technique of implying terms the judges have been able, since as early as the mid-nineteenth century, to incorporate relevant parts of collective agreements into individual contracts while leaving individuals free, in theory, to negotiate and enforce their own contracts. The British approach differs from that in the United States because the collective agreement does not provide all the terms, and from that in most European countries, because the collective agreement does not provide compulsory minimum terms. In theory individual employer and employee are free to contract for less advantageous terms than those of the collective agreement; in practice they are more likely to contract for better terms.

The link between collective regulation and the individual contract is not an automatic one (Hepple and O'Higgins, 1981:124–31). The mere fact that a trade union is described as the 'agent' or 'representative' of its members does not generally make the agreements it negotiates binding so far as those members are concerned. Conversely, the fact that certain employees are not members of the bargaining union does not prevent the agreement from applying to them: in practice, agreements usually apply to members and non-members alike. The incorporation may be by an express provision to this effect in the individual contract. Proof of this has been facilitated since 1963 by legislation (currently EPCA s.2(3)) which requires the employer to give a written statement of employment terms to each employee which may include a reference to a 'document' where such terms can be seen, but this does not mean that the employer, either with or without the union's concurrence, can alter the terms of the contract of employment by referring to a collective agreement if the employee has not agreed to its incorporation. More frequently, since the parties are unlikely to have expressly agreed, the incorporation will be by way of implying the 'usual' or 'customary' terms, and a collective agreement may be regarded as 'crystallised custom'.

The two main problems which arise with the implied term technique are those of bridging the gap between the collective agreement and the individual contract, and the translation of terms of the collective agreement into terms appropriate to the individual contract. The courts have not always recognised or dealt satisfactorily with these problems. The answer to the bridging problem should have nothing to do with the issue of legal enforceability between the collective parties because the legislative function of the collective agreement is quite distinct from its contractual (or 'peace-treaty') function, but sometimes the courts have confused the functions and refused to imply a term from a 'gentlemen's agreement'. Such decisions are regarded in the academic literature as erroneous (Hepple and O'Higgins, 1981:124–33). The bridge depends, above all, upon the way in which the court formulates the term to be implied. For example, if the courts ask 'Did the employee agree to work on the terms of any collective agreement as altered from time to time?' the employee's knowledge of the detailed terms of the agreement will be irrelevant, but the employee would need to know that there was an agreement of some kind. On the other hand if the question is 'Did the employee agree to work on the usual terms?' then the agreement may be binding even though the employee is ignorant of its very existence.

The translation question raises the issue as to which terms of the collective agreement are appropriate in the case of an individual. For example, the collective agreement may confer rights on a person other than the individual party to the contract of employment in question. Mary Smith, a machinist, even if she is a shop steward, cannot legally enforce a term in a collective agreement that the non-machinists in her plant will be paid £x per week. She can enforce only her own right to be paid the machinist's wage of £y. The collective agreement may impose obligations on someone who is not party to the individual contract, such as an employers' association, and this cannot be enforced as part of the individual contract either. The agreement may also contain terms which are essentially collective in nature: in particular, collective disputes procedures. It would be highly unusual to regard these as appropriate for individual incorporation. In one situation, that of 'peace' obligations in collective agreements, judicial doubts led Parliament, in section 18(4) of the Trade Union and Labour Relations Act 1974 (TULRA), to provide that terms of a collective agreement which prohibit or restrict the right of workers to engage in a strike or other industrial action shall not form part of an individual contract unless a number of stringent conditions are met.

What has been said about the incorporation of collective agreements also applies generally to the incorporation of awards under voluntary arbitration. Where the Central Arbitration Committee (CAC) makes an award following the failure of an employer to provide information for bargaining to a recognised union, this becomes, by virtue of EPA s.21, a compulsory term of the individual contracts of employees to whom they apply and can be replaced only by a subsequent award or collective agreement or a more favourable individual contract.

The discrepancy between the actual state of affairs in a largely voluntarist collective bargaining system and the legal model has thus been reconciled by use of a common law technique. Since the common law is the product of judicial decisions this has strengthened the rule-making power of judges. So long as the system remained essentially voluntarist this did not matter much because workers, either as individuals or with the support of their unions, very rarely resorted to the courts and, with few exceptions, it was not the practice of employers to do so. The common law model survived the protective legislation of the nineteenth and early twentieth centuries because, as indicated later, the legislation largely operated extra-contractually and much of its enforcement depended upon inspectorates rather than upon civil proceedings by individuals. However, the fundamental weaknesses of that model have been exposed when subjected to the demands of the new employment protection legislation since the mid-1960s. Before exploring this view the nature of the regulatory legislation must be examined.

REGULATORY LEGISLATION

Auxiliary and Regulatory Legislation Distinguished

The legislation discussed in this section is called regulatory because it directly lays down rules of employment on matters such as wages, hours, safety, and termination of the contract. It is used to restrict the power of management and applies irrespective of whether or not the workers are organised. The policy of the law in this and the previous century has been not to regulate by statute the terms of employment of those who are considered capable of protecting themselves. The nineteenth-century factories legislation applied primarily to women and children and not to adult men. In the twentieth century, the principle has been to cover by direct regulation only those who are not protected by collective bargaining and to deal only with those subjects which do not appear to lend themselves to collective bargaining. Even where there is regulatory legislation, it has often been designed to allow for its replacement by approved collective agreements which are at least as good in content as the regulatory legislation. In any event, legislation can always be supplemented by collective bargaining on the same subject.

The primacy of voluntary collective bargaining has meant that regulatory legislation has tended to take second place to other legislation which is auxiliary to collective bargaining, that is which is used to promote negotiation, agreement and observance of agreements (as discussed in Chapter 15). The content of the regulatory legislation and the sanctions by which it is enforced, as well as its importance relative to collective bargaining, has changed and is still changing.

Three 'layers' or 'models' of legislation (Kahn-Freund, 1977a:24) may be distinguished. The first, and earliest, although some of the specific statutes are of recent vintage, is that of the nineteenth century, mainly concerned with the hours and welfare of women, young persons, and children, with safety at work, and also with the method of wage payment and the calculation of wages. The second model is the early twentieth-century minimum wage legislation, now consolidated in the Wages Councils Act 1979 and the Agricultural Wages Act 1948 and Agricultural Wages (Scotland) Act 1949. This legislation is discussed in Chapter 8; here it need be noted only that although the terms of orders by Wages Councils and Agricultural Wages Boards are compulsorily implied in the relevant contracts of employment and can be enforced by individuals in the civil courts, the more important legal sanction is that a wages inspector can enforce the contract on behalf of the worker by obtaining an order for the payment of up to two years' arrears of wages. The third model is that of the late twentieth century concerning job and income security, and discrimination on grounds of sex and race. Discrimination is considered in Chapter 13; here it is observed that the Equal Pay Act 1970, the Sex Discrimination

Act 1975, and the Race Relations Act 1976 rely heavily on individual enforcement through industrial tribunals.

Factories Acts Model

Writing in 1882 Jevons took the view that there were no principles of industrial legislation—'legislation must proceed on the grounds of experience, legislation must be Baconian' (cited by Tillyard, 1936:16). That view was shared by many early twentieth-century writers, such as Sidney Webb (1926:ix) who described a 'century of experiment in factory legislation' as a 'typical example of English practical empiricism'. The implication that there was some kind of process of 'trial and error' is now generally regarded as mistaken (Kahn-Freund, 1977a:33; Wedderburn, 1971:238). Instead, it is in the ebb and flow of struggle by unions and reform groups inside and outside Parliament, and the resistance by powerful groups of employers and the intellectual supporters of laissez-faire that the key must be found to the patchy character of the still influential protective legislation which began with the Regulation of Chimney Sweepers Act of 1788 and the Health and Morals of Apprentices Act of 1802.

The initial aim of the short-time committees from 1831 onwards was the ten-hour day for all employees, regardless of sex or age, but after 1840 the committees modified their aims to concentrate on the hours of work of adult women. There were many reasons for this important change of strategy. The political reality of the time meant that the main aim was not achievable. Moreover male trade unionists saw their skilled jobs threatened by technical advances, such as the 'self-acting mule', and increasingly took defensive positions against the employment of semi-skilled and unskilled women, as is reflected in the demands of some short-time committees for the withdrawal of women from factories. A new conception was emerging of man as the breadwinner and wife as the child rearer also undertaking temporary unskilled work to supplement family earnings, and the position of working women was being seen by the Victorian middle classes as a 'social problem' worthy of their concern (Creighton, 1979:19).

The opposition to reform came from some industrialists and the political devotees of laissez-faire. They argued that the evils were exaggerated, that protective legislation was an unwarranted interference with the freedom to trade, and that British industry would be exposed to unfair competition from foreign firms who had no such restrictions upon them. In the 1850s the Women's Rights Opposition also opposed the legislation as a threat to women's employment. Against this the early socialists argued that legislation was needed because women were far too weak economically and socially to achieve change through trade unions alone. A similar debate can be heard today on the issue of whether the special protection for women should be removed (Equal Opportunities Commission, 1979).

The first major victory for the short-time committees was the Factories

Act of 1844, which equated women with young persons and restricted their hours, and required dangerous parts of machinery to be fenced, as well as strengthening the powers of the inspectorate which had been established by the Factories Act of 1833. The opportunities for evasion were many and some loopholes were closed in seven Acts passed between 1844 and 1856. Most important of all was the 'Ten Hours Act' of 1847 which conceded the main demand of the short-time committees.

In the second half of the nineteenth century this legislation, which applied only to textile factories, was gradually extended to cover factories and workshops over a wide range of old and new manufacturing industries. There were overlapping and sometimes contradictory Acts applying to different types and sizes of establishment, which led to a consolidating Act in 1878. This ended the division between larger and smaller establishments and gave a general definition of 'factory' premises which has survived, with few changes, into modern legislation. The history of the legislation after 1878 is one of alterations of detail and periodic consolidation, with the principles established by this legislation being retained, currently in the Factories Act 1961. The tendency towards minute regulation of particular manufacturing processes was accentuated by the power which has been given to ministers since 1891 to do this by delegated legislation. At different times, activities outside manufacturing industry were also regulated: mines from 1842 (but with effective inspection only from 1860), shops from 1886 (although the health and safety aspects of shop work remained largely outside statutory control until the enactment of the Offices, Shops, and Railway Premises Act 1963). It was not until 1956 that standards comparable to factory legislation were extended to agriculture.

Surveying the scene in 1972, an official committee of inquiry under the Chairmanship of Lord Robens found that there were nine main groups of statutes controlling different industrial activities and these were supported by over 500 subordinate statutory instruments. These contained a mass of intricate and ill-assorted detail. They showed neither internal logic nor consistency and were far from comprehensive. Some five million of the twenty-three million workers in Britain were employed in premises not subject to any occupational health or safety legislation. A result of the recommendations of the Committee was the comprehensive Health and Safety at Work Act 1974, in force from 1975. The existing legislation relating to health, safety, and welfare is very slowly being replaced by this new comprehensive system.

The basic philosophy of the new system is self-regulation. The Robens Report stated: 'our present system encourages rather too much reliance on state regulation, and rather too little on personal responsibility and voluntary, self-generating effort' (Robens, 1972: para.28). One avenue towards this has been the Safety Representatives and Safety Committees Regulations 1977 (in force since 1978) which give recognised trade unions the power to appoint safety representatives who have the right to request the creation of safety committees. Another avenue has been the emphasis on the responsibility of line management for the health and safety of those under their supervision, as well as the stress on individual responsibility (Dawson et al., 1981a, 1981b; Codrington and Henley, 1981).

Despite this very important shift of emphasis towards self-regulation in health and safety matters, it would be a mistake to regard this primarily as an extension of collective bargaining in place of statutory regulation. The Robens view (1972: para.66) was that there was a 'greater natural identity of interests between "the two sides" in relation to safety and health problems than in most other matters' and the legislation is based on the concept of consultation rather than bargaining over such matters. The legislation does not rely only on autonomous sanctions but offers safety representatives externally enforceable rights, for example the right of complaint to an industrial tribunal regarding failure by an employer to allow time off for carrying out duties as a representative. Moreover, self-regulation takes place in a framework of strengthened state inspection and enforcement. The various inspectorates were brought together under the policy direction of the Health and Safety Commission and the administration of the Health and Safety Executive. Inspectors were given increased enforcement powers, including the flexible preventive measures of improvement notices, requiring specific changes in workplace practices, and prohibition notices barring the use of hazardous plant or premises. The 1974 Act continues the nineteenth-century pattern of imposing positive legal obligations on the employer to observe certain minimum standards, but it does so more comprehensively than before, placing general duties of affirmative action (including training and supervision) and also obliges others such as designers, manufacturers, and suppliers of equipment to control hazards at their source. The legal obligations are still central. At best, the incentive given by the Act and regulations towards more efficient management and worker participation, express a hope that apathy about safety can be overcome. But it remains an open question whether this kind of incentive will prove to be an appropriate model for the improvement of health and safety standards in poorly unionised industries and small or medium-sized establishments.

The nineteenth-century legacy of common law and legislation continues to dominate the area of health, safety, and welfare. There is a close link between the health and safety legislation and the question of compensation for industrial injuries, another area in which individual legal enforcement maintains a powerful hold (Robens, 1972:app.7; Pearson, 1978: ch.17). Relics may be found in other fields as well, such as the Truck legislation; despite many pleas for reform Britain is almost unique in having no comprehensive legislation on the methods of payment of wages. But perhaps the most important consequence of the nineteenth-century model has been the absence of the kind of comprehensive regulation that is to be found in other industrial countries of such basic matters as hours and holidays for all employees. There is specific regulation of the hours of women and young persons in certain activities, but with few exceptions the hours of adult men are regulated unilaterally by the employer or by collective bargaining.

The reason for the selective use of the 'method of legal enactment' as a means of worker protection, even when the trade unions were in a position to demand comprehensive statutory regulation in the period after 1914, must be found in the pragmatic approach of the trade unions. As Kahn-Freund (1968:4) explained, protective legislation cautiously expanded was seen as no more than a supplement to collective bargaining, useful in areas such as health, safety, and welfare where practical experience taught that negotiations and enforcement by union representatives were ineffective. For those who were strongly unionised minimum standards could be achieved without the help of legislation.

Employment Protection Legislation

Since 1963 there has been a spate of legislation mainly designed to give employees a measure of security against abrupt or unfair dismissal and to provide compensation when jobs disappear for certain economic reasons. The main measures are: the Contracts of Employment Act 1963 which introduced minimum periods of notice to terminate the contract of employment and income guarantees during the notice period; the Redundancy Payments Act 1965 which gave employees dismissed because of the closure or movement of their place of work, or a reduction in the requirements for certain categories of employees, the right to lump sum compensation; and the unfair dismissals provisions introduced by the Industrial Relations Act 1971. All these measures have been the subject of amendment and are now consolidated in the Employment Protection (Consolidation) Act 1978 (EPCA), itself subsequently amended. The 1978 Act also consolidates a number of supplementary provisions, such as the right of the employee to receive a written statement of the main terms of employment (ss.1–7), a note of grievance and disciplinary procedures (s.1(4)), and itemised pay statements (ss.8–10), and incorporates certain measures to maintain employees' income such as guarantee payments when work is not available (ss.12–18), maternity pay (ss.33–44), and the protection of wages on the insolvency of the employer (ss.121–127), as well as rights to time off work (ss.27–30).

A variety of imprecise concepts has been applied to this legislation. One is the idea of 'property in the job' which Meyers (1964:1) defines as the right to undisturbed possession of a job which cannot be taken away without due process of law. This, as Turner et al. (1967:337) have remarked, is the 'employee's compensation for his relative lack of property in the capital which employs him'. But in reality there is no market for job-property rights: job holders, unlike property owners cannot dispose of their jobs, and the financial compensation which they receive from the employers bears little relation to market fluctuations and is arbitrarily limited in amount by the legislation.

Another concept is the 'right to work' which, in this context, means the right to remain continuously employed including the right to re-employment in the event of unjustified termination (Hepple, 1981:76). The central measure is the law against unfair dismissal. The statistics reveal the startling fact that only a tiny proportion of those who complain to industrial tribunals that they have been unfairly dismissed are re-employed, and that the proportion has declined since the legislation was amended, with effect from June 1976, to make re-employment the primary remedy. In 1973, 4·2 per cent of those whose cases were settled before a hearing were given back their jobs. This has fallen each year and was only 1·6 per cent in 1980. Of those who went to a hearing, 2·3 per cent had a recommendation for reinstatement in 1973; by 1980 orders for re-employment were made in only 0·8 per cent of such cases. The median level of compensation in 1980 was £598 (about five weeks' wages at the average wage).[4] This may be compared with the theoretical maximum figure (in 1980) of £16,910. The reasons for this remarkable failure to provide a 'right to work' through unfair dismissals legislation have been the subject of investigation (Dickens et al., 1981a:160; Williams and Lewis, 1981; Lewis, 1981:316). Among the most widely supported reasons are that employers will not accept re-employment and the tribunals are reluctant to conclude that it is 'practicable' for the employer to comply with an order, and that the tribunals and ACAS conciliation officers only pay lip service to the statutory requirement to give priority to re-employment. Moreover, the majority of dismissed workers are not, by the time their cases come up for hearing, seeking re-employment. It is interesting to compare the situation in the United States where grievance arbitrators, under collective agreements, reinstate about half of the employees whose cases are brought to arbitration, and employees wrongfully discharged for union activities are normally reinstated under the provisions of the National Labor Relations Act (Elkouri and Elkouri, 1973:648). A reasonable inference from this, and also the common practice of securing reinstatement in Britain where voluntary procedures are used or industrial action is resorted to, is that for an effective 'right to work' there generally has to be solid trade union backing at the workplace.

The primary purpose of legislation on unfair dismissals then, like that on redundancy payments, is to provide certain dismissed workers with compensation. As indicated above, the level of unfair dismissal awards is relatively low and this reflects not only the fact that low wage earners are the main users of the tribunal system, but also (since loss of earnings is the main element in the award of compensation) that those who are eligible to present a complaint (at present with at least one year of service with the same employer or two years if there are twenty or fewer employees) are usually able to find new employment within a relatively short period. The

---

[4] The statistics are derived from the *Employment Gazette*, 1977, p.1078; 1978, p.555; 1979, p.866; 1981, p.82; 1981, p.539.

compensation is a lump sum rather than a periodical payment, and where the employee is not in employment at the date of assessment the compensation almost inevitably either underestimates or overestimates the actual loss suffered. The redundancy payments provisions are also based on the lump sum principle, but here there is a scale of payments assessed according to age and length of continuous employment, subject to a maximum (£4,050 in 1982). Fryer (1973b:12) estimated that only about a quarter to a third of all employees made redundant had been eligible to claim payments under the Act (there is a two-year qualifying period) and the average lump sum paid to each employee was approximately one-fifth of median adult male annual earnings. The payments are made by the employer who can claim a rebate (originally two-thirds, later half, and since 1977 41 per cent) from a Redundancy Fund to which all employers contribute. The stated purposes of the Redundancy Payments Act included the mitigation of the economic consequences of redundancy, compensation for the loss of job property rights, and the encouragement of mobility. A survey of the main groups actually or potentially involved in redundancy by Parker et al. (1971) found that the Act has had some impact on attitudes and behaviour, increasing flexibility and mobility of labour and reducing the level of dispute activity over redundancies. One of the most important demonstrated consequences of the Act has been to increase the significance of age as a criterion for redundancy because the larger payments to older workers with long service acts as a mechanism to induce them to leave employment (Department of Employment, 1978c:1038). In this sense the Act has facilitated movement out of the labour force, rather than mobility between jobs.

Studies of the impact of the employment protection legislation have shown that a secondary function has been to make managements more careful in recruiting and shedding labour (Daniel and Stilgoe, 1978; Clifton and Tatton-Brown, 1979). From the individual worker's viewpoint this has meant an important improvement in procedural justice at the workplace. Jobs no longer exist simply at the whim of the employer. Britain was the last industrialised European country to adopt statutory minimum periods of notice. At common law the employer was free to dismiss for any reason, or without assigning a reason, simply by giving the period of notice prescribed by the contract or the custom of the trade (e.g. as little as two hours on a Friday in the construction industry) or, in the absence of this, whatever period of notice the courts considered reasonable. So far as manual workers were concerned the length of notice depended not so much on legal conceptions of reasonableness as on the relative strengths of organised labour and management. Before 1963 few collective agreements dealt with notice periods, and appeals against dismissals through agreed procedures were relatively rare. The statutory minimum periods of notice, still short by European standards, have been lengthened from time to time since 1963, currently being one week for up to two years' service, then one week for each year's service up to twelve weeks for those with twelve years' or more service. It is significant that the legislation was not asked for by the unions and arose largely from a concern about unofficial strikes. Its main function has been to make dismissals of long-serving employees more expensive for the employer (Hepple, 1980:477).

The unfair dismissals legislation focuses attention on the fairness of the employer's decision to dismiss the particular employee. Studies of the impact of the legislation are unanimous in their verdict that the greatest effect has been on reforming and formalising disciplinary and dismissals procedures (Daniel and Stilgoe, 1978; Brown, 1981:41). However, this impact is uneven since in highly unionised establishments the findings are that procedures are likely to have pre-dated the legislation. The basic standards are not to be found in the legislation itself, which simply adopts the broad and open-ended criterion of reasonableness. Certain ground rules are encouraged by the ACAS Code of Practice on Disciplinary Practice and Procedures in Employment, but it is the industrial tribunals, under the guidance of the appellate courts, which have developed the principle that the employer must have adequate factual grounds on which to reach his decision, after a reasonably careful investigation following a fair procedure (Hepple and O'Higgins, 1981:ch.17). In this case the law satisfies Meyers' notion (1964:1) of 'due process' in the context of job security, and also interprets the statutory concept of 'equity' as guaranteeing the equal treatment of all those belonging to a relevant category. The importance of these procedural safeguards as a basic individual civil liberty should not be underestimated.

At the same time the unfair dismissals legislation is seen by many as serving a third function, that of legitimating 'the existing structure of authoritarian control and inequality of reward in industry' (Bercusson, 1981:33). The critique by Hyman and Brough (1975) of the ideological function of notions of 'fairness' in general has been applied in the context of unfair dismissal. The law, while appearing to control or regulate the power of management to dismiss, has been seen as having in its application 'an essentially managerial perspective' (Weekes et al., 1975:28), and as having been diluted by conservative judicial interpretations in its impact on employment security (Boothman and Denham, 1981:14).

In order to assess these views of the legislation it must be made clear that Parliament entrusted the task of deciding whether the employer acted fairly to industrial tribunals, two of whose three members hearing each case are appointed by virtue of their knowledge and experience of industrial relations. The expertise of the lay members, one of them drawn from a panel of employers' organisation nominees, and the other from a panel of trade union nominees, is supposed to be the source of the definition of 'fairness'. In practice 96 per cent of tribunal decisions are unanimous (COIT, 1981). There are, however, a number of limitations on the exercise of this expertise. One is that the legal chairman of the tribunal generally controls the procedure and is the 'expert' source of knowledge on the law which includes the guidance given by the appellate courts on the correct approach to the issues. It is that guidance which is another fetter on the expertise of the tribunal. There is a right of appeal on a question of law. Initially this was to the National Industrial Relations Court, then between 1974 to 1976 to the High Court, and since then to the Employment Appeal Tribunal (EAT), itself a tripartite body. Further appeals may go to the Court of Appeal and the House of Lords (Hepple and O'Higgins, 1981: ch.22). The EAT has given a broad interpretation to the notion of an error of law so as to enable itself to review a wide range of tribunal decisions (Elias, 1981:201), and to lay down guidelines on 'reasonableness' in specific situations such as suspected dishonesty, sickness, incompetence, redundancy, and so on. The general approach is that tribunals may not usurp managerial decisions to dismiss simply because they disagree with them: the test is whether the decision is within the range of responses which a reasonable employer could adopt. This severely limits the tribunal's powers of intervention, and may be one of the reasons why the proportion of employees who are successful in cases going to a hearing has been consistently low (30·8 per cent in 1977, 27·7 per cent in 1980).[5] The conception has been of certain 'enlightened' management styles, such as a corrective rather than a punishment-centred view of discipline. By being told to look at how a reasonable body of employers might behave, the tribunal's application of fairness has become norm-reflecting rather than norm-setting (Elias, 1981:213). Not surprisingly, therefore, tribunal decisions reflect current conceptions of 'good' practice rather than more radical notions of worker control of jobs.

A fourth function of the legislation is that of providing a 'floor of rights' upon which collective bargaining may improve. The design of the legislation (e.g. EPCA ss.18,65,96) has been to allow collective agreements to replace the statutory provisions with ministerial approval where the standards in the agreement are at least as high as those in the legislation. In fact these exemption provisions have rarely been used: only three exempted agreements for redundancy payments in seventeen years, one for unfair dismissal in ten years, and just over twenty for guarantee payments in seven years. The reasons are complex. In the case of redundancy payments it is difficult to spread the burden evenly across an industry where only one or two employers agree to an exempted scheme, and it is difficult to maintain flexibility because of the practical limitations within one enterprise of offering suitable alternative employment instead of a payment. The standards for exemption in the case of unfair dismissal are stringent. Most national agreements do not allow appeal to an independent arbitrator or tribunal, and employers have been reluctant to provide enforceable rights at least as beneficial as those in the legislation (Bourn, 1979:85). As a result collective agreements have played a supplementary role to the legislation, covering voluntary payments in addition to the statutory minima or prescribing procedures for selection,

---

[5] *Employment Gazette*, 1977, p.1078; 1981, p.539.

but not replacing the legislation (Labour Research Department, 1981). The core of job security is now to be found in law and not in collective bargaining.

FUTURE TRENDS

Is Legalism Inevitable?

As has been shown, there is widespread criticism that the growth of statutory rights has imported excessive formalism into the disputes settlement process. Against this it has been argued that tribunals must inevitably 'interpret law in legal fashion' (Munday, 1981:159). These different views reflect a clash of legal values and the values of an industrial relations system. The industrial tribunals are now an established part of the legal system, suffering as do other parts of that system from over-complex statute law, and a bewildering and growing volume of precedents. The danger, as Lord Denning said in one case, is that 'if we are not careful, we shall find the industrial tribunals bent down under the weight of the law books or, what is worse, asleep under them'.[6] Even more dangerous, from the industrial relations viewpoint, is the tendency, so often associated with lawyers but not confined to them, to narrow-minded formalism.

Part of the problem is the illusion, created by the founders of the tribunals, that they are significantly different from courts. In fact they are court-substitutes since like the ordinary courts they have a regular and permanent existence with the function of adjudicating disputes by the application of legal rules. The real distinction is between those bodies such as the High Court which have general jurisdiction over disputes, and those with specialised jurisdictions. It is the specialised jurisdiction of the industrial tribunals, rather than their relatively informal procedures, which distinguish them from ordinary courts. Special jurisdictions are nothing new: indeed they can be said to be fundamental to the whole of English legal history, as shown by the development of the Court of Chancery in overcoming the rigidity of the common law courts and the host of special jurisdictions over the centuries. The historical tendency has been to subject these special jurisdictions to the demands of the legal profession. The statutes are framed by parliamentary draftsmen who expect them to be interpreted by professional judges according to established principles of interpretation known only to lawyers. Legal advisers want predictability and hence judicial guidelines so that they can confidently advise clients. They adopt the jargon and conventions of their profession which are closed to laymen. Moreover, the pressures of conflict lead to a kind of ritual-isation which takes special forms in individual employment litigation, through the use of technical legal points, deliberate delays, and various forms of 'gamesmanship'. The adversarial system on which the tribunals

---

[6] *Walls Meat Co. Ltd.* v. *Khan* [1978] I.R.L.R. 499 at p.501.

are modelled is suited to the system of trial by a jury who know nothing in advance about the facts and places heavy reliance on oral presentation, cross-examination and what Lord Devlin (1981:58) called 'verbal pugilism' and 'display fighting'. Despite some procedural reforms of the tribunals in 1980 (Hepple and O'Higgins, 1981:ch.22), none of this can work entirely satisfactorily where one or both of the parties lacks professional representation, and the tribunal is not a true 'industrial jury' (as it is often misleadingly called) but is appointed because of its expertise. The adversarial basis of tribunal litigation is contradicted by the demands placed on the tribunals by the lack of adequate representation, and also by some parts of the legislation (e.g. the removal in 1980 of the burden of proving reasonableness by the employer), to adopt a more investigative or inquisitorial approach. However, the tribunals are denied the power to carry through such an approach because they cannot, save on the application of a litigant, compel the attendance of witnesses or the production of documents. It is the individual litigants who control the proceedings.

Against these pressures of the legal system, are the demands of the industrial relations system. The Donovan Report (1968:para.568) placed its faith in collective bargaining as the best way to give improved facilities for the speedy and informal settlement of disputes. But the Commission recognised that for a large number of employees no voluntary machinery exists and that statutory rights need judicial machinery for their enforcement. The tribunals can claim to have met some of the original aims. They are accessible, conducting hearings in some twenty-five centres, and relatively cheap and speedy compared to the ordinary courts, with cases coming to hearing, on average, within eight to ten weeks of application (COIT, 1981). Moreover, they seem to have reached many employees outside the scope of effective bargaining. Statistics published by the Department of Employment in 1976[7] indicate that the legislation has been most effective in those industries where union density is low and collective bargaining weak, in particular in small undertakings where pay and employment standards are low. A (relatively small) survey by Dickens (1979:18) found that there was a reasonable degree of satisfaction on the part of applicants and respondents in the tribunal system.

However, distrust of the law and of legalism remains. The introduction of tripartism into the judicial process, first used in the courts of referees under the National Insurance Act 1911, and then in the Munitions of War Tribunals during the First World War (Rubin, 1977:149) has not overcome all the criticisms of the ideology and decisions of tribunals. In part these criticisms reflect unrealistic expectations about a statutory system which inevitably involves, even with tripartism, the application of radical legislation by a conservative judiciary. Industrial tribunals may be categorised, adapting Devlin's analysis (1981:8), as activist rule-makers in the

---

[7] *Employment Gazette,* June 1976, p.590, and see D. Jackson, 'The Use of the Law of Unfair Dismissal', University of Aston Working Paper No. 95, May 1978.

sense that they keep pace with the current ideological consensus among industrial relations practitioners. But they are not, and it would be unrealistic to expect them to be, dynamic or creative rule-makers, using the law to generate changes in the consensus. Underlying the criticisms is a confusion between social justice and individual justice, and a lack of appreciation of the fact that judges, by the very nature of their role in the British system, are not pliable instruments of social reform.

The fundamental question for the future of individual rights is therefore how, within the limits of a system of industrial relations largely structured and determined by collective bargaining, the law can best serve the demand for speedy, informal, and accessible adjudication. Three models exist. The first is that of the ordinary courts, which are used for this purpose for example in the Netherlands and Italy. This is an unlikely development in Britain because of the traditional hostility of unions to the legal profession and the relative success which the tripartite tribunals have already achieved. A second model is that of specialised bipartite labour courts, as in France (since 1806) where *conseils de prud 'hommes* elected from the ranks of workers and employers are 'guided' by a legal secretary. It seems that even in this system legalism is as much a problem as in Britain, and there are no clear advantages over the tripartite British system (Napier, 1979:270; Van Noorden, 1980:1098). A third model is that of grievance arbitration, that is a procedure by which the parties agree to submit individual grievances to third-party decision, as found in the United States. The strengths of this model are that the parties are able to fashion the arbitration procedure, to agree upon the issues the arbitrator is to decide, and that the union 'owns' the grievance and so is able to reconcile individual and collective interests. The weaknesses of the model, as it operates in the United States, are high cost and delays, the possibility of abuse by the sole bargaining agent, and the fact that it applies only to organised workers. Such a model could have been, but was not, developed in Britain and the legislation has had no significant effect in stimulating such a development. Thus the conclusion emerges that in the short- and medium-term at least, industrial tribunals will continue to fill a gap where collective bargaining has failed. Within the tribunal system there will be ample scope for a continuing battle against the worst excesses of legalism, by lawyers who are trained to understand industrial relations, by other practitioners who grasp the fundamentals of legal technique, by draftsmen who learn to speak clearly and not subtly, and by judges who respect the expertise of the lay members and create informal and efficient procedures.

Individual Rights and Collective Bargaining

As argued above, the legal model of the individual contract no longer reflects the norms of industrial life. The dissolution of the collective entity of the establishment and undertaking into a series of individual contracts, without formal legal recognition of the organs of workers' representation and collective bargaining, did not matter a great deal so long as the legal framework was essentially voluntarist. 'The voluntary principle', said Kahn-Freund (1954b:51), 'is sufficiently valuable to be purchased at the price of a lack of realism in the law'. But the transformation of the legal framework by the introduction of a host of individual legal rights prompts the question whether this lack of realism can be sustained.

The statute law is complex in structure, partly because it utilises the contract of employment as the vehicle for the new individual rights. Judicial interpretations have relied heavily on the concepts of the common law of contract. For example, an employee's right to complain of being forced to resign by the employer's conduct ('constructive dismissal') has been made to turn upon whether or not the employee can prove a breach of a fundamental term of the contract of employment (Hepple and O'Higgins, 1981:ch.15). This in turn has led to the revival of expansive implied obligations such as that of mutual trust and confidence or cooperation between employer and employee redolent of a unitary perspective of individual labour relations (Hepple and O'Higgins, 1981:ch.9). The common law concepts are themselves ambiguous, leaving much scope for judicial inventiveness. As yet the 'social' rights of employees to control their jobs have proved no match for the property rights of employers upon which the common law rests. Even matters where the collective interest is paramount, such as the right to organise, are enforced through a series of individual rights (see Chapter 15) and these are limited to those with existing contracts of employment, so excluding those on the 'lump' and those seeking work.

This chapter has demonstrated that the unfair dismissals legislation gave an important impetus to unilateral rule-making on disciplinary practice and procedures, and has done relatively little to bring about an expansion of collective bargaining in this field. A key question is whether procedural control over managerial discretion will in future give greater recognition to the collective interest, for example by a general right for trade unions at the workplace to be consulted about any type of dismissal and not only about proposed redundancies, as at present, and by more direct encouragement of independent systems of internal appeals against disciplinary decisions. It is doubtful whether collective involvement of this kind can be effective so long as the statutory employment protections rest on contractual foundations.

More or Less Legislation?

Kahn-Freund's generalisation that 'regulatory legislation is apt to prevail over collective bargaining where and when the political pressure power of the workers exceeds their industrial pressure power' (1977a:39) was evident in the period of the Labour Government's 'Social Contract' with the TUC (1974–9) when the Employment Protection Act, with its motley collection of individual rights, was traded against agreement to a voluntary incomes policy. Pressure by employers against the legislation led to a number of restrictions in the Conservative Government's Employment Acts of 1980 and 1982. There remains a wide area of consensus about the central areas of legal regulation, and there would undoubtedly be great resistance to any attempt to take away rights now firmly established.

There will continue to be pressures for the extension of individual rights. One source of pressure is the EEC, whose directives on matters such as collective redundancies[8] and workers' rights on the transfer of undertakings,[9] have already resulted in important changes in British law. Other EEC initiatives, reflecting the higher social standards in most other member states, on subjects such as temporary and part-time work and protection of workers in respect of the introduction of new technologies, may compel changes in British law. Even if Britain's continued membership of the EEC were to be put in doubt, the pressure by multinational corporations for equality of competition in the countries in which they operate will encourage this process of 'harmonisation upwards'. Other pressure groups include the women's rights movement, demanding an extension of the equal pay and sex discrimination legislation, and civil liberties groups wanting the protection of the worker's privacy and against discrimination on grounds such as age, political opinion, sexual preferences, and physical and mental disability.

Whatever specific changes are made, an underlying problem is the effect of legislation of this kind on the operation of labour markets. Individual rights are unlikely to enlarge access to jobs particularly for those in low-paid, discontinuous employment without the benefit of strong collective organisations. In a market economy the law cannot guarantee the right to productive employment, only the right to social assistance (Hepple, 1981:73). What the law can do is guarantee individuals the right to equal treatment and equal respect, and so future strategies against poverty and unemployment might be expected to include a strengthening of legislation against racial and sexual discrimination and its extension to other disadvantaged groups such as the disabled, older members of the working population who suffer from age discrimination, and generally to discrimination on grounds of social origin. A strategy for maintaining continuous employment might include measures for widening the coverage of the law, and would make re-employment a more attractive remedy, for example, by the statutory continuation of contracts of employment until disputes about their termination are resolved by conciliation or, failing this, by decision of an industrial tribunal. However, even the extension of individual rights in ways such as this cannot be expected to transcend the economic and social structure of the labour market. 'Law', as Kahn-Freund (1977a:2) said, 'is a secondary force in human affairs, and especially in labour relations.'

[8] *Official Journal*, L48/29, 22 February 1975, implemented in EPA Part IV.
[9] *Official Journal*, L61,26, 5 March 1977, implemented by the Transfer of Undertakings (Protection of Employment) Regulations 1982, S.I. 1982 No. 1794.

17 Incomes and Anti-Inflation Policy

Robert J. Davies

Inflation and recurrent balance of payments crises have been regular features of Britain's economic life since World War II. Unfortunately, the conventional demand management tools of monetary and fiscal policy have often proved inadequate in tackling these problems, producing instead a 'stop-go' pattern in the nation's economic activity. Policy makers have sought new tools with which to control the economy. One example is incomes policy, an administrative device designed to restrain directly the growth of money incomes so that they do not rise faster than the rate of growth of real output. Achieving this purpose successfully would offer policy makers the happy prospect of reconciling the so called 'magic triangle' of full employment, price stability, and a competitive level of economic growth. Therein, of course, lies its attraction.

As is often the case, performance has fallen short of promise. Nevertheless, over the past two decades incomes policies have become a more or less permanent feature of British life, even during the term of governments initially opposed to them. This chapter describes and analyses the nature of these policies. The first section considers the economic rationale for incomes policy against the background of an analysis of the causes of inflation. Subsequent sections consider the institutional character of British policies, the key issues that have arisen in their operation, the economic and institutional impact they have had, and their future prospects. Finally, a brief chronology of incomes policy intervention over the post-war period is provided as an appendix.

ECONOMIC RATIONALE FOR INCOMES POLICY

Wage and Price Inflation and the Simple Phillips Curve

The most useful point of departure for any analysis of inflation in the context of incomes policy is the simple Phillips curve (Phillips, 1958). The empirical basis for this curve derives from the existence of an inverse relationship between the rate of change of money wages ($\dot{W}$) and the level of unemployment (U). That is:

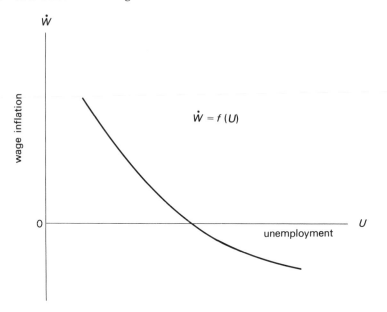

FIGURE 17.1: The Simple Phillips Curve

The theoretical justification for the curve is the simple principle that wages will be bid upwards by excess demand for labour.

This construct appealed strongly to policy-makers during the 1960s because it explained why price stability had proved so illusive relative to the achievement of full employment. Put simply, higher employment could be achieved only at the expense of higher wage inflation. In addition to its value as a tool of diagnosis, the construct also proved useful as an instrument of prescription, since it focuses attention on the possibility of designing so called 'supply-side' policies that shift the Phillips curve downwards and thereby improve the inflation-unemployment trade-off. Incomes policy, which allows policy-makers to intervene directly in the labour market to limit the growth of money incomes, is an obvious example of supply-side intervention. Thus if demand-side policies are used to achieve the desired unemployment level, incomes policy can be used to restrain the consequent upward pressures on wages, costs, and prices. Needless to say, incomes policies are not the only method of influencing the supply-side. Other possibilities include manpower programmes, measures to improve the mobility of labour, various forms of regional policy, and policies to promote greater competition in product and factor markets (see Chapter 14).

A potential source of confusion over the use of the Phillips curve in the analysis of inflation is that whereas concern over inflation is typically expressed in terms of prices, the Phillips curve expresses a relationship between unemployment and wages. Implicit in the analysis, therefore, is the idea that there is a strong link between wage changes and price changes. This implicit connection is made explicit in the widely held view (for which there is significant empirical support in Britain; see Sargan, 1980) that prices are determined as a simple 'mark-up' over costs, with wages by far the largest element. Formally,

$$\dot{P} = a(\dot{W}) - b(\dot{Q}) + c(\dot{M}) + d(\dot{D}) + e(\dot{T}) \quad (1)$$

| price changes | wage changes | changes in labour productivity | changes in import prices | changes in profit share | changes in indirect taxes |

This simple mark-up model suggests that if import prices do not change, if employers maintain constant profit margins, if indirect taxes such as VAT do not change, and if pricing decisions are made only by reference to the cost elements in equation (1) rather than by responding to fluctuations in demand, then price stability can be achieved if wages grow at the same rate as labour productivity (i.e. if $\dot{W}=\dot{Q}$). In the current state of the economy this is clearly a big 'if', but it does give a strong clue as to why productivity criteria have figured so prominently in most incomes policies. The equation also provides a good explanation for the concern expressed by companies over policies that include rigid price restraint; for if wages are not in fact restrained, or import prices increase substantially, a tight squeeze will be put on profits with disturbing long-term implications for investment and growth.

Monetarists and Inflation

The simple Phillips curve and its attendant rationale for incomes policy have been subject to challenge on both empirical and theoretical grounds. On an empirical level the recent experience of stagflation casts considerable doubt on the idea that inflation and unemployment are, in fact, alternatives. On a theoretical level the apparent breakdown of the Phillips relationship has been explained on the grounds that the true relationship is not between unemployment and *money* wages, but between unemployment and *real* wages (Friedman, 1968). That is, wage bargains are struck on the basis of anticipated *real* returns, and hence implicitly include expectations about future price movements. This produces what is frequently referred to as the 'expectations Phillips curve'. Formally,

$$\dot{W} = g(\dot{P}^e) + f(U) \quad (2)$$

| wage changes | expected price changes | unemployment |

Equation (2) implies the existence of a family of Phillips curves, with one for each level of price expectations. For example, as Figure 17.2 illustrates, an increase in price expectations from price stability at $\dot{P}^e=0$ (the state implicitly assumed by the simple Phillips curve) to inflation at 5 per cent will shift the curve up parallel to itself, with further shifts occurring as expected inflation accelerates to 10 per cent, 15 per cent and so on.

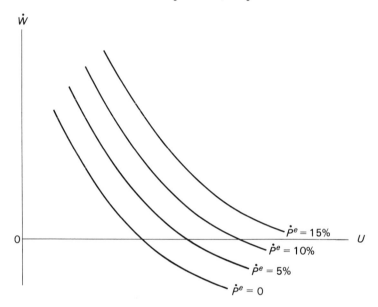

FIGURE 17.2: A Family of 'Expectations Phillips Curves'

This analysis has important consequences for the role of incomes policy as an anti-inflation device. Figure 17.3 helps illustrate this. Suppose the economy is initially at position A in Figure 17.3 with an unemployment rate of U^0, wage growth of 3 per cent and expectations of price stability ($\dot{P}^e=0$), an outcome that is possible so long as labour productivity is growing at a rate sufficient to offset the growth in money wages (i.e. 3 per cent). Now suppose the government decides that the existing level of unemployment U^0 is too high and uses monetary or fiscal policy to expand the level of aggregate demand in the economy in an effort to reduce unemployment to U^1. One way of achieving this expansion would be to increase the money supply at a rate in excess of the long-term growth in output. Figure 17.3 suggests that on the basis of the original Phillips curve this policy manoeuvre is associated with an increase in wage inflation to 10 per cent. Equation (1) indicates that unless productivity increases to offset this wage inflation (or unless there are offsetting changes in profits or import prices) the wage increases will eventually cause price increases. As domestic prices rise, so too will price expectations, causing a parallel shift in the Phillips curve. This will continue until the full increase in prices is

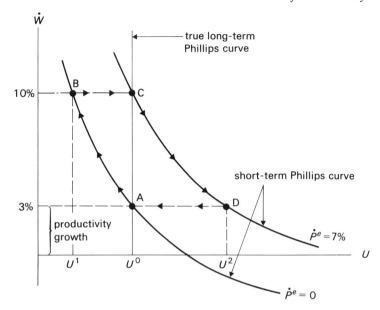

FIGURE 17.3: Monetarism and the True Long-Term Phillips Curve

reflected in expectations. If the authorities maintain their monetary policy at the higher level of demand stimulus, the economy will eventually find itself at a position such as C with the same unemployment rate but higher inflation. If the authorities expand demand further in an attempt to maintain an unemployment rate as low as U^1, they will simply move the economy on to higher and higher expectations Phillips curves, thereby producing an ever accelerating inflation rate.

The above analysis provides the basis of the monetarist position. Attempts to move the economy beyond its so called 'natural rate' of unemployment (in this example U^0) by expanding the money supply will in the long term only increase inflation, with no effect on either output or employment. Thus the initial effect of the monetary stimulus in moving the economy from U^0 to U^1 is a purely short-run phenomenon which will disappear once price expectations have fully adjusted. Expressed another way, the argument is that the true long-term Phillips curve is vertical at the natural rate of unemployment.

The monetarist analysis leaves little room for incomes policy. It suggests that the level of unemployment is largely independent of the government's demand management policy, being determined instead by the operation of the real forces of supply and demand in the labour market. If left to themselves, these forces will automatically produce full employment. In the context of inflation, all that is required is an appropriate monetary policy. If the authorities decide that inflation is too high, all they need do is reduce the rate of monetary expansion to bring it back into line with the growth in the economy's real productive capacity.

The mechanics of this process are illustrated in Figure 17.3. This time the economy starts from C, and it is assumed that the government wants to get back to A. The monetarist prescription is that the growth of the money supply should be reduced to dampen excess demand and so raise unemployment to a rate such as U^2, at which wage increases are brought back into line with the growth in labour productivity. Lest this increase in unemployment offend anybody there is the assurance that this state of affairs is only temporary, for as wage inflation falls so will price inflation, and with it price expectations, so that unemployment will eventually fall back towards the natural rate. The dynamic adjustment path of the economy through the complete inflation cycle is thus described by the path A→B→C→D→A in Figure 17.3.

The monetarist analysis leaves unanswered three important questions. First, how much additional unemployment will be required before wage and price inflation come down? This is equivalent to asking how *flat* the *short-run* Phillips curve is. Second, to what extent do wage increases actually respond to price expectations? This is equivalent to asking how *steep* the *long-run* Phillips curve is, or, to put it more technically, how close the coefficient on the price expectations term in equation (2) is to the value of one. (If it equals one, the long-term Phillips curve is vertical.) Third, how long does it take for price expectations to adjust? This is equivalent to asking about the dynamic path of adjustment through the inflation cycle depicted in Figure 17.3.

In principle the first two questions can be answered by reference to the accumulated evidence. Unfortunately, as a practical matter things are not quite so simple, since there are two major problems with the empirical work that are yet to be fully resolved. The first arises because the relationship between unemployment and excess demand seems to have changed significantly during the mid-1960s. This change, associated by some economists with the introduction of earnings-related unemployment benefits, has made consistent estimation of the expectations Phillips curve extremely difficult.

The second problem is how a concept such as price expectations is to be measured empirically. This has involved considerable controversy about the sort of mechanisms people use in forming their expectations. Do they, for example, base their forecasts on some weighted average of past rates (adaptive expectations)? Or do they learn that history alone is a poor guide and become more sophisticated by looking at the stance of monetary policy, the size of the budget deficit, interest and exchange rate movements and so on, and thereby reach a more 'rational' forecast (rational expectations)? The issue is of more than merely semantic interest, for if bargainers adjust quickly to changes in the expected rate of inflation, and forecast it accurately, the dynamic adjustment path illustrated in Figure 17.3 will be accomplished much more quickly and with smaller variations in unemployment than otherwise.

These problems suggest that the empirical evidence needs to be treated with some caution. With this caveat in mind, most studies which include the 1970s find unemployment to be insignificant as a determinant of wage changes (Artis, 1981); indeed, some even report a perverse positive relationship (Henry et al., 1976). Moreover, these findings appear unaffected by the substitution of more sophisticated indicators of excess demand such as the output-gap (the difference between the economy's full employment potential output and its actual output) for the unemployment variable (Gordon, 1981). While the inflation expectations variable invariably carries a positive sign, it often has a coefficient of significantly less than one (Laidler and Parkin, 1975). Roughly translated this means that changes in price expectations (usually measured according to an adaptive scheme) are not fully reflected in money wage changes, implying that the long-term Phillips curve, while steeper than the short-term curve, is not vertical. This finding is, however, contested (Parkin, 1975; Parkin et al., 1976).

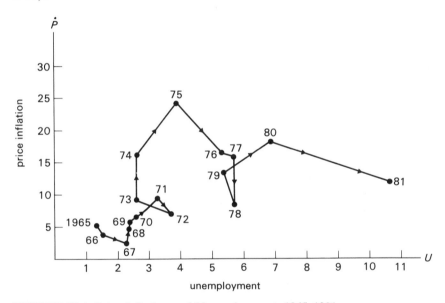

FIGURE 17.4: Price Inflation and Unemployment, 1965–1981

Source: Central Statistical Office, *Economic Trends* (London: HMSO, monthly issues), 38 and 42.

None of these studies gives a clue to the nature of the long-term adjustment path involved in reducing inflation. Some evidence on this is provided in Figure 17.4, which plots actual unemployment/price inflation combinations for each year from 1965 to 1981. The contrast with the hypothetical pattern depicted in Figure 17.3 is striking.

Taken together, these results have disturbing implications for anti-inflation policy. First, they suggest that increasing unemployment is likely to have little impact in slowing wage inflation, unless the government is prepared to tolerate unemployment levels considerably in excess of those experienced in the 1960s and 1970s. Second, they suggest that expectations are both slow to adjust to changes in the actual rate of inflation, and are not always fully incorporated into wage-setting behaviour. Moreover, it seems intuitively plausible that this inertia in the adjustment process is likely to be more marked during the deceleration phase of the inflation cycle than during the acceleration phase. Thus not only are anti-inflation policies based purely on monetary restraint likely to involve excessively high unemployment levels (as Figure 17.4 indicates), they are also likely to involve the maintenance of these levels for a significant amount of time before bargainers adjust to a low-inflation psychology. This gloomy prognosis explains the scepticism of many British economists, especially those in the institutionalist or 'Keynesian' tradition, towards a purely monetarist anti-inflation programme; for them incomes policies are an essential feature of any fight against inflation for social as much as economic reasons.

'Institutionalist', 'Keynesian', and 'Eclectic' Theories of Inflation

The basic principle behind the so-called institutionalist analysis of inflation is the idea that wages are determined more by social and political forces than by economic forces such as excess demand in labour markets. The primary actors in the process of wage determination are the trade unions, which are seen as being able to increase wages, and hence costs, independently of the pressure of demand in the labour market. According to this 'cost-push' view, there is no guarantee that increasing unemployment will have any meaningful effect on either wages or prices.

Somewhat confusingly, this approach is also often referred to as 'Keynesian', partly because it seems to accord with Keynes's own thinking on the subject of money wage determination, but also because subsequent writers in the 'Keynesian' tradition have greatly elaborated on it (Worswick, 1944; Hicks, 1974). While the argument varies in detail from author to author, its essential features remain broadly the same. In general, the argument is that the maintenance of full employment over the post-war period removed from the trade unions any major restraints on their ability, or willingness, to press for higher wages. Decentralised bargaining and inter-union rivalry have, moreover, combined to obscure the ultimately self-defeating nature of this competitive wage scramble. As a consequence, with individual wages heavily influenced by comparability, the aggregate level of wages, and hence the inflation rate, is largely determined independently of market forces. The final element in the causal chain is the government, or more precisely the monetary authorities, who are obliged to expand the money supply to finance the unions' inflationary wage gains to avoid increasing the level of unemployment.

The logic of this argument leads inexorably towards the need for an incomes policy, with its precise form depending upon the factors that are identified as motivating the unions' competitive wage behaviour. If wage competition is seen to derive from conflict over income shares, then the appropriate policy is one directed towards the alleviation of such conflict through the achievement of a more consensual or egalitarian distribution of income. Alternatively, if wage inflation derives from the operation of some form of 'wage leadership' mechanism, such as one in which large wage increases are transmitted from a leading productivity sector (Jackson et al., 1972; Eatwell et al., 1974), then the appropriate task of incomes policy is the relatively more straightforward one of simply restraining the 'key' sector.

The plausibility of many aspects of the institutionalist analysis is not to be denied. What is less certain is whether it adds up to a convincing theory of inflation. It is, for example, unable to account for the sudden and rapid acceleration of inflation in Britain in the early 1970s (Jackman et al., 1981). It is also unable to account for the international character of recent inflation experience, including the broadly simultaneous acceleration of inflation rates across Western industrialised countries from the mid-1960s, and the striking similarity in these countries' inflation rates, at least until 1972. These characteristics seem to be more convincingly explained by excess demand and its transmission across national boundaries under a system of fixed exchange rates (Zis, 1975).

The more 'eclectic' cost-push approaches perform rather better in an international context, since they accept that wages do depend upon excess demand but argue that the nature of this relationship is strongly influenced by trade union action. More specifically, either the slope or the level of the Phillips curve may be altered by trade union pressure. Expressed formally,

$$\dot{W} = g(\dot{P}^e) + f(U) + h(F) \tag{3}$$

$$\text{wage changes} \qquad \begin{array}{c}\text{expected}\\\text{price changes}\end{array} \qquad \text{unemployment} \qquad \begin{array}{c}\text{union}\\\text{pushfulness}\end{array}$$

In this equation, unions may influence wages either by altering the relationship between wage changes and unemployment, by influencing the adjustment of price expectations, or through the additional union push-fulness variable.

There are two schools of thought about the influence of unions on the wage change-unemployment relationship. One points to the ability of unions to gain more accurate information than individual workers can about market conditions, enabling them to adjust more quickly to changes in the demand for labour. This implies that the 'unionised' Phillips curve will be steeper than the 'non-unionised' Phillips curve. The other argues that they slow down the response to market forces because they engage in collective bargaining over wages only at periodic intervals (Friedman, 1951). This implies a flatter Phillips curve.

The evidence for Britain appears more consistent with the view that unions make the short-run Phillips curve flatter, thus reducing the responsiveness of wage changes to labour market forces (Thomas, 1977). This flattening seems most pronounced at higher levels of unemployment, however, which suggests that unions can insulate wage bargaining from the pressures of unemployment (Layard, Metcalf and Nickell, 1978). In addition, the evidence suggests that unions may actually *speed up* the adjustment to increases in the inflation rate. Thus the implication is that unions introduce a high degree of asymmetry or downward inertia into the wage bargaining system.

In the context of the ability of unions to *shift* the Phillips curve upwards, a variety of indicators have been suggested as proxies for some type of union pressure index. The two most popular have been the rate of change in the proportion of the labour force unionised (Hines, 1964, 1971) and strike frequency (Godfrey, 1971; Taylor, 1972; Laidler, 1976). Empirical evidence has been found both for and against the significance of these variables. Even where the evidence has been supportive, however, critics have emphasised the lack of any convincing theoretical rationale for including such variables. Indeed, they have often suggested that where these additional variables are significant they are merely acting as additional proxies for excess demand, the effects of inflation, or both.

For those convinced that union pushfulness is a significant source of inflationary pressure – and the evidence is certainly not strong enough to reject such a proposition – incomes policies again come into their own. By imposing some form of wage ceiling they can be used directly to restrain the ability of unions to push wages upward. They may also be useful in restraining the growth of inflation expectations during the upswing of an inflationary cycle, or of speeding their downward revision during the downswing. In both cases they represent an important anti-inflation device.

These justifications for incomes policy are not, however, universally accepted. Given inflation expectations, an effective incomes policy must either reduce the actual inflation rate (by, for example, imposing direct and immediate restraints on wages and prices) and thereby reduce expectations that are formed adaptively, or it must lead people who form their expectations rationally to believe that the future will be different from the past. The policy, in other words, must be credible. Supporters of the rational expectations view point to past experience to indicate that to the extent that incomes policy has any effect at all, it is only temporary, with inflation taking off again as soon as the policy is lifted or breaks down. Thus even if expectations fall initially, they will simply jump up again as soon as the policy comes to an end. Second, given the chequered history of incomes policies, there is no real reason to suppose that the public will place any more faith in their anti-inflation powers than in the announcement of a firm commitment to monetary restraint. This leads to the suggestion that in practice incomes policy can add little to the effectiveness of an appropriate monetary policy in reducing inflation expectations.

Even if these arguments are accepted and the idea that incomes policy can be a useful anti-inflation device is rejected (Brittan, 1981), a rationale may still be found for the policy as an anti-unemployment device. This proposition is usefully illustrated in the context of a wage inflation model which assumes that unions bargain to achieve a certain target increase in their real wage. The model may be expressed formally as follows:

$$\dot{W} \quad = \quad (\dot{P}^e) \quad + \quad a(Y-Y^*) \quad + \quad \dot{R} \quad (4)$$

wage changes	expected price changes	actual output	potential output	target growth in real wages

This model differs in three major respects from the Phillips curves considered earlier. First, the coefficient on price expectations is assumed to be unity. Second, wage changes are explained in terms of excess demand as measured by the 'output-gap' (that is, by deviations of actual output from its potential or full employment level) rather than by unemployment. Third, a new variable ($\dot{R}$) is added to represent the target or desired growth in real wages. Several factors might cause unions to revise this variable upwards. These include increases in direct taxes, which reduce net take-home pay; and previous shortfalls from the real wage target, which might prompt catch-up demands.

Empirically, operational specifications of the target real-wage model have stood up well to econometric tests. Recent research seems to confirm that current wage increases respond positively to previous shortfalls in real after-tax income from their target level (usually measured by a time trend), as well as to past increases in prices; but they do not, apparently, respond significantly to changes in unemployment (Henry et al., 1976). Even though more recent evidence has cast some doubt over the performance of this model beyond 1975 when Phase I of the Social Contract was introduced with its £6 limit, it nevertheless remains one of the more plausible explanations of Britain's wage inflation experience. Indeed, its failure after 1975 is perhaps not too surprising given that a major goal of the £6 policy and its immediate descendants was that of persuading workers to forego real wage increases.

If the target real wage model is in fact correct in the British context, it has important implications for macroeconomic policy. This is clearly illustrated if equation (4) is considered in conjunction with the simple mark-up price model. In the absence of any change in the profit share or the rate of indirect taxation, and if import prices rise in line with domestic prices, then:

$$\dot{P} \quad = \quad \dot{W} \quad - \quad \dot{Q} \quad (5)$$

price changes	wage changes	changes in labour productivity

Now if the target real wage equation (4) is substituted for $\dot{W}$ in the price equation, the resulting expression can be easily rearranged to produce an expression for actual output (Y) relative to its full employment level (Y*). That is:

$$\underset{\substack{\text{actual}\\\text{output}}}{Y} \quad = \quad \underset{\substack{\text{potential}\\\text{output}}}{Y^*} \quad - \quad \underset{\substack{\text{expected minus}\\\text{actual price}\\\text{changes}}}{b(\dot{P}^e-\dot{P})} \quad - \quad \underset{\substack{\text{employment}\\\text{implications of the}\\\text{real wage target}}}{b(\dot{R}-\dot{Q})} \qquad (6)$$

where b=1/a.

This expression carries a fairly straightforward message. It suggests that if the government wishes to prevent wage-push forces from producing an inflationary spiral, then it must operate the economy at below its full employment potential (Y*). The extent of this required shortfall will, moreover, be increased if actual inflation is to fall below the expected rate in order to produce a downward spiral in inflation rates. The required shortfall between actual and potential output will also be increased if the real wage growth target pursued by the unions ($\dot{R}$) exceeds the growth in labour productivity ($\dot{Q}$), or if it remains unchanged in the face of increases in either import prices or indirect taxes, *unless* the gains in real wages are made at the expense of profits. In fact, the evidence strongly suggests that many of these things have actually happened during the 1970s. The OPEC oil cartel and a depreciating currency combined to produce higher import prices; productivity growth slowed significantly; and the share of profits in national income roughly halved.

Equation (6) provides a fairly good explanation of recent economic developments, and of the policy dilemma facing governments caught between inflation and unemployment, and also highlights two potentially important roles for incomes policy. The first is the now familiar idea that such policies might be used to reduce inflation expectations. The second is that they provide a means for bringing the unions' real wage target back into line with the economy's productive potential and the realities of higher world prices for energy. Both offer the prospect of lower unemployment.

Once again these justifications for incomes policy are not universally accepted. With regard to their presumed ability to reduce union wage aspirations, it is argued that incomes policy may have just the opposite effect. In part this is because they attract attention to inequities that were previously only poorly perceived. But it is also argued that they merely emphasise the objective of cutting real wages, and thereby stoke the fires of dissent and resistance all the more. Thus, even if an incomes policy has some initial success in producing below-target settlements, once the policy is removed workers will simply increase their demands again in an effort to catch-up.

Alternative Rationales: Redistribution, Productivity, and Planning

Incomes policies have also been advocated as a means of achieving a broader range of economic and social objectives. One of the most important of these relates to their potential impact on the distribution of income. Incomes policies can never be distributionally neutral. Any policy that seeks to establish some kind of pay norm must decide whether this should be expressed as a flat rate or as a percentage. The choice has important implications for income distribution. Flat-rate policies in particular have the effect of favouring the low paid relative to other income earners, and in so doing tend to compress income differentials. Despite their justification on egalitarian grounds, such policies have usually failed to gain universal acceptance, particularly within the ranks of skilled workers, who resent the erosion of their relative position. The consensus among economists is that incomes policies are not the appropriate device for helping the low paid, a task they believe should be left to the tax-social-security system.

The distributional implications of incomes policy do, however, go beyond the issue of merely redistributing income *among* wage and salary earners. For example, in so far as the recent inflation has been associated with an increase in labour's share in national income relative to profits, its control, especially through wage restraint, is likely to imply a reverse shift. There are many, the CBI included, who would see this as an essential element in Britain's long-term recovery, and as a necessary condition for an improvement in the climate for investment. Nevertheless, any such move could clearly serve to increase distributional conflict, unless it was based upon broadly based social consent. In this sense it is extremely difficult to isolate discussions of the various rationales for incomes policy from the question of the precise form that such policies take.

Productivity and efficiency improvement have also been important strands in the development of British incomes policies. Indeed, it has been argued that the work of bodies such as the National Board for Prices and Incomes (1965–70) amounted to a form of free compulsory management consultancy service (Clegg, 1979:360). The case for incomes policy has therefore received some stimulus from the perceived need to boost Britain's flagging productivity performance and stimulate international competitiveness.

Finally, incomes policies have been advocated as an important adjunct to the development of a system of indicative planning. The National Plan of 1965, for example, sought to create a coordinated and consistent set of macroeconomic projections of how the economy was likely to develop over the coming five years. As an integral part of this exercise incomes policy was seen as a device for limiting wage growth to keep it broadly in line with the projected growth in output per worker. The major flaw was that the forecasts all too often turned out to be wrong, typically erring on the side of excessive optimism (Smith, 1968).

The Rationale: A Brief Summary

The discussion so far has illustrated the divergence of opinion among economists on the desirability of incomes policy. Its rationale as a means of controlling inflation, restraining union pushfulness, influencing inflation expectations, or producing permanent reductions in the union's real wage target have all been criticised. Incomes policies have also been accused of distorting market signals, leading to a loss of efficiency in allocating resources. One obvious answer to this accusation is that such distortions are swamped by the losses associated with high unemployment – an apparently inevitable adjunct to unbridled monetarism. Moreover, the modern mixed economy is already characterised by so many so-called distortions that it is an open question whether the imposition of an incomes policy actually makes things any worse.

The essential point is that the case for incomes policy is based as much on the failure or inadequacy of the alternatives as on the policy's own particular merits. For its supporters, the hope has always been that the policies of tomorrow will be better than those of yesterday and today. For governments, moreover, the policy has the major virtue that it has an immediate and visible impact, indicating that at least something is being done. In this sense the most convincing rationale for incomes policy is to be found more in the realm of political economy than of economics.

FORMS OF INCOMES POLICY INTERVENTION

Britain has not been alone in its reliance on incomes policies. In practice there are few Western industrialised countries that have not succumbed to its siren call at some time or another. It is therefore instructive to consider British policies in a broader international context, and to seek to establish why they have taken the particular form they have.

The International Context

While the goals of incomes policy can be stated relatively simply, this is not true of the means employed to achieve them. Incomes policies in Britain and elsewhere have appeared in an almost bewildering array of guises, a fact which makes classification difficult. One useful typology that successfully imposes some order on the international diversity displayed by the policy is, however, provided by Braun (1975:3–4). Following this scheme six distinct categories of policy may be identified. First, efforts to influence or inform public opinion on the need for restraint. Though the precise mechanism may vary, involving the use of national advisory bodies or councils of experts, the main objective remains the generation of voluntary national consensus. Second, the implementation of more formal guidelines for restraint on a voluntary or mandatory basis. Third, attempts to restrain cost pressures in specific sectors, especially 'key sectors', where wage and price decisions are highly visible (e.g. the public sector, basic or nationalised industries, rental housing, food prices). Fourth, short-term government intervention to freeze or severely restrain wage and price increases, either to buy time or influence inflation expectations. Fifth, the operation of a longer-term coordinated system of income determination, with or without government involvement (as in Scandinavian countries) or compulsory arbitration (as in Australia and New Zealand). Sixth, 'institutional engineering' including the long-term reform of bargaining structures to lessen the pressure from competitive wage bargaining; labour market policies to improve mobility and ease inflationary bottlenecks; and reform of the legal framework to control strikes, improve mediation and arbitration, or limit union power.

In an international context, incomes policies have also varied according to the institutional framework within which they operate. This offers a further means of classification: direct government intervention (as in Britain, France, Canada, and the United States); compulsory arbitration (as in Australia and New Zealand); employer coordination (as in West Germany); bi-partite cooperation between employers and trade unions (as in Sweden); and tri-partite cooperation between government, employers, and the trade unions (as in Austria and Norway, and the Netherlands until the early 1960s).

The British Context

The precise form that incomes policy takes will depend on the economic, political, and institutional constraints that face the country concerned. In Britain, for example, incomes policy has typically been instituted in situations of crisis, most often in relation to the balance of payments (1948–50; 1956; 1961–2; 1966–7; 1972; 1975–6), with the primary aim of restraining wages and reducing unit labour costs. This has implied that the policy has frequently been based, at least initially, on the introduction of a short-term freeze. Other features of the British experience also stand out. These include the existence of incomes policy as a more or less continuous fact of economic life over the past twenty years, a strong reliance on direct government intervention, and recourse to statutory rather than voluntary means of control. All of these features can be explained by the constraints that have faced British policy makers.

The more or less continuous nature of incomes policy intervention, for example, is closely related to Britain's economic performance. This includes slow growth, accelerating inflation, a steady decline in competitive position, and an aggregate unemployment rate which, though low until recently by historical standards, has shown both a disturbing tendency to increase and an unacceptable degree of regional variation.

The reliance on government intervention may be related to two important features of the institutional environment. First, the size of the public sector (accounting for nearly one-third of all employees) where collective bargaining is both centralised and highly visible. This implies not only that there will always be some form of public sector pay policy, but also that a key determinant of the success of an incomes policy will be how well it works among the government's own employees. In part this represents the influence of the public sector on the overall pattern, or going rate of settlements, but equally important is the impact that public sector pay has on the government's ability to control the level of public expenditure, itself an important element of anti-inflation policy. The second feature of the institutional environment is the decentralised character of collective bargaining in the private sector. As argued above, this characteristic makes individual unions highly unlikely to restrain their wage demands without some form of government intervention, even though they may recognise that attempts by all unions to gain large money increases will ultimately be self defeating. Moreover, if the private sector is not restrained, the heavy reliance placed on comparability in determining public sector pay will make it virtually impossible for the government to control its own pay bill without generating tremendous resentment.

These arguments are also relevant to explaining why governments in Britain have often had to rely upon statutory rather than voluntary controls. In particular, international experience points to three important prerequisites for a successful long-term voluntary policy. First, a centralised or at least well coordinated bargaining structure, preferably with powerful centralised confederations of unions and employers. In addition to the familiar argument that the larger size of the bargaining units makes them better able to perceive the macroeconomic consequences of their actions, there is the simple point that the smaller number of wage decisions implied by this structure makes voluntary coordination and administration a good deal easier. Similarly, the existence of centralised decision-making power within union and employer federations makes the policy easier to impose at the rank and file or individual firm level. In Britain, by contrast, the relative autonomy of workplace union organisation is associated with a pattern of relations between leaders and the rank and file that would make it extremely difficult for the leaders, even if they were willing to do so, to commit their unions to long-term restraint.

A second prerequisite is the existence of a close and stable link between the trade union movement and the government. In particular, left-wing governments appear to have a better chance of achieving voluntary consensus on incomes policy, not least because they are better able to convince the unions that these policies are not simply a means of depressing labour income relative to profits. Though the condition of closeness has been reasonably approximated under Labour governments, its stability has inevitably been undermined by the rise and fall of Labour's electoral fortunes.

The third prerequisite relates to the economic background to incomes policy. For example, while short-term voluntary restraint has often been possible against a background of economic crisis (as with the policies of 1948–50 and Phases I and II of the Social Contract), long-term voluntary policies seem to require a background of reasonably sustained economic growth. This implies that the goal of incomes policy is to determine, or at worst moderate, the distribution of real income gains rather than to impose real incomes losses, as has recently been the unenviable task of British policies.

One final feature of the British context that has militated against a successful voluntary policy in anything other than the short term is the attitude of the public sector. Public sector unions have frequently been in the forefront of opposition to voluntary restraint. They have also been prominent in the large pay claims often associated with the demise of incomes policies (as in 1969–70, 1974–5, and 1978–9). One explanation for this undoubtedly lies in the justified fear among public sector workers that incomes policies will be imposed most tightly against them, partly because of their greater visibility, but also because their scope for wage drift is restricted relative to that in the private sector. This latter factor was particularly important in the late 1960s and helps to explain the pay explosion in the public sector in the early 1970s.

THE OPERATION OF INCOMES POLICY IN BRITAIN

The detailed characteristics of British incomes policies have changed substantially over time, reflecting increased experience and adaptation in the face of previous difficulties. Certain key issues have nevertheless arisen over and over again. These may be conveniently classified under three headings: the specification and development of criteria, the role of exceptions, and administrative machinery and enforcement.

Specification and Development of Criteria

The precise criteria adopted for guiding an incomes policy obviously depend upon the goals of the policy: whether, for example, it is a response to a short-term crisis or is based upon a longer-term attempt to modify wage-price behaviour. Whatever the goal, the criteria must make some sort of economic sense; they must be simple enough to be easily understood; and if they are to be in place for some time, they must also be flexible enough to encompass broadly accepted notions of fairness. The latter element in particular is essential if the policy is to achieve any kind of consensus about its operation, and most commentators agree that the ideal policy is based upon consent. This, of necessity, introduces a highly pragmatic element into the design of policy criteria: they must be formulated with a view to securing acceptance from the key participants, and most importantly from the trade unions. As well as providing for controls on wages and salaries, criteria have therefore also been designed to include controls on prices, profits, dividends, and rents.

In terms of specific criteria the simplest policy is obviously an outright freeze. But this can only be a very short-term expedient. Over the longer-term there has to be some room left for discretion. This has usually been accomplished by specifying a wage 'target', 'guiding light', or 'norm' together with a small list of exceptions. During the period 1962 to mid-1966 the conventional wisdom held that incomes should only be allowed to rise in line with the growth in national output, on the assumption that this would lead to a broadly stable price level. Determining the appropriate growth rate proved more difficult than expected, however, with the specified target invariably turning out to be an over-estimate. This created a tendency for the published target to raise expectations about the scope for real income gains, which was then further compounded by its tendency to be seen as a minimum entitlement. Because of these problems the simple criterion of national productivity growth fell from favour, being replaced in March 1968 after a year of standstill and severe restraint by a ceiling on 'group' earnings (3½ per cent) and subsequently by a maximum range (2½–4½ per cent). An important feature of the latter criterion, evident in its emphasis on group earnings rather than simple wage rates, was the more explicit recognition of the problem of plant and company level wage drift – a problem that had become increasingly acute with the shift in the structure of collective bargaining towards increased workplace negotiation in the early 1960s.

With output growth falling below an annual average of 2 per cent and inflation climbing inexorably into double figures, the goal for the 1970s shifted from one of price stability to one of inflation containment. The first criterion to emerge under the Heath Government of 1970–74 aimed simply at encouraging the voluntary de-escalation of settlements. Known as the 'n–1' policy, it was intended to bring about a 1 per cent reduction in successive settlements by public sector workers, with the hope that this would have a useful demonstration effect in the private sector. Unfortu-nately, these demonstration effects only seem to work from high to low wage sectors, not *vice versa*.

Following the relative simplicity of a six-month freeze (November 1972 – March 1973) a more complex set of compulsory criteria was introduced in April 1973. This specified a part flat rate, part percentage increase (£1 a week plus 4 per cent) up to a given ceiling (£250 a year) which was to be used to determine the allowable increase in the group pay bill. With the maximum increase in the earnings 'kitty' determined in this way, some flexibility was then allowed in its distribution, subject to the £250 ceiling. Under Stage 3 of the Heath policy the criteria became a percentage or flat rate (7 per cent or £2.25 a week) whichever was the larger, again applied to the total pay bill and again with a specified maximum (£350 a year). This time, to complicate matters further, a flexibility margin of 1 per cent on the group wage bill was added for the adjustment of anomalies.

The major innovation in the Stage 3 policy, however, was the introduction of 'threshold agreements', which effectively provided for full wage indexation for any increase in inflation beyond 7 per cent. Unfortunately this innovation, normally a potentially useful device for neutralising the impact of inflation expectations, was introduced just as world oil and commodity prices began to rise. The outcome was a 17 per cent increase in the retail price index which triggered no less than eleven 'threshold payments'.

By the spring of 1975 threshold payments and a rush of large public sector settlements had combined to produce an annual rate of increase in average earnings of 30 per cent. Meanwhile, inflation was running at over 20 per cent. All this undermined foreign confidence and with it the strength of sterling. The response on the wage front was the £6 limit of the Social Contract, introduced with strong TUC support in the Autumn of 1975. The emergence of this policy represented a return to a simple flat-rate criterion, severed from any links with either productivity or the prevailing inflation rate. Apart from its obvious simplicity, one potential virtue of this criterion, at least in the eyes of the TUC, was that it favoured the low paid, a group generally perceived to have suffered most from inflation.

Under Phase II of the Social Contract, introduced in August 1976, the target was switched back to a percentage (5%) with both a minimum (£2.50) and a maximum (£4). Like the £6 policy the overriding aim was to reduce inflation and few exceptions were allowed.

As usual, strains began to show as the Social Contract moved into its third year. The limit was raised to 10 per cent on earnings plus an allowance for self-financing productivity deals. With the growth in earnings down to about 9 per cent and inflation falling rapidly towards single figures, the rationale behind the choice of target seemed less informed by the needs of an effective anti-inflation policy than by the hope of promoting a third year of union acquiescence. Success on this score proved limited, and the government was forced to have recourse to the device of cash limits to restrain the public sector and to the threat of sanctions to restrain the private sector.

By the fourth year of the policy, due to begin in the Autumn of 1978, support from both the TUC and the CBI had totally evaporated. A 5 per cent target was declared unilaterally by the government, but the policy was beginning to crumble, with its ultimate demise heralded by a series of bitter public-sector disputes. Once again, balancing the requirements of a successful anti-inflation target with the need for consent, particularly in the later stages of a policy, had proven highly illusive.

Exceptions

This discussion of the evolution of policy criteria highlights the problems involved in longer-term attempts at restraint. Either the overall criteria must be eased, or an ever increasing barrage of exceptions allowed. This range of exceptions must, moreover, be broad enough to allow for some flexibility and the correction of anomalies, but not so broad as to undermine totally the goal of the policy in restraining income growth. The trade-off is clearly an awkward one.

One of the most comprehensive statements of exceptions was that provided under the Labour Government's incomes policy of April 1965. This allowed four exceptions to the national productivity norm: where the employees concerned had made a direct contribution towards increasing productivity; where it was essential in the national interest to secure a change in the distribution of manpower and a pay increase was necessary for the purpose; where there was a general recognition that existing levels of remuneration were too low to maintain a reasonable standard of living; and where there was widespread recognition that certain groups had fallen seriously out of line with the level of remuneration for similar work and it was in the national interest that these should be improved. For convenience these are often termed the productivity, manpower, low-pay, and comparability exceptions respectively.

Subsequent lists of exceptions have generally been variations on these themes, the variations depending upon the severity of the policy. During strict phases of incomes policy, for example, most exceptions have typically been suspended, as during Phases I and II of the Social Contract. At other times new exceptions have been added, such as equal pay for women following the 1970 Equal Pay Act, and an allowance for the restoration or adjustment of relativities (January – June 1970).

The potential incompatibility of certain of these exceptions is obvious. Any attempt to improve the position of the low paid, for example, is bound to disturb some relativities and thereby generate considerable pressure for further exceptions. Similarly, as a tool of incomes policy the productivity exception has often disrupted relativities, or comparability in a way that has undermined the long-term stability of the policy. The problem is that productivity grows at different rates in different industries for reasons that are quite unrelated to the relative attributes of the labour force. Moreover, in some sectors, including the service and public sectors, productivity is difficult or impossible to measure, and even where it can be measured there is considerable scope for 'bogus' deals. Thus, despite the superficial appeal of the productivity exception in anchoring wage changes firmly to real output changes and offering scope for 'buying out' restrictive practices, its practical difficulties are considerable.

Two additional reasons for exceptional treatment have been provided by the need to provide extra remuneration for 'unsocial hours' and 'special cases'. The rationale behind these exceptions has typically been either the need to placate some group with sufficient bargaining power to destroy an incomes policy (such as the miners) or to reward some group which can command widespread public sympathy (such as the nurses). The need for such exceptions adds yet another dimension to the incomes policy problem and highlights the immense difficulties involved in reconciling efficiency, economic need, social equity, and disparate bargaining strength within a stable framework for income growth and distribution.

Administrative Machinery and Enforcement

Just as the ideal incomes policy is a voluntary one based upon the active support of those affected, so the ideal machinery for implementation is undoubtedly one largely administered by the parties themselves. Only two policies can be said to have approached this ideal. The first was the policy of 1948–50, the second the Social Contract of 1975–9. Both were operated under Labour governments, had broad union support, and were instituted at times of recognised economic crisis. Under the remaining policies, particularly where active restraint was required from the private sector, reliance has typically been placed upon some form of independent body appointed by government. These bodies have shown considerable variety through successive policies as lessons have been learned about their composition and role. For the most part, this evolution has derived from adaption to past success or failure, but there has also been a marked reluctance among governments to rely on the machinery bequeathed by their predecessors.

The first bodies to be appointed were the Council on Prices, Productivity and Incomes – also known as the 'Three Wise Men' – (1957), and the National Incomes Commission (1962). The first to play a fully active role in the operation of a comprehensive incomes policy, however, was the National Board for Prices and Incomes (NBPI), which was established as an advisory and consultative body to help administer the Labour incomes policy of 1965–9. The success of the Board as both advisor and consultant is is undoubted. What is less clear are its achievements as an instrument of pay restraint. In this area the policy, and by implication also the Board, is generally regarded as something of a failure, although this probably owed less to its own shortcomings than to its restricted powers. The problem was that under the 1965–9 policy overall control and interpretation remained with the (then) Ministry of Labour, so that not all settlements were referred to the Board. In these cases the Ministry often proved a far less adequate judge in its scrutiny of excessive settlements.

Following the election of the Heath Government in 1970 the NBPI was disbanded, only to be replaced within two years by two new bodies: the Pay Board and the Price Commission. Several important lessons had apparently been learned, and the Pay Board was designed to be much more difficult to bypass than the NBPI had been, and hence to be a much more effective mechanism of restraint. The Pay Board was, moreover, charged with administering a pay code that actively sought to eliminate as much as practicable all possible loopholes. Included among these was an obvious and recognised bane of the 1965–9 policy: the emergence of significant plant level wage drift. Several problems nevertheless remained. For example, throughout the 1972–4 policy the Department of Employment retained its responsibility for conciliation and arbitration while still significantly implicated in the task of formulating the restraint policy. These roles obviously make uneasy bed-fellows, and it would have been better had they been separated as occurred subsequently under the Social Contract. Here the Advisory, Conciliation and Arbitration Service (ACAS) operated as an independent agent untainted by the role of policy formulator or interpreter, with the latter role being undertaken jointly by the Department of Employment and the General Council of the TUC.

Under the first two phases of the Social Contract (1975–7), administration was carried out without the use of any formal independent machinery. It was based instead on self-discipline and self-policing, albeit backed up by the powers of the Price Commission as a potential sanction against over indulgence in the private sector. The task of administration was made substantially easier by the relative simplicity of the £6 limit and the subsequent 5 per cent/£4 ceiling, and by the absence of allowable exceptions. Nevertheless, the relative success of the policy does highlight the need for voluntary consensus, particularly at shop-floor level. Without it, especially under Britain's highly decentralised system of private-sector bargaining, no machinery, however well designed, can possibly hope to monitor all private bargains struck at plant level.

This last point raises the thorny issue of sanctions. Even under a voluntary policy there are few who would anticipate universal adherence without some form of enforcement mechanism. In this context there is a widespread belief that overt sanctions against workers who breach the policy are likely to be self defeating. As an alternative, where sanctions have been imposed they have been aimed primarily against employers. Under Phases III and IV of the Social Contract (1977–9) the government threatened sanctions against firms who breached the policy in the form of loss of export credit guarantees and the removal of government contracts. In the public sector strict cash limits were enforced to achieve similar results. The desirability of such sanctions has nevertheless been questioned. Indeed, the private-sector sanctions in the Social Contract were removed in December 1978 following a parliamentary refusal to endorse their imposition against the Ford Motor Company. If penal sanctions against both workers and employers are ruled out, however, the main alternatives are the familiar techniques of 'moral suasion', and the threat of exposure and public censure. The deterrent effect of such devices is clearly open to question.

One further piece of administrative machinery established by the Labour Government of 1974–9 that deserves mention is the Standing Commission on Pay Comparability. It was set up following the 'winter of discontent' in March 1979 to consider the issue of public-private sector comparability and was abolished by the Thatcher Government early in 1981. A simple lesson emerged for the short life of this body: the extreme difficulty of reconciling comparability and public-sector restraint in the absence of effective restraints on the private sector and in the presence of expenditure cuts in the public sector.

ECONOMIC AND INSTITUTIONAL IMPACT OF INCOMES POLICY

Seen simply against the background of the performance of the British economy in the 1960s and 1970s, with inflation, unemployment, and growth getting worse, incomes policy must surely be judged a failure. In practice, matters are not quite so simple. Isolating the true effects of incomes policy ideally involves comparing the actual pattern of events with the pattern that would have prevailed had the policy not been introduced. Forced reliance on estimates or projections of the 'what would have happened if' variety, even though they may be based upon techniques of some statistical sophistication, obviously leaves a great deal of room for error. The evidence presented below must therefore be treated with some caution. In considering this evidence it is useful to make some distinctions between the broad economic effects of incomes policy, including its impact on wages, wage structure, profits, and unemployment; its effects on specific groups such as the public sector and the low paid; and finally, its more general impact on industrial relations institutions and their operation, and on the pattern of strike activity.

Economic Impact

The consensus among early studies was that the incomes policies introduced up until the mid-1960s had had some success in lowering the rate of wage inflation, although curiously this conclusion did not seem to extend to price inflation. But this generally favourable view was subsequently questioned in a well known study by Lipsey and Parkin (1970). Their findings suggest that incomes policy replaces the trade-off relationship between wages and unemployment with what amounts to a constant (possibly because the norm becomes the minimum target). One implication of the Lipsey-Parkin study is that incomes policies are likely to be successful only if operated at a relatively high level of aggregate demand (low unemployment), and this led them to suggest that with the exception of the policy of 1948–50 the incomes policies operated until 1968 had actually made things worse.

These findings and the policy prescription based on them have been subject to considerable criticism, some elements of which are also relevant to other studies. These revolve around the problems of deciding whether or not a policy is in force, the fact that different episodes of incomes policy are far from homogeneous, and the need to allow for anticipation and re-entry effects. In any event, the Lipsey-Parkin findings have not proven empirically robust when subjected to more rigorous econometric tests (Parkin et al., 1972:3–13).

Considerable doubt also exists over the proposition that incomes policies are best operated at high levels of aggregate demand. Indeed, on the contrary, it has been argued that particularly in the early 1970s incomes policy was not always accompanied by a sufficiently restrictive monetary policy. The inevitable consequence was the release of pent-up liquidity as soon as the policy ended, an outcome which provides one explanation for the inflationary aftermath of the policy in 1969–71 and 1974–5 (Stevenson and Trevithick, 1977). Figure 17.5, which plots wage and price inflation, the share of profits in national income, and unemployment over the period

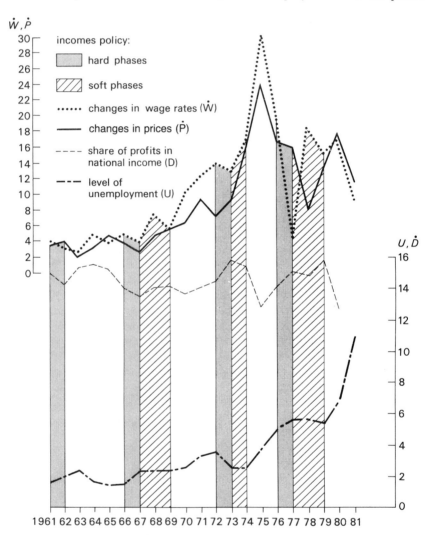

FIGURE 17.5: Incomes Policy, Wages, Prices, Profits and Unemployment

Source: Central Statistical Office, *Economic Trends* (London: HMSO, monthly issues), 38, 40, and 42; and *Economic Trends: Annual Supplement* (London: HMSO, 1982), 38.

1960 to 1981, clearly illustrates these post-incomes policy inflationary episodes.

More systematic confirmation of the existence of a 'rebound effect' following the demise of incomes policy is provided by Henry and Ormerod (1978), who, on the basis of their estimation of a target real wage equation, report a significant upsurge in wage inflation after incomes policy is removed. Their general conclusion is that the beneficial effects on wage inflation of introducing an incomes policy are at best only temporary, and are largely offset by a rebound effect once the policy comes to an end. Whether this is an inevitable consequence of incomes policy or largely the result of an inappropriate mix of macroeconomic policies remains an open question.

One additional point that should be made is that even if incomes policies are unsuccessful in controlling the magnitude of pay settlements, they may still exert some restraining influence through generally reducing the frequency of their occurrence. Indeed, one important feature of incomes policy since the late 1960s has been their insistence on the 'twelve-month rule' to limit pay settlements to once a year. Recent estimates for the coal industry (Pencavel, 1982) suggest that wage freezes have, in fact, had a significant impact in reducing the probability of a new wage settlement occurring.

The impact of incomes policy on wages is not simply confined to changes in their absolute level. There is also the question of wage structure. Indeed, in this context there is a popular belief that incomes policies, and especially those since 1972 which have included flat rate elements, have led to a significant degree of earnings compression. Aggregate data reveal that one of the most striking aspects of this compression has been that between male and female earnings. It is, however, incorrect to attribute this primarily to incomes policy rather than to the equal pay legislation of 1970.

In terms of occupational differentials, recent aggregate earnings data confirm the compression from the late 1960s (Elliott and Fallick, 1977), though the correspondence between this compression and the timing of incomes policy is not close (Dean, 1978). Analysis by Brown (1976, 1979) at a more disaggregated level for the West Midlands' engineering industry tends to confirm that incomes policy was not the prime factor in compressing differentials. In fact, differentials appeared to narrow more during years of relatively free collective bargaining (August 1974 – July 1975, for example) than under 'policy on' periods; while under Phases I and II of the Social Contract (August 1975 – July 1977) differentials were actually partially restored. The explanation advanced is that neither set of pay constraints was universally respected, with negotiators apparently seeking to bend the rules to weaken the redistributive bias of the policy. But some aspects of these results are contentious. Based upon a national case study of engineering, Chater (1981) has argued that Brown's results are applicable only to the West Midlands, and though incomes policy has probably not been the only influence at work during the 1970s, it has nevertheless been the strongest single factor in promoting compression, at least in the engineering industry. Unfortunately, it is not possible to generalise from these results to draw conclusions about the effects of incomes policy on the overall pattern of occupational differentials, for according to a recent study of earnings dispersion within manual and non-manual groups (Ashenfelter and Layard, 1979) the engineering industry is a special case. Outside engineering, it appears that there was a 'remarkable absence of equalisa-tion' over the period 1970–77.

Incomes policies may also affect profits. One possibility, especially since the restraining impact of incomes policy on wages does not always seem to feed through into prices, is an enlargement of the share of profits in national income. But in practice, as Figure 17.5 suggests, incomes policy does not seem to have had any systematic impact on profits. The profit share fell during the hard phases of incomes policies in the 1960s, but rose during the hard phases of the 1970s. The results during the soft phases are equally ambiguous. One clear tendency during the 1970s, however, was the tendency for the profit share to fall dramatically as wages rebounded during the demise of incomes policy.

The last aspect of the economic impact of incomes policy to be con-sidered is unemployment. Figures 17.4 and 17.5 both reveal a steady upward trend in the aggregate unemployment rate and a progressive worsening of the inflation-unemployment 'trade-off'. There is, however, no clear evidence to suggest that incomes policy intervention has actually made unemployment worse, unless it is argued that higher unemployment has been necessary following the demise of incomes policy as a means of restraining the size of the rebound effect in wage settlements. The evidence presented in Figure 17.5 is consistent with such an interpretation (unemployment does seem to increase following an incomes policy), although it is also consistent with the argument that incomes policy acts to stabilise or reduce the level of unemployment (as in 1967–70, 1971–4, and 1976–9). Given the enormous unemployment cost of the 1979–82 anti-inflation experiment, however, a preference for the latter interpretation, and as a corollary the advocacy of incomes policy as an anti-unemployment device, is easy to understand.

Public Sector and the Low Paid

The usual method of determining pay in the public sector has several distinctive characteristics. First, there is the importance of comparability, a fact which derives largely from the general absence of any readily measurable or marketed output from public service employees. This introduces enormous problems because comparability is not a precise concept, and may even be an inappropriate pay criterion if productivity is changing at markedly different rates between the public and private sectors or if supply and demand conditions are changing. Second, comparability inevitably implies a lag in the wage adjustment process. The longer this lag the more disruptive it becomes, partly because it creates resentment among those groups which are left behind, but also because it often produces large settlements to correct anomalies which, when taken out of context, have a disruptive impact on the overall system of pay bargaining. These features provide the key to the impact of incomes policy on the public sector.

As usual the evidence needs to be treated with caution, not least because the labour force in the public sector is extremely heterogeneous and different elements fared differently under successive policies. Nevertheless, incomes policies have generally been applied more strictly in the public sector, particularly against non-manual workers, and large public-sector settlements have followed periods of incomes policy during which public sector workers have felt discriminated against. For example, after the demise of the Heath policy in 1974 public-sector pay rose significantly during the 1974–5 pay round relative to the private sector, though this was reversed over the following four years (Dean, 1981). This apparently destabilising impact of incomes policy on public-sector pay movements, both through its initial disturbance of comparability and via its effect on the lag in the adjustment process, is a serious problem. Not only has it helped to undermine the last two major attempts at incomes policy, it has also greatly increased the problem of public expenditure control, producing large movements in nominal public spending and attendant cuts in the volume of public services.

Turning to the issue of low pay, every formal policy since 1965 has acknowledged the problem and included it at some stage, either explicitly in the list of exceptions or implicitly through the use of a flat-rate pay criterion. Even so, the evidence suggests that the policies of the late 1960s did nothing to help the low paid and, indeed, in some cases were actually detrimental (R. Steele, 1981). The most successful were the 'flat-rate' policies of 1975–7 which did, while in force, produce some improvement in the relative position of the low paid. Removal of the policies undid much of this, however, as more powerful groups moved to restore relativities. The evidence also suggests that this temporary success was achieved through compression within industries rather than by improving the lot of low-paying industries relative to others (R. Steele, 1981:149). One problem with using an incomes policy to improve the position of the low paid is that even where a flat rate is specified there is no guarantee that the low paid will actually receive it in full. Moreover, the relative position of the low paid can only be improved at the cost of smaller increases for the higher paid, an outcome that more powerful groups in the wage hierarchy often strongly resist.

Institutional Impact

One of the more important areas of the institutional impact of incomes policy is on bargaining structure. The rapid spread of productivity bargaining, especially under the policies of 1965–70, provided an impetus to plant-level bargaining. Moreover, through its influence on bargaining structure, incomes policy could also be advanced as an instrument of change in trade union structure, most notably in relation to the internal restructuring that occurred to take account of the developments in workplace organisation. Too much should not be made of this, however, as a far more plausible explanation is that in many industries these changes were a response to the growth in the power of shop stewards (Clegg 1979:376).

A case could also be made for the proposition that incomes policy, most notably in the form of the Social Contract, was instrumental in increasing the status and authority of the TUC and its General Council. Once again, however, cause and effect are hard to disentangle since the Social Contract could equally be argued to have been made possible by the increased authority of the leadership of the General Council following their successful defeat of the Industrial Relations Act of 1971.

Incomes policies also seem to have had a significant impact on strike activity (Davies, 1979). The imposition of incomes policy seems to have reduced the number of strikes over pay issues but, especially during its 'hard' phases, to have increased the number over non-pay issues. Moreover, the reduction in pay strikes is apparently achieved only at the expense of a sharp upsurge in such strikes as soon as the policy is removed. This result is consistent with workers and their unions attempting to make up lost ground and to rectify perceived inequities and anomalies. Thus when an incomes policy is considered over its complete 'life cycle' – from restraint through to re-entry into normal collective bargaining – it appears to have been associated with a significant increase in the overall frequency of strike activity.

In addition to their impact on the number of strikes, incomes policies also seem to have influenced their size, particularly in the public sector. For most of the post-war period the public sector (with the exception of mining) was characterised by relatively low strike rates, a record which may be partly attributed to a desire under centralised bargaining to avoid major trials of strength. This record was shattered in 1969–70, heralding the emergence of a climate of public sector militancy that has carried over into the 1980s, undermining both incomes policies and the electoral performance of governments.

One final institutional impact of incomes policy, and particularly of the Social Contract, that deserves some mention relates to the nature of the concessions made by governments in return for union acquiescence. Brittan (1981:176), in particular, has argued that these concessions – which include state encouragement of the closed shop; the extension of union immunities from the normal processes of contract law; price, profit-margin, and dividend controls; increased council house and mortgage subsidies; and the tightening of rent controls – have had a seriously detrimental impact on the economy by increasing unemployment, discouraging risk investment, and creating capacity shortage. Evaluating the empirical validity of this argument is difficult if not impossible. But whether the concessions mentioned by Brittan have been as detrimental as he and others have claimed is very much open to question. To take the example of the closed shop, employers have often granted it in order to eliminate the possibility of inter-union rivalry and to promote greater order and stability in their industrial relations. Similarly, any losses resulting from the concessions granted to achieve cooperative incomes policies have to be balanced against the costs associated with the unemployment resulting from the use of restrictive monetary policy to restrain wage growth.

FUTURE PROSPECTS FOR INCOMES POLICY

The possibilities that exist for future incomes policy include a 'new' social contract; traditional proposals for a norm plus exceptions; proposals for synchronisation of settlements or compression of the bargaining round; the reform of public-sector pay determination, including the formation of some central arbitral or review body; proposals to alter the balance of bargaining power either by weakening the unions or strengthening employers; a variety of tax-based incomes policies; and finally a series of more radical proposals starting with the establishment of an 'Industrial Parliament' and ranging through a 'National Council for the Regulation of Differentials' and a 'National Arbitration Court', to various systems for taxing back excessive settlements from workers. All these proposals have been discussed in detail elsewhere (Blackaby, 1980b). Here, therefore, attention is concentrated on a critical review of a narrower range of proposals broadly corresponding to the policy stances adopted by the three major political parties. These include the no incomes policy/monetarist stance of the Thatcher government, the Labour Party/TUC proposals for a 'new' social contract or National Economic Assessment, and the combination tax-based incomes policy/National Arbitration Court proposed by some leading members of the Social Democratic–Liberal Alliance.

The policy position of the Conservative Government amounts to a rejection of incomes policy on the basis of its past failures, with reliance placed instead on the strict control of public expenditure and tight monetary policy. These policies have in fact brought down pay settlements and inflation, but their unemployment cost (as Figures 17.4 and 17.5 illustrate) has been enormous. Indeed, it is worth remembering that a reduction of only 1 per cent in unemployment would increase output by about £2 billion (Jackman and Layard, 1982:48). There is, moreover, no guarantee that wage inflation will not simply surge again when monetary policy is eased, just as it has done following the demise of past incomes policies. In short, there is no indication that anything has been done to alter permanently the inherently inflationary character of Britain's decentralised wage-setting institutions.

The Labour Party is also only too well aware of the shortcomings of past incomes policies. This is particularly true of those introduced as short-term crisis measures in support of fiscal and monetary austerity. Discussion has therefore centred around a 'new' social contract or National Economic Assessment. This amounts to a return to a form of national economic planning that seeks to win workplace union support and encompasses the share of national incomes going to profits, earnings from employment, rents, social benefits, and so on. The ultimate objective is the creation of a more consensual bargaining climate. In one version (Basnett, 1982) union-government cooperation, including the operation of a National Economic Forum, is seen as requiring a firm government commitment to improving the lot of the low paid through a 'Minimum Terms and Conditions Act'.

More than enough evidence has been presented in this chapter to question both the effectiveness and stability of this type of centralised voluntary policy as a means of restraining inflationary wage pressure in the British institutional context, particularly in the face of expansionary monetary and fiscal policies. Yet if such policies are pursued as a means of reducing unemployment, some means of effectively restraining wage settlements will undoubtedly be required. This is most effectively illustrated by a recent forecast (utilising the Treasury's macroeconomic model) of the outcome of two alternative expansionary strategies aimed at reducing unemployment to below one million by 1986 (Huhne, 1982). Both strategies assume identical tax reductions, increases in public spending, and some depreciation in the external value of the pound, but one forecast overrides the normal equations in the model by assuming an incomes policy which effectively keeps average pay rises to about 8 per cent. The results are presented in Table 17.1. It reveals that the *successful* imposition of an incomes policy leaves the economy in a much stronger position with lower unemployment and much lower inflation. But it also leaves workers with a significantly lower increase in real take-home pay, which leads many to question whether any incomes policy can ever be successful in anything other than the short-run.

One scheme, recently embraced by certain sections of the SDP-Liberal

TABLE 17.1: THE IMPACT OF ALTERNATIVE REFLATIONARY STRATEGIES

	1982	1983	1984	1985	1986
Reflation with Incomes Policy					
Unemployment (000s)	2929	2577	1934	1379	993
Inflation rate (per cent)	9.2	10.3	4.7	5.3	6.9
Real take-home pay	−1.6	−0.7	+3.5	+2.1	+0.9
Reflation without Incomes Policy					
Unemployment (000s)	2932	2598	2020	1565	1263
Inflation rate (per cent)	9.4	12.7	12.4	15.5	18.5
Real take-home pay	−1.2	+1.7	+5.9	+3.0	+2.1

Source: Huhne (1982:19).

Alliance, that claims to offer a much better prospect for success on this score is the tax-based incomes policy proposed by Layard (Jackman and Layard, 1982). The economic rationale for an incomes policy underlying this scheme derives from a target real wage model similar to that discussed in the first section of this chapter. This model suggests that only a permanent incomes policy is likely to be effective in reducing the unions' real wage target to an extent sufficient to reduce substantially the non-inflationary level of unemployment. And the advocates of the tax-based scheme believe that a policy which allows the parties to engage in 'free' collective bargaining, but subject to an additional constraint on their behaviour in the form of a wage inflation tax, is more likely than conventional policies to remain a permanent feature of the process of wage determination.

The mechanics of the scheme involve the government declaring at the beginning of the bargaining round a norm for the growth of hourly earnings. Any employer exceeding this norm would then be liable for a tax of 100 per cent on the excess (i.e. if the norm was 5 per cent and the employer paid 8 per cent, then the tax would be equal to 3 per cent of the new wage bill). To avoid the deflationary consequences of the tax all revenues would be returned to firms at appropriate intervals (say through the adjustment of the national insurance surcharge) in an amount proportional to each firm's total wage bill. The net effect would be not only to impose a penalty on firms that breached the norm, but also to reward those who settled below it. The hope is, therefore, that the tax would strengthen the resistance of employers to excessive settlements.

Several features of this scheme are worthy of note. It requires no elaborate enforcement machinery or centralised agreement and avoids the politicisation of the wage decision by leaving it at the local level. The scheme also focuses on the actual increase in hourly earnings rather than on the wage rates laid down in collective agreements, and is therefore immune from the problem of wage drift. A further significant feature of the policy is that it is not totally undermined if it is breached; indeed any firm is at liberty to pay above the norm if it desires, but by doing so it will incur a tax penalty in the year in which the excessive settlement is made.

The scheme does, nevertheless, have a number of drawbacks. For example, if the going-rate becomes established above the norm (as seems to have occurred frequently with previous more conventional policies), then only firms paying above the going rate (rather than the lower norm) will suffer a penalty in the long term. This emphasises the need from the outset for some significant consensus about the size of the norm. Failing this, one solution would be to distribute the proceeds from the tax only among those firms that pay at or below the established norm. The problem with this, however, is that it would only serve to compound an additional drawback of the Layard scheme, namely its discouragement of productivity improvements. Thus, in marked contrast to previous incomes policies, the tax-based scheme actually penalises firms who pay above the norm to reward workers for improvements in their productive performance.

This last criticism is important, for as the analysis of the first section of the chapter shows, productivity improvement offers an equally potent but preferable means of combating the inflationary effects of large money wage increases. One potential solution would be to exempt productivity based increases above the norm from the tax. This clearly complicates the scheme and involves the establishment of some form of central productivity review agency which many would view as yet another bureaucratic irrelevance. In defence of such an agency, however, it could be argued that the most successful example of previous incomes policy machinery was the National Board for Prices and Incomes, not, as indicated above, in its role as an instrument of wage restraint, but rather in its role as adviser and consultant. A strong case could therefore be made for recreating such an agency and charging it only with the task of monitoring, reviewing and promoting productivity improvement schemes – operating in other words as a sort of publicly funded management consultancy firm.

A further criticism of the Layard policy is that firms may simply pass on the inflation tax in higher prices, making it ultimately self-defeating. The answer here is that inter-firm competitive pressure should serve to prevent such behaviour. Unfortunately, a number of areas of the private sector and most areas of the public sector are not highly competitive. Indeed, in the public sector the tax-based policy is clearly of limited relevance, although given the importance of comparability in determining public sector pay, any scheme which effectively restrains the private sector will also have some beneficial impact on the public sector. Nevertheless, some form of central public-sector review agency would probably be required.

One example of such an agency might be a 'National Arbitration Court' or 'Pay Commission' of the type advocated by Meade (1982). The basis of this proposal (which has also found favour with the SDP) is a government commitment to monetary and fiscal policies that permit money demand to grow at a predetermined rate (5 per cent). Within this overall framework the wage bargaining machinery then determines the level of employment, with excessive settlements leading inevitably to lower employment levels. In the event of disagreements, or of excessive settlements, cases would be referred to the National Arbitration Court, which would be charged with choosing between the employer's final offer and the union's final demand according to which would maximise employment.

The idea is that this 'final offer selection' process would encourage the parties to reach voluntary agreements within the 5 per cent framework. The problem is that the criterion of maximising employment would, at least in the present economic climate, invariably involve choosing the employer's position, and such an outcome is unlikely to endear the scheme to the unions. Further, the court would have to be extremely large to cope with a concerted plant-level challenge to the policy. Its feasibility as a viable private-sector mechanism is thus open to question. As a public-sector control agency charged with the task of assessing comparability, however, it could provide a useful adjunct to a decentralised tax-based private-sector policy, backed up by an appropriate fiscal and monetary stance.

CONCLUSIONS

Arriving at a balanced assessment of incomes policy is extremely difficult. Opinion remains sharply divided on both the policy's economic rationale and its operational impact. The evidence, moreover, is sufficiently ambiguous to lend more than adequate support to proponents and opponents alike. Yet while agnosticism might be the safest course, it is little help to policy makers charged with formulating a practical response to the problem of achieving more employment and faster growth without generating more inflation. What then, in the light of the foregoing analysis, is the best course for policy makers to follow?

The most convincing explanation of recent British wage behaviour is the target real wage or real wage resistance model, specified in terms of desired growth in real after-tax incomes. This model implies the existence of a high degree of inertia in the system of wage bargaining, with unions eager both to resist current shortfalls from their real wage target and to catch-up for previous shortfalls, including those brought about by incomes policy. Moreover, given the apparent insensitivity of wage inflation to moderate levels of excess demand, conventional deflationary policies, including tight monetary policy, seem to require much higher levels of unemployment than previously to restrain inflationary wage pressure. Yet there is no guarantee that even a sustained period of extensive unemployment will have any permanent impact on wage bargaining and, as Table 17.1 suggests, wage inflation is likely to take off again as soon as the economy is reflated.

It is against this background that the need for some form of incomes policy is cast into sharp relief. The point is not that such policies represent the ideal solution, but rather that they represent one additional weapon in an arsenal of less than adequate alternatives. Appropriately formulated, incomes policy offers one potential means of reducing the unemployment cost of a non-inflationary monetary policy. The social desirability of this outcome is obvious, but even on purely economic grounds the benefits of lower unemployment and higher output vastly outweigh the implied costs of a less efficient allocation of resources in the economy.

The key question is what constitutes an 'appropriately formulated' incomes policy. Here the lessons of the past are instructive. Highly centralised policies, whether statutory or voluntary, that have sought to monitor and control thousands of separate private-sector pay settlements have never lasted. They have merely served to politicise wage bargaining decisions and, to the extent that they have achieved restraint, it has often been only at the expense of a rebound effect when the policy has been removed. In the public sector, where bargaining is more centralised and wage decisions are by their nature more political, central monitoring and control of pay is more feasible. Nevertheless, given the importance attached to wage comparability, public-sector restraint cannot be achieved in anything other than the short term in the absence of effective restraint in the private sector.

If a highly centralised private-sector policy is ruled out, the most promising alternative appears to be a decentralised tax-based policy levied on hourly earnings. Such a policy has several advantages. These include the preservation of some semblance of 'free' collective bargaining, and hence scope for the adjustment of relativities through decentralised agreement rather than administrative fiat, a reduced susceptibility to collapse if the policy is breached, and less prospect that wage decisions will be shifted from the economic to the political arena. All these factors contribute to the policy's potential for survival as a more permanent feature of the system of wage bargaining than previous more conventional policies.

Administrative problems and uncertainties remain, as they do with all incomes policy proposals. A tax-based policy still requires an agency to establish an appropriate and credible norm and, if productivity improvement is to be actively encouraged and rewarded, some form of central productivity review body. Although public-sector pay must also be dealt with, the goal of comparability, and hence the task of a future comparability commission, would be much more compatible with a restraint policy if private-sector settlements were under control.

A final requirement is an appropriate monetary and fiscal stance. Past attempts at incomes policy have often created a 'pressure cooker effect' by being used to restrain inflation in an economy that is already overheated. No incomes policy, however constituted, can hope to achieve this task for long. Thus to complement a tax-based policy, monetary policy should be set to allow money demand to grow broadly in line with the growth of potential output. Similarly, fiscal policy must recognise the potentially inflationary impact of high and increasing direct and indirect taxes on wage demands and resist the temptation to finance large budget deficits through money creation. While acknowledging that many of Britain's current economic problems are basically structural in character, such a policy combination nevertheless offers the best prospect for a return to a low-inflation economy at more tolerable levels of unemployment.

APPENDIX TO CHAPTER 17

GOVERNMENT INTERVENTION IN PAY BARGAINING IN THE POST-WAR PERIOD

Labour Governments 1945–51

September 1947—Minister of Labour writes to trade unions and employers in selected industries urging restraint.

February 1948—*Statement on Personal Incomes, Costs and Prices.* TUC gives support.

January 1950—Stafford Cripps proposes wages standstill but TUC rejects it in September.

Conservative Governments 1951–64

1952–4—Undeclared attempt to influence pay movements by arbitration.

May 1954—Macmillan seeks support for 'price plateau' policy; public and private employers asked to impose price and pay stability. Opposition from TUC.

1957–61—Council on Prices, Productivity and Incomes ('Three Wise Men') sits; produces four annual reports but is boycotted by TUC.

1961–2—Selwyn Lloyd introduces temporary 'pay pause'.

1962—*Incomes Policy: the Next Step* recommends 2–2½% 'guiding light' but is ignored. National Incomes Commission (NIC) and National Economic Development Council (NEDC) set up.

Labour Governments 1964–70

November 1964—NIC abolished.

December 1964—*Joint Statement of Intent on Productivity, Prices and Incomes.*

February 1965—National Board for Prices and Incomes (NBPI) set up March 1971. *(Machinery of Prices and Incomes Policy.)*

April 1965—*Prices and Incomes Policy.* (3–3½% norm and four criteria for exceptional pay increases.)

November 1965—'Early Warning System' to review key wage decisions.

July 1966—*Prices and Incomes Standstill.* (Pay and price freeze for six months followed by six months 'severe restraint'; the introduction followed a balance of payments crisis.)

March 1967—*Prices and Incomes Policy after 30 June 1967.* (No norm; increases need to be justified against 1965 criteria.)

April 1968—*Productivity, Prices and Incomes Policy in 1968 and 1969.* (3½% ceiling except for genuine productivity agreements and major revisions of pay structures.)

December 1969—*Productivity, Prices and Incomes Policy after 1969.*
(Norm of 2½–4½%.)

Conservative Government 1970–74

July 1970—Undeclared policy of diminishing levels of pay settlements in
public sector (n–1).
January 1971—Office of Manpower Economics (to service pay reviews and
enquiries).
July 1971—Voluntary undertakings by the Confederation of British
Industry to restrain price increases to 5% per annum.
November 1972—*A Programme for Controlling Inflation: the First Stage.*
Stage 1 of Counter Inflation Policy: Freeze.
April 1973—Stage 2 of Counter Inflation Policy: £1 a week+4% with
upper limit of £250 a year. Some flexibility on moves towards equal pay.
November 1973—Stage 3 of Counter Inflation Policy: 7% or £2.25 a week,
1% for flexibility, upper limit of £350 a year. Threshold Agreements:
40p for each full 1% rise in Retail Price Index. Pay Board established
with power to fine offenders.
December 1973—Price Commission established.

Labour Governments 1974–9

July 1974—Pay Board and all associated controls on pay disbanded.
Threshold payments continue to November 1974. Price Commission and
statutory price controls retained.
September 1974—Social Contract endorsed by TUC. Wage increases to be
in line with increase in cost of living and 12-month intervals between
settlements.
July 1975—*The Attack on Inflation.* Phase I: limit of £6 per week for the
year to August 1976 with no increases to those over £8,500.
August 1976—Phase II: Limit of £2.50 for those earning up to £50 per
week; 5% for those earning between £50 and £80; and a maximum of £4
for higher earners. Tied to tax concessions.
July 1977—*The Attack on Inflation after 31st July 1977.* Government
unable to reach agreement with TUC on Phase III. Declares 10%
maximum with exceptions for self-financing productivity schemes.
July 1978—*Winning the Battle Against Inflation.* Government unable to
reach agreement with TUC on Phase IV. Unilaterally declares 5%
maximum with exceptions for self-financing productivity schemes and
rigidly defined special cases.
December 1978—Government withdraws sanctions against private companies which breach policy.
March 1979—Following so-called 'winter of discontent', government sets
up the Standing Commission on Pay Comparability to examine terms
and conditions of referred public service workers.

Conservative Government 1979

1979–82—Cash limits used to control wage increases in public sector. 'Expected increases' in private sector suggested by Government and Treasury officials. Standing Commission is disbanded. Emphasis on strict monetary control to reduce wage settlements.

Bibliography

Aaronovitch, S., and M. Sawyer. 1975. *Big Business: Theoretical and Empirical Aspects of Concentration and Mergers in the United Kingdom.* London: Macmillan.
——, and R. Smith. 1981. *The Political Economy of British Capitalism.* London: McGraw-Hill.
Abel-Smith, B., and P. Townsend. 1965. *The Poor and the Poorest: A New Analysis of the Ministry of Labour's Family Expenditure Surveys of 1953-54 and 1960.* London: Bell.
Addison, J.T. 1975 'Sex Discrimination: Some Comparative Evidence'. *British Journal of Industrial Relations,* XIII, 263–5.
——, and J. Burton. 1978. 'Wage Adjustment Processes: A Synthetic Treatment'. *British Journal of Industrial Relations,* XVI, 208–23.
——, and W. S. Siebert. 1979. *The Market for Labor: An Analytical Treatment.* Santa Monica: Goodyear.
Advisory Conciliation and Arbitration Service (ACAS). 1978. *Button Manufacturing Wages Council.* Report 11. London: HMSO.
——. 1980. *Industrial Relations Handbook.* London: HMSO.
——. 1981a. *Annual Report 1980.* London: HMSO.
——. 1981b. *The Contract Cleaning Industry.* Report 20. London: HMSO.
——. 1982. *Annual Report 1981.* London: HMSO.
Aldred, Chris. 1981. *Women at Work.* London: Pan.
Allen, V.L. 1960. *Trade Unions and the Government.* London: Longmans.
——. 1981. *The Militancy of British Miners.* Shipley: Moor Press.
Anderman, Steve. 1981. 'Labour Law in Sweden: A Comment'. *Law and the Weaker Party: An Anglo-Swedish Comparative Study.* Vol. 1. Ed. Alan C. Neal. Abingdon: Professional Books, 193–207.
Anderson, Alan. 1971. 'The Labour Laws and the Cabinet Legislative Committee of 1926–27'. *Society for the Study of Labour History Bulletin,* XXIII, 37–54.
Anthony, Peter D. 1977. *The Conduct of Industrial Relations.* London: Institute of Personnel Management.
Armstrong, Eric George Abbott. 1969. *Industrial Relations: An Introduction.* London: Harrap.
Armstrong, M. 1978. 'The History and Organisation of the Broad Left in the AUEW (Engineering Section)'. MA dissertation, University of Warwick.
Armstrong, P.J. 1982. 'If It's Only Women It Doesn't Matter So Much'. *Work, Women and the Labour Market.* Ed. J. West. London: Routledge & Kegan Paul, 27–43.
——, J. F. B. Goodman and J. D. Hyman. 1981. *Ideology and Shop-Floor Industrial Relations.* London: Croom Helm.

Arnison, Jim. 1974. *The Shrewsbury Three: Strikes, Pickets and 'Conspiracy'.* London: Lawrence & Wishart.

Arrow, K.J. 1972a. 'Models of Job Discrimination'. *Racial Discrimination in Economic Life.* Ed. A. H. Pascal. Lexington: Heath, 83–102.

——. 1972b. 'Some Mathematical Models of Race Discrimination in the Labor Market'. *Racial Discrimination in Economic Life.* Ed. A. H. Pascal. Lexington: Heath, 187-203.

——. 1973. 'The Theory of Discrimination'. *Discrimination in Labor Markets.* Eds. O. Ashenfelter and A. Rees. Princeton University Press, 3–33.

——, and F. Hahn. 1971. *General Competitive Analysis.* New York: Holden Day.

Artis, M.J. 1981. 'Incomes Policies: Some Rationales'. *Incomes Policies, Inflation and Relative Pay.* Eds. J. L. Fallick and R. F. Elliott, 6–22.

——, and M. H. Miller. 1979. 'Inflation, Real Wages and the Terms of Trade'. *Inflation, Development and Integration.* Ed. J. K. Bowers. Leeds: Leeds University Press, 55–85.

Ashdown, R.T., and K.H. Baker. 1973. *In Working Order: A Study of Industrial Discipline.* Manpower Papers 6. London: HMSO.

Ashenfelter, O. 1973. 'Racial Discrimination and Trade Unionism'. *Journal of Political Economy,* LXXX, no. 3(1), 435–64.

——, and R. Layard. 1979. 'The Effects of Incomes Policy upon Differentials'. Discussion Paper 44. London: London School of Economics, Centre for Labour Economics.

Atkinson, A.B. 1973. 'Low Pay and the Cycle of Poverty'. *Low Pay.* Ed. F. Field. London: Arrow Books, 101–17.

——. 1975. *The Economics of Inequality.* Oxford: Oxford University Press.

——. 1981. 'Unemployment Benefits and Incentives'. *The Economics of Unemployment in Great Britain.* Ed. John Creedy. London: Butterworth, 128–49.

——, J. Micklewright and H. Sutherland. 1982. *Low Pay: A Preliminary Look at the Evidence from the Family Expenditure Survey.* Discussion Series no. 3. London: Low Pay Unit.

Bacon, Robert, and Walter Eltis. 1976. *Britain's Economic Problem: Too Few Producers.* London: Macmillan.

Bagwell, P.S. 1974. *Industrial Relations.* Government and Society in Nineteenth Century Britain: Commentaries on British Parliamentary Papers. Dublin: Irish University Press.

Bain, George Sayers. 1967. *Trade Union Growth and Recognition.* Research Paper 6, Royal Commission on Trade Unions and Employers' Associations. London: HMSO.

——. 1970. *The Growth of White-Collar Unionism.* Oxford: Clarendon Press.

——. 1971. 'Management and White-Collar Unionism'. *Conflict at Work.* Eds. S. Kessler and B. Weekes. London: BBC Publications, 15–31.

——, David Coates and Valerie Ellis. 1973. *Social Stratification and Trade Unionism: A Critique.* London: Heinemann.

——, and Farouk Elsheikh. 1976. *Union Growth and the Business Cycle: An Econometric Analysis.* Oxford: Blackwell.

——, and Farouk Elsheikh. 1979. 'An Inter-Industry Analysis of Unionisation in Britain'. *British Journal of Industrial Relations,* XVII, 137–57.

——, and Farouk Elsheikh. 1981. 'An Industrial Analysis of Union Growth in Britain: The Data Base'. Discussion Paper. Coventry: SSRC Industrial Relations Research Unit, University of Warwick.

Bain, George Sayers, and Farouk Elsheikh. 1982. 'Union Growth and the Business Cycle: A Disaggregated Study'. *British Journal of Industrial Relations*, XX, 34–43.

——, and Robert Price. 1980. *Profiles of Union Growth: A Comparative Statistical Portrait of Eight Countries*. Oxford: Blackwell.

Balfour, C. 1972. *Incomes Policy and the Public Sector*. London: Routledge & Kegan Paul.

Banks, J.A. 1974. *Trade Unionism*. London: Collier-Macmillan.

Baran, Paul, and Paul Sweezy. 1968. *Monopoly Capital*. Harmondsworth: Penguin.

Barber, A. 1980. 'Ethnic Origin and the Labour Force'. *Employment Gazette*, LXXXVIII, 841–8.

Barker, Terry. 1982. 'Long-Term Recovery: A Return to Full Employment?'. *Lloyds Bank Review*, no. 143, 19–35.

Barrett, Brian, Ed Rhodes and Ronald John Beishon (eds.). 1975. *Industrial Relations and the Wider Society: Aspects of Interaction*. London: Collier-Macmillan.

Bartrip, Peter W.J., and P. T. Fenn. 1980. 'The Conventionalisation of Factory Crime: A Reassessment'. *International Journal for the Sociology of Law*, VIII, 175–86.

Basnett, D. 1982. *The Future of Collective Bargaining*. London: Fabian Society.

Batstone, Eric. 1980. 'What have Personnel Managers Done for Industrial Relations?'. *Personnel Management*, June, 36–41.

——, Ian Boraston and Stephen Frenkel. 1977. *Shop Stewards in Action: The Organization of Workplace Conflict and Accommodation*. Oxford: Blackwell.

——, Ian Boraston and Stephen Frenkel. 1978. *The Social Organization of Strikes*. Oxford: Blackwell.

Bayliss, F.J. 1962. *British Wages Councils*. Oxford: Blackwell.

Beardwell, I., D. Miles and E. Worman. 1981. *The Twilight Army: A Study of Civil Service Cleaners*. London: CSU/Low Pay Unit.

Beaumont, Phil, and Mary Gregory. 1980. 'The Role of Employers in Collective Bargaining in Britain'. *Industrial Relations Journal*, XI, no. 5, 46–52.

Becker, Gary S. 1971. *The Economics of Discrimination*. 2nd edn. Chicago: University of Chicago Press.

——. 1975. *Human Capital: A Theoretical and Empirical Analysis, with Special Reference to Education*. 2nd edn. Chicago: National Bureau of Economic Research. 1st edn. 1964. New York: National Bureau of Economic Research.

Beechey, V. 1978. 'Women and Production: A Critical Analysis of Some Sociological Theories of Women's Work'. *Feminism and Materialism*. Eds. A. Kuhn and A. M. Wolpe. London: Routledge & Kegan Paul, 155–97.

Bell, J.D.M. 1975. 'The Development of Industrial Relations in Nationalized Industries in Post-War Britain'. *British Journal of Industrial Relations*, XIII, 1–13.

Bennett, F. 1981. 'Family Wage'. *Low Pay Review*, no. 4, 10–15.

Bercusson, Brian. 1978. *Fair Wages Resolutions*. London: Mansell.

——. 1981. 'Employment Protection'. *The Employment Acts 1974–1980 with Commentary*. Charles D. Drake and Brian Bercusson. London: Sweet & Maxwell, 4–42.

Berger, S., and M. Piore. 1980. *Dualism and Discontinuity in Industrial Societies*. Cambridge: Cambridge University Press.

Bevan, G., K. Sisson and P. Way. 1981. 'Cash Limits and Public Sector Pay'. *Public Administration*, LIX, 379–98.

Beynon, Huw. 1973. *Working for Ford*. Harmondsworth: Penguin.

——, and Hilary Wainwright. 1979. *The Workers' Report on Vickers*. London: Pluto.

Black, B., et al. 1980. *Low Pay in Northern Ireland.* London: Low Pay Unit.

Blackaby, Frank T. (ed.). 1980a. *The Future of Pay Bargaining.* London: Heinemann.

——. 1980b. 'An Array of Proposals'. *The Future of Pay Bargaining.* Ed. F. T. Blackaby, 64–91.

Blackburn, R.M. 1967. *Union Character and Social Class.* London: Batsford.

——, and M. Mann. 1979. *The Working Class in the Labour Market.* London: Macmillan.

Blinder, Alan S. 1972. 'Who Joins Unions?'. Working Paper no. 36. Princeton: Princeton University, Department of Economics, Industrial Relations Section.

Bolton. 1971. Department of Trade and Industry. Committee of Inquiry on Small Firms. *Report.* Cmnd 4811. London: HMSO.

Bootham, F., and D. Denham. 1981. 'Industrial Tribunals: Is There an Ideological Background?'. *Industrial Relations Journal,* XII, no. 3, 6–14.

Boraston, Ian, Hugh Armstrong Clegg and Malcolm Rimmer. 1975. *Workplace and Union: A Study of Local Relationships in Fourteen Unions.* London: Heinemann.

Bosanquet, N., and P. Doeringer. 1973. 'Is There a Dual Labour Market in Britain?'. *Economic Journal,* LXXXIII, 421–35.

Boston, S. 1980. *Women Workers and the Trade Union Movement.* London: Davis-Poynter.

Bourn, C. 1979. 'Statutory Exemptions for Collective Agreements'. *Industrial Law Journal,* VIII, 85–99.

Bowers, J.K., and D. Harkess. 1979. 'Duration of Unemployment by Age and Sex'. *Economica,* XLVI, 239–60.

Braun, A.R. 1975. 'The Role of Incomes Policy in Industrial Countries Since World War II'. *International Monetary Fund Staff Papers,* XXII, 1–36.

Braverman, H. 1974. *Labor and Monopoly Capital: The Degradation of Work in the Twentieth Century.* New York: Monthly Review Press.

Brittan, S. 1981. 'Why British Incomes Policies Have Failed'. *Incomes Policy.* Eds. R. E. J. Chater, A. Dean and R. F. Elliott. Oxford: Oxford University Press, 104–27.

Brossard, M., and M. Maurice. 1974. 'Existe-t-il un modele universel de l'organisation'. *Sociologie du Travail,* XVI, no. 4, 402–26.

Brown, William Arthur. 1972. 'A Consideration of "Custom and Practice" '. *British Journal of Industrial Relations,* X, 42–61.

——. 1973. *Piecework Bargaining.* London: Heinemann.

——. 1976. 'Incomes Policy and Pay Differentials'. *Oxford Bulletin of Economics and Statistics,* XXXVIII, 27–49.

——. 1979. 'Engineering Wages and the Social Contract, 1975–1977'. *Oxford Bulletin of Economics and Statistics,* XLI, 51–61.

——. 1980. 'The Structure of Pay Bargaining in Britain'. *The Future of Pay Bargaining.* Ed. F. T. Blackaby, 129–47.

—— (ed.). 1981. *The Changing Contours of British Industrial Relations: A Survey of Manufacturing Industry.* Oxford: Blackwell.

——, Robert Ebsworth and Michael Terry. 1978. 'Factors Shaping Shop Steward Organisation in Britain'. *British Journal of Industrial Relations,* XVI, 139-59.

——, and Keith F. Sisson. 1983. 'Industrial Relations in the Next Decade: Current Trends and Future Possibilities'. *Industrial Relations Journal* (forthcoming).

——, and Michael Terry. 1978. 'The Changing Nature of National Wage Agreements'. *Scottish Journal of Political Economy,* XXV, 119–34.

Buchanan, R.T. 1974. 'Merger Waves in British Unionism'. *Industrial Relations Journal,* V, no. 2, 37–45.

Buchanan, R.T. 1981. 'Mergers in British Trade Unions, 1949–79'. *Industrial Relations Journal,* XII, no. 3, 40–49.

Bullock. 1977. Committee of Inquiry on Industrial Democracy. *Report.* Cmnd 6706. London: HMSO.

Bullock, Alan. 1967. *The Life and Times of Ernest Bevin: Minister of Labour 1940–1945.* London: Heinemann.

Burawoy, Michael. 1979. *Manufacturing Consent: Changes in the Labor Process under Monopoly Capitalism.* Chicago: University of Chicago Press.

Business Statistics Office. 1978. *Historical Record of the Census of Production 1907–1970.* London: HMSO.

Cairnes, J.E. 1887. *Some Leading Principles of Political Economy.* London: Macmillan.

Carlson, J.A., and J. M. Parkin. 1975. 'Inflation Expectations'. *Economica,* XLII, 123–38.

Carpenter, M.J. 1983. 'The Development of Trade Union Activity Among Nurses'. PhD thesis, University of Warwick.

Carson, W.G. 1974. 'Symbolic and Instrumental Dimensions of Early Factory Legislation: A Case Study in the Social Origins of Criminal Law'. *Crime, Criminology and Public Policy.* Ed. R. Hood. London: Heinemann, 107–38.

——. 1979. 'The Conventionalisation of Early Factory Crime'. *International Journal for the Sociology of Law,* VII, 37–60.

——. 1980. 'Early Factory Inspectors and the Viable Class Society: A Rejoinder'. *International Journal for the Sociology of Law,* VIII, 187–91.

Central Office of Industrial Tribunals (COIT). 1981. 'Fact Sheet'. London: COIT.

Central Policy Review Staff (CPRS). 1975. *The Future of the British Car Industry.* London: HMSO.

——. 1980. *People and their Families.* London: HMSO.

Central Training Council. 1969. 'Training for Skill: The Time for Change'. *Third Report to the Secretary of State.* London: HMSO, Appendix VIII.

Certification Office for Trade Unions and Employers' Associations. 1981. *Annual Report of the Certification Officer 1980.* London: The Office.

Chandler, A.D. 1977. *The Visible Hand: The Managerial Revolution in American Business.* Cambridge, Mass.: Harvard University Press.

Chater, R.E.J. 1981. 'The Earnings Dilemma'. *Incomes Policy.* Eds. R. E. J. Chater, A. Dean and R. F. Elliott. Oxford: Oxford University Press, 104–28.

Cheshire, P.C. 1973. 'Regional Unemployment Differences in Great Britain'. *National Institute of Economic and Social Research Regional Papers,* II, 1–40.

Child, J., R. Loveridge and M. Warner. 1973. 'Towards an Organizational Study of Trade Unions'. *Sociology,* VII, no. 1, 71–91.

Chiplin, B. 1979. 'An Evaluation of Sex Discrimination: Some Problems and a Suggested Reorientation'. *Women in the Labor Market.* Eds. C. B. Lloyd, E. S. Andrews and C. L. Gilroy. New York: Columbia University Press, 246–70.

——. 1981. 'An Alternative Approach to the Measurement of Sex Discrimination: An Illustration from University Entrance'. *Economic Journal,* XCI, 988–97.

——, M. M. Curran and C. J. Parsley. 1980. 'Relative Female Earnings in Great Britain and the Impact of Legislation'. *Women and Low Pay.* Ed. P. J. Sloane. London: Macmillan, 57–126.

——, and P. J. Sloane. 1974. 'Sexual Discrimination in the Labour Market'. *British Journal of Industrial Relations,* XII, 371–402.

——, and P. J. Sloane. 1976a. *Sex Discrimination in the Labour Market.* London: Macmillan.

Chiplin, B., and P. J. Sloane. 1976b. 'Personal Characteristics and Sex Differentials in Professional Employment'. *Economic Journal*, LXXXVI, 729–45.

Chiswick, B.R. 1980. 'The Earnings of White and Coloured Male Immigrants in Britain'. *Economica*, XLVII, 81–7.

Clark, Jon, et al. 1980. *Trade Unions, National Politics and Economic Management: A Comparative Study of the TUC and the DGB*. London: Anglo-German Foundation.

——, and *Lord* Wedderburn. 1983. 'Modern Labour Law: Problems, Functions and Policies'. *Labour Law and Industrial Relations: Building on Kahn-Freund*. Eds. *Lord* Wedderburn, R. Lewis and J. Clark (forthcoming).

Clegg. 1980. Standing Commission on Pay Comparability. *General Report*. Report no. 9. Cmnd 7995. London: HMSO.

Clegg, Hugh Armstrong. 1970. *The System of Industrial Relations in Great Britain*. Oxford: Blackwell. (2nd edn. 1972.)

——. 1971. *How to Run an Incomes Policy and Why We Made Such a Mess of the Last One*. London: Heinemann.

——. 1975. 'Pluralism in Industrial Relations'. *British Journal of Industrial Relations*, XIII, 309–16.

——. 1976a. *The System of Industrial Relations in Great Britain*. 3rd edn. Oxford: Blackwell.

——. 1976b. *Trade Unionism under Collective Bargaining: A Theory Based on Comparisons of Six Countries*. Oxford: Blackwell.

——. 1976c. 'Are Strikes in the Public Sector Inevitable?'. *International Conference on Trends in Industrial and Labour Relations*. Eds. F. Bairstow and S. Bochner. Montreal: n.p., 49–61.

——. 1979. *The Changing System of Industrial Relations in Great Britain*. Oxford: Blackwell.

——. 1982. 'Reflections on Incomes Policy and the Public Sector in Britain'. *Labour and Society*, VII, 3–12.

——, Alan Fox and A. F. Thompson. 1964. *A History of British Trade Unions Since 1889*. Volume I, 1889–1910. Oxford: Clarendon Press.

——, A. J. Killick and Rex Adams. 1961. *Trade Union Officers*. Oxford: Blackwell.

Cliff, Tony. 1970. *The Employers' Offensive: Productivity Deals and How to Fight Them*. London: Pluto.

Clifton, J. 1977. 'Competition and the Evolution of the Capitalist Mode of Production'. *Cambridge Journal of Economics*, I, no. 2, 137–51.

Clifton, R., and C. Tatton-Brown. 1979. *Impact of Employment Legislation on Small Firms*. Research Paper no. 6. London: Department of Employment.

Coates, Ken (ed.). 1979. *What Went Wrong? Explaining the Fall of the Labour Government*. Nottingham: Spokesman.

——. 1981. *Work-ins, Sit-ins and Industrial Democracy*. Nottingham: Spokesman.

——, and Tony Topham. 1977. *The Shop Steward's Guide to the Bullock Report*. Nottingham: Spokesman.

——, and Tony Topham. 1980. *Trade Unions in Britain*. Nottingham: Spokesman.

Coates, R.D. 1972. *Teachers' Unions and Interest Group Politics*. Cambridge: Cambridge University Press.

——. 1980. *Labour in Power?* London: Longman.

Codrington, C., and J. S. Henley. 1981. 'The Industrial Relations of Injury and Death: Safety Representatives in the Construction Industry'. *British Journal of Industrial Relations*, XIX, 297–316

Commission for Racial Equality. 1980. *Annual Report*. London: HMSO.

Commission for Racial Equality. 1981a. *Annual Report.* London: HMSO.
——. 1981b. *Report of a Formal Investigation into BL Cars Ltd. and Two Shop Stewards.* London: The Commission.
Commission on Industrial Relations (CIR). 1971. *The Hotel and Catering Industry: Part 1, Hotels and Restaurants.* Report 23. Cmnd 4789. London: HMSO.
——. 1972. *Employers' Organisations and Industrial Relations.* Study no. 1. London: HMSO.
——. 1973. *Industrial Relations at Establishment Level: A Statistical Survey.* Study no. 2. London: HMSO.
——. 1974a. *Clothing Wages Councils.* Report 77. London: HMSO.
——. 1974b. *Small Firms and the Code of Industrial Practice.* Report 69. London: HMSO.
——. 1974c. *Trade Union Recognition: CIR Experience.* Study no. 5. London: HMSO.
——. 1974d. *Retail Distribution.* Report 89. London: HMSO.
Confederation of British Industry. 1965. *Evidence to the Royal Commission on Trade Unions and Employers' Associations.* London: CBI.
——. 1972. *Report of the Commission of Inquiry into Industrial and Commercial Representation.* London: CBI.
——. 1977a. *The Future of Pay Determination: A Discussion Document.* London: CBI.
——. 1977b. *In Place of Bullock.* London: CBI.
——. 1979. *Pay: The Choice Ahead.* London: CBI.
Conservative Party. 1968. *Fair Deal at Work: The Conservative Approach to Modern Industrial Relations.* London: Conservative Political Centre.
Cooper, Bruce M., and A. F. Bartlett. 1976. *Industrial Relations: A Study in Conflict.* London: Heinemann.
Coote, Anna, and B. Campbell. 1982. *Sweet Freedom: The Struggle for Women's Liberation.* London: Picador.
——, and Peter Kellner. 1980. *Hear this, Brother.* London: New Statesman.
Cowling, Keith. 1982. *Monopoly Capitalism.* London: Macmillan.
Craig, C., et al. 1980a. *Abolition and After: The Cutlery Wages Council.* Research Paper no. 18. London: Department of Employment.
——, et al. 1980b. *Abolition and After: The Jute Wages Council.* Research Paper no. 15. London: Department of Employment.
——, et al. 1980c. *Abolition and After: The Paper Box Wages Council.* Research Paper no. 12. London: Department of Employment.
——, et al. 1980d. 'After the Wages Council: Industrial and Staff Canteens'. Cambridge: University of Cambridge, Department of Applied Economics. (Mimeographed.)
——, et al. 1980e. 'Minimum Wage Legislation and Labour Market Segmentation: Final Report to the Department of Employment on "the Effect of the Abolition of Wages Councils" '. *Low Pay and Labour Market Segmentation in Advanced Industrial Countries.* Vol. 1. Cambridge: University of Cambridge, Department of Applied Economics. (Mimeographed.)
——, et al. 1982. *Labour Market Structure, Industrial Organisation and Low Pay.* Cambridge: Cambridge University Press.
Creigh, Stephen, Nigel Donaldson and Eric Hawthorn. 1980. 'Stoppage Activity in OECD Countries'. *Employment Gazette,* LXXXVIII, 1174–81.
Creighton, W.B. 1979. *Working Women and the Law.* London: Mansell.
Cressey, Peter, et al. 1981. *Industrial Democracy and Participation: A Scottish Survey.* Research Paper no. 28. London: Department of Employment.
Crine, S. 1981. *The Great Pay Robbery.* London: Low Pay Unit.

Cripps, T.F., and R. J. Tarling. 1974. 'An Analysis of the Duration of Male Unemployment in Great Britain 1932–73'. *Economic Journal*, LXXXIV, 289–316.

Crossley, J.R. 1966. 'Collective Bargaining, Wage Structure and the Labour Market in the United Kingdom'. *Wage Structure in Theory and Practice*. Ed. Hugh Jones. Amsterdam: North Holland, 157–235.

——. 1968. 'The Donovan Report: A Case Study in the Poverty of Historicism'. *British Journal of Industrial Relations*. VI, 296–302.

Crouch, Colin. 1977. *Class Conflict and the Industrial Relations Crisis: Compromise and Corporatism in the Policies of the British State*. London: Heinemann.

——. 1979. *The Politics of Industrial Relations*. London: Fontana.

Cuthbert, Norman H., and Kevin H. Hawkins. 1973. *Company Industrial Relations Policies: The Management of Industrial Relations in the 1970s*. London: Longman.

Daniel, W.W. 1976. *Wage Determination in Industry*. London: Political and Economic Planning.

——. 1980a. *Maternity Rights: The Experience of Women*. London: Policy Studies Institute.

——. 1980b. 'Influences on the Level of Wage Settlements in Manufacturing Industry'. *The Future of Pay Bargaining*. Ed. F. T. Blackaby, 148–62.

——. 1981a. *Maternity Rights: The Experience of Employers*. London: Policy Studies Institute.

——. 1981b. 'A Clash of Symbols: The Case of Maternity Legislation'. *Policy Studies*, II, 74–85.

——. 1981c. 'Why is High Unemployment Still Somehow Acceptable?'. *New Society*, LV, 19 March, 495–7.

——, and E. Stilgoe. 1978. *The Impact of Employment Protection Laws*. London: Policy Studies Institute.

Daubigney, J.P., and J. J. Silvestre. 1972. *Comparaison de hiérarchie des salaires entre l'Allemagne et la France*. Aix-en-Provence: Laboratoire d'Economie et de Sociologie du Travail. Another version was published as 'Structure des salaires dans les entreprises françaises et allemandes'. *Les Documents du Centre d'Etude des Revenus et des Côuts*, no. 23, Documentation Française, Paris, 1974.

Davies, Paul. 1973. 'In Search of Jobs and Defendants'. *Modern Law Review*, XXXVI, 78–89.

——, and Mark Freedland. 1979. *Labour Law: Text and Materials*. London: Weidenfeld & Nicolson.

——, and *Lord* Wedderburn. 1977. 'The Land of Industrial Democracy'. *Industrial Law Journal*, VI, 197–211.

Davies, Robert J. 1979. 'Economic Activity, Incomes Policy and Strikes: A Quantitative Analysis'. *British Journal of Industrial Relations*, XVII, 205–23.

Dawson, S., P. Poynter and D. Stevens. 1981a. 'Self-Regulation and Safety at Work: The Hopes and the Reality'. DSES Working Paper. London: Imperial College.

——, P. Poynter and D. Stevens. 1981b. 'Strategies for Controlling Hazards at Work'. DSES Working Paper. London: Imperial College.

Dean, Andrew. 1978. 'Incomes Policies and Differentials'. *National Institute Economic Review*, LXXXV, 40–48.

——. 1981. 'Public and Private Sector Pay and the Economy'. *Incomes Policies, Inflation and Relative Pay*. Eds. J. L. Fallick and R. F. Elliott, 45–71.

Deaton, David. 1980. 'On Testing Theories of Labour Market Segmentation'. *Low Pay and Labour Market Segmentation in Advanced Industrial Countries*. Vol. 1.

Cambridge: University of Cambridge, Department of Applied Economics. (Mimeographed.)

Deaton, David, and P. Beaumont. 1980. 'The Determinants of Bargaining Structure: Some Large Scale Evidence for Britain'. *British Journal of Industrial Relations*, XVIII, 202–16.

Department of Employment. Annual. *New Earnings Survey*. London: HMSO.

——. 1970. *Industrial Relations Bill: Consultative Document*. London: The Department.

——. 1972. *Training for the Future: A Plan for Discussion*. London: The Department.

——. 1973. *Employment and Training: Government Proposals*. Cmnd 5250. London: HMSO.

——. 1975. *Women and Work: A Review*. Research Paper no. 11. London: The Department.

——. Unit for Manpower Studies. 1976. *The Role of Immigrants in the Labour Market*. London: The Department.

——. 1977. 'How Individual People's Earnings Change'. *Employment Gazette*, LXXXV, 19–24.

——. 1978a. *Industrial Democracy*. Cmnd 7231. London: HMSO.

——. 1978b. Royal Commission on the Distribution of Income and Wealth. *Selected Evidence Submitted to the Royal Commission for Report 6: Lower Incomes*. London: HMSO.

——. 1978c. 'Age and Redundancy'. *Employment Gazette*, LXXXVI, 1032–9.

——. 1978d. 'Engagement and Vacancies Survey Results'. *Employment Gazette*, LXXXVI, 655.

——. 1980a. 'Large Industrial Stoppages, 1960–1979'. *Employment Gazette*, LXXXVIII, 994–9.

——. 1980b. 'Racial Discrimination at Work'. *Employment Gazette*, LXXXVIII, 1124–5.

——. 1981a. *A New Training Initiative: A Programme for Action*. Cmnd 8455. London: HMSO.

——. 1981b. *Trade Union Immunities*. Cmnd 8128. London: HMSO.

——. 1981c. 'Patterns of Pay: Early Results of the 1981 NES'. *Employment Gazette*, LXXXIX, 443–9.

——. 1981d. 'Race Relations at Work'. *Employment Gazette*, LXXXIX, 431–2.

—— and Manpower Services Commission. 1976. *Training for Vital Skills: A Consultative Document*. London: The Department.

Department of Employment and Productivity. 1969. *In Place of Strife: A Policy for Industrial Relations*. Cmnd 3888. London: HMSO.

Department of Health and Social Security (DHSS). 1982. 'Low Income Families – 1979'. (Mimeographed.)

Devlin, *Lord* Patrick. 1981. *The Judge*. Oxford: Oxford University Press.

Diamond. 1978. Royal Commission on the Distribution of Income and Wealth. *Lower Incomes*. Report 6. Cmnd 7175. London: HMSO.

Dickens, Linda. 1979. 'Unfair Dismissal Applications and the Industrial Tribunal System'. *Industrial Relations Journal*, IX, no. 4, 4–18.

——, et al. 1979. 'A Response to the Government's Working Papers on Amendments to Employment Protection Legislation'. Discussion Paper. Coventry: SSRC Industrial Relations Research Unit, University of Warwick.

——, et al. 1981a. 'Re-employment of Unfairly Dismissed Workers: The Lost Remedy'. *Industrial Law Journal*, X, 160–75.

——, et al. 1981b. 'Statutory Protection against Unfair Dismissal in Great Britain'. Paper presented to workshop zu Fragen der Kündigungspraxis, November 1981. To be published in Germany under the auspices of the Free University, Berlin.

Dixit, A. 1978. 'The Balance of Trade in a Model of Temporary Equilibrium with Rationing'. *Review of Economic Studies*, XLV, 393–404.

Doeringer, P.B., and M. J. Piore. 1971. *Internal Labour Markets and Manpower Analysis*. Lexington: Heath.

Donovan. 1968. Royal Commission on Trade Unions and Employers' Associations. *Report*. Cmnd 3623. London: HMSO.

Dowling, M.J., et al. 1981. *Employee Participation: Practice and Attitudes in North-West Manufacturing Industry*. Research Paper no. 27. London: Department of Employment.

Doyle, Brian. 1980. 'A Substitute for Collective Bargaining?: The Central Arbitration Committee's Approach to Section 16 of the Employment Protection Act 1975'. *Industrial Law Journal*, IX, 154–66.

Drucker, P. 1951. *The New Society: The Anatomy of the Industrial Order*. London: Heinemann.

Druker, J. 1980. 'One Big Union? Structural Change in Building Trade Unionism'. PhD thesis, University of Warwick.

Duncan, C. 1982. *Low Pay: Its Causes and the Post-War Trade Union Response*. Chichester: Research Studies Press.

Dunn, Stephen. 1981. 'The Growth of the Post-Entry Closed Shop in Britain since the 1960s: Some Theoretical Considerations'. *British Journal of Industrial Relations*, XIX, 275–96.

Durcan, J.W., and W. E. J. McCarthy. 1972. 'What is Happening to Strikes?' *New Society*, 2 November, 267–9.

Dutton, P. A. 1982. 'The New Training Initiative: What are Its Chances?' Discussion Paper 18. Coventry: University of Warwick, Institute for Employment Research.

Eaton, Jack, and Colin Gill. 1981. *The Trade Union Directory*. London: Pluto.

Eatwell, John. 1982. *Whatever Happened to Britain?* London: British Broadcasting Corporation.

——, J. Llewellyn and R. Tarling. 1974. 'Money Wage Inflation in Industrial Countries'. *Review of Economic Studies*, XLI, no. 4, 515–23.

Edelstein, J.D., and M. Warner. 1975. *Comparative Union Democracy: Organisation and Opposition in British and American Unions*. London: Allen & Unwin.

Edgeworth, F.Y. 1922. 'Equal Pay to Men and Women for Equal Worth'. *Economic Journal*, XXXI, 431–57.

Edmund-Davies. 1978. Committee of Inquiry on the Police. *Reports on Negotiating Machinery and Pay*. Cmnd 7283. London: HMSO.

Edwards, Paul K. 1977. 'The Kerr-Siegel Hypothesis of Strikes and the Isolated Mass: A Study of the Falsification of Sociological Knowledge'. *Sociological Review*, n.s. XXV, 551–74.

——. 1981. 'The Strike-Proneness of British Manufacturing Establishments'. *British Journal of Industrial Relations*, XIX, 135–48.

——. 1982. 'Britain's Changing Strike Problem?' *Industrial Relations Journal*, XIII, no. 2, 5–20.

——, and Hugh Scullion. 1982a. *The Social Organization of Industrial Conflict: Control and Resistance in the Workplace*. Oxford: Blackwell.

——, and Hugh Scullion. 1982b. 'The Local Organization of a National Dispute: The British 1979 Engineering Strike'. *Industrial Relations Journal*, XIII, no. 1, 57–63.

Edwards, Richard C. 1975. 'The Social Relations of Production in the Firm and Labor Market Structure'. *Labor Market Segmentation*. Eds. R. Edwards, M. Reich and D. M. Gordon. Lexington: Lexington Books, 3–26.

——. 1979. *Contested Terrain: The Transformation of the Workplace in the Twentieth Century*. London: Heinemann.

Edwards, Ronald Stanley, and R. D. V. Roberts. 1971. *Status, Productivity and Pay: A Major Experiment*. London: Macmillan.

Elias, P. 1973. 'Trade Union Amalgamations: Patterns and Procedures'. *Industrial Law Journal*, II, 125–36.

——. 1981. 'Fairness in Unfair Dismissal: Trends and Tensions'. *Industrial Law Journal*, X, 201–17.

Elkouri, Frank, and Edna Asper Elkouri. 1973. *How Arbitration Works*. 3rd edn. Washington D.C.: Bureau of National Affairs.

Elliott, J. 1978. *Conflict or Co-operation? The Growth of Industrial Democracy*. London: Kogan Page.

Elliott, R.F. 1977. 'Public Sector Wage Movements: 1950–1973'. *Scottish Journal of Political Economy*, XXIV, no. 2, 133–51.

——, and J. L. Fallick. 1977. 'Pay Differentials in Perspective: A Study of Manual and Non-Manual Workers' Pay over the Period 1951–1975'. Occasional Paper 77-07. Aberdeen: University of Aberdeen, Department of Political Economy.

——, and J. L. Fallick. 1981. *Pay in the Public Sector*. London: Macmillan.

Ellis, J., and R. W. Johnson. 1973. *Members from the Unions*. London: Fabian Society.

Ellis, V. 1981. *The Role of Trade Unions in the Promotion of Equal Opportunities*. Manchester: Equal Opportunities Commission.

Elsheikh, Farouk, and George Sayers Bain. 1979. 'The Determination of the Rate of Change of Unionization in the U.K.: A Comment and Further Analysis'. *Applied Economics*, XI, 452–63.

——, and George Sayers Bain. 1980. 'Unionisation in Britain: An Inter-Establishment Analysis Based on Survey Data'. *British Journal of Industrial Relations*, XVIII, 169–78.

England, Joe. 1979. 'How UCATT Revised Its Rules: An Anatomy of Organisational Change'. *British Journal of Industrial Relations*, XVII, 1–18.

——. 1981. 'Shop Stewards in Transport House: A Comment on the Incorporation of the Rank and File'. *Industrial Relations Journal*, XII, no. 5, 16–29.

Equal Opportunities Commission (EOC). 1979. *Health and Safety Legislation: Should We Distinguish between Men and Women?* Manchester: EOC.

Ewing, Keith. 1982. 'Industrial Action: Another Step in the Right Direction?' *Industrial Law Journal*, XI, 207–26.

Eyraud, F. 1981. 'Action syndicale et salaire: une comparaison France/Grande-Bretagne'. Doctoral thesis, University of Aix-Marseille II.

Fallick, J.L., and R.F. Elliott (eds.). 1981a. *Incomes Policies, Inflation and Relative Pay*. London: Allen & Unwin.

——, and R. F. Elliott. 1981b. 'Incomes Policy and the Public Sector'. *Incomes Policies, Inflation and Relative Pay*. Eds. J. L. Fallick and R. F. Elliott, 100–127.

Farnham, David, and John Pimlott. 1979. *Understanding Industrial Relations*. London: Cassell.

Feather, Victor. 1968. 'The Royal Commission's Analysis: A Trade Union Appraisal'. *British Journal of Industrial Relations*, VI, 339–46.

Field, F. 1979. *One in Eight: A Report on Britain's Poor*. London: Low Pay Unit.

Fine, B. 1980. *Economic Theory and Ideology*. London: Edward Arnold.

——. 1982. 'Multinational Corporations, the British Economy and the Alternative Economic Strategy'. Discussion Paper no. 111. London: Birkbeck College.

——, and L. Harris. 1983. *The Peculiarities of the British Economy*. London: Lawrence & Wishart (forthcoming).

Fisher, M.R. 1973. *Measurement of Labour Disputes and their Economic Effects*. Paris: OECD.

Flanders, Allan D. 1952. *Trade Unions*. London: Hutchinson.

Flanders, Allan D. 1964. *The Fawley Productivity Agreements: A Case Study of Management and Collective Bargaining.* London: Faber.

———. 1967. *Collective Bargaining: Prescription for Change.* London: Faber. (Reprinted in Flanders, 1970a.)

———. 1970a. *Management and Unions: The Theory and Reform of Industrial Relations.* London: Faber.

———. 1970b. 'Collective Bargaining: Prescription for Change'. *Management and Unions,* 155–211.

———. 1970c. 'Collective Bargaining: A Theoretical Analysis'. *Management and Unions,* 213–40.

———. 1970d. 'Industrial Relations: What is Wrong with the System?' *Management and Unions,* 83–128.

———. 1974. 'The Tradition of Voluntarism'. *British Journal of Industrial Relations,* XII, 352–70.

———, and Hugh Armstrong Clegg (eds.). 1954. *The System of Industrial Relations in Great Britain: Its History, Law and Institutions.* Oxford: Blackwell.

Forde, M. 1982. 'The "Closed Shop" Case'. *Industrial Law Journal,* XI, 1–15.

Fowler, A. 1975. *Personnel Management in Local Government.* London: Institute of Personnel Management.

Fox, Alan. 1966. *Industrial Sociology and Industrial Relations.* Research Paper 3, Royal Commission on Trade Unions and Employers' Associations. London: HMSO.

———. 1973. 'Industrial Relations: A Social Critique of Pluralist Ideology'. *Man and Organisation.* Ed. J. Child. London: Allen & Unwin, 185–234.

———. 1974. *Beyond Contract: Work, Power and Trust Relations.* London: Faber.

Freedland, Mark. 1976. 'Employment Protection: Redundancy Procedures and the EEC'. *Industrial Law Journal,* V, 24–34.

Friedman, Andrew L. 1977. *Industry and Labour: Class Struggle at Work and Monopoly Capitalism.* London: Macmillan.

Friedman, H., and S. Meredeen. 1980. *The Dynamics of Industrial Conflict: Lessons from Fords.* London: Croom Helm.

Friedman, M. 1951. 'Some Comments on the Significance of Labor Unions for Economic Policy'. *The Impact of the Union.* Ed. D. McC. Wright. New York: Harcourt Brace.

——— 1968. 'The Role of Monetary Policy'. *American Economic Review,* LVIII, 1–17.

Fröbel, F., J. Heinrichs and O. Kreye. 1980. *The New International Division of Labour.* London: Cambridge University Press.

Fryer, R.H. 1973a. 'The Myths of the Redundancy Payments Act'. *Industrial Law Journal,* II, 1–16.

———. 1973b. 'Redundancy, Values and Public Policy'. *Industrial Relations Journal,* IV, no. 2, 2–19.

———. 1979. 'British Trade Unions and the Cuts'. *Capital and Class,* VIII, 96–112.

———, Andy Fairclough and Tom Manson. 1974. *Organisation and Change in the National Union of Public Employees.* London: NUPE.

Gallie, Duncan. 1978. *In Search of the New Working Class: Automation and Social Integration within the Capitalist Enterprise.* Cambridge: Cambridge University Press.

Garside, W.R. 1980. *The Measurement of Unemployment.* Oxford: Blackwell.

Gennard, John, Stephen Dunn and Michael Wright. 1979. 'The Content of British Closed Shop Agreements'. *Employment Gazette,* LXXXVII, 1088–92.

———, Stephen Dunn and Michael Wright. 1980. 'The Extent of Closed Shop Arrangements in British Industry'. *Employment Gazette,* LXXXVIII, 16–22.

Gennard, John, and M. D. Steuer. 1971. 'The Industrial Relations of Foreign-Owned Subsidiaries in the United Kingdom'. *British Journal of Industrial Relations*, IX, 143–59.

Gill, Ken. 1981. Contribution to *The Forward March of Labour Halted?* Eds. Martin Jacques and Francis Mulhern. London: Verso, 20–23.

Gintis, H. 1976. 'The Nature of Labour Exchange and the Theory of Capitalist Production'. *Review of Radical Political Economics*, VIII, no. 2, 36–54.

Glucklich, P., and M. Snell. 1982. *Women: Work and Wages*. Discussion Series no. 2. London: Low Pay Unit.

Glyn, Andrew, and John Harrison. 1980. *The British Economic Disaster*. London: Pluto.

——, and Bob Sutcliffe. 1972. *British Capitalism, Workers and the Profits Squeeze*. Harmondsworth: Penguin.

Godfrey, L.G. 1971. 'The Phillips Curve: Incomes Policy and Trade Union Effects'. *The Current Inflation*. Eds. H. G. Johnson and A. R. Nobay. London: Macmillan, 99–124.

Goldman, Alvin L. 1979. 'United States of America'. *International Encyclopedia for Labour Law and Industrial Relations*. Ed. R. Blanpain. 8 vols. Daventer: Kluwer.

Goldthorpe, John H. 1974. 'Industrial Relations in Great Britain: A Critique of Reformism'. *Politics and Society*, IV, 419–52.

——, and K. Hope. 1974. *The Social Grading of Occupations: A New Approach and Scale*. Oxford: Oxford University Press.

Goodhart, A.L. 1927. 'The Legality of the General Strike'. *Yale Law Journal*, XXXVI, 464–85.

Goodman, G. 1979. *The Awkward Warrior: Frank Cousins, His Life and Times*. London: Davis-Poynter.

Goodman, J.F.B., and T. G. Whittingham. 1973. *Shop Stewards*. London: Pan. First published 1969 under the title *Shop Stewards in British Industry*.

——, et al. 1977. *Rule-Making and Industrial Peace: Industrial Relations in the Footwear Industry*. London: Croom Helm.

Gordon, D.M. 1972. *Theories of Poverty and Underemployment*. Lexington: Lexington Books.

——. 1976. 'Capitalist Efficiency and Socialist Efficiency'. *Monthly Review*, XXVIII, no. 3, 19–39.

Gordon, R.J. 1981. 'International Monetarism, Wage Push and Monetary Accommodation'. *Inflation, Depression and Economic Policy in the West*. Ed. A. S. Courakis. London: Mansell, 1–64.

Gospel, Howard. 1974. 'An Approach to a Theory of the Firm in Industrial Relations'. *British Journal of Industrial Relations*, XI, 211–28.

——, and Paul Willman. 1981. 'Disclosure of Information: The CAC Approach'. *Industrial Law Journal*, X, 10–22.

Gramsci, A. 1977. *Selections from Political Writings, 1910–20*. Ed. Quintin Hoare. London: Lawrence & Wishart.

Grant, Ronald M. 1977. *Industrial Relations*, Manchester: Ginn.

Grant, Wyn, and David Marsh. 1977. *The Confederation of British Industry*. London: Hodder & Stoughton.

Greenhalgh, C. 1980. 'Male-Female Wage Differentials in Great Britain: Is Marriage an Equal Opportunity?'. *Economic Journal*, CXC, 751–75.

Greenwood, J.A. 1972. 'On the Abolition of Wages Councils'. *Industrial Relations Journal*, III, no. 4, 30–42.

Gronau, R. 1974. 'Wage Comparisons: A Selective Bias'. *Journal of Political Economy*, LXXXII, 1119–43.

Hall, K., and Isobel Miller. 1971. 'Industrial Attitudes to Skill Dilution'. *British Journal of Industrial Relations,* IX, 1–20.

Hall, Robert E. 1971. 'Prospects for Shifting the Phillips Curve through Manpower Policy'. *Brookings Papers on Economic Activity,* no. 3, 659–701.

Hallas, D. 1974. 'White Collar Workers'. *International Socialism,* LXXII, 14–22.

Halsbury. 1974. Committee of Inquiry into the Pay and Related Conditions of Nurses and Midwives. *Report.* London: HMSO for DHSS.

Hansard. 1980. H. C. Deb., 21 May. Col. 203. London: HMSO.

Harrison, M. 1960. *Trade Unions and the Labour Party.* London: Allen & Unwin.

Hart, R. A., and D. I. MacKay. 1975. 'Engineering Earnings in Britain, 1914–1968'. *Journal of the Royal Statistical Society,* Ser. A, CXXXVIII, no. 1, 32–50.

Hawes, W.R., and C. C. P. Brookes. 1980. 'Change and Renewal: Joint Consultation in Industry'. *Employment Gazette,* LXXXVIII, 353–61.

——, and David Smith. 1981. 'Employee Involvement Outside Manufacturing'. *Employment Gazette,* LXXXIX, 265–71.

——, and G. Smith. 1981. *Patterns of Representation of the Parties in Unfair Dismissal Cases: A Review of the Evidence.* Research Paper no. 22. London: Department of Employment.

Hawkins, Kevin H. 1972. *Conflict and Change: Aspects of Industrial Relations.* London: Holt, Rinehart & Winston.

——. 1976. *British Industrial Relations, 1945–1975.* London: Barrie & Jenkins.

——. 1981. *Trade Unions.* London: Hutchinson.

HAY-MSL Limited. 1976. *Analysis of Managerial Remuneration in the United Kingdom and Overseas.* Background Paper 3. Royal Commission on the Distribution of Income and Wealth. London: HMSO.

Hemingway, John. 1978. *Conflict and Democracy: Studies in Trade Union Government.* Oxford: Clarendon Press.

Henderson, J., and R. Quandt. 1980. *Microeconomic Theory.* London: McGraw-Hill.

Henry, S.G.B., and Ormerod, P. 1978. 'Incomes Policy and Wage Inflation: Empirical Evidence for the U.K. 1961–77'. *National Institute Economic Review,* LXXXV, 31–9.

——, M. C. Sawyer and P. Smith. 1976. 'Models of Inflation in the United Kingdom: An Evaluation'. *National Institute Economic Review,* LXXVII, 31–9.

Hepple, B.A. 1972. 'Union Responsibility for Shop Stewards'. *Industrial Law Journal,* IV, 197–211.

——. 1980. 'A Functional Approach to Dismissal Laws'. *International Collection of Essays in Memoriam Sir Otto Kahn-Freund.* Eds. F. Gamillscheg et al. Munich: C. H. Beck, 477–91.

——. 1981. 'A Right to Work?' *Industrial Law Journal,* X, 65–83.

——. 1982. 'The Transfer of Undertakings (Protection of Employment) Regulations'. *Industrial Law Journal,* XI, 29–40.

——, and P. O'Higgins. 1971. *Public Employee Trade Unionism in the United Kingdom: The Legal Framework.* Ann Arbor: Institute of Labor and Industrial Relations.

——, and P. O'Higgins (eds.). 1972. *Encyclopedia of Labour Relations Law.* 3 vols. London: Sweet & Maxwell. [Looseleaf, regularly updated.]

——, and P. O'Higgins. 1981. *Employment Law.* 4th edn. B. A. Hepple. London: Sweet & Maxwell.

Herding, R.G. 1972. *Job Control and Union Structure.* Rotterdam: Rotterdam University Press.

Hicks, J.R. 1963. *The Theory of Wages.* 2nd edn. London: Macmillan.

——. 1974. *The Crisis in Keynesian Economics.* Oxford: Blackwell.

Hill, Stephen, and Keith Thurley. 1974. 'Sociology and Industrial Relations'. *British Journal of Industrial Relations*, XII, 147–70.

Hindess, B. 1971. *The Decline of Working Class Politics*. London: Paladin.

Hines, A.G. 1964. 'Trade Unions and Wage Inflation in the United Kingdom: 1893–1961'. *Review of Economic Studies*, XXXI, no. 88, 221–52.

——. 1971. 'The Determinants of the Rate of Change of Money Wage Rates and the Effectiveness of Incomes Policy'. *The Current Inflation*. Eds. H. G. Johnson and A. R. Nobay. London: Macmillan, 143–78.

Hobsbawm, Eric, et al. 1981. *The Forward March of Labour Halted?* Eds. M. Jacques and F. Mulhern. London: Verso.

Holden, K. 1978. 'A Cross-Section Study of the Relationship between Strikes and Market Structure in the United Kingdom'. *Journal of Economic Studies*, n.s. V, 37–49.

Houghton. 1974. Committee of Inquiry into the Pay of Non-University Teachers. *Report*. Cmnd 5848. London: HMSO.

Hughes, John. 1967. *Trade Union Structure and Government: Structure and Development*. Research Paper 5, Part 1, Royal Commission on Trade Unions and Employers' Associations. London: HMSO.

——. 1968. *Trade Union Structure and Government: Membership Participation and Trade Union Government*. Research Paper 5, Part 2, Royal Commission on Trade Unions and Employers' Associations. London: HMSO.

Huhne, C. 1982. 'Economic Forecast'. *Guardian*, 20 April, 19.

Hunt, Dennis D. 1977. *Common Sense Industrial Relations*. Newton Abbot: David & Charles.

Hunt, J. 1982. 'A Woman's Place is in Her Union'. *Women, Work and the Labour Market*. Ed. J. West. London: Routledge & Kegan Paul, 154–71.

——, and S. Adams. 1980. *Women, Work and Trade Union Organisation*. London: Workers' Educational Association.

Hunter, L.C. 1973. 'The Economic Determination of Strike Activity: A Reconsideration'. Discussion Papers in Economics no. 1. Glasgow: University of Glasgow, Department of Social and Economic Research.

Hurstfield, J. 1978. *The Part-Time Trap: Part-Time Workers in Britain Today*. London: Low Pay Unit.

——. 1980. 'Part-Time Pittance'. *Low Pay Review*, no. 1, 1–15.

Hyman, Richard. 1971. *Marxism and the Sociology of Trade Unionism*. London: Pluto.

——. 1972. *Disputes Procedure in Action: A Study of the Engineering Industry Disputes Procedure in Coventry*. London: Heinemann.

——. 1975. *Industrial Relations: A Marxist Introduction*. London: Macmillan.

——. 1977. *Strikes*. 2nd edn. London: Fontana-Collins.

——. 1978. 'Pluralism, Procedural Consensus and Collective Bargaining'. *British Journal of Industrial Relations*, XIII, 16–40.

——. 1979. 'The Politics of Workplace Trade Unionism'. *Capital and Class*, VIII, 54–67.

——. 1981. 'Green Means Danger?' *Politics and Power*, IV, 129–45.

——, and Ian Brough. 1975. *Social Values and Industrial Relations*. Oxford: Blackwell.

——, and Tony Elger. 1981. 'Job Controls, the Employers' Offensive and Alternative Strategies'. *Capital and Class*, XV, 115–49.

——, and R. H. Fryer. 1975. 'Trade Unions: Sociology and Political Economy'. *Processing People*. Ed. J. McKinlay. New York: Holt, Rinehart & Winston, 150–213.

Institute for Employment Research. 1982. *Review of the Economy and Employment*. Coventry: University of Warwick, Institute for Employment Research.

Institute of Personnel Management. 1977. *Staff Status for All*. London: IPM.

Jackman, R., and R. Layard. 1982. 'An Inflation Tax'. *Fiscal Studies*, III, 47–59.

——, C. Mulvey and J. Trevithick. 1981. *The Economics of Inflation*. Oxford: Martin Robertson.

Jackson, Dudley, H. A. Turner and Frank Wilkinson. 1972. *Do Trade Unions Cause Inflation? Two Studies: With a Theoretical Introduction and Policy Conclusion*. University of Cambridge, Department of Applied Economics, Occasional Papers 36. Cambridge: Cambridge University Press.

Jackson, Michael P. 1982. *Industrial Relations: A Textbook*. 2nd edn. London: Croom Helm.

Jackson, Peter, and Keith F. Sisson. 1976. 'Employers' Confederations in Sweden and the UK and the Significance of Industrial Infrastructure'. *British Journal of Industrial Relations*, XIV, 306–23.

James, Bernard. 1977. 'Third Party Intervention in Recognition Disputes: The Role of the Commission on Industrial Relations'. *Industrial Relations Journal*, VIII, no. 2, 29–40.

Jenkins, Peter. 1970. *The Battle of Downing Street*. London: Charles Knight.

Johnston, T.L. 1981. *An Introduction to Industrial Relations*. Plymouth: Macdonald & Evans.

Jones, J.L. 1969. *Trade Unionism in the Seventies*. London: Transport and General Workers Union.

Jones, Michael. 1980. 'CAC and Schedule 11: The Experience of Two Years'. *Industrial Law Journal*, IX, 28–44.

Kahn-Freund, Otto. 1943. 'Collective Agreements under War Legislation'. *Modern Law Review*, VI, 112–43.

——. 1954a. 'Intergroup Conflicts and their Settlement'. *British Journal of Sociology*, V, 193–227. Reprinted in O. Kahn-Freund, *Selected Writings*, 1978, 41–77.

——. 1954b. 'The Legal Framework'. *The System of Industrial Relations in Great Britain*. Eds. A. D. Flanders and H. A. Clegg, 42–127.

——. 1959. 'Labour Law'. *Law and Opinion in England in the 20th century*. Ed. M. Ginsberg. London: Stevens, 215–63. Reprinted in O. Kahn-Freund, *Selected Writings*, 1978, 1–40.

——. 1967. 'A Note on Status and Contract in British Labour Law'. *Modern Law Review*, XXX, 635–44. Reprinted in O. Kahn-Freund, *Selected Writings*, 1978, 78–86.

——. 1968. *Labour Law: Old Traditions and New Developments*. Toronto: Clark, Irwin.

——. 1970. 'Trade Unions, the Law and Society'. *Modern Law Review*, XXXIII, 241–67. Reprinted in O. Kahn-Freund, *Selected Writings*, 1978, 128–53.

——. 1972. *Labour and the Law*. London: Stevens.

——. 1977a. *Labour and the Law*. 2nd edn. London: Stevens.

——. 1977b. 'Blackstone's Neglected Child: The Contract of Employment'. *Law Quarterly Review*, XCIII, 508–28.

——. 1977c. 'Industrial Democracy'. *Industrial Law Journal*, VI, 65–84.

——. 1978. *Selected Writings*. London: Stevens.

——. 1979. *Labour Relations: Heritage and Adjustment*. Oxford: Oxford University Press.

——. 1981. *Labour Law and Politics in the Weimar Republic*. Ed. and intr. by R. Lewis and J. Clark. Oxford: Blackwell.

Kelly, J.E., and C. W. Clegg. 1982. *Autonomy and Control at the Workplace*. London: Croom Helm.

Kelsall, R.K., D. Lockwood and A. Tropp. 1956. 'The New Middle Class in the

Power Structure of Great Britain'. *Transactions of the Third World Congress of Sociology*, III, 320-29.

Kerr, Clark, and Abraham Siegel. 1954. 'The Inter-Industry Propensity to Strike'. *Industrial Conflict*. Eds. A. Kornhauser, R. Dubin and A. M. Ross. New York: McGraw-Hill, 186–212.

Keynes, John Maynard. 1936. *The General Theory of Employment, Interest and Money*. London: Macmillan.

Kilpatrick, A., and T. Lawson. 1980. 'On the Nature of Industrial Decline in the UK'. *Cambridge Journal of Economics*, IV, 85–102.

Kinnie, N. 1982. 'Local versus Centralised Bargaining: The Dangers of a "Halfway House" '. *Personnel Management*, January, 32–6.

Knowles, K.G.J.C., and D. J. Robertson. 1951. 'Differences between the Wages of Skilled and Unskilled Workers, 1880–1950'. *Oxford University Institute of Economics and Statistics Bulletin*, XIII, no. 4, 109–27.

Kogan, M. 1981. 'Education in Hard Times'. *Big Government in Hard Times*. Eds. C. Hood and M. Wright. Oxford: Martin Robertson, 152–73.

Labour Research Department. 1981. *Redundancy Agreements*. Bargaining Report 14. London: LRD.

Laidler, D. 1976. 'Inflation: Alternative Explanations and Policies: Tests and Data Drawn from Six Countries'. *Institutions, Policies and Economic Performance*. Eds. K. Brunner and A. Metzler. New York: North Holland, 251–306.

——, and J. M. Parkin. 1975. 'Inflation: A Survey'. *Economic Journal*, LXXXV, no. 4, 741–809.

Lawson, T. 1981. 'Paternalism and Labour Market Segmentation Theory'. *The Dynamics of Labour Market Segmentation*. Ed. F. Wilkinson. London: Academic Press, 47–66.

Layard, Richard. 1982. 'Is Income Policy the Answer to Unemployment?'. *Economica*, XLIX, 219–39.

——, D. Metcalf and S. Nickell. 1978. 'The Effect of Collective Bargaining on Relative and Absolute Wages'. *British Journal of Industrial Relations*, XVI, 287–302.

——, D. Piachaud and M. Stewart. 1978. *The Causes of Poverty*. Background Paper 5, Royal Commission on the Distribution of Income and Wealth. London: HMSO.

Lazonick, W. 1983. 'Technological Change and the Control of Work: The Development of Capital-Labour Relations in US Mass Production Industries'. *Managerial Strategies and Industrial Relations*. Ed. H. Gospel. London: Heinemann (forthcoming).

Lees, Dennis, and Brian Chiplin. 1970. 'The Economics of Industrial Training'. *Lloyds Bank Review*, April, 29–41.

Leggatt, Andrew. 1979. *Report of Inquiry into Certain Trade Union Recruitment Activities*. Cmnd 7706. London: HMSO.

Lerner, Shirley. 1961. *Breakaway Unions and the Small Trade Union*. London: Allen & Unwin.

——, and John Bescoby. 1966. 'Shop Steward Combine Committees in the British Engineering Industry'. *British Journal of Industrial Relations*, IV, 154–64.

Lewenhak, S. 1977. *Women and Trade Unions*. London: Benn.

Lewin, D., P. Feuille and T. A. Kochan (eds.). 1977. *Public Sector Labor Relations: Analysis and Readings*. New Jersey: Thomas Horton & Daughters.

Lewis, H.G. 1974. 'Comments on Selectivity Biases in Wage Comparisons'. *Journal of Political Economy*, LXXXII, 1145–55.

Lewis, Paul. 1981. 'An Analysis of Why Legislation Has Failed to Provide Employment Protection for Unfairly Dismissed Workers'. *British Journal of Industrial Relations*, XIX, 316–26.

Lewis, Roy. 1970. 'The Legal Enforceability of Collective Agreements'. *British Journal of Industrial Relations*, VIII, 313–33.

——. 1976. 'The Historical Development of Labour Law'. *British Journal of Industrial Relations*, XIV, 1–17.

——. 1979a. 'Collective Agreements: The Kahn-Freund Legacy'. *Modern Law Review*, XLII, 613–22.

——. 1979b. 'Kahn-Freund and Labour Law: An Outline Critique'. *Industrial Law Journal*, VIII, 202–21.

——, and Jon Clark. 1977. 'The Bullock Report'. *Modern Law Review*, XL, 323–38.

——, and Jon Clark. 1981. 'Introduction'.*Labour Law and Politics in the Weimar Republic*. Otto Kahn Freund. Oxford: Blackwell.

——, and Bob Simpson. 1981. *Striking a Balance? Employment Law After the 1980 Act*. Oxford: Martin Robertson.

——, and Bob Simpson. 1982. 'Disorganising Industrial Relations: An Analysis of Sections 2–8 and 10–14 of the Employment Act 1982'. *Industrial Law Journal*, XI, 227–46.

Liddle, R.J., and W. E. J. McCarthy. 1972. 'The Impact of the Prices and Incomes Board on the Reform of Collective Bargaining'. *British Journal of Industrial Relations*, X, 412–39.

Lindley, R.M. (ed.). 1978. *Britain's Medium-Term Employment Prospects*. Coventry: University of Warwick, Manpower Research Group.

——. 1980. 'Employment Policy in Transition'. *Economic Change and Employment Policy*. Ed. R. M. Lindley. London: Macmillan, 330–82.

——. 1981. 'Education, Training and the Labour Market in Britain'. *European Journal of Education*, XVI, no. 1, 7–27.

——. 1982. 'Occupational Choice and Investment in Human Capital'. *The Labour Market in Britain*. Eds. J. Creedy and R. B. Thomas. London: Butterworth, 91–129.

Lipset, S.M., M. Trow and J. Coleman. 1956. *Union Democracy: The Internal Politics of the International Typographical Union*. Glencoe, Ill.: Free Press.

Lipsey, R.G., and J. M. Parkin. 1970. 'Incomes Policy: A Reappraisal'. *Economica*, XXXVII, 115–38.

Littler, C., and G. Salaman. 1982. 'Bravermania and Beyond: Recent Theories of the Labour Process'. *Sociology*, XVI, 251–69.

Lloyd, Penelope A. 1976. *Incentive Payment Systems*. Management Survey Report 34. London: British Institute of Management.

Lockwood, David. 1958. *The Blackcoated Worker: A Study in Class Consciousness*. London: Allen & Unwin.

Low Pay Unit. 1975. *Who Will Protect the Low Paid?* London: Low Pay Unit.

——. 1980. 'Profile of the Low Paid in Britain'. *Wealth, Income and Inequality*. Ed. A. B. Atkinson. 2nd edn. Oxford: Oxford University Press, 370–81.

——. 1982a. *The Case for a National Minimum Wage*. London: Low Pay Unit.

——. 1982b. *Wages Councils: An Evaluation, Briefing*. London: Low Pay Unit.

Lowndes, Richard. 1972. *Industrial Relations: A Contemporary Survey*. London: Holt, Rinehart & Winston.

Lydall, H. 1968. *The Structure of Earnings*. Oxford: Clarendon Press.

McCall, J.J. 1973. *Income Mobility, Racial Discrimination and Economic Growth*. New York: Heath.

McCarthy, W.E.J. 1964. *The Closed Shop in Britain*. Oxford: Blackwell.

McCarthy, W.E.J. 1966. *The Role of Shop Stewards in British Industrial Relations.* Research Paper 1, Royal Commission on Trade Unions and Employers' Associations. London: HMSO.

—— (ed.). 1969. *Industrial Relations in Britain: A Guide for Management and Unions.* London: Lyon, Grant & Green.

——. 1970. 'The Nature of Britain's Strike Problem'. *British Journal of Industrial Relations,* VIII, 224–36.

——. 1976. *Making Whitley Work: Review of the Operation of the National Health Service Whitley Council System.* London: DHSS.

——, and N. Ellis. 1973. *Management by Agreement: An Alternative to the Industrial Relations Act.* London: Hutchinson.

——, and S. R. Parker. 1968. *Shop Stewards and Workplace Relations.* Research Paper 10, Royal Commission on Trade Unions and Employers' Associations. London: HMSO.

McCormick, B.J., and P.S. Manley. 1967. 'The Industrial Training Act'. *Westminster Bank Review,* February, 44–56.

Macdonald, D.E. 1960. *Trade Unions and the State.* London: Macmillan.

Machlup, F. 1967. 'Theories of the Firm: Marginalist, Behavioral, Managerial'. *American Economic Review,* LVII, no. 1, 1–33.

MacKay, D.I., et al. 1971. *Labour Markets under Different Employment Conditions.* London: Allen & Unwin.

MacKenzie, R.T. 1955. *Political Parties.* London: Heinemann.

McKersie, R.B., and L. Hunter. 1973. *Pay, Productivity and Collective Bargaining.* London: Macmillan.

Mackie, L., and P. Pattullo. 1977. *Women at Work.* London: Tavistock.

MacLennan, E. 1980. *Minimum Wages for Women.* London: Low pay Unit/EOC.

McNabb, Robert, and George Psacharopoulos. 1981. 'Racial Earnings Differentials in the UK'. *Oxford Economic Papers,* n.s. XXXIII, no. 3, 415–25.

McNay, M., and C. Pond. 1980. *Low Pay and Family Poverty.* London: Study Commission on the Family.

Maitland, I. 1980. 'Disorder in the British Workplace: The Limits of Consensus'. *British Journal of Industrial Relations,* XVIII, 353–64.

Makeham, P. 1980. *Youth Unemployment.* Research Paper no. 10. London: Department of Employment.

Maki, D.R., and Z. A. Spindler. 1975. 'The Effect of Unemployment Compensation on the Rate of Unemployment in Great Britain'. *Oxford Economic Papers,* XXVII, 440–54.

Malinvaud, Edmond. 1977. *The Theory of Unemployment Reconsidered.* Oxford: Blackwell.

——. 1980a. *Profitability and Unemployment.* Cambridge: Cambridge University Press.

——. 1980b. 'Macroeconomic Rationing of Employment'. *Unemployment in Western Countries.* Eds. E. Malinvaud and Jean-Paul Fitoussi. London: Macmillan, 173–205.

Manpower Services Commission. 1978a. *TOPS Review.* London: MSC.

——. 1978b. *Training for Skills: A Programme for Action.* London: MSC.

——. 1980. *Outlook on Training: Review of the Employment and Training Act 1973.* London: MSC.

——. 1981a. *A Framework for the Future: A Sector by Sector Review of Industrial and Commercial Training.* London: MSC.

——. 1981b. *Labour Market Quarterly Report,* November.

——. 1981c. *A New Training Initiative: A Consultative Document.* London: MSC.

——. 1981d. *A New Training Initiative: An Agenda for Action.* London: MSC.

Marchington, Mick. 1982. *Managing Industrial Relations.* Maidenhead: McGraw Hill.

Marglin, S. 1974. 'What Do Bosses Do?: The Origins and Functions of Hierarchy in Capitalist Production'. *The Division of Labour*. Ed. A. Gorz. Brighton: Harvester Press, 13–54.

Marsden, David. 1980. *Study of the Changes in the Wage Structure of Manual Workers in Industry in Six Community Countries Since 1966*. Eurostat C2/80032. Luxembourg: Statistical Office of the European Communities.

——. 1981. 'Vive la Différence: Pay Differentials in Britain, West Germany, France and Italy'. *Employment Gazette*, LXXXIX, 309–18, 324.

——. 1982. 'Career Structures and Training in Internal Labour Markets in Britain – and Comparisons with West Germany'. *Manpower Studies*, IV, 10–17.

Marsh, A.I. 1965. *Industrial Relations in Engineering*. London: Pergamon.

——. 1982. *Employee Relations Policy and Decision Making*. Aldershot: Gower.

——, and E. E. Coker. 1963. 'Shop Steward Organisation in the Engineering Industry'. *British Journal of Industrial Relations*, I, 170–90.

——, E. O. Evans and P. Garcia. 1971. *Workplace Industrial Relations in Engineering*. London: Kogan Page.

——, and W. E. J. McCarthy. 1968. *Disputes Procedures in Britain*. Research Paper 2, Part 2, Royal Commission on Trade Unions and Employers' Associations. London: HMSO.

Marshall, A. 1920. *Principles of Economics*. 8th edn. London: Macmillan.

Martin, Roderick. 1968. 'Union Democracy: An Explanatory Framework'. *Sociology*, II, no. 2, 205–20.

——. 1981. *New Technology and Industrial Relations in Fleet Street*. Oxford: Clarendon Press.

Martin, Ross M. 1980. *TUC: The Growth of a Pressure Group 1868–1976*. Oxford: Clarendon Press.

Marx, K., and F. Engels. 1848. 'Manifesto of the Communist Party'. *The Revolutions of 1848: Political Writings*. Vol. 1. Ed. and intr. by David Fernbach, 1973. Harmondsworth: Penguin, 62-98.

Massey, D. 1978. 'Capital and Locational Change: The UK Electrical Engineering and Electronics Industries'. *Review of Radical Political Economics*, X, no. 3, 39–54.

Maurice, M., F. Sellier and J. J. Silvestre. 1978. *Production de la hiérarchie dans l'enterprise: recherche d'un effet sociétal France-Allemagne*. Aix-en-Provence: Laboratoire d'Economie et de Sociologie du Travail. A revised version published as *Politique d'éducation et organisation industrielle en France et en Allemagne*. Paris: Presses Universitaires de France, 1982.

——, A. Sorge and M. Warner. 1980. 'Societal Differences in Organizing Manufacturing Units: A Comparison of France, West Germany and Great Britain'. *Organization Studies*, I, no. 1, 59–86.

Mayhew, K. 1979. 'Economics and Strikes'. *Oxford Bulletin of Economics and Statistics*, XLI, 1–19.

——, and B. Rosewell. 1978. 'Immigrants and Occupational Crowding in Great Britain'. *Oxford Bulletin of Economics and Statistics*, XL, 223–48.

——, and B. Rosewell. 1979. 'Labour Market Segmentation in Britain'. *Oxford Bulletin of Economics and Statistics*, XLI, 81–115.

Meade, James. 1982. *Wage-Fixing*. Vol. I of *Stagflation*. London: Allen & Unwin.

Megaw, 1982. *Report of an Inquiry into Civil Service Pay*. Cmnd 8590. London: HMSO.

Mellish, M., and N. Collis-Squires. 1976. 'Legal and Social Norms in Discipline and Dismissal'. *Industrial Law Journal*, V, 164–77.

Metcalf, D. 1977. 'Unions, Incomes Policy and Relative Wages in Britain'. *British Journal of Industrial Relations*, XV, 157–75.

Metcalf, D. 1981. *Low Pay, Occupational Mobility, and Minimum Wage Policy in Britain.* Washington D.C.: American Enterprise Institute for Policy Research.

Meyers, Frederick. 1964. *Ownership of Jobs: A Comparative Study.* Los Angeles: University of California, Institute of Industrial Relations.

Michels, Robert. 1915. *Political Parties.* New York: Hearsts. New edition published New York: Dover, 1959.

Middlemas, Keith. 1979. *Politics in Industrial Society: The Experience of the British System Since 1911.* London: André Deutsch.

Miles, R., and A. Phizacklea. 1978. 'The TUC and Black Workers 1974–1976'. *British Journal of Industrial Relations,* XVI, 195–207.

Miliband, R. 1971. *Parliamentary Socialism.* London: Allen & Unwin.

Miller, Kenneth. 1982. 'Factory Occupations in Scotland'. *Industrial Law Journal,* XI, 115–17.

Milne-Bailey, W. 1934. *Trade Unions and the State.* London: Allen & Unwin.

Mincer, J. 1962. 'On-the-Job Training: Costs, Returns and Some Implications'. *Journal of Political Economy,* LXX, no. 5, pt. 2 (supplement).

——. 1974. *Schooling, Experience and Earnings.* New York: National Bureau of Economic Research.

——, and S. W. Polachek. 1974. 'Family Investments in Human Capital: Earnings of Women'. *Journal of Political Economy,* LXXXII, no. 2(2), S76–S108.

——, and S. W. Polachek. 1978. 'Women's Earnings Re-examined'. *Journal of Human Resources,* XIII, 118–34.

Ministry of Labour. 1962. *Industrial Training: Government Proposals.* Cmnd 1892. London: HMSO.

——. National Joint Advisory Council. Committee on Dismissal Procedures. 1967. *Dismissal Procedures: Report.* London: HMSO.

Ministry of Labour and National Service. 1958. *Training for Skill: Recruitment and Training of Young Workers in Industry. Report by a Sub-Committee of the National Joint Advisory Council.* (Carr Report.) London: HMSO.

Minkin, L. 1974. 'The British Labour Party and the Trade Unions'. *Industrial and Labor Relations Review,* XXVIII, no. 1, 7–37.

——. 1978. 'The Party Connection'. *Government and Opposition,* XIII, no. 4, 458–84.

——. 1980. *The Labour Party Conference: A Study in the Politics of Intra-Party Democracy.* Manchester: Manchester University Press.

Moore, William J., and Robert J. Newman. 1975. 'On the Prospects for American Trade Union Growth: A Cross-Section Analysis'. *Review of Economics and Statistics,* LVII, 435–45.

Moran, Michael. 1974. *The Union of Post Office Workers: A Study in Political Sociology.* London: Macmillan.

——. 1977. *The Politics of Industrial Relations.* London: Macmillan.

Mortimer, James Edward. 1968. *Industrial Relations.* London: Heinemann for the Institute of Supervisory Management.

Moylan, S., and B. Davies. 1981. 'The Flexibility of the Unemployed'. *Employment Gazette,* LXXXIX, 29–33.

Muller, W.D. 1979. *The 'Kept Men'? The First Century of Trade Union Representation in the British House of Commons, 1874–1975.* Brighton: Harvester.

Müller-Jentsch, W. 1981. *Gewerkschaften als Intermediäre Organisationen.* Frankfurt a.M.: Institut für Sozialforschung. Published in English as *Trade Unions as Intermediary Organisations.* 1982. Frankfurt a.M.: Institut für Sozialforschung.

Mulvey, C. 1976. 'Collective Agreements and Relative Earnings in UK Manufacturing in 1973'. *Economica,* XLIII, 419–27.

Munday, Roderick. 1981. 'Tribunal Lore: Legalism and the Industrial Tribunals'. *Industrial Law Journal*, X, 146–59.

Munns, V.G., and W. E. J. McCarthy. 1967. *Employers' Associations: The Results of Two Studies*. Research Paper 7, Royal Commission on Trade Unions and Employers' Associations. London: HMSO.

Myrdal, G. 1964. *An American Dilemma: The Negro in America*. Condensed version by Arnold Rose. New York: Harper & Row.

Napier, B.W. 1977. 'Judicial Attitudes to the Employment Relationship: Some Recent Developments'. *Industrial Law Journal*, VI, 1–18.

——. 1979. 'The French Labour Courts: An Institution in Transition'. *Modern Law Review*, XLII, 270–84.

National Board for Prices and Incomes (NBPI). 1966. *Productivity and Pay During the Period of Severe Restraint*. Report 23. Cmnd 3167. London: HMSO.

——. 1967. *Productivity Agreements*. Report 36. Cmnd 3311. London: HMSO.

——. 1968a. *Job Evaluation*. Report 83. Cmnd 3772. London: HMSO.

——. 1968b. *Payment of Results Systems*. Report 65. Cmnd 3627. London: HMSO.

——. 1969. *Productivity Agreements*. Report 123. Cmnd 4136. London: HMSO.

——. 1971. *General Problems of Low Pay*. Report 169. Cmnd 4648. London: HMSO.

National Federation of the Self-Employed. 1981. *Priced Out: The Effect of Wages Councils on Jobs*. London: The Federation.

Neal, Leonard Francis, and Andrew Robertson. 1968. *The Manager's Guide to Industrial Relations*. London: Allen & Unwin.

Nell, E.J. 1980. 'Competition and Price-Taking Behaviour'. *Growth, Profits,and Property*. Ed. E. J. Nell. Cambridge: Cambridge University Press, 99–117.

Newman, G., and E. Smythe. 1982. *Path to Maturity*. London: Co-operative Press.

Newman, N. 1980. 'Britain's Non-Union Leaders'. *Management Today*, July, 59–64, 112–18.

Nichols, Theo, and Huw Beynon. 1977. *Living with Capitalism: Class Relations in the Modern Factory*. London: Routledge & Kegan Paul.

Nickell, S. 1977. 'Trade Unions and the Position of Women in the Industrial Wage Structure'. *British Journal of Industrial Relations*, XV, 192–210.

——. 1979. 'The Effect of Unemployment and Related Benefits on the Duration of Unemployment'. *Economic Journal*, LXXXIX, 34–49.

Nightingale, Martyn. 1980. 'UK Productivity Dealing in the 1960s'. *Capital and Labour*. Ed. Theo Nichols. Glasgow: Fontana, 316–33.

Nolan, Peter and W. A. Brown. 1983. 'Competition and Workplace Wage Determination'. *Oxford Bulletin of Economics and Statistics*, XLV, 269–87.

Oatey, M. 1970. 'The Economics of Training with Respect to the Firm'. *British Journal of Industrial Relations*, VIII, 1–21.

Offe, C., and H. Wiesenthal. 1980. 'Two Logics of Collective Action'. *Political Power and Social Theory, 1980*. Vol. 1, 67–115.

Office of Manpower Economics. 1973. *Measured Daywork*. London: HMSO.

——. 1976. Royal Commission on the Distribution of Income and Wealth. *Selected Evidence Submitted to the Royal Commission for Report 1: Initial Report on the Standing Reference*. London: HMSO.

Ogden, S. G. 1981. 'The Reform of Collective Bargaining: A Managerial Revolution?'. *Industrial Relations Journal*, XII, no. 5, 30–42.

Oi, W. 1962. 'Labor as a Quasi-Fixed Factor'. *Journal of Political Economy*, LXX, no. 6, 538–55.

Organisation for Economic Cooperation and Development (OECD). 1965. *Wages and Labour Mobility*. Paris: OECD.

Panitch, Leo. 1976. *Social Democracy and Industrial Militancy: The Labour Party, the Trade Unions and Incomes Policy 1945–1974.* Cambridge: Cambridge University Press.

——. 1977. 'The Development of Corporatism in Liberal Democracies'. *Comparative Political Studies*, X, 61–90.

——. 1980. 'Recent Theorizations of Corporatism'. *British Journal of Sociology*, XXXI, no. 2, 159-87.

——. 1981. 'Trade Unions and the Capitalist State'. *New Left Review*, no. 125, 21–60.

Parker, P.A.L., W. R. Hawes and A. L. Lumb. 1971. *The Reform of Collective Bargaining at Plant and Company Level.* Department of Employment, Manpower Papers 5. London: HMSO.

Parker, S.R. 1974. *Workplace Industrial Relations 1972.* London: HMSO.

——. 1975. *Workplace Industrial Relations 1973.* London: HMSO.

——, et al. 1971. *Effects of the Redundancy Payments Act.* London: HMSO.

Parkin, J.M. 1975. 'The Causes of Inflation: Recent Contributions and Current Controversies'. *Current Economic Problems.* Eds. J. M. Parkin and A. R. Nobay. Cambridge: Cambridge University Press, 243–73.

——, and M. T. Sumner (eds.). 1972. *Incomes Policy and Inflation.* Manchester: Manchester University Press.

——, M. T. Sumner and R. Ward. 1976. 'The Effects of Excess Demand, Generalized Expectations and Wage-Price Controls on Inflation in the U.K.: 1956–71'. *The Economics of Price and Wage Controls.* Eds. K. Brunner and A. H. Meltzer. Amsterdam: North Holland, 193-221.

Parsley, C.J. 1980. 'Labor Union Effects on Wage Gains: A Survey of Recent Literature'. *Journal of Economic Literature*, XVIII, 1–31.

Partington, Martin. 1980. 'Unemployment, Industrial Conflict and Social Security'. *Industrial Law Journal*, IX, 243–53.

Pearson. 1968. *Report of a Court of Inquiry under Lord Pearson into the Dispute between the British Steel Corporation and Certain of their Employees.* Cmnd 3754. London: HMSO.

Pearson. 1978. Royal Commission on Civil Liability and Compensation for Personal Injury. *Report.* Cmnd 7054. 3 vols. London: HMSO.

Pencavel, John H. 1970. 'An Investigation into Industrial Strike Activity in Britain'. *Economica*, n.s. XXXVII, 239–56.

——. 1974. 'Relative Wages and Trade Unions in the United Kingdom'. *Economica*, n.s. XLI, 194–210.

——. 1982. 'The Effects of Incomes Policies on the Frequency and Size of Wage Changes'. *Economica*, n.s. XLIX, 149–59.

Phelps, Edmund S. 1971. 'Money Wage Dynamics and Labor Market Equilibrium'. *Microeconomic Foundations of Employment and Inflation Theory.* Ed. E. S. Phelps. London: Macmillan, 124–66.

——. 1972. 'The Statistical Theory of Racism and Sexism'. *American Economic Review*, LXII, 659-61.

Phelps Brown, Ernest Henry. 1977. *The Inequality of Pay.* Oxford: Oxford University Press.

——, and M. H. Browne. 1962. 'Earnings in Industries of the United Kingdom, 1948–59'. *Economic Journal*, LXXII, 517–49.

——, and S. Hopkins. 1955. 'Seven Centuries of Building Wages'. *Economica*, n.s. XXII, 195–206.

Phillips, A. W. 1958. 'The Relation betwen Unemployment and the Rate of Change of Money Wage Rates in the United Kingdom, 1861–1957'. *Economica*, n.s. XXV, 283–99.

Phillips, G.A. 1976. *The General Strike: The Politics of Industrial Conflict*. London: Weidenfeld & Nicolson.

Piore, M.J. 1971. 'The Dual Labour Market: Theory and Implications'. *Problems in Political Economy: An Urban Perspective*. Ed. D. M. Gordon. Lexington: Heath, 93–7.

Pissarides, C. 1978. 'The Role of Relative Wages and Excess Demand in the Sectoral Flow of Labour'. *Review of Economic Studies*, XLV, 453–67.

Playford, C. 1980. *Low Pay Policies?* London: Low Pay Unit.

——. 1981. *In the Shadow of Decline: Low Pay in the Inner City*. London: Low Pay Unit.

Pliatzky, L. 1982. 'Cash Limits and Pay Policy'. *Political Quarterly*, LIII, 16–23.

Polacheck, S.W. 1975. 'Potential Biases in Measuring Male–Female Discrimination'. *Journal of Human Resources*, X, 105–229.

Pond, C. 1980a. 'Low Pay and Unemployment'. *Low Pay Review*, no. 2, 1–12.

——. 1980b. 'Policy Programmes for the Low Paid: The Low Pay Unit'. *Low Pay and Labour Market Segmentation in Advanced Industrial Countries*. Vol. 1. Cambridge: University of Cambridge, Department of Applied Economics. (Mimeographed.)

——. 1981. 'Low Pay: 1980s Style'. *Low Pay Review*, no. 4, 1–10.

——. 1982. 'Youth Unemployment: Are Wages to Blame?'. *Low Pay Review*, no. 8, 6–13.

——, F. Field and S. Winyard. 1976. *Trade Unions and Taxation*. Studies for Trade Unionists 6. London: Workers' Educational Association.

Prais, S.J. 1976. *The Evolution of Giant Firms in Britain*. Cambridge: Cambridge University Press.

Price, Robert, and George Sayers Bain. 1976. 'Union Growth Revisited: 1948–1974 in Perspective'. *British Journal of Industrial Relations*, XIV, 339–55.

——, and George Sayers Bain. 1983. 'Union Growth in Britain: Retrospect and Prospect'. *British Journal of Industrial Relations*, XXI, 46–68.

Priestley. 1955. Royal Commission on the Civil Service 1953–55. *Report*. Cmnd 9613. London: HMSO.

Psacharopoulos, G., and R. Layard. 1979. 'Human Capital and Earnings: British Evidence and a Critique'. *Review of Economic Studies*, XLVI, 485–503.

Purcell, John. 1979a. 'The Lessons of the Commission on Industrial Relations' Attempts to Reform Workplace Industrial Relations'. *Industrial Relations Journal*, X, no. 2, 4–22.

——. 1979b. 'A Strategy for Management Control in Industrial Relations'. *The Control of Work*. Eds. J. Purcell and R. Smith. London: Macmillan, 27–58.

——. 1981. *Good Industrial Relations: Theory and Practice*. London: Macmillan.

Reddaway, W. B. 1959. 'Wage Flexibility and the Distribution of Labour'. *Lloyds Bank Review*, n.s. LIV, 32–48.

Reder, M. W. 1955. 'The Theory of Occupational Wage Differentials'. *American Economic Review*, XLV, no. 5, 833–52.

Rehmus, C. M. (ed.). 1975. *Public Employment Labor Relations: An Overview of Eleven Nations*. Ann Arbor: Institute of Labor and Industrial Relations.

Renner, Karl. 1949. *The Institutions of Private Law and their Social Functions*. Ed. and intr. by O. Kahn-Freund. London: Routledge & Kegan Paul.

Rice, M. 1981. 'The 1979 National Engineering Dispute'. MA dissertation, University of Warwick.

Richardson, John Henry. 1954. *An Introduction to the Study of Industrial Relations*. London: Allen & Unwin.

Richardson, Ray, and Steve Catlin. 1979. 'Trade Union Density and Collective Agreement Patterns in Britain'. *British Journal of Industrial Relations*, XVII, 376–85.

Rimmer, L., and J. Popay. 1982. *Employment Trends and the Family*. London: Study Commission on the Family.

Robarts, S. 1981. *Positive Action for Women: The Next Step in Education, Training and Employment*. London: NCCL.

Robens. 1972. Department of Employment. Committee on Safety and Health at Work. *Report of the Committee 1970–72*. Cmnd 5034. 3 vols. London: HMSO.

Roberts, Benjamin Charles. 1956. *Trade Union Government and Administration in Great Britain*. London: Bell.

—— (ed.). 1962. *Industrial Relations: Contemporary Problems and Perspectives*. London: Methuen. Revised edition 1968.

Robertson, Norman, and J. L. Thomas. 1968. *Trade Unions and Industrial Relations*. London: Business Books.

Robinson, D. (ed.). 1970. *Local Labour Markets and Wage Structures*. London: Gower.

Robinson, O. 1979. 'Part-Time Employment in the European Community'. *International Labour Review*, CXVIII, no. 3, 299–314.

Roeber, J. 1975. *Social Change at Work: The ICI Weekly Staff Agreement*. London: Duckworth.

Rogaly, J. 1977. *Grunwick*. Harmondsworth: Penguin.

Routh, G. 1980a. *Occupation and Pay in Great Britain 1906–79*. London: Macmillan.

——. 1980b. 'The Morals of Pay'. *The Roots of Pay Inequalities*. G. Routh, D. Wedderburn and B. Wootton, 4–11.

——, D. Wedderburn and B. Wootton. 1980. *The Roots of Pay Inequalities*. Discussion Series No. 1. London: Low Pay Unit.

Rowe, J. W. F. 1928. *Wages in Practice and Theory*. London: Routledge.

Rowthorn, Bob. 1977. 'Conflict, Inflation and Money'. *Cambridge Journal of Economics*, I, 197–220.

Rubery, Jill. 1978. 'Structured Labour Markets, Worker Organisation and Low Pay'. *Cambridge Journal of Economics*, II, 17–36.

——, Roger Tarling and Frank Wilkinson. 1982. 'Industrial Relations Issues in the 1980s'. University of Cambridge, Department of Applied Economics. (Unpublished paper.)

——, and Frank Wilkinson. 1981. 'Outwork and Segmented Labour Markets'. *The Dynamics of Labour Segmentation*. Ed. F. Wilkinson. London: Academic Press, 115–32.

Rubin, G. R. 1977. 'The Origins of Industrial Tribunals: Munitions of War Tribunals during the First World War'. *Industrial Law Journal*, VI, 149–64.

Runnymede Trust and the Radical Statistics Race Group. 1980. *Britain's Black Population*. London: Heinemann.

Sabel, C. F. 1981. 'The Internal Politics of Trade Unions'. *Organizing Interests in Western Europe*. Ed. S. Berger. Cambridge: Cambridge University Press, 209–44.

Salter, W. E. G. 1966. *Productivity and Technical Change*. 2nd edn. Cambridge: Cambridge University Press.

Samuelson, P. 1957. 'Wages and Interest: A Modern Dissection of Marxian Economic Models'. *American Economic Review*, XLVII, no. 6, 884–913.

Sargan, J. D. 1980. 'The Consumer Price Equation in the Post-War British Economy: An Exercise in Equation Specification and Testing'. *Review of Economic Studies*, XLVII, 113–35.

Saunders, C., and D. Marsden. 1979. *A Six-Country Comparison of the Distribution of Industrial Earnings in the 1970s*. Background Paper 8, Royal Commission on the Distribution of Income and Wealth. London: HMSO.
——, and D. Marsden. 1981. *Pay Inequalities in the European Community*. London: Butterworth.
——, Santosh Mukherjee, David Marsden and Alison Donaldson. 1977. *Winners and Losers: Pay Patterns in the 1970s*. Brighton: Sussex University, Centre for Contemporary European Studies. PEP Broadsheet no. 570.
Saville, J. 1973. 'The Ideology of Labourism'. *Knowledge and Belief in Politics*. Eds. R. Benewick, R. N. Berki and B. Parekh. London: Allen & Unwin, 213–26.
Schmitter, Philippe, and Gerhard Lehmbruch (eds.). 1979. *Trends Towards Corporatist Intermediation*. London: Sage.
Shalev, Michael. 1978. 'Lies, Damned Lies and Strike Statistics: The Measurement of Trends in Industrial Conflict'. *The Resurgence of Class Conflict in Western Europe Since 1968*. Vol. 1. Eds. C. Crouch and A. Pizzorno. London: Macmillan, 1–19.
Shapiro, N. 1976. 'The Neoclassical Theory of the Firm'. *Review of Radical Political Economics*, VIII, no. 4, 17–29.
Sharp, Ian. 1950. *Industrial Conciliation and Arbitration in Great Britain*. London: Allen & Unwin.
Shister, Joseph. 1953. 'The Logic of Union Growth'. *Journal of Political Economy*, LXI, 413–33.
Shorey, John. 1975. 'The Size of the Work Unit and Strike Incidence'. *Journal of Industrial Economics*, XXIII, 175–88.
——. 1976. 'An Inter-Industry Analysis of Strike Frequency'. *Economica*, XLIII, 349–65.
——. 1977. 'Time Series Analysis of Strike Frequency'. *British Journal of Industrial Relations*, XV, 63–75.
Siebert, W. S., and P. J. Sloane. 1981. 'The Measurement of Sex and Marital Status Discrimination at the Workplace'. *Economica*, XLVIII, 125–41.
Sieff, *Lord*. 1981. 'It's People Who Matter'. *Sunday Times*, 13 December.
Silver [Shalev], Michael. 1973. 'Recent British Strike Trends: A Factual Analysis'. *British Journal of Industrial Relations*, XI, 66–104.
Simon, Daphne. 1954. 'Master and Servant'. *Democracy and the Labour Movement*. Ed. J. Saville. London: Lawrence & Wishart, 160–200.
Simpson, Bob. 1969. 'In Place of Strife: A Policy for Industrial Relations'. *Modern Law Review*, XXXII, 420–26.
——. 1979. 'Judicial Control of ACAS'. *Industrial Law Journal*, VIII, 69–84.
——. 1982. 'Unforgettable – or a Repeat Performance?'. *Modern Law Review*, XLV, 447–54.
——, and John Wood. 1973. *Industrial Relations and the 1971 Act*. London: Pitman.
Singleton, Norman. 1975. *Industrial Relations Procedures*. London: HMSO.
Sinzheimer, Hugo. 1927. 'The Essence of Labour Law' ('Das Wesen des Arbeitsrechts'). *Grundfragen des Arbeitsrechts*. Ed. G. Hermes. Berlin, 4–9.
Sisson, Keith F. *The Management of Collective Bargaining: An International Comparison*. Oxford: Blackwell (forthcoming).
Skeels, J. W. 1971. 'Measures of US Strike Activity'. *Industrial and Labor Relations Review*, XXIV, 515–25.
Sloane, P. J. (ed.). 1980a. *Women and Low Pay*. London: Macmillan.
——. 1980b. 'The Structure of Labour Markets and Low Pay for Women'. *Women and Low Pay*. Ed. P. J. Sloane, 127–64.

Sloane, P.J., and W. S. Siebert. 1980. 'Low Pay Amongst Women: The Facts'. *Women and Low Pay*. Ed. P. J. Sloane, 9–56.

Smith, C. T. B., et al. 1978. *Strikes in Britain: A Research Study of Industrial Stoppages in the United Kingdom*. Department of Employment, Manpower Papers 15. London: HMSO.

Smith, D. C. 1968. 'Incomes Policy'. *Britain's Economic Prospects*. Ed. R. E. Caves. London: Allen & Unwin, 104–46.

Smith, David J. 1976. *The Facts of Racial Disadvantage*. London: Political and Economic Planning.

——. 1977. *Racial Disadvantage in Britain*. Harmondsworth: Penguin.

——. 1980. 'Unemployment and Racial Minority Groups'. *Employment Gazette*, LXXXVIII, 602–6.

Snell, M. W., P. Glucklich and M. Povall. 1981. *Equal Pay and Opportunities: A Study of the Implementation and Effects of the Equal Pay and Sex Discrimination Acts in 26 Organisations*. Research Paper no. 20. London: Department of Employment.

Social Democratic Party (SDP). 1982a. *Democracy at Work: Green Paper No. 6*. London: SDP.

——. 1982b. *Reforming the Trade Unions: Green Paper No. 7*. London: SDP.

——. 1982c. *Towards Full Employment: Green Paper No. 1*. London: SDP.

Somerton, M. 1977. *Trade Unions and Industrial Relations in Local Government*. Studies for Trade Unionists, III, 11. London: Workers' Educational Association.

Spence, M. 1973. 'Job Market Signalling'. *Quarterly Journal of Economics*, LXXXVII, 355–74.

Spoor, A. 1967. *White-Collar Union: Sixty Years of NALGO*. London: Heinemann.

Stanton, D. 1977. 'The Take Up Debate on the UK Family Income Supplement'. *Policy and Politics*, V, no. 4, 27–45.

Starr, G. 1981. *Minimum Wage Fixing*. Geneva: International Labour Office.

Steele, R. 1981. 'Incomes Policy and Low Pay'. *Incomes Policies, Inflation and Relative Pay*. Eds. J. L. Fallick and R. F. Elliott, 128–54.

Steele, Richard. 1982. 'Northern Ireland's Low Wages'. *Low Pay Review*, no. 8, 1–5.

Steer, P., and J. Cable. 1978. 'Internal Organisation and Profit: An Empirical Analysis of Large UK Companies'. *Journal of Industrial Economics*, XXVII, 13–30.

Stevenson, J., and J. Trevithick. 1977. 'On the Complementarity of Monetary Policy and Incomes Policy'. *Scottish Journal of Political Economy*, XXIV, 19–31.

Stiglitz, J. E. 1973. 'Approaches to the Economics of Discrimination'. *American Economic Review, Papers and Proceedings*, LXIII, no. 2, 287–95.

Storey, John. 1980. *The Challenge to Management Control*. London: Kogan Page.

Sweet, T. G., and D. Jackson. 1977. 'The Changing Nature of British Strikes'. Working Paper Series no. 79. Birmingham: University of Aston Management Centre.

Tarling, Roger, and Frank Wilkinson. 1977. 'The Social Contract: Post-War Incomes Policies and their Social Impact'. *Cambridge Journal of Economics*, I, 395–414.

——, and Frank Wilkinson. 1982. 'Inflation and Unemployment: A Critique of Meade's Solutions'. *Cambridge Economic Policy Review*, VIII, no. 1, 39–43.

Taussig, F. W. 1927. *Principles of Economics*. 3rd edn. London: Macmillan.

Taylor, J. 1972. 'Incomes Policy, the Structure of Unemployment and the Phillips Curve: The United Kingdom Experience: 1953–70'. *Incomes Policy and Inflation*. Eds. J. M. Parkin and M. T. Sumner, 182–200.

Taylor, Robert. 1980. *The Fifth Estate: Britain's Unions in the Modern World.* Revised edn. London: Pan Books.

Terry, Michael. 1977. 'The Inevitable Growth of Informality'. *British Journal of Industrial Relations,* XV, 75–90.

——. 1979. 'The Emergence of a Lay Elite?'. *Sociologie du Travail,* XXI, 380–96. Also published as Discussion Paper. 1978. Coventry: SSRC Industrial Relations Research Unit, University of Warwick.

——. 1982. 'Organising a Fragmented Workforce: Shop Stewards in Local Government'. *British Journal of Industrial Relations,* XX, 1–19.

Thakur, M., and D. Gill. 1976. *Job Evaluation in Practice.* London: Institute of Personnel Management.

Thirlwall, A. P. 1981. 'Keynesian Employment Theory is Not Defunct'. *Three Banks Review,* no. 131, 14–29.

——. 1982. 'De-Industrialisation in the United Kingdom'. *Lloyds Bank Review,* no. 144, 22–37.

Thomas, R. L. 1977. 'Unionization and the Phillips Curve: Time Series Evidence from Seven Industrial Countries'. *Applied Economics,* IX, 33–49.

Thomson, A. W. J., and P. B. Beaumont. 1978. *Public Sector Bargaining: A Study of Relative Gain.* Farnborough: Saxon House.

——, and S. Engleman. 1975. *The Industrial Relations Act: A Review and Analysis.* London: Martin Robertson.

——, and L. C. Hunter. 1975. 'The Level of Bargaining in a Multi-Plant Company'. *Industrial Relations Journal,* VI, no. 2, 23–40.

——, C. Mulvey and M. Farbman. 1977. 'Bargaining Structure and Relative Earnings in Great Britain'. *British Journal of Industrial Relations,* XV, 176–91.

Thurley, K. 1981. 'Personnel Management in the UK: A Case for Urgent Treatment?'. *Personnel Management,* August, 24–30.

Thurow, L. C. 1969. *Poverty and Discrimination.* Washington: Brookings Institution.

——. 1970. *Investment in Human Capital.* London: Wadsworth.

——. 1975. *Generating Inequality: Mechanisms of Distribution in the U.S. Economy.* London: Macmillan.

Tillyard, Frank. 1936. *The Worker and the State.* 2nd edn. Tillicoultry: NCLC Publishing Society.

Tobin, James. 1980. *Asset Accumulation and Economic Activity.* Oxford: Blackwell.

Torrington, Derek P. 1972. *Handbook of Industrial Relations.* Epping: Gower.

Townsend, P. 1979. *Poverty in the United Kingdom: A Survey of Household Resources and Living Standards.* Harmondsworth: Penguin.

Trades Union Congress (TUC). 1981. *Improving Industrial Relations in the National Health Service: A Report by the TUC Health Services Committee.* London: TUC.

——. 1982. *Annual Report 1982.* London: TUC.

Trades Union Congress-Labour Party Liaison Committee. 1982. *Economic Planning and Industrial Democracy: The Framework for Full Employment.* London: TUC.

Trainor, R. 1982. 'The Management of Industrial Relations'. *Health Services Manpower Review,* VIII, 11–16.

Trevithick, James. 1977. *Inflation: A Guide to the Crisis in Economics.* Harmondsworth: Penguin.

Turner, H. A. 1952. 'Trade Unions, Differentials and the Levelling of Wages'. *Manchester School of Economic and Social Studies,* XX, 227–82.

Turner, H.A. 1957. 'Inflation and Wage Differentials in Great Britain'. *The Theory of Wage Determination.* Ed. J. T. Dunlop. London: Macmillan, 123–35.
——. 1962. *Trade Union Growth, Structure and Policy: A Comparative Study of the Cotton Unions in England.* London: Allen & Unwin.
——. 1963. *The Trend of Strikes.* Leeds: Leeds University Press.
——. 1969a. *Is Britain Really Strike-Prone?* University of Cambridge, Department of Applied Economics, Occasional Papers 20. Cambridge: Cambridge University Press.
——. 1969b. 'The Donovan Report'. *Economic Journal, LXXIX,* 1–10.
——. 1982. 'Blueprints for Survival'. *Times Higher Education Supplement,* 12 February, 12.
——, Garfield Clack and Geoffrey Roberts. 1967. *Labour Relations in the Motor Industry: A Study of Industrial Unrest and an International Comparison.* London: Allen & Unwin.
——, Geoffrey Roberts and David Roberts. 1977. *Management Characteristics and Labour Conflict: A Study of Managerial Organization, Attitudes and Industrial Relations.* University of Cambridge, Department of Applied Economics, Papers in Industrial Relations and Labour no. 3. Cambridge: Cambridge University Press.
Undy, R. 1978. 'The Devolution of Bargaining Levels and Responsibilities in the TGWU, 1965–75'. *Industrial Relations Journal, IX,* no. 3, 44–56.
——. 1979. 'The Electoral Influence of the Opposition Party in the A.U.E.W. Engineering Section 1960–75'. *British Journal of Industrial Relations, XVII,* 19–33.
——, et al. 1981. *Change in Trade Unions: The Development of UK Unions Since the 1960s.* London: Hutchinson.
Union of Shop, Distributive and Allied Workers (USDAW). 1982. *35th Annual Report, 1981.* Manchester: USDAW.
Utton, M. A. 1975. 'British Merger Policy'. *Competition Policy in the UK and EEC.* Eds. K. D. George and C. Joll. Cambridge: Cambridge University Press, 95–121.
Van Noorden, Sally. 1980. 'French Labour Courts and Unfair Dismissal Law'. *Employment Gazette, LXXXVIII,* 1098–1102.
Walton, Richard, and R. B. McKersie. 1965. *A Behavioral Theory of Labor Negotiations: An Analysis of a Social Interaction System.* New York: McGraw Hill.
Ward, Terry. 1981. 'The Case for an Import Control Strategy in the UK'. *Socialist Economic Review.* Eds. D. Currie and R. Smith. London: Merlin Press, 93–108.
Watters, F. 1981. Interview (with Peggy Kahn). *Society for the Study of Labour History Bulletin, XLIII,* 54–67.
Webb, Sidney. 1926. 'Preface'. *A History of Factory Legislation.* B. L. Hutchins and A. Harrison. 3rd edn. London: King and Son.
——, and Beatrice Webb. 1894. *The History of Trade Unionism.* London: Longman.
——, and Beatrice Webb. 1897. *Industrial Democracy.* London: Longman.
——, and Beatrice Webb. 1920. *Industrial Democracy.* New edn. London: Longman.
Wedderburn, Dorothy. 1980. 'Inequalities in Pay'. *The Roots of Pay Inequalities.* G. Routh, D. Wedderburn and B. Wootton, 12–17.
Wedderburn, K. W. (*Lord*). 1971. *The Worker and the Law.* 2nd edn. Harmondsworth: Penguin.
——. 1972. 'Labour Law and Labour Relations in Britain'. *British Journal of Industrial Relations, X,* 270–90.
——. 1976. 'The Employment Protection Act 1975: Collective Aspects'. *Modern Law Review, XXXIX,* 168–83.

Wedderburn, K.W. (*Lord*). 1978. 'The New Structure of Labour Law in Britain'. *Israel Law Review*, XIII, 435–58.

——. 1980. 'Industrial Relations and the Courts'. *Industrial Law Journal*, IX, 65–94.

——. 1981. 'Secondary Action and Gateways to Legality: A Note'. *Industrial Law Journal*, X, 113–18.

——. 1982a. 'Secondary Action and Primary Values'. *Modern Law Review*, XLV, 317–22.

——. 1982b. 'Tory Boot Goes In'. *New Socialist*, May/June, 17–22.

——. 1983. 'Otto Kahn-Freund and British Labour Law'. *Labour Law and Industrial Relations: Building on Kahn-Freund*. Eds. Lord Wedderburn, R. Lewis and J. Clark (forthcoming).

——, and P. L. Davies. 1969. *Employment Grievances and Disputes Procedures in Britain*. Berkeley and Los Angeles: University of California Press.

——, R. Lewis and J. Clark (eds.). 1983. *Labour Law and Industrial Relations: Building on Kahn-Freund*. Oxford: Oxford University Press (forthcoming).

Weekes, Brian, et al. 1975. *Industrial Relations and the Limits of Law: The Industrial Effects of the Industrial Relations Act, 1971*. Oxford: Blackwell.

Weintraub, E. R. 1979. *Microfoundations: The Compatibility of Microeconomics and Macroeconomics*. Cambridge: Cambridge University Press.

Weiss, L. W. 1966. 'Concentration and Labor Earnings'. *American Economic Review*, LVI, no. 1. 96–117.

Wellens, J. 1963. *The Training Revolution*. London: Evans Brothers.

White, Michael. 1981. *Payment Systems in Britain*. Aldershot: Gower.

Whitehead, Ken. 1977. *Industrial Relations*. London: Teach Yourself Books.

Wigham, E. 1973. *The Power to Manage: A History of the Engineering Employers' Federation*. London: Macmillan.

Wilkinson, F., and H. A. Turner. 1972. 'The Wage-Tax Spiral and Labour Militancy'. *Do Trade Unions Cause Inflation?* D. Jackson, H. A. Turner and F. Wilkinson, 63–103.

Williams, Gertrude. 1957. *Recruitment to Skilled Trades*. London: Routledge & Kegan Paul.

——. 1963. *Apprenticeship in Europe*. London: Chapman & Hall.

Williams, Kevin, and D. Lewis. 1981. *The Aftermath of Tribunal Reinstatement and Re-engagement*. Research Paper no. 23. London: Department of Employment.

Williamson, O. 1981. 'The Modern Corporation: Origins, Evolution, Attributes'. *Journal of Economic Literature*, XIX, no. 4, 1537–68.

Willman, P. 1980. 'Leadership and Trade Union Principles'. *Industrial Relations Journal*, XI, no. 4, 39–49.

——. 1981. 'The Growth of Combined Committees: A Reconsideration'. *British Journal of Industrial Relations*, XIX, 1–13.

Wilson, A. W., and Stanley R. Hill. 1968. *Industrial Relations, Law and Economics*. London: Longman.

Windolf, P. 1981. 'Strategies of Enterprises in the German Labour Market'. *Cambridge Journal of Economics*, V, 351–67.

Winkler, J. T. 1974. 'The Ghost at the Bargaining Table: Directors and Industrial Relations'. *British Journal of Industrial Relations*, XII, 191–212.

Winyard, S. 1976. *Policing Low Wages: A Study of the Wages Inspectorate*. London: Low Pay Unit.

Wootton, Barbara Frances, Baroness Wootton of Abinger. 1955. *The Social Foundations of Wage Policy: A Study of Contemporary British Wage and Salary Structure*. London: Allen & Unwin.

Workers' Educational Association. 1980. 'Editorial Comment'. *Trade Union Studies Journal,* I, 2.

Worswick, G. D. N. 1944. 'The Stability and Flexibility of Full Employment'. *The Economics of Full Employment.* Oxford University Institute of Statistics. Oxford: Blackwell, 59–84.

Wright, M. 1981. 'Big Government in Hard Times: The Restraint of Public Expenditure'. *Big Government in Hard Times.* Eds. C. Hood and M. Wright. Oxford: Martin Robertson, 3–31.

Ziderman, Adrian. 1975. 'Costs and Benefits of Manpower Training Programmes in Great Britain'. *British Journal of Industrial Relations,* XIII, 223–43.

——. 1978. *Manpower Training: Theory and Policy.* London: Macmillan.

Zis, G. 1975. 'Inflation: An International Monetary Phenomenon or Domestic Social Phenomenon'. *British Journal of International Studies,* I, no. 2, 98–118.

Index